Cross-Border Transfers and Redundancies

Cross-Border Transfers and Redundancies

General Editor
Susan Mayne
Solicitor, CMS Cameron McKenna, London

Editors
Caroline Humphries
Solicitor, CMS Cameron McKenna, London
Andreas Tinhofer
Rechtsanwalt, CMS Reich-Rohrwig Hainz, Vienna
Ian Watson
Solicitor, CMS Cameron McKenna, London

With specialist contributors

Tottel
publishing

Tottel Publishing
Maxwelton House
41-43 Boltro Road
Haywards Heath
West Sussex
RH16 1BJ

A CIP Catalogue record for this book is available from the British Library.

ISBN 1 84592 016 3

Typeset by Columns Design Ltd, Reading, Berkshire
Printed and bound in Great Britain by CPI Bath

Foreword

This is an extremely useful book, and fills a real gap in the bookshelves of law libraries and practitioners' offices. So far as the UK is concerned, it comes at a particularly crucial time, with changes to TUPE finally on the agenda and the imminent implementation of the Information and Consultation Directive into Regulations which are likely to have a substantial impact on employers and employees, all of whom will be in need of guidance. Indeed, at the CAC, where we have not been much visited by disputes relating to European Works Councils, we are about to be in the forefront of Information and Consultation, and I have no doubt we will be leafing through the pages of Mayne, unless the parties have done so already!

The book's coverage is geographically broad and jurisprudentially deep, and its approach and its language are concise and comprehensible. It will be widely welcomed.

Sir Michael Burton
President, EAT and Chairman, CAC

Preface

We have written this book with legal practitioners and those involved in cross-border transactions in mind. These are interesting and busy times: throughout Europe, there has been a steady surge in corporate mergers and acquisitions over the last couple of decades. This activity has raised some interesting points of law that are often glossed over – not to mention some difficult industrial relations issues.

We in the world of Employment Law have become familiar with the outsourcing of call centres and other services to India; less immediately newsworthy but equally notable is the high level of corporate activity crossing national boundaries in Europe. Despite the stated aim of the Acquired Rights Directive being the protection of the employment of workers in the European Union, employees in one European jurisdiction whose work transfers to another European jurisdiction (whether by way of outsourcing, merger, acquistion or any other method) are often in no better a situation than those employees whose work is transferred to New Delhi, for example. Confusion exactly about what the law in relation to such transfers says is often simply worked out in the course of negotiations between the parties to a particular transaction. The employees who are likely to be affected often do not have much of a say in this process, despite the growth in strength of European Works Councils, staff councils and other representative bodies in the European Union.

As a result of this increase in European cross-border mergers and acquisitions, the European Parliament has called for more thought to be addressed to the rights of workers. However, despite the large body of European and domestic legislation and case law in place, there are, as we discovered, still a large number of 'grey areas' and a significant degree of uncertainty. Such uncertainty is often addressed pragmatically on a case-by-case basis to all parties' mutual satisfaction – but not always. In this book, we set out to examine the 'grey areas' of cross-border transfer law in the European Union and to find answers to them. We have liaised closely with our colleagues in other CMS offices to produce a comprehensive review of the legal treatment of cross-border transfers in each of the named jurisdictions. We have tried to be as helpful as possible to the reader by producing very detailed case studies with Question and Answer sections, which address the problems most commonly faced in cross-border transactions. Each contributor has produced their responses to these case studies. For the reader who requires further information or guidance, we have provided cross-references, footnotes and, where appropriate, a list of useful literature and websites.

Whilst many of the issues addressed in this book are complex, we have tried to make the material easily readable in order to leave the reader with a firm grasp of the main principles. We have addressed local issues and custom and practice to ensure that the work goes further than a mere recitation of the law in each country.

Without the resilience and conviction of our CMS colleagues who have contributed to it, this book would never have been written and we would like to offer our thanks to them first. For his invaluable input and critical eye, we would like to thank Simon Jeffreys. For their patience and hard work, our thanks also go to our secretaries Terri Samuel, Mary Economou and Michelle Demaio.

Finally, but not least, we are grateful to Simon Jeffreys and Anthony Fincham, partners in the London employment team for encouraging and supporting this work, and to our spouses and partners Marc Meryon, Charles Humphries, Kate Singer and Marianne Tinhofer and our children Rory, Elsa, Justin and Jakob for their forebearance whilst this book was being written.

The law is stated as at 1 August 2004. Where possible, we have sought to highlight any relevant changes in law or practice which are thought to be forthcoming at the time of publication.

Susan Mayne

Andreas Tinhofer

Ian Watson

Caroline Humphries

September 2004

Contents

List of contributors

Editors
Susan Mayne
Caroline Humphries
Ian Watson
CMS Cameron McKenna, London
Phone: +44 (0)20 7367 3000
Fax: +44 (0)20 7367 2000
E-mail: susan.mayne@cmck.com
caroline.humphries@cmck.com
ian.watson@cmck.com
Website: www.law-now.com

Dr Andreas Tinhofer LLM
CMS Reich-Rohrwig Hainz, Vienna
Phone: +43 1 40 443 0
Fax: +43 1 40 443 9000
E-mail: andreas.tinhofer@cmslegal.at
Website: www.cmslegal.at

The Acquired Rights Directive
Ian Watson
CMS Cameron McKenna, London
Phone: +44 (0)20 7367 3000
Fax: +44 (0)20 7367 2000
E-mail: ian.watson@cmck.com
Website: www.law-now.com

Collective redundancies
Emma Frost
CMS Cameron McKenna, London
Phone: +44 (0)20 7367 3000
Fax: +44 (0)20 7367 2000
E-mail: emma.frost@cmck.com
Website: www.law-now.com

Information and consultation
Amanda Sheridan
CMS Cameron McKenna, London
Phone: +44 (0)20 7367 3000
Fax: +44 (0)20 7367 2000
E-mail: amanda.sheridan@cmck.com
Website: www.law-now.com

Jurisdiction and governing law
Layla Bunni
CMS Cameron McKenna, London
Phone: +44 (0)20 7367 3000
Fax: +44 (0)20 7367 2000
E-mail: layla.bunni@cmck.com
Website: www.law-now.com

Martin Fodder
Littleton Chambers, London
Phone: +44 (0)20 7797 8600
Fax: +44 (0)20 7797 8699
E-mail:
clerks@littletonchambers.co.uk

Case studies
Susan Mayne
Caroline Humphries
CMS Cameron McKenna, London
Phone: +44 (0)20 7367 3000
Fax: +44 (0)20 7367 2000
E-mail: susan.mayne@cmck.com
caroline.humphries@cmck.com
Website: www.law-now.com

Austria
Dr Andreas Tinhofer LLM
CMS Reich-Rohrwig Hainz, Vienna
Phone: +43 1 40 443 0
Fax: +43 1 40 443 9000
E-mail: andreas.tinhofer@cmslegal.at
Website: www.cmslegal.at

Belgium
Stanislas van Wassenhove
Michaël De Leersnyder
Alexis Ceuterick
CMS Lexcelis, Brussels
Phone: +00 32 2 626 22 32
Fax: +00 32 2 626 22 55
E-mail:
stanislas.vanwassenhove@cmslegal.be
michael.deleersnyder@cmslegal.be
alexis.ceuterick@cmslegal.be
Website: www.cmslegal.be

France
Nicolas de Sevin
Caroline Froger-Michon
Catherine Delanoë-Daoud
CMS Bureau Francis Lefèbvre, Paris
Phone: +00 33 1 47 38 55 00
Fax: +00 33 1 47 38 55 55
Email: n.de.sevin@bfl-avocats.com
c.froger@bfl-avocats.com
Website: www.bfl-avocats.com

Germany
Dr Barbara Bittmann
CMS Hasche Sigle, Düsseldorf
Phone: +49 (0) 211 4934–418
Fax: +49 (0) 211 4934–126
E-mail:
barbara.bittmann@cmslegal.de
Website: www.cmslegal.de

Astrid Wellhöner LLM Eur
CMS Hasche Sigle, Stuttgart
Phone: +49 (0) 711 9764–650
Fax: +49 (0) 711 97 64–921
E-mail:
astrid.wellhoener@cmslegal.de
Website: www.cmslegal.de

Dr Wolfgang Schmiedl
CMS Hasche Sigle, Munich
Phone: +49 (0) 89 23807–248
Fax: +49 (0) 89 23807–170
E-mail:
wolfgang.schmiedl@cmslegal.de
Website: www.cmslegal.de

Hungary
Dr Gabriella Ormai
Dr Péter K Bán LLM
Ormai es Tarsai CMS Cameron
McKenna, Budapest
Phone: +36 1 483 4800
Fax: +36 1 483 4801
E-mail: gabriella.ormai@cmck.com
peter.karoly.ban@cmck.com
Website: www.law-now.com

Italy
Massimo Donna LLM Eur
CMS Adonnino Ascoli & Cavasola
Scamoni, Rome
Phone: +39 06 478151
Fax: +39 06 483755
E-mail: massimo.donna@aacs.it
Website: www.aacs.it

The Netherlands
Mr Jos W M Pothof
CMS Derks Star Busmann, Utrecht
Phone: +31 (0) 30 2121 645
Fax: +31 (0) 30 2121 165
E-mail: j.pothof@cmsderks.nl
Website: www.cmsderks.nl

Ms Solveigh B Bijkerk-Verbruggen
CMS Derks Star Busmann, Utrecht
Phone: +31 (0) 30 2121 672
Fax: +31 (0) 30 2121 165
E-mail: s.bijkerk@cmsderks.nl
Website: www.cmsderks.nl

Ms Rachida el Johari
CMS Derks Star Busmann,
Amsterdam
Phone: +31 (0) 20 3016 307
Fax: +31 (0) 20 3016 330
E-mail: r.eljohari@cmsderks.nl
Website: www.cmsderks.nl

Spain
Francisco Fernández
CMS Bureau Francis Lefèbvre,
Madrid
Phone: +0034 91 436 45 31
Fax: +0034 91 436 43 02
E-mail: fernandez@bfl-abogados.com
Website: www.bfl-avocats.com

Switzerland
Dr Stefan Gerster LLM
Dr Matthias Leemann LLM
CMS von Erlach Klainguti Stettler
Wille, Zurich
Phone: +41 44 285 11 11
Fax: +41 44 285 11 22
E-mail: s.gerster@cmslegal.ch
m.leemann@cmslegal.ch
Website: www.cmslegal.ch

United Kingdom
Susan Mayne
CMS Cameron McKenna, London
Phone: +44 (0)20 7367 3000
Fax: +44 (0)20 7367 2000
E-mail: susan.mayne@cmck.com
Website: www.law-now.com

Table of statutes

References in the right-hand column are to paragraph numbers. Paragraph references printed in **bold** type indicate where the statute is set out in part or in full.

Table of statutory instruments

References in the right-hand column are to paragraph numbers.

Table of EU legislation

References in the right-hand column are to paragraph numbers. Paragraph references printed in **bold** type indicate where the text is set out in part or in full.

Table of cases

A

B

C

D

xl *Table of cases*

E

EC Commission v Belgium: 237/84 [1986] ECR 1247,
[1988] 2 CMLR 865, ECJ A3.3
EC Commission v Italy: 235/84 [1986] ECR 2291,
[1987] 3 CMLR 115, ECJ A5
EC Commission v United Kingdom: C-382/92 [1994] ECR
I-2435, [1995] 1 CMLR 345, [1994] ICR 664, [1994] IRLR
392, ECJ J1.7
EC Commission v United Kingdom: C-383/92 (1992) OJ C316,
1992, p 15; on appeal [1994] ECR I-2479, [1995] 1 CMLR
345, [1994] ICR 664, [1994] IRLR 412, ECJ A2.7, B1.9, M2.4, S1.2
Europièces SA (in liquidation) v Sanders: C-399/96 [1998] ECR
I-6965, [1999] All ER (EC) 831, [2001] 1 CMLR 667,
[1998] All ER (D) 574, ECJ A2.4, A3.2
Evenas-Baro v SA Sonauto, Supreme Court, 2 May 2001 .... L1.3
Expro Gulf Ltd v Birnie (UKEAT/0222/04/DA) D3.2, D5, D9.2

F

Federal Employment Court, 21 October 1980, AP No 8 on s 111 .... M2.6
Federal Employment Court, 12 February 1987, AP No 67 on
s 613A M1.2
Federal Employment Court, 20 April 1989, DB 1989, 2334 .... M1.2
Federal Employment Court, 13 June 1989, BAGE 62, 88 .... M2.4
Federal Employment Court, 24 August 1989, DB 1990, 1666 .... M2.1
Federal Employment Court, 29 October 1992, DB 1993, 743 .... M1.1
Federal Employment Court, 24 October 1996, DB 1997, 630 .... M2.4
Federal Employment Court, 22 May 1997, NZA 1997, 1050 .... M1.2
Federal Employment Court, 11 March 1999, DB 1999, 1274 .... M2.4
Federal Employment Court, 13 April 2000, DB 2000, 2175 .... M2.4
Federal Employment Court, 20 November 2001, DB 2002, 950 .... M2.4
Federal Employment Court, 21 February 2002, BB 2002, 2335 .... M2.2
Financial Times v Bishop (EAT/0147/03/ZT) D9.2
Foreningen af Arbejdsledere i Danmark v A/S Danmols Inventar:
105/84 [1985] ECR 2639, [1986] 1 CMLR 316, ECJ A3.2, B1.2, S1.4
Foreningen af Arbejdsledere i Danmark v Daddy's Dance Hall
A/S: 324/86 [1988] ECR 739, [1989] 2 CMLR 517,
[1988] IRLR 315, ECJ A2, A2.1, A3.1, J3.2, P1.5, P3.2
Francovich and Bonifaci v Italy: C-6, 9/90 [1991] ECR I-5357,
[1993] 2 CMLR 66, [1995] ICR 722, [1992] IRLR 84, ECJ S1.2
Frankfurt Regional Court, 27 February 2003, 11 Sa 799/02 .... M1.2

G

GMB v Susie Radin Ltd [2004] EWCA Civ 180, [2004] 2 All ER
279, [2004] ICR 893, 148 Sol Jo LB 266, [2004] All ER (D)
353 (Feb), sub nom Radin (Susie) Ltd v GMB [2004] IRLR
400, (2004) Times, 16 March B1.9, S2.4

H

I

J

K

L

M

N

O

P

R

S

T

Decisions of the European Court of Justice are listed below numerically.
These decisions are also included in the preceding alphabetical list.

PART I

Common European framework

A The Acquired Rights Directive

Ian Watson

A1 Introduction

Prior to the introduction of Council Directive 77/187/EEC on the approximation of the laws of the member states relating to the safeguarding of employees' rights in the event of transfers of undertakings, businesses or parts of businesses (the '1977 Directive'), the common law position in a number of countries within the European Community was that, when ownership of an entity's business (ie its assets, both tangible and intangible, its goodwill etc) transferred, the employment relationships to which the transferor was party on the date the transaction was completed (ie its workforce) did not transfer to the transferee, unless the parties specifically contracted to that effect.

The 1977 Directive, which changed this common law position, was adopted to standardise the legal treatment of workers when the undertakings or businesses in relation to which they are employed are transferred to new owners within the European Community. By providing that employees in such situations were to remain in employment with the transferee on the same terms and conditions as they had agreed with the transferor, the 1977 Directive (as amended by Council Directive 98/50/EC and Council Directive 2001/23/EC, hereinafter the 'Directive'[1]) aimed to bind employers in such a way that the rights of those employees were safeguarded. In addition to ensuring that this basic principle was enshrined in their national laws, the Directive specifically obliged member states to introduce legislation which provided:

- that transferees would observe the provisions of any collective agreements that had been entered into by transferors;

- that transferors and transferees would only legitimately be able to effect dismissals arising out of, or in connection with, transfers for economic, technical or organisational reasons entailing changes in the workforce;

- that the position of employees' representatives would be preserved where the undertaking or business or part thereof being transferred retained its autonomy; and

- that the representatives of employees likely to be affected by a transfer would be informed and, in certain circumstances, consulted by their employers in advance.

The stipulations made by the Directive with regard to the protection of employees' rights in connection with transfers are minimum requirements. Member states are free either to 'apply or introduce laws, regulations or administrative provisions' or 'promote or permit collective agreements or agreements between social partners' that are 'more favourable to employees'[2]. Indeed, the Directive was, and is, intended only as a means of achieving the 'partial harmonisation' of the national laws of the member states, rather than as a means of establishing a uniform level of protection throughout the European Community. This is something that the European Court of Justice ('ECJ') has explicitly acknowledged in its jurisprudence. Accordingly, the court has given the governments and courts of the member states a significant degree of discretion when implementing and applying the Directive.

1   References to articles within the Directive, unless otherwise indicated, are to those within Council Directive 2001/23/EC. All quotations are taken directly from the English translations of the Directives.
2   Council Directive 2001/23/EC, art 8.

A2 Scope of the Directive

The Directive applies to 'any transfer of an undertaking, business, or part of an undertaking or business to another employer as a result of a legal transfer or merger'[1]. Article 1(1)(b) of the Directive defines the transfer of an undertaking or business, or part of an undertaking or business as 'a transfer of an economic entity which retains its identity, meaning an organised grouping of resources which has the objective of pursuing an economic activity, whether or not that activity is central or ancillary.'

Initially, the ECJ took the literal view that a 'transfer of an undertaking' had to occur as a direct consequence of a 'legal transfer or merger'[2]. The court reassessed the inter-relationship between these three key concepts in *Dr Sophie Redmond Stichting v Hendrikus Bartol*[3] (*'Bartol'*), suggesting that a national court considering whether a 'non-merger' transfer within the terms of the Directive has taken place must first consider whether the scenario constitutes a 'legal transfer' and, if so, then whether it satisfies the criteria for a 'transfer of an undertaking' set out by the ECJ in *Spijkers v Gebroeders Benedik Abattoir CV*[4] (*'Spijkers'*). Whilst the ECJ seems content to continue providing national courts with guidance in relation to the definition of the term 'legal transfer' and the scenarios that fall within it, by setting out a detailed framework for member states to establish whether a 'transfer of an undertaking' has taken place, the court has effectively delegated decision-making in this regard. Thus, once the ECJ has given judgment as to whether a particular scenario may constitute a 'legal transfer' within the terms of the Directive, it is up to the national courts to determine whether a 'transfer of an undertaking' has taken place on the facts by referring to the *Spijkers* criteria. The ECJ took this approach in *Foreningen af Arbejdsledere i Danmark v Daddy's Dance Hall A/S*[5] (*'Daddy's Dance Hall'*), for example.

1   Council Directive 2001/23/EC, art 1(1)(a).
2   *Abels v Bedrijfsvereniging voor de Metaalindustrie en de Electrotechnische Industrie*:135/83 [1985] ECR 469, ECJ (*'Abels'*).
3   C-29/91 [1992] ECR I-3189, ECJ.
4   24/85 [1986] 2 CMLR 296, ECJ.
5   324/86 [1988] ECR 739, ECJ.

A2.1 Legal transfers

It was initially assumed that, in the context of the Directive, the term 'legal transfer' only covered a change in the identity of an employer carried out by contract. However, the ECJ adopted a purposive approach to the interpretation of the term, providing that it can also apply to changes in the identity of the person or body responsible for carrying on a business or undertaking arising from legislative or administrative acts, for example. Thus, the absence of a direct contractual link between the transferor and the transferee does not, of itself, prevent a transfer from falling within the terms of the Directive[1]. In *Merckx and Neuhuys v Ford Motors Co Belgium SA*[2] (*'Merckx'*), the ECJ held that the termination of a motor vehicle dealership arrangement with one undertaking and the award of that motor vehicle dealership to another undertaking pursuing the same activities in the same area constituted a 'legal transfer' for the purposes of the Directive. Further, the ECJ has held that the term 'legal transfer' could also apply to a transfer carried out in two distinct stages with the involvement of a third party, provided the undertaking or business in question retained its identity throughout[3].

1 C-51/00: *Temco Service Industries SA v Samir Imzilyen* [2002] ECR I-969.
2 C-171/94 [1996] IRLR 467, ECJ.
3 *P Bork International A/S (in liquidation) v Foreningen af Arbejdsledere i Danmark, acting on behalf of Birger E Petersen, and Jens E Olsen v Junckers Industrier A/S* (*'Bork'*): 101/87 [1988] ECR 3057, ECJ.

Legislative or administrative acts

As stated at *A2.1* above, the ECJ has accepted the proposition that the Directive could apply to a change in the identity of an employer arising from a legislative or administrative act. In *Bartol*[1], the court ruled that a local authority's decision to discontinue grant-based funding to one organisation and switch that funding to another organisation pursuing the same activities and operating in the same area could constitute a 'legal transfer' for the purposes of the Directive. Although the court in *Bartol* did not consider other scenarios where it felt there could be a 'legal transfer' without there being a direct contractual relationship between the transferor and the transferee, it has been suggested by commentators that, in the light of its decision, the Directive could apply where the identity of an employer changes due to a judicial decision or as a consequence of succession by operation of law.

1 C-29/91: *Dr Sophie Redmond Stichting v Hendrikus Bartol* [1992] ECR I-3189, ECJ.

Contracting-out

The ECJ first considered whether the 'contracting-out' of a service (ie the process by which third parties are given the opportunity to bid to carry out an activity previously carried out internally) could constitute a 'legal transfer' within the meaning of the Directive in *Rask and Christensen v ISS Kantineservice A/S*[1] (*'Rask'*). It held that the Directive could, in principle, apply to such a situation, adding that it was of no consequence that the 'contracted-out' activity in question had been only ancillary to the transferor's business or if the agreement reached between the parties required the transferee to provide the 'contracted-out' service exclusively for the benefit of the transferor.

The ECJ approved the principles it had set out in *Rask*, in the case of *Schmidt v Spar und Leihkasse der früheren Amter Bordesholm, Kiel und Cronshagen*[2] (*'Schmidt'*). Here, the court held that the Directive could apply where an activity was 'contracted-out', even where a single employee of the transferor had previously performed that activity. The number of employees engaged in carrying out a particular activity prior to it being 'contracted-out' to a third party is therefore irrelevant to the determination of whether the Directive applies to a specific transaction.

Although *Rask* and *Schmidt* both concerned the 'contracting-out' of activities in the private sector, the ECJ confirmed in *Hernandez Vidal SA v Gomez Perez*[3] (*'Hernandez Vidal'*) that the Directive could also apply, in principle, to the 'contracting back in' of activities that had previously been outsourced. Further, the court has confirmed that the Directive could apply to the 'contracting-out' and 'contracting back in' of services in the public sector, as well as the private sector[4].

1   C-209/91 [1992] ECR I-5755, ECJ.
2   C-392/92 [1994] ECR I-1311, ECJ.
3   Joined Cases C-127/96, C-229/96 and C-74/977 [1998] ECR I-8179, ECJ.
4   C-127/96, C-229/96 and C-74/97: *Hernandez Vidal* and Joined Cases C-173/96 and C-247/96: *Sanchez Hidalgo v Associacion de Servicio Aser* (*'Sanchez Hidalgo'*) [1998] ECR I-8237, ECJ.

Leasing arrangements

In *Landsorganisationen i Danmark for Tjenerforbundet i Danmark v Ny Molle Kro*[1], the ECJ held that employees of an undertaking, the identity of whose employer changes without there being a change in the ownership of that undertaking (in this case, the owner of a leased undertaking resumed the running of the business following a breach of covenant by the lessee), are entitled to the same level of protection as employees who are employed by an undertaking that is sold. That the termination of a leasing arrangement and its subsequent reassignment could constitute a 'legal transfer' within the terms of the Directive was confirmed by the ECJ in *Daddy's Dance Hall*[2].

1   287/86 [1987] ECR 5465, ECJ.
2   *Foreningen af Arbejdsledere i Danmark v Daddy's Dance Hall A/S*: 324/86 [1988] ECR 739, ECJ.

A2.2 Mergers

Whilst art 1(1)(a) of the Directive expressly provides that a 'transfer of an undertaking' may take place as a result of a 'merger', it does not define the term. However, art 12 of Council Directive 78/855/EEC, concerning mergers of public limited liability companies, states that the 'protection of the rights of the employees of each of the merging companies shall be regulated in accordance with Directive77/187/EEC' (ie the 1977 Directive). It is therefore assumed that the term 'merger' in the context of the Directive should be construed in accordance with the definitions set out in arts 3(1) and 4(1) of Council Directive 78/855/EEC. Article 3(1) defines a 'merger by acquisition' as a transaction 'whereby one or more companies are wound up without going into liquidation and transfer to another all their assets and liabilities in exchange for the issue to the shareholders of the company or companies being acquired of shares in the acquiring company and a cash payment, if any ...', whilst art 4(1) defines a 'merger by the formation of a new company' as a transaction 'whereby several companies are wound up without going into liquidation and transfer to a company that they set up all their assets and liabilities in exchange for the issue to their shareholders of shares in the new company and a cash payment, if any ...'. Thus, for a transaction to be considered a 'merger' for the purposes of Council Directive 78/855/EEC (and therefore the Directive), it would appear that there must be a change in the identity of the employer. Accordingly, 'share sales' (ie where control of a company is acquired via the purchase of its share capital) are excluded from the scope of the Directive. This is because, in such situations, there is only a change in the identity of the owner of the company's share capital and not a change in the identity of the employer of the company's workforce. Thus, the operation of the Directive is confined to 'mergers' by way of 'asset sales' (ie where control of a company is acquired via the purchase of its individual assets), where the identity of the employer of the company's workforce changes.

A2.3 Transfers of undertakings or businesses, or parts of undertakings or businesses

As stated in **A2** above, the first question for national courts to consider is whether a 'legal transfer' or 'merger' has taken place within the terms of the Directive. The courts in member states must then determine whether the facts give rise to a 'transfer of an undertaking or business' or a part thereof. The ECJ has yet to define comprehensively what is meant by 'part of' an undertaking or business. However, this will always be a question of fact and degree.

In *Spijkers*[1], the ECJ held that, in order for a national court to determine whether an undertaking or business has been transferred as a 'going concern' and retained its identity such that the Directive applies, it is necessary for it to consider all the facts characterising the transaction, including but not limited to:

- the type of undertaking or business;

- whether its tangible and intangible assets are transferred;

- the value of its intangible assets at the time of transfer;

- whether the majority of its employees are taken on by the new owner;

–   whether its customers are transferred;

–   the degree of similarity between the activities carried out before and after the transfer; and

–   the period, if any, for which those activities were suspended.

The ECJ has confirmed that no single factor is decisive to the overall determination[2] and that national courts should consider all the facts characterising a particular transaction together, rather than each aspect in isolation, before making an assessment as to whether the business or undertaking in question has retained its identity following a transfer.

The court has reaffirmed the importance of the seven criteria it set out in *Spijkers* in a number of subsequent cases. However, it has seemed to focus more on the 'degree of similarity between the activities carried out before and after the transfer' element of the formula than any other. Prior to its judgment in *Süzen*, the ECJ tended to concentrate on the extent to which the transferee of an undertaking or business continued carrying out the same or similar activities as the transferor following a transfer. The court applied this approach in *Schmidt*, stating that this was the most significant determinant of whether an undertaking or business had retained its identity such that 'a transfer of an undertaking' had taken place. In its judgment, the ECJ confirmed that the transfer of tangible assets to a transferee was not a necessary pre-requisite for a 'transfer of an undertaking' to have taken place.

The ECJ developed this approach in *Ledernes Hovedorganisation (acting for Ole Rygaard) v Dansk Arbejdsgiverforening*[3] ('*Rygaard*'), stating that the transfer of a specific works contract to a third party by an undertaking whose business activities were not limited to that one contract would only constitute a 'transfer of an undertaking' under the terms of the Directive to the extent that a body of assets sufficient to enable the transferee to carry out, in a stable way, the same or similar activities as the transferor, were also transferred (rather than simply made available by the transferor to the transferee following the transfer). However, the ECJ did not totally abandon the approach it took in *Schmidt*, applying it in *Merckx*[4] to hold that a 'transfer of an undertaking' had taken place where a motor vehicle dealership contract was terminated and awarded to another undertaking pursuing the same activities in the same area, even though no tangible assets had been transferred and the business activities of the two undertakings were carried out from different premises and under different names.

The ECJ changed the emphasis of the test for determining whether a 'transfer of an undertaking' has taken place in *Süzen*, holding that the extent to which the relevant entity retained its identity was the crucial consideration. Building on the reasoning it adopted in *Rygaard*, the ECJ stated in *Süzen* that, for the Directive to apply, the undertaking or business being transferred has to be a 'stable economic entity' (ie an organised grouping of people and assets that enables a particular economic activity to be carried out) whose activities are not limited to performing a specific works contract. The ECJ stressed that an 'economic entity' cannot be reduced to the activity entrusted to it, as its identity can also emerge from other factors such as its workforce, its management staff, the assets and operational resources available to it and the operating methods it employs. In so doing, the court seemed to suggest that the loss by a service provider of a contract to a third party, which subsequently continued or resumed the same or similar business activities as that service provider, did not, of itself, constitute a 'transfer of an undertaking' under the Directive; it thereby apparently rejected the approach it took in *Schmidt*.

The ECJ approved the reasoning it adopted in *Süzen* in the subsequent cases of *Hernandez Vidal*[5] and *Sanchez Hidalgo*[6], confirming that, in order for the Directive to apply to the transfer of an undertaking or business, the undertaking or business in question must constitute and remain a 'stable economic entity'. In its judgment in *Hernandez Vidal*, which involved a labour-intensive undertaking, the court added that, although such a 'stable economic entity' must be sufficiently structured and autonomous, it need not have significant assets.

In focusing more on whether the undertaking in question has retained its identity as a 'stable economic entity' following a change in the legal or natural person who is responsible for carrying on its business following *Süzen*, the ECJ has emphasised the importance of examining the characteristics of the particular undertaking (ie the type of business carried on, its assets, the production or operating methods employed etc). For instance, where a business requires specific tangible or intangible assets in order to operate effectively, the ECJ has suggested that a transfer of that business in accordance with the Directive can only take place if a significant portion of those assets is transferred. Further, the ECJ has suggested, for example in its judgment in *Sanchez Hidalgo*, that whilst the transfer of the majority of a workforce is not necessarily indicative of a 'transfer of an undertaking' having taken place, the fact that none of the workforce of a former employer are taken on, does not, of itself, preclude the possibility that a transfer within the terms of the Directive has occurred. An overall assessment of the situation is required. This approach was taken in the recent case of *Abler v Sodexho MM Catering Gesellschaft mbH*[7], where the re-tendering of a contract to provide catering services was held to be a 'transfer of an undertaking', even though the new contractor took on only the premises and equipment, and not the materials, stock or staff that the old contractor had employed.

The ECJ's case law following *Süzen*, with its emphasis on whether an undertaking or business retains its identity as a 'stable economic entity' following a transfer, was adopted in the definition of 'transfer of an undertaking' in art 1(1)(b) of Council Directive 98/50/EC (the '1998 Directive') and subsequently in Council Directive 2001/23/EC (the '2001 Directive'). Accordingly, for a 'transfer of an undertaking' to take place in accordance with the Directive, there must be an 'economic entity', 'meaning an organised grouping of resources which has the objective of pursuing an economic activity'[8], which is organised in a stable manner and not limited to the performance of one particular works contract. Further, there must be a change in the identity of the legal or natural person responsible for carrying out the business of the 'economic entity' and employing its workforce, which does not result in the 'economic entity' losing its identity in terms of the activities it carries out, the way in which those activities are organised, the resources available to it, its workforce, its management and its operating methods.

1   *Spijkers v Gebroeders Benedik Abattoir CV*: 24/85 [1986] 2 CMLR 296, ECJ.
2   See C-392/92: *Schmidt v Spar und Leihkasse der früheren Amter Bordesholm, Kiel und Cronshagen* [1994] ECR I-1311, ECJ, and C-13/95: *Süzen v Zehnacker Gebäudereinigung GmbH Krankenhausservice* [1997] ECR I-1259, ECJ, for example.
3   C-48/94 [1995] ECR I-2745, ECJ.
4   C-171/94: *Merckx and Neuhuys v Ford Motors Co Belgium SA* [1996] IRLR 467, ECJ.
5   Joined Cases C-127/96, C-229/96 and C-74/97: *Hernandez Vidal SA v Gomez Perez* [1998] ECR I-8179, ECJ.
6   Joined Cases C-173/96 and C-247/96: *Sanchez Hidalgo v Associacion de Servicio Aser* [1998] ECR I-8237, ECJ.
7   C-340/01 [2004] IRLR 168
8   Council Directive 2001/23/EC, art 1(1)(b).

A2.4   Insolvency proceedings

Although the 1977 Directive did not expressly preclude the possibility that transfers arising out of insolvency proceedings could fall within its scope, the ECJ held in *Abels*[1] that the Directive would not apply to such transfers in the absence of an express provision to the contrary. The court reasoned that, should the Directive automatically apply in such situations, potential transferees of undertakings in financial difficulty might be dissuaded from acquiring them in a form and on conditions that were acceptable to their creditors. The ECJ, influenced by the social objectives of the Treaty of Rome and the Directive's expressed purpose of safeguarding the rights of employees in the event that the undertaking or business in relation to which they are employed is transferred, suggested that the interests of workers might be better served if the Directive did not automatically apply to transfers arising out of such insolvency proceedings, as there was a risk that, should it do so, potential transferees might attempt to avoid its application by offering to purchase the individual assets of the undertaking in question, rather than its business as a 'going concern', with the result that all of its employees would be left without jobs. However, the ECJ confirmed in *Abels* that member states had the discretion to provide that the Directive applied to transfers arising out of such insolvency proceedings, should they so wish.

In reaching its decision in *Abels*, the ECJ distinguished 'insolvency' proceedings, instituted with a view to liquidating the assets of an undertaking and under the supervision of a competent national authority, from 'pre-insolvency' procedures, whereby an undertaking in financial difficulty is transferred to a third party to enable it to suspend payments to its creditors with a view to reaching a settlement with them, and to prevent the liquidation of its assets. In so doing, the court emphasised the importance of judicial and administrative supervision during 'insolvency' proceedings, in contrast to the relative lack of such supervision in 'pre-insolvency' procedures. However, in *Giuseppe d'Urso v Ercole Marelli Elettromeccanica Generale SpA*[2] (*'d'Urso'*), the ECJ held that the nature and extent of such supervision is not conclusive in establishing whether the Directive applies to transfers arising out of particular proceedings. Rather, the sole determinant in this regard is the objective the proceedings seek to achieve. As such, the court held that, whilst the Directive did not apply to transfers arising out of settlements made with creditors with a view to liquidating the assets of undertakings, it did apply to transfers arising out of agreements or declarations that have the purpose of enabling undertakings to continue in business.

The ECJ approved this approach in *Luigi Spano v Fiat Geotech SpA and Fiat Hitachi Excavators SpA*[3] and provided further clarification in *Jules Dethier Equipement SA v Jules Dassy & Sovam SPRL*[4] (*'Jules Dethier'*), where it held that, although the form of the proceedings in question is relevant to the determination of whether the Directive applies to transfers arising in relation to them, the most important factor is their purpose. This reasoning was utilised by the ECJ in *Europièces SA v Sanders & Automotive Industries Holding Co SA*[5] (*'Europièces'*), where the court stated that the Directive applied to a transfer arising out of a voluntary liquidation.

The position reached by the ECJ was consolidated in the 1998 Directive, which stated that:

> 'unless Member States provide otherwise, [the Articles within the Directive dealing with the safeguarding of employees' rights] shall not apply to any transfer of an undertaking, business or part of an undertaking or business where the transferor is the subject of bankruptcy proceedings or analogous insolvency proceedings which have been instituted with a view to the liquidation of the assets of the transferor and are under the supervision of a competent public authority.[6]'

This wording was subsequently replicated in the 2001 Directive[7]. Therefore, unless member states provide otherwise, employees' rights are not safeguarded when the undertaking in relation to which they are employed is transferred where it is subject to insolvency proceedings under the supervision of a competent national authority that has, as its sole purpose, the liquidation of that undertaking's assets.

Against this background, it should be noted that the Directive requires member states to 'take appropriate measures with a view to preventing misuse of insolvency proceedings in such a way as to deprive employees of the rights provided for (by the) Directive[8].' However, the ECJ has yet to set out conclusively what character these 'measures' should have.

---

1   *Abels v Bedrijfsvereniging voor de Metaalindustrie en de Electrotechnische Industrie*: 135/83 [1985] ECR 469, ECJ.
2   C-362/89 [1991] ECR I-4105, ECJ.
3   C-472/93 [1995] ECR I-4321, ECJ.

4   C-319/94 [1998] ECR I-1061, ECJ.
5   C-399/96 [1998] ECR I-6965, ECJ.
6   Council Directive 98/50/EC, art 4A.
7   Council Directive 2001/23/EC, art 5(1).
8   Council Directive 2001/23/EC, art 5(4).

A2.5 Public sector transfers

The ECJ, in response to the uncertainty that existed as to whether the Directive applied to transfers of entities within the public sector, has developed a distinct set of rules in this regard. In the case of *Annette Henke v Gemeinde Schierke and Verwaltungsgemeinschaft Brocken*[1], the court held that the transfer of administrative functions between different government authorities, or the reorganisation of such functions within the public sector, did not fall within the scope of the Directive. In so doing, the ECJ drew a distinction between the transfer of an economic activity and the transfer of an activity involving the exercise of public authority within the public sector. The court stated that, whilst the latter activity may involve aspects of an economic nature, those aspects could only ever be ancillary to the exercise of public authority. Thus, it appeared that the Directive would apply in a situation where a public sector function of an economic nature, but not involving the exercise of public authority, was transferred. This contention was apparently supported by the ECJ's subsequent decisions in *Oy Liikenne AB v Liskojärvi & Juntunen*[2] and *Mayeur v Association Promotion de l'Information Messine*[3], where it held, respectively, that the provision of transport services and the provision of information services within the public sector constituted 'economic activities', such that their transfer would be covered by the terms of the Directive.

The position has been clarified somewhat by the 2001 Directive, which states that it 'shall apply to public and private undertakings engaged in economic activities ... An administrative reorganisation of public administrative authorities, or the transfer of administrative functions between public administrative authorities, is not a transfer within the meaning of the Directive.[4]'

1   C-298/94 [1996] ECR I-4989, ECJ.
2   C-172/99 [2002] ECR I-745, ECJ.
3   C-175/99 [2000] ECR I-7755, ECJ.
4   Council Directive 2001/23/EC, art 1(c).

A2.6 Affected employees

The Directive applies only to 'employees', who are defined as 'any person who, in the Member State concerned, is protected as an employee under national employment law.[1]' However, whilst the Directive provides that it 'shall be without prejudice to national law as regards the definition of the contract of employment or employment relationship', it confirms that:

'Member States shall not exclude from [its] scope ... contracts of employment or employment relationships solely because:

(a)   of the number of working hours performed or to be performed;

(b)   they are employment relationships governed by a fixed-duration
contract of employment …; or

(c)   they are temporary employment relationships … and the undertaking, business or part of the undertaking or business transferred
is, or is part of, the temporary employment business which is the
employer.[2]'

It has been argued that the relatively wide discretion given to member states
in determining the application of the Directive (eg public sector workers are
not covered by its terms, in so far as they are not defined as 'employees' and
not protected by the employment law in force in particular member states)
reflects the fact that it was only ever intended to achieve 'partial harmonisation' of their laws in this area.

In *Botzen v Rotterdamsche Droogdok Maatschappij BV*[3], the ECJ stated that it
was the link between an employee and the undertaking or part of the
undertaking in relation to which he/she carries out his/her duties that
characterised an employment relationship. The court added that, in order for
a transfer to fall within the scope of the Directive, the employee(s) in
question must be party to an employment relationship with the transferor
immediately beforehand. In this regard, it is of no consequence that a
particular employee is, for example, on sick leave or maternity leave at the
time of a transfer, as he/she would still be party to an employment
relationship with the transferor.

The Directive only confers rights on those employees who are 'wholly
engaged in' or 'assigned' to the undertaking or part of the undertaking that is
transferred at the time of transfer. This does not, however, preclude the
application of the Directive to an employee who is required to perform
activities in relation to other parts of the same undertaking or to other
undertakings within the same overall structure that are not transferred, which
could properly be described as *de minimis*. However, if an employee is
required to perform more substantive activities with regard to several parts of
the same undertaking, or several undertakings within the same overall
structure (eg an employee in a human resources department), then he/she
cannot, for the purposes of the Directive, be regarded an 'employee' of the
particular part of the undertaking or of the particular undertaking that is
transferred.

1   Council Directive 2001/23/EC, art 2(1)(d).
2   Council Directive 2001/23/EC, art 2(2).
3   186/83 [1985] ECR 519, ECJ.

A2.7 Employees' representatives

The Directive defines employees' representatives as 'the representatives of
the employees provided for by the laws or practices of the Member States.'[1]'
Accordingly, the Directive does not stipulate any rules in relation to their
election, status or function. The original implementing legislation adopted by

the UK government provided that the information and consultation procedures within the Directive (see **A4** below for more detail) applied only to trade unions recognised voluntarily by employers (with the consequence that an employer would not be subject to a duty to inform and consult in the context of a transfer, if it did not recognise a trade union in its workplace). In *European Commission v United Kingdom*[2], the ECJ held that the UK government had failed to transpose the Directive correctly, as it had not provided a mechanism whereby employees could elect or appoint representatives to take part in information and consultation procedures on their behalf where their employer did not recognise a trade union. Whilst acknowledging that the Directive had not been introduced to bring about 'full harmonisation' of national systems for the representation of employees in the workplace, the ECJ was concerned to ensure that its provisions were not deprived of their effectiveness by the laws and practices of the individual member states. Although the UK government was therefore obliged to amend its employee representation structures, the fact that the Directive does not require 'full harmonisation' of the laws of the member states meant that it had considerable latitude in deciding how to do so.

The representatives of employees affected by the transfer of an undertaking or business are afforded a defined role and given particular rights by the Directive. It provides that 'if the term of office of the representatives … expires as a result of the transfer, the representatives shall continue to enjoy the protections provided by the laws, regulations, administrative provisions or practice of the Member States' against any actions that may be taken against them by employers[3]. Further, the Directive provides that 'if the undertaking, business or part of an undertaking or business preserves its autonomy' and 'the conditions necessary for the constitution of the employees' representation are fulfilled', then 'the status and function of the representatives or of the representation of the employees affected … shall be preserved on the same terms and subject to the same conditions as existed before the date of the transfer by virtue of law, regulation, administrative provision or agreement.[4]'

If, on the other hand, the entity transferred does not 'preserve its autonomy' (ie it ceases to exist independently of the transferee), the Directive provides that 'the Member States shall take the necessary measures to ensure that the employees transferred who were represented before the transfer continue to be properly represented during the period necessary for the reconstitution or reappointment of the representation … in accordance with national law and practice.[5]' Again, this gives the member states a considerable degree of discretion.

However, if the 'conditions necessary for the reappointment of the representatives of the employees or for the reconstruction of the representation of the employees are fulfilled', the status and function of the representatives or of the representation of the employees affected by the transfer, will not be preserved[6]. This may happen, for example, where the undertaking in question is amalgamated into a much larger organisation, which operates a completely different system of representation for its employees.

1   Council Directive 2001/23/EC, art 2(1)(c).
2   C-382/92 [1994] ECR I-2479, ECJ.
3   Council Directive 2001/23/EC, art 6(2).
4   Council Directive 2001/23/EC, art 6(1).
5   Council Directive 2001/23/EC, art 6(1).
6   Council Directive 2001/23/EC, art 6(1).

A2.8 Territorial scope

The Directive applies 'where and in so far as the undertaking, business or part of the undertaking or business to be transferred is situated within the territorial scope of the Treaty (of Rome).[1]' It is where the relevant undertaking is 'situated' (ie its physical location) and not where the legal person or body that owns that undertaking is 'situated' (ie its registered office) that is important. Thus, the Directive does not apply to transfers of undertakings that are physically located outside of the European Community, even if they are owned by individuals or companies who reside or have their registered offices in a member state.

1   Council Directive 2001/23/EC, art 1(2).

A3 Consequences for affected employees

A3.1 Transfer of employment

Transfer of rights and obligations arising from an employment contract

The Directive states that 'the transferor's rights and obligations arising from a contract of employment or from an employment relationship existing on the date of a transfer shall, by reason of such transfer, be transferred to the transferee.[1]' The employment relationships of the affected employees of the transferor are therefore transferred automatically to the transferee, without the need for any of the parties involved to specifically consent to the same[2]. The ECJ reaffirmed this basic principle in *Claude Rotsart de Hertaing v J Benoidt SA (in liquidation) and IGC Housing Service SA*[3] ('*Rotsart*'), holding that the contract of employment of an affected employee of the transferor could not be maintained with the transferor following a transfer, as it was automatically continued with the transferee. In addition, the court confirmed that this process could not be made conditional on the wishes of the parties or be obstructed by the refusal of a transferee to comply with the obligations it inherited as a consequence of a transfer.

Thus, the Directive limits the autonomy of transferees by requiring them to act in accordance with the rights and obligations of transferors vis-à-vis their employees that existed on the date of transfer. Although the ECJ initially interpreted this principle strictly, it held in *Schmidt*[4] that the Directive did not preclude a transferee varying the rights and obligations it inherited from a transferor, in so far as this is permitted by the laws of the relevant member state in situations other than business transfers. The court subsequently reaffirmed this reasoning in *Daddy's Dance Hall*[5] and *Rask*[6], adding the important proviso that the transfer itself must not constitute the principal reason for the variation of terms and conditions (in which case it will be ineffective).

The ECJ developed this approach in *Serene Martin v South Bank University*[7] ('*Martin*'), where it held that, if a transferee offers transferring employees new and less favourable terms and conditions to bring them 'into line' with those of its existing workforce following a transfer, any consent to such variation that is purported to be given by the transferring employees is invalid. Further, transferring employees cannot waive their rights under the Directive nor have them restricted, even if they consent and are compensated by being awarded new benefits by the transferee that mean that, taken as a whole, they are in a better position than prior to the transfer[8]. However, it is possible that transferring employees may be deemed by their conduct to have consented to a variation in their terms and conditions of employment by a transferee, if they continue to work for their new employer on that basis without complaint for a substantial period of time.

In addition to acquiring the transferor's rights and obligations arising from those employment relationships existing on the date of transfer (eg the entitlement of the transferring employees to receive outstanding wages, take accrued annual leave etc)[9], a transferee inherits all liabilities connected with those employment relationships at that point in time (in the UK, such liabilities might include, for example, liability in relation to unfair dismissal, discrimination and personal injury claims). The corollary of this position is that, upon completion of a transfer, the transferor is released from its obligations as employer vis-à-vis the transferring employees[10]. Although this is the 'default position', the Directive confirms 'Member States may provide that, after the date of transfer, the transferor and the transferee shall be jointly and severally liable in respect of obligations which arose before the date of transfer ...[11]'. Certain member states have therefore adopted the principle of joint and several liability for pre-transfer obligations for a set period of time following completion of a transfer.

1   Council Directive 2001/23/EC, art 3(1)
2   Joined Cases 144/87 and 145/87: *Harry Berg and Johannes Theodorus Maria Busschers v Ivo Martin Besselsen* ('*Berg*') [1988] ECR 2559, ECJ.
3   C-305/94: [1996] ECR I-5927, ECJ.
4   C-392/92: *Schmidt v Spar und Leihkasse der früheren Amter Bordesholm, Kiel und Cronshagen* [1994] ECR I-1311, ECJ.
5   *Foreningen af Arbejdsledere i Danmark v Daddy's Dance Hall A/S*: 324/86 [1988] ECR 739, ECJ.
6   C-209/91: *Rask and Christensen v ISS Kantineservice A/S* [1992] ECR I-5755, ECJ.
7   C-4/01 [2004] 1 CMLR 472, ECJ.
8   *Foreningen af Arbejdsledere i Danmark v Daddy's Dance Hall A/S*: 324/86 [1988] ECR 739, ECJ.
9   *Abels v Bedrijfsvereniging voor de Metaalindustrie en de Electrotechnische Industrie*: 135/83 [1985] ECR 469, ECJ.

10   Joined Cases 144/87 and 145/87: *Harry Berg and Johannes Theodorus Maria Busschers v Ivo Martin Besselsen ('Berg')* [1988] ECR 2559, ECJ.
11   Council Directive 2001/23/EC, art 3(1).

Transfer of terms and conditions agreed in collective agreements

In many member states, terms and conditions of employment regulated by collective agreements are automatically incorporated into individual contracts of employment. The Directive states that, following a transfer, 'the transferee shall continue to observe the terms and conditions agreed in any collective agreements on the same terms applicable to the transferor under that agreement, until the date of termination or expiry of the collective agreement or the entry into force or application of another collective agreement.[1]' However, the Directive adds that 'Member States may limit the period for observing such terms and conditions with the proviso that it shall not be less than one year.[2]' The Directive may therefore have the effect, following a transfer, of making the contracts of employment of different parts of a transferee's workforce subject to the terms and conditions of different collective agreements, albeit only for a certain period of time. Notwithstanding this, transferees will obviously not be bound by any post-transfer collective agreements negotiated between transferors and trade unions.

1   Council Directive 2001/23/EC, art 3(3).
2   Council Directive 2001/23/EC, art 3(3).

Occupational pension schemes

The Directive states that 'unless Member States provide otherwise ... employees' rights to old-age, invalidity or survivors' benefits under supplementary company or intercompany pension schemes outside the statutory social security schemes in Member States' are excluded from the protection it confers[1]. However, it also provides that 'Member States shall adopt the measures necessary to protect the interests of employees and of persons no longer employed in the transferor's business at the time of the transfer in respect of rights conferring on them immediate or prospective entitlement to old age benefits ...[2]'.

Unless otherwise required by member states, transferees are not obliged to maintain contributions to transferring employees' occupational pension schemes (with transferors remaining responsible for any liabilities in this regard in accordance with the rules of their schemes). Accrued pension rights are, of course, protected. According to ECJ case law, the exception in the Directive in relation to 'immediate or prospective entitlement(s) to old age benefits' under occupational schemes must be interpreted strictly, as it constitutes an exception to the general rule that all a transferor's rights and obligations arising from its employment relationships with the transferring employees are transferred to the transferee. Only benefits that may be paid from the time an employee reaches the end of his/her 'normal' working life (as laid down by the rules of the relevant occupational scheme) can properly be classified as 'old-age benefits' within the meaning of the Directive. An employer's obligation to pay an employee early retirement benefits in the event of his/her dismissal, in accordance with his/her employment contract or an appropriate collective agreement, for example, does not therefore fall within the exception and will generally transfer to a transferee[3]. The ECJ has confirmed that this is also true of early retirement benefits that are specifically triggered by redundancy[4].

1   Council Directive 2001/23/EC, art 4(a).
2   Council Directive 2001/23/EC, art 4(b).
3   C-164/00: *Katia Beckman v Dynamco Whicheloe Macfarlane Ltd* [2002] ECR I-4893, ECJ.
4   C-4/01: *Serene Martin v South Bank University* [2004] 1 CMLR 472, ECJ.

A3.2 Right to object

As is explained at *A3.1* above, the transfer of employment relationships from a transferor to a transferee occurs automatically, simply by reason of a 'transfer of an undertaking' having taken place. It follows from the stated objective of the Directive to safeguard 'employees' rights in the event of transfers of undertakings (and) businesses' that employers should not be able to prevent the automatic transfer of employment relationships[1]. It is, however, questionable whether employees are obliged to accept the transfer of their employment to another employer upon a transfer.

Whilst the Directive itself does not explicitly afford employees the right to object to the transfer of their employment, the ECJ made it clear in its ruling in *Foreningen af Arbejdsledere i Danmark v A/S Danmols Inventar (in liquidation) ('Mikkelsen')*[2] that an employee's contract of employment does not automatically transfer where he/she decides of his/her own accord to object to the change in the identity of his/her employer and indicate that he/she does not wish to continue his/her employment relationship with the new employer. Indeed, the ECJ has stated on numerous occasions that to oblige employees to accept the transfer of their employment would infringe their fundamental right to choose who they work for[3].

In *Grigorios Katsikas v Angelos Konstantinidis*[4] (*'Katsikas'*), the ECJ confirmed that employees have the 'option' of objecting to the transfer of their contracts of employment upon a 'transfer of an undertaking'. Thus, whilst the Directive protects employees' rights to remain employed by a transferee on the same terms and conditions as they had agreed with a transferor, it does not oblige them to continue their employment relationships with a transferee if they do not wish to do so.

The Directive does not set out the legal consequences of an employee objecting to the transfer of his/her employment relationship (ie it does not state whether, should an employee object to the transfer of his/her employment to the transferee, such employment will continue with the transferor following a transfer). Regulation of this issue is therefore left to the member states. In the UK, for example, a mutual agreement to terminate an employee's contract of employment is deemed to have occurred where he/she objects to its transfer to a transferee. Thus, an employee's somewhat limited right to object to the transfer of his/her employment in the UK, if exercised, has the effect of terminating his/her employment at that point and leaving him/her with no right to claim he/she has been dismissed, unfairly or otherwise, by the transferor.

1   C-305/94: *Claude Rotsart de Hertaing v J Benoidt SA (in liquidation) and IGC Housing Service SA* [1996] ECR I-5927, ECJ; and C-362/89: *d'Urso v Ercole Marelli Elettromeccanica Generale SpA* [1991] ECR I-4105, ECJ.
2   105/84 [1986] 1 CMLR 316, ECJ.
3   See C-171/94: *Merckx and Neuhuys v Ford Motors Co Belgium SA* [1996] IRLR 467, ECJ and C-399/96: *Europièces SA v Sanders & Automotive Industries Holding Co SA* [1998] ECR I-6965, ECJ, for example.
4   C-132/91 [1992] ECR I-6577, ECJ.

A3.3 Protection against dismissal

The Directive provides that 'the transfer of (an) undertaking (or) business or part of (an) undertaking or business shall not in itself constitute grounds for dismissal by the transferor or the transferee.[1]' Dismissals, whether carried out before or after a transfer, are therefore prohibited where the principal reason for them is the transfer itself or a connected reason. Whilst this provision does not protect 'certain specific categories of employees who are not covered by the laws or practice of the Member States in respect of protection against dismissal'[2], the ECJ has stated that this exception must be construed restrictively and stressed that member states must not deprive employees of such protection in so far as they enjoy security, no matter how limited, against dismissal under their national laws[3].

This basic prohibition has the aim of preventing employers frustrating the Directive's objective of safeguarding employees' rights on transfers by terminating their employment. However, the Directive adds an important caveat: 'this provision shall not stand in the way of dismissals that may take place for economic, technical or organisational reasons entailing changes in the workforce.[4]' Whilst the ECJ has given no explicit guidance on what might constitute valid 'economic, technical or organisational reasons' for such dismissals, it is clear that, to fall within the ambit of the exception, an employer must genuinely be motivated by a reason of this nature and have acted fairly in all the circumstances, as well as reasonably, in treating that reason as sufficient reason for a dismissal. The ECJ has confirmed that both transferors and transferees can rely upon the exception [5].

Thus, where there is a transfer-related dismissal for 'economic, technical or organisational reasons entailing changes in the workforce' of either the transferor or the transferee, the dismissal is, prima facie, lawful. In *Bork*[6], the ECJ held that it was for the national courts to determine, considering all the circumstances, the true reason for an employer dismissing an employee. In this regard, the court stated that they should take particular note of whether the dismissal in question took place at a time close to that of the relevant transfer and whether the employee in question was subsequently re-engaged by the transferee. In practice, transferees are sometimes advised to wait until 12 months have passed following a transfer before dismissing employees or substantially amending their contracts of employment (and therefore risking claims of 'constructive dismissal') in the absence of 'economic, technical or organisational reasons entailing changes in the workforce', as, after this time, it is supposedly less likely that such dismissals or variations will be found to be connected with the transfer. However, it should be remembered that the passage of time is only an indicator in this regard and there is no guarantee as to how a particular court or tribunal will decide such issues.

If a national court decides that an employee has been dismissed as a consequence of a business transfer and not for an 'economic, technical or organisational reason', or that he/she has been dismissed for such a reason, yet the dismissal was nonetheless unfair, the dismissal is, on the face of it, in breach of the Directive. In the majority of member states, a dismissal in breach of the Directive is deemed void, such that if a transferor attempts to carry one out prior to a planned transfer, the affected employee will remain an employee of the relevant undertaking up to the date of transfer, and the transferor's rights and obligations in relation to him/her will be automatically transferred to the transferee at that point. However, member states such as the UK do not recognise the concept of nullity in relation to dismissals in breach of the Directive. Accordingly, if a transferor in the UK attempted to carry out such a dismissal before a planned transfer, it would be effective, but the affected employee would be entitled to claim he/she had been unfairly dismissed, and liability in this regard would transfer to the transferee.

It is therefore unclear whether, in a pre-transfer situation where an employer attempts to dismiss an employee for something other than an 'economic, technical or organisational reason entailing changes in the workforce', that dismissal should properly be classified as void or whether, in accordance with the Directive's aim of achieving only 'partial harmonisation' of the laws of the member states, the legal consequences of such a dismissal should be left to be regulated by the national courts. The ECJ has not yet confirmed which is the preferred approach.

1   Council Directive 2001/23/EC, art 4(1).
2   Council Directive 2001/23/EC, art 4(1).
3   *European Commission v Belgium*: 237/84 [1986] ECR 1247, ECJ.
4   Council Directive 2001/23/EC, art 4(1).
5   C-319/94: *Jules Dethier Equipement SA v Jules Dassy & Sovam SPRL* [1998] ECR I-1061, ECJ.
6   *P Bork International A/S (in liquidation) v Foreningen af Arbejdsledere i Danmark, acting on behalf of Birger E Petersen, and Jens E Olsen v Junckers Industrier A/S*: 101/87 [1988] ECR 3057, ECJ.

A3.4 Constructive dismissal

In a provision that appears to have been modelled on the UK concept of 'constructive dismissal', the Directive states that 'if the contract of employment or the employment relationship is terminated because the transfer involves a substantial change in working conditions to the detriment of the employee, the employer shall be regarded as having been responsible for termination of the contract of employment or of the employment relationship.[1]' Thus, if an employee of a transferor resigns in anticipation of a 'substantial' and detrimental change in his/her terms and conditions of employment as a consequence of a proposed transfer, he/she will have been 'constructively dismissed' and will potentially have a claim against his/her current employer.

Obviously, the key question is what amounts to a 'substantial change in working conditions'. Ultimately, this is a matter for the national courts to decide, having considered the relevance of the working condition in question, as well as the degree of change involved. Although there is little ECJ case law on this issue, the court has held that a change in the level of an employee's remuneration could potentially satisfy this requirement[2]. In the UK, constructive dismissals in response to 'substantial' changes in working conditions upon transfers are classified as 'automatically unfair' for the purposes of unfair dismissal legislation[3].

1   Council Directive 2001/23/EC, art 4(2).
2   C-171/94: *Merckx and Neuhuys v Ford Motors Co Belgium SA* [1996] IRLR 467, ECJ.
3   Transfer of Undertakings (Protection of Employment) Regulations 1981, reg 8(1).

A4 Information and consultation

A4.1 Duty of the transferor and the transferee to inform

In order that the relevant employees are aware of the potential impact on them of a proposed transfer, the Directive requires the transferor and the transferee 'to inform the representatives of their respective employees affected by the transfer of the following:

–   the date or proposed date of the transfer;

–   the reasons for the transfer;

–   the legal, economic and social implications of the transfer for the employees; and

–   any measures envisaged in relation to the employees.[1]'

This requirement extends to all employees who are likely to be affected by a proposed transfer or by any 'measures' taken in connection with it, whether they are employed by the transferor or the transferee. For the transferor, this might include employees who are not actually transferred, but retained following a transfer. For the transferee, it might include employees who are likely to be affected by the influx of transferred employees following a transfer.

The Directive requires that both the transferor and the transferee 'give such information to the representatives of his employees in good time before the transfer is carried out[2]', although it does not impose a specific time limit in this regard or specify the sanction(s) that member states should apply in the event of a failure to inform and consult. The Directive imposes an additional obligation on the transferee to provide its employees' representatives with such information 'before his employees are directly affected by the transfer as regards their conditions of work and employment.[3]'

1   Council Directive 2001/23/EC, art 7(1).
2   Council Directive 2001/23/EC, art 7(1).
3   Council Directive 2001/23/EC, art 7(1).

A4.2   Duty of the transferor and the transferee to consult

Where the transferor or the transferee 'envisages measures in relation to his employees' will be taken with regard to a transfer, the Directive requires that they provide the necessary information to, and 'consult [with] the representatives of [those] employees in good time on such measures with a view to reaching an agreement'[1]. Thus, employees' representatives only have the right to be consulted in relation to 'measures' (eg changes to terms and conditions of employment, a reduction in the workforce etc) envisaged by employers that are likely to affect the employees they represent. A transferor's obligation to consult with regard to 'measures' might extend to those which it foresees the transferee will take in relation to the transferring employees following the transfer (such details having been provided by the transferee) as well as those the transferor foresees it will take.

Consultation must take place regardless of whether an employer anticipates staff will be dismissed and information must be provided to employees' representatives far enough in advance to ensure consultation will be meaningful. The Directive provides for a degree of employee participation in the decision-making process by stipulating that consultation must be carried out 'with a view to reaching an agreement' in relation to the proposed 'measures'. Although an employer is obliged to consider any representations made by the employees' representatives and reply to them (ie if suggestions from the employees' representatives are rejected by an employer, reasons should be given), the employees' representatives do not have the right to veto any decisions made by a transferor or transferee in this regard.

The Directive provides that, where a member state's laws, regulations or administrative provisions 'provide that representatives of the employees may have recourse to an arbitration board to obtain a decision on the measures to be taken in relation to employees', that member state may limit the duties of information and consultation set out above 'to cases where the transfer carried out gives rise to a change in the business likely to entail serious disadvantages for a considerable number of employees.[2]' However, the Directive states that the transferor's and transferee's information and consultation processes in such situations must still 'cover at least the measures envisaged in relation to the employees' and 'take place in good time before the change in the business … is effected.[3]'

1   Council Directive 2001/23/EC, art 7(2).
2   Council Directive 2001/23/EC, art 7(3).
3   Council Directive 2001/23/EC, art 7(3).

A4.3 Transnational companies

The Directive makes it clear that the duties of information and consultation it imposes 'shall apply irrespective of whether the decision resulting in the transfer is taken by the employer or an undertaking controlling the employer', adding that 'in considering alleged breaches (of these duties), the argument that such a breach occurred because the information was not provided by an undertaking controlling the employer shall not be accepted as an excuse'[1]. The potential impact of these provisions on transnational companies is obvious.

1   Council Directive 2001/23/EC, art 7(4).

A4.4 Small businesses

To ensure that employees are adequately informed in all situations, the Directive stipulates 'Member States shall provide that, where there are no representatives of the employees in an undertaking or business through no fault of their own, the employees concerned must be informed in advance' of the details set out at *A4.1* above[1]. This provision was included within the Directive to ensure that workers employed in relation to small businesses or businesses without sophisticated systems of representation are still informed where they are likely to be affected by a transfer. The Directive does not, however, impose a duty for the transferor or the transferee to inform the employees 'in good time' or to consult with them in these circumstances.

1   Council Directive 2001/23/EC, art 7(6).

A5 Implementation

Member states must ensure that, whichever methods they adopt in order to do so, they fully implement the terms of the Directive. Accordingly, in *European Commission v Italy*[1], whilst the ECJ accepted that collective agreements were a legitimate means of establishing information and consultation procedures with regard to transfers, it held that, since the collective agreements in question only covered certain economic sectors, the Italian Government was obliged to introduce further legislation to ensure full compliance with the provisions of the Directive. Further, as set out at **A1** above, member states are free to apply or introduce laws, regulations or administrative provisions that are more favourable to employees than those contained in the Directive.

The Directive imposes an obligation on member states to 'introduce into their national legal systems such measures as are necessary to enable all employees and representatives of employees who consider themselves wronged by failure to comply with the obligations arising from [it] to pursue claims by judicial process after possible recourse to other competent authorities.[2]' It is in this way that employees and their representatives are expected to enforce their rights in the event that transferors or transferees do not adequately recognise or protect them.

1   235/84 [1986] ECR 2291, ECJ.
2   Council Directive 2001/23/EC, art 9.

A6 Conclusion

The introduction and application of the Directive has been extremely controversial, both legally and politically. Whilst the very subject matter of the Directive means that it is always likely to be politically contentious, the legal controversies surrounding it have been heightened by the fact that the ECJ's case law in this area is particularly complicated and has not been entirely consistent. Further, that the Directive was only ever intended as a means of achieving 'partial harmonisation' of national laws has led to a considerable divergence in implementing legislation, regulations and administrative provisions across member states. This has, in turn, led to a divergence in the level of protection provided for employees in the European Community.

A more extensive analysis of the impact of the Directive and its implementation and application in the member states can be found in Chapters **J–S**.

B Collective redundancies

Emma Frost

B1 The Collective Redundancies Directive

B1.1 Background

The Collective Redundancies Directive 75/129/EEC (the '1975 Directive') introduced the obligation for employers to inform and consult with workers' representatives on collective redundancies. It recognised the importance of employers establishing procedures for informing and consulting workers' representatives in the event of collective redundancies (defined to mean the dismissal of workers above a specified minimum number, effected by an employer for one or more reasons not related to the individual workers concerned) and sought to approximate the laws of the member states, who were required to implement the directive within two years following its notification (ie by 17 February 1977). The 1975 Directive aimed to provide workers with greater protection in the event of mass redundancies.

In June 1992, the Council of Member States adopted a further Directive (1992/56/EEC) (the '1992 Directive') which amended the 1975 Directive in order to make the information and consultation obligations for employers more comprehensive. The 1992 Directive was implemented pursuant to the Community Charter of the Fundamental Social Rights of Workers, which was adopted at the European Council meeting held in Strasbourg on 9 December 1989.

The current obligations for informing and consulting on collective redundancies are governed by Council Directive 98/59/EC of 20 July 1998 on the approximation of the laws of the member states relating to collective redundancies (the 'Directive'). The Directive consolidated the 1975 Directive, as subsequently amended in 1992. A key principle behind the Directive is that employers should consult workers' representatives at an early stage, with the aim of reaching an agreement regarding collective redundancies and their implementation. The Directive attempts to strike a balance between the economic needs of employers and the social requirements of workers. Employers contemplating mass redundancies are required to take part in a meaningful information and consultation process with workers' representatives. The intention is to provide workers' representatives with a realistic chance of influencing an employer's decisions regarding collective redundancies before they are finally made. This means that, before any major business restructuring plans are publicly announced by an employer, the information and consultation process should have been followed.

Member states were granted some discretion when transposing the Directive into their national legislation and, accordingly, the laws relating to collective redundancies in each member state differ. A purposive approach needs to be taken when interpreting domestic legislation enacted to implement the directives mentioned above – domestic legislation must be applied in such a way that it conforms with Community law. This rule was expressed in wide terms in the case of *Marleasing SA v La Comercial Internacional de Aliment-ación SA*[1] where the ECJ stated that 'in applying national law, a national court must interpret it, as far as possible, in the light of the wording and purpose of any relevant EEC directive, whether the national law originated before or after adoption of the directive.'

The Directive also expressly states that member states may introduce or apply provisions with regard to collective redundancies which are more favourable to workers than those contained within it. This has added to the inevitable differences between the obligations imposed on employers by each member state. However, the Directive did not seek to harmonise member states' laws in this area completely, but rather to approximate the laws. Member states were given a degree of flexibility when implementing the Directive, so that they could do so in the most suitable way according to their national laws and practice.

1   C-106/89 [1992] 1 CMLR 305.

B1.2 The scope of the Directive

'Collective redundancies' are defined in the Directive as:

'dismissals effected by an employer for one or more reasons not related to the individual workers concerned where, according to the choice of the Member States, the number of redundancies is:

(i) either, over a period of 30 days:
- at least 10 in establishments normally employing more than 20 and less than 100 workers,
- at least 10% of the number of workers in establishments normally employing at least 100 but less than 300 workers,
- at least 30 in establishments normally employing 300 workers or more;

(ii) or, over a period of 90 days, at least 20, whatever the number of workers normally employed in the establishments in question' (art 1(1)(a)).

When calculating the 'number of redundancies' (referred to within art 1(1)(a)), 'terminations of an employment contract due to the employer's initiative for one or more reasons not related to the individual workers concerned shall be assimilated to redundancies, provided that there are at least five redundancies.' This means that employees leaving an employer due to voluntary early retirement and negotiated terminations should be included in the number of dismissals for the quantitative part of the definition for 'collective redundancies'.

The Directive does not define the term 'worker'. However, Lord MacKenzie Stuart, in *Mikkelsen v Danmols Inventar A/S*[1], when considering the Directive and the Acquired Rights Directive 2001/23/EC, stated that 'the question as to whether a person is to be regarded as a "worker" is to be decided according to the law of each Member State'.

1 [1986] 1 CMLR 316.

B1.3 Meaning of 'establishment'

When assessing whether or not the Directive applies, it is necessary to look at the number of redundancies planned at a particular 'establishment'. The term 'establishment' is not defined in the Directive, despite the meaning of this term being key to its interpretation. The term 'establishment' was also used in the 1975 Directive and arguments subsequently ensued over its precise meaning. It was therefore decided that all member states needed to have a uniform interpretation of the term 'establishment' in the context of the Directive. As a term of Community law, it could not be defined by reference to the laws of the member states.

In *Rockfon A/S v Specialarbejderforbundet i Danmark*[1], the ECJ decided that the concept of an 'establishment' for the purposes of the Directive should be interpreted as meaning the unit to which workers who it is anticipated will be made redundant are assigned to carry out their duties. It is not essential, in order for it to be classified as an establishment, for the unit in question to have a management which can independently effect collective redundancies (as defined in the Directive). This interpretation was determined by the ECJ by reference to the purpose and general principles of the Directive and the circumstances in which the Directive was adopted.

1 [1996] IRLR 168.

B1.4 Application of the Directive

The Directive does not apply to:

'(a) collective redundancies effected under contracts of employment concluded for limited periods of time or for specific tasks except where such redundancies take place prior to the date of expiry or the completion of such contracts;

(b) workers employed by public administrative bodies or by establishments governed by public law (or, in Member States where this concept is unknown, by equivalent bodies);

(c) the crews of seagoing vessels' (art 1(2)).

The obligations on employers to inform, consult and notify workers' representatives apply regardless of whether the decision on collective redundancies is made by the worker's employer or its parent company. This prevents companies belonging to the same group making it more difficult for the Directive to apply to them by transferring the power to make decisions relating to collective redundancies to separate decision-making bodies.

Employers are not therefore able to use the defence that the necessary information was not provided by the controlling undertaking which took the decision on the redundancies.

The Directive also applies in principle to collective redundancies resulting from a cessation of activities due to a court judgment (ie insolvency situations).

B1.5 Information and consultation

Where an employer is contemplating collective redundancies, he must begin consultations with workers' representatives in good time with a view to reaching an agreement (art 2(1)).

The term 'workers' representatives' must be interpreted in accordance with each member state's laws and/or practices. In general, such representatives tend to be trade union representatives or elected employee representatives.

The representatives consult on behalf of all workers 'affected' by the proposed collective redundancies. This is a broad requirement, as the employer has a duty to consult with representatives on how the remaining workers will be affected by the proposed redundancies as well as in relation to those workers who may actually be dismissed.

To enable workers' representatives to make constructive proposals, employers are obliged to supply them with all relevant information in good time during the course of the consultation, and to notify them in writing of:

- the reasons for the proposed redundancies;

- the number of categories of workers to be made redundant;

- the number and categories of workers normally employed;

- the period over which the proposed redundancies are to be effected;

- the criteria proposed for the selection of workers to be made redundant;

- the method for calculating any redundancy payments (art 2(3)).

The Directive sets a high standard of disclosure for the employer by requiring that 'all relevant information' be given to the workers' representatives during the consultation process.

The Directive gives member states the option, when implementing the Directive, to provide for workers' representatives to be able to request assistance from experts on the grounds of the technical complexity of the matters on which the information and consultation process is based.

B1.6 Timing of the consultation

The Directive utilises the phrase 'contemplating collective redundancies'. This phrase was also used in the 1975 Directive and attention following its implementation focused on the precise date on which the employer was supposed to commence consultation. UK domestic legislation (at that time) stated that consultation should begin as soon as the employer 'proposed' collective redundancies. UK case law focused on the distinction between the Directive requiring consultation to begin when collective redundancies were 'contemplated' and the requirement under UK legislation for consultation to begin when collective redundancies were 'proposed'. There was considerable debate over the exact meaning of these words and the appropriate time for consultation to commence, given that an employer could face a claim for a 'protective award' if consultation was delayed. A protective award is an award of pay for a 'protected period' to the workers affected by an employer's failure to consult properly. The maximum 'protected period' is 90 days. In the UK case of *Re Hartlebury Printers Ltd*[1], the judge stated that 'the range of mental states included within the word "contemplation" is wide and would extend from merely "thinking about" to "having in view or expecting".' In the UK case of *R v British Coal Corpn and Secretary of State for Trade and Industry, ex p Vardy*[2], Judge Glidewell determined that the wording in the UK legislation ('proposed') was not compatible with the wording in the 1975 Directive ('contemplated'). He stated that the verbs could not be interpreted as having an equivalent meaning. Judge Glidewell interpreted the requirement to consult when collective redundancies are 'contemplated' as being 'at an early stage when the employer is first envisaging the possibility that he may have to make employees redundant', whereas the requirement to consult under UK legislation when collective redundancies are 'proposed' was interpreted as meaning when the employer has decided that 'it is his intention, however reluctant, to make employees redundant.'

The UK case law illustrates the difficulties experienced by courts in interpreting the 1975 Directive, as transposed into national legislation, with regard to the precise timing of the consultation process. It is submitted that the use of the word 'contemplating' means that consultation with workers' representatives must begin before an irrevocable decision to carry out redundancies has been taken by an employer. This raises the question of when the consultation process has actually begun. Commentators suggest that consultation can only be deemed to have commenced when the workers' representatives have been provided with sufficient information by the employer to enable meaningful consultation to take place. This is essentially a question of fact to be determined in each particular case. However, the obligation to consult is capable of being triggered before the employer is in a position to provide workers' representatives with 'all relevant information'.

In addition (due to the 1992 amendments), the Directive states that consultation should begin 'in good time'. This changes the focus from the precise time at which consultation should commence to the adequacy of the time given for the consultation process. The wording in the Directive does not provide employers with a definitive answer as to exactly when the consultation process should start. However, provided the consultation process has started in good time to allow all the issues to be properly addressed with the workers' representatives, the employer will have complied with its duty to consult.

As mentioned at *B1.4* above, the Directive applies to collective redundancies 'where the establishment's activities are terminated as a result of a judicial decision'. The employer is under a duty to consult as soon as collective redundancies are contemplated. Therefore, if the employer does not foresee the closure of the relevant establishment due to a court judgment, it does not have within its contemplation the resulting collective redundancies and, accordingly, no obligation to consult arises. In the case of *Dansk Metal v Nielsen*[3], the ECJ held that there 'is no implied obligation under the Directive to foresee collective redundancies. It does not stipulate the circumstances in which the employer must contemplate collective redundancies and in no way affects his freedom to decide whether and when he must formulate plans for collective dismissals.' However, if the employer does foresee the making of a judicial decision and therefore contemplates collective redundancies, it would be under an obligation to consult.

1   [1992] IRLR 516.
2   [1993] 1 CMLR 721.
3   [1986] 1 CMLR 91.

B1.7 Scope of the consultation

It is important for an employer to understand the full extent of the consultation exercise it is obliged to carry out in accordance with the Directive. It is hard to assess the extent of the requirement to consult 'with a view to reaching an agreement'. Whilst it cannot be classed as a duty to bargain, it definitely means more than giving workers' representatives notice of the projected redundancies and then listening to their responses. Although the Directive does not require an agreement to be reached, the employer and the workers' representatives must consult in good faith, engaging in serious and substantive discussions that give the representatives the opportunity to make constructive proposals. The use of the phrase 'with a view to reaching an agreement' highlights that consultation should not just be procedural. An employer should begin consultation with an open mind and make a real effort to take into account the concerns of the workers' representatives. It may be the case that the employer and the workers' representatives cannot reach an agreement. The consultation process is not open-ended and there may come a point when the employer will want to implement the proposed redundancies. As long as the employer has shown a willingness to take account of the workers' representatives' proposals and the possibility of reaching an agreement has been exhausted, the employer will have complied with its duty to consult.

The consultation should at least 'cover ways and means of avoiding collective redundancies or reducing the number of workers affected, and of mitigating the consequences by recourse to accompanying social measures aimed, inter alia, at aid for redeploying or retraining workers made redundant' (art 2(2)).

The wording 'by recourse to accompanying social measures aimed, inter alia, at aid for redeploying or retraining workers made redundant' was introduced by the 1992 amendments, thereby widening the scope of the consultation required to include the alleviation of the consequences of redundancy.

There is no clear judicial authority on whether the employer is required to consult over the reasons for making the proposed redundancies. Although the employer must consult on whether any redundancies should be made, this does not necessarily mean that workers' representatives have the right to a participative role in the commercial decision-making process. The Directive does not stipulate that representatives have the right to participate in the actual formulation of the employer's commercial plans. Although the management of an employer is still responsible for making the ultimate decision, it should bear in mind that engaging with its workforce in this process can lead to better decisions being made and industrial relations being improved.

B1.8 Procedure for collective redundancies

An employer must notify the competent public authority (the 'Authority') in writing of any collective redundancies it proposes to make. For example, in the UK the employer must send written notification of any planned collective redundancies to the Secretary of State for Trade and Industry. This notification must include all the relevant information concerning the proposed redundancies and the consultations held with workers' representatives. A copy of the notification must be sent to the workers' representatives, who may then send any comments they have to the Authority (art 4).

The earliest that proposed collective redundancies can take effect is 30 days after the requisite notification has been given to the Authority. This 30-day period is to be used by the Authority to seek solutions. The Directive therefore envisages an interventionist role on the part of the Authority.

Under the Directive, member states may grant the Authority either the power to reduce this 30-day period or, if the problems raised by the proposed collective redundancies are not likely to be resolved within this time frame, the power to extend the period to 60 days. The employer must be informed (before the initial period has expired) of any such extension and the reasons for it. The Directive also gives member states the discretion to grant wider powers of extension to the Authority.

The Directive states that it is not compulsory for member states to apply this 30-day period to collective redundancies due to a cessation of activities resulting from a court judgment. However, if a member state does choose to apply the requirements of art 4 of the Directive in these circumstances (ie the cessation of an establishment's activities as a result of a court judgment), the notification of the collective redundancies is only necessary if the Authority specifically requests it.

The Directive states that the duty to consult arises when collective redundancies are 'contemplated' (see *B1.6* above) and that the duty to notify the

Authority arises when there are 'any projected collective redundancies'. The Directive seems to envisage that these will arise at different stages of the employer's thought process, with the notification to the Authority taking place when the employer has made the decision to carry out the redundancies following consultation.

It is crucial for employers to comply with the proper notification process, because the timetable for effecting any proposed redundancies is not set in motion until the requisite notification has been given to the Authority.

B1.9 Enforcement

Member states must ensure that judicial and/or administrative procedures for enforcing the obligations under the Directive are available to workers' representatives and/or workers (art 6).

The Directive does not stipulate any financial sanctions for non-compliance by employers with the information and consultation obligations. It simply states that member states must have legal or administrative procedures in place for enforcement of the Directive by workers' representatives or workers.

> 'Where a Community Directive does not specifically provide any penalty for an infringement or refers for that purpose to national laws, regulations and administrative provisions, Article 5 of the Treaty requires the Member States to take all measures necessary to guarantee the application and effectiveness of Community law. For that purpose, while the choice of penalties remains within their discretion, they must ensure in particular that infringements of Community law are penalised under conditions which, in any event make the penalty effective, proportionate and dissuasive[1].'

There are significant differences between the sanctions imposed by member states for breach of information or consultation obligations under the Directive. In some states (eg France and Spain), if the employer has breached its duties in this regard, the dismissals are rendered void, whereas in other countries (eg the UK and Denmark) the employees would only have a financial sanction imposed on them. In the UK, the employment tribunals/courts have the discretion to make a protective award against the employer for a maximum period of 90 days for failing to inform and consult on collective redundancies in accordance with the Directive (see *B1.6* above). In the recent UK case of *Susie Radin Ltd v GMB*[2], the Court of Appeal established the presumption that an employer's failure to inform and consult on collective redundancies should automatically attract the maximum protective award (and should only be reduced if there are mitigating factors justifying a reduction). In his judgment, Gibson LJ states that, whilst the employment tribunals/courts have a 'wide discretion to do what is just and equitable in all the circumstances ... the focus should be on the seriousness of the employer's default'. The case reiterates that the purpose of the protective award is to ensure that employers carry out proper consultation processes and makes the sanction for breach by employers of their legal obligations in this regard, more dissuasive.

It has been questioned whether the level of fines implemented by member states for breach of the Directive by employers is high enough to act as a deterrent. The new Information and Consultation Directive 2002/14/EC requires the sanctions applied by member states to be 'effective, proportionate and dissuasive'. The decision of the Court of Appeal in *Susie Radin Ltd v GMB* shows that the UK is taking a stricter approach to deter employers from failing to consult with workers' representatives in relation to collective redundancies. This change reflects the importance of the information and consultation process. However, it remains to be seen if the sanctions applied in other member states will be increased as a result of the changing culture.

1   *European Commission v United Kingdom* [1994] IRLR 412.
2   [2004] EWCA Civ 180, [2004] IRLR 400.

B2 Developments

In a resolution on 18 February 2000, the European Parliament directed the European Commission to evaluate the application of the Directive and to propose financial sanctions for infringement by employers, together with proposals for the general improvement of the Directive. There was also a call for the Commission to reform Community legislation and its directives to allow affected workers to contest (within local courts) the economic grounds of financially motivated plans for collective redundancies put forward by employers, before the redundancies put forward by employers are actually announced.

Despite the fact that collective redundancies have been controlled by a European Directive since 1975, there are still significant differences between the member states' laws in this area. However, given the flexibility built into the original directive and the subsequent directives, this is not surprising. At the moment, it is difficult for multinational employers to draw up integrated restructuring plans that span different European countries, as the legal framework in relation to collective redundancies varies so widely between member states.

In May 2001, the European Commission announced a package of measures designed to help reduce the impact on workers of corporate restructuring decisions. This included a commitment to certain legislative measures. It also included the following checklist of best practices for companies that are considering major restructuring:

●   Inform and consult employees at the earliest opportunity on the anticipated business environment and business prospects.

●   Involve all stakeholders in the design of restructuring plans.

- Keep redundancies to a minimum through redeployment within the company or, failing that, securing alternative employment in spin-off or other enterprises.

- Promote the employability of employees and life-long learning, at all times.

- Provide additional specific training at times of restructuring for those likely to be adversely affected.

- Be prepared to help fund the creation of alternative employment opportunities through supporting specific projects or establishing a special development fund.

- Be willing, where necessary, to use outside mediation to achieve solutions acceptable to all parties.

Since the Directive came into being, the information and consultation duties of employers have been enhanced generally by the European Works Council Directive and the European Company Statute (see Chapter **C**).

The Information and Consultation Directive 2002/14/EC essentially requires employers to inform workers' representatives on an ongoing basis about matters such as strategic planning and the company's economic performance, with a specific duty to consult on proposed measures affecting job security, terms and conditions of employment or work organisation (see Chapter **C**). Its introduction may lead to greater harmonisation of the obligations imposed on employers by each member state.

Over the next few years, it is expected that there will be gradual changes in management practices, reflecting the evolving information and consultation culture, with increased employee involvement in commercial decision-making processes.

C Information and consultation

Amanda Sheridan

C1 Introduction

The promotion of communication between management and labour is an important objective of the European Union, as set out in the Treaty of Rome (art 136). This objective has been pursued against a background of conflict, not only between individual member states, but also between employers and employee representatives within those member states. A major problem has been widespread resistance to giving employees a legal right to participate in their employers' decision-making processes. Difficulties have arisen because of the wide variety of information and consultation structures that already exist in member states. For example, in the United Kingdom and Ireland, there is very little governmental control of employee representation, and most companies are run by management boards on which workers are not represented. In other countries, notably France and Germany, there are well-established traditions of state regulation in this area, and employees generally have a legal right to be represented on management boards,

Despite these problems, the European Union has passed legislation to increase employee representation in the management of the entities in which they are employed and to broaden employers' duties to inform and consult their workforces. There are now a number of European Directives setting out minimum requirements for informing and consulting employees in certain situations:

- The Acquired Rights Directive 2001/23/EC

- The Collective Redundancies Directive 98/59/EC

- The European Works Council Directive 94/45/EC

- The Information and Consultation Directive 2002/14/EC

- The Employee Involvement Directive 2001/86/EC

In order to take account of existing cultural and legal differences in respect of information and consultation, these Directives tend to set out a basic framework, leaving member states to clarify the detail in the way that is best suited to their national laws and practices. Part 4 of this book illustrates the differences in the way in which the member states have implemented the Directives. Varying interpretations of European legislation by national courts account for further differences in the laws and practices of member states.

The latest Directives to come into force are indicative of a trend towards giving employees greater rights to information and consultation about their employer's general economic situation and its possible impact on their employment, sometimes even before commercial decisions are taken. This is in addition to employees' existing rights to be consulted in particular situations such as collective redundancies or business transfers. There is also a trend towards implementing transnational arrangements for employee consultation, as seen in the European Works Council Directive and the Employee Involvement Directive, although the Employee Involvement Directive is voluntary in the sense that it applies only to companies who choose to set up a new form of European company. Inevitably, there is some overlap in the scope of these Directives. However, the requirements in each Directive constitute separate obligations and a new Directive cannot be used as an excuse to reduce employees' rights to a level below that which exists under their national law.

C2 The European Works Council Directive

Council Directive 94/45/EC of 22 September 1994 on the establishment of a European Works Council or a procedure in Community-scale undertakings and Community-scale groups of undertakings for the purpose of informing and consulting employees.

C2.1 Background

The European Works Council Directive ('the EWC Directive') came into force on 22 September 1994 and its provisions had to be incorporated into the laws of the member states by 22 September 1996. A European Works Council ('EWC') is essentially a council set up in accordance with the EWC Directive to inform and consult employees, although it is often forgotten that, under the EWC Directive, an alternative procedure for informing and consulting employees ('ICP') can be set up. The EWC Directive has a long and difficult history and talks during its negotiation broke down several times, not least because the United Kingdom government was fundamentally opposed to its introduction. The EWC Directive arose out of the recognition that there was no efficient structure in place to cover the increasing number of companies operating across several EU countries, and the consequent increase in the number of cross-border transfers of employees within the EU. There was a concern that corporate decisions could be taken in one member state that would have a fundamental impact on employees in another member state, and that these situations were not covered by the existing Acquired Rights Directive or the Collective Redundancies Directive. The purpose of the EWC Directive was therefore to improve the right to information and consultation for employees in certain types of undertaking operating in more than one member state, but only if those employees wanted to benefit from that improvement. The structure of the EWCs envisaged in the EWC Directive is taken, to a large degree, from the French and German models of works councils, although the EWC Directive itself is not particularly prescriptive, since it had to take into account the wide differences in national information and consultation structures.

A key principle behind the EWC Directive is that the central management of an entity and its EWC must work together in a spirit of co-operation, with due regard to their reciprocal rights and obligations (art 9). This provision reflects the fear that management could seek to control an EWC.

As mentioned above, it is possible under the EWC Directive to establish a different transnational procedure for informing and consulting employees (an 'ICP') rather than an EWC. Central management and employees' representatives are under a similar duty to work in a spirit of co-operation, with due regard for each other's rights, in relation to an ICP arrangement (art 9).

The EWC Directive is being reviewed by the European Commission during 2004. This may result in some amendments being made, which would probably be adopted in Spring 2005. Some of the legal and practical problems highlighted by the European Commission and other interested parties during the consultation process that has taken place as part of this review include:

- the absence of any provision in the EWC Directive requiring an adaptation clause in agreements to cover changes in the structures of undertakings or groups of undertakings;

- the lack of clarity in relation to the timescale for informing and consulting employees;

- the lack of training (including language training) or rights to take time off for such training for relevant employees and employees' representatives;

- weaknesses in enforcement mechanisms at national and European level;

- weaknesses in the protection and rights of employees' representatives;

- in addition, the existing threshold in respect of the size of workforces may be reduced to bring a greater number of undertakings within the scope of the EWC Directive; and

- the minimum and maximum numbers of members of an EWC may be changed as a result of the expansion of the EU in May 2004.

C2.2 The territorial scope of the EWC Directive

The EWC Directive applies to the EU countries and to three EEA members: Norway, Lichtenstein and Iceland. References to member states in this section of the chapter therefore include these additional countries.

When the EWC Directive came into force in 1994, it did not apply to the United Kingdom because the United Kingdom government had not signed the Social Chapter of the 1992 Maastricht Treaty. In 1997, the United Kingdom's opt-out from the Social Chapter ended with the Amsterdam Treaty, and the scope of the EWC Directive was extended to cover the United Kingdom.

Member states have to ensure that the management of undertakings in their territory complies with the EWC Directive regardless of whether the entity in question is managed centrally in that territory (art 11).

C2.3 Community-scale undertakings and groups of undertakings

The EWC Directive provides that an EWC or an ICP must be established in every 'Community-scale undertaking' and every 'Community-scale group of undertakings'.

For the purposes of the EWC Directive, a 'Community-scale undertaking' means any undertaking with at least 1,000 employees within the member states, of which at least 150 employees must be employed in each of at least two member states (art 2(1)(a)). The EWC Directive therefore only affects very large transnational businesses.

A 'group of undertakings' is defined as a 'controlling undertaking' and its 'controlled undertakings' (art 2(1)(b)). A 'controlling undertaking' is 'an undertaking which can exercise a dominant influence over another undertaking' (ie 'the controlled undertaking'), for example by virtue of ownership, financial participation or its governing rules (art 3(1)). The ability to exercise a dominant influence, and therefore control, is presumed (unless proved otherwise) when an undertaking:

(a)   holds a majority of another undertaking's subscribed capital; or

(b)   controls a majority of the votes attached to that undertaking's issued share capital; or

(c)   can appoint more than half the members of that undertaking's administrative, management or supervisory body.

A dominant influence will not be presumed where an office holder is exercising his functions in insolvency proceedings or arrangements with creditors (art 3(5)). In most corporate structures, it will be clear which is the 'controlling undertaking'. However, the position may be less clear in partnerships, franchises and other commercial structures. If two or more undertakings satisfy one or more of the criteria set out in (a), (b) and (c) above, point (c) will be the decisive factor (art 3(7)).

The law to be applied when determining whether an undertaking is a 'controlling undertaking' is the law of the member state which governs that undertaking. If this governing law is the law of a non-EU state, the applicable law is:

•   the law of the member state where the representative of the undertaking is situated; or, if there is no representative,

•   the law of the member state where the 'central management' of the group undertaking that employs the greatest number of employees is situated (art 3(6)).

'Central management' is defined in the EWC Directive as the central management of the 'Community-scale undertaking' or, in the case of a 'Community-scale group of undertakings', of the 'controlling undertaking' (art 2(1)(e)).

A 'Community-scale group of undertakings' means a group of undertakings with:

- at least 1,000 employees within the member states; and

- at least two group undertakings in different member states; and

- at least one group undertaking with at least 150 employees in one member state and at least one other group undertaking with at least 150 employees in another member state (art 2(1)(c)).

The EWC Directive states that thresholds for determining the size of a workforce must be based on the average number of employees (including part-time employees) employed during the two years prior to the calculation. However, the method of calculating that number is set by national legislation and/or practice (art 2(2)). This means that there are varying methods of calculation across the member states, reflecting different approaches to 'atypical' workers, e g part-timers, casual workers and contractors.

Member states may provide that the terms of the EWC Directive do not apply to merchant navy crews (art 1(5)).

The EWC Directive allows member states to lay down particular provisions for the central management of undertakings in their territories that directly pursue the aim of 'ideological guidance' with respect to the provision of information and the expression of opinions, if such provisions already existed at 22 September 1994 (art 8(3)).

C2.4 Establishing a European Works Council ('EWC') or an alternative Information and Consultation Procedure ('ICP')

An EWC or an ICP can be established in three ways under the EWC Directive:

- Under a voluntary agreement that was already in force as at 22 September 1996 (or 15 December 1999 in the case of the United Kingdom) (art 13); or

- By voluntary negotiations between central management and a 'special negotiating body' ('SNB') set up for that purpose; or

- If no voluntary agreement can be reached, under the default provisions of the Annex to the EWC Directive, as implemented into the relevant national legislation.

These three processes are considered in more detail at *C2.5* to *C2.7* below. It should be noted that if neither the management nor the employees of an entity initiate the negotiation process, there is no obligation to start negotiations, or to set up an EWC or an ICP.

C2.5 Existing voluntary agreements

The provisions of the EWC Directive do not apply if, as at 22 September 1996 (or 15 December 1999 in the case of the United Kingdom), there was an agreement already in existence that covered the whole of the relevant workforce and which provided for the transnational informing and consulting of employees. This was the reason why so many voluntary agreements (sometimes known as 'Article 13 agreements') were signed up in advance of the September 1996 deadline and, in fact, most EWCs stem from Article 13 agreements. When those agreements expire, the parties can agree to renew them. If they are not renewed, the provisions of the EWC Directive will then apply (art 13). In theory, the only requirements for voluntary agreements are that they must cover the whole of the relevant workforce in the member states and provide for transnational information and consultation. In practice, however, many voluntary agreements have followed the basic format of an EWC.

C2.6 Voluntary negotiations between central management and a Special Negotiating Body ('SNB')

The second method of establishing an EWC or an ICP is by voluntary negotiation between management and an SNB, each of which is under a duty to negotiate in a spirit of co-operation and with a view to reaching agreement. The SNB and management must determine the scope, composition, functions and terms of office of the EWC or the arrangements for the ICP. This type of agreement is sometimes known as an 'Article 6 agreement'.

The central management of an undertaking is responsible for creating the conditions and means necessary to set up an EWC or an ICP. If central management is situated in a member state outside the EU, a representative agent in an EU state must take on that responsibility. If there is no such representative agent, management in the EU state employing the greatest number of the undertaking's employees must take on the responsibility (art 4).

Negotiations for setting up an EWC or an ICP can be commenced by:

- central management on its own initiative; or

- at the written request of at least 100 employees or their representatives in at least two undertakings or establishments in at least two different member states (art 5(1)).

Therefore, if an employer does not wish to initiate the process, it does not have to unless expressly requested to do so.

Although a 'Community-scale undertaking' is defined for the purposes of the EWC Directive by art 2(1)(a), the Directive does not include a definition of an 'establishment'.

The EWC Directive provides that member states must ensure employees in undertakings and/or establishments in which there are no employees' representatives have the right to elect an SNB (art 5(2)). However, the EWC Directive does not deal with the situation where employees of an entity in one member state want to set up an ICP or an EWC, and their colleagues in another country do not. Consequently, this is not generally dealt with in the relevant national legislation.

An SNB may decide, by at least a two-thirds majority, not to open negotiations for the establishment of an EWC or an ICP at all, or to stop any negotiations that have already started. If negotiations are stopped in this way, the whole procedure is terminated and the default provisions set out in the Annex to the EWC Directive do not need to be applied. A new request to convene an SNB can then only be made, at the earliest, two years after this vote took place (unless the parties agree an earlier date) (art 5.5).

Central management must fund the operation of an SNB and member states are free to set detailed budgetary rules for this purpose.

C2.7 Election or appointment of SNB members

Member states must provide rules in their national legislation covering the method of election or appointment of SNB members in their territory. An SNB must have a minimum of three and a maximum of 17 members. Each relevant member state must be represented by at least one SNB member, and there must be additional members in proportion to the number of employees of the relevant entity working in other member states, calculated according to the rules set by the country in which central management is situated. Central and local management of the relevant entity must be informed of the composition of any SNB (art 5(2)).

C2.8 The role of the SNB

Central management and the SNB (acting by a simple majority vote of its members) must determine by written agreement:

- the undertakings or establishments to be covered by the agreement;

- the composition of the EWC, the number of members, the allocation of seats and the term of office;

- the procedure for management to inform and consult the EWC;

- the venue, frequency and duration of meetings of the EWC;

- the financial and material resources to be allocated to the EWC; and

- the duration of the agreement and the procedure for its renegotiation (art 6(2)).

For the purpose of these negotiations, the SNB may be assisted by experts of its choice.

Central management and the SNB (again acting by a simple majority vote of its members) may decide in a written agreement to establish one or more ICPs instead of an EWC. This agreement must stipulate how the employees' representatives will meet to discuss the information conveyed to them. The information must include, in particular, transnational issues that significantly affect workers' interests (art 6(3)). Other than this, there are no set requirements as to the form or substance of an ICP.

C2.9 Default agreements under the Annex to the EWC Directive

The third way of establishing an EWC is in accordance with a 'default procedure', as set out in the Annex to the EWC Directive. These default provisions (or more detailed provisions set by individual member states) may, in accordance with art 7 of the EWC Directive, apply if:

- central management and the SNB decide that those provisions should apply; or

- where central management refuses to recommence negotiations within six months of a request from the SNB, which is made at least two years after it has voted to stop negotiating with central management; or

- where, after three years from the date of that request, central management and the SNB are unable to conclude an agreement.

The Annex to the EWC Directive sets out the minimum requirements for the establishment, composition and operation of an EWC. However, member states may provide for more detailed or more onerous provisions in national legislation (art 7). Because the Annex is so prescriptive, most employers prefer to negotiate voluntary agreements.

C2.10 Composition

The Annex to the EWC Directive states that an EWC must be composed of employees of a Community-scale undertaking, or a Community-scale group of undertakings, who have been elected by employees' representatives or, if there are none, by the entire workforce (Annex, 1(b)). There must be a minimum of three members and a maximum of 30. If justified by the size of the EWC, a select committee can be elected from the EWC's members, comprising a maximum of three members (Annex, 1(c)). Once decided upon, management must be informed of the composition of an EWC.

The EWC Directive left the method of election and appointment to EWCs to be set by national legislation and/or practice. However, each relevant member state must be represented by at least one employee on an EWC. The number of additional members must be proportionate to the number of employees working in the establishments, the controlling undertaking or the controlled undertakings, as set by the national legislation of the member state where central management is situated (Annex, 1(d)).

C2.11 Operation and procedure

The Annex to the EWC Directive states that EWCs must adopt their own rules of procedure, but gives EWCs the following minimum rights (which can be enhanced by member states):

- to meet with central management once a year to review at least the following issues: the structure, economic and financial situation of the business; the probable development of the business (including production and sales); the situation and probable trend of employment; investments; substantial organisational changes; the introduction of new working methods or production processes; transfers of production; mergers, cut-backs or closures of undertakings or establishments (or parts of them); and collective redundancies (Annex, 2);

- to meet without management before any planned meeting between the EWC and management (Annex, 4);

- to be informed and consulted on the basis of reports drawn up by central management on the progress of the business and its prospects (Annex, 2);

- to be assisted by experts of their choice, if this is necessary to enable them to carry out their tasks (although member states may provide that management can limit funding to cover one expert only) (Annex, 6 and 7);

- to be provided with appropriate financial and other resources by central management to enable them to perform their functions (in accordance with budgetary rules, if set by member states). Expenses should cover, in particular, the cost of organising meetings, arranging interpretation facilities, accommodation and travel expenses (Annex, 7); and

- if there are exceptional circumstances affecting employees' interests to a considerable extent, to be informed (via a select committee, if there is one). 'Exceptional circumstances' envisaged by the EWC Directive include relocations, business closures and collective redundancies. Members of an EWC who are employed in relation to the establishment or undertaking directly concerned by the measures in question must also have the right to participate in a meeting between the select committee (if any) and management. This meeting must take place as soon as possible after, and on the basis of, a report prepared by management (Annex, 3).

Member states can lay down rules on the chairing of information and consultation meetings between EWCs and management, if they so wish (Annex, 4).

EWCs are obliged to report back to employees' representatives (or, if there are none, to the workforce as a whole) the content and outcome of information and consultation procedures (Annex, 5).

Four years after an EWC is established, it can decide whether to continue to apply the provisions of the Annex to the EWC Directive or to open negotiations for a separate voluntary agreement (Annex, 1(f)).

C2.12 Confidentiality

Member states must provide that members of SNBs or EWCs, any experts who assist them and any employees' representatives, must not reveal any information that has been expressly provided to them in confidence. This obligation applies even after they have left office (art 8(1)). Member states must also provide that, in specific cases, and to the extent possible under national legislation, central management does not have to disclose information to SNBs, EWCs, employees' representatives or any experts, where this would seriously harm the functioning of, or be prejudicial to, the undertakings concerned (art 8(2)).

The EWC Directive states that member states must make provision for administrative or judicial appeal procedures which employees' representatives may initiate when central management expressly requires confidentiality or does not provide information and is in breach of the Directive (art 11). Use of these procedures may result in management being ordered to disclose the information in question.

C2.13 Enforcement

The EWC Directive provides that members of SNBs and EWCs and employees' representatives involved in ICPs, must have the same employment protection and guarantees as are set by existing national legislation and practice in the country in which they are employed. This should include appropriate guarantees to cover attendance at meetings and pay for absences connected with their duties under the EWC Directive (art 10). In many countries, this means that the relevant employees will be protected against dismissal or other detriment for reasons connected to their duties, and entitled to enhanced compensation rights if they are dismissed for such a reason.

Member states must also provide for appropriate procedures to enforce the EWC Directive in their territory and sanctions for failure to comply with the requirements of the EWC Directive (art 11).

C3 The Information and Consultation Directive

Directive 2002/14/EC of the European Parliament and of the Council of 11 March 2002 establishing a general framework for informing and consulting employees in the European Community.

C3.1 Background

The EC Information and Consultation Directive ('the Consultation Directive') came into force on 23 March 2002, after years of difficult debate. The principles behind the Consultation Directive are:

- to establish a European-level framework of minimum standards for informing and consulting employees about business decisions which affect them directly;

- to allow member states to adapt this framework to their own national law and industrial relations practice; and

- to ensure that the interests of both employers and employees are taken into account.

The idea of the Consultation Directive was first formally proposed in April 1995. Difficulties arose largely because member states, employers' organisations and trade unions did not agree on the desirability of having an EU framework for information and consultation. Opposition to the proposals came, in particular, from the United Kingdom, Germany and Ireland. The degree of opposition generally correlated to the likely impact of the Consultation Directive on existing national information and consultation systems. In some countries, such as France and the Netherlands, there will be limited impact. In others, such as the United Kingdom and Ireland, its effects are likely to be much greater.

C3.2 Implementation

National legislation to implement the provisions of the Consultation Directive must generally be adopted by 23 March 2005. However, there are transitional provisions allowing implementation to be phased for countries where the introduction of the Consultation Directive will mean a significant change in workplace culture (mainly the United Kingdom and Ireland).

The transitional provisions apply only to member states where, as at 23 March 2002, there was:

- no general, permanent and statutory system of informing and consulting employees; and

- no general, permanent and statutory system of employee representation in the workplace (eg works councils or trade union-based bodies) (art 10).

The Consultation Directive and the transitional provisions distinguish between 'undertakings' and 'establishments'. These terms are defined in detail at *C3.3* below. Broadly, an 'undertaking' is a corporate entity and an 'establishment' is a business unit. Countries that are able to take advantage of the transitional provisions may apply national legislation implementing the Consultation Directive in three stages, according to the number of employees employed in 'undertakings' or 'establishments':

● 'Undertakings' with at least 150 employees or 'establishments' with at least 100 employees must be covered by 23 March 2007.

● 'Undertakings' with at least 100 employees or 'establishments' with at least 50 employees must be covered by 23 March 2008.

● There must be full application of the Consultation Directive from 23 March 2008 (ie by that date its provisions must apply to 'undertakings' with at least 50 employees or establishments with at least 20 employees) (arts 10 and 11).

C3.3 The scope of the Consultation Directive

The Consultation Directive does not apply to small 'undertakings', because it was felt that its requirements might hinder their creation and development. Member states may choose whether to apply the provisions of the Consultation Directive to:

● 'undertakings' employing at least 50 employees in any one member state; or to

● 'establishments' employing at least 20 employees in any one member state.

The Consultation Directive leaves it up to individual member states to decide the method for calculating these thresholds (art 3(1)). An 'employee' is defined, for the purposes of the Directive, as 'any person who, in the Member State concerned, is protected as an employee under national employment law and in accordance with national practice' (art 2(d)). Again, therefore, this is left to each member state to clarify in their legislation implementing the Directive.

An 'undertaking' is defined in the Consultation Directive as 'a public or private undertaking carrying out an economic activity, whether or not operating for gain, which is located within the territory of the Member States' (art 2(a)). Although the scope of this definition is not entirely clear, it is generally understood to cover legal entities such as incorporated companies. However, there have been varying interpretations, of how it should be applied to complex corporate structures. Many corporate structures consist of individual subsidiaries, which would presumably be considered as groups of connected undertakings for these purposes.

An 'establishment' means, for the purposes of the Consultation Directive, 'a unit of business defined in accordance with national law and practice, and located within the territory of a Member State, where an economic activity is carried out on an ongoing basis with human and material resources' (art 2(b)). This is generally understood to mean a physical entity such as a factory, office or shop. An 'undertaking' could therefore theoretically carry out business at one or more 'establishments'. If the Consultation Directive is applied to 'undertakings' rather than 'establishments', this would avoid the requirement of setting up consultation procedures in separate parts of businesses, focusing instead on more centralised systems for informing and consulting.

If similar provisions already existed in national legislation on 23 March 2002, special provisions may be made for 'undertakings' or 'establishments' which mainly pursue:

- political, professional organisational, religious, charitable, educational, scientific or artistic aims; or

- aims involving information and the expression of opinions (eg the media) (art 3(2)).

Member states may also derogate from the Consultation Directive by making particular provisions for the crews of seagoing vessels (art 3(3)).

C3.4 Information and consultation

The Consultation Directive does not set out detailed practical arrangements for informing and consulting employees, although it is clearly envisaged that this will take place through employees' representatives. Detailed procedures must be determined by individual member states in compliance with the broad principles set out in the Consultation Directive.

Member states have existing legislation and/or practices for informing and consulting employees' representatives, based on the requirements of the Acquired Rights Directive and the Collective Redundancies Directive. Accordingly, employees' representatives are defined as the 'representatives provided for by national laws and/or practices' (art 2(e) (which are generally elected representatives, trade union representatives or individual representatives). Deciding the practical arrangements in this regard should therefore be relatively straightforward for the member states (art 4(1)).

The Consultation Directive allows member states to use their national systems to require employees in a particular workplace to indicate their collective support for information and consultation, before they have a right to it (Recital 15).

The Consultation Directive provides that the information and consultation process must include:

- information on the recent and probable development of the 'undertaking's' or 'establishment's' activities and economic situation; and

- information and consultation on the situation, structure and probable development of employment and on any anticipatory measures envisaged, particularly where there is a threat to employment; and

- information and consultation on decisions which are likely to lead to substantial changes in work organisation or contractual relations, including collective redundancies (art 4(2)).

There is therefore some overlap with the Collective Redundancies Directive, the Acquired Rights Directive and the EWC Directive.

'Information' is defined in the Consultation Directive as the 'transmission by the employer to employees' representatives of data in order to enable them to acquaint themselves with the subject matter and to examine it' (art 2(f)). However, there is very little guidance within the Directive on how and when information has to be provided. It has to be given:

- at such time;

- in such a manner; and

- with such content

as are appropriate to enable employees' representatives to study the information adequately and, where necessary, to prepare for consultation. Member states therefore have considerable discretion to decide how information procedures should be organised (art 4(3)).

'Consultation' is defined in the Consultation Directive as 'the exchange of views and establishment of dialogue between the employees' representatives and the employer' (art 2(g)). Although some requirements for the consultation process are specified in the Directive, they are very broad. Consultation must take place:

- with a view to reaching an agreement on decisions within the scope of the employer's powers which are likely to lead to substantial changes in work organisation or in contractual relations;

- at an appropriate time;

- by an appropriate method;

- with appropriate content;

- at the relevant level of management and representation, depending on the subject under discussion;

- on the basis of information supplied by the employer and the opinions formulated by the employees' representatives; and

- in such a way as to enable employees' representatives to meet the employer and obtain a response to their opinion(s) and the reason(s) for that response (art 4(4)).

Details of the precise form and timing of the consultation process therefore need to be set by individual member states. Accordingly, in practice, processes could vary considerably, since they will be drawn from existing national provisions and practices.

The Consultation Directive also gives member states the freedom to specify that the practical arrangements for informing and consulting employees can be set by voluntarily negotiated agreements (including pre-existing agreements) between management and the workforce (art 5). Such agreements can contain arrangements for information and consultation that differ from those set out in the Directive. However, the arrangements agreed (including those set out in agreements that are renewed) must comply with the underlying objectives and principles of the Consultation Directive; that is:

- they must be effective;

- they must have been agreed as part of a process that involved the employer and employees' representatives working in a spirit of co-operation and with due regard for their reciprocal rights and obligations; and

- they must take into account the interests of the employer and the employees (art 1).

This effectively means that arrangements should not be imposed by management, and that employees must be involved in the process (through their representatives).

C3.5 Confidentiality

Many employers will be concerned about releasing sensitive and confidential information to employees' representatives as part of the information and consultation process. The Consultation Directive therefore offers protection for employers against disclosure of particularly sensitive information.

The Directive asserts that member states must incorporate provisions that prevent employees' representatives, and any experts who may be assisting them, from disclosing to employees or third parties any information which has been provided to them expressly in confidence, provided this has been done in the legitimate interests of the employer. This obligation of confidentiality continues even after the representatives or experts have completed their term of office or assignment.

Member states may authorise employees' representatives, and anyone assisting them, to pass on confidential information to employees and to third parties who are bound by obligations of confidentiality (art 6(1)). They may also provide for procedures designed to safeguard confidentiality of information (art 6(3)).

Member states must ensure, in specific cases and within limits laid down by national legislation, that employers in their territory are not obliged to communicate information or undertake consultation which would seriously harm the functioning of the 'undertaking' or 'establishment' in question, or be prejudicial to it (art 6(2)).

The Consultation Directive provides that employers' requirements for confidentiality and any withholding of prejudicial information must be open to review via national administrative or judicial review procedures (art 6(3)).

C3.6 Enforcement

Member states must ensure employees' representatives have adequate legal protection and guarantees to enable them to perform their duties properly (art 7). Usually, this means that they must be given protection against dismissal or suffering any other detriment for a reason connected to their duties.

There must also be adequate procedures in place at national level to enable the requirements of the Consultation Directive to be enforced in the event of non-compliance by employers or employees' representatives (art 8(1)).

The Consultation Directive further requires that member states must set out adequate sanctions to be applied if employers or employees' representatives infringe its terms. These sanctions must be effective, proportionate and dissuasive (for example, fines payable by employers to employees) (art 8(2)).

C4 The European Company Statute and Employee Involvement Directive

Council Regulation (EC) No 2157/2001 of 8 October 2001 on the Statute for a European Company (SE) and Council Directive 2001/86/EC of 8 October 2001 supplementing the Statute for a European Company with regard to the involvement of employees.

C4.1 Background

The Regulation establishing the European Company Statute ('the ECS Regulation') and the accompanying Directive on the Involvement of Employees in the European Community ('the Employee Involvement Directive') were adopted on 8 October 2001. The ECS Regulation came into force on 8 October 2004, and the Employee Involvement Directive must have been transposed into national legislation by that date. Like other pieces of European legislation on employee consultation, these have been the subject of many years of debate and controversy since they were first proposed in 1970. Both the ECS Regulation and the Employee Involvement Directive will apply throughout the EEA (ie the EU member states and Norway, Iceland and Lichtenstein) (art 70). In contrast to the other Directives considered in this book, the operation of the Employee Involvement Directive is voluntary, as it applies only to the 'SE' form of company.

The ECS Regulation gives companies in the EEA the option of forming a European Company (also known as a 'Societas Europaea' or 'SE') and sets out the company law applicable to such an entity. Since the ECS Regulation is directly applicable in all member states, the SE will, in principle, be governed by EU company law, rather than by national company law. However, the ECS Regulation does not cover all areas of law. For example, it does not cover tax, intellectual property, insolvency or employment law, as well as some corporate governance issues. All these areas will therefore be covered by the national laws of the member state where the SE is registered.

The accompanying Employee Involvement Directive sets out the requirements for the involvement of employees in relation to SEs, which must be agreed before they can be established. This Directive should have been implemented in each member state, but only covers SEs. Companies which operate as multinationals across Europe in the 'traditional' manner will be subject to the European Works Council Directive.

The underlying aim of the ECS Regulation is to enable companies that operate in several different member states to set up one company which can validly operate in all of those states. The European Commission hopes that the introduction of the SE will bring administrative and cost benefits to companies by having one set of rules and a unified management structure. An SE should also be able to expand or restructure more easily (eg by engaging in cross-border mergers or joint ventures with companies based in other member states). However, it remains to be seen whether the SE structure will be popular in practice. Companies may be put off by the complexity of the legislation, the requirements on employee involvement, and the fact that many substantive legal matters affecting the SE will still be governed by the national laws of the member state where it is registered (notably tax, which is often a key factor in deciding corporate structure). It may therefore be that the SE is popular mainly with companies that engage frequently in cross-border transactions such as joint ventures.

The main underlying principles behind the Employee Involvement Directive, as set out in its recitals, are:

- to ensure that the establishment of an SE does not entail the disappearance or reduction of employee involvement practices in the companies that are participating in the SE;

- to ensure that transnational information and consultation procedures are set up when an SE is created, whilst allowing for the continuing diversity of rules and practices that exist in different member states; and

- to provide for default requirements in the event that employees' representatives and management do not reach agreement.

C4.2 The ECS Regulation

A summary of the ECS Regulation is set out in this chapter. However, its detailed provisions and its implications in terms of corporate law are beyond the scope of this book.

C4.3 Formation of an SE

An SE can be created from two or more commercial bodies, at least two of which must be resident in different member states. There are five forms of SE, each of which is subject to different rules. An SE cannot be registered in any of these five forms unless arrangements for employee involvement have been finalised in accordance with the Employee Involvement Directive, or a decision has been taken not to proceed with an employee involvement agreement and to rely instead on national information and consultation rules. The five ways in which an SE can be set up are:

- the merger of two or more EEA-based companies, provided at least two of them are governed by the laws of different member states (art 17);

- forming an SE as a holding company for public or private limited companies with registered offices and head offices within the EEA. At least two of those companies must be governed by the laws of different member states or have had a subsidiary governed by the laws of different member states for the previous two years. The participating companies then become majority-owned by the SE;

- forming an SE as a subsidiary by subscription for its shares by other entities. At least two of these entities must be governed by the laws of different member states or have had a subsidiary governed by the law of different member states for the previous two years. The SE would be wholly owned by the entities setting it up, but they do not have to have equal shareholdings in it;

- transforming an existing public company, if it has had a subsidiary company in another member state for at least two years. If an SE is formed in this way, any voluntary arrangements for employee involvement must be at least at the same level as existing arrangements in the public company to be transformed into an SE (Employee Involvement Directive, art 4); and

- an SE may itself set up one or more subsidiaries in the form of SEs (art 3.2).

C4.4 The characteristics of an SE

Broadly, an SE will have the following characteristics:

- Separate 'legal personality' (art 1).
- A minimum subscribed capital of €120,000 (art 4).

- A registered office located within the EU in the same member state as its head office. Member states have the option of providing that the registered office of an SE and head office of an SE must be situated in the same place (art 7).

- A name preceded or followed by the letters 'SE' (art 11).

- Registration in the member state in which it has its registered office. However, registration of an SE will be published in the Official Journal of the European Communities (arts 12 and 14).

- The adoption of either a two-tier management system (consisting of a supervisory body and a management body) or a one-tier system (consisting of an administrative body) (art 38). This broadly reflects the two types of management system used in Europe. Each member state must make both systems available to an SE. In a two-tier system, the management body is responsible for managing the SE, and its members are appointed, removed and supervised by the supervisory body (or the shareholders in general meeting, if member states so choose). Every three months, the management body must provide a progress report to the supervisory body. There are detailed rules in the ECS Regulation on the operation of one-tier and two-tier management systems, which are outside the scope of this book.

C4.5 The law applicable to an SE

Most of the provisions of the ECS Regulation state that SEs are to be governed by the national legislation applicable to public companies in the member states where they are registered (art 5). However, in some cases, the laws of other member states will apply. For example, the rules for the appointment of SNB members (art 3.2) and for the protection of employees' representatives (art 10) will be those of the member state in which the relevant employees or their representatives are situated. It is likely that determining the law applicable to a particular aspect of an SE's operation will be a complex issue requiring specialist advice.

C4.6 The Employee Involvement Directive

The Employee Involvement Directive states that, where the establishment of an SE has been proposed, a company's or group's management or administration must start negotiations with an SNB representative of the participating companies' employees in order to establish arrangements for the involvement of employees in the SE (art 3). These negotiations may continue for six months, unless extended by agreement to one year. If no agreement is concluded by that deadline, a set of standard rules will apply. The Employee Involvement Directive provides that these standard rules must be incorporated into national legislation in such a way as to comply with the minimum rules set out in the Annex to the Directive.

An SE cannot be validly formed unless arrangements have been made for employee involvement in one of three ways:

- by an agreement between an SNB and management (an 'Article 4 voluntary agreement'); or

- by a decision of an SNB to rely on national information and consultation rules (an 'Article 3(6) decision'); or

- acceptance by management of default rules on employee involvement based on the Annex to the Employee Involvement Directive.

'Involvement of employees' is defined in the Employee Involvement Directive as any mechanism – including information, consultation and participation – through which employees' representatives may exercise an influence on decisions to be taken within a company (art 2(h)). 'Information', 'consultation' and 'participation' are all defined in the Employee Involvement Directive.

'Information' is defined as:

- the informing of a body representing employees and/or employees' representatives by an SE on questions which concern the SE and any of its subsidiaries or establishments situated in other member states;

- at a time, in a manner, and with a content, which allows the employees' representatives to undertake an in-depth assessment of the possible impact on an SE and, where appropriate, to prepare for consultation with that SE (art 2(i)).

This is a new definition of 'information', which has not been seen in previous directives such as the European Works Council Directive.

'Consultation' is defined in the Employee Involvement Directive as:

- the establishment of dialogue and an exchange of views between a body representing employees and/or the employees' representatives and an SE;

- at a time, in a manner, and with a content, which allows the employees' representatives, on the basis of the information provided to them, to express an opinion on measures envisaged by an SE that may be taken into account in the decision-making process within that SE (art 2(j)).

This is a more detailed definition than has been seen in other Directives such as the European Works Council Directive, which states simply that consultation is 'the exchange of views and establishment of dialogue.'

'Participation' is defined in the Employee Involvement Directive as the influence of a body representing employees and/or the employees' representatives in the affairs of a company by way of:

- the right to elect or appoint some of the members of the company's supervisory or administrative body, or

- the right to recommend and/or oppose the appointment of some or all of the members of the company's supervisory or administrative body (art 2(k)).

'Participation' is a new concept and has not been used in other Directives. The definition in the Employee Involvement Directive attempts to cover all the forms of employee participation that exist across the EU (such as the German and Dutch dual board model and the Swedish single board model). Where employees of one or more of the companies participating in the establishment of an SE have participation rights, there is a presumption that the same level of participation rights will be granted to all the SE's employees (including those that did not previously have them), except in certain circumstances when it is agreed by at least a two-thirds majority of an SNB.

'Employees' representatives' are not defined in detail in the Employee Involvement Directive. They are the 'employees' representatives provided for by national law and/or practice' (art 2(e)).

C4.7 The Special Negotiating Body ('SNB')

An SNB must be created as soon as possible after a draft plan to set up an SE has been published (art 1). The management or administrative bodies of the SE then have an obligation to take steps to negotiate with the SNB to establish the arrangements for the involvement of employees within the SE. These arrangements can consist of the establishment of a representative body, or one or more alternative information and consultation procedures.

Some requirements for the establishment and operation of an SNB are set out in the Employee Involvement Directive, although much of the detail is left to member states to determine in their implementing legislation. An SNB must be made up of representatives of employees in all 'participating companies' and of any 'concerned subsidiaries or establishments' (art 3.2). 'Participating companies' are the companies that directly participate in establishing an SE (art 2(b)). A 'concerned subsidiary or establishment' is a subsidiary or 'establishment' of a 'participating company' that will become a subsidiary or 'establishment' of the proposed SE once it has been established (art 2(d)).

C4.8 Composition of an SNB

SNB members must be elected or appointed by employees in proportion to the number of employees employed in each member state by the 'participating companies'. The employees in different member states must have one seat on an SNB for every 10 per cent (or fraction thereof) of the total number employees employed across the EEA (art 3(2)(a)).

Where an SE has been formed by a merger, there must be additional SNB members from each member state to ensure the SNB includes at least one member from each company that participated in the establishment of the SE which is registered and has employees in that member state, and which will cease to exist as a separate legal entity following the SE's registration. However:

- the number of such additional members must not exceed 20 per cent of the number of members designated as per *C4.7* above; and

- the composition of the SNB must not give rise to the 'double representation' of the employees concerned.

If the number of participating companies is higher than the number of additional seats available on the SNB, those additional seats must be allocated to companies in different member states by decreasing order of the number of employees they employ (art 3(2)(a)(ii)).

C4.9   Method of election

The method for electing or appointing members of an SNB in the territory of an individual member state must be determined by that member state. Member states have to take measures to ensure that, as far as possible, these arrangements provide for at least one member of an SNB representing each participating company that has employees in the member state concerned. However, the measures must not increase the overall number of members of an SNB (art 3(2)(b)).

Member states may provide in their implementing legislation that SNB members can include trade union representatives, even if they are not employees of a participating company, as well as members elected by employee ballot. This again is in contrast to the European Works Council Directive, which does not provide for trade union representation. The Employee Involvement Directive states that there must also be provision for employees in 'undertakings' or 'establishments' in which there are no employees' representatives (through no fault of their own) to have the right to elect or appoint SNB members (art 3(2)(b)).

C4.10   Decision-making in an SNB

The Employee Involvement Directive states that an SNB generally has to take decisions by an absolute majority of its members, provided that this majority also represents an absolute majority of the employees. Each member has one vote (art 3(4)).

However, a two-thirds majority of SNB members is required for a decision to approve an agreement for a reduced number of employees on the board of an SE, and that majority must represent at least two-thirds of employees and include the votes of members representing employees in at least two different member states. This applies in the case of an SE to be established by merger, if participation covers at least 25 per cent of the overall number of employees of the participating companies. If an SE is to be established by way of a holding company or formation of a subsidiary, this applies if participation covers at least 50 per cent of the overall number of employees of the participating companies (art 3(4)). Employee participation rights cannot be reduced where a company has transformed into an SE, if employees of that company had such rights. These provisions reflect the underlying aim of the Employee Involvement Directive, namely to ensure that voting rules in these circumstances are proportionate to the risk of disappearance or reduction of existing participation systems and practices. This risk is obviously greater where an SE is formed by transformation or merger.

C4.11 Experts

For the purpose of negotiations, an SNB can request experts of its choice to assist generally and to attend meetings in an advisory capacity where this is appropriate 'to promote coherence and consistency at Community level' (which is not defined). These experts could be, for example, representatives of appropriate Community-level trade union organisations (art 3(5)).

C4.12 Expenses

The expenses of an SNB and its members must be paid by the participating companies so as to enable it and them to carry out their functions in an appropriate manner. Member states may, however, lay down budgetary rules regarding the operation of SNBs, including limiting their funding to cover the involvement of one expert only (art 3(7)).

C4.13 National information and consultation rules: an 'Article 3(6) decision'

Under art 3(6) of the Employee Involvement Directive, an SNB can decide not to open negotiations with management or to terminate negotiations already opened, and to rely instead on existing national rules on information and consultation in force in each member state where the relevant SE has employees. Such a decision must be taken by a two-thirds majority of the members of the SNB representing at least two-thirds of the employees, which must include the votes of members representing employees employed in at least two different member states. An 'Article 3(6) decision' cannot be taken if an SE is to be established by way of transformation and the employees in the company to be transformed have participation rights (see *C4.3* above).

An SNB has to be reconvened if at least 10 per cent of the employees of the relevant SE or its subsidiaries or their representatives request it, no earlier than two years after an 'Article 3(6) decision' has been taken (or sooner if all parties agree). If an SNB does not reach a voluntary agreement with management as a result of further negotiations, the standard default provisions set out in the Annex to the Employee Involvement Directive do not apply.

All member states will have national rules for information and consultation as a result of the Information and Consultation Directive which will be in force from March 2005.

C4.14 Voluntary agreements on employee involvement

A voluntary agreement on employee involvement between an SNB and management has to be reached within a period of six months from the start of negotiations (or a period of 12 months if the parties agree to extend it) (art 5).

The agreement reached between the management of an SE and an SNB has to specify:

- the scope of the agreement;

- the composition, number of members and allocation of seats on the representative body that will consult with the SE's management in connection with the information and consultation arrangements;

- the functions of, and the procedure for the information and consultation of, the representative body;

- the frequency of meetings of the representative body;

- the financial and material resources to be allocated to the representative body;

- the arrangements for implementing an alternative information and consultation procedure ('ICP'), if that is to be established instead of a representative body;

- if the parties have decided to establish arrangements for participation, the substance of those arrangements (including the number of relevant administrative or supervisory board members the employees will be entitled to elect, appoint, recommend or oppose) and the associated procedures;

- the date on which the agreement will commence, its duration, and the situations where the agreement should be renegotiated; and

- if an SE is established by transformation, that at least the same level of employee involvement as existed in the companies to be transformed will exist in the SE (art 4).

C4.15 The Annex to the Employee Involvement Directive

If no voluntary agreement has been reached before the end of a set negotiating period, or if the parties agree, the minimum standard rules set out in the Annex to the Information and Consultation Directive (as implemented in the relevant national legislation) will apply to the SE. These standard rules establish a representative body to inform and consult employees, and set out procedures for its operation and management.

C4.16 Composition of the representative body

Part 1 of the Annex to the Employee Involvement Directive states that a representative body has to be set up in accordance with the following rules:

(a)   A representative body must be composed of employees of an SE and its subsidiaries and establishments, elected or appointed by the employees' representatives, or, if there are none, by all employees of the SE.

(b)   Members must be elected or appointed according to national legislation and/or practice. Member states must set rules to ensure that the number of members of, and allocation of seats on, the representative body will be adapted to take account of changes occurring within the SE and its subsidiaries and establishments.

(c)   Members must be elected or appointed in proportion to the number of employees employed in each member state by the entities participating in an SE. This has to be done by allocating each member state one seat per portion of employees employed in that member state which equals 10 per cent (or a fraction of 10 per cent) of the number of employees employed by all the participating entities.

(d)   If warranted by its size, the representative body shall elect a select committee from among its members which can have a maximum of three members.

(e)   An SE's management must be informed of the composition of an SNB.

(f)   After the representative body has been established for four years, it must consider whether to conclude a voluntary agreement or to continue to apply the rules set out in the Annex.

C4.17 Standard Annex rules for information and consultation

(a)   A representative body has the right to be informed and consulted. For that purpose, it has the right to meet with an SE's management at least once a year on the basis of regular management reports on the progress of the business and its prospects.

(b)   An SE's management has to provide a representative body with the agenda for meetings of the administrative, management or supervisory organ and with copies of all documents submitted to the general meeting of its shareholders.

(c)   The annual consultation meeting with a representative body has to relate in particular to:

- the structure, economic and financial situation of the SE;

- the probable development of the business and of production and sales;

- the situation and probable trend of employment;

- investments;

- substantial changes concerning organisation, the introduction of working methods or production processes, transfers of production, mergers, cut-backs or closure; and

- collective redundancies.

(d)   A representative body has a right to be informed and to meet management at any time if there are exceptional circumstances affecting the employees' interests to a considerable extent. This applies, for example, in the case of relocations, transfers, closures of businesses, and collective redundancies.

(e)   Member states can set their own rules on the chairing of information and consultation meetings.

(f)   Members of a representative body must inform the representatives of employees of an SE, its subsidiaries and establishments about the content and outcome of information and consultation procedures.

(g)   A representative body (and its select committee, if any) can be assisted by experts of its (or their) choice, although member states may choose to set a limit on funding to the cost of one expert.

(h)   Members of a representative body are entitled to time off work for training connected with their duties, without suffering any loss of wages.

(i)   The costs of a representative body must be met by the relevant SE. This includes the cost of material resources such as interpretation facilities, as well as accommodation and travelling expenses. Member states can, if they wish, lay down budgetary rules for these purposes.

C4.18 Standard Annex rules for participation

Part 3 of the Annex to the Employee Involvement Directive states that employee participation in an SE shall be subject to the following rules:

(a)   In the case of an SE established by transformation, if the rules of a member state relating to employee participation in the administrative or supervisory body of the relevant company applied before registration of the SE, all aspects of participation must continue to apply in relation to that SE.

(b)   With regard to other methods of establishing an SE, the employees of the SE, its subsidiaries and establishments and/or their representative body shall have the right to elect, appoint, recommend or oppose the appointment of a number of members of the administrative or supervisory body of the SE equal to the highest proportion in force in the participating companies concerned before its registration. The rules set out in the Annex do not specify exactly how members are to be elected or appointed.

(c) If none of the companies participating in the establishment of an SE was governed by participation rules before registration of the SE, the SE is not required to provide for employee participation.

(d) A representative body must decide on the allocation of seats within the administrative or supervisory body and on the way in which an SE's employees may recommend or oppose the appointment of members in proportion to the number of the SE's employees in each member state. Each member state may determine the allocation of seats it is given within an SE's administrative or supervisory body.

(e) Every member of the administrative or supervisory body of an SE who has been appointed by the representative body, or by the employees, must be a full member with the same rights and obligations as members representing shareholders (including the right to vote).

C4.19 Confidentiality

Member states have to provide in their national legislation that members of an SNB or representative body, employees' representatives, and any experts assisting them, are not authorised to reveal any information that has been given to them in confidence. This obligation must continue to apply even after they have left office or completed their assignment (art 8(1)).

Member states may set out in their national legislation that an SE does not have to provide information if, according to objective criteria, to do so would seriously harm the functioning of the SE or its subsidiaries, or would be prejudicial to them. This could be subject to prior administrative or judicial authorisation (art 8(2)).

The Employee Involvement Directive asserts that there must be administrative or judicial appeal procedures in place which employees' representatives can use if they disagree with the withholding of information or the confidentiality required by an SE (art 8(4)). As a result of these procedures, an SE could be ordered to disclose the information in question.

C4.20 Protection for employees' representatives

The members of an SNB or employees involved in an alternative information and consultation procedure, and any employees' representatives, must have the same protection and guarantees provided for employees' representatives in other national legislation and/or practice. This must include the payment of wages for time spent carrying out their duties (art 10).

C4.21 Misuse of procedures

Each member state is required to implement appropriate measures to prevent the misuse of the SE structure for the purpose of depriving employees of their rights to be involved in the businesses in relation to which they are employed (art 11).

C4.22 Compliance and enforcement

Member states must implement appropriate measures to ensure that employees (and employees' representatives, where relevant) comply with the Employee Involvement Directive, including appropriate administrative and legal procedures. These measures must apply, regardless of whether an SE has its registered office within the territory of a particular member state (art 12).

D Jurisdiction and governing law

Layla Bunni
Martin Fodder

D1 Introduction

This chapter will deal with two related but distinct areas in an international employment arrangement:

- which court or courts will have jurisdiction to hear any dispute between the parties; and

- which law will the court that hears the dispute apply?

D2 Diversity of legal systems

The concept of law developed independently in communities around the world at very early stages of civilisation to regulate the various aspects of human behaviour and relationships between one individual and another and thus achieve a balance between the freedom of choice of the individual and the control of this freedom for the protection of others. Societies aspired to have laws that mirrored justice so as to eliminate the necessity to resort to force except for the purpose of upholding the supremacy of the law itself.

Rules were written in the form of legal codes as early as 1700 BC and, as communities sprang up, grew and later declined, the legal rules changed from a few basic simple codes to sophisticated, complex and voluminous systems of law. Legal concepts developed from what was earlier considered to be the law of the gods into a three-tier hierarchy. At the top, the law of the gods changed to the law of God due to the evolution of religion. The second tier was represented by natural law or the law of reason and common sense, and the third tier by man-made law. The latter has been subject to evolution from time to time and from place to place while endeavouring to respect the boundaries laid down by the divine and natural laws.

Given that these developments in the law took different directions in different cultures around the world, it is now practically impossible to achieve international standardisation of the law dealing with legal relationships of individuals and their employers across international boundaries. The contemporary legal systems of the world have evolved differently across societies, cultures and political systems. Because they are rooted in different cultures, they are written in different languages, influenced by different religious beliefs and formed under different customs. Given such socio-cultural variety, it may be easier and more acceptable to reach international agreement on the basic concepts and rules which should govern contractual relationships in an international field. However, the fact remains that as soon as a contract of employment with an international aspect to it is entered into, a diversity of laws governing the contract between the employer and employee is automatically introduced.

D3 Contemporary legal systems

D3.1 Background

There are two main legal systems in the EU which apply today. These are:

–   the Romano-Germanic group; and

–   the common law group.

There are of course other groups in existence, some of which are totally distinct from the two mentioned above, whilst others share some of their concepts.

The Romano-Germanic group owes its origin to Roman law during the times of Caesar Augustus (63 BC to 14 AD). The term 'civil law' is often used in the English-speaking world to denote the Romano-Germanic group of legal systems and to indicate that the origin of these laws is the Roman law. Romano-Germanic laws, are in principle, based on the judicial application of a certain legal code to a particular case by learned jurists and theorists, in conformity with logical and systematic deduction. Under this group, the rules of law have developed as rules of conduct linked to ideas of 'justice and morality'.

The common law group on the other hand, originated as the law 'common' to all of England after the Norman conquest in 1066. It developed from a body of law which is almost entirely the product of judicial decisions by courts which applied custom and reason to everyday disputes, aided by only a few formal enactments of law. The common law continued to be developed in England by judges, rather than by legislators, through the accumulation of tradition expressed by upholding certain principles. The resultant case law continues at present to fill gaps in the law, or to change the law in a certain direction, or to interpret the meaning of the large number of legislative enactments, by declaring precedents which impose authority on future judicial decisions. Such authority is not granted to decided cases in the Romano-Germanic systems: a volume of reports of judicial decisions in common law has a similar authority to that of an authoritative legal text book in Romano-Germanic systems.

D3.2 Jurisdiction and governing law in more detail: European legislation and common law

Rules as to jurisdiction operate in two distinct ways. On the one hand, such rules will operate to distribute, as between two or more rival national forums, in which of those forums a dispute should be heard. Rules in this category do not of themselves create rights for individual employees: they determine the forum in which a claim may be brought[1]. On the other hand, rules as to jurisdiction may operate within a particular state to determine whether a particular right can be asserted by an individual in a particular court or tribunal[2]. Rules as to jurisdiction of this second variety will often have nothing to do with the territorial aspects of the dispute. They may relate to the time within which a claim has to be brought, or perhaps the legal status ('employee', 'self employed person' or 'worker') of the individual claimant.

Rules as to the applicable or governing law determine which substantive legal rules are to be applied by a national court to determine a particular dispute once it is determined that the court or tribunal has jurisdiction. The High Court of England and Wales frequently applies foreign substantive law in determining disputes between parties before it, having determined that the governing law is that of a foreign country. It is worth pointing out at this preliminary stage that there are limits to this form of judicial activity. A United Kingdom employment tribunal is a creature of statute. Nobody has yet argued that a UK employment tribunal can adjudicate on a claim for the French equivalent of unfair dismissal compensation, although as a matter of construction of the relevant convention (ie the Rome Convention – as to which see below) it should be able to do so. It should be noted that neither Council Regulation (EC) 44/2001 (the 'Regulation') nor the Brussels Convention contains any provisions on jurisdiction as to rights arising out of mandatory rules.

However, a UK employment tribunal would appear to have power to determine a contractual claim where the law of France is the governing law[3]. This is because the (albeit financially limited) contractual jurisdiction of the employment tribunal is expressly stated to be equivalent to that of the ordinary courts[4].

In order to understand the new jurisdictional rules which are imposed by international conventions and European legislation that apply to both civil and commercial matters, it is important to recognise the connection between those rules and the common law system. The law relating to jurisdiction is contained in the Brussels Convention and Council Regulation (EC) 44/2001 and the law as to governing law in the Rome Convention. These form the basic framework in determining whether the court of a member state has jurisdiction to hear a claim, or which state's laws govern the terms of the contract.

The Brussels Convention and Council Regulation (EC) 44/2001 require the national courts of a member state to apply that state's own jurisdictional rules, thus providing 'indirect' delegated jurisdictional rules for each member state. It follows, therefore, that common law rules still continue to determine jurisdiction where the Brussels Convention and the Regulation delegate such power to the common law rules. The common law rules, however, only govern civil and commercial matters when permitted to do so by the Convention or the Regulation.

1   See e g Council Regulation (EC) 44/2001 (OJ L12/1), as explained below.

2   In *Lawson v Serco* [2004] EWCA Civ 12, [2004] 2 All ER 200, considered in detail below, the Court of Appeal held, reversing the EAT, that the rules contained in reg 11 of the Employment Tribunals (Constitution and Rules of Procedure) Regulations 2001 only distribute as between England and Wales on the one hand and Scotland on the other the jurisdiction to hear claims of unfair dismissal etc. The rules did not confer on any particular individual the right not to be unfairly dismissed.

3   Subject to rules as to service (as to which, see *D9.1* below). For an example of case where the employment tribunal applied – or should have applied – foreign law in a contractual dispute, see *Bryant v Foreign and Commonwealth Office* (EAT/174/02).

4   See Employment Tribunals Act 1996, s 3 and the Employment Tribunals Extension of Jurisdiction (England and Wales) Order 1994. See the consolidated cases *SSAFA Forces Help v McClymont* (UKEAT/0164/03/DA); *Croft v Cathay Pacific Airways* (UKEAT/0367/03/DA; *Veta Ltd v Croft* (UKEAT/03680/03/DA); *Sysdeco Ireland Ltd v Atkins* (UKEAT/0080/04/DA); and *Expro Gulf Ltd v Birnie* (UKEAT/0222/04/DA) ('*SSAFA*') at paras 50–1 to the effect that the employment tribunal's jurisdiction precisely shadows the civil court's jurisdiction.

D4 Jurisdiction

When determining which country's court may hear a dispute arising out of an employment relationship with an international aspect to it, the first step is to identify the nature of the claim. If the matter is contractual and the employer is based in the UK, then the Brussels Convention and Council Regulation (EC) 44/2001 may apply. If it is a statutory claim, then the domestic laws of each relevant country will need to be examined to determine which jurisdiction applies.

If the employee is based outside the EU, eg in the USA or Japan, the contract of employment needs to be considered to see if there is an express jurisdiction clause, what the laws of the relevant countries are and, if it is proposed that proceedings are to be initiated in the UK against an overseas defendant, whether the UK court is likely to grant leave out of jurisdiction: this is considered in more detail below. If, however, both parties to the dispute are in the EU and both countries are contracting states, the Convention on Jurisdiction and the Enforcement of Judgments in Civil and Commercial Matters[1] (the Brussels Convention) will apply in determining the jurisdiction of the courts.

The Brussels Convention was enacted into UK law by the Civil Jurisdiction and Judgments Act 1982. It only applies where the case involves a 'civil or commercial matter' and where there is a conflict as to jurisdiction between two or more contracting states. Employment claims are deemed to be both civil and commercial matters. Council Regulation (EC) 44/2001 came into force in March 2002. It replaces and overrides the provisions and application of the Brussels Convention (save where the Regulation leaves gaps) in relation to all proceedings instituted on or after 1 March 2002. The texts of the Regulation and the Brussels Convention are therefore now the primary source of the direct jurisdictional and judgment recognition rules.

If the Regulation gives jurisdiction to the courts in the UK, those courts must exercise that jurisdiction when called upon to do so by the claimant in the case. If the Regulation allocates jurisdiction to courts in another member state as well as the courts in England, then either England or that member state may exercise jurisdiction, but not both.

1   Brussels, 27 September 1968.

D5 Articles 18–21 of Council Regulation (EC) 44/2001: jurisdiction over individual contracts of employment

By section 5 of Ch II, art 18 of the Regulation it is provided that 'in matters relating to individual contracts of employment, jurisdiction shall be determined by that Section'. The rules contained in s 5 relating to employment contracts give a certain degree of choice for employees in relation to where they can sue their employers.

Articles 18–21 of the Regulation contain the jurisdictional rules in relation to employment contracts and basically provide as follows:

(1)   If the defendant (this can be either employee or employer) enters or intends to enter into appearance in one member state, the courts of that member state will have jurisdiction.

(2)   If the Posted Workers Directive 96/71/EC applies to the case, the jurisdiction provided for under the Directive will apply[1].

(3)   If the defendant is not domiciled in a member state, jurisdiction may be claimed on the basis of art 4 of the Regulation, which, in the case of the UK, provides for the common law rules of jurisdiction to apply.

(4)   An employer not domiciled in a member state is treated as being domiciled in a member state where it has a branch, agency or other establishment, if the dispute arises out of that establishment;

(5)   The employee may bring proceedings either:

(a)   in the court of the member state where the employer is domiciled; or

(b)   in the court of another member state where the employee habitually carries out his work[2] or the last place that he did so; or

(c)   in another member state if this was where the employee was engaged by the employer and the employee does not habitually carry out his work in any one country.

(6)   The employer may only bring proceedings in the member state where the employee is domiciled.

(7)   Any court which has jurisdiction in accordance with these rules will also have jurisdiction to hear a counterclaim relating to the same case.

(8)   An agreement on choice of court will only apply if it is entered into after the dispute has arisen (though query how easy it would be to determine the exact point in time when the dispute actually arose) or it

allows the employee to bring the claim in a jurisdiction other than (and therefore in addition to) one which applies under these rules.

A difficulty arises when attempting to interpret (5) above which relates to art 19 of the Regulation. The use of the word 'place' in this rule is slightly misleading and it has been suggested that 'place' should be interpreted as meaning 'member state'. Similarly, the reference in art 19 to ' any one country' should also be interpreted as meaning 'member state'.

1   See Posted Workers Directive 96/71/EC, art 6.
2   See the decision of the ECJ in *Weber v Universal Ogden Services Ltd*: C-37/00 [2002] QB 1189; and *SSAFA Forces Help v McClymont* (UKEAT/0164/03/DA); *Croft v Cathay Pacific Airways* (UKEAT/0367/03/DA; *Veta Ltd v Croft* (UKEAT/03680/03/DA); *Sysdeco Ireland Ltd v Atkins* (UKEAT/0080/04/DA); and *Expro Gulf Ltd v Birnie* (UKEAT/0222/04/DA), para 45.

D6   Governing law: the Rome Convention

The law which governs a contract between certain parties and by which questions as to the validity, application and interpretation of its terms are addressed is referred to as the 'applicable law of the contract'. In some jurisdictions, the terms 'proper law' and 'governing law' are used instead. Where there is no certainty as to the applicable law of the contract, the applicable law will be selected in accordance with the principles of a branch of law known as 'private international law' sometimes called 'the conflict of laws'. This is a body of principles which attempts to provide answers as to what law is the most appropriate to apply and which forum is appropriate to determine a particular issue with an international dimension. This branch of law forms part of the legal system of every jurisdiction and, therefore, there are as many systems of conflict of laws as there are jurisdictions. There are three alternatives in respect of determination of the applicable law of the contract, as follows.

D6.1   An express choice of the applicable law

For the UK, the Rome Convention on the Law Applicable to Contractual Obligations (the 'Rome Convention') will apply when determining the question as to what law will apply to the contract of employment. The Rome Convention was enacted into UK law by the Contracts (Applicable Law) Act 1990. The Rome Convention applies to contractual obligations involving a choice of law between the laws of two different countries (art 1(1)). On the face of things, it makes no difference that one of those countries is not a signatory to the Rome Convention.

Where the parties have expressly or impliedly agreed in the employment contract that it should be governed by the laws of a particular country, the Rome Convention recognises that choice of law (art 3(1)). This recognition is subject to the imposition of so-called 'mandatory rules'. Article 3(3) introduces the 'mandatory rules' concept[1] and provides that the chosen law of a contract can be overridden by the mandatory rules of a country where all the other elements relevant to the situation are connected with that one country. This means that even though the law of a foreign jurisdiction may be chosen as the law governing an employment contract, certain statutory rights (in practice, rights of an employee) which would apply to a contract governed by the law of the country with which the contract was really most connected will still apply to that contract. The employee may therefore have his cake and eat it too: where a mandatory rule which would apply but for an express or inferred choice of proper law gives greater protection, then that mandatory rule can be invoked by the employee. Equally, where a rule of law of the system of law chosen by the parties under the contract gives greater protection than the equivalent mandatory rule the system of the law that has been chosen will apply.

1   And Rome Convention, art 6 develops it.

D6.2 An inferred choice of the applicable law

Where there is no express and clear choice of the applicable law of the contract, it may be possible to infer a choice of law from the other provisions of the contract and the relevant circumstances. Factors from which a choice of the applicable law of the contract may be inferred include the residence of the employer/employee, the currency in which payment of the employee's salary is being made and the location where the employee is required to carry out his duties under the employment contract. If the contract of employment contains an arbitration clause, inference as to the applicable law of the contract may be taken as being where the place for the arbitration has been selected. The rules as to mandatory rules apply in the case of an inferred choice of this sort.

D6.3 No choice of the applicable law

If no law has been chosen by the parties to the contract and no inference can be made to establish such law, the principles of conflict of laws are used to select the legal system which should apply. In contracts involving the laws of member states of the EU, the applicable law is determined in accordance with the art 6(2) principles of the Rome Convention which provides that the applicable law will be:

(a)   that of the country where the employee habitually carries out his work under the contract, even though the employee may be temporarily employed in another country; or

(b)   where the employee works in several jurisdictions, that of the country in which the employer's place of business through which the employee was hired is situated.

These principles are subject to a proviso that the applicable law may yet be decided to be that of the country with which the contract is 'more closely connected' if a consideration of this question leads to a country other than that determined by reference to principles (a) or (b) above. This would involve considering matters such as the place or places from which and the mechanism by which the employee was managed, paid and disciplined.

An employee who is employed by a company based in one EU member state and is required to perform his duties in a different member state will therefore be connected with at least two countries as a result. The applicable law of the contract may be determined:

(a)   by the country in which the employing company's place of business through which the employee was hired is situated; or

(b)   where the employee predominantly delivers performance under the contract at the time of the dispute; or

(c)   as being that which is stated in the contract as being the governing law which should be applied.

D6.4 Posted Workers Directive

Although the Posted Workers Directive 96/71/EC has not been brought into force by positive legislation (as opposed to the repeal and amendment of certain enactments – as to which see below), it is important to appreciate that the Posted Workers Directive is superior to the Convention when and if they conflict. The preamble to the Posted Workers Directive makes it clear that the purpose of the Directive is to 'lay down a nucleus of mandatory rules for the minimum protection' of posted workers. The key provision is art 3(1), which provides that member states must ensure that, whatever the law that would otherwise apply to the employment relationship, workers who are posted to a member state must be entitled to the minimum levels of protection that otherwise apply in that member state regarding maximum work periods and minimum rest periods; minimum rates of pay (including overtime rates); conditions for temporary and hired out workers; health and safety at work; protections for pregnant women, those women who have just given birth, children and young people; equality of treatment between the sexes (and other provisions on non discrimination).

D7 Practical considerations

When determining what governing law to apply to the contract, some practical considerations include the following:

(a)   If the organisation is familiar with a certain legal system which is usually applied to the organisation's commercial contracts, to ensure consistency this legal system should not be deviated from when applying a system to the organisation's contracts for expatriates.

(b)   How stable is the organisation's choice of legal system? How well respected is that legal system internationally?

(c)   What level of protection does the organisation's choice of legal system have for employees? Some countries' laws are more employee-friendly than others.

(d)   Consider the difference of approach between legal systems under common law and those under civil law. Common law is almost entirely the product of judicial decisions by courts which apply custom and reason to disputes, aided by formal enactments of law, whilst civil law is based on the judicial application of a legal code only. There is a greater risk of employees having unfair dismissal and/or redundancy rights if the choice of legal system is based on common law, as these rights are conferred on individuals by statute, as are a lot of employment rights.

(e)   What are the formal requirements of the chosen law that need to be complied with before and after entering into the contract? For example, under the chosen law, how many people are required to sign to contract on behalf of the company? Will the contract be required to be executed in the language of the host country? Does the contract need to be notarised or executed by way of a deed?

D8 Jurisdiction and related issues as to common law contractual rights for employees working outside or partly outside the UK

As already noted, the fact that a contract is governed by eg Italian law does not mean that it has to be sued on in Italy. It can be sued on in the UK. Although it is right that, by virtue of art 5 of the Brussels Convention, there is jurisdiction and, perhaps, the normal jurisdiction, in relation to a contract of employment, in the courts of the country where the employment is ordinarily performed, art 2 of the Convention provides a fall-back.

Consequently, by virtue of ordinary rules of jurisdiction, the High Court or county court can hear claims against UK domiciliaries, such as the UK Government, for claims of breach of a contract governed by foreign law. It may be more unsatisfactory for it to be tried here, given the fact that many witnesses may be abroad; but it can be tried here in the ordinary courts and now, by virtue of s 3 of the Employment Tribunals Act 1996, and delegated legislation, any such claim (with specified exceptions) which the High Court can hear can also be tried in the employment tribunal[1].

There is of course a risk of competing or co-ordinate jurisdictions. It would seem that an employment tribunal has an equivalent jurisdiction to that of the High Court to stay an action on the ground of forum non conveniens. This jurisdiction is considered in more detail below. This possibility was acknowledged by the EAT in *Bryant v Foreign and Commonwealth Office*[2] and confirmed in *SSAFA Forces Help v McClymont*[3].

1   Although the amount recovered will be limited to £25,000.
2   EAT/174/02.
3   UK EAT/0164/03/DA.

D8.1 Jurisdiction in respect of claims in the English courts where there is a foreign element; Civil Procedure Rules 1998 ('CPR'); service in and out of the jurisdiction

This section deals with the common law claims that are heard in English courts (as opposed to employment tribunals[1]). Jurisdiction in respect of common law claims is a function of service: the English civil courts do not have jurisdiction to hear a claim unless the defendant can be validly served (whether inside or outside the jurisdiction). The relevant provisions are in CPR, Pt 6.

A foreign company may be validly served without the permission of the court where:

(a)   it has a place within the jurisdiction where the corporation carries on its activities; or

(b)   it has a place of business within the jurisdiction[2].

If neither of these applies, then in order to effectively serve a defendant outside the jurisdiction *without* the permission of the court the claim must be one which the court has power to determine under the Civil Jurisdiction and Judgments Act 1982 (ie the Brussels Convention and Council Regulation (EC) 44/2001 – see above). There must be no pending proceedings between the parties concerning the same claim in any other UK court, or the courts of any other Convention territory, and the defendant must be domiciled in the UK or another Convention territory.

If neither of these routes is available, the permission of the court will have to be sought.

CPR 6.3 contains the relevant rules requirement for permission for service out of jurisdiction. The claimant makes an application for service out of jurisdiction without the defendant to the claim being notified of it. If the court grants permission to the claimant to serve proceedings on the defendant out of the jurisdiction, the defendant may apply under CPR Pt 11 to have the court declare that it has no jurisdiction and will therefore apply to have service set aside. This will require a full review as to whether the court should have granted permission to serve out of jurisdiction in the first place.

When deciding whether or not to grant permission to serve out of jurisdiction, the court will have to consider the following:

(i)   Whether the claim(s) made falls within the types of proceedings set out at CPR 6.20, which includes:

   (1)   claims for a remedy against a person domiciled within the jurisdiction[3];

   (2)   claims for injunctions ordering the defendant to do or refrain from doing an act within the jurisdiction;

(3) claims where there is a real issue for the court to try and the claimant wants to serve the claim form on a third party who is part of the claims;

(4) claims for interim remedies;

(5) claims relating to contracts where the contract was made within the jurisdiction[4] by or through an agent trading or resident within the jurisdiction[5], and is governed by English law[6] or contains a term which gives the court jurisdiction to hear the claim[7];

(6) contract claims which are made in respect of a breach of contract committed within the jurisdiction[8];

(7) claims that are made for a declaration that no contract exists where, if the contract was found to exist, it would comply with the conditions set out at (5) above;

(8) claims in tort where damage was sustained within the jurisdiction or the damage sustained resulted from an act committed within the jurisdiction; and

(9) claims made to enforce any judgment or tribunal award.

(ii) If the claim falls within the scope of CPR 6.20, the court will have jurisdiction to grant permission to serve out, otherwise there is no power to grant leave to serve out and the permission and service may be set aside.

(iii) Written evidence in support of the application for permission is required. This evidence must specify the paragraph(s) of CPR 6.20 on which the claimant is basing his application. This will assist in providing the defendant with what he will need to argue his case if he wants to have the permission to serve out and set aside.

The further factor that the court may have to consider (assuming it has the power to grant permission under CPR 6.20) is whether the case was a proper one for the court to exercise its discretion in favour of granting such permission. There are three elements in this:

(a) Is England the proper place to bring the claim?

(b) Is there any overriding injustice in bringing the defendant to England?

(c) Does the claimant show a serious issue to be tried upon the merits of the claim?

If any of these elements are decided against the claimant, there is the possibility that permission to serve out may be set aside.

CPR 6.20(5)–(7) deal with contractual claims. For any of these to apply there must be an actual contract. If the question that needs to be determined is whether or not a contract exists, the rules of the English conflict of laws will need to be applied[9]. To determine this, the defendant must firstly be asked whether he admits that there is a contract. If he says that a contract does not exist, English law must be applied. This involves the application of the rules of the Contracts (Applicable Law) Act 1990 (see *D6.1* above). If there is a contract when the rules of the Act are applied, the claim will fall within CPR 6.20. Similarly, if there is no contract when the rules of the Act are applied, the claim will not fall within CPR 6.20.

The requirement that England be the proper forum in which a claimant can bring a claim is contained at CPR 6.21(2A). The leading case dealing with this issue, *Spiliada Maritime Corpn v Cansulex Ltd*[10], established that the burden of proof is on the claimant to persuade the court that England is the appropriate forum for the trial of the action.

Even if England is not the natural forum for the trial of the action, in rare cases it may be that the proper place to bring the claim is England. Under certain circumstances the court may still make an order granting permission to serve out. There are two grounds where this may be the case:

1.   If there has to be a choice of court agreement between the parties. This is, however, subject to the case falling within the Brussels Convention (see **D5** above). This also ensures that there is conformity with applying the law that relates to choice of court agreements.

2.   If England is not the natural forum but there is no other forum available, England may still be the proper place to bring the claims.

Under what circumstances would it be unjust to require the defendant to come to England? This would be where England was said to be the proper forum to bring the claim but not the proper place. Loss of an accrued defence by way of limitation in a foreign court may also be a reason. However, matters such as differences in the level of damages or procedural matters will not be factors which will be considered.

A court will not grant permission to serve out of jurisdiction unless the claimant raises a serious issue to be tried. Prior to the new Civil Procedure Rules this rule was established in the House of Lords case *Seaconsar Far East Ltd v Bank Markazi Jomhouri Islami Iran*[11]. This imposed the burden of proof on the claimant to show that he had a proper case that could be tried.

CPR 6.21(1)(b) simply requires the claimant to provide written evidence stating that he believes that his case has a reasonable prospect of success. This could be interpreted to mean that it is sufficient if the claimant has a genuine belief in the prospects of success even if this belief is ill-founded. Notwithstanding this, however, there is the argument that the *Seaconsar* case remains reliable and that its principles should continue to apply. However, this is not intended to place an additional hurdle in the claimant's way if he has already established that England is the natural forum and that it is not unjust to require the defendant to come to England to defend the claim. As long as the claim is sufficiently strong on its merits to survive an application to strike it out, that should be enough.

As already noted, the employment tribunal has a (financially limited) jurisdiction to determine breach of contract claims. The international dimension of this jurisdiction has been the subject of two recent decisions at EAT level[12]. In the *SSAFA* case the EAT ruled that the forum non conveniens principles set out above applied to ET proceedings in breach of contract claims because the ET jurisdiction precisely shadows the jurisdiction of the ordinary civil courts to hear such claims[13].

1   Note, however, that employment tribunals have a limited common law jurisdiction, as to which see below.
2   See CPR 6.5(6).
3   This means domicile as set out in Sch 1 to the Civil Jurisdiction and Judgments Order 2001.
4   A contract is made in England if, applying the English domestic law rules governing when, where and how contracts are made, the contract in question was made in England. If acceptance is made by post, the contract will be deemed to be made where the letter of acceptance is posted; if by electronic means (ie telephone, telex or fax), it will be deemed to be made at the place where the acceptance is received.
5   It is not necessary that the agent concluded the contract himself. It is sufficient that he acted as an intermediary to formalise the contract between the principal and the claimant.
6   English law is the proper law of the contract for contracts made before 2 April 1991. For contracts made after 1 April 1991, the contract is governed by English law in accordance with the Contracts (Applicable Law) Act 1990.
7   Jurisdiction is likely to be conferred under Council Regulation (EC) 44/2001 and permission to serve out will not be needed.
8   The contract does not have to fit with CPR 6.20(5); so long as the breach is committed within the jurisdiction, the court may authorise service out.
9   *Amin Rasheed Shipping Corp v Kuwait Insurance Co* [1984] AC 50 (by applying the choice of law of the common law).
10   [1987] 1 AC 460.
11   [1994] 1 AC 438.
12   *Bryant v Foreign and Commonwealth Office* (EAT/174/02) and *SSAFA Forces Help v McClymont* (UKEAT/0164/03/DA).
13   *SSAFA Forces Help v McClymont* (UKEAT/0164/03/DA), para 50. The EAT declined to overturn the ET's conclusion that it was not appropriate to allow claims by Cathay Pacific pilots who lived in and were based in Hong Kong during their employments to be tried in London (as opposed to Hong Kong).

D9 Jurisdiction to hear statutory claims; general considerations; construction of the relevant statute

The question of whether a particular statute confers a right on a particular individual is a question as to the construction of the statute in question. Modern statutes expressly state to which territories they *extend*, ie the territories within which the courts must apply the statute[1]. A statute may or may not expressly state to which persons or relationships it *applies*[2]. Because people, unlike territories, can move around, the problem of application will often raise questions as to whether a statute has application outside the territories to which it extends. So it is in employment law.

1   For example, s 244 of the Employment Rights Act 1996 provides that the Act extends to England and Wales and Scotland. See further below. For a more detailed examination of the concepts of and distinction between extent and application see Bennion *Statutory Interpretation* (4th edn), Part V, p 275 et seq.
2   As will be shown in the next section, the Employment Rights Act 1996 formerly contained an application provision. That provision was repealed and not replaced.

D9.1   Service of documents: a preliminary hurdle?

Before turning to more substantive issues, there is one procedural issue to which little attention has been paid as yet[1]. Rule 23(4)(e) of the 2001 Employment Tribunals Rules of Procedure provides that, in the case of a notice or document directed to a party, the notice or document may be sent by post or delivered to or at:

(i) the address specified in the originating application or notice of appearance to which notices and documents are to be sent, or in a notice pursuant to r 23(5), which amends the address to which notices and documents are to be sent; or

(ii) if no such address has been specified, or if a notice sent to such an address has been returned, then it can be sent to any other known address or place of business in the United Kingdom or, if the party is a corporate body, the body's registered or principal office in the United Kingdom or, in any case, such address or place outside the United Kingdom as the President or a Regional Chairman may allow.

Although anecdotal experience suggests that service abroad routinely takes place without reference to a Regional Chairman or the President, there is considerable force in the argument that such service is invalid. If this is correct, then what principle or principles should guide the Regional Chairman or President when he or she considers whether to 'allow' service abroad? In default of any other guidance, the obvious candidate would be the regime provided by CPR 6.17–6.21 (see above). This point awaits consideration, however. In the meantime, someone who receives a notice of application outside of the United Kingdom might well be advised to take points as to whether the service has been effective.

1   See 'Case report' ELA Briefing, vol 10, no 3 (April 2003) for an article on this issue. The point has yet to be considered by the EAT, though it has been taken at employment tribunal level.

D9.2   Unfair dismissal

The Employment Rights Act 1996 affords various rights to employees, including, perhaps most significantly, the right not to be unfairly dismissed, which is contained in Pt X and specifically s 94(1). See more generally Chapter S as to UK employment rights. The territorial application of the Employment Rights Act 1996 (ERA 1996) was formerly regulated by s 196. ERA 1996, s 196(2) provided that Pt X of ERA 1996, which deals with unfair dismissal, did not apply to any employment arrangement where the employee was engaged wholly or mainly outside Great Britain.

Section 196 of ERA 1996 was repealed by s 32(3) of the Employment Relations Act 1999 with effect from 25 October 1999 against the background of the need to implement the Posted Workers Directive, which requires that member states of the EU ensure that in certain circumstances, workers posted to another member state in the EU are entitled to at least the same basic terms and conditions of employment as workers habitually employed in that member state, and of the perception that the Court of Appeal's decision in *Carver v Saudi Arabian Airlines*[1] created – or rather confirmed – an unjust anomaly.

Mrs Carver worked as an air hostess under a written contract of employment, which was stated to be subject to the laws of the Kingdom of Saudi Arabia, provided for the place of employment to be Jeddah, and was summarily terminable in the event of Mrs Carver becoming pregnant. After a while, Mrs Carver came to be based at Heathrow Airport and for several years preceding the termination of her employment that situation continued. When she was dismissed upon notifying her pregnancy, Mrs Carver brought a claim of unfair dismissal. The Court of Appeal ruled that the employment tribunal had no jurisdiction. Although she had been based in the UK at her employer's base at Heathrow Airport in the UK for a number of years, the contract provided that the ordinary place in which her work was performed was Jeddah (from where she had originally worked). The Court of Appeal approved a 'contract test' in determining where jurisdiction lay, and followed earlier decisions in *Wilson v Maynard Shipbuilding Consultants*[2] and *Janata Bank v Ahmed*[3].

As interpreted in those cases, ERA 1996, s 196 required the tribunal to consider the position as a matter of construction of the contract as it appeared at the date that the contract was entered into, and not what actually happened regarding the location of the work during the lifetime of the contract.

A rival interpretation, advocated by Lord Denning MR in *Todd v British Midland Airways*[4] and christened 'the base test', had required the tribunal to have regard to where the employee 'should be regarded as working, even though he may spend days, weeks or months working overseas'. The *Carver* Court of Appeal took the view that the base test failed to take into account the words 'under the employee's contract of employment' in s 196.

The confirmation that the 'contract test' was the correct test had the result that employees who might have worked for some years in Great Britain were excluded from the protection of ERA 1996. This was at least part of the reason for the repeal of s 196. However, s 196 was not replaced with a new express statutory test. In explaining this approach, the Minister of State said that 'international law and the principles of our domestic law are enough to ensure that our legislation does not apply in inappropriate circumstances.[5]'

A number of conflicting decisions were generated at employment tribunal level following the repeal, and four of these[6] reached the Employment Appeal Tribunal, resulting in three distinct and irreconcilable, approaches. We move straight to a consideration of the Court of Appeal's subsequent decision in one of those cases, *Lawson v Serco Ltd*[7].

Serco was registered and had its head office in England and Wales. Serco provided support services for the RAF and civilian police on Ascension

Island in the South Atlantic. Ascension Island is a dependency of St Helena, which is in turn an overseas territory of the United Kingdom. Ascension Island is therefore not part of the United Kingdom. Mr Lawson, who was British and domiciled in England, was appointed as a security supervisor to work on Ascension Island. No mention was made of any law other than that of England applying to his contract. After a few months on Ascension Island Mr Lawson resigned and claimed in the (Watford) employment tribunal that he had been unfairly dismissed for asserting a statutory right under the Working Time Regulations 1998. The employment tribunal ruled that it had no jurisdiction.

The Employment Appeal Tribunal allowed Mr Lawson's appeal holding that, with the repeal of ERA 1996, s 196, the only fetter on the jurisdiction of an employment tribunal was supplied by reg 11(5) of the Employment Tribunals (Constitution and Rules of Procedure) Regulations 2001. This provides that the Rules of Procedure (in Sch 1 of the Regulations) should 'apply in proceedings to which they relate where: (a) the respondent ... resides or carries on business in England and Wales'. Thus, held the EAT, 'it is the proximity of the respondent to the United Kingdom that provides the yardstick for determining jurisdiction.' Since Serco was resident in and carried on business in England and Wales, the Watford employment tribunal had jurisdiction notwithstanding that the employment had been entirely on Ascension Island.

The Court of Appeal allowed Serco's appeal. They said:

> 'Section 94(1) provides that "an employee has the right not to be unfairly dismissed by his employer". The question is: what are the employments covered by the section? The answer, in our judgment, is straightforward though it may be difficult to apply in some cases: employment in Great Britain[8].
> ...
> We are in no doubt that the Employment Tribunal had no jurisdiction to consider a claim for unfair dismissal by [Mr Lawson]. On the evidence he was not employed in Great Britain within the meaning of section 94(1) of the 1996 Act. He was employed on Ascension Island, however strong were his and his employer's British connection. The test applied by the EAT is not the correct one. Save where there is express provision to the contrary[9], the Act covers employment in Great Britain[10].
> ...
> We accept the need for a degree of flexibility in applying the test. The Posting of Workers Directive provides protection in a jurisdiction visited. Protection in a jurisdiction from which there is a temporary absence is not necessarily excluded and the existence of the Directive points to the need for a degree of flexibility in deciding where the employment is. A dismissal during a single, short absence from Great Britain would not normally exclude the protection of the 1996 Act. In

most cases it will not be difficult to decide whether an employment is in Great Britain; borderline cases will depend on an assessment of all the circumstances of the employment in the particular case. The residence of the parties may be relevant to where the employment is, but the emphasis must be upon the employment itself.[11]'

Having rejected the argument that jurisdiction was determined by the rules of procedure in the 2001 Regulations, the Court of Appeal also rejected the test of whether the employment had a 'sufficient or substantial connection' with Great Britain which had been approved by the EAT in *Jackson v Ghost Inc*[12] (Clarke J presiding) and *Financial Times Ltd v Bishop*[13] (Burke J presiding). The 1996 Act did not, in the view of the Court of Appeal, permit the adoption of the sufficient connection test considered by Sir Donald Nicholls V-C in the 'quite different circumstances of jurisdiction in bankruptcy' in *Re Paramount*[14]. Neither could the courts return to the 'base test' which had been approved in *Todd* because this was 'irrevocably linked' to the working of s 196 and earlier legislation and the concept of 'ordinarily working' and was not appropriate to a statutory regime which no longer included that section[15].

It is worth noting that the *Lawson v Serco Ltd* decision does not explore the relationship between the 'European' measures – ie Council Regulation (EC) 44/2001 and the Rome Convention on the Law Applicable to Contractual Obligations beyond remarking that 'the Rome Convention does not assist in the construction of the 1996 Act'[16].

The decision of the Court of Appeal removes one uncertainty by its rejection of the test based on reg 11(5) of the 2001 Regulations. It is now clearly not sufficient that the respondent be resident or carrying on business in England and Wales to found jurisdiction in any particular case. At the other extreme, it is also clearly not necessary that employer and employee be at all times located within territories to which the Act extends, ie England and Wales, and Scotland[17]. These points aside, *Lawson v Serco Ltd* gives little guidance to tribunals who will have to decide the question on the facts of particular cases.

If the facts are effectively on all fours with those of Mr Lawson's case, where the employment was envisaged to be and was in fact one that from start to finish took place wholly in a single place outside Great Britain, then presumably tribunals will have little hesitation in saying that the test of 'employment in Great Britain' is not satisfied. In less extreme cases the position is much more problematic. What are 'the circumstances of the case' which have to be assessed in order to arrive at the answer? In the light of the passages quoted above, the employee's place of residence appears to be one of the factors; where the employer was resident is another. But residence is far from being conclusive either way. That the employee was only abroad for what was envisaged to be a 'single, short absence' would apparently not normally contraindicate a finding of 'employment in Great Britain'; this will prevent employers posting an employee abroad for a short period in order to dismiss them and thus avoid a claim under ERA 1996. But what of the employee who works 'out of' Britain but spends most of her time abroad, either in one place or several places and either for relatively short periods of time or for extended periods of time. In such a case the employee might argue that her 'base' was in Great Britain if only because nowhere else could be said to be her base. Whilst a test focused exclusively on the employee's 'base' is rejected by the Court of Appeal, 'the location of the employee's base may throw some light on where the employment is'[18].

Presumably a choice of a law other than that of a part of Great Britain[19] cannot, at least on its own, defeat a right to bring a claim of unfair dismissal because of the provision in ERA 1996, s 204(1) that it is 'immaterial for the purposes' of ERA 1996 whether the law which governs the contract of employment is the law of the United Kingdom or not[20]. From this it would appear to follow that a choice of law clause makes no difference whatsoever, even in a case where all the other factors – whatever the relevant factors might be – are precisely balanced. Would a choice of jurisdiction clause which appeared to confer exclusive jurisdiction on, say, the courts of New York State, be of any weight? It might be argued that it should not be, because of the provisions that prevent parties from contracting out of the protection of ERA 1996[21]. But if the contract contains an express choice of New York law and a jurisdiction clause in favour of the courts of that state, then are these choices not part of 'all the circumstances of the case' which need to be considered on the question as to whether ERA 1996 applies at all? This is a logically anterior question to the question of whether the parties are attempting to oust a jurisdiction which would otherwise exist.

Does a term in a contract specifying the place where the employee (ordinarily) works carry any weight? Applying the reasoning deployed by the Court of Appeal in rejecting the base test (the statutory regime no longer includes the words from which it sprang) then contractual expressions as to the place of work cannot be conclusive but, again, would they be one of 'the circumstances' to be considered?

Although the Court of Appeal expressly rejected the test of substantial or sufficient connection, it may well be that in practice this will be the test that tribunals will come to apply. Presumably the EAT will take the line that the question is one of fact for the tribunal and will allow a degree of latitude such that it will recognise that on the same facts different tribunals will be permitted to reach opposite conclusions.

At the time of going to press, Mr Lawson had just been given leave to appeal to the House of Lords. It is not known on what grounds the appeal is being made or when the House of Lords will hear the case but, in the meantime, what will take some considerable working out is what factors can and cannot be included in the consideration, and in particular the extent to which any agreement will determine the result. For the moment advisers will need to consider the extent to which the terms of an employment contract should anticipate a future dispute as to jurisdiction by including express terms as to place(s) and base of working, choice of law[22] and jurisdiction. Many will no doubt conclude that there may be something to be gained for an employer from including terms which may have the effect of persuading a tribunal that ERA 1996 does not apply, especially in a case where the factual background is unlikely to drive the conclusion inexorably one way or the other. It may be thought desirable to use precedents other than UK-style precedents (which might include reference to rights to notice being those applying under ERA 1996, s 86 or less explicit pointers towards the United Kingdom). Possible consequences for jurisdiction issues may also provide an imperative to pay employees in a particular place or in a particular currency, or to provide for taxation in a particular country other than the United Kingdom.

The way in which the test laid down in *Lawson v Serco Ltd* should be applied was one of the issues considered by the EAT in the *SSAFA* cases[23]. The EAT said that the task was not dissimilar to that which tribunals faced when they had to decide whether or not the applicant was an employee: 'identify the relevant factors and make an overall judgement as to which side of the line the particular facts fall'[24]. Two of the decisions (one involving pilots employed by international airlines and the other an employee who spent periods of time working both in Ireland and at home in England) were remitted to the ET to decide in accordance with the new test. In a third, where the employee worked wholly in Germany, it was held, unsurprisingly, that she could not claim when the *Serco* test of employment in Great Britain was applied.

1   [1999] IRLR 370, CA.
2   [1977] IRLR 491, CA.
3   [1981] IRLR 457, CA.
4   [1978] ICR 959
5   *Hansard*, 26 July 1999, Col 32, Mr McCartney, Minister of State, DTI.
6   *Lawson v Serco Ltd* [2004] EWCA Civ 12; *Bryant v Foreign and Commonwealth Office* (EAT/174/02); *Jackson v Ghost Inc* [2003] IRLR 824 and *Financial Times v Bishop* EAT/0147/03/ZT, 25 November 2003.
7   [2004] EWCA Civ 12, [2004] 2 All ER 200.
8   Pill LJ giving the judgment of the court at [8].
9   This is a reference to s 201, which confers a power to extend the protection of the Act to offshore employees 'even where' this may apply to activities outside the United Kingdom, and to s 199(7) applying the Act to mariners on British registered ships.
10   Pill LJ at [22].
11   Pill LJ at [29].
12   [2003] IRLR 824.
13   (EAT/0147/03/ZT) 25 November 2003.
14   [1993] Ch 223 at 239–40.
15   Pill LJ at [27].
16   See Pill LJ at [19].
17   Pill LJ at [15] rejecting the submission on behalf of Serco that the territorial limitation in ERA 1996, s 244 concluded the issue. It follows that Bennion's general principle in *Statutory Interpretation* (4th edn), section 128, p 206, that an Act 'applies to all persons and matters within the territory to which it extends but not to any other persons and matters' is not applicable here.
18   Pill LJ at [27].
19   Or, more precisely, England and Wales or Scotland: see ERA 1996, s 244, which extends the Act to those territories ('but not to Northern Ireland').
20   Pill LJ at [18] and [19].
21   ERA 1996, s 203(1).

22   Note that in *SSAFA Forces Help v McClymont* (UKEAT/0164/03/DA) the EAT said (at
     para 32) that the proper law of the contract was immaterial to the issue because of ERA
     1996, s 204(1), which provided that the parties could not, by consent, confer on the
     tribunal a jurisdiction which it did not possess. *Quaere*, however, whether choice of law
     might not be a relevant factor (albeit not a conclusive one), especially where all other
     factors were evenly balanced.
23   *SSAFA Forces Help v McClymont* (UKEAT/0164/03/DA); *Croft v Cathay Pacific Airways*
     (UKEAT/0367/03/DA; *Veta Ltd v Croft* (UKEAT/03680/03/DA); *Sysdeco Ireland Ltd v
     Atkins* (UKEAT/0080/04/DA); and *Expro Gulf Ltd v Birnie* (UKEAT/0222/04/DA).
24   See para 19.

D9.3 The anti-discrimination statutes and regulations

The position is not uniform either as between the various statutory prohibitions against discrimination or as between those statutes and the unfair
dismissal regime, as explained in *Lawson v Serco Ltd*[1] and discussed above.

1   [2004] EWCA Civ 12, [2004] 2 All ER 200.

The Race Relations Act 1976

By s 4(1) of the the Race Relations Act 1976 ('RRA 1976') the Act applies
only in relation to employment at an establishment in Great Britain (including territorial waters (s 78(1)[1]) and accordingly overseas employees are
outside the protection of RRA 1976. Section 8(1) formerly provided that an
employment was to be regarded as being at an establishment in Great Britain
unless the employee did his work wholly outside Great Britain. This section
and the corresponding provision in s 6(1) of the Sex Discrimination
Act 1975 ('SDA 1975') had been amended in 1999[2] so as to delete the words
'or mainly' formerly contained in that section. Section 6(1) of SDA 1975
had, in its pre-amended form, been interpreted in *Carver v Saudi Arabian
Airlines*[3], referred to at *D9.1* above. The Race Relations Act 1976 (Amendment) Regulations 2003[4] made further amendments by expanding the
meaning of employment at an establishment in Great Britain to include
employees who do their work wholly outside it. Instead of taking an
exclusionary form, the section now brings within the scope of RRA 1976 any
employee who (a) does his work wholly or partly in Great Britain; or (b) does
his work wholly outside Great Britain, but where s 1A applies. Section 1A
applies if in a case involving discrimination on grounds of race or ethnic or
national origins, or harassment:

'(a)   the employer has a place of business at an establishment in Great
       Britain;
 (b)   the work is for the purposes of the business carried on at that
       establishment; and
 (c)   the employee is ordinarily resident in Great Britain –
       (i) at the time when he applies for or is offered the employment,
           or
       (ii) at any time during the course of the employment.'

In *Carver* the Court of Appeal said that the tribunal had to consider where at
the time of the alleged discrimination the applicant was wholly (or, then,

mainly) working. In the *Saggar* [5] case the EAT gave further consideration to the relationship between the location of the employee at various points in time and the discrimination complained of; discrimination at the stage where there is not yet a contract (where it was conceded that the test must be by reference to the putative contract[6]); a 'one off' incident of discrimination; discrimination taking place over a period and, finally, post-employment discrimination. As to 'one off' incidents and discrimination over a period, the EAT considered that the *Carver* test was capable of being adequately operated: it was necessary for the tribunal to identify the relevant period of the employment to which the *Carver* test should be applied[7].

In the *Saggar* case, which was based on the wording of RRA 1976 prior to its amendment in 2003 but will be of some continuing relevance, the EAT also considered the meaning of 'working', since one of the applicants contended that she was working when she attended a training course in the United Kingdom and the other that he was working when he came for the purposes of a retreat, a wedding and a funeral. The EAT said that the relevant questions were:

–   What was the contractual position? Was the applicant doing the activity because he was required to do it under the contract, expected to, or simply permitted (and, if so, whether in his own time or by taking time off)?

–   What was the content of the activity?

–   What was the duration of it and what was its regularity[8]?

The third and final point in issue in the *Saggar* case was whether the 'de minimis' rule applies to the concept of working 'wholly outside Great Britain'. The EAT held that it did. An applicant could not claim jurisdiction on the basis of a one-day visit by reference to a period of discrimination which was otherwise in relation to employment which was entirely abroad. Instead, the relevant period should be identified depending on the facts of the particular case, eg since the last move or transfer, since the last promotion or, possibly, since the commencement of the employment contract[9].

1   On the meaning of 'employment at an establishment in Great Britain', see RRA 1976, s 8 and SDA 1975, s 10.
2   By the Equal Opportunities (Employment Legislation) (Territorial Limits) Regulations 1999. See also the amendments made by the Race Relations Act 1976 (Amendment) Regulations 2003.
3   [1999] IRLR 370, CA.
4   SI 2003/1626.
5   *Saggar v Ministry of Defence; Lucas v Ministry of Defence; Ministry of Defence v Gandiya* (Appeal Nos UKEAT/1385/01, 0506/02 and 1059/02).
6   And see *Deria v General Council of British Shipping* [1986] IRLR 108.
7   See *Saggar v Ministry of Defence*, paras 31–32.
8   See *Saggar v Ministry of Defence*, paras 34–42.
9   See *Saggar v Ministry of Defence*, paras 48–49.

The Sex Discrimination Act 1975

So far as the Sex Discrimination Act 1975 (SDA 1975) is concerned, the relevant provision is contained in s 6(1), which provides that 'It is unlawful for a person, in relation to employment by him at an establishment in Great Britain, to discriminate against a woman'. There is a deeming provision in s 10(1) so that: 'For the purposes of this Part and section 1 of the Equal Pay Act 1970, employment is to be regarded as being at an establishment in Great Britain unless the employee does his work wholly ... outside Great Britain.' As already noted, this was amended into its present form in 1999. By s 10(4) of SDA 1975, 'where work is not done at an establishment at all, it shall be treated, for the relevant purposes as done at the establishment from which it is done or (where it is not done from any establishment) at the establishment with which it has the closest connection.'

The Disability Discrimination Act 1995 (Amendment) Regulations 2003

From 1 October 2004 the Disability Discrimination Act 1995 (Amendment) Regulations 2003 amend the Disability Discrimination Act 1995, s 68(2)(a) so that employees are deemed to work at an establishment in Great Britain if they work 'wholly or partly in Great Britain', and s 68(2)(b) provides that employees who do their work 'wholly outside' Great Britain can claim under identical qualifying criteria in s 68(2A).

Employment Equality (Religion or Belief) Regulations 2003 and Employment Equality (Sexual Orientation) Regulations 2003

The territorial scope for both of these Regulations is contained at reg 9. An employee is protected under both of these Regulations if he does his work 'wholly or partly in Great Britain', but will also be protected under reg 9(1)(b) if he does his work 'wholly outside' Great Britain. Regulation 9(2) contains the qualifying criteria which apply to both reg 9(1)(a) and (b).

D9.4 Other employment rights

ERA 1996, s 196 formerly regulated the territorial application of various other rights, ie rights to statements of employment particulars (ss 1–7) and rights as to minimum notice (ss 86–91) which did not apply in relation to employment during any period when the employee was engaged in work wholly or mainly outside Great Britain, unless the employee ordinarily worked in Great Britain and the work outside Great Britain was for the same employer, or the law which governed his contract of employment was the law of England and Wales or the law of Scotland[1].

ERA 1996, ss 8–10 provide employees with the right to itemised pay statements.

ERA 1996, Pt II provides employees with the right not to suffer unauthorised deductions; rights not to have to make payments to the employer; limits on amount and time of deductions in retail employment; and rights as to wages determined by reference to shortages etc.

As already noted, ERA 1996, s 196 was totally repealed by s 32(3) of the Employment Relations Act 1999. Accordingly, there is no express regulation as to the territorial application of these various rights. The Court of Appeal's decision in *Lawson v Serco Ltd*[2] does not directly assist. Any distinction as regards rights to statements of employment particulars will now have to be implied rather than express. The issue awaits consideration by the appellate courts.

1   ERA 1996, s 196(1): note that this was *not* the same test as that contained in s 196(2), which concerned, amongst other things, the right to bring a claim of unfair dismissal. See above.
2   [2004] EWCA Civ 12, [2004] 2 All ER 200.

EC Directives

E Acquired Rights Directive 2001/23/EC

COUNCIL DIRECTIVE 2001/23/EC

of 12 March 2001

on the approximation of the laws of the Member States relating to the safeguarding of employees' rights in the event of transfers of undertakings, businesses or parts of undertakings or businesses

E1

THE COUNCIL OF THE EUROPEAN UNION,

Having regard to the Treaty establishing the European Community, and in particular Article 94 thereof,

Having regard to the proposal from the Commission,

Having regard to the opinion of the European Parliament,

Having regard to the opinion of the Economic and Social Committee,

Whereas:

(1) Council Directive 77/187/EEC of 14 February 1977 on the approximation of the laws of the Member States relating to the safeguarding of employees' rights in the event of transfers of undertakings, businesses or parts of undertakings or businesses has been substantially amended. In the interests of clarity and rationality, it should therefore be codified.

(2) Economic trends are bringing in their wake, at both national and Community level, changes in the structure of undertakings, through transfers of undertakings, businesses or parts of undertakings or businesses to other employers as a result of legal transfers or mergers.

(3) It is necessary to provide for the protection of employees in the event of a change of employer, in particular, to ensure that their rights are safeguarded.

(4) Differences still remain in the Member States as regards the extent of the protection of employees in this respect and these differences should be reduced.

(5) The Community Charter of the Fundamental Social Rights of Workers adopted on 9 December 1989 ('Social Charter') states, in points 7, 17 and 18 in particular that: 'The completion of the internal market must lead to an improvement in the living and working conditions of workers in the European Community. The improvement must cover, where

necessary, the development of certain aspects of employment regulations such as procedures for collective redundancies and those regarding bankruptcies. Information, consultation and participation for workers must be developed along appropriate lines, taking account of the practice in force in the various Member States. Such information, consultation and participation must be implemented in due time, particularly in connection with restructuring operations in undertakings or in cases of mergers having an impact on the employment of workers'.

(6)   In 1977 the Council adopted Directive 77/187/EEC to promote the harmonisation of the relevant national laws ensuring the safeguarding of the rights of employees and requiring transferors and transferees to inform and consult employees' representatives in good time.

(7)   That Directive was subsequently amended in the light of the impact of the internal market, the legislative tendencies of the Member States with regard to the rescue of undertakings in economic difficulties, the case law of the Court of Justice of the European Communities, Council Directive 75/129/EEC of 17 February 1975 on the approximation of the laws of the Member States relating to collective redundancies and the legislation already in force in most Member States.

(8)   Considerations of legal security and transparency required that the legal concept of transfer be clarified in the light of the case law of the Court of Justice. Such clarification has not altered the scope of Directive 77/187/EEC as interpreted by the Court of Justice.

(9)   The Social Charter recognises the importance of the fight against all forms of discrimination, especially based on sex, colour, race, opinion and creed.

(10) This Directive should be without prejudice to the time limits set out in Annex I Part B within which the Member States are to comply with Directive 77/187/EEC, and the act amending it,

HAS ADOPTED THIS DIRECTIVE:

E2

CHAPTER I

Scope and definitions

Article 1

1.

(a)   This Directive shall apply to any transfer of an undertaking, business, or part of an undertaking or business to another employer as a result of a legal transfer or merger.

(b)   Subject to subparagraph (a) and the following provisions of this Article, there is a transfer within the meaning of this Directive where there is a transfer of an economic entity which retains its identity, meaning an organised grouping of resources which has the objective of pursuing an economic activity, whether or not that activity is central or ancillary.

(c)   This Directive shall apply to public and private undertakings engaged in economic activities whether or not they are operating for gain. An administrative reorganisation of public administrative authorities, or the transfer of administrative functions between public administrative authorities, is not a transfer within the meaning of this Directive.

2. This Directive shall apply where and in so far as the undertaking, business or part of the undertaking or business to be transferred is situated within the territorial scope of the Treaty.

3. This Directive shall not apply to seagoing vessels.

Article 2

1. For the purposes of this Directive:

(a)   'transferor' shall mean any natural or legal person who, by reason of a transfer within the meaning of Article 1(1), ceases to be the employer in respect of the undertaking, business or part of the undertaking or business;

(b)   'transferee' shall mean any natural or legal person who, by reason of a transfer within the meaning of Article 1(1), becomes the employer in respect of the undertaking, business or part of the undertaking or business;

(c)   'representatives of employees' and related expressions shall mean the representatives of the employees provided for by the laws or practices of the Member States;

(d)   'employee' shall mean any person who, in the Member State concerned, is protected as an employee under national employment law.

2. This Directive shall be without prejudice to national law as regards the definition of contract of employment or employment relationship.

However, Member States shall not exclude from the scope of this Directive contracts of employment or employment relationships solely because:

(a)   of the number of working hours performed or to be performed,

(b)   they are employment relationships governed by a fixed-duration contract of employment within the meaning of Article 1(1) of Council Directive 91/383/EEC of 25 June 1991 supplementing the measures to encourage improvements in the safety and health at work of workers with a fixed-duration employment relationship or a temporary employment relationship, or

(c)   they are temporary employment relationships within the meaning of

Article 1(2) of Directive 91/383/EEC, and the undertaking, business or part of the undertaking or business transferred is, or is part of, the temporary employment business which is the employer.

E3

CHAPTER II

Safeguarding of employees' rights

Article 3

1. The transferor's rights and obligations arising from a contract of employment or from an employment relationship existing on the date of a transfer shall, by reason of such transfer, be transferred to the transferee.

Member States may provide that, after the date of transfer, the transferor and the transferee shall be jointly and severally liable in respect of obligations which arose before the date of transfer from a contract of employment or an employment relationship existing on the date of the transfer.

2. Member States may adopt appropriate measures to ensure that the transferor notifies the transferee of all the rights and obligations which will be transferred to the transferee under this Article, so far as those rights and obligations are or ought to have been known to the transferor at the time of the transfer. A failure by the transferor to notify the transferee of any such right or obligation shall not affect the transfer of that right or obligation and the rights of any employees against the transferee and/or transferor in respect of that right or obligation.

3. Following the transfer, the transferee shall continue to observe the terms and conditions agreed in any collective agreement on the same terms applicable to the transferor under that agreement, until the date of termination or expiry of the collective agreement or the entry into force or application of another collective agreement.

Member States may limit the period for observing such terms and conditions with the proviso that it shall not be less than one year.

4.

(a) Unless Member States provide otherwise, paragraphs 1 and 3 shall not apply in relation to employees' rights to old-age, invalidity or survivors' benefits under supplementary company or intercompany pension schemes outside the statutory social security schemes in Member States.

(b) Even where they do not provide in accordance with subparagraph (a) that paragraphs 1 and 3 apply in relation to such rights, Member States shall adopt the measures necessary to protect the interests of employees and of persons no longer employed in the transferor's business at the time of the transfer in respect of rights conferring on them immediate or prospective entitlement to old age benefits, including survivors' benefits, under supplementary schemes referred to in subparagraph (a).

Article 4

1. The transfer of the undertaking, business or part of the undertaking or business shall not in itself constitute grounds for dismissal by the transferor or the transferee. This provision shall not stand in the way of dismissals that may take place for economic, technical or organisational reasons entailing changes in the workforce.

Member States may provide that the first subparagraph shall not apply to certain specific categories of employees who are not covered by the laws or practice of the Member States in respect of protection against dismissal.

2. If the contract of employment or the employment relationship is terminated because the transfer involves a substantial change in working conditions to the detriment of the employee, the employer shall be regarded as having been responsible for termination of the contract of employment or of the employment relationship.

Article 5

1. Unless Member States provide otherwise, Articles 3 and 4 shall not apply to any transfer of an undertaking, business or part of an undertaking or business where the transferor is the subject of bankruptcy proceedings or any analogous insolvency proceedings which have been instituted with a view to the liquidation of the assets of the transferor and are under the supervision of a competent public authority (which may be an insolvency practitioner authorised by a competent public authority).

2. Where Articles 3 and 4 apply to a transfer during insolvency proceedings which have been opened in relation to a transferor (whether or not those proceedings have been instituted with a view to the liquidation of the assets of the transferor) and provided that such proceedings are under the supervision of a competent public authority (which may be an insolvency practitioner determined by national law) a Member State may provide that:

(a) notwithstanding Article 3(1), the transferor's debts arising from any contracts of employment or employment relationships and payable before the transfer or before the opening of the insolvency proceedings shall not be transferred to the transferee, provided that such proceedings give rise, under the law of that Member State, to protection at least equivalent to that provided for in situations covered by Council Directive 80/987/EEC of 20 October 1980 on the approximation of the laws of the Member States relating to the protection of employees in the event of the insolvency of their employer, and, or alternatively, that,

(b) the transferee, transferor or person or persons exercising the transferor's functions, on the one hand, and the representatives of the employees on the other hand may agree alterations, in so far as current law or practice permits, to the employees' terms and conditions of employment designed to safeguard employment opportunities by ensuring the survival of the undertaking, business or part of the undertaking or business.

3. A Member State may apply paragraph 20(b) to any transfers where the transferor is in a situation of serious economic crisis, as defined by national law, provided that the situation is declared by a competent public authority and open to judicial supervision, on condition that such provisions already existed in national law on 17 July 1998.

The Commission shall present a report on the effects of this provision before 17 July 2003 and shall submit any appropriate proposals to the Council.

4. Member States shall take appropriate measures with a view to preventing misuse of insolvency proceedings in such a way as to deprive employees of the rights provided for in this Directive.

Article 6

1. If the undertaking, business or part of an undertaking or business preserves its autonomy, the status and function of the representatives or of the representation of the employees affected by the transfer shall be preserved on the same terms and subject to the same conditions as existed before the date of the transfer by virtue of law, regulation, administrative provision or agreement, provided that the conditions necessary for the constitution of the employee's representation are fulfilled.

The first subparagraph shall not apply if, under the laws, regulations, administrative provisions or practice in the Member States, or by agreement with the representatives of the employees, the conditions necessary for the reappointment of the representatives of the employees or for the reconstitution of the representation of the employees are fulfilled.

Where the transferor is the subject of bankruptcy proceedings or any analogous insolvency proceedings which have been instituted with a view to the liquidation of the assets of the transferor and are under the supervision of a competent public authority (which may be an insolvency practitioner authorised by a competent public authority), Member States may take the necessary measures to ensure that the transferred employees are properly represented until the new election or designation of representatives of the employees.

If the undertaking, business or part of an undertaking or business does not preserve its autonomy, the Member States shall take the necessary measures to ensure that the employees transferred who were represented before the transfer continue to be properly represented during the period necessary for the reconstitution or reappointment of the representation of employees in accordance with national law or practice.

2. If the term of office of the representatives of the employees affected by the transfer expires as a result of the transfer, the representatives shall continue

to enjoy the protection provided by the laws, regulations, administrative provisions or practice of the Member States.

E4

CHAPTER III

Information and consultation

Article 7

1. The transferor and transferee shall be required to inform the representatives of their respective employees affected by the transfer of the following:

– the date or proposed date of the transfer,

– the reasons for the transfer,

– the legal, economic and social implications of the transfer for the employees,

– any measures envisaged in relation to the employees.

The transferor must give such information to the representatives of his employees in good time, before the transfer is carried out.

The transferee must give such information to the representatives of his employees in good time, and in any event before his employees are directly affected by the transfer as regards their conditions of work and employment.

2. Where the transferor or the transferee envisages measures in relation to his employees, he shall consult the representatives of his employees in good time on such measures with a view to reaching an agreement.

3. Member States whose laws, regulations or administrative provisions provide that representatives of the employees may have recourse to an arbitration board to obtain a decision on the measures to be taken in relation to employees may limit the obligations laid down in paragraphs 1 and 2 to cases where the transfer carried out gives rise to a change in the business likely to entail serious disadvantages for a considerable number of the employees.

The information and consultations shall cover at least the measures envisaged in relation to the employees.

The information must be provided and consultations take place in good time before the change in the business as referred to in the first subparagraph is effected.

4. The obligations laid down in this Article shall apply irrespective of whether the decision resulting in the transfer is taken by the employer or an undertaking controlling the employer.

In considering alleged breaches of the information and consultation requirements laid down by this Directive, the argument that such a breach occurred because the information was not provided by an undertaking controlling the employer shall not be accepted as an excuse.

5. Member States may limit the obligations laid down in paragraphs 1, 2 and 3 to undertakings or businesses which, in terms of the number of employees, meet the conditions for the election or nomination of a collegiate body representing the employees.

6. Member States shall provide that, where there are no representatives of the employees in an undertaking or business through no fault of their own, the employees concerned must be informed in advance of:

–   the date or proposed date of the transfer,

–   the reason for the transfer,

–   the legal, economic and social implications of the transfer for the employees,

–   any measures envisaged in relation to the employees.

E5

CHAPTER IV
Final provisions
Article 8

This Directive shall not affect the right of Member States to apply or introduce laws, regulations or administrative provisions which are more favourable to employees or to promote or permit collective agreements or agreements between social partners more favourable to employees.

Article 9

Member States shall introduce into their national legal systems such measures as are necessary to enable all employees and representatives of employees who consider themselves wronged by failure to comply with the obligations arising from this Directive to pursue their claims by judicial process after possible recourse to other competent authorities.

Article 10

The Commission shall submit to the Council an analysis of the effect of the provisions of this Directive before 17 July 2006. It shall propose any amendment which may seem necessary.

Article 11

Member States shall communicate to the Commission the texts of the laws, regulations and administrative provisions which they adopt in the field covered by this Directive.

Article 12

Directive 77/187/EEC, as amended by the Directive referred to in Annex I, Part A, is repealed, without prejudice to the obligations of the Member States concerning the time limits for implementation set out in Annex I, Part B.

References to the repealed Directive shall be construed as references to this Directive and shall be read in accordance with the correlation table in Annex II.

Article 13

This Directive shall enter into force on the 20th day following its publication in the Official Journal of the European Communities.

Article 14

This Directive is addressed to the Member States.

Done at Brussels, 12 March 2001.

For the Council

The President

B Ringholm

E6

ANNEX I

PART A

Repealed Directive and its amending Directive

(referred to in Article 12)

Council Directive 77/187/EEC (OJ L61, 5.3.1977, p 26)

Council Directive 98/50/EC (OJ L201, 17.7.1998, p 88)

PART B

Deadlines for transposition into national law

(referred to by Article 12)

Directive	Deadline for transposition
77/187/EEC	16 February 1979
98/50/EC	17 July 2001

E7

ANNEX II

Correlation table

Directive 77/187/EEC	This Directive
Article 1	Article 1
Article 2	Article 2
Article 3	Article 3
Article 4	Article 4
Article 4a	Article 5
Article 5	Article 6
Article 7	Article 8
Article 7a	Article 9
Article 7b	Article 10
Article 8	Article 11
—	Article 12
—	Article 13
—	Article 14
—	ANNEX I
—	ANNEX II

F Collective Redundancies Directive 98/59/EC

COUNCIL DIRECTIVE 98/59/EC

of 20 July 1998

on the approximation of the laws of the Member States relating to collective redundancies

F1

THE COUNCIL OF THE EUROPEAN UNION,

Having regard to the Treaty establishing the European Community, and in particular Article 100 thereof,

Having regard to the proposal from the Commission,

Having regard to the opinion of the European Parliament,

Having regard to the opinion of the Economic and Social Committee,

(1) Whereas for reasons of clarity and rationality Council Directive 75/129/EEC of 17 February 1975 on the approximation of the laws of the Member States relating to collective redundancies should be consolidated;

(2) Whereas it is important that greater protection should be afforded to workers in the event of collective redundancies while taking into account the need for balanced economic and social development within the Community;

(3) Whereas, despite increasing convergence, differences still remain between the provisions in force in the Member States concerning the practical arrangements and procedures for such redundancies and the measures designed to alleviate the consequences of redundancy for workers;

(4) Whereas these differences can have a direct effect on the functioning of the internal market;

(5) Whereas the Council resolution of 21 January 1974 concerning a social action programme made provision for a directive on the approximation of Member States' legislation on collective redundancies;

(6) Whereas the Community Charter of the fundamental social rights of workers, adopted at the European Council meeting held in Strasbourg on 9 December 1989 by the Heads of State or Government of 11 Member States, states, inter alia, in point 7, first paragraph, first sentence, and second paragraph; in point 17, first paragraph; and in point 18, third indent:

'7.   The completion of the internal market must lead to an improvement in the living and working conditions of workers in the European Community (...).

The improvement must cover, where necessary, the development of certain aspects of employment regulations such as procedures for collective redundancies and those regarding bankruptcies.

(...)

17.   Information, consultation and participation for workers must be developed along appropriate lines, taking account of the practices in force in the various Member States.

(...)

18.   Such information, consultation and participation must be implemented in due time, particularly in the following cases:

(– ...)

(– ...)

– in cases of collective redundancy procedures;

(– ...)'

(7)   Whereas this approximation must therefore be promoted while the improvement is being maintained within the meaning of Article 117 of the Treaty;

(8)   Whereas, in order to calculate the number of redundancies provided for in the definition of collective redundancies within the meaning of this Directive, other forms of termination of employment contracts on the initiative of the employer should be equated to redundancies, provided that there are at least five redundancies;

(9)   Whereas it should be stipulated that this Directive applies in principle also to collective redundancies resulting where the establishment's activities are terminated as a result of a judicial decision;

(10) Whereas the Member States should be given the option of stipulating that workers' representatives may call on experts on grounds of the technical complexity of the matters which are likely to be the subject of the informing and consulting;

(11) Whereas it is necessary to ensure that employers' obligations as regards information, consultation and notification apply independently of whether the decision on collective redundancies emanates from the employer or from an undertaking which controls that employer;

(12) Whereas Member States should ensure that workers' representatives and/or workers have at their disposal administrative and/or judicial procedures in order to ensure that the obligations laid down in this Directive are fulfilled;

(13) Whereas this Directive must not affect the obligations of the Member States concerning the deadlines for transposition of the Directives set out in Annex I, Part B,

HAS ADOPTED THIS DIRECTIVE:

F2

SECTION I

Definitions and scope

Article 1

1. For the purposes of this Directive:

(a) 'collective redundancies' means dismissals effected by an employer for one or more reasons not related to the individual workers concerned where, according to the choice of the Member States, the number of redundancies is:

 (i) either, over a period of 30 days:

 – at least 10 in establishments normally employing more than 20 and less than 100 workers,

 – at least 10% of the number of workers in establishments normally employing at least 100 but less than 300 workers,

 – at least 30 in establishments normally employing 300 workers or more,

 (ii) or, over a period of 90 days, at least 20, whatever the number of workers normally employed in the establishments in question;

(b) 'workers' representatives' means the workers' representatives provided for by the laws or practices of the Member States.

For the purpose of calculating the number of redundancies provided for in the first subparagraph of point (a), terminations of an employment contract which occur on the employer's initiative for one or more reasons not related to the individual workers concerned shall be assimilated to redundancies, provided that there are at least five redundancies.

2. This Directive shall not apply to:

(a) collective redundancies effected under contracts of employment concluded for limited periods of time or for specific tasks except where such redundancies take place prior to the date of expiry or the completion of such contracts;

(b) workers employed by public administrative bodies or by establishments governed by public law (or, in Member States where this concept is unknown, by equivalent bodies);

(c)   the crews of seagoing vessels.

F3

SECTION II

Information and consultation

Article 2

1.   Where an employer is contemplating collective redundancies, he shall begin consultations with the workers' representatives in good time with a view to reaching an agreement.

2.   These consultations shall, at least, cover ways and means of avoiding collective redundancies or reducing the number of workers affected, and of mitigating the consequences by recourse to accompanying social measures aimed, inter alia, at aid for redeploying or retraining workers made redundant.

Member States may provide that the workers' representatives may call on the services of experts in accordance with national legislation and/or practice.

3.   To enable workers' representatives to make constructive proposals, the employers shall in good time during the course of the consultations:

(a)   supply them with all relevant information and

(b)   in any event notify them in writing of:

   (i)   the reasons for the projected redundancies;

   (ii)   the number of categories of workers to be made redundant;

   (iii)   the number and categories of workers normally employed;

   (iv)   the period over which the projected redundancies are to be effected;

   (v)   the criteria proposed for the selection of the workers to be made redundant in so far as national legislation and/or practice confers the power therefor upon the employer;

   (vi)   the method for calculating any redundancy payments other than those arising out of national legislation and/or practice.

The employer shall forward to the competent public authority a copy of, at least, the elements of the written communication which are provided for in the first subparagraph, point (b), subpoints (i) to (v).

4.   The obligations laid down in paragraphs 1, 2 and 3 shall apply irrespective of whether the decision regarding collective redundancies is being taken by the employer or by an undertaking controlling the employer.

In considering alleged breaches of the information, consultation and notification requirements laid down by this Directive, account shall not be taken of any defence on the part of the employer on the ground that the necessary information has not been provided to the employer by the undertaking which took the decision leading to collective redundancies.

F4

SECTION III

Procedure for collective redundances

Article 3

1. Employers shall notify the competent public authority in writing of any projected collective redundancies.

However, Member States may provide that in the case of planned collective redundancies arising from termination of the establishment's activities as a result of a judicial decision, the employer shall be obliged to notify the competent public authority in writing only if the latter so requests.

This notification shall contain all relevant information concerning the projected collective redundancies and the consultations with workers' representatives provided for in Article 2, and particularly the reasons for the redundancies, the number of workers to be made redundant, the number of workers normally employed and the period over which the redundancies are to be effected.

2. Employers shall forward to the workers' representatives a copy of the notification provided for in paragraph 1.

The workers' representatives may send any comments they may have to the competent public authority.

Article 4

1. Projected collective redundancies notified to the competent public authority shall take effect not earlier than 30 days after the notification referred to in Article 3(1) without prejudice to any provisions governing individual rights with regard to notice of dismissal.

Member States may grant the competent public authority the power to reduce the period provided for in the preceding subparagraph.

2. The period provided for in paragraph 1 shall be used by the competent public authority to seek solutions to the problems raised by the projected collective redundancies.

3. Where the initial period provided for in paragraph 1 is shorter than 60 days, Member States may grant the competent public authority the power to extend the initial period to 60 days following notification where the problems raised by the projected collective redundancies are not likely to be solved within the initial period.

Member States may grant the competent public authority wider powers of extension.

The employer must be informed of the extension and the grounds for it before expiry of the initial period provided for in paragraph 1.

4.   Member States need not apply this Article to collective redundancies arising from termination of the establishment's activities where this is the result of a judicial decision.

F5

SECTION IV

Final provisions

Article 5

This Directive shall not affect the right of Member States to apply or to introduce laws, regulations or administrative provisions which are more favourable to workers or to promote or to allow the application of collective agreements more favourable to workers.

Article 6

Member States shall ensure that judicial and/or administrative procedures for the enforcement of obligations under this Directive are available to the workers' representatives and/or workers.

Article 7

Member States shall forward to the Commission the text of any fundamental provisions of national law already adopted or being adopted in the area governed by this Directive.

Article 8

1.   The Directives listed in Annex I, Part A, are hereby repealed without prejudice to the obligations of the Member States concerning the deadlines for transposition of the said Directive set out in Annex I, Part B.

2.   References to the repealed Directives shall be construed as references to this Directive and shall be read in accordance with the correlation table in Annex II.

Article 9

This Directive shall enter into force on the 20th day following its publication in the Official Journal of the European Communities.

Article 10

This Directive is addressed to the Member States.

Done at Brussels, 20 July 1998.

For the Council

The President

W MOLTERER

F6

ANNEX I

PART A

Repealed Directives

(referred to by Article 8)

Council Directive 75/129/EEC and its following amendment:

Council Directive 92/56/EEC.

PART B

Deadlines for transposition into national law

(referred to by Article 8)

Directive	Deadline for transposition
75/129/EEC (OJ L48, 22.2.1975, p 29)	19 February 1977
92/56/EEC (OJ L245, 26.8.1992, p 3)	24 June 1994

F7

ANNEX II

Correlation table

Directive 75/129/EEC	This Directive
Article 1(1), first subparagraph, point (a), first indent, point 1	Article 1(1), first subparagraph, point (a)(i), first indent
Article 1(1), first subparagraph, point (a), first indent, point 2	Article 1(1), first subparagraph, point (a)(i), second indent
Article 1(1), first subparagraph, point (a), first indent, point 3	Article 1(1), first subparagraph, point (a)(i), third indent

Article 1(1), first subparagraph, point (a), second indent	Article 1(1), first subparagraph, point (a)(ii)
Article 1(1), first subparagraph, point (b)	Article 1(1), first subparagraph, point (b)
Article 1(1), second subparagraph	Article 1(1), second subparagraph
Article 1(2)	Article 1(2)
Article 2	Article 2
Article 3	Article 3
Article 4	Article 4
Article 5	Article 5
Article 5a	Article 6
Article 6(1)	—
Article 6(2)	Article 7
Article 7	—
—	Article 8
—	Article 9
—	Article 10
—	Annex I
—	Annex II

G European Works Council Directive 94/45/EC

COUNCIL DIRECTIVE 94/45/EC

of 22 September 1994

on the establishment of a European Works Council or a procedure in Community-scale undertakings and Community-scale groups of undertakings for the purposes of informing and consulting employees

GI

THE COUNCIL OF THE EUROPEAN UNION,

Having regard to the Agreement on social policy annexed to Protocol 14 on social policy annexed to the Treaty establishing the European Community, and in particular Article 2(2) thereof,

Having regard to the proposal from the Commission,

Having regard to the opinion of the Economic and Social Committee,

Acting in accordance with the procedure referred to in Article 189c of the Treaty,

Whereas, on the basis of the Protocol on Social Policy annexed to the Treaty establishing the European Community, the Kingdom of Belgium, the Kingdom of Denmark, the Federal Republic of Germany, the Hellenic Republic, the Kingdom of Spain, the French Republic, Ireland, the Italian Republic, the Grand Duchy of Luxembourg, the Kingdom of the Netherlands and the Portuguese Republic (hereinafter referred to as 'the Member States'), desirous of implementing the Social Charter of 1989, have adopted an Agreement on Social Policy;

Whereas Article 2(2) of the said Agreement authorises the Council to adopt minimum requirements by means of directives;

Whereas, pursuant to Article 1 of the Agreement, one particular objective of the Community and the Member States is to promote dialogue between management and labour;

Whereas point 17 of the Community Charter of Fundamental Social Rights of Workers provides, inter alia, that information, consultation and participation for workers must be developed along appropriate lines, taking account of the practices in force in different Member States; whereas the Charter states that 'this shall apply especially in companies or groups of companies having establishments or companies in two or more Member States';

Whereas the Council, despite the existence of a broad consensus among the majority of Member States, was unable to act on the proposal for a Council

Directive on the establishment of a European Works Council in Community-scale undertakings or groups of undertakings for the purposes of informing and consulting employees, as amended on 3 December 1991;

Whereas the Commission, pursuant to Article 3(2) of the Agreement on Social Policy, has consulted management and labour at Community level on the possible direction of Community action on the information and consultation of workers in Community-scale undertakings and Community-scale groups of undertakings;

Whereas the Commission, considering after this consultation that Community action was advisable, has again consulted management and labour on the content of the planned proposal, pursuant to Article 3(3) of the said Agreement, and management and labour have presented their opinions to the Commission;

Whereas, following this second phase of consultation, management and labour have not informed the Commission of their wish to initiate the process which might lead to the conclusion of an agreement, as provided for in Article 4 of the Agreement;

Whereas the functioning of the internal market involves a process of concentrations of undertakings, cross-border mergers, take-overs, joint ventures and, consequently, a transnationalisation of undertakings and groups of undertakings; whereas, if economic activities are to develop in a harmonious fashion, undertakings and groups of undertakings operating in two or more Member States must inform and consult the representatives of those of their employees that are affected by their decisions;

Whereas procedures for informing and consulting employees as embodied in legislation or practice in the Member States are often not geared to the transnational structure of the entity which takes the decisions affecting those employees; whereas this may lead to the unequal treatment of employees affected by decisions within one and the same undertaking or group of undertakings;

Whereas appropriate provisions must be adopted to ensure that the employees of Community-scale undertakings are properly informed and consulted when decisions which affect them are taken in a Member State other than that in which they are employed;

Whereas, in order to guarantee that the employees of undertakings or groups of undertakings operating in two or more Member States are properly informed and consulted, it is necessary to set up European Works Councils or to create other suitable procedures for the transnational information and consultation of employees;

Whereas it is accordingly necessary to have a definition of the concept of controlling undertaking relating solely to this Directive and not prejudging definitions of the concepts of group or control which might be adopted in texts to be drafted in the future;

Whereas the mechanisms for informing and consulting employees in such undertakings or groups must encompass all of the establishments or, as the case may be, the group's undertakings located within the Member States, regardless of whether the undertaking or the group's controlling undertaking has its central management inside or outside the territory of the Member States;

Whereas, in accordance with the principle of autonomy of the parties, it is for the representatives of employees and the management of the undertaking or the group's controlling undertaking to determine by agreement the nature, composition, the function, mode of operation, procedures and financial resources of European Works Councils or other information and consultation procedures so as to suit their own particular circumstances;

Whereas, in accordance with the principle of subsidiarity, it is for the Member States to determine who the employees' representatives are and in particular to provide, if they consider appropriate, for a balanced representation of different categories of employees;

Whereas, however, provision should be made for certain subsidiary requirements to apply should the parties so decide or in the event of the central management refusing to initiate negotiations or in the absence of agreement subsequent to such negotiations;

Whereas, moreover, employees' representatives may decide not to seek the setting-up of a European Works Council or the parties concerned may decide on other procedures for the transnational information and consultation of employees;

Whereas, without prejudice to the possibility of the parties deciding otherwise, the European Works Council set up in the absence of agreement between the parties must, in order to fulfil the objective of this Directive, be kept informed and consulted on the activities of the undertaking or group of undertakings so that it may assess the possible impact on employees' interests in at least two different Member States; whereas, to that end, the undertaking or controlling undertaking must be required to communicate to the employees' appointed representatives general information concerning the interests of employees and information relating more specifically to those aspects of the activities of the undertaking or group of undertakings which affect employees' interests; whereas the European Works Council must be able to deliver an opinion at the end of that meeting;

Whereas certain decisions having a significant effect on the interests of employees must be the subject of information and consultation of the employees' appointed representatives as soon as possible;

Whereas provision should be made for the employees' representatives acting within the framework of the Directive to enjoy, when exercising their functions, the same protection and guarantees similar to those provided to employees' representatives by the legislation and/or practice of the country of employment; whereas they must not be subject to any discrimination as a result of the lawful exercise of their activities and must enjoy adequate protection as regards dismissal and other sanctions;

Whereas the information and consultation provisions laid down in this Directive must be implemented in the case of an undertaking or a group's controlling undertaking which has its central management outside the territory of the Member States by its representative agent, to be designated if necessary, in one of the Member States or, in the absence of such an agent, by the establishment or controlled undertaking employing the greatest number of employees in the Member States;

Whereas special treatment should be accorded to Community-scale undertakings and groups of undertakings in which there exists, at the time when this Directive is brought into effect, an agreement, covering the entire workforce, providing for the transnational information and consultation of employees;

Whereas the Member States must take appropriate measures in the event of failure to comply with the obligations laid down in this Directive,

HAS ADOPTED THIS DIRECTIVE:

G2

SECTION I

General

Article 1
Objective

1. The purpose of this Directive is to improve the right to information and to consultation of employees in Community-scale undertakings and Community-scale groups of undertakings.

2. To that end, a European Works Council or a procedure for informing and consulting employees shall be established in every Community-scale undertaking and every Community-scale group of undertakings, where requested in the manner laid down in Article 5(1), with the purpose of informing and consulting employees under the terms, in the manner and with the effects laid down in this Directive.

3. Notwithstanding paragraph 2, where a Community-scale group of undertakings within the meaning of Article 2(1)(c) comprises one or more undertakings or groups of undertakings which are Community-scale undertakings or Community-scale groups of undertakings within the meaning of Article 2(1)(a) or (c), a European Works Council shall be established at the level of the group unless the agreements referred to in Article 6 provide otherwise.

4. Unless a wider scope is provided for in the agreements referred to in Article 6, the powers and competence of European Works Councils and the scope of information and consultation procedures established to achieve the purpose specified in paragraph 1 shall, in the case of a Community-scale undertaking, cover all the establishments located within the Member States and, in the case of a Community-scale group of undertakings, all group undertakings located within the Member States.

5. Member States may provide that this Directive shall not apply to merchant navy crews.

Article 2
Definitions

1. For the purposes of this Directive:

(a) 'Community-scale undertaking' means any undertaking with at least 1,000 employees within the Member States and at least 150 employees in each of at least two Member States;

(b) 'group of undertakings' means a controlling undertaking and its controlled undertakings;

(c) 'Community-scale group of undertakings' means a group of undertakings with the following characteristics:

 –   at least 1,000 employees within the Member States,

 –   at least two group undertakings in different Member States, and

 –   at least one group undertaking with at least 150 employees in one Member State and at least one other group undertaking with at least 150 employees in another Member State;

(d) 'employees' representatives' means the employees' representatives provided for by national law and/or practice;

(e) 'central management' means the central management of the Community-scale undertaking or, in the case of a Community-scale group of undertakings, of the controlling undertaking;

(f) 'consultation' means the exchange of views and establishment of dialogue between employees' representatives and central management or any more appropriate level of management;

(g) 'European Works Council' means the council established in accordance with Article 1(2) or the provisions of the Annex, with the purpose of informing and consulting employees;

(h) 'special negotiating body' means the body established in accordance with Article 5(2) to negotiate with the central management regarding the establishment of a European Works Council or a procedure for informing and consulting employees in accordance with Article 1(2).

2. For the purposes of this Directive, the prescribed thresholds for the size of the workforce shall be based on the average number of employees, including part-time employees, employed during the previous two years calculated according to national legislation and/or practice.

Article 3
Definition of 'controlling undertaking'

1. For the purposes of this Directive, 'controlling undertaking' means an undertaking which can exercise a dominant influence over another undertaking ('the controlled undertaking') by virtue, for example, of ownership, financial participation or the rules which govern it.

2. The ability to exercise a dominant influence shall be presumed, without prejudice to ʼproof to the contrary, when an undertaking, in relation to another undertaking, directly or indirectly:

(a)   holds a majority of that undertaking's subscribed capital; or

(b)   controls a majority of the votes attached to that undertaking's issued share capital; or

(c)   can appoint more than half of the members of that undertaking's administrative, management or supervisory body.

3. For the purposes of paragraph 2, a controlling undertaking's rights as regards voting and appointment shall include the rights of any other controlled undertaking and those of any person or body acting in his or its own name but on behalf of the controlling undertaking or of any other controlled undertaking.

4. Notwithstanding paragraphs 1 and 2, an undertaking shall not be deemed to be a 'controlling undertaking' with respect to another undertaking in which it has holdings where the former undertaking is a company referred to in Article 3(5)(a) or (c) of Council Regulation (EEC) 4064/89 of 21 December 1989 on the control of concentrations between undertakings.

5. A dominant influence shall not be presumed to be exercised solely by virtue of the fact that an office holder is exercising his functions, according to the law of a Member State relating to liquidation, winding up, insolvency, cessation of payments, compositions or analogous proceedings.

6. The law applicable in order to determine whether an undertaking is a 'controlling undertaking' shall be the law of the Member State which governs that undertaking.

Where the law governing that undertaking is not that of a Member State, the law applicable shall be the law of the Member State within whose territory the representative of the undertaking or, in the absence of such a representative, the central management of the group undertaking which employs the greatest number of employees is situated.

7. Where, in the case of a conflict of laws in the application of paragraph 2, two or more undertakings from a group satisfy one or more of the criteria laid down in that paragraph, the undertaking which satisfies the criterion laid down in point (c) thereof shall be regarded as the controlling undertaking, without prejudice to proof that another undertaking is able to exercise a dominant influence.

G3

SECTION II

Establishment of a European Works Council or an employee information and consultation procedure

Article 4

Responsibility for the establishment of a European Works Council or an employee information and consultation procedure

1. The central management shall be responsible for creating the conditions and means necessary for the setting up of a European Works Council or an information and consultation procedure, as provided for in Article 1(2), in a Community-scale undertaking and a Community-scale group of undertakings.

2. Where the central management is not situated in a Member State, the central management's representative agent in a Member State, to be designated if necessary, shall take on the responsibility referred to in paragraph 1.

In the absence of such a representative, the management of the establishment or group undertaking employing the greatest number of employees in any one Member State shall take on the responsibility referred to in paragraph 1.

3. For the purposes of this Directive, the representative or representatives or, in the absence of any such representatives, the management referred to in the second subparagraph of paragraph 2, shall be regarded as the central management.

Article 5

Special negotiating body

1. In order to achieve the objective in Article 1(1), the central management shall initiate negotiations for the establishment of a European Works Council or an information and consultation procedure on its own initiative or at the written request of at least 100 employees or their representatives in at least two undertakings or establishments in at least two different Member States.

2. For this purpose, a special negotiating body shall be established in accordance with the following guidelines:

(a) The Member States shall determine the method to be used for the election or appointment of the members of the special negotiating body who are to be elected or appointed in their territories.

Member States shall provide that employees in undertakings and/or establishments in which there are no employees' representatives through no fault of their own, have the right to elect or appoint members of the special negotiating body.

The second subparagraph shall be without prejudice to national legislation and/or practice laying down thresholds for the establishment of employee representation bodies.

(b)   The special negotiating body shall have a minimum of three and a maximum of 17 members.

(c)   In these elections or appointments, it must be ensured:

–   firstly, that each Member State in which the Community-scale undertaking has one or more establishments or in which the Community-scale group of undertakings has the controlling undertaking or one or more controlled undertakings is represented by one member,

–   secondly, that there are supplementary members in proportion to the number of employees working in the establishments, the controlling undertaking or the controlled undertakings as laid down by the legislation of the Member State within the territory of which the central management is situated.

(d)   The central management and local management shall be informed of the composition of the special negotiating body.

3. The special negotiating body shall have the task of determining, with the central management, by written agreement, the scope, composition, functions, and term of office of the European Works Council(s) or the arrangements for implementing a procedure for the information and consultation of employees.

4. With a view to the conclusion of an agreement in accordance with Article 6, the central management shall convene a meeting with the special negotiating body. It shall inform the local managements accordingly.

For the purpose of the negotiations, the special negotiating body may be assisted by experts of its choice.

5. The special negotiating body may decide, by at least two-thirds of the votes, not to open negotiations in accordance with paragraph 4, or to terminate the negotiations already opened.

Such a decision shall stop the procedure to conclude the agreement referred to in Article 6. Where such a decision has been taken, the provisions in the Annex shall not apply.

A new request to convene the special negotiating body may be made at the earliest two years after the abovementioned decision unless the parties concerned lay down a shorter period.

6. Any expenses relating to the negotiations referred to in paragraphs 3 and 4 shall be borne by the central management so as to enable the special negotiating body to carry out its task in an appropriate manner.

In compliance with this principle, Member States may lay down budgetary rules regarding the operation of the special negotiating body. They may in particular limit the funding to cover one expert only.

Article 6
Content of the agreement

1. The central management and the special negotiating body must negotiate in a spirit of co-operation with a view to reaching an agreement on the detailed arrangements for implementing the information and consultation of employees provided for in Article 1(1).

2. Without prejudice to the autonomy of the parties, the agreement referred to in paragraph 1 between the central management and the special negotiating body shall determine:

(a) the undertakings of the Community-scale group of undertakings or the establishments of the Community-scale undertaking which are covered by the agreement;

(b) the composition of the European Works Council, the number of members, the allocation of seats and the term of office;

(c) the functions and the procedure for information and consultation of the European Works Council;

(d) the venue, frequency and duration of meetings of the European Works Council;

(e) the financial and material resources to be allocated to the European Works Council;

(f) the duration of the agreement and the procedure for its renegotiation.

3. The central management and the special negotiating body may decide, in writing, to establish one or more information and consultation procedures instead of a European Works Council.

The agreement must stipulate by what method the employees' representatives shall have the right to meet to discuss the information conveyed to them.

This information shall relate in particular to transnational questions which significantly affect workers' interests.

4. The agreements referred to in paragraphs 2 and 3 shall not, unless provision is made otherwise therein, be subject to the subsidiary requirements of the Annex.

5. For the purposes of concluding the agreements referred to in paragraphs 2 and 3, the special negotiating body shall act by a majority of its members.

Article 7
Subsidiary requirements

1. In order to achieve the objective in Article 1(1), the subsidiary requirements laid down by the legislation of the Member State in which the central management is situated shall apply:

– where the central management and the special negotiating body so decide, or

– where the central management refuses to commence negotiations within six months of the request referred to in Article 5(1), or

– where, after three years from the date of this request, they are unable to conclude an agreement as laid down in Article 6 and the special negotiating body has not taken the decision provided for in Article 5(5).

2. The subsidiary requirements referred to in paragraph 1 as adopted in the legislation of the Member States must satisfy the provisions set out in the Annex.

G4

SECTION III

Miscellaneous provisions

Article 8
Confidential information

1. Member States shall provide that members of special negotiating bodies or of European Works Councils and any experts who assist them are not authorised to reveal any information which has expressly been provided to them in confidence.

The same shall apply to employees' representatives in the framework of an information and consultation procedure.

This obligation shall continue to apply, wherever the persons referred to in the first and second subparagraphs are, even after the expiry of their terms of office.

2. Each Member State shall provide, in specific cases and under the conditions and limits laid down by national legislation, that the central management situated in its territory is not obliged to transmit information when its nature is such that, according to objective criteria, it would seriously harm the functioning of the undertakings concerned or would be prejudicial to them.

A Member State may make such dispensation subject to prior administrative or judicial authorisation.

3. Each Member State may lay down particular provisions for the central management of undertakings in its territory which pursue directly and essentially the aim of ideological guidance with respect to information and the expression of opinions, on condition that, at the date of adoption of this Directive such particular provisions already exist in the national legislation.

Article 9
Operation of European Works Council and information and consultation procedure for workers

The central management and the European Works Council shall work in a spirit of co-operation with due regard to their reciprocal rights and obligations.

The same shall apply to co-operation between the central management and employees' representatives in the framework of an information and consultation procedure for workers.

Article 10
Protection of employees' representatives

Members of special negotiating bodies, members of European Works Councils and employees' representatives exercising their functions under the procedure referred to in Article 6(3) shall, in the exercise of their functions, enjoy the same protection and guarantees provided for employees' representatives by the national legislation and/or practice in force in their country of employment.

This shall apply in particular to attendance at meetings of special negotiating bodies or European Works Councils or any other meetings within the framework of the agreement referred to in Article 6(3), and the payment of wages for members who are on the staff of the Community-scale undertaking or the Community-scale group of undertakings for the period of absence necessary for the performance of their duties.

Article 11
Compliance with this Directive

1. Each Member State shall ensure that the management of establishments of a Community-scale undertaking and the management of undertakings which form part of a Community-scale group of undertakings which are situated within its territory and their employees' representatives or, as the case may be, employees abide by the obligations laid down by this Directive, regardless of whether or not the central management is situated within its territory.

2.   Member States shall ensure that the information on the number of employees referred to in Article 2(1)(a) and (c) is made available by undertakings at the request of the parties concerned by the application of this Directive.

3.   Member States shall provide for appropriate measures in the event of failure to comply with this Directive; in particular, they shall ensure that adequate administrative or judicial procedures are available to enable the obligations deriving from this Directive to be enforced.

4.   Where Member States apply Article 8, they shall make provision for administrative or judicial appeal procedures which the employees' representatives may initiate when the central management requires confidentiality or does not give information in accordance with that Article.

Such procedures may include procedures designed to protect the confidentiality of the information in question.

Article 12
Link between this Directive and other provisions

1.   This Directive shall apply without prejudice to measures taken pursuant to Council Directive 75/129/EEC of 17 February 1975 on the approximation of the laws of the Member States relating to collective redundancies, and to Council Directive 77/187/EEC of 14 February 1977 on the approximation of the laws of the Member States relating to the safeguarding of employees' rights in the event of transfers of undertakings, businesses or parts of businesses.

2.   This Directive shall be without prejudice to employees' existing rights to information and consultation under national law.

Article 13
Agreements in force

1.   Without prejudice to paragraph 2, the obligations arising from this Directive shall not apply to Community-scale undertakings or Community-scale groups of undertakings in which, on the date laid down in Article 14(1) for the implementation of this Directive or the date of its transposition in the Member State in question, where this is earlier than the abovementioned date, there is already an agreement, covering the entire workforce, providing for the transnational information and consultation of employees.

2.   When the agreements referred to in paragraph 1 expire, the parties to those agreements may decide jointly to renew them.

Where this is not the case, the provisions of this Directive shall apply.

Article 14
Final provisions

1.   Member States shall bring into force the laws, regulations and administrative provisions necessary to comply with this Directive no later than

22 September 1996 or shall ensure by that date at the latest that management and labour introduce the required provisions by way of agreement, the Member States being obliged to take all necessary steps enabling them at all times to guarantee the results imposed by this Directive. They shall forthwith inform the Commission thereof.

2. When Member States adopt these measures, they shall contain a reference to this Directive or shall be accompanied by such reference on the occasion of their official publication. The methods of making such reference shall be laid down by Member States.

Article 15
Review by the Commission

Not later than 22 September 1999, the Commission shall, in consultation with the Member States and with management and labour at European level, review its operation and, in particular examine whether the workforce size thresholds are appropriate with a view to proposing suitable amendments to the Council, where necessary.

Article 16

This Directive is addressed to the Member States.

Done at Brussels, 22 September 1994.

For the Council
The President
N BLUEM

G5

ANNEX

Subsidiary requirements referred to in Article 7 of the Directive

1. In order to achieve the objective in Article 1(1) of the Directive and in the cases provided for in Article 7(1) of the Directive, the establishment, composition and competence of a European Works Council shall be governed by the following rules:

(a) The competence of the European Works Council shall be limited to information and consultation on the matters which concern the Community-scale undertaking or Community-scale group of undertakings as a whole or at least two of its establishments or group undertakings situated in different Member States.

  In the case of undertakings or groups of undertakings referred to in Article 4(2), the competence of the European Works Council shall be limited to those matters concerning all their establishments or group undertakings situated within the Member States or concerning at least two of their establishments or group undertakings situated in different Member States.

(b)   The European Works Council shall be composed of employees of the Community-scale undertaking or Community-scale group of undertakings elected or appointed from their number by the employees' representatives or, in the absence thereof, by the entire body of employees.

The election or appointment of members of the European Works Council shall be carried out in accordance with national legislation and/or practice.

(c)   The European Works Council shall have a minimum of three members and a maximum of 30.

Where its size so warrants, it shall elect a select committee from among its members, comprising at most three members.

It shall adopt its own rules of procedure.

(d)   In the election or appointment of members of the European Works Council, it must be ensured:

-   firstly, that each Member State in which the Community-scale undertaking has one or more establishments or in which the Community-scale group of undertakings has the controlling undertaking or one or more controlled undertakings is represented by one member,

-   secondly, that there are supplementary members in proportion to the number of employees working in the establishments, the controlling undertaking or the controlled undertakings as laid down by the legislation of the Member State within the territory of which the central management is situated.

(e)   The central management and any other more appropriate level of management shall be informed of the composition of the European Works Council.

(f)   Four years after the European Works Council is established it shall examine whether to open negotiations for the conclusion of the agreement referred to in Article 6 of the Directive or to continue to apply the subsidiary requirements adopted in accordance with this Annex.

Articles 6 and 7 of the Directive shall apply, *mutatis mutandis*, if a decision has been taken to negotiate an agreement according to Article 6 of the Directive, in which case 'special negotiating body' shall be replaced by 'European Works Council'.

2. The European Works Council shall have the right to meet with the central management once a year, to be informed and consulted, on the basis of a

report drawn up by the central management, on the progress of the business of the Community-scale undertaking or Community-scale group of undertakings and its prospects. The local managements shall be informed accordingly.

The meeting shall relate in particular to the structure, economic and financial situation, the probable development of the business and of production and sales, the situation and probable trend of employment, investments, and substantial changes concerning organisation, introduction of new working methods or production processes, transfers of production, mergers, cut-backs or closures of undertakings, establishments or important parts thereof, and collective redundancies.

3.   Where there are exceptional circumstances affecting the employees' interests to a considerable extent, particularly in the event of relocations, the closure of establishments or undertakings or collective redundancies, the select committee or, where no such committee exists, the European Works Council shall have the right to be informed. It shall have the right to meet, at its request, the central management, or any other more appropriate level of management within the Community-scale undertaking or group of undertakings having its own powers of decision, so as to be informed and consulted on measures significantly affecting employees' interests.

Those members of the European Works Council who have been elected or appointed by the establishments and/or undertakings which are directly concerned by the measures in question shall also have the right to participate in the meeting organised with the select committee.

This information and consultation meeting shall take place as soon as possible on the basis of a report drawn up by the central management or any other appropriate level of management of the Community-scale undertaking or group of undertakings, on which an opinion may be delivered at the end of the meeting or within a reasonable time.

This meeting shall not affect the prerogatives of the central management.

4.   The Member States may lay down rules on the chairing of information and consultation meetings.

Before any meeting with the central management, the European Works Council or the select committee, where necessary enlarged in accordance with the second paragraph of point 3, shall be entitled to meet without the management concerned being present.

5.   Without prejudice to Article 8 of the Directive, the members of the European Works Council shall inform the representatives of the employees of the establishments or of the undertakings of a Community-scale group of undertakings or, in the absence of representatives, the workforce as a whole, of the content and outcome of the information and consultation procedure carried out in accordance with this Annex.

6. The European Works Council or the select committee may be assisted by experts of its choice, in so far as this is necessary for it to carry out its tasks.

7. The operating expenses of the European Works Council shall be borne by the central management.

The central management concerned shall provide the members of the European Works Council with such financial and material resources as enable them to perform their duties in an appropriate manner.

In particular, the cost of organising meetings and arranging for interpretation facilities and the accommodation and travelling expenses of members of the European Works Council and its select committee shall be met by the central management unless otherwise agreed.

In compliance with these principles, the Member States may lay down budgetary rules regarding the operation of the European Works Council. They may in particular limit funding to cover one expert only.

H Information and Consultation Directive 2002/14/EC

Directive 2002/14/EC of the European Parliament and of the Council

of 11 March 2002

establishing a general framework for informing and consulting employees in the European Community

H1

THE EUROPEAN PARLIAMENT AND THE COUNCIL OF THE EUROPEAN UNION,

Having regard to the Treaty establishing the European Community, and in particular Article 137(2) thereof,

Having regard to the proposal from the Commission,

Having regard to the opinion of the Economic and Social Committee,

Having regard to the opinion of the Committee of the Regions,

Acting in accordance with the procedure referred to in Article 251(4), and in the light of the joint text approved by the Conciliation Committee on 23 January 2002,

Whereas:

(1) Pursuant to Article 136 of the Treaty, a particular objective of the Community and the Member States is to promote social dialogue between management and labour.

(2) Point 17 of the Community Charter of Fundamental Social Rights of Workers provides, inter alia, that information, consultation and participation for workers must be developed along appropriate lines, taking account of the practices in force in different Member States.

(3) The Commission consulted management and labour at Community level on the possible direction of Community action on the information and consultation of employees in undertakings within the Community.

(4) Following this consultation, the Commission considered that Community action was advisable and again consulted management and labour on the contents of the planned proposal; management and labour have presented their opinions to the Commission.

(5) Having completed this second stage of consultation, management and labour have not informed the Commission of their wish to initiate the process potentially leading to the conclusion of an agreement.

(6) The existence of legal frameworks at national and Community level

intended to ensure that employees are involved in the affairs of the undertaking employing them and in decisions which affect them has not always prevented serious decisions affecting employees from being taken and made public without adequate procedures having been implemented beforehand to inform and consult them.

(7) There is a need to strengthen dialogue and promote mutual trust within undertakings in order to improve risk anticipation, make work organisation more flexible and facilitate employee access to training within the undertaking while maintaining security, make employees aware of adaptation needs, increase employees' availability to undertake measures and activities to increase their employability, promote employee involvement in the operation and future of the undertaking and increase its competitiveness.

(8) There is a need, in particular, to promote and enhance information and consultation on the situation and likely development of employment within the undertaking and, where the employer's evaluation suggests that employment within the undertaking may be under threat, the possible anticipatory measures envisaged, in particular in terms of employee training and skill development, with a view to offsetting the negative developments or their consequences and increasing the employability and adaptability of the employees likely to be affected.

(9) Timely information and consultation is a prerequisite for the success of the restructuring and adaptation of undertakings to the new conditions created by globalisation of the economy, particularly through the development of new forms of organisation of work.

(10) The Community has drawn up and implemented an employment strategy based on the concepts of 'anticipation', 'prevention' and 'employability', which are to be incorporated as key elements into all public policies likely to benefit employment, including the policies of individual undertakings, by strengthening the social dialogue with a view to promoting change compatible with preserving the priority objective of employment.

(11) Further development of the internal market must be properly balanced, maintaining the essential values on which our societies are based and ensuring that all citizens benefit from economic development.

(12) Entry into the third stage of economic and monetary union has extended and accelerated the competitive pressures at European level. This means that more supportive measures are needed at national level.

(13) The existing legal frameworks for employee information and consultation at Community and national level tend to adopt an excessively a posteriori approach to the process of change, neglect the economic aspects of decisions taken and do not contribute either to genuine anticipation of employment developments within the undertaking or to risk prevention.

(14) All of these political, economic, social and legal developments call for changes to the existing legal framework providing for the legal and practical instruments enabling the right to be informed and consulted to be exercised.

(15) This Directive is without prejudice to national systems regarding the exercise of this right in practice where those entitled to exercise it are required to indicate their wishes collectively.

(16) This Directive is without prejudice to those systems which provide for the direct involvement of employees, as long as they are always free to exercise the right to be informed and consulted through their representatives.

(17) Since the objectives of the proposed action, as outlined above, cannot be adequately achieved by the Member States, in that the object is to establish a framework for employee information and consultation appropriate for the new European context described above, and can therefore, in view of the scale and impact of the proposed action, be better achieved at Community level, the Community may adopt measures in accordance with the principle of subsidiarity as set out in Article 5 of the Treaty. In accordance with the principle of proportionality, as set out in that Article, this Directive does not go beyond what is necessary in order to achieve these objectives.

(18) The purpose of this general framework is to establish minimum requirements applicable throughout the Community while not preventing Member States from laying down provisions more favourable to employees.

(19) The purpose of this general framework is also to avoid any administrative, financial or legal constraints which would hinder the creation and development of small and medium-sized undertakings. To this end, the scope of this Directive should be restricted, according to the choice made by Member States, to undertakings with at least 50 employees or establishments employing at least 20 employees.

(20) This takes into account and is without prejudice to other national measures and practices aimed at fostering social dialogue within companies not covered by this Directive and within public administrations.

(21) However, on a transitional basis, Member States in which there is no established statutory system of information and consultation of employees or employee representation should have the possibility of further restricting the scope of the Directive as regards the numbers of employees.

(22) A Community framework for informing and consulting employees should keep to a minimum the burden on undertakings or establishments while ensuring the effective exercise of the rights granted.

(23) The objective of this Directive is to be achieved through the establishment of a general framework comprising the principles, definitions and arrangements for information and consultation, which it will be for the Member States to comply with and adapt to their own national situation, ensuring, where appropriate, that management and labour have a leading role by allowing them to define freely, by agreement, the arrangements for informing and consulting employees which they consider to be best suited to their needs and wishes.

(24) Care should be taken to avoid affecting some specific rules in the field of employee information and consultation existing in some national laws, addressed to undertakings or establishments which pursue political, professional, organisational, religious, charitable, educational, scientific or artistic aims, as well as aims involving information and the expression of opinions.

(25) Undertakings and establishments should be protected against disclosure of certain particularly sensitive information.

(26) The employer should be allowed not to inform and consult where this would seriously damage the undertaking or the establishment or where he has to comply immediately with an order issued to him by a regulatory or supervisory body.

(27) Information and consultation imply both rights and obligations for management and labour at undertaking or establishment level.

(28) Administrative or judicial procedures, as well as sanctions that are effective, dissuasive and proportionate in relation to the seriousness of the offence, should be applicable in cases of infringement of the obligations based on this Directive.

(29) This Directive should not affect the provisions, where these are more specific, of Council Directive 98/59/EC of 20 July 1998 on the approximation of the laws of the Member States relating to collective redundancies and of Council Directive 2001/23/EC of 12 March 2001 on the approximation of the laws of the Member States relating to the safeguarding of employees' rights in the event of transfers of undertakings, businesses or parts of undertakings or businesses.

(30) Other rights of information and consultation, including those arising from Council Directive 94/45/EEC of 22 September 1994 on the establishment of a European Works Council or a procedure in Community-scale undertakings and Community-scale groups of undertakings for the purposes of informing and consulting employees, should not be affected by this Directive.

(31) Implementation of this Directive should not be sufficient grounds for a reduction in the general level of protection of workers in the areas to which it applies,

HAVE ADOPTED THIS DIRECTIVE:

H2

Article 1

Object and principles

1. The purpose of this Directive is to establish a general framework setting out minimum requirements for the right to information and consultation of employees in undertakings or establishments within the Community.

2. The practical arrangements for information and consultation shall be defined and implemented in accordance with national law and industrial relations practices in individual Member States in such a way as to ensure their effectiveness.

3. When defining or implementing practical arrangements for information and consultation, the employer and the employees' representatives shall work in a spirit of co-operation and with due regard for their reciprocal rights and obligations, taking into account the interests both of the undertaking or establishment and of the employees.

Article 2

Definitions

For the purposes of this Directive:

(a) 'undertaking' means a public or private undertaking carrying out an economic activity, whether or not operating for gain, which is located within the territory of the Member States;

(b) 'establishment' means a unit of business defined in accordance with national law and practice, and located within the territory of a Member State, where an economic activity is carried out on an ongoing basis with human and material resources;

(c) 'employer' means the natural or legal person party to employment contracts or employment relationships with employees, in accordance with national law and practice;

(d) 'employee' means any person who, in the Member State concerned, is protected as an employee under national employment law and in accordance with national practice;

(e) 'employees' representatives' means the employees' representatives provided for by national laws and/or practices;

(f) 'information' means transmission by the employer to the employees' representatives of data in order to enable them to acquaint themselves with the subject matter and to examine it;

(g)   'consultation' means the exchange of views and establishment of dialogue between the employees' representatives and the employer.

Article 3

Scope

1.   This Directive shall apply, according to the choice made by Member States, to:

(a)   undertakings employing at least 50 employees in any one Member State, or

(b)   establishments employing at least 20 employees in any one Member State.

Member States shall determine the method for calculating the thresholds of employees employed.

2.   In conformity with the principles and objectives of this Directive, Member States may lay down particular provisions applicable to undertakings or establishments which pursue directly and essentially political, professional, organisational, religious, charitable, educational, scientific or artistic aims, as well as aims involving information and the expression of opinions, on condition that, at the date of entry into force of this Directive, provisions of that nature already exist in national legislation.

3.   Member States may derogate from this Directive through particular provisions applicable to the crews of vessels plying the high seas.

Article 4

Practical arrangements for information and consultation

1.   In accordance with the principles set out in Article 1 and without prejudice to any provisions and/or practices in force more favourable to employees, the Member States shall determine the practical arrangements for exercising the right to information and consultation at the appropriate level in accordance with this Article.

2.   Information and consultation shall cover:

(a)   information on the recent and probable development of the undertaking's or the establishment's activities and economic situation;

(b)   information and consultation on the situation, structure and probable development of employment within the undertaking or establishment and on any anticipatory measures envisaged, in particular where there is a threat to employment;

(c)   information and consultation on decisions likely to lead to substantial changes in work organisation or in contractual relations, including those covered by the Community provisions referred to in Article 9(1).

3. Information shall be given at such time, in such fashion and with such content as are appropriate to enable, in particular, employees' representatives to conduct an adequate study and, where necessary, prepare for consultation.

4. Consultation shall take place:

(a) while ensuring that the timing, method and content thereof are appropriate;

(b) at the relevant level of management and representation, depending on the subject under discussion;

(c) on the basis of information supplied by the employer in accordance with Article 2(f) and of the opinion which the employees' representatives are entitled to formulate;

(d) in such a way as to enable employees' representatives to meet the employer and obtain a response, and the reasons for that response, to any opinion they might formulate;

(e) with a view to reaching an agreement on decisions within the scope of the employer's powers referred to in paragraph 2(c).

Article 5

Information and consultation deriving from an agreement

Member States may entrust management and labour at the appropriate level, including at undertaking or establishment level, with defining freely and at any time through negotiated agreement the practical arrangements for informing and consulting employees. These agreements, and agreements existing on the date laid down in Article 11, as well as any subsequent renewals of such agreements, may establish, while respecting the principles set out in Article 1 and subject to conditions and limitations laid down by the Member States, provisions which are different from those referred to in Article 4.

Article 6

Confidential information

1. Member States shall provide that, within the conditions and limits laid down by national legislation, the employees' representatives, and any experts who assist them, are not authorised to reveal to employees or to third parties, any information which, in the legitimate interest of the undertaking or establishment, has expressly been provided to them in confidence. This obligation shall continue to apply, wherever the said representatives or experts are, even after expiry of their terms of office. However, a Member State may authorise the employees' representatives and anyone assisting them to pass on confidential information to employees and to third parties bound by an obligation of confidentiality.

2.   Member States shall provide, in specific cases and within the conditions and limits laid down by national legislation, that the employer is not obliged to communicate information or undertake consultation when the nature of that information or consultation is such that, according to objective criteria, it would seriously harm the functioning of the undertaking or establishment or would be prejudicial to it.

3.   Without prejudice to existing national procedures, Member States shall provide for administrative or judicial review procedures for the case where the employer requires confidentiality or does not provide the information in accordance with paragraphs 1 and 2. They may also provide for procedures intended to safeguard the confidentiality of the information in question.

Article 7

Protection of employees' representatives

Member States shall ensure that employees' representatives, when carrying out their functions, enjoy adequate protection and guarantees to enable them to perform properly the duties which have been assigned to them.

Article 8

Protection of rights

1.   Member States shall provide for appropriate measures in the event of non-compliance with this Directive by the employer or the employees' representatives. In particular, they shall ensure that adequate administrative or judicial procedures are available to enable the obligations deriving from this Directive to be enforced.

2.   Member States shall provide for adequate sanctions to be applicable in the event of infringement of this Directive by the employer or the employees' representatives. These sanctions must be effective, proportionate and dissuasive.

Article 9

Link between this Directive and other Community and national provisions

1.   This Directive shall be without prejudice to the specific information and consultation procedures set out in Article 2 of Directive 98/59/EC and Article 7 of Directive 2001/23/EC.

2.   This Directive shall be without prejudice to provisions adopted in accordance with Directives 94/45/EC and 97/74/EC.

3.   This Directive shall be without prejudice to other rights to information, consultation and participation under national law.

4. Implementation of this Directive shall not be sufficient grounds for any regression in relation to the situation which already prevails in each Member State and in relation to the general level of protection of workers in the areas to which it applies.

Article 10

Transitional provisions

Notwithstanding Article 3, a Member State in which there is, at the date of entry into force of this Directive, no general, permanent and statutory system of information and consultation of employees, nor a general, permanent and statutory system of employee representation at the workplace allowing employees to be represented for that purpose, may limit the application of the national provisions implementing this Directive to:

(a) undertakings employing at least 150 employees or establishments employing at least 100 employees until 23 March 2007, and

(b) undertakings employing at least 100 employees or establishments employing at least 50 employees during the year following the date in point (a).

Article 11

Transposition

1. Member States shall adopt the laws, regulations and administrative provisions necessary to comply with this Directive not later than 23 March 2005 or shall ensure that management and labour introduce by that date the required provisions by way of agreement, the Member States being obliged to take all necessary steps enabling them to guarantee the results imposed by this Directive at all times. They shall forthwith inform the Commission thereof.

2. Where Member States adopt these measures, they shall contain a reference to this Directive or shall be accompanied by such reference on the occasion of their official publication. The methods of making such reference shall be laid down by the Member States.

Article 12

Review by the Commission

Not later than 23 March 2007, the Commission shall, in consultation with the Member States and the social partners at Community level, review the application of this Directive with a view to proposing any necessary amendments.

Article 13

Entry into force

This Directive shall enter into force on the day of its publication in the *Official Journal of the European Communities*.

Article 14

Addresses

This Directive is addressed to the Member States.

Done at Brussels, 11 March 2002.

For the European Parliament

The President

P Cox

For the Council

The President

J Piqué i Camps

Case studies

1 Structure of the case studies

Susan Mayne
Caroline Humphries

1.1 Introduction

The application of the laws of different member states across national borders can be a difficult matter, both technically and in practice.

In order to demonstrate how the laws of different member states operate in practice, we have devised three case studies.

Case Study 1 deals with the acquisition by a company situated in one EU state of a 'business' situated in another EU state. This is an asset deal, with no relocation issues. The purpose of this case study is to show how different EU countries deal with the acquisition of a 'business' outside their own country, where that 'business' will remain in another EU country.

Case Study 2 deals with the situation where a parent company decides to close down part of the business of one of its subsidiaries (based in one EU country) and transfer this to another subsidiary (based in another EU country). The purpose of this case study is to show how different EU countries deal with the transfer of a 'business' from their own country to another EU country, including a physical move.

Case Study 3 deals with the outsourcing of an ancillary activity of a business from an EU country to a non-EU country. The purpose of this case study is to show how different national laws operate outside the EU.

Each case study is based on a common fact scenario, which sets out the core information on which responses are based. Although the case studies to which each of the contributors have responded are substantially the same, there are slight differences between them to reflect the fact that each contributor has set out responses from his own country's perspective. The case studies have therefore been tailored to ensure that the scenarios described are appropriate for each contributor (for example, in Case Study 1, Dormir, the prospective new manager of the hotels, must be located in the country of each contributor for the scenarios to make any sense). Notwithstanding these variations, the scenarios upon which the case studies are based have been kept substantially the same, so that clear contrasts and comparisons can be made between the approaches taken in different EU states.

1.2 Standard questions – local perspectives

Each case study includes a number of questions, so that each contributor can discuss a broad range of cross-border issues from a practical perspective. As with the scenarios in the case studies, these questions have been amended slightly to reflect the fact that each contributor has answered them from his country's perspective. Similarly, variations within the questions have been kept to a minimum, to illustrate the differences in approach between different countries.

This section of the book simply sets out the standard fact scenario and questions for each case study, in unamended form. Each chapter in Part 4 of the book sets out the exact scenarios and questions to which the contributors have responded (amended as indicated above). These have been reproduced in full in each chapter, so that each contributor's response is self-contained.

13 Case studies

13.1 Case study 1
(Acquisition of a 'business' situated in another EU state; asset deal; no relocation)

Slumber Ltd, a hotel management company incorporated in the UK and based in Manchester, UK, has been in financial difficulties for some time. Slumber operates nine exclusive hotels in the main British cities (London, Manchester, Birmingham, Leeds, Glasgow, Edinburgh, Liverpool, Cardiff and Bristol) under the 'Slumber' brand. Slumber is 100 per cent owned by UK hotel chain Ezeroom plc, also incorporated in the UK. Each hotel has about 50 staff: five in management, 20 in the restaurant and 25 in house service. Slumber does not own the hotels itself; instead it has a seven-year management agreement with Hotel Investment plc ('HIP'), the owner of the hotels, which is incorporated and based in London, UK. Under this contract Slumber runs the fully equipped hotels on its own risk and has to pay a fixed fee to HIP.

In its central management centre in Manchester, Slumber has another 30 staff. These are 10 managers (including Marketing, Managing, Finance, Sales and Operations Directors) and 20 secretaries, clerks and administrators.

A number of staff are members of the trade union, The Association of Hotel Workers ('AHW'), which has been formally recognised by Slumber as having bargaining rights for hourly paid hotel staff. This is a particularly active union and there is a collective agreement in force. Due to increasing staff costs and the declining demand for expensive hotel accommodation, Slumber is making bigger and bigger operating losses. Slumber is obliged to cut jobs in all the hotels and thus dismisses 40 members of staff as redundant. As a consequence, the service worsens and customer complaints become more frequent. When the board of HIP realises how serious the situation has become, it starts to look for a new operator of its hotels.

Some weeks later, while Slumber is still operating the hotels, a [*each contributor inserts his/her own country here*] company is found which seems able to manage the hotels in a much more profitable way for HIP than Slumber. The company, which is called Dormir, is based in [*capital of the contributor's own country*] but has already gathered some experience of running hotels in the UK. It operates hotels under the 'Dormir' brand. The board of HIP enters into discussions with Dormir for it to replace Slumber as manager of the hotels.

1. Acquisition of the hotels

It is anticipated that Dormir will want to manage all nine of the hotels under a single management agreement with HIP.

(a) **Would this be a business transfer (defined as a transfer within the meaning of TUPE) under UK law?**

(ONLY TO BE ANSWERED BY UK CONTRIBUTOR)

(b) **Even though Slumber will not transfer any of its activities to [*the country of the specific chapter*], would the acquisition of the hotels in this way constitute a business transfer under [*the contributor's own country's*] law?**

(c) **Would it make any difference to whether this constituted a business transfer, under TUPE, if Dormir only wanted to manage the six English hotels (excluding the hotels in Glasgow, Edinburgh and Cardiff)?**

(ONLY TO BE ANSWERED BY UK CONTRIBUTOR)

(d) **Would it make any difference to [*the contributor's answer*] to (b) above if Dormir only wanted to manage six hotels (for example only the English hotels, excluding those in Scotland and Wales, i e the hotels in Glasgow, Edinburgh and Cardiff)?**

(ANSWER UNDER THE CONTRIBUTOR'S OWN COUNTRY'S LEGISLATION)

2. Employees who work only partly in the business

What is the position of those staff who work partly in Slumber and partly in Ezeroom? For example, the human resources director of Slumber is also the human resources director of Ezeroom and he has his employment agreement with Ezeroom. He spends approximately 40 per cent of his time dealing with Slumber's personnel matters and the remainder of his time on the human resources affairs of Ezeroom.

(a) **If this is a TUPE transfer, can he be said to have transferred under TUPE in the UK?**

(UK CONTRIBUTOR TO ANSWER)

(b) **What is the law on employees who work only partly in the undertaking to be transferred in [*the contributor's country*]?**

(EACH CONTRIBUTOR TO RESPOND ACCORDING TO THEIR OWN NATIONAL LAWS)

3. Staff who work outside the UK in another EU country

It transpires that some Slumber central management staff are actually working and based in [the country the chapter is about]. *Two are* [that country's] *nationals.*

(a)   **Would these staff transfer to Dormir under TUPE if there was a TUPE transfer?**

(UK CONTRIBUTOR TO ANSWER THIS. OTHER CONTRIBU-TORS COMMENT ON UK RESPONSE)

(b)   **Would the position be different if there was a branch office of Ezeroom in [*the contributor's own country*], which directly employed these staff?**

(UK TO ANSWER, BUT OTHER CONTRIBUTORS COMMENT ON THE UK RESPONSE)

4. Dismissal of employee

One of the Slumber staff, Mr X, was dismissed by Slumber after HIP had given notice to terminate the contract with Slumber and whilst negotiations were ongoing with Dormir. Mr X is owed two months' back pay and unpaid holiday.

Against whom can Mr X bring a claim, and where, if Mr X is a UK national based in [*the contributor's own country*]?

5. Transfer of employee outside the UK

Mr Y (the marketing director) has been vital to the success of Slumber and has been responsible for many successful ideas. Dormir would like to retain his services and move him to Dormir's headquarters in [the contributor's own country]. *Mr Y has no wish to live in* [the contributor's country].

(a)   **How does TUPE impact on Mr Y: is he obliged to transfer against his will?**

(UK ONLY TO ANSWER)

(b)   **What is the law on objection to a transfer in [*the contributor's own country*]?**

(c)   **Can Mr Y claim constructive dismissal on the basis that he would be expected to work and be based in [*the contributor's own country*] and this is nowhere near his home?**

(UK TO ANSWER AND OTHER CONTRIBUTORS TO COM-MENT)

6. Dormir's business strategy

What is the best way of structuring the transfer of the hotels to Dormir from [*the contributor's own country's*] perspective? Would

the contributor advise Dormir to set up a subsidiary company registered in the UK specifically to purchase Slumber and thereby avoid any cross-border element?

(NOT FOR UK TO ANSWER – ONLY TO BE ANSWERED BY OTHER CONTRIBUTORS)

13.2 Case study 2
(Production moves from one EU country to another EU country; physical move)

Alpha Incorporated is a multinational car tyre manufacturing and distribution business based in Europe. Alpha's headquarters are in [*a different EU country from the one the chapter is about*]. Alpha has tyre plants in [*the contributor's own country, eg UK*], [*another EU country, eg Germany*] and [*a third EU country, eg France*]. Each of the tyre plants is a wholly owned and independently operated subsidiary of Alpha. Alpha has a European Works Council.

The subsidiary in [*the contributor's country*] is Beta. Beta employs about 250 employees, mostly in the direct production of tyres. The employees are on standard basic contracts which do not contain any mobility clauses. Due to increased competition from cheaper producers in the Far East, Alpha is having to reduce its own production costs. Beta has the highest production costs of all Alpha's European operations. Alpha has decided to end the production of tyres in [*the contributor's country*] and move production to Gamma, another subsidiary, not far away but across the national border in [*a different EU country but one already mentioned above, eg France or Germany*] which has more modern plant and equipment. Beta will continue to exist, but as a sales and marketing organisation only, with about 30 staff.

Most of Beta's tyre-making plant and machinery is transferred to Gamma, but Gamma will only need an extra 125 staff to increase its output to the required level to supply Beta's market. Those employees from Beta who are required to work for Gamma will be expected to accept the terms and conditions and working practices of the Gamma plant, which are very different from those in operation at the Beta plant. For example, Gamma pays its employees considerably lower hourly wages and they work longer hours than those at Beta. Gamma does not want to pay more to the employees transferred to it from Beta than it does to its current employees. Gamma operates a different type of pension scheme.

1. Does this transaction constitute a 'business transfer'?

(a)   **As Beta's tyre-making plant and machinery have transferred to Gamma, will this constitute a business transfer under the Acquired Rights Directive implementing legislation of [*the contributor's own country*] ('business transfer')?**

(b)   **Does it make any difference to whether this is a business transfer if employees of Beta transfer across to Gamma?**

(c)   **Can the transfer of plant and machinery coupled with the transfer of half the employees (125) constitute a business transfer under [*the contributor's own country's*] legislation if the other 125 employees are dismissed prior to the transfer?**

(d)   **Does the fact that the business will transfer to a different country make any difference to whether this is a business transfer?**

(e)   **Is [*the contributor's own country's*] business transfer law concerned with the actual distance moved (irrespective of whether this means a change of country)?**

2. Relocation, but no business transfer

(a)   **Assuming the move does NOT constitute a business transfer (because the business of Beta does not adequately retain its identity) but instead is deemed to be a straightforward relocation, are any of Beta's employees obliged or entitled to transfer?**

(b)   **If employees do nevertheless relocate, what will happen to their employment contracts? Will these continue, or will Gamma be entitled to provide new contracts?**

(c)   **What will be the law applicable to the contracts of the employees who relocate?**

3. Dismissals

(a)   **Assuming the move does constitute a business transfer:**

(i)   **are any dismissals in connection with the transfer lawful?**

(ii) **what are the rights and remedies (including applicable law and appropriate jurisdiction) of any employees dismissed:**

a.   **before the transfer?**

b.   **after the transfer?**

(b)   **Would these rights and remedies change if this was not a business transfer?**

4. European Works Council and other employees' representatives

(a)   **Will Alpha be required to inform and consult the European Works Council about the transfer or any redundancies?**

(b)   **Are any other employee representatives required to be involved in the transfer or any redundancies (ie at national or local level)?**

5. Collective agreements

What is the effect of the business transfer on any collective agreements affecting Beta's employees?

6. Change of terms and conditions

(a) If this is a business transfer, how can Gamma lawfully harmonise employment contracts and change the terms and conditions of the employees currently on the more generous Beta contracts of employment?

(b) If this is a business transfer, can Gamma reduce the wages of the former Beta employees?

(c) If this is a business transfer, what will happen to the former Beta employees as regards their private pension arrangements?

(d) Is it easier to change terms and conditions of employment if the changes are made six months after the transfer?

13.3 Case study 3
(Outsourcing of an ancillary activity to a non-EU country)

A large multinational (ABC) based in [*the contributor's own country*] has decided to outsource its entire internal IT function to a third party provider in Romania, as the costs of hiring competent IT personnel in Romania are far lower than in [*the contributor's own country*], largely because wages are so much lower. At present 200 employees are employed by ABC in its IT function in [*the contributor's own country*]. It is anticipated that exactly the same IT function will be required in Romania with approximately the same number of people required to run it. There will be no difference in the service or approach for those requiring IT assistance and even the internal telephone number will be automatically diverted. The Romanian third party provider has no assets or presence in [*the contributor's own country*].

1. Business transfer

Will this be a business transfer within the scope of [*the contributor's own country's*] law applying ARD?

2. Effect on employees

(a) What will happen to the employees currently employed in the IT function at ABC? Will they transfer across?

(b) If the employees do transfer, what will the applicable law be for their employment contracts with the third party provider? Where can they make any claims?

3. Data protection

Will there be special data protection issues on the transfer of knowledge and information outside [*the contributor's own country*] to Romania?

4. Transfer to India

Please comment on any differences there would be to your answers if the function was transferred to India rather than Romania.

PART 4

Country by country guide

J Austria

Dr Andreas Tinhofer

J1 Business transfers

J1.1 Background

General issues

Before the implementation of the Acquired Rights Directive 77/187/EEC ('ARD') in Austria, the transfer of an undertaking (or part thereof) by way of singular succession (ie sale, lease, etc) did not automatically give rise to the transfer or the termination of the employment relationships that existed in connection with that undertaking prior to the transfer. Instead, the employees stayed with the transferor, who in most cases could dismiss them due to lack of available work. According to the Austrian Supreme Court of Justice, it was only the employment contracts of the workers' representatives in relation to an undertaking that were (in certain circumstances) automatically transferred to the transferee, in order to guarantee workers continuing representation. Accordingly, the transfer of a regular employee required the consent of all three parties (ie employee, transferor and transferee), which could be implied by 'conclusive conduct' (eg where the transferee continues to employ the employee following the transfer of the undertaking). However, the transfer of an undertaking by virtue of universal succession (ie succession to the estate of a deceased former employer or the merger of two or more companies) generally meant that the transferee succeeded the transferor in relation to all the employment contracts he had entered into prior to the transfer.

Notwithstanding the lack of statutory protection for contractual terms and conditions, 'collective employment rights' were safeguarded to a limited extent under the old law. In Austria, individual employees as well as their representatives can rely upon collective employment rights. These rights derive mainly from collective agreements and works agreements. The former are generally concluded at 'industry' level between the relevant Federal Trade Union (*Österreichischer Gewerkschaftsbund* – 'ÖGB') and relevant Chamber of Commerce (*Wirtschaftskammer*), the statutory bodies that represent employees and employers respectively. The latter are agreements between employers and works councils (*Betriebsrat*), which are also established by statute. In the rare event that a transferee was not covered by a collective agreement, he was obliged, following the transfer, to comply with the terms of the collective agreement that covered the transferor. As far as works agreements were concerned, they continued to apply in the same way to a transferee following the transfer, unless the business was amalgamated into the transferee's undertaking.

The ARD was implemented in Austria in 1993, to coincide with the entry into force of the Agreement on the European Economic Area ('EEA') on 1 January 1994. The implementation was effected by a new statute, the Employment Contract Law Adaptation Act 1993 (*Arbeitsvertragsrechts-Anpassungsgesetz* – 'AVRAG') and by amendments to the Collective Employment Regulatory Act (*Arbeitsverfassungsgesetz* – 'ArbVG'). These provisions came into force on 1 July 1993. The only substantial amendment to Austrian business transfer law since then occurred in 2002, when Directive 98/50/EEC regarding employee information and consultation was implemented. The implementing legislation also reduced the transferor's potential liability in business transfer situations, after legal commentators had raised concerns that Austrian law might have infringed transferors' fundamental human rights (see *J1.4* below for more detail).

In the 10 years following the implementation of the ARD, the new business transfer legislation in Austria has generated a considerable amount of case law. The majority of the cases that have come before the Supreme Court concern the concept of a 'business transfer' and the termination of employment contracts before or after such a transfer. In considering the cases arising from Austrian business transfer legislation, the Supreme Court has not hesitated to ask the European Court of Justice for preliminary rulings on the correct interpretation of the ARD, if it considers European case law in a particular area is unclear or completely absent[1]. The new business transfer legislation has also inspired a large amount of legal commentary, which, in Austria, tends to influence the legal reasoning of the courts.

By and large, the Austrian implementing legislation and the case law of the Supreme Court seem to be in compliance with the ARD. However, there is one exception: certain public servants are excluded from the scope of the AVRAG, regardless of the fact that they are considered to be 'employees' under Austrian law. In several cases the Supreme Court has remedied this shortcoming by applying the ARD directly to such employees. However, as these rulings do not exempt the Austrian Parliament from its obligation to correctly and fully implement the ARD, it remains to be seen whether the European Commission will take action against Austria for failing to do so.

In practice, business transfers sometimes raise legal issues that have yet to be tackled by the Austrian courts. Some of these issues are not dealt with in the ARD or are only dealt with in very general terms, and therefore stem from the Austrian implementing legislation. For example, an employee's right to object to the transfer of his employment is not dealt with in the ARD (see *J1.4* below) and the effect of a business transfer on collective agreements is dealt with only in general terms, which has led to a great deal of debate amongst legal commentators (see *J1.4* below). Other issues are more general and arise from the interpretation of the ARD. An example is whether employees can validly agree with a transferor that they are 'hired out' to a transferee, whilst remaining in employment relationships with the transferor (see *J1.4* below). In practice, this issue arises almost exclusively in relation to business transfers within groups of companies.

1   For example, C-340/01: *Abler v Sodexho MM Catering Betriebsgesellschaft mbH* [2004] IRLR 168, ECJ.

Cross-border issues

Although it would appear that cross-border business transfers are occurring more and more often, there is virtually no case law in Austria in this regard. Likewise, there is very little legal writing dealing explicitly with the legal problems that arise in relation to such transactions and, of course, the solutions proposed are not always the same. However, due to the similarity of the legal systems in Austria and Germany, the case law of the German Federal Employment Court (*Bundesarbeitsgericht*) and the arguments put forward in German legal writing on this topic have influenced the legal debate in Austria and are likely to have an impact on the rulings of the Austrian courts in the future.

In practice, cross-border business transfers raise two fundamental jurisdictional issues as regards employment rights. First, which national court will accept jurisdiction to hear a case against an employer that is domiciled in state A, where the affected employee is domiciled in state B? Second, which national law will the court apply?

In Austria, the first question must be answered by reference to art 19 of Council Regulation (EC) 44/2001 on jurisdiction and the recognition and enforcement of judgments, which came into force on 1 March 2002. Article 19 provides that an employer domiciled in a member state within the European Union may be sued:

  (i)   in the courts of the member state where he is domiciled; or

  (ii) in the courts of the member state where the affected employee habitually carries out his work or where he last did so.

If a business situated in Austria is acquired by a German company by way of an 'asset deal', the employees of that business may argue that the acquiring company assumes all the rights and obligations arising from the employment relationships with their existing employer, pursuant to the applicable business transfer law (see *J1.4* below for more detail). Further, as such a change in the identity of the employer would not, of itself, change the employees' regular place of work, it is likely that they would be able to sue the German company in both Austria and Germany. The position would, of course, be the same where the transferee of the Austrian business is domiciled in any other member state of the European Union, excluding Denmark. However, as there is currently no case law dealing with this specific issue, it remains to be seen what stand the Austrian courts would take in this regard.

The second question is governed by the EC Convention on the law applicable to contractual obligations 1980 (the 'Rome Convention'). The Rome Convention, which came into force in Austria on 1 December 1998 and has been directly applicable ever since, applies 'to contractual obligations in any situation involving a choice between the laws in different countries' (art 1(1)). In the absence of a choice of law within an employment contract, the Rome Convention provides that it shall be governed by the law of the country where the employee 'habitually carries out his work in performance of the contract' (art 6(2)(a)). If the employee does not habitually carry out his work in any one country, his employment contract is deemed to be subject to the law of the country in which the business through which he is engaged is situated (art 6(2)(b)). If, however, the employment contract is more closely connected with another country, the Rome Convention states that it shall be governed by the law of that country (art 6(2) final limb). In such an exceptional case, the employee's regular place of work is irrelevant, as is the location of the business through which he is engaged.

Where a German company acquires an Austrian business by way of an 'asset deal' (as described above), the relevant employment relationships continue to be governed by Austrian law as long as the employees habitually carry out their work in Austria, provided that the transaction qualifies as a 'business transfer' under business transfer legislation.

The jurisdictional issues are much more complex where a 'business transfer' involves the relocation of an undertaking. In accordance with the general principles outlined above, the legal treatment of such a transaction boils down to the question of whether the relocation of the business changes where the employees habitually carry out their work. Although there is no case law in relation to this issue in Austria, some legal commentators have argued that the mere relocation of a business does not automatically change the 'regular place of work' of its employees. Others have advocated a specific right for employees to object to relocating to another country with the business in relation to which they are employed. Raising such an objection would, of course, mean that the employees remained employed by the transferor, who would be entitled to dismiss them by reason of redundancy. If, however, the employees agreed to move to the transferee's place of business in another country, it is generally assumed that this would become their 'regular place of work' and the national law applicable to their employment contracts would change accordingly.

It is fair to say that business transfer law is one of the most complex areas of Austrian employment law. Accordingly, any employer who is planning to acquire or dispose of a business (or part of one) or who intends to become involved in an outsourcing scenario, especially where the proposed transaction has a 'cross-border' element, should seek legal advice.

The following sections aim to outline the most important features of Austrian business transfer law, whilst serving as a basic introduction to Austrian employment law as a whole for readers who are unfamiliar with it. This chapter should serve as a gateway to a more detailed study of Austrian business transfer law, if this is necessary (see J4 below for lists of key books and websites).

J1.2 Identifying a relevant transfer

As mentioned above, most Austrian case law and a great deal of legal commentary in this area have focused on the concept of a 'business transfer'. The wide interpretation given to certain provisions of the ARD by the ECJ, which culminated in the *Christel Schmidt*[1] case, caused considerable concern and even irritation in Austria (as well as in Germany). One possible reason for this concern was the apparent conflict between the Austrian and German system of works councils and the 'functional' approach to business transfers espoused by the ECJ. However, since the ECJ reaffirmed the importance of an 'economic entity' retaining its identity following a 'business transfer' in *Süzen*[2], the Supreme Court has referred to European case law much more frequently. The broad statutory definition of a 'relevant transfer' in s 3(1) of the AVRAG has facilitated a purposive approach, whereby the Austrian courts interpret the ARD in accordance with ECJ case law.

Austrian business transfer law encompasses all kinds of transactions that have been considered 'business transfers' by the ECJ. The Supreme Court has consistently held that a 'business transfer' occurs whenever an 'economic entity' is transferred to another employer whilst retaining its identity. The 'economic entity' itself is defined by the Supreme Court as 'an organised grouping of persons and assets exercising an economic activity which pursues a specific objective'[3]. The economic activity does not necessarily have to be pursued for a profit, although it must be more than a 'one-off' activity, such as the construction of a building[4]. Whilst there is no test for determining whether a grouping of persons and assets is 'organised' within this definition, it would seem that at least one employee must be assigned to the specific activity being carried out.

Unlike the ARD, the AVRAG does not specifically require that there be a 'contractual transfer' or a 'merger' in order for a 'business transfer' to occur. The legislative materials produced in relation to the AVRAG show that Parliament intended that it cover any form of legal transaction by virtue of which a transferor can dispose of an economic entity to a transferee. There is no need for a direct contractual link between the transferor and the transferee under the AVRAG[5]. Therefore, transfers involving three parties, such as the change of the lessee of a restaurant[6] or the change of service providers to a particular business[7], fall within Austrian business transfer legislation. In addition, it is not necessary that ownership of the business be transferred under Austrian business transfer law[8].

Although it appears from the legislative materials produced in relation to the AVRAG that Parliament considered that the privatisation of public services would fall within the concept of a 'business transfer', it nevertheless excluded almost all civil servants from the scope of the AVRAG (s 1(1), (2)). However, the European Community does not consider such a situation a problem, so long as there are equivalent safeguards in place in respect of the affected employees. In Austria, the majority of the legislation that provides for the transfer of certain public services to wholly state-owned companies also provides for the transfer of the employees concerned. However, in those cases where Austrian privatisation legislation does not specifically implement the principles of the ARD, the affected civil servants can rely directly on the Directive, and must be taken on by the transferee[9]. It goes without saying that the direct application of the ARD in Austria cannot remedy the government's failure to correctly and fully implement art 1(1)(c) of the Directive (codifying the case law of the ECJ)[10]. Hence, it would not come as a surprise to this author if the European Commission were to start infringement proceedings against Austria in the near future.

The AVRAG does not apply if the transferor is involved in a certain kind of insolvency proceeding (*Konkursverfahren*) (s 3(2)). A *Konkursverfahren* does not aim to liquidate the assets of the business that is in financial difficulties, and the court handling the matter is obliged to explore whether the business can be rescued so that the jobs of its employees are saved. As a consequence of the exclusion within the AVRAG, potential buyers of insolvent undertakings in Austria commonly wait until after a *Konkursverfahren* has been instituted before attempting to take them over. In many cases, the business can still be acquired as a 'going concern'. The exclusion within the AVRAG was introduced in the light of the ECJ's early case law[11], which has now been clarified and supplemented by the current art 5 of the ARD. Although Austrian legal commentators have raised concerns that s 3(2) of the AVRAG does not comply with the ARD, the Supreme Court has recently held that it does[12].

1   See C-392/92: *Schmidt v Spar- und Leihkasse der früheren Ämter Bordesholm, Kiel und Cronshagen* [1994] ECR I-1311, ECJ.
2   C-13/95: *Süzen v Zehnacker Gebäudereinigung GmbH Krankenhausservice* [1997] ECR I-1259, ECJ.
3   OGH 21.10.1999, 8 Ob A 143/98g.
4   Compare C-48/94: *Ledernes Hovedorganisation (acting for Ole Rygaard) v Dansk Arbejdsgiverforening* [1995] ECR I-2745, ECJ.
5   OGH 7.10.1998, 8 Ob A 193/98t, RdW 1999, 220.
6   OGH 1.9.1999, 9 Ob A 192/99x, RdW 2000/144.
7   OGH 23.1.2004, 8 Ob A 122/03d.
8   OGH 1.9.1999, 9 Ob A 192/99x, RdW 2000/144.
9   OGH 15.4.1999, 8 Ob A 221/98b, ZAS 2000, 108; 26.6.2003, 8 Ob A 41/03t, RdW 2003/573.
10   C-343/98: *Collino and Chiappero v Telecom Italia SpA* [2000] ECR I-6659, ECJ; C-175/99: *Mayeur* [2000] ECR I-7755, ECJ.
11   *Abels v Bedrijfsvereniging voor de Metaalindustrie en de Electrotechnische Industrie*: 135/83 [1985] ECR 469, ECJ; C-362/89: *d'Urso v Ercole Marelli Elettromeccanica Generale SpA* [1991] ECR I-4105, ECJ; C-472/93: *Luigi Spano v Fiat Geotech SpA and Fiat Hitachi Excavators SpA* [1995] ECR I-4321, ECJ.
12   OGH 16.10.2003, 8 Ob S 7/03t, RdW 2004/136.

J1.3 Affected employees

As is discussed in Chapter **A**, the ARD does not define who is to be considered an 'employee' for the purposes of business transfer law. Instead, it refers to the national laws of the member states and their concepts of employment contracts and employment relationships (art 2(2)). Under Austrian law, an employment contract is deemed to exist if a person (the 'employee') undertakes to provide services to another person (the 'employer') for a period of time, in a state of 'personal dependence'. Essentially, 'personal dependence' means that the employee cannot do what he likes during his working hours – he is integrated into the employer's organisation, he has to comply with the employer's instructions, and he is subject to the employer's supervision and disciplinary measures. However, not all of these factors must exist at the same time for a person to be considered an 'employee', as it is an overall assessment of the situation that decides whether he works under an employment contract or a contract for services.

The ARD provides that part-time workers, those on fixed-term contracts and those employed on a temporary basis must not be excluded from the scope of business transfer laws in member states. In Austria, such workers are covered by the AVRAG and the relevant provisions of the ArbVG. In general, it is sufficient for a person to be considered an 'employee' for the purposes of Austrian business transfer law if he has a valid employment contract at the time of the transfer, even if he has already been given notice (see *J1.5* below for more details of the restrictions on dismissal). Indeed, the Supreme Court has held that even employees who have only a legally binding offer of engagement by the transferor have to be taken on by the transferee[1].

In Austria, public sector workers can be divided into two main groups. First, there are officials appointed by decree (*Beamte* – career public servants), who are not therefore considered 'employees'. Second, there are workers employed under employment contracts, the content of which is highly regulated by statute (*Vertragsbedienstete* – contract public employees), who are considered 'employees'. As is mentioned at *J1.2* above, the AVRAG explicitly excludes almost all public servants from its scope, regardless of the nature of their employment. As 'career public servants' are not considered 'employees' under Austrian employment law, their employment would never transfer with the undertaking in relation to which they are employed. As is also mentioned in *J1.2* above, in the event that the rights of 'contract public employees' are not safeguarded by equivalent legislation in Austria, upon the transfer of the undertaking in relation to which they are employed, they can rely directly on the provisions of the ARD[2].

Workers employed on a temporary basis in Austria commonly enter into employment contracts with employment agencies, rather than their end clients (for whom they actually work). Therefore, their employment relationships are only affected when the businesses of the employment agencies are transferred to other employers. Transfers of the businesses of the employment agencies' end clients do not affect the employment relationships of temporary workers.

Whilst there is no specific case law in Austria on this point yet, legal commentators have questioned whether the hiving-off of the whole or part of an undertaking from a parent company to one of its subsidiaries would automatically trigger the transfer of the employees employed in relation to that undertaking to the subsidiary company. It has been argued that it is often more favourable for the employees concerned to remain employed by the parent company and be seconded to work for the subsidiary company, rather than have their employment relationships transfer automatically to the subsidiary (on the basis that the parent company is generally more credit-worthy than the subsidiary company and that the hiving-off might result in a change in the applicable collective agreement and/or works agreement, which could lead to a worsening in the terms and conditions of the employees concerned).

In situations where only part of an undertaking is being transferred, the Supreme Court (in accordance with the case law of the ECJ) applies an 'organisational' test to determine which employees transfer with it (ie it considers to which department a particular employee is assigned and whether that department is being transferred)[3]. In doing so, the Supreme Court makes an overall assessment of the situation. No single factor is conclusive.

Austrian business transfer law does not automatically exclude non-Austrian nationals or non-EU citizens from its scope. Further, unlike the UK legislation implementing the ARD, the AVRAG does not contain a provision limiting its scope to transfers of undertakings or businesses situated in Austria immediately before the transfer. It is therefore conceivable that the courts of other member states could apply the provisions of the AVRAG in accordance with the principles of the Rome Convention (see *J1.1* above).

1   OGH 12.7.2000, 9 Ob A 93/00t, RdW 2001/184.
2   OGH 15.4.1999, 8 Ob A 221/98b, ZAS 2000/11.
3   See OGH 28.8.1997, 8 Ob A 91/97h, ZAS 1998, 143.

J1.4 Effects of the transfer

Under AVRAG, s 3, the employment relationships that exist in relation to an undertaking or business at the time it is transferred transfer to the transferee, along with all rights and obligations. Therefore, it is often said that a transferee in such a situation 'steps into the shoes of the transferor'. The substance of the relevant individual employment contracts (whether the terms and conditions are specified in writing, agreed verbally or implied by practice) will remain the same.

As a result of AVRAG, s 3, the transferee is obliged to pay any outstanding wages owed to transferring employees for services rendered prior to the transfer. Further, the time an employee has spent with the transferor prior to a transfer must be recognised by the transferee for the purpose of any rights that depend on length of service (eg redundancy payments, notice periods, sick pay, etc).

The precise impact of a business transfer on the occupational pension scheme in place within an undertaking depends on its legal basis. If the entitlement to a company pension is founded upon the terms of a collective agreement or a works agreement, the rules for these kinds of agreements apply. If, on the other hand, such a pension is promised in the transferring employees' employment contracts, a transferee can refuse to take over the transferor's obligations in this regard, in which case the employees generally are entitled to a lump sum payment representing the loss of their rights in this regard from the transferor. However, a transferee cannot refuse to take over the transferor's obligations in relation to an occupational pension scheme if the business transfer in question is the result of a 'universal succession', such as the merger of two (or more) companies or a succession to the estate of a deceased employer (AVRAG, s 5(1)).

Collective agreements and works agreements

As pointed out at *J1.1* above, it is important, for the purposes of Austrian law, to distinguish between the two kinds of agreement that can be concluded with employee representatives. In practice, collective agreements are concluded by trade unions with the Chamber of Commerce and generally apply to all employers within a certain industry. As a matter of principle, a single employer cannot be a party to a collective agreement in Austria. Collective agreements can regulate all material aspects of the employment relationship so that the individual contract is only relevant in generating an employment relationship between two parties. As collective agreements operate in the same way as statutory law, they need not be (expressly or implicitly) incorporated into individual employment contracts. However, individual employment contracts can supplement collective agreements where the latter do not regulate a particular aspect of the employment relationship exhaustively. More importantly, as trade unions generally aim to set only a minimum standard of working conditions, the parties to an individual employment contract may depart from a collective agreement in favour of the employee (the so-called 'favourability principle').

As regards the consequences of a business transfer in relation to an employee's rights and duties arising from a collective agreement, one must distinguish between two factual situations:

(i)   Where the transferee is bound by another collective agreement when the business (or part thereof) in question is transferred to it.

Prior to the implementation of the ARD in Austria, it was widely assumed amongst legal commentators that, in such a situation, the collective agreement to which the transferee was bound superseded that which the transferor had entered into, even if its terms and conditions were less favourable for the transferring employees. Presumably because it was unclear whether such a solution complied with the terms of the ARD, the Austrian Legislator in 1993 implemented the terms of what is now art 3(3) of the Directive in AVRAG, s 4(1), which provides that transferees must observe the terms and conditions agreed in any collective agreement with the transferor until the termination or expiry of that agreement or the entry into force of another collective agreement. However, one year after the transfer the parties of the employment contract may agree to deviate from such a collective agreement, even if this is to the employee's disadvantage. As the Supreme Court has given little guidance as to how it should be interpreted, s 4(1) is ignored in practice.

Much more relevant is AVRAG, s 4(2), which maintains the protection given to employees by collective agreements entered into by transferors in at least two regards. First, it provides that the transferring employees are entitled to the minimum wages (for standard working hours) set by the collective agreement to which the transferor was party if, and so long as, the collective agreement entered into by the transferee provides for lower minimum wages. This rule does not apply where higher wages are provided for in the individual employment contracts entered into with the transferor. Second, s 4(2) provides that any terms within a collective agreement entered into by a transferor that afford the transferring employees a certain level of protection against dismissal (eg restriction of the reasons for dismissal) are statutorily incorporated into their employment contracts if the transferor ceases to operate a business following the business transfer.

(ii) Where the transferee is not bound by any other collective agreement when the business (or part thereof) in question is transferred to it.

Even before the implementation of the ARD, Austrian law provided that the collective agreement to which the transferor was party automatically transferred to the transferee in such a situation. Accordingly, the transferring employees were, and are, guaranteed the protection provided by that collective agreement until it expired or was terminated, or until another collective agreement was concluded by (one of) the employers' organisation(s) to which the transferee belonged. As most employers in Austria are obliged to be members of the Chamber of Commerce or another employers' organisation that is able to conclude collective agreements, this scenario is very rare in practice.

In contrast to collective agreements, works agreements are concluded by individual employers and works councils. However, they operate in much the same way as collective agreements (and therefore statutory laws) in that they are legally binding on employers and employees without needing to be incorporated into individual employment contracts. Works agreements can regulate issues arising out of the organisation of work in a particular workplace (eg the introduction of wage-incentive plans or supervisory systems), but not minimum wages or working hours (unless a statute or collective agreement explicitly so provides).

Works agreements generally stick to the businesses to which they relate without much regard for their owner, such that if a particular business is being transferred, the new employer would be bound by the works agreements his predecessor has concluded with the works council. Thus, employers must generally honour pre-existing works agreements following business re-organisations or business transfers and cannot 'start with a clean slate'. In practice, however, it is often extremely difficult to determine whether, and to what extent, transferring employees are entitled to rely on a pre-existing works agreement where after the transfer the business (or part thereof) is fully integrated into the transferee's business.

The precise effects of a cross-border transfer on pre-existing collective agreements and works agreements have still yet to be determined by the Supreme Court. Further, legal commentators in Austria have only considered certain aspects of this complex area. However, in analysing how an Austrian court may deal with this issue in the future, one must first distinguish between two possible scenarios:

(i) Where the business (or part thereof) in question is acquired by a company domiciled in another country without being relocated.

In such a situation, providing the organisational structure of the business was not substantially altered, the foreign transferee would normally be bound by any pre-existing works agreements in the same way as a domestic transferee. The effect of the business transfer on any pre-existing collective agreements would depend on whether the foreign transferee were subject to a collective agreement in its own country that also applied to employees located abroad. In such an (admittedly unlikely) situation, the transferee would not be obliged to observe the terms and conditions of the pre-existing collective agreement, except those that related to a minimum wage or protection for employees against dismissal. If, however, the foreign transferee were party to a collective agreement in its own country that did not apply to employees located abroad or were not party to a collective agreement at all, the terms and conditions of the pre-existing collective agreement would continue to apply following the business transfer, subject to the provisos outlined above.

(ii) Where the business (or part thereof) in question is acquired by a company domiciled in another country and, at the same time, relocated to that country.

The majority of legal commentators in Austria submit that the transferring employees would not be entitled to rely on the terms and conditions of any pre-existing collective agreements or works agreements in such a situation, on the basis that the business in connection with which they are employed would need to be situated in Austria for them to do so. However, some Austrian legal commentators have suggested that the relocation of a business (or part thereof) to another country would necessarily alter the national law that applied to those employees. If this were the case, the extent to which they would be protected by any pre-existing collective agreements or works agreements would depend on whether the laws of the country to which the business were relocated recognised foreign collective agreements and/or works agreements.

Right to object

Section 3(1) of the AVRAG provides for the automatic transfer of all the employment relationships that exist in relation to a business at the time it is transferred. However, AVRAG, s 3(4) allows the affected employees (but not the transferee) to object to this automatic transfer in two situations, in both cases within a period of one month:

(i) Where the transferee refuses to take on a transferor's obligations in relation to an occupational pension scheme arising from individual employment contracts, in accordance with AVRAG, s 5(1).

(ii) Where a pre-existing collective agreement is superseded by a collective agreement to which the transferee is party that provides for a weaker level of protection against dismissal and the transferee refuses to incorporate the provisions of the pre-existing collective agreement in this regard into the individual employment contracts of the transferring employees. However, transferring employees can only object to a business transfer on this basis if the transferor continues to operate a business subsequently, as otherwise the relevant provisions of the pre-existing collective agreement would automatically be incorporated into their employment contracts by statute.

Austrian legal commentators agree that, in both situations, an employee utilising his/her right to object to a business transfer would leave his/her employment relationship with the transferor unchanged, but this could lead to the transferor making him/her redundant due to lack of work.

It is debatable whether, notwithstanding AVRAG, s 3(4), there is a general right for affected employees to object to business transfers in Austria. Although the ECJ has held on a number of occasions that employees cannot be forced to work for employers they have not chosen themselves[1], the Supreme Court, which has indicated that the right of employees to object to business transfers may not be restricted to the two situations covered by s 3(4), has yet to confirm the position in this regard. However, the Supreme Court has confirmed that employee members of works councils have the right to object to the transfer of their employment as, otherwise, employers could end their involvement in the works councils by simply disposing of the part of the business in relation to which they were employed[2].

1   See also C-132/91: *Grigorios Katsikas v Angelos Konstantinidis* [1992] ECR I-6577, ECJ; C-171/94: *Merckx v Ford Motors Co Belgium SA* [1996] ECR I-1253, ECJ; OGH 25.4.2001, 9 Ob A 272/00s, infas 2001, A 88.
2   OGH 23.5.1997, 8 Ob A 105/97t, RdW 1997, 612.

Employers' liability

In implementing the ARD, the Austrian Legislator has provided for the joint liability of transferors and transferees in relation to business transfers (which is, of course, optional under art 3(1) of the Directive). Accordingly, AVRAG, s 6(1) states that both employers are jointly and severally liable vis-à-vis the transferring employees in respect of any obligations (eg accrued wages or bonuses not paid by the transferor) that arose before the business transfer. Thus, the risks to transferring employees of being hived-off to insolvent employers are reduced.

The principle of joint and several liability in Austria does not extend to obligations arising after a business transfer. Therefore, if a transferee fails to pay the wages of the transferring employees for the services they have provided after a business transfer, they cannot look to the transferor for payment in this regard.

Liability for redundancy pay and contributions to occupational pensions schemes

Austrian law limits the liability of transferors in respect of severance payments and contributions to company pension schemes. These entitlements, whether contractual or statutory, are considered to be a special kind of remuneration for the services employees provide throughout the course of their employment relationships, even if they become payable only at the end of those relationships. Therefore, transferors are only liable, under AVRAG, s 6(2), for the notional value of these entitlements at the time of a business transfer. In response to concerns that making the liability of transferors unlimited in this regard would infringe their fundamental rights, s 6(2) has recently been amended so that they are only liable for entitlements in respect of severance payments and contributions to company pension schemes that accrue within five years of a business transfer. Further, it is now open to the parties to a business transfer to contract to the effect that only the transferee is responsible for any liabilities that arise in this regard, provided he receives adequate securities from the transferor.

J1.5 Dismissal of employees

Austria has not yet implemented ARD, art 4(1), which provides that the parties to a business transfer cannot dismiss employees purely by reason of that business transfer. However, the Supreme Court has indicated on a number of occasions that any dismissal having as its 'principal reason' a business transfer will be null and void. It has also made it clear that this principle applies equally to dismissals carried out by transferors and transferees[1] and that the burden of proof in establishing that a particular dismissal was motivated by a reason other than a business transfer is on the employer who carried it out[2]. Which employer a dismissed employee proceeds against will obviously depend on whether the employee takes legal action before or after a business transfer[3].

The concept of an unwarranted dismissal being deemed null and void is a familiar one in Austrian law. Although there is no statutory time limit for employees dismissed in this fashion to claim that their dismissals are null and void, the Austrian courts have held that they must do so without 'undue delay'. In making an assessment as to whether a dismissed employee's complaint in this regard is time-barred, the Austrian courts will consider all the circumstances, including, in particular, the reason(s) for any delay. In one case, the Supreme Court held that employees who had waited 10 months to bring such a claim were time-barred[4].

Not all dismissals that coincide with business transfers are unlawful. Austrian law provides that employers are free to terminate employment relationships, provided they observe the general rules of dismissal legislation. For instance, an employer may legitimately dismiss an employee on grounds of misconduct immediately before or after a business transfer[5]. Moreover, dismissals carried out close to the time of business transfers can, under certain circumstances, be justified for economic or organisational reasons, provided they would have been carried out in any case[6]. In practice, however, the Austrian courts seem willing to sanction such dismissals only if they are carried out by transferees and not transferors.

In AVRAG, s 3(5) and (6), the Austrian Legislator has implemented ARD, art 4(2), which entitles employees to terminate their employment with transferees where their terms and conditions of employment are 'substantially' worsened as a result of changes to the collective agreements or works agreements that apply to them. An employee who resigns in such a situation is, prima facie, treated as if the transferee had dismissed him/her and is generally entitled to a severance payment (see *J2.4* for further details). Although the Supreme Court has yet to define exactly what constitutes a 'substantial' change to an employee's working conditions, there is a consensus amongst legal commentators in Austria that such a change must:

(i)   affect terms and conditions of employment that are 'essential' by their very nature (eg remuneration, working time, paid leave, etc); and

(ii)   be noticeable in quantitative terms.

The Austrian courts have accordingly been granted a wide discretion to apply this provision on a case-by-case basis.

1   OGH 5.6.2002, 9 Ob A 97/02h, RdW 2003/33.
2   OGH 28.8.1997, 8 Ob A 91/97h, RdW 1997, 739, and many more.
3   OGH 10.6.1998, 9 Ob A 55/98y, RdW 1999, 222.
4   OGH 30.6.1999, 9 Ob A 160/99s, SZ 72/112.
5   OGH 22.10.1997, 9 Ob A 274/97b, RdW 1998, 217.
6   OGH 28.8.1997, 8 Ob A 91/97h, RdW 1997, 739.

J1.6 Harmonisation and variation of contract

As has been pointed out above, terms and conditions of employment in Austria are not only provided for in individual employment contracts, but also in collective agreements and, to a lesser extent, in works agreements. The parties to a business transfer cannot determine the effect it has on these 'collective rights', as this is strictly regulated by statutory law (see *J1.4* for further details). However, this does not prevent a transferee from amending the terms and conditions of employment of the transferring employees by individual agreement after a business transfer. Although the Austrian courts have accepted that transferees and transferring employees may validly agree to improvements in the employees' pay and/or working conditions, it is debatable whether a general right to change employees' terms and conditions following a business transfer exists. However, the Supreme Court has indicated that a change in terms and conditions may be compatible with the purpose of the ARD, to the extent that the agreement reached is, on balance, more favourable to the employees than the previous arrangement[1]. Transferees wishing to negotiate such post-transfer arrangements should avoid putting undue pressure on the transferring employees or their representatives, as this might invalidate any agreement that is reached.

1   OGH 24.9.2003, 9 Ob A 17/03w.

J1.7 Duty to inform and consult

Effect of a business transfer on employee representatives

In Austria, the statutory representation of employees within a particular workplace must reflect the organisation of the business in question. Thus, if a business comprises two or more distinct organisational entities with at least five employees each, there must be a separate works council in respect of each entity (*Betrieb*). These organisational entities, which shall be called 'establishments' for the purposes of this chapter, are defined in Austria by statute and must be distinguished from the businesses themselves, which are over-arching economic entities. Employees of such establishments generally pursue defined activities that are ancillary to the main activities of the business, whilst their managers tend to enjoy a certain degree of independence from the management of the business, at least on a day-to-day basis.

Works councils tend to follow the legal 'destiny' of the establishments in relation to which they exist. Accordingly, the transfer of an establishment that retains its identity does not generally affect the status of any works council that exists in relation to it. Where part of an establishment is transferred and becomes an establishment in its own right following a business transfer, any works council that existed in relation to that establishment would continue to represent the transferred employees in the new establishment for a maximum period of four months, until a works council has been established (although this four-month period can be extended by a works agreement until the day on which the works council's terms of office expires). In the case of a merger of two (or more) establishments (or parts thereof), resulting in the creation of a new establishment, the works councils that existed in the establishments prior to the merger would join together to form a 'provisional' works council until a new one could be elected. This election would need to take place within a period of one year from the date of the merger (ArbVG, s 62(c)).

Sections 120–122 of the ArbVG provide special protection for employee representatives against dismissal, even after their terms of office have ended.

Information and consultation of the employee representatives

In addition to the general duty to inform and consult works councils on all matters affecting employees' interests (ArbVG, ss 91–92), employers are also obliged to provide detailed information to works councils in relation to business transfers (ArbVG, s 108(2a)). Such information must be provided 'on time' and before the transfer in question has taken place. The employer must inform the relevant works council of the 'measures' it intends to take in relation to the proposed business transfer, the reason(s) for those 'measures' and their likely legal, economic and social impact on the employees (ArbVG, s 108(2a)). Where there is no works council in place, the transferor or the transferee must give the information specified above (including the proposed date of the transfer) in writing to the employees likely to be affected (AVRAG, s 3(a)).

Austrian law does not impose a duty on employers in such situations to 'seek agreement' with employee representatives. It is therefore arguable that the Austrian Legislator has not fully implemented the ARD[1]. However, employers can be fined if they do not comply with their duties to inform employee representatives with regard to collective dismissals (ArbVG, s 160).

1   C-382/92: *Commission v United Kingdom* [1994] ECR I-2435.

J2 Redundancy

J2.1 Background

In practice, business transfers often create redundancy situations. In many cases, especially takeovers and transfers involving undertakings competing in the same industry, the business transferred is integrated into an existing undertaking so that the work can be organised more efficiently. The transferee will generally have its own ideas as to how the transferred business should be organised and managed. As has been pointed out above (see *J1.5* for further details), an employer is entitled to 'lay-off' transferring employees or members of its pre-transfer workforce in accordance with the general principles of dismissal law. However, employers considering making employees redundant should consider the following issues before doing so:

–   Statutory protection against dismissals.

–   Notice periods and termination dates.

–   Information and consultation.

–   Severance payments.

–   Settlement agreements.

J2.2 Statutory protection against dismissals

An employer can give an employee notice of his/her dismissal, either in writing or orally, without specifying any reason. However, employees who have been employed for at least six months in an establishment (*Betrieb*) with at least five employees are entitled to challenge such a dismissal before the Austrian courts on the ground that it is 'socially unjust' (*sozialwidrig*). Such a claim may be brought by the dismissed employee or by a works council, either of which must prove that the dismissal is prejudicial to the employee's 'essential interests'. In practice, the Austrian courts use expert evidence to assess the chances of the dismissed employee getting another job with similar pay and working conditions.

Even if an employee is able to show that the dismissal is prejudicial to his/her 'essential interests', the employer can still justify it by demonstrating, for example, that the dismissal was related to the employee's capability or conduct (eg inability to work, lack of punctuality, etc) or to operational reasons. A redundancy situation clearly falls into the latter category. To prove that a genuine redundancy situation exists, an employer must show, at the very least, that:

(i)   the employee's position has ceased to exist; and

(ii) there is no suitable alternative employment.

The term 'suitable alternative employment' is not always restricted to the jobs that are available within an establishment at the time an employee is dismissed. If, for example, an employee is willing and able to do the job of a colleague working in the same establishment that has a similar job description, a works council could challenge the dismissal on the basis that the employer has made an 'unfair selection' (ie because the dismissed employee's colleague is less in need of protection). In practice, however, works councils rarely proceed in this manner.

If an employee is able to show that a dismissal is prejudicial to his/her 'essential interests' and his/her employer cannot justify it on the grounds set out above, an Austrian court will hold that the dismissal is null and void. Accordingly, the employment relationship will be deemed never to have been terminated. In cases where an employee's notice period has already expired by the time the court makes its decision (as is almost always the case), he/she will be entitled to payment of the arrears immediately and subsequently to his/her regular pay on the contractual payment dates.

Austrian law considers certain groups of employees (eg works council members, pregnant women, those who are disabled, etc) especially vulnerable to the termination of their employment and therefore affords them a higher degree of protection against dismissal. Generally, these employees can only validly be dismissed for reasons prescribed by law and with the prior consent of a court (or another public authority).

As to cross-border situations, the general view is that the provisions for protection against dismissal described above do not stipulate 'contractual obligations'. Instead, they refer to the statutory 'works constitution law' which is considered to apply only to establishments situated in Austria (territorial principle). Therefore, where a business is transferred to another employer in a different country without being relocated to that country, the transferring employees would still be afforded statutory protection against being unjustly dismissed. However, if that business were relocated to a different country upon transfer, it is likely that this protection would be lost.

J2.3 Notice periods and termination dates

In Austria, only employment relationships for unspecified durations can generally be terminated by giving notice. In so doing, employers must observe statutory notice periods and statutory termination dates (see below). Although the relevant statutory notice period is normally determined by an employee's length of service with his/her current employer, periods of employment with previous or associated employers may sometimes be taken into account by agreement. Although the notice periods and termination dates that apply to particular employment relationships can be determined in collective agreements and individual employment contracts, works agreements can only ever set notice periods. In accordance with the 'favourability principle' (see *J1.4* for further details), agreements in respect of notice periods and termination dates may only differ from the statutory provision in this regard to the extent that they are more favourable for employees.

For historic reasons, the Austrian workforce is divided into two categories: 'white-collar' workers and 'blue-collar' workers. Although the two groups enjoy almost the same rights these days, white-collar workers are still treated more favourably in some areas of the law, such as termination of employment. The Act on White Collar Workers (*Angestelltengesetz* – 'AngG') provides that employers in Austria must respect the following notice periods when terminating the employment of white-collar workers:

Years of service	Notice period
Less than two	Six weeks
At least two but less than five	Two months
At least five but less than 15	Three months
At least 15 but less than 25	Four months
More than 25	Five months

As stated above, Austrian law provides for certain termination dates. Section 20(2) of the AngG states that employers can only terminate employment relationships at the end of each quarter (ie on 31 March, 30 June, 30 September and 31 December). However, AngG, s 20(4) provides that the parties to an individual employment contract may validly agree that their employment relationship can also be terminated on the fifteenth day or at the end of each month. It should be noted that some collective agreements exclude this possibility after the employment has lasted for a certain number of years.

The relevant notice periods and termination dates for blue-collar workers in Austria are usually set in collective agreements. If no collective agreement applies, or if one does but does not regulate notice periods, both parties must generally observe a 14-day notice period unless they agree otherwise in an employment contract (s 77 of the Trade Act (*Gewerbeordnung* – 'GewO')).

Any failure by an employer or employee to comply with prescribed notice periods or termination dates would constitute 'untimely notice' (*zeitwidrige Kündigung*) under Austrian law. Although a termination carried out with 'untimely notice' would have the effect of prematurely ending the employment relationship, the dismissed employee would, prima facie, be entitled to claim pay in lieu of notice (*Kündigungsentschädigung*). This remedy, which originates from the law of damages, aims to compensate an employee for the loss he/she has suffered as a consequence of the premature termination of his/her employment. By providing that the dismissed employee receives the remuneration he/she would have been paid during the period between the date the employer prematurely terminated his/her employment and the actual date of termination, this remedy attempts to put him/her in the same financial situation he/she would have been in had the employer given notice in accordance with the relevant statute, collective agreement, works agreement or employment contract. An employee dismissed in this fashion is entitled to receive the full payment in lieu of notice up to a maximum period of three months. If, however, the period in relation to which compensation is due exceeds three months, any amount the employee has saved by not working, has earned from working or has deliberately failed to earn, will be set off against the compensation to which the employee is entitled from the fourth month onwards.

J2.4 The duty to inform and consult prior to redundancy

General rules on information and consultation

Although all establishments in Austria employing at least five employees are required to set up works councils, there is no sanction provided by law for a failure to do so. Accordingly, there are many businesses in Austria that do not have works councils, in circumstances where they should.

A works council must be informed in advance of an employer's intention to carry out a dismissal and may demand that it is consulted by the employer and given the opportunity to state its opinion in this regard within a period of five working days from the date on which it is first informed. If the works council makes such a demand, the employer may not carry out the proposed dismissal before the works council has stated its opinion or the five working days period has elapsed. Should an employer do so, or should it fail to inform a works council in the first place, the dismissal will be deemed null and void under Austrian law (see *J1.5* for further details).

Collective dismissals

If an employer plans to carry out dismissals exceeding a certain number of employees within 30 days ('collective dismissals'), it must give the Employment Service advance warning in accordance with a procedure generally referred to as the 'redundancies notification procedure' (*Kündigungs-frühwarnsystem*). The employer is obliged to forward a copy of this notification to the relevant works council, which must also be consulted on the matter. This procedure aims to give the Employment Service, the employer and the works council sufficient time to explore the potential ways in which the proposed dismissals could be avoided.

The thresholds for determining whether an employer must notify the Employment Service of its intention to carry out dismissals generally relate to the number of employees who work in the establishment in question:

Number of employees in establishment	Threshold for notification
21–99 employees	At least five employees to be dismissed
100–600 employees	At least 5 per cent of the workforce to be dismissed
More than 600 employees	At least 30 employees to be dismissed
Irrespective of the size of the establishment	At least five employees aged over 50 to be dismissed

Mutual agreements on the dissolution of employment relationships upon the employer's initiative must also be taken into account in determining whether a particular threshold has been exceeded.

If a particular threshold is exceeded and the employer fails to notify the Employment Service at least 30 days before it carries out the first dismissal, all of the collective dismissals are deemed null and void.

J2.5 Severance payments

The old system of statutory severance payments

Until 2003 Austrian law generally required employers to make statutory severance payments (*Abfertigung*) to employees upon the termination of their employment, provided they had been employed for a period of at least three years at the date of termination. However, employers were not obliged to make statutory severance payments where:

(i)   the employee had resigned without justification; or

(ii) the employee had been summarily dismissed for reasons relating to his/her conduct.

The amount of the severance payment to which a particular employee was entitled depended on the length of his/her service. After three years' service, a dismissed employee was prima facie entitled to a statutory severance payment equal to two months' pay, with the amount of the payment which the employee could claim rising to three, four, six, nine and 12 months' pay after five, 10, 15, 20 and 25 years of service, respectively. Statutory severance payments were not subject to social insurance contributions and were only liable to income tax at a flat rate of 6 per cent.

These regulations in respect of statutory severance payments in Austria are still applicable to all employment relationships that were entered into before 1 January 2003.

The new system of statutory severance payments

The system of statutory severance payments in Austria has recently been reformed (*Abfertigung Neu*). Employers are now required to make contributions to a special 'severance fund' equalling 1.53 per cent of the monthly remuneration of each employee whose employment started after 31 December 2002. Upon the termination of these employees' employment, they will generally be entitled to the accrued balance of their employer's contributions to the fund (either to receive it as a lump sum or to have the amount transferred to a fund maintained by a future employer). In such cases, employers will not be required to make statutory severance payments. In the case of some dismissals (eg summary dismissals with good cause), an employer's contributions are 'frozen' so that the balance remains within the relevant severance fund until such time as the employee's employment with another employer is terminated in a way that entitles him/her to it.

Payments under a social plan

Where employers anticipate making collective dismissals or major changes to the organisation of establishments entailing serious disadvantages for significant proportions of the workforce, they can conclude so-called 'social plans' (*Sozialplan*) with the relevant works councils. Social plans, which mainly cover financial arrangements for employees attending or organising re-training schemes and higher severance payments for employees who have been or are to be made redundant, are generally treated as works agreements under Austrian law. However, if there are at least 20 employees working in a particular establishment, any social plan concluded with the works council there can also be enforced before the Public Mediation and Arbitration Board (*Schlichtungsstelle*).

J2.6 Settlement agreements

It is quite common for the parties to a dispute in relation to the termination of an employee's employment to reach an agreement whereby the employer pays the employee a certain amount of money calculated as a multiple of his/her monthly salary. Such an agreement is completely voluntary and an employee cannot be forced to enter into one, either by his/her employer or a court. Although there is no 'rule of thumb' as regards the calculation of the 'voluntary severance payment' (*freiwillige Abfertigung*) an employer makes, the employee's length of service and his/her chances of finding suitable alternative employment, as well as the financial situation of the employer, are obviously relevant to its determination.

J3 Case studies

J3.1 Case study 1
(Acquisition of a 'business' situated in another EU state; asset deal; no relocation)

Slumber Ltd, a hotel management company incorporated in the UK based in Manchester, UK, has been in financial difficulties for some time. Slumber operates nine exclusive hotels in the main British cities (London, Manchester, Birmingham, Leeds, Glasgow, Edinburgh, Liverpool, Cardiff and Bristol) under the 'Slumber' brand. Slumber is 100 per cent owned by UK hotel chain Ezeroom plc, also incorporated in the UK. Each hotel has about 50 staff: five in management, 20 in the restaurant and 25 in house service. Slumber does not own the hotels itself; instead it has a seven-year management agreement with Hotel Investment plc ('HIP'), the owner of the hotels, which is incorporated and based in London, UK. Under this contract Slumber runs the fully equipped hotels on its own risk and has to pay a fixed fee to HIP.

In its central management centre in Manchester, Slumber has another 30 staff. These are 10 managers (including Marketing, Managing, Finance, Sales and Operations Directors) and 20 secretaries, clerks and administrators.

A number of staff are members of the trade union, The Association of Hotel Workers ('AHW'), which has been formally recognised by Slumber as having bargaining rights for hourly paid hotel staff. This is a particularly active union and there is a collective agreement in force. Due to increasing staff costs and the declining demand for expensive hotel accommodation, Slumber is making bigger and bigger operating losses. Slumber is obliged to cut jobs in all the hotels and thus dismisses 40 members of staff as redundant. As a consequence, the service worsens and customer complaints become more frequent. When the board of HIP realises how serious the situation has become, it starts to look for a new operator of its hotels.

Some weeks later, while Slumber is still operating the hotels, an Austrian company is found which seems able to manage the hotels in a much more profitable way for HIP than Slumber. The company, which is called Dormir, is based in Vienna but has already gathered some experience of running hotels in the UK. It operates hotels under the 'Dormir' brand. The board of HIP enters into discussions with Dormir for it to replace Slumber as manager of the hotels.

1. Acquisition of the hotels

It is anticipated that Dormir will want to manage all nine of the hotels under a single management agreement with HIP.

(a) **Would this be a business transfer (defined as a transfer within the meaning of TUPE) under UK law?**

(ONLY TO BE ANSWERED BY UK CONTRIBUTOR)

(b) **Even though Slumber will not transfer any of its activities to Austria, would the acquisition of the hotels in this way constitute a business transfer under Austrian law?**

Answer

Yes, it would.

Legal reasoning

As stated at *J1.2* above, the Austrian courts generally apply the criteria that have been developed by the European Court of Justice in order to determine whether a specific transaction constitutes a business transfer under the Austrian legislation that implements the Acquired Rights Directive ('ARD'). Hence, the crucial questions for an Austrian court would be: whether Slumber has operated an 'economic entity' (which is beyond any doubt) and whether this 'economic entity' retains its identity upon being transferred to Dormir. The latter condition is likely to be fulfilled on the basis that Dormir will continue the same activity (ie the management of hotels) following the transfer. The lack of a direct contractual link between Slumber and Dormir is irrelevant under Austrian law, as is the fact that Dormir does not own the hotels in question.

(c) **Would it make any difference to whether this constituted a business transfer, under TUPE, if Dormir only wanted to manage the six English hotels (excluding the hotels in Glasgow, Edinburgh and Cardiff)?**

(ONLY TO BE ANSWERED BY UK CONTRIBUTOR)

(d) **Would it make any difference to your answer to (b) above if Dormir only wanted to manage six hotels (for example only the English hotels, excluding those in Scotland and Wales, ie the hotels in Glasgow, Edinburgh and Cardiff)?**

Answer

No, it would not.

Legal reasoning

The management of each hotel can be considered a severable 'economic entity', as it falls within the ECJ's definition of 'an organised grouping of persons and assets exercising an economic activity which pursues a specific objective'.

2. Employees who work only partly in the business

What is the position of those staff who work partly in Slumber and partly in Ezeroom? For example, the human resources director of Slumber is also the human resources director of Ezeroom and he has his employment agreement with Ezeroom. He spends approximately 40 per cent of his time dealing with Slumber's personnel matters and the remainder of his time on the human resources affairs of Ezeroom.

(a) **If this is a TUPE transfer, can he be said to have transferred under TUPE in the UK?**

(UK CONTRIBUTOR TO ANSWER)

(b) **What is the law on employees who work only partly in the undertaking to be transferred in Austria?**

Under Austrian law, only employees who have employment contracts with the undertakings being transferred can rely on the national business transfer legislation. Thus, it would appear to be irrelevant how much time the human resources director spends dealing with Slumber's personnel matters if he has an employment contract with Ezeroom. Accordingly, it is likely that an Austrian court would hold that his employment relationship with Ezeroom would not be affected by the transfer of Slumber's hotel management business to Dormir.

3. Staff who work outside the UK in another EU country

It transpires that some Slumber central management staff are actually working and based in Austria already. Two are Austrian nationals.

(a) **Would these staff transfer to Dormir under TUPE if there was a TUPE transfer?**

(TO BE ANSWERED BY UK CONTRIBUTOR. PLEASE COMMENT ON UK RESPONSE)

Answer

In theory yes, although this would depend on a number of factors, including their contracts of employment.

Legal reasoning

TUPE applies to undertakings or parts of undertakings situated in the UK immediately prior to transfer. These employees work for and are employed by Slumber, the undertaking to be transferred, but they are simply based in Austria. The undertaking of Slumber is situated in the UK immediately before the transfer (even if some staff work outside the UK). Therefore, members of Slumber central management who are working in Austria will technically transfer. The important point is that TUPE in principle applies to undertakings or a part of an undertaking which is situated in the UK immediately before the transfer. The fact that some of the employees are not actually located in the UK is irrelevant.

*Difficulties may arise in practice. For example, the employees may no longer be required to continue working in the same place and there may be potential breaches of contract. If their employment is terminated, this is likely to be in connection with the transfer and potentially unfair. Whether or not they have claims in the UK, or indeed in Austria, will depend on conflicts of laws issues (see Chapter **D**).*

Comment: Where employees habitually carry out their work in Austria, they can generally rely on Austrian law (art 6(2)(a) of the Rome Convention). As it is likely that this transaction could constitute a business transfer under the Austrian legislation implementing the ARD, the affected employees could sue Dormir in the Austrian courts for payment of wages, etc, since their employment would have been transferred.

(b) **Would the position be different if there was a branch office of Ezeroom in Austria, which directly employed these staff?**

(UK TO ANSWER, BUT PLEASE COMMENT)

Answer

The position may be the same.

Legal reasoning

TUPE is likely to apply if the branch office qualifies as an associated employer and the employees are 'assigned' (Botzen v Rotterdamsche Droogdok Maatschappij BV: 186/83 [1985] ECR 519, ECJ) to Slumber (in other words, they carry out all their functions for Slumber which is their de facto employer). In such a case the courts are likely to pierce the corporate veil and treat Slumber as the employer for those purposes.

Comment: As the branch office would still be part of Slumber, the position would not be any different. If, on the other hand, the employees in Austria were employed by a separate legal entity (eg an associated company of Slumber), they would not be affected by the transfer of Slumber to Dormir under Austrian law, even if they had been assigned to work for Slumber on a full-time basis.

4. Dismissal of employee

One of the Slumber staff, Mr X, was dismissed by Slumber after HIP had given notice to terminate the contract with Slumber and whilst negotiations were ongoing with Dormir. Mr X is owed two months' back pay and unpaid holiday.

Against whom can Mr X bring a claim, and where, if Mr X is a UK national based in Austria?

Provided that Mr X's regular place of work has been in Austria, he could, in principle, bring a claim before the competent Austrian court against any employer that is domiciled within the EU (excluding Denmark) (art 19 of Council Regulation (EC) 44/2001; see *J1.1* above for more details). Further, in the absence of a choice of law provision in Mr X's employment contract, he would be subject to Austrian law to the extent that he habitually carried out his work in Austria (art 6 of the Rome Convention; see *J1.1* above). It is therefore possible that Mr X could sue Dormir, submitting that he had been dismissed on the grounds of the envisaged business transfer (as defined under Austrian business transfer legislation), which would render the purported dismissal null and void under Austrian law if the courts found in his favour. As the transferee of a business assumes all the rights and obligations arising from the employment relationships with the transferor, Dormir would be liable to pay transferring employees any outstanding holiday pay and any arrears of salary.

5. Transfer of employee outside the UK

Mr Y (the marketing director) has been vital to the success of Slumber and has been responsible for many successful ideas. Dormir would like to retain his services and move him to Dormir's headquarters in Austria. Mr Y has no wish to live in Austria.

(a)   **How does TUPE impact on Mr Y: is he obliged to transfer against his will?**

(UK ONLY TO ANSWER)

(b)   **What is the law on objection to a transfer in Austria?**

Section 3(1) of the Employment Contract Law Adaptation Act 1993 (*Arbeitsvertragsrechts-Anpassungsgesetz* – 'AVRAG') provides for the automatic transfer of all the employment relationships that exist in relation to a business at the time it is transferred. However, AVRAG, s 3(4) allows the affected employees (but not the transferee) to object to this automatic transfer in two situations, in both cases within a period of one month:

(i)   Where the transferee refuses to take on a transferor's obligations in relation to an occupational pension scheme arising from individual employment contracts, in accordance with AVRAG, s 5(1).

(ii)   Where a pre-existing collective agreement is superseded by a collective agreement to which the transferee is party that provides for a weaker level of protection against dismissal and the transferee refuses to incorporate the provisions of the pre-existing collective agreement in this regard into the individual employment contracts of the transferring employees. However, transferring employees can only object to a business transfer on this basis if the transferor continues to operate a business subsequently, as otherwise the relevant provisions of the pre-existing collective agreement would automatically be incorporated into their employment contracts in accordance with AVRAG, s 4(2).

Austrian legal commentators agree that, in both situations, an employee utilising his/her right to object to a business transfer would leave his/her employment relationship with the transferor unchanged, but could lead to the transferor making him/her redundant, eg if it ceases to operate a business following the transfer.

It is debatable whether, notwithstanding AVRAG, s 3(4), there is a general right for affected employees to object to business transfers in Austria. Although the ECJ has held on a number of occasions that employees cannot be forced to work for employers they have not chosen themselves, the Supreme Court, which has indicated that the right of employees to object to business transfers may not be restricted to the two situations covered by s 3(4), has yet to confirm the position in this regard. However, the Supreme Court has confirmed that employee members of works councils have the right to object to the transfer of their employment as, otherwise, employers could end their involvement in the works councils by simply disposing of the part of the business in relation to which they are employed.

(c) **Can Mr Y claim constructive dismissal on the basis that he would be expected to work and be based in Austria and this is nowhere near his home?**

(UK TO ANSWER, BUT PLEASE COMMENT)

Answer

Possibly, if this amounts to a fundamental breach of his contract or if being expected to work and be based abroad amounts to a substantial change in working conditions and is to the employee's detriment.

Legal reasoning

In addition to general common law tests for constructive dismissal, reg 5(5) provides that an employee has the right 'to terminate his contract of employment without notice if a substantial change is made in his working conditions to his detriment'. It is important therefore that the change is substantial and to the employee's detriment. Such a claim is likely to lie against the transferee (Dormir). Only in rare circumstances such as where the transferor (Slumber) has not been open with the employee about the change in working conditions is a claim likely to succeed against the transferor (Slumber). Case law is of importance here.

In Merckx and Neuhuys v Ford Motors Co Belgium SA [1996] IRLR 467, Anfo Motors SA transferred its Ford dealership to an independent dealer.

There was no transfer of assets and only 14 out of Anfo's 60 employees were taken on. The ECJ identified a community right to claim constructive dismissal where there was a 'substantial change in working conditions to the detriment of the employee' because of the transfer.

In Rossiter v Pendragon [2002] IRLR 483, Mr Rossiter argued that he had suffered a detriment through changes in the calculation of commission, that his holiday pay was no longer based on commission and that he was made to assume lesser duties. The Court of Appeal held that in order to claim constructive dismissal there would have to be a repudiatory breach of contract, which there was not in this case.

The use of mobility clauses is limited in long-distance transfers, as the test for redundancy (see above) is where the employee actually carries out his work.

Comment: As it would appear that Mr Y's regular place of work has been in the UK, it may be assumed that Austrian law would not, in the absence of a choice of law, apply to his employment, even after a business transfer had taken place. However, if the scenario were to be adjudicated under Austrian law, Mr Y could not be required to move to Austria under his employment contract, since he could generally rely on the (at least implicit) agreement that his habitual place of work is situated in the UK. If, however, Mr Y had a mobility clause in his contract of employment which covered Austria, he would be required to relocate there by his new employer and could not claim constructive dismissal.

6. Dormir's business strategy

What is the best way of structuring the transfer of the hotels to Dormir from an Austrian perspective? Would you advise Dormir to set up a subsidiary company registered in the UK specifically to purchase Slumber and thereby avoid any cross-border element?

From a pure employment law perspective, it should not make much difference whether it is the Austrian company, Dormir, that takes over the management of the hotels or its English subsidiary. Under the common European rules on the applicable law for contractual obligations (Rome Convention of 1980), the applicable law depends primarily on the regular place of work, not in which member state an employer is situated. The same principle is to be applied in order to determine where employees can make their claims. Consequently, in structuring the transfer of the hotels to Dormir, other factors such as tax and liability would need to be considered. Furthermore, UK administrative law could require Dormir to be established in the UK.

J3.2 Case study 2
(Production moves from one EU country to another EU country; physical move)

Alpha Incorporated is a multinational car tyre manufacturing and distribution business based in Europe. Alpha's headquarters are in France. Alpha has tyre plants in Austria, Germany and France. Each of the tyre plants is a wholly owned and independently operated subsidiary of Alpha. Alpha has a European Works Council.

The subsidiary in Austria is Beta. Beta employs about 250 employees, mostly in the direct production of tyres. The employees are on standard basic contracts which do not contain any mobility clauses. Due to increased competition from cheaper producers in the Far East, Alpha is having to reduce its own production costs. Beta has the highest production costs of all Alpha's European operations. Alpha has decided to end the production of tyres in Austria and move production to Gamma, another subsidiary not far away but across the national border in Germany which has more modern plant and equipment. Beta will continue to exist, but as a sales and marketing organisation only, with about 30 staff.

Most of Beta's tyre-making plant and machinery is transferred to Gamma, but Gamma will only need an extra 125 staff to increase its output to the required level to supply Beta's market. Those employees from Beta who are required to work for Gamma will be expected to accept the terms and conditions and working practices of the Gamma plant, which are very different from those in operation at the Beta plant. For example, Gamma pays its employees considerably lower hourly wages and they work longer hours than those at Beta. Gamma does not want to pay more to the employees transferred to it from Beta than it does to its current employees. Gamma operates a different type of pension scheme.

1. Does this transaction constitute a 'business transfer'?

(a) **As Beta's tyre-making plant and machinery have transferred to Gamma, will this constitute a business transfer under the Acquired Rights Directive implementing legislation of Austria?**

Answer

Probably yes, although the transfer of Beta's material assets is not, of itself, conclusive of the transaction constituting a 'business transfer'.

Legal reasoning

Although there is not yet any Austrian case law on this particular point, the case law of the ECJ has been adopted by the Austrian courts. In order for a business transfer to take place in accordance with the ARD, it is necessary that the 'economic entity' being transferred retain its identity. The determination of this issue can be extremely difficult, especially in the case of a relocation. Nevertheless, in assessing whether a particular transaction constitutes a business transfer, all the facts must be assessed. Such assessment should include consideration of: the type of undertaking or business in question; whether or not its tangible assets (such as buildings and movable property) are transferred; the value of its intangible assets at the time of the transfer; whether or not the majority of its employees are taken on by the new employer; whether or not its customers are transferred; the degree of similarity between the activities carried on before and after the transfer, and the period, if any, for which those activities are suspended. However, these individual factors are part of a much longer overall assessment and cannot therefore be considered in isolation (see *Spijkers v Gebroeders Benedik Abattoir CV*: 24/85 [1986] 2 CMLR 296 and *Süzen v Zehnacker*: C-13/95 [1997] ECR I-1259; see *A2.3* for more details).

In the present case, important material assets (ie the tyre-making plant and machinery) have been transferred to Gamma in Germany. Further, the activities carried on before and after the transfer (ie the production of car tyres) are almost certainly going to be the same. However, it is not certain whether Beta's customers will transfer to Gamma, how long it will be after the transfer before the plant and machinery transferred can be used in Germany to produce tyres again, or how many of Beta's employees will actually transfer to Gamma. According to the latest case law of the ECJ, however, the latter criterion would probably have less weight than the transfer of material assets, since the production of tyres cannot be regarded as an activity based essentially on manpower. (See the answer to question 1(**b**) below for more details.)

(**b**)   **Does it make any difference to whether this is a business transfer if employees of Beta transfer across to Gamma?**

Answer

No.

Legal reasoning

As is mentioned in the response to question 1(**a**) above, the recruitment of employees who have been employed in an 'economic entity' (eg a plant for the production of car tyres) by another employer is one factor to consider in the overall assessment of whether or not that economic entity has been transferred whilst retaining its identity (ie whether the transaction constitutes a transfer under the ARD). According to the ECJ's case law, the weight to be attached to the various factors depends on the type of business in question (see *A2.3* for more details). In *Carlito Abler v Sodhexho MM Catering Gesellschaft mbH*: C-340/01 [2004] IRLR 168, the ECJ held that a change of contractors entrusted to provide catering services to a hospital, with the new contractor using substantial parts of the tangible assets previously used by the old contractor, fell within the terms of the ARD, even though the new contractor did not offer employment to any of the old contractor's employees. The court reasoned that catering could not be regarded 'as an activity based essentially on manpower since it required a significant amount of equipment', in contrast to cleaning services (see *Süzen v Zehnacker*: C-13/95 [1997] ECR I-1259). On the basis of this case law, it seems safe to conclude that the production of car tyres does not depend 'essentially' on manpower either, since the activity is inconceivable without access to expensive material assets (eg premises, machinery, etc).

(c) **Can the transfer of plant and machinery coupled with the transfer of half the employees (125) constitute a business transfer under Austrian legislation if the other 125 employees are dismissed prior to the transfer?**

Answer

Without prejudice to the response to question 1(a) above, yes it can.

Legal reasoning

First, as has been pointed out in the response to question 1(b) above, due to the nature of the business in question (ie the production of car tyres), it would appear to be irrelevant whether Gamma offers employment to any of Beta's employees. Second, under Austrian law, any dismissals effected by a transferor in order to avoid the application of the business transfer legislation are null and void.

(d) **Does the fact that the business will transfer to a different country make any difference to whether this is a business transfer?**

Answer

No.

Legal reasoning

Under Austrian law, the cross-border element would not be a relevant factor in determining whether the transaction constitutes a 'business transfer'. However, the actual distance between the former and the new place of business would be important in the overall assessment of whether or not the identity of the business has been retained (see response to question 1(a) above).

(e) **Is Austrian business transfer law concerned with the actual distance moved (irrespective of whether this means a change of country)?**

Answer

Yes.

Legal reasoning

The distance that a business moves is taken into account by the Austrian courts when assessing whether the economic entity being transferred has retained its identity. Whilst there is no specific case law on this point, the Austrian Supreme Court has implicitly accepted that the relocation of a business over a distance of 55km (without a change in the identity of the employer) did not affect its identity (OGH 14.6.2000, 9 Ob A 48/00z).

2. Relocation, but no business transfer

(a) **Assuming the move does NOT constitute a business transfer (because the business of Beta does not adequately retain its identity) but instead is deemed to be a straightforward relocation, are any of Beta's employees obliged or entitled to transfer?**

Answer

No. Under Austrian law, the employees would be neither obliged nor entitled to transfer to Gamma, unless the two employers reached an agreement with them to that effect.

Legal reasoning

According to the freedom of contract principle, an employment relationship is based on the free will of the two parties concerned. Any exception to this rule must be provided for by statutory law, such as s 3(1) of the Employment Contract Law Adaptation Act 1993 (*Arbeitsvertragsrechts-Anpassungsgesetz* – 'AVRAG') in relation to business transfers.

(b) **If employees do nevertheless relocate, what will happen to their employment contracts? Will these continue, or will Gamma be entitled to provide new contracts?**

Such a situation would generally be governed by German law, as the employees' 'regular place of work' would be in Germany (art 6 of the Rome Convention; see *J1.1* above.)

(c) **What will be the law applicable to the contracts of the employees who relocate?**

See the response to question 2(b) above. The parties could, however, choose that the law of a different jurisdiction applies to the contracts of employment, although this would not deprive the employees of the protection afforded to them by the 'mandatory rules' of the law that would apply to their contracts in the absence of a choice of law (art 6(1) of the Rome Convention).

3. Dismissals

(a) **Assuming that the move does constitute a business transfer:**

(i)   **are any dismissals in connection with the transfer lawful?**

Answer

Yes, but only if they can be justified.

Legal reasoning

In accordance with Austrian case law, any dismissals connected with a business transfer are null and void unless they can be justified by a reason related to the capability or the conduct of the employee in question or the specific needs of the relevant business. However, for a dismissal to be deemed null and void, the affected employee must assert that it is invalid within a reasonable period following the purported dismissal. Although the Austrian Supreme Court has held that a period of 10 months was too long a period to wait before raising such an assertion, it has stressed that the period of time after which the validity of a dismissal can no longer be questioned depends on the specifics of the individual case (OGH 30.6.1999, DRdA 2000, 311).

(ii)   **what are the rights and remedies (including applicable law and appropriate jurisdiction) of any employees dismissed:**

   a.   before the transfer?

   Employees who were dismissed before the business transfer could sue Beta or Gamma before an Austrian court, since their regular place of work was in Austria. For the same reason, in the absence of a choice of law within the employees' contracts of employment, the court would have to apply Austrian law (art 6 of the Rome Convention; see *J1.1* above). The employees could claim that they had been dismissed in connection with the proposed business transfer, which would render the purported dismissals null and void. If the employees succeeded, they would be reinstated as employees of Beta. However, if the business transfer had occurred in the meantime, Gamma would be identified as their new employer. Whoever was identified by a court as the employees' employer would be liable to pay any outstanding wages owed to them.

   b.   after the transfer?

   The first question one must ask is whether the employment relationships would still be governed by Austrian law (see *J1.1* above). If the change of employers is accompanied by the relocation of the business in question, one must establish where the employees 'habitually carry out their work' (art 6(2)(a) of the Rome Convention).

   If the employees consented to working in a new place of business in Germany after the transfer, their employment relationships could become subject to German law, including its rules on dismissals of employees by transferees (see **M2**). If this was to happen, the employees could no longer sue Gamma before an Austrian court, since their regular place of work would be in Germany (art 19 of Council Regulation (EC) 44/2001).

If, on the other hand, the employees refused to move to Germany following the business transfer, their employment would continue to be governed by Austrian law. If Gamma is no longer be able to employ them in Austria on the basis of their employment contract, the employees can be made redundant in accordance with the general principles of Austrian dismissal law.

(b)   Would these rights and remedies change if this was not a business transfer?

Answer

Yes.

Legal reasoning

In such a case, Beta's employees would not be able to rely on Austrian business transfer law and could not therefore claim to be taken on by Gamma after the completion of the transaction. The employees could potentially be dismissed by Beta for lack of work, provided they are genuinely redundant and cannot be employed for other purposes (eg sales and marketing). In selecting which employees it wished to retain, Beta would have to take account of the social characteristics (ie age, marital status, etc) of the employees concerned (rather than simply their qualifications). If it did not do so, the dismissed employees could appeal against their dismissals as 'socially unjust' (*Sozialwidrigkeit*), provided that the relevant works council had rejected them beforehand (see *J2.1* above).

If Beta wished to make at least five per cent of its staff redundant within a period of 30 days, the statutory regulations on 'collective dismissals' would have to be observed. Under these provisions, an employer must notify the Employment Service Agency of its intention to make redundancies at least 30 days before the first dismissal is declared, otherwise any dismissals are null and void. In addition, any Beta works council would have to be informed and consulted on this issue.

4. European Works Council and other employees' representatives

(a)   Will Alpha be required to inform and consult the European Works Council about the transfer or any redundancies?

As the central management of the Alpha group of companies is situated in France, this question can only be answered under French law.

However, it may be assumed that the French implementing legislation of the European Works Council Directive 94/45/EC generally provides for information and consultation in such a case of cross-border transfer and redundancies.

(b) **Are any other employee representatives required to be involved in the transfer or any redundancies (ie at national or local level)?**

Answer

Assuming that there is a works council at Beta (as it employs about 250 employees), it would need to be involved in both the business transfer and any resulting redundancies.

Legal reasoning

Under Austrian law, works councils must be elected by the workforce in all establishments employing five or more employees. Works councils in Austria are afforded certain rights, ranging from information and consultation to co-determination (see *J2.3* above).

In the event of a 'business transfer', Beta would have to inform its works council of the reason(s) for the transfer, the legal, economic and social consequences for the staff, and any personnel measures it envisaged.

In cases of 'individual redundancies', the works council would need to be informed in advance and could state its opinion on Beta's proposals within a period of five working days (see *J2.3* above). However, even if the works council rejected the proposed dismissals, Beta would still be able to go ahead with them, but the dismissals would be open to challenge on the grounds that they were 'socially unjust'.

If Beta plans to carry out 'collective dismissals' (see *J2.3* above), its works council must be informed of the reason(s) for the planned dismissals, the number and occupational groups of the employees to be made redundant (including their qualification, their period of service and the criteria for their selection), the number and occupational groups of the regular employees, the period during which the redundancies are to take place and any planned measures which might alleviate the adverse effects for the employees. The works council would also have a right to be consulted in such a situation. As Beta employs more than 20 employees and a substantial part of its workforce are likely to lose their jobs, the works council would have the power to negotiate and conclude a 'social plan' (*Sozialplan*) with Beta. The purpose of such a plan would be to prevent or mitigate the negative consequences of the proposed redundancies for the employees concerned. In practice, employers provide voluntary severance payments, finance training schemes, etc. If the parties did not reach agreement on a 'social plan', either of them could apply for a binding decision by the public 'mediation and conciliation board' (*Schlichtungsstelle*), which would be established at the competent employment court in Austria.

5. Collective agreements

What is the effect of the business transfer on any collective agreements affecting Beta's employees?

In Austria, there is a distinction between collective agreements and works agreements (see *J1.4* above). Most legal commentators feel that both agreements require the relevant business to be situated in Austria, such that the employees in the scenario would not be able to rely on Beta's collective agreements and/or works agreements following a business transfer to another country. However, if the employees' regular place of work changed as a result of the relocation, the national law that applies to them would generally change, too (see response to question 3(a)(ii)b). In such a case, one would need to consider whether the law of the country to which the business has relocated provides for the observance of foreign collective agreements and/or works agreements (see *M1.4*).

6. Change of terms and conditions

(a)   **If this is a business transfer, how can Gamma lawfully harmonise employment contracts and change the terms and conditions of the employees currently on the more generous Beta contracts of employment?**

Again, one must first determine whether the employees would be subject to Austrian or German law. If, even after the relocation of the employees' regular place of work to Germany, Austrian law applied (eg by a choice of law) Gamma could attempt to negotiate a mutual change of the contractual terms and conditions. In this context, however, the case law of the ECJ would need to be observed. Accordingly, the business transfer itself would not constitute a valid ground for a change in terms and conditions (see *Serene Martin v South Bank University*: C-4/01 [2004] IRLR 74). Further, disadvantageous new terms and conditions would not be able to be set-off against other advantages (*Foreningen af Arbejdsledere i Danmark v Daddy's Dance Hall A/S*: 324/86 [1988] ECR 739, ECJ).

If the employees did not agree to a change in their terms and conditions, Gamma could consider issuing dismissals pending a change of contract (*Änderungskündigung*). However, Gamma's desire to harmonise the employment conditions of its workforce would not be sufficient to justify any dismissals it decided to make. In addition, under art 6 of the Rome Convention, the German provisions on protection against dismissal (see **M2**) would probably apply, regardless of any choice of law the parties had.

(b) **If this is a business transfer, can Gamma reduce the wages of the former Beta employees?**

Assuming that the employees' wages are set out in their employment contracts, this would only be possible under Austrian law by mutual agreement, or by a dismissal pending a change of contract (see response to question **6(a)** above for more details).

(c) **If this is a business transfer, what will happen to the former Beta employees as regards their private pension arrangements?**

Under Austrian law, the answer to this question depends on the legal basis of the relevant occupational pension scheme. The transferee could refuse to take on the transferor's commitments as regards a contractual pension scheme. In this case, the employees would be entitled to a lump sum payment from the transferor reflecting the value of their pension rights. The situation may be different if German law applies.

(d) **Is it easier to change terms and conditions of employment if the changes are made six months after the transfer?**

Answer

In theory, no. In practice, maybe yes.

Legal reasoning

As pointed out in the response to question **6(a)** above, the ECJ's case law regarding harmonisation of terms and conditions is very strict. This case law applies, regardless of when the purported changes are introduced. However, it would probably be easier to argue that it was not the business transfer as such, but objective business reasons that triggered them if Gamma waited six months before attempting to introduce changes to the employees' terms and conditions.

J3.3 Case study 3
(Outsourcing of an ancillary activity to a non-EU country)

A large multinational (ABC) based in Austria has decided to outsource its entire internal IT function to a third party provider in Romania, as the costs of hiring competent IT personnel in Romania are far lower than in Austria, largely because wages are so much lower. At present 200 employees are employed by ABC in its IT function in Austria. It is anticipated that exactly the same IT function will be required in Romania with approximately the same number of people required to run it. There will be no difference in the service or approach for those requiring IT assistance and even the internal telephone number will be automatically diverted. The Romanian third party provider has no assets or presence in Austria.

1. Business transfer

Will this be a business transfer within the scope of Austria's law applying the ARD?

Answer

No, provided that the Romanian contractor is merely awarded the contract without any assets being transferred and without taking over any employees of the Austrian undertaking.

Legal reasoning

According to the ECJ's case law, which the Austrian Supreme Court has adopted, the mere contracting out of an activity does not, of itself, constitute a business transfer (see *Süzen v Zehnacker Gebäudereinigung GmbH Krankenhausservice*: C-13/95 [1997] ECR I-1259, ECJ).

Provided that the activities of the IT function can properly be classified as 'labour-intensive', it is likely that it would, based on the ECJ's reasoning in *Süzen*, be classified as an 'economic entity', ie a group of workers engaged in a joint activity on a permanent basis. If, therefore, the Romanian contractor takes over 'a major part, in terms of their numbers and skills, of the employees specially assigned by his predecessor to that task', the transaction would fall within the terms of the ARD and, therefore, the Austrian business transfer legislation.

2. Effect on employees

(a)   **What will happen to the employees currently employed in the IT function at ABC? Will they transfer across?**

Answer

No.

Legal reasoning

As this scenario would not constitute a business transfer, the employees of ABC's IT department would not be entitled to rely on the Austrian legislation implementing the ARD. It is likely that, as a consequence of ABC's IT function being contracted out, the employees currently employed in that function would be redundant. If so, ABC would be entitled to dismiss them if there was no suitable alternative employment available.

(b)   **If the employees do transfer, what will the applicable law be for their employment contracts with the third party provider? Where can they make any claims?**

Answer

Subject to the assumptions set out below, the employees could sue the Romanian service provider in Austria. In such a case, the employees would be able to rely on Austrian law.

Legal reasoning

As long as Romania is not a member of the EU, Council Regulation (EC) 44/2001 on jurisdiction and the recognition and enforcement of judgments does not apply. Therefore, the 'national' rules on jurisdiction must be applied, under which an Austrian court could be designated by the Austrian Supreme Court as competent to hear the employees' claims, provided they were Austrian citizens (or domiciled in Austria) and the enforcement of their rights in Romania would not be possible or inequitable (s 28(1) no 2 of the Austrian Jurisdictional Code – *Jurisdiktionsnorm*).

The question of which law has to be applied must be answered in accordance with the rules on conflict of laws. Even if Romania has yet to accede to the Rome Convention 1980 on the law applicable to contractual obligations, it would still be binding on the Austrian courts. Therefore, in the absence of a choice of law clause in the employees' contracts of employment, their employment relationships would be governed by Austrian law, so long as they habitually carry out their work here (art 6(2)(a) of the Rome Convention). It is generally assumed that a mere change in the identity of an employee's employer does not affect his/her regular place of work. Consequently, it is likely that the employees could rely on Austrian business transfer law in their action against a (new) Romanian employer before an Austrian court.

3. Data protection

Will there be special data protection issues on the transfer of knowledge and information outside Austria to Romania?

Answer

Yes.

Legal reasoning

Under Austrian law, data protection issues are regulated by the Data Protection Act 2000 (*Datenschutzgesetz* – 'DSG'), which implements EC Directive 95/46/EC. According to this Act, the transfer of data from Austria to non-EU countries generally requires the prior permission of the Austrian Commission on Data Protection (*Datenschutzkommission*), unless the affected employees have given their explicit and informed consent to the transfer (DSG, s 12). The Austrian Commission on Data Protection can only give the required permission if the non-EU country in question is able to ensure an adequate level of data protection in the particular case, or if the Commission feels that there are adequate safeguards in place, in particular appropriate contractual clauses.

4. Transfer to India

Please comment on any differences there would be to your answers if the function was transferred to India rather than Romania.

Answer

There would be no differences to the answers above.

Legal reasoning

As long as Romania is not a member of the EU, it will not be subject to the common European rules on jurisdiction, as laid down in Council Regulation (EC) 44/2001. Therefore, as far as issues of jurisdiction are concerned, they are dealt with in accordance with the same rules, regardless of whether the IT function is outsourced to Romania or India. The issues surrounding the transfer of data to another country are dealt with in the same way in both scenarios. The same is true for the question of which law applies to the employees affected by the outsourcing of the IT function, although in this case, the Rome Convention must always be applied, regardless of whether the other country is a party to that Convention or not.

J4 Additional information

J4.1 Useful websites

www.ris.bka.gv.at
(Legal Information System of the Austrian State – *Rechtsinformationssystem des Bundes*: eg legal texts, draft bills, case law of the Supreme Court of Justice, the Constitutional Court and the Supreme Administrative Court; free of charge)

www.parlinkom.gv.at
(Austrian Parliament; free of charge)

www.rdb.at
(legal database – *Rechtsdatenbank*: eg case law, legal journals; charges)

J4.2 Useful literature

Business transfers

Binder *Arbeitsvertragsrechts-Anpassungsgesetz* (Manz, 2001)

Holzer & Reissner *Arbeitsvertragsrechts-Anpassungsgesetz* (ÖGB-Verlag, 1998)

Redundancies

Tinhofer *Kündigung aus wirtschaftlichen Gründen – Ein Handbuch für die Praxis* (LexisNexis, 2002)

General books on employment law

Mazal & Risak *Das Arbeitsrecht – System und Praxiskommentar* (LexisNexis, looseleaf)

K Belgium

Stanislas van Wassenhove

Michaël De Leersnyder

Alexis Ceuterick

K1 Business transfers

K1.1 Background

The main principles of the EU directives were implemented by the Collective Bargaining Agreement (CBA) no 32*bis* of 7 June 1985:

- Automatic transfer of the employment contracts of the transferred employees and maintenance of the terms and conditions – CBA no 32*bis*, art 7.

- Protection against dismissal in connection with the business transfer – CBA no 32*bis*, art 9.

The obligation to inform and consult with employees is not regulated by CBA no 32*bis* itself (except in the absence of a Works Council and Trade Union delegation – see below). However, these obligations result from the CBA of 9 March 1972 concerning the Works Council, the Royal Decree of 27 November 1973 concerning the economic and financial information to be provided to the Works Council, and CBA no 5 of 24 May 1971 concerning Trade Union delegations.

K1.2 Identifying a relevant transfer

The Collective Bargaining Agreement no 32*bis* of 7 June 1985 (as modified by CBA no 32*ter* to CBA no 32*quinquies*), concluded within the National Labour Council, concerns the transfer of acquired rights in the event of a change of employer resulting from the transfer of undertakings effected by contract. This CBA also regulates the rights of employees transferred in the event of repossession of assets after a bankruptcy order. This CBA was concluded by the National Labour Council in execution of EU Directive 77/187/EEC of 14 February 1977, which has been modified by Directive 98/50/EC and Directive 2001/23/EC. It is applicable to any change of employer resulting from the transfer of undertakings or businesses of whatever kind effected by contract (including a change in the legal status of the company, formation of a partnership, disposal, merger and take-over), except for a change of employer caused by death.

An enterprise (undertaking) is 'either a legal entity, or a technical work/ production unit, or a department thereof'. According to legal experts, the change of employer involves that the legal employer has to change. Therefore, the selling of shares does not fall under the scope of CBA no 32*bis*.

The criteria identified by the European Court of Justice for determining whether there is a transfer within the meaning of art 1(1) of Directive 77/187/EEC are:

–   an economic entity, defined as an organised unit of persons, tangible and intangible elements, making possible the exercise of an economic activity pursuing a well-defined objective, organised in a stable manner and not limited to performing one specific works contract;

–   there must be a change, in terms of contractual relations, in the legal or natural person who is responsible for carrying on the business and who incurs the obligations of an employer towards employees of the entity;

–   the economic entity must retain its identity, which is marked both by the continuation by the new employer of the same activities and by the continuity of its workforce, its management staff, the way in which its work is organised, its operating methods or the operational resources available to it.

A transfer within the meaning of CBA no 32*bis* is defined in art 6 of that CBA as follows:

'When a transfer is considered, the transfer of an economic entity is defined as an organised unit of assets, which maintains its identity to pursue an economic activity.'

According to the CBA there should always be a change of employer.

The commentary on art 6 of CBA no 32*bis*, as expressed by the negotiators of CBA no 32*bis*, defines an undertaking as either a legal entity, or an autonomous business unit[1]. Even a part of the undertaking, as intended in the Law of 28 June 1966 regarding the indemnification ('compensation': note that in Belgium payments for compensation or on the termination of employment are known as 'indemnities') of the dismissed workers in the case of the closure of an undertaking, could be considered as an undertaking. According to the Law of 28 June 1966, in defining its applicability, a part of an undertaking should have at least 20 workers. Some authorities consider, therefore, that CBA no 32*bis* would only be applicable to transfers of undertakings having at least 20 workers[2]. This interpretation has been criticised because it would not be in accordance with the European Directives. Furthermore, as the Law of 28 June 1966 is to be repealed by the Law of 26 June 2002, the above-mentioned interpretation should be disregarded[3].

If one of the undertakings that are involved in the transaction is not located in Belgian territory, the question is then whether CBA no 32*bis* will be applicable.

It must be taken into consideration that CBA no 32*bis* is applicable to any employer who falls within the scope of the Law of 5 December 1968 on the collective bargaining agreements and the joint committees. This law applies to any employer located within Belgian territory, even if he is a foreigner. If only the transferee is located in Belgium, only he will have to comply with the existing CBA, including CBA no 32*bis*. If only the transferor is located in Belgium, only he will have to comply with CBA no 32*bis*.

1　Within the meaning of the Law of 20 September 1948 on the organisation of business.
2　Cl Wantiez 'Transferts conventionnels d'entreprise et droit du travail' (1996) EDS 31.
3　L Peltzer 'Transfert conventionnel d'entreprise' (2003) EDS 31–2.

Examples[1]

1. An undertaking located in the USA is to be transferred to Belgium. As the Directive is not applicable, CBA no 32*bis* would not be applicable to the transferor, even if the transferee is located in Belgium. However, the (Belgian) employees of the transferee should be informed about the transaction.

2. An undertaking located in the UK is to be transferred to Belgium. In this case, the Directive applies on the transfer. It means that the transferor located in the UK must comply with the British rules that transpose the Directive, while the transferee located in Belgium must comply with CBA no 32*bis*.

1　L Peltzer 'Transfert conventionnel d'entreprise' (2003) EDS 19.

K1.3 Affected workers

The term 'employee' can cover different meanings. In Belgium, an employee is:

> 'a person bound by an employment contract who works under the authority of another person, the employer.'

CBA no 32*bis* is also applicable to every person working, otherwise than by an employment contract, under the authority of another person.

Self-employed workers and persons employed by 'statute' are excluded. Persons working for the Belgian Government and most public undertakings are principally employed by statute. This means that the legal employment position of these persons is governed by specific rules (the statute), from the moment that they are appointed or hired by the government or the public undertaking. These persons are not employed under an employment contract and the rules on employment contracts are not applicable to them.

Moreover, according to the Law of 5 December 1968 on Collective Bargaining Agreements and Joint Committees, CBAs are not applicable to persons, regardless of whether they are bound by an employment contract or a statute, employed by the Belgian Government or by most public undertakings. This means that such persons are not subject to CBA no 32*bis* and cannot rely on it.

However, persons working for the Belgian Government and for most public undertakings can appeal to the European directives to preserve their rights. The 'private' transferor or transferee, on the other hand, will have to comply with CBA no 32*bis*.

The employment contract or employment relationship must exist at the moment of the transfer.

In the case of business transfers, all workers of the transferred company or part of the company will be affected. The transferee is obliged to take over all the workers who belong to (the part of) the undertaking which was transferred.

K1.4 Effects of the transfer

By virtue of CBA no 32*bis* and the Directives 77/187/EEC and 2001/23/EC, the transferor's rights and obligations arising from a contract of employment or from an employment relationship existing on the date of the transfer shall, by reason of such transfer, be transferred to the transferee.

This means that the employment contract is not terminated and that no new contract has to be concluded: the contract itself is transferred to the new employer. The original employment contracts will have to be honoured by the transferee.

The most important consequence of the automatic transfer of the employment contract is the maintenance of the working conditions existing with the transferor: seniority, salary, responsibilities, working time, etc. The place of work is part of the contract and is therefore a 'working condition'. There is a lot of case law about the question whether it is an 'essential working condition'. According to case law, transfer of an employment contract to another country may be regarded as an illegal breach of the employment contract, except when the business is transferred to the country of origin of the employee and if the parties agreed upon it during the employment. Other relocations (within the same country) are often qualified as a change of an 'essential working condition' if the change is important. In Belgium, a change of location to another linguistic area generally qualifies as a change of an essential working condition. To avoid employees filing claims, it is advisable for an employer to sign a contract of transfer with them after the transfer.

The Law of 5 December 1968 on Collective Bargaining Agreements and Joint Committees expressly provides for the maintenance of collective bargaining agreements applicable to the transferor in the case of a legal transfer. This has important consequences, since many working conditions (eg remuneration, working hours, thirteenth month salary, etc) are governed by CBAs, either agreed at national level, in the joint committee or in the company itself. After the expiry of these CBAs, they will continue to apply to the employment contracts unless the contracts expressly provide otherwise: their provisions are deemed to be incorporated into the individual employment contract.

There is controversy surrounding the question whether such rules would apply to CBAs concluded at an industrial level, within the joint committee, where the joint committee of the employer would be different after the transfer.

Automatic transfer does not, however, apply to old age, invalidity and pension benefits payable under schemes supplementing the official social security system. However, if the system is contained in a CBA, the transferee must maintain it. In the case of other schemes, if the new employer decides not to maintain a scheme, some authorities consider that the employees must be granted similar benefits instead of the original scheme, since pension benefits are part of the remuneration of the employee which has to be maintained in the event of a transfer.

According to art 37, § 2, al 1 of the Law of 28 April 2003 on Complementary Pensions, a transfer cannot result in the reduction of the amount of pension reserves (at the time of the transfer) that the members acquired. The pension reserves are the rights that are built up by the employees' and employer's contributions to the pension system. This article also stipulates that a change of joint committee cannot result in the reduction of pension obligations, unless the legal procedures of creation or modification of a pension plan are respected.

Right to object

Belgian law has no rule that allows the employee to refuse the change of employer.

Is it possible for an employee to consider that by the imposition of a transfer the employer acted as if he terminated the employment contract with the employee (can the employee consider that he has been dismissed)?

Most Belgian authorities and courts consider that if a worker refuses to be transferred, he may be considered as having terminated his contract[1] or he may be dismissed for serious cause by the employer[2].

If the place of work of the employee has been changed, he will have a good argument for objecting to the transfer. Indeed, the place of work could be considered as an essential element of the employment contract. According to case law, the transfer of the employment contract to another country may be regarded as an illegal breach of the employment contract, except when the business is transferred to the country of origin of the employee[3] and if the parties agreed upon it during the employment.

1   T T Liège, 10 January 1990, (1990) JTT 221. See also C T Liège, 10 June 1993, (1993) JTT 371; T T Namur, 28 November 1994, (1995) Chron DS 347.
2   L Peltzer 'Transfert conventionnel d'entreprise' (2003) EDS 112.
3   C Trav Bruxelles, 23 October 1996, (1997) JTT 38.

Liability for redundancy pay

According to art 8 of CBA no 32*bis* the transferor and transferee are jointly liable for the debts that exist at the time of the transfer.

If an employee is dismissed prior to the transfer for a reason that is not connected with the transfer, he may claim redundancy pay in the normal way against the transferor.

If a dismissal is connected with the transfer, the obligation for redundancy pay will be extended to the transferee. The transferor remains *in solidum* liable for any redundancy payment. This means that there is joint liability between the transferor and the transferee for the debts that exist at the time of the transfer and for redundancy payments.

KI.5 Dismissal of employees

According to art 9 of CBA no 32*bis*, a change of employer does not in itself constitute, either for the transferor or for the transferee, a ground for the dismissal of employees. Employees transferred to a new employer, however, can be dismissed for serious cause or for economic, technical or organisational reasons which involve changes in the undertaking's employment structure.

A business transfer will always be accompanied by structural changes. There could be 'double employment' (two employees for the same function) as a consequence of the transfer. It seems logical that dismissals in this context are stated to be for 'organisational reasons'. Of course, this does not mean that these dismissals are always legitimate. Otherwise, it would make the prohibition of dismissals meaningless. The employer must still act reasonably in all the circumstances in dismissing the relevant employees.

If a contract of employment is terminated because the transfer has resulted in a significant change in the terms and conditions of employment to the employees' disadvantage, the termination of the employment relationship is deemed to have taken place because of the action of the employer, normally the transferee employer.

Belgian legislation does not foresee a specific penalty for the non-respect of art 9 of CBA no 32*bis*, but the breach by an employer of collective bargaining agreements in general is a criminal offence. However, until now, we are not aware of proceedings brought on this basis. The risk is, therefore, rather small. The employee who is dismissed in violation of art 9 of CBA no 32*bis* could claim for additional damages on top of his severance indemnity[1].

Note that the transferor and the transferee are jointly liable for the debts existing at the time of the transfer. This means that the employee can act either against the transferor or the transferee, or against both, for the totality of his claim. The one that pays the totality of the claim can ask to be (partly) reimbursed by the other debtor.

The transferee is held liable for the debts existing after the transfer.

In the event of the transfer of an undertaking which is the subject of a bankruptcy order or an arrangement with creditors decreed by the court, special provisions apply[2].

1   See *K1.6* below.
2   See below.

K1.6 Variation and termination of contract

As explained above, the transfer of an undertaking, a business or a part of a business does not in itself constitute grounds for dismissal by the transferor or the transferee. That provision does not, however, prevent dismissals that may take place for economic, technical or organisational reasons entailing changes in the workforce.

Article 9 of CBA no *32bis* protects the right of employees not to be dismissed where the only reason is the transfer, against both the transferor and the transferee.

According to the European Court of Justice (ECJ), the contract of employment with the employee 'unlawfully dismissed' by the transferor shortly before the transfer must be regarded as still existing even if the 'dismissed' employee has not been taken on after the transfer of the undertaking. In other words, the dismissal will have no effect[1].

The fact that the ECJ considers that the contract should be regarded as still existing is an important difference from Belgian law. According to Belgian redundancy legislation, a dismissal (even when illegal) always terminates an employment contract immediately and definitively[2].

The rules of the Directives and the CBAs, in particular those concerning the protection of workers against dismissal by reason of transfer, must be considered to be mandatory, so that it is not possible to derogate from them in a manner unfavourable to employees. Therefore, since CBA no *32bis* does not provide for a sanction in case of violation of art 9 of the CBA, the Belgian Government did not comply with the Community obligations. This could justify a claim for damages against the Belgian Government.

Where no legislation provides for specific sanctions in case of non-compliance with the prohibition of dismissal, the worker who is unlawfully dismissed solely by reason of the transfer could claim for an additional payment on top of the severance indemnity. However, the chances of success of such a claim are limited.

A difference should be made between blue-collar workers[3] and white-collar workers[4].

1   Motif 18, CJEC, 15 June 1988, (1989) JTT 40; Motif 40, 41 42, CJEC, 12 March 1998, (1998) JTT 221; Motif 28, CJEC, 24 January 2002, (2002) JTT 185.
2   Case law of the Belgian Supreme Court – Cour de Cassation. Cass, 25 March 1991, (1991) JTT 324; Cass, 12 September 1988, (1988) JTT 477.

3   Mainly involved in manual work.
4   Mainly involved in intellectual work.

Blue-collar workers

According to art 63 of the Law of 3 July 1978 on Employment Contracts, the employer should pay an indemnity of six months of remuneration to the employee if the employer cannot prove that the dismissal is fair. A dismissal will be unfair if it is not for reasons of the worker's performance or for the company's needs.

A worker who is dismissed because of a transfer could claim the payment of the indemnity of six months, unless his employer can prove that the dismissal is fair[1].

1   C Trav Liège, 7 February 2001 (not published) RG no 3355/00, as mentioned in L Peltzer *Transfert conventionnel d'entreprise* (2003) Kluwer, p 132.

White-collar workers

White-collar workers can only claim an indemnity on the basis of the rules of common law.

The worker will have to prove that the reason for his dismissal is linked to the transfer, and he will have to establish the extent of his damages.

The employee should, however, be aware that the termination indemnity that he is entitled to after his dismissal is a lump sum. This sum is supposed to cover all damages (moral and material) he suffers because of the dismissal. Therefore, the employee will have to prove that he suffered a separate damage which is not covered by the termination indemnity, which is supposed to cover all damages resulting from the dismissal.

Furthermore, it should be noted that art 10 of CBA no 32*bis* stipulates that if the contract of employment or the employment relationship is terminated because the transfer involves a substantial change in the working conditions to the detriment of the employee, the employer is to be regarded as having been responsible for the termination.

K1.7 Duty to inform and consult

The following applies to companies having workers' representatives (works council or trade union delegation).

Royal Decree of 27 November 1973

This Royal Decree imposes on the employer an obligation to communicate to the works council, at regular intervals, the economic and financial information, the nature and content of which are detailed in the Royal Decree. Besides the regular information, additional information shall be provided occasionally to the works council, ie without waiting for periodical information to be provided:

(i) whenever events occur which are likely to lead to major consequences for the undertaking;

(ii) in every case where internal decisions are taken, which are likely to have significant implications on the undertaking. Such decisions should, if possible, be communicated to the works council before their implementation.

Where occasional information is provided, the employer must comment on the expected effects of the event or decision, on the development of the undertaking and on the employees' situation.

The information is given to the works council or, in the absence of a works council, to the trade union delegation.

A transfer of a business unit, which entails the transfer of all personnel working in that business unit, must be analysed as an event which is likely to lead to major consequences for the undertaking and for its employees. As a consequence, such a decision should, if possible, be communicated to the works council before its implementation.

Collective Bargaining Agreement no 9 of 9 March 1972

If there is a works council, the business decision to transfer which has an effect on employment may be taken and disclosed only after the works council has been informed and consulted in the manner laid down by arts 3 and 11 of CBA no 9. If the business decision to transfer has no effect on employment, the works council must be informed in due time and before any disclosure of the decision.

Article 3, al 1 provides that the obligation to inform and consult the works council must be complied with before the decision is taken, and that it 'must allow discussions in the Works Council, in full knowledge of the facts, during which the members may give their opinion, make suggestions or raise objections'.

As the works council must be given the opportunity to ask questions and receive appropriate answers, it should be consulted a reasonable time before the decision is taken by the employer. Article 11 provides that:

'in the case of merger, concentration, purchase or closure, the Works council must be informed in due time and before any disclosure of the decision. It must be consulted effectively and in advance, in relation to amongst others the consequences for staff employment, work organisation and, generally speaking, the employment policy'.

The concept of concentration is a general notion which covers different kinds of operations, such as the transfer of all or parts of the shares or parts of an undertaking with the transfer of control of the undertaking as a consequence, the transfer of business, or all of the assets of the undertaking, and all other grouping arrangements whereby the undertakings concerned maintain their individuality. Following the guidance relating to art 11, the obligation to inform and consult the works council must be complied with as soon as possible between the moment that the board agrees with the decision to transfer and the moment that the general meeting of shareholders is convened to discuss the decision that will be taken. This procedure must be complied with before any decision is made public.

In order to ensure continuity of dialogue within the works council, the employer must provide, either immediately or at the following meeting, the response he wants to make regarding the opinions, suggestions and objections made by the members in accordance with CBA no 9 regarding the consequences on employment.

The information that must be given to the works council must be sufficient, so that discussion in the works council is made possible. The transaction must also be put in its economic context (in its scale within the country) and in its industrial context. It must include information relating to the region or relating to the group. The purpose is to give the employees objective and complete information on how the transaction will affect the company and the employees.

Belgian law does not compel the employer to provide written information, but it is strongly advisable for the employer to do so. In the case of a cross-border transfer, the following information should be prepared: balance sheets, status and graphics, time schedule taking into account the local specifics, and strategy and tactics for the consultations of the works council.

If written information is given, it must be supported by a verbal explanation from the employer or from his delegate.

In case of non-compliance with that rule, criminal penalties (rather theoretical) are provided.

Collective Bargaining Agreement no 62 of 6 February 1996

For those undertakings which have established a European Works Council (EWC) in accordance with Council Directive 94/45/EC, it is necessary for them to consult this council, if the transfer affects at least two undertakings of the group located in two different EC member states. Directive 94/45/EC is partly implemented in Belgian law through an industry-wide Collective Bargaining Agreement no 62.

According to art 27 of CBA no 62, the EWC should deal with the information and consultation with regard to matters that concern at least two groups of undertakings in different member states.

According to art 37 of CBA no 62, the undertaking or controlling undertaking must be required to communicate to the employees' appointed representatives general information concerning the interests of employees, and information relating more specifically to those aspects of the activities of the undertaking or group of undertakings which affect employees' interests.

Companies having no workers' representatives

For undertakings having no works council or trade union delegation, CBA no 32*bis* does impose on the employer an obligation to inform the employees of:

– the date considered or fixed for the transfer;

– the reason for the transfer;

– the legal, economic and social consequences of the transfer or asset purchase for the employees;

– the measures considered for the employees.

Other rules apply for companies in bankruptcy[1].

1   See *K1.9.*

K1.8 Notification to the authorities

According to employment law, a transfer of a business does not entail any duty of notification to (or authorisation from) the national authorities, unless it entails a collective dismissal or a closure of the company[1].

If the transfer is accompanied or followed by a collective dismissal or a closure, the collective dismissal and the closure have to fulfil some notification requirements, but the authorities may not forbid the dismissals/closure from being carried out[2].

In the case of collective dismissal, the employees may file a complaint if the information and consultation procedure has not been observed, unless the employees' representatives have not raised objections in due time.

The cost of a business transfer depends upon various factors: the remuneration to be paid and the working conditions to be ensured by the transferee for the employees previously employed by the transferor, the possible relocation of the undertaking, the re-negotiation of various contracts signed by the transferor, the tax regime of the transferor, etc.

1   Applicable to companies having at least 20 employees: see below.
2   See below.

K1.9 Transfer following insolvency or judicial agreement with creditors

Article 2 of CBA no 32*quinquies* modifies art 1 of CBA no 32*bis* in the sense that transfers that are executed in the framework of a 'judicial agreement' can be considered as transfers by contract. The regulations, however, are tempered by art 8*bis* of CBA no 32*bis*.

In the event of the transfer of an undertaking subject to a bankruptcy order, special provisions apply. The main purpose of CBA no 32*bis*, ie to maintain the rights of the workers when they are transferred to another employer, is no longer strictly followed. Indeed, the main purpose is then to maintain employment by ensuring the continuation of the company.

If the transfer takes place within a period of six months after the bankruptcy order, there is no automatic transfer of the employment relationship: the prospective employer is free to choose which employees are to be transferred. For those who are 'chosen', the collectively agreed terms and conditions of employment[1] and seniority remain in force. An employee's length of service under the former employer and the period between the bankruptcy order and the new contract of employment are both included in any subsequent calculations for the period of notice[2].

If the transferee wants to change the conditions that were applicable collectively or agreed collectively with the transferor, he must negotiate with the organisations represented in the trade union delegation.

CBA no 32*bis*, as modified by CBA no 32*quinquies* of 13 March 2002, provides that for companies having no workers' representatives, the workers concerned must be notified in advance of:

–   the date considered or fixed for the transfer;

–   the reason for the transfer;

–   the legal, economic and social consequences of the transfer for the employees;

–   measures contemplated with respect to the workers.

1   Stipulated by collective agreement or negotiated arrangements at company level.
2   Except in the case of termination during the probationary period with the new employer.

K1.10 Competent jurisdiction

In the event of an individual claim against a cross-border transfer of business, the competent jurisdiction must be determined following the rules of Council Regulation (EC) 44/2001 of 22 December 2000. According to s 5 (jurisdiction over individual contracts of employment), an employer domiciled in a member state may be sued:

–   before the courts of the member state where the employer is domiciled (ie where he has his registered office) or;

–   in another member state:

  •   before the courts of the place where the employee usually carries out his work or in the courts of the last place where he did so, or

  •   if the employee does not or did not habitually carry out his work in one country, before the courts of the place where the business which hired the employee is or was situated.

K2 Redundancy

K2.1 Background

As mentioned above, the transfer of an undertaking, business or part of a business does not in itself constitute a ground for dismissal by the transferor or the transferee (art 9 of CBA no 32*bis*). That provision does not, however, prevent dismissals that may take place for economical, technical or organisational reasons entailing changes in the workforce. It protects the rights of employees against a dismissal whose only reason is the transfer, in relation to both the transferor and the transferee. It does not restrict the power of the transferor any more than that of the transferee to effect dismissals for the reasons which it allows.

Belgian legislation provides several regulations to terminate a contract:

–   It is possible that a collective dismissal occurs in accordance with the rules as mentioned hereinafter. For the rules of collective dismissals to be effective, a company ('undertaking') must employ an average of more than 20 employees over the calendar year preceding the year during which the company dismisses a certain number of employees within a 60-day period. These rules force the employer to consult and provide employees' representatives with appropriate information *before any decision is taken*[1], to notify the director of the regional office of the State Employment Agency of the planned collective dismissal and to pay the employees an indemnity for the collective dismissal[2].

    Furthermore, the employer must observe a minimum period of one month from the date of notification of collective dismissal before he can proceed with notification of the termination of the employment contracts.

–   Under some conditions, a collective dismissal may lead to a closure. Other specific rules will then be applicable[3].

    In both cases (collective dismissal and closure), indemnities might have to be paid. These indemnities are on top of any termination indemnity, indemnity for protected employees, unemployment allowances, etc.

    Both procedures must also be observed in compliance with the linguistic rules applicable to each undertaking, taking into account the linguistic region where it undertakes its activities[4]. Notwithstanding specific rules that apply to some municipalities[5], the procedure must be in French when the operational headquarters is located in the French-speaking Region[6], in Dutch when it is located in the Dutch-speaking Region[7], in German when it is located in the German-speaking Region, and in the language of the employee (French or Dutch) when it is located in Brussels[8].

- In all cases which are neither situations of closure nor collective dismissal, the general rules with regard to termination of employment contracts will be applicable[9].

- Finally, special rules apply in cases of the dismissal of protected workers[10].

1   It is always referred to the intention, as the decision has not been taken yet but has only been contemplated.
2   See *K2.2* below.
3   See *K2.2* below.
4   'Operational headquarters' or 'siège d'exploitation'.
5   So-called 'communes à facilités'.
6   Decree of the French Community of 30 June 1982.
7   Decree of the Flemish Community of 19 July 1973.
8   Law of 18 July 1966.
9   See *K2.2* below.
10   See *K2.2* below.

K2.2 Redundancy payments

Collective dismissal

Legislation applicable to collective dismissals

The rules that apply to collective dismissals in Belgium are as follows:

- Royal Decree of 5 December 1969 and Royal Decree of 24 May 1976 regarding the notification of the collective dismissal and the notification of vacancies

- Collective Bargaining Agreement no 24 of 2 October 1975 regarding the procedure for information and consultation of the employees' representatives in case of collective dismissal

- Collective Bargaining Agreement no 10 of 8 May 1973 regarding collective dismissal (regarding the payment of special indemnities)

- Collective Bargaining Agreement no 9 of 9 March 1972 co-ordinating the national agreements and the Collective Bargaining Agreement regarding the works councils

- Law of 13 February 1998 regarding rules relating to improvement of employment (related to the procedure of information and consultation and the sanctions in case of non-compliance with the different rules)

- See also collective bargaining agreements (CBA) concluded within some joint committees.

Scope of application

Principle

The procedure of consulting and giving appropriate information to the employees' representatives provided for by the Law of 13 February 1998 applies only to undertakings having an average of more than 20 employees during the calendar year preceding the collective dismissal[1]. The undertaking is defined as any autonomous technical unit[2] within a company, or any of its departments[3]. For undertakings having a works council, the obligations of information provided by CBA no 9 have also to be complied with[4].

1 Article 63 of the Law of 13 February 1998.
2 'Unité technique d'exploitation'.
3 Article 62, 3° of the Law of 13 February 1998 refers to the definition given in art 14 of the Law of 20 September 1948, but includes also any department of the undertaking.
4 See below.

The autonomous technical unit

As a rule, the autonomous technical unit[1] refers to economic and social criteria provided for in art 14 of the Law of 20 September 1948.

Economic autonomy refers to the independence of each entity. It can be reinforced when production and distribution do not occur in the same location, or when the separate entities have considerable freedom to develop their activities in an independent way[2].

Social autonomy refers to the existence of a single social environment for each entity[3]. Conversely, the fact that the accountancy of every entity is centralised into one company, or that every entity is located at the same address, indicates that there is no social autonomy.

The supreme judicial court in Belgium (*Cour de Cassation – Hof van Cassatie*) considers the social criteria to be more important than economic autonomy[4].

1 Unité technique d'exploitation.
2 T T Bruxelles, 18 February 1983, (1983) JTT 201; N Beaufils, P Denis, P Pype and O Vanbellinghen (eds) *Les élections sociales 2000* (1999) FEB, p 24.
3 For example, different addresses, different languages, autonomy for human resources management.
4 Cass, 22 October 1979, (1980) JTT 58; Cass, 12 November 1979, (1981) JTT 7; Cass, 19 December 1983, (1984) JTT 82 ; N Beaufils, P Denis, P Pype and O Vanbellinghen (eds) *Les élections sociales 2000* (1999) FEB, p 24.

A department ('division de l'entreprise')

The Law of 13 February 1998 does not give any definition of a department. But legal scholars have defined this word as follows: 'any part of an undertaking, having a technical activity sufficiently distinct from the whole undertaking, but without having as complete economic and social autonomy as the autonomous technical unit'[1].

The following could be considered departments:

–   an activity performed by separate plants and machinery which represents a high proportion of the global production of the undertaking[2];

–   cleaning and kitchen departments[3];

–   a restaurant belonging with a number of other restaurants to a company[4].

Only those departments having more than 20 employees in the *calendar year* preceding the collective dismissal must be taken into consideration for a collective dismissal.

1   P Denis 'La protection des représentants du personnel au conseil d'entreprise et au comité de sécurité, d'hygiène et d'embellissement des lieux de travail' (1996) Doc FEB, p 60; see also Fr Robert (ed) *Le licenciement collectif* (2000) Kluwer, p 35.
2   C T Liège, 14 July 1992, (1993) JLMB 738.
3   C T Antwerp, 25 June 1992 and Cass, 19 April 1993, (1993) JTT 305.
4   T T Brussels, 10 March 1994, (1994) Chron DS 417.

Definition of collective dismissal

Collective dismissal can be defined as:

–   any dismissal of a certain number of employees, depending on the total number of employees in the company[1];

–   that takes place during a 60-day period; and

–   has been decided for *economic* or *technical* reasons, or is not related to the employees' behaviour or conduct[1].

To have a collective dismissal one needs, over a period of 60 days:

–   the dismissal of a minimum of 10 employees if the employer employs an average of less than 100 employees;

–   the dismissal of a minimum of 20 employees if the employer employs between 100 and 200 employees;

–   the dismissal of a minimum of 30 employees if the employer employs more than 300 employees.

1   Article 2 of CBA no 24.

Extension

The Law of 3 February 1998 provides that a collective dismissal occurs in the following cases:

–   when dismissals take place during the 60-day period as referred to above;

–   when dismissals take place during the 60-day period that follows the 60-day period as referred to above, when the closure of the undertaking is not intended;

–   when dismissals take place between the 60-day period and the date of the closure[1], when the closure of an undertaking is intended;

In some cases, a collective dismissal can lead to a closure of a company[2] which is subject to specific rules[3].

1   The date of the closure being the date defined by the Law of 28 June 1966 (see below).
2   When it ceases its main activity and proceeds to the dismissal of a certain number of employees.
3   See 'Closure' below.

Procedure

Information and consultation on the intention to carry out a collective dismissal

The employer must inform and consult the employees' representatives on his intention to proceed with a collective dismissal.

He must keep all the evidence that the requirements have been met[1] and that he has convened the works council/trade union representatives/employees or their representatives, as required by law or internal regulation.

It should be kept in mind that the procedure is intended to allow the works council to give its opinion, to make suggestions and to allow discussions before the employer takes a decision. The employer has also to inform the works council/trade union representatives/employees or their representatives of the follow-up he intends to give to their opinion[2].

Information and consultation of the workers' representatives must be made in compliance with the following four steps.

1   Article 66, § 1, al 3 of the Law of 13 February 1998.
2   Article 3 of CBA no 9.

(i) Convening a notification meeting

The employer must provide the employees' representatives[1] with a written report stating that he *intends*[2] to carry out a collective dismissal[3]. Such a report should be communicated and commented on at a notification meeting, in order to let the employees' representatives have an oral explanation on this report[4].

The written report must state:

–   the reasons for proposing the collective dismissal;

–   the proposed criteria for choosing the employees who would be dismissed;

–   the number and the categories of employees to be dismissed;

–   the number and the categories of employees who have been employed by the undertaking;

–   the method of calculating any additional severance indemnity which is not provided by law or by collective bargaining agreement;

–   the intended period for dismissals.

This should allow the employees' representatives to formulate their opinion and suggestions in due time in order for the employer to examine them[5]. Normally, consultation, which will have to take place, will cover the possibility of avoiding or limiting dismissals as well as the possibility of mitigating their consequences.

The works council must be convened in accordance with its internal rules. Failing the works council, the trade union representatives must be convened. Written notifications to attend the notification meeting, possibly sent by registered mail, and written minutes of the meeting should qualify as relevant proof of such a meeting.

When there is no works council and no trade union delegation, the employees should be informed. They should also have the opportunity to ask questions about the operation.

It is advisable that, during the first meeting, the parties agree on an agenda for the meetings.

1   Members of the works council, or trade union delegation if there is no works council, or in
    cases where there is no works council or trade union delegation, the employees.
2   As opposed to 'decides'.
3   Law of 13 February 1998 (art 66) and CBA no 24.
4   Article 3, al 3 of CBA no 9.
5   Article 3 of CBA no 24.

(*ii*) *Consultation meeting(s) focused on the worker representatives' position*

The employer has to meet the works council/trade union representatives/ employees or their representatives as often as necessary for information and consultation.

Written notifications to attend the consultation meeting, possibly sent by registered mail, and written minutes of the meeting should qualify as relevant proof of such a meeting.

The worker representatives must have the opportunity to formulate:

–   questions to the employer;

–   arguments and counter-proposals;

–   remarks, suggestions and complaints;

–   alternatives to the intended dismissals.

(*iii*) *Questions and answers meeting(s)*

The employer has to examine the proposals and answer the questions. But the employer takes the final decision.

Written notifications to attend the 'answering' meeting, possibly sent by registered mail, and written minutes of the meeting should qualify as relevant proof of such a meeting.

An effective consultation must take place with the workers' representatives with regard to:

–   the impact of the intended collective dismissal on the employment prospects;

–   the organisation of the work and the employment policy;

– questions to the employer, arguments and counter-proposals, remarks, suggestions, complaints and/or alternatives formulated during the first consultation meeting(s);

– the possibility of avoiding or reducing the intended collective dismissal;

– alternatives to the intended dismissals and measures which could mitigate the social consequences of the intended dismissals in order to contribute to the workers' outplacement and/or retraining.

(iv) End of the information and consultation procedure

The employer should note officially in the minutes that the procedure of collective dismissal has ended, and that rules regarding notification and consultation have been observed.

As the case may be, a social plan may be agreed between the parties after the closing of the consultation procedure. Sometimes this is an obligation that is stipulated by a CBA.

If the social plan is agreed with the contribution of the employees' representatives, the plan has the status of a CBA.

Notification to the sub-regional office of the State Employment Agency

The employer has to inform the director of the sub-regional office of the State Employment Agency[1] where the undertaking is located by giving him simultaneously a copy of the information given to the works council/trade union representatives/employees or their representatives[2].

After meeting the requirements mentioned above, the employer has to notify the director of the regional office of the State Employment Agency of his *plan* (*intention*) to carry out a collective dismissal.

This notification has to mention:

– the name and the address of the company;

– the kind of activity of the undertaking;

– the joint committee of the undertaking;

– the number of employees;

– the reasons for the dismissal;

– the number of employees to be dismissed (listing by the following categories: sex, age, professional categories, departments);

– the period during which the dismissals will take place;

– the written documents proving consultation with the employees' representatives has taken place[3].

On the day of the notification to the director of the (sub-)regional office of the State Employment Agency, the employer must:

- hand over to the employees' representatives a copy of that notification, in order to allow them to communicate their eventual comments to the director of the sub-regional service for employment[4];

- post the notification in a location where it can be seen, within the premises of the undertaking;

- send a copy of such notification by registered mail to the employees who fall within the scope of the collective dismissal and whose employment contracts have been terminated on the day of the notification.

1   The 'Regional Committee of Employment'.
2   Article 7 of the Royal Decree of 24 May 1976 on collective dismissals.
3   Article 7 of the Royal Decree of 24 May 1976; art 66, § 2 of the Law of 13 February 1998.
4   Article 8 of the Royal Decree of 24 May 1976; art 66, § 2 of the Law of 13 February 1998.

Cooling-off period

The employees' representatives[1] or, failing that, the individual employees have the opportunity to notify the employer (as well as the director of the (sub-)regional office of the State Employment Agency) of their possible objections where the employer has failed to comply with the collective dismissal procedure. These objections should be notified within a 30-day time period as from the date of the posting of the above notification.

The employer is prohibited from implementing any dismissals or giving notice until this 30-day period has elapsed from the date of the notification to the regional office of the State Employment Agency[2].

In some cases, the regional office of the State Employment Agency has to be informed by the employer of any job vacancy within the company[3].

1   Works council or union representatives.
2   The period may be extended to 60 days under certain circumstances.
3   Royal Decree of 5 December 1969.

Indemnity

Scope

In addition to the normal indemnity or notice, an indemnity could be due when the employer dismisses more than 10 per cent of the employees of the undertaking during a 60-day period, if the dismissal has been decided for *economic* or *technical* reasons.

The scope of application is the same as described by the Law of 13 February 1998[1]. Nevertheless, for undertakings ranging from 20 to 59 employees, there is a collective dismissal when the dismissal concerns at least *six* employees[2].

The indemnity is not due for some categories of employees. Employees employed for a definite period[3] and interim[4] employees[5] do not benefit from this system.

Article 7 of CBA no 10 extends the right to an indemnity for collective dismissal to the following employees:

(1) unemployed employees who are precluded from the unemployment allowances for a reason that they are not responsible for;

(2) employees having concluded a new employment contract and earning less than they previously did with the employer who carried out the collective dismissal;

(3) employees attending training for adults and who receive an indemnity which is less than they previously earned;

(4) a dismissed employee who is entitled to unemployment allowances.

1 The definition of the undertaking refers to any autonomous technical unit ('unité technique d'exploitation') in the company. Article 10 of CBA no 10 refers to the definition given in art 14 of the Law of 20 September 1948 (see above).
2 Article 2 of CBA no 10.
3 'Fixed term'.
4 'Temporary'.
5 'Travailleurs intérimaires'.

Amount

The indemnity for collective dismissal amounts to half of the difference between the monthly net salary (with a maximum of €2,630.66 gross[1]), after payment of social and fiscal contributions, and the monthly unemployment allowance.

The indemnity shall be added to the monthly unemployment allowance and shall never be paid for more than four months.

The indemnity is due for a period of four months beginning at the date of the dismissal or, as the case may be, the day following the period covered by the severance pay. If the period of notice[2] exceeds three months, the indemnity shall be reduced for each month exceeding this period[3].

1 Since 1 June 2003.
2 Or the indemnity paid in lieu thereof.
3 Article 11 of CBA no 10.

Sanctions

Neither CBA no 24 nor the Royal decree of 24 May 1976 provides for civil sanctions. However, non-compliance with the rules of CBA no 24 and the Royal Decree of 24 May 1976 can result in criminal penalties[1] or administrative fines[2].

However, the Law of 13 February 1998 covers protection for employees and sanctions against the employer.

If the dismissal has been notified to employees without complying with the rules mentioned above, specific rights exist for these employees. The rules can be summarised as follows.

Within 30 days following the dismissal or following the date that the dismissals are considered to be collective dismissals, the representatives of the employees can notify the employer, by registered mail, that they raise objections to the procedure of consultation and information with the employees[3]. Once this has been done, the employees who have been dismissed can challenge the termination, within the same time period.

If the claim is considered well-founded, the notice period for the employees will be suspended during a period starting from the third business day after the issue of the registered mail to the employer. The employer will have to restart the whole procedure of collective dismissal and the above-mentioned period will run until 60 days following the notification of the collective dismissal to the director of the regional office of the State Employment Agency. If the employer has terminated the contract of employment without a notice period, but with the payment of a severance indemnity, the employees may claim to be reinstated. Should the employer refuse to reinstate an employee, he will have to pay an indemnity amounting to the salary accruing between the termination and the 60th day following the new and correct notification of the collective dismissal to the administration.

However, the dismissed employees may not challenge alleged non-compliance with steps (i) to (iv) of the procedure[4] if the employees' representatives failed to file complaints challenging those steps of the procedure within a 30-day period following the day of displaying the notification within the premises of the undertaking.

The Law of 8 April 2003 stipulates that an employer who is convicted for not respecting the information and consultation procedure, also should be fined a sum of €1,000 to €5,000 per employee who was employed by the closed company, at the moment that the decision to close was taken. This fine should be paid to the National Office of Social Security[5].

In addition to the sanctions applicable in the case where the employer infringes the rules regarding collective dismissal, the employer may be held liable for criminal charges and fines if he fails to respect the legal obligations concerning closure of the undertaking[6].

1   Article 56 et seq of the Law of 5 December 1968 concerning collective bargaining agreements.
2   Article 1, 14° of the Law of 30 June 1971 concerning administrative fines.
3   Article 67 of the Law of 13 February 1998.
4   Article 66, § 1er, al 2.
5   *Rijksdienst voor Sociale Zekerheid – Office National de Sécurité Sociale.*
6   Articles 27–31 of the Law of 28 June 1966.

Closure[1]

Legislation applicable to closure of an undertaking

Notwithstanding the rules applicable to collective dismissals, additional rules apply to closures of undertakings, with respect to the requirements mentioned below. The most important are:

–   Law of 28 June 1966 regarding compensation of dismissed employees in the event of closure of an undertaking;

–   Law of 30 June 1967 regarding the extension of the Fund for Closure of an undertaking;

–   Royal Decree of 6 July 1967 implementing art 6 of the Law of 30 June 1967 regarding the extension of the Fund for Closure of an undertaking;

–   Royal Decree of 20 September 1967 implementing art 3, al 4; art 5; art 15, al 2; and art 17 of the Law of 28 June 1966 regarding indemnification of dismissed employees in the event of closure of an undertaking;

–   Royal Decree of 20 February 1968 determining the way to calculate the average number of employees during a 'civil year';

–   See also the CBAs that are applicable in some joint committees;

–   New Law of 26 June 2002. This Law will come into force after a Royal Decree has determined the date.

1   Law of 28 June 1966.

Scope of application

Further requirements have to be met if the undertaking, and divisions thereof (hereafter referred to as an 'undertaking' – see above), have employed at least 20 employees on average during the calendar year preceding the closure. The average number of employees is computed on the basis of the total number of employees registered with the social security administration during the reference year.

The undertaking is defined as any autonomous technical unit within a company, or any of its departments. For undertakings having a works council, the provisions of information set out by CBA no 9 also have to be complied with.

As a rule, the autonomous technical unit refers to economic and social criteria provided in art 14 of the Law of 20 September 1948[1].

1   The Law of 28 June 1966 refers to the definition given in art 14 of the Law of 20 September 1948, but includes also any department of the undertaking which employed at least 20 employees on an average during the calendar year preceding the closure.

Definition of closure

A closure of an undertaking occurs when it ceases its main activity or closes a department of the company *and* if it reduces simultaneously the number of employees to a figure below 25 per cent of the average number of employees employed during the calendar year preceding the closure[1].

The law provides that the closure happens on the first day of the month following the month during which the number of employees has been reduced below the aforementioned 25 per cent.

1   The Closure of Undertakings Fund, a public agency within the Ministry of Employment and Labour, may qualify the geographical transfer, merger and/or sale of an undertaking, or certain cases of major restructuring not leading to a reduction of the staff by more than 75 per cent as being equivalent to a closure of an undertaking.

Procedure

Information and consultation

CBA no 9 provides that information and consultation regarding some decisions must occur before the decision is taken. Article 3 of CBA no 9 allows members of the works council to discuss, give opinions, and formulate suggestions or objections about the information. It provides that written information must be coupled with an oral comment from the employer or from the employer's representative. But this CBA does not lay down specific rules regarding collective dismissals and closures.

In the event of closure of an undertaking leading to collective dismissal, the procedure as described above must be complied with[1].

In the event that an effective consultation has commenced, it will be continued, if possible, until the conclusion between the parties of agreements, including an agreement on the social measures to be taken.

In the event that an effective consultation is not possible regarding the proposed social measures, owing to obstruction from the employee representatives, the employer should inform the employee representatives as to whether or not it maintains its intention to close down and carry out a collective dismissal.

In both cases, employees' representatives should be invited to a consultation meeting. The purpose of this meeting will be the announcement by the employer of the notification of the project for a collective dismissal resulting from an intended closure, regardless of the possible objections of the employee representatives.

1   And written evidence that the different steps have been observed must be kept.

Notification

At the outcome of such a meeting, the employer must notify the director of the regional employment office, by registered mail, of its collective dismissal plan resulting from an intended closure, together with the data mentioned above.

On the day of the notification to the director of the (sub-)regional office of the State Employment Agency, the employer must :

–   hand over to the employees' representatives a copy of that notification, in order to allow them to communicate their eventual comments to the director of the sub-regional service for employment[1];

– publish the notification within the premises of the undertaking;

– send a copy of such notification by registered mail to the employees who fall within the scope of the collective dismissal and whose employment contract has already been terminated on the day of the notification and of its posting.

1   Article 8 of the Royal Decree of 24 May 1976; art 6, § 2 of the Law of 13 February 1998.

Cooling-off period

The same rules as mentioned above apply to the closure of an undertaking. Nevertheless, the director may not extend the 30-day period in case of a project for a collective dismissal resulting from an intended closure. On the contrary, in such a case, the director may in principle reduce the 30-day cooling-off period.

Notification of the decision to close down to the employee representatives, employees and authorities

After the 30-day cooling-off period, and not earlier, once the decision to close down is taken – as opposed to an intention – the employer must convene a meeting with the employee representatives[1] and:

– must post a dated and signed notice in a location where it will be seen, within the premises of the undertaking, informing the employees of its decision to close down the undertaking;

– must inform the works council or, in absence thereof, the union representatives of its decision;

– must notify its decision and certain specific data to a number of authorities, by registered mail.

The following data must be provided:

– name and address of the undertaking;

– nature of its activities;

– anticipated date of cessation of the principal activities of the undertaking;

– complete list of personnel employed on the date of notification, indicating for each person:

  • family name, first name and address;

  • date of birth;

  • date of hiring;

  • the statutory minimum notice period applicable;

- marital status;
- function(s) the employee could exercise in addition to his/her past occupation.

The authorities to whom the closure decision and the above-mentioned data must be notified are:

- The Minister of Employment and Labour;
- The federal and regional Ministers of Economic Affairs;
- The National Employment Office;
- The Closure of Undertaking Fund;
- The President of the Joint Committee.

1   Works council or, in the absence thereof, union representatives.

Specific notification to the Closure of Undertaking Fund

(**a**) On the fifteenth day following the date of the *closure*[1], the employer must notify the Closure of Undertaking Fund of the following data by registered mail:

- name and address of the undertaking;
- nature of its activities;
- competent Joint Committee;
- number of employees employed during each of the 12 months preceding the date of closure[2];
- alphabetical list of the employees having at least five years of seniority and whose employment contract of unlimited duration was terminated either during the 12 months preceding the closure or at the time of the closure. For each employee, the list must contain:
  - family name, first name and address;
  - date of hiring;
  - how and by whom the employment contract was terminated;
  - starting date of the notice period or, in the case of immediate termination, the date of such termination;
  - amount and date of payment of the closure of undertaking indemnity;
  - bank account number of the employee for the payment of any indemnities.

The notifications and lists referred to above must be signed by the employer and his signature must be preceded by the following affidavit[3]:

'I certify on my honour that this declaration is sincere and complete.'

(**b**) On the fifteenth day following the date of the *termination of the employment contract*, the employer must notify the Closure of Undertaking Fund of the following data by registered mail: alphabetical list of the employees having at least five years of seniority and whose employment contract of unlimited duration was terminated during the 12 months following the closure. For each employee, the list must contain information referred to under (**a**) above. For those workers who participate in the liquidation of the company, the above-mentioned 12-month time period is extended to three years.

The notifications and lists referred to above must be signed by the employer and his signature must be preceded by the following affidavit[4]:

'I certify on my honour that this declaration is sincere and complete.'

1   The closure is considered to take place on the first day of the month following that during which the number of employees has decreased to below 25 per cent of the average number of employees employed during the year preceding that of the cessation of activity.
2   For those employees who participate in the liquidation of the undertaking, the above-mentioned 12-month time period is extended to three years.
3   In principle, in French or in Dutch.
4   In principle, in French or in Dutch.

Indemnity

If they meet the necessary requirements, employees dismissed at the occasion of the closure[1] are entitled to receive a closing indemnity. This indemnity amounts to €126.17[2] per year of seniority in the undertaking, up to 20 years, or a maximum of €2,523.40.

In addition, every employee who is aged over 45 years receives an indemnity of €126.17 (since 1 June 2003) for every year over the age of 45. The amount is limited to €2,523.40 (since 1 June 2003).

Some exceptions exist, depending on the (industry-related) joint committee of the company. The competent joint committee of the company depends upon the company's main activity.

Please note that these indemnities have to be paid on top of other indemnities such as termination indemnities, unemployment allowances, indemnities due to protected employees (see below), etc.

1   Or 18 months before for white-collar employees.
2   Indemnity on 1 June 2003.

Sanctions

In addition to the sanctions applicable in the case where the employer infringes the rules regarding collective dismissal, the employer may be held liable for criminal charges and fines if he fails to respect the legal obligations concerning the closure of an undertaking[1].

The Law of 8 April 2003 stipulates that an employer who is convicted for not respecting the information and consultation procedure should also be fined a sum of €1,000 to €5,000 per employee who was employed by the closed company, at the moment that the decision to close was taken. This fine should be paid to the National Office of Social Security (*Rijksdienst voor Sociale Zekerheid – Office National de Sécurité Sociale*).

1   Articles 27–31 of the Law of 28 June 1966.

Termination of employment contracts of non-protected workers

Employment contracts for a definite duration or a specific task

Employment contracts for a definite duration or a specific task automatically expire at the *end* of the contractual term or when the task has been *achieved*. *No indemnity* is due in this case.

Employment contracts entered into for a specific task or a definite duration may not be terminated at any time except for a serious cause.

If the employer or employee terminates the employment contract, he has to pay an *indemnity* equal to the remuneration that should have been paid until the end of the employment contract. This indemnity may not, however, be higher than double the indemnity that should have been paid if the contract had been for an indefinite period[1].

1   Article 40 of the Law of 3 July 1978.

Employment contracts concluded for an indefinite period

Employment contracts concluded for an indefinite period may be terminated at any time (except for the special category of protected employees: see hereunder).

The terminating party must, however, give the other party *a notice of termination in writing and in the appropriate language.*

If the employer or employee fails to give a correct notice, he shall be liable to pay an *indemnity* equal to the salary and benefits (including holiday pay, bonus, thirteenth month, etc) that the employee would have been entitled to during the correct period of notice, based on the last monthly salary[1].

1   Article 39 of the Law of 3 July 1978.

Notice period given by the employer

(a) *Manual employees (blue-collar)* [1]

–   with less than six months of service: notice period of 28 calendar days;

–   with more than six months but less than five years: 35 calendar days;

–   with more than five years but less than 10 years: 42 calendar days;

–   with more than 10 years but less than 15 years: 56 calendar days;

–　with more than 15 years but less than 20 years: 84 calendar days;

–　with more than 20 years of service: 112 calendar days.

In many sectors, there are collective agreements providing for longer (or shorter) notice periods. A notice properly served is generally effective the Monday of the week following the one during which it is served.

1　Royal Decree of 10 February 2000.

(*b*)　*Intellectual employees (white-collar)*[1]

–　Employees earning less than €26,418[2] gross[3] per year at the date of the dismissal: the applicable notice is three months per period of five years of service.

–　Employees earning more than €26,418 gross per year (figure valid for 2004): the notice period is determined by mutual agreement concluded at the earliest when the notice is given, or, in the absence of agreement, by the Labour Court. No general rules are provided by statute in order to determine the length of the notice, but the main factors taken into account by the courts are the employee's age, seniority[4], position and salary. Courts often use calculation formulae. The most frequently applied formula is the so-called 'Claeys' formula based on computer calculation.

–　There is a special rule for employees earning more than €52,836 gross[5] per year and who have been hired after 1 April 1994. In that case, parties may determine the notice period that will have to be respected in the event that the employer terminates the contract. The length of notice cannot, however, be shorter than the notice period provided for employees earning less than €26,418 gross[6] per year: three months per period of five years of service.

Notice is effective from the first day of the month following the one during which it is validly served (except in case of suspension of the contract).

1　Article 82 of the Law of 3 July 1978.
2　The salary in the context of a termination: monthly gross x 13.92 (thirteenth month and holiday allowances) + all benefits in kind (bonus earned during the 12 months preceding the termination, private use of car, meal vouchers, group insurance, etc).
3　Figure valid for 2004.
4　The employer should check whether any 'conventional' seniority has been granted: in employment contracts, the parties stipulate a fictive seniority in favour of the employee. In the event of dismissal, the employee will be entitled to longer notice.
5　2004 figure.
6　2004 figure.

(*c*)　*Procedure*

Any notice given by the employer can only be validly served by means of a registered letter or a bailiff's writ containing the duration of the notice period and the day such period starts to run[1].

When notice is served by means of a registered letter, it will have effect on the third working day after the day of sending. For white-collar employees, the notice period becomes effective from the first day of the month following the month during which the notice has been served. Therefore, in order to be effective without delay, the letter will have to be sent at the latest three working days before the end of the month.

For blue-collar employees, a notice which has been properly served is effective as of the Monday of the week following the week in which notice has been served.

1   Article 37 of the Law of 3 July 1978.

(d) Yearly premiums, holidays allowances, thirteenth month and bonus

The employer who terminates an employment contract has to pay yearly premiums, holiday allowances (only for white-collar employees) and thirteenth month salary in proportion to the date of termination (pro rata temporis). The employee may be entitled to a pro rata of a bonus (if there is a bonus plan in the employment contract), or that the complete bonus may have to be paid.

In some sectors of industry and commerce, an identical regulation applies even if it is the employee who has terminated the employment agreement.

(e) Non-competition clause

Individual contracts must be checked to see if there is any non-competition clause which stipulates a subsequent indemnification that has to be paid by the employer when he terminates an employment contract. This clause must be checked carefully to be sure of the validity. The employer may relinquish his rights under this clause within two weeks after the termination and, therefore, will not have to pay the non-competition indemnity.

(f) Clientele indemnity

A special clientele indemnity has also to be paid by the employer who terminates the employment agreement of a sales representative. The indemnity is only due if the terminated employment was the sales representatives' main activity and if the sales representative has at least one year of seniority. It amounts to three months' salary for a seniority of less than five years. If the seniority exceeds five years, the indemnity will be raised by one month's salary for each additional period of five years' seniority.

Furthermore, the indemnity is only due if the sales representative can establish that he brought in clients[1]. Attracting/recruiting clients is legally presumed when the employment contract contains a non-competition clause.

1   Which need not necessarily be significant or important.

(g) Stability clause

Some employment contracts or collective bargaining agreements[1] may contain stability clauses or conventional seniority clauses[2] which may affect the duration of the notice period.

These clauses, which hinder the possibility of the employer dismissing people, or limit this possibility in time, are accepted in Belgian law, eg:

– prohibition from dismissing the employee for economic or technical reasons within a period of 29 months;

– an employment contract that grants a fictive (contractual) seniority ('seniority clause') to the employee; in the case of dismissal, a longer notice should be granted.

1 In, for example, the insurance sector.
2 Where a 'conventional' seniority has been granted in an employment contract, the parties stipulate a fictive seniority in favour of the employee. In the event of dismissal, the employee will be entitled to longer notice.

(h) Outplacement rights

The Law of 5 September 2001 covers a right for out-placement services for elderly employees (minimum age of 45 years). CBA no 51 of 10 February 1992 and CBA no 82 of 10 July 2002 contain rules regarding out-placement measures.

The employee aged 45 or more and who has a seniority of one year, and who is not dismissed for serious cause, can benefit from 3 x 20 hours out-placement during one year.

If the employer does not respect the out-placement obligations, he must pay a penalty. The amount is set out by Royal Decree.

(i) Early retirement

To qualify for an early retirement[1] indemnity, any employee must be at least 60 years old and must have been dismissed by the employer[2]. The indemnity is paid by the employer in addition to unemployment benefits until the employee reaches the age of 65. An employee taking advantage of a '*prépension* scheme' must be replaced with an unemployed person.

For companies recognised as being in economic difficulties or restructuring, the age may be reduced to 52 years (exceptionally 50) by the Minister of Employment, a shorter notice period may apply and the duty of replacement may be lifted.

Economic difficulties can be evidenced where the company registered running losses (before taxes) in its last two accountancy reports.

Restructuring companies are those that carry out a collective dismissal in compliance with CBA no 24 and the Royal Decree of 24 May 1976. In case of reorganisation, the collective dismissal has to take place within a six-month period following the date the company has been recognised as restructuring.

For the authorisation to be granted by the Minister of Employment, there are several requirements, such as:

-   a CBA providing early retirement in the company;

-   evidence of economic difficulties or reorganisation;

-   evidence that employees' representatives have been consulted;

-   positive measures for women;

-   measures for a better organisation of the work within the company;

-   a financial commitment in writing by a bank that confirms that early retirement indemnities will be paid in case of bankruptcy.

1   'Pre-pension'.
2   The system of early retirement under 60 years has to be laid down in a joint committee's collective bargaining agreement, and the collective bargaining agreement may reduce the age to 58 years.

(j)   Statutory claims – unfair dismissal

In Belgian employment law, normally the employer does not have to justify the termination of the employment contract of a white-collar worker. Therefore, there is no unfair dismissal, unless the employee proves that there is specific damage above the damage caused by the termination[1]. The employee will have to prove fault by the employer, the damage, and the link between the fault and the damage. This is very difficult to establish and the amounts allocated are not very high compared to the termination indemnity[2].

When the employer wants to terminate the contract of a blue-collar worker, he will have to substantiate the termination[3].

The termination of the contract of manual employees has to be linked to the performance or conduct of the worker, or to company needs.

The performance or conduct of the employee could be unacceptable conduct, eg verbal abuse, insubordination, etc. Even no proper 'misconduct', such as absence for illness, can be a fair reason for dismissal if such absence is of such duration that it creates problems within the company, or when the performance of the worker does not meet the employer's needs.

Company needs are determined by the employer and relate to financial grounds or the company's organisation.

The employer will be the sole person competent to evaluate the performance or the conduct. Tribunals and courts will only check whether the motive for the dismissal is substantiated.

The employer does not have to state the reasons for the dismissal at the time he terminates the contract, but can do it for the first time in court. Normally it happens earlier, because social documents[4] will have to state the reason for termination of the contract in order to check if the worker has a right to unemployment benefits[5]. If the blue-collar worker challenges the dismissal, the worker has to prove that the dismissal is linked to the performance or conduct of the employee, or to company needs. Otherwise, an indemnity of six months' salary will be due to the worker.

1   For example, in the case of termination combined with insults, threats, etc.
2   Ranging from €1,000 up to €10,000, or sometimes more.
3   Article 63 of the Law of 3 July 1978.
4   For example, redundancy form C4.
5   In an involuntary unemployment situation.

Trial period

Any employment contract may contain a trial period clause allowing either party to terminate the contract during the trial period with a reduced period of notice. To be enforceable, the trial period clause must be in writing and signed before the employee starts his employment.

For manual employees, the trial period is a minimum of seven days and a maximum of 14 days. However, the contract may not be terminated during the first seven days, except for serious causes. Thereafter, it may be terminated at the end of any working day during the trial period without notice or compensation in lieu thereof.

For white-collar workers and sales representatives, the trial period is a maximum of six months, and 12 months if the employee's annual remuneration exceeds €31,669[1]. During the trial period, the contract may be terminated at any time by giving seven days' notice. However, a notice given during the first month of employment will be considered as given only at the end of that month. Notice must be given in accordance with various formal requirements.

1   2004 figure.

Special rules for the dismissal of protected workers

Protected employees, ie mainly elected (and non-elected) nominated employees for the works council, Committee for Protection and Prevention at Work ('Comité pour la prévention et la protection au travail') and the trade union representatives are entitled to a special protection against dismissal[1].

Trade union representatives can be nominated at any time by the unions. If nominated, they will benefit from protection against dismissal[2]. In case of dismissal, the procedure is as follows: the employer has first to inform all the members of the trade union delegation of the undertaking as well as the concerned trade unions, by registered letter. This mail is effective from only the third business day after being posted. A seven-day period follows this notification, during which the trade union may refuse the envisaged dismissal. In case of refusal, the employer may file the same request before the conciliation service[3] of the joint committee, which has to give its opinion within 30 days. The employer may file an appeal before the Labour Court if the 'Bureau de conciliation' has not reached a unanimous decision[4]. The employer may not execute the decision of dismissal during this procedure.

Trade union representatives who have been dismissed without compliance with the procedure are entitled to a special protection indemnity equal to one year's gross salary.

For elected (and non-elected) nominated employees for the works council or Committee for Protection and Prevention at Work, dismissal is only allowed for economic or technical reasons[5], or for serious cause[6].

The procedure in case of dismissal for economic or technical reason is as follows: the employer must send a registered mail to the chairman of the joint committee in order to ascertain that economic or technical reasons for dismissal are recognised and subsequently dismiss the employees' representatives (or candidates) for the works council or Committee for Prevention and Protection at Work. The joint committee must take a decision within a two-month period following the request.

If the joint committee does not take its decision within this time period, the employer may dismiss the employees' representatives (or candidates) *only in the case of a closure of the undertaking or in the case of dismissal of a category of employees*. This decision may be challenged by the employees.

If the procedure has been infringed, the dismissed employee[7] may require, by registered mail, to be reinstated under the same working standards as before the dismissal.

If the employee does not require to be reinstated, he/she can require the payment of an indemnity ranging from two years' gross remuneration up to four years', depending upon the seniority in the company.

If the employee requires to be reinstated and the reinstatement has not been accepted by the employer within 30 days after the request, he/she may require the payment of an indemnity ranging from two years' gross remuneration up to four years', depending upon the seniority in the company. Furthermore, he/she is also entitled to obtain the payment of *the remuneration until the next social elections* (even if he/she was not elected).

Amongst others, the following employees are also entitled to special protection:

- pregnant women;
- employees who filed a complaint about sexual harassment;
- employees who are candidates for a political function;
- employees who opted for a long-term leave ('crédit-temps');
- employees who have opted for parental leave;
- employees who are entitled to time off for training;

–   internal medical doctors.

1   Law of 19 March 1991 and CBA no 5.
2   The same protection as the employees' representatives may be granted to union delegates in undertakings without a Committee for Protection and Prevention at Work.
3   'Bureau de conciliation'.
4   Article 18, al 6 of CBA no 5.
5   With the agreement of the joint committee.
6   With the agreement of the Chairman of the Labour Court.
7   Or his trade union.

K2.3 (Alternative) settlement agreements

According to art 2044 of the Civil Code, a settlement agreement is an agreement whereby parties end a conflict or avoid a conflict arising.

In labour law matters, these agreements are often used as an instrument to end definitively a conflict arising on the termination of employment. The objective of this agreement is to settle for once and for ever the conflict and to avoid, by the integration of renunciation of rights by both parties, future discussions.

Most rules concerning employment contracts are mandatory. Thus, an employee can only renounce his rights after the right has been acquired.

It is important to know that agreements regarding the notice period can be concluded at the earliest when the notice is given[1].

[1] See above, 'Special rules for the dismissal of protected workers'.

K2.4 The duty to inform and consult prior to redundancy

The obligation to inform and consult in the event of a transfer of undertaking (CBA no 32*bis*) has been examined at **K1** above.

According to Belgian law, there is an obligation to consult and inform in case of:

–   collective dismissals: see *K2.2* above;

–   closure: see *K2.2* above.

For individual redundancies, there is no legal obligation to consult or inform. CBAs, concluded on industry or company level, can provide for a procedure in case of individual dismissals.

In the case of the dismissal of a protected worker (for serious cause, or for economic or technical reasons) a specific procedure should be respected[1].

[1] See *K2.2* above.

K2.5 Offer of alternative work

In Belgium there is no obligation for the dismissed employee to accept a work offer by the employer after notice of dismissal has been given. The refusal of the employee will not affect his entitlement to redundancy pay.

K2.6 Unfair redundancy

A difference should be made between blue-collar workers (mainly manual work) and white-collar workers (mainly intellectual work).

Blue-collar workers

According to art 63 of the Law of 3 July 1978 on Employment Contracts, the employer should pay an indemnity of six months of remuneration to the worker if the employer cannot prove that the dismissal is fair. A dismissal will be unfair if it is not given for reasons of the worker's performance or for company needs.

A worker who is dismissed can claim for payment of the six months' indemnity. His employer will then have to prove that he dismissed the worker for reasons of his performance or for company needs.

White-collar workers

White-collar workers who claim that their dismissal is unfair can only claim an indemnity on the basis of the rules of common law (abuse of the right to dismiss).

The worker will have to prove that his dismissal was unreasonable, wrongful and unfair. He will have to establish the extent of his damage.

The employee should, however, be aware that the termination indemnity he is entitled to after his dismissal is a lump sum. This sum is supposed to cover all damage (moral and material) he suffers because of the dismissal. Therefore, he will have to prove that he suffered separate damage which is not covered by the termination indemnity, which is held to cover all damage resulting from the dismissal.

K3 Case studies

K3.1 Case study 1
(Acquisition of a 'business' situated in another EU state; asset deal; no relocation)

Slumber Ltd, a hotel management company incorporated in the UK and based in Manchester, UK, has been in financial difficulties for some time. Slumber operates nine exclusive hotels in the main British cities (London, Manchester, Birmingham, Leeds, Glasgow, Edinburgh, Liverpool, Cardiff and Bristol) under the 'Slumber' brand. Slumber is 100 per cent owned by UK hotel chain Ezeroom plc, also incorporated in the UK. Each hotel has about 50 staff: five in management, 20 in the restaurant and 25 in house service. Slumber does not own the hotels itself; instead it has a seven-year management agreement with Hotel Investment plc ('HIP'), the owner of the hotels, which is incorporated and based in London, UK. Under this contract Slumber runs the fully equipped hotels on its own risk and has to pay a fixed fee to HIP.

In its central management centre in Manchester, Slumber has another 30 staff. These are 10 managers (including Marketing, Managing, Finance, Sales and Operations Directors) and 20 secretaries, clerks and administrators.

A number of staff are members of the trade union, The Association of Hotel Workers ('AHW'), which has been formally recognised by Slumber as having bargaining rights for hourly paid hotel staff. This is a particularly active union and there is a collective agreement in force. Due to increasing staff costs and the declining demand for expensive hotel accommodation, Slumber is making bigger and bigger operating losses. Slumber is obliged to cut jobs in all the hotels and thus dismisses 40 members of staff as redundant. As a consequence, the service worsens and customer complaints become more frequent. When the board of HIP realises how serious the situation has become, it starts to look for a new operator of its hotels.

Some weeks later, while Slumber is still operating the hotels, a Belgian company is found which seems able to manage the hotels in a much more profitable way for HIP than Slumber. The company, which is called Dormir, is based in Brussels, but has already gathered some experience of running hotels in the UK. It operates hotels under the 'Dormir' brand. The board of HIP enters into discussions with Dormir for it to replace Slumber as manager of the hotels.

1. Acquisition of the hotels

It is anticipated that Dormir will want to manage all nine of the hotels under a single management agreement with HIP.

(a) **Would this be a business transfer (defined as a transfer within the meaning of TUPE) under UK law?**

(ONLY TO BE ANSWERED BY UK CONTRIBUTOR)

(b) **Even though Slumber will not transfer any of its activities to Belgium, would the acquisition of the hotels in this way constitute a business transfer under Belgian law?**

CBA no 32*bis* applies when there is a 'relevant transfer' of a business or a part thereof. According to art 6 of CBA no 32*bis*, a transfer is the transfer of an economic entity defined as an organised unit of assets, which maintains its identity after the transfer. This covers a wide variety of transactions.

To determine if there is a relevant transfer, the central issue is whether there is an economic entity that retains its identity following the acquisition. This is largely a question of fact.

In the case *Spijkers v Gebroeders Benedik Abattoir CV*: 24/85 [1986] 2 CMLR 296, the ECJ held:

'It is necessary to determine whether what has been sold is an economic entity which is still in existence, and this will be apparent from the fact that its operation is actually being continued or has been taken over by the new employer, with the same economic or similar activity.'

The ECJ held that factors to be taken into account include the type of undertaking, the similarity of activities before and after the transfer, if any customers are transferred, the value of any intangible assets, if and how many staff were taken on, and the duration or any interruption of services.

Conclusion

If following the transfer the same business will be operating in the same premises, but in different ownership, there will be a relevant transfer under CBA no 32bis.

(c) **Would it make any difference to whether this constituted a business transfer, under TUPE, if Dormir only wanted to manage the six English hotels (excluding the hotels in Glasgow, Edinburgh and Cardiff)?**

(ONLY TO BE ANSWERED BY UK CONTRIBUTOR)

(d) **Would it make any difference to your answer to (b) above if Dormir only wanted to manage six hotels (for example only the English hotels, excluding those in Scotland and Wales, ie the hotels in Glasgow, Edinburgh and Cardiff)?**

Answer

It depends. There would not be any difference in the application of the law, as the test would be exactly the same. However, different conclusions may be drawn.

Legal reasoning

According to arts 1 and 6, CBA no 32*bis* applies when there is a relevant transfer of a business or part of a business. Therefore the acquisition of only six of the hotels would still mean that CBA no 32*bis* potentially applies to that part which is transferred. The key question would again be whether the six hotels (or each of them) constitute an economic entity which retains its identity following the transfer.

Since there are different staff for each of the six hotels, CBA no 32*bis* (as far as there is a relevant transfer) will apply to the (local) staff of the relevant hotel. As regards central management, the question will be more delicate, since the members of that staff work for all of the nine hotels, of which the majority (six out of nine) will be transferred. It is therefore possible (but this has to be examined on a case-by-case basis) that part of the central management will transfer too.

2. Employees who work only partly in the business

What is the position of those staff who work partly in Slumber and partly in Ezeroom? For example, the human resources director of Slumber is also the human resources director of Ezeroom and he has his employment agreement with Ezeroom. He spends approximately 40 per cent of his time dealing with Slumber's personnel matters and the remainder of his time on the human resources affairs of Ezeroom.

(a) **If this is a TUPE transfer, can he be said to have transferred under TUPE in the UK?**

(UK CONTRIBUTOR TO ANSWER)

(b) **What is the law on employees who work only partly in the undertaking to be transferred in Belgium?**

The specific facts of each case will have to be analysed.

The ECJ (Motif 13, ECJ, 14 April 1994, (1994) JTT 282; Motif 16, ECJ, 12 November 1992, (1993) Chron DS 102) decided that the Directive is applicable to the workers assigned to the transferred part of the undertaking, since the working relationship is essentially characterised by the link existing between the worker and the part of the undertaking he is assigned to for the performance of his job.

However, the fact that the employee exercises some activity within the transferred part of the undertaking is not sufficient to make the legislation on transfer of undertakings applicable. It is also necessary that the employee is actually 'employed' in the relevant part (Motif 19, ECJ, 7 February 1985, (1985) JTT 163).

3. Staff who work outside the UK in another EU country

It transpires that some Slumber central management staff are actually working and based in Belgium. Two are Belgian nationals.

(a) **Would these staff transfer to Dormir under TUPE if there was a TUPE transfer?**

Answer

In theory, yes, although this would depend on a number of factors, including their contracts of employment.

Legal reasoning

TUPE applies to undertakings or parts of undertakings situated in the UK immediately prior to transfer. These employees work for and are employed by Slumber, the undertaking to be transferred, but they are simply based in Belgium. The undertaking of Slumber is situated in the UK immediately before the transfer (even if some staff work outside the UK). Therefore members of Slumber central management who are working in Belgium will technically transfer. The important point is that TUPE in principle applies to an undertaking, or a part of an undertaking, which is situated in the UK immediately before the transfer. The fact that some of the employees are not actually located in the UK is irrelevant.

Difficulties may arise in practice. For example, the employees may no longer be required to continue working in the same place and there may be potential breaches of contract. If their employment is terminated, this is likely to be in connection with the transfer and potentially unfair. Whether or not they have claims in the UK, or indeed in Belgium, will depend on conflicts of laws issues (see Chapter D).

(b)   Would the position be different if there was a branch office of Ezeroom in Belgium, which directly employed these staff?

(UK TO ANSWER, BUT PLEASE COMMENT)

Answer

The position may be the same.

Comment: Courts in Belgium are likely to treat Slumber as the employer in this case.

4. Dismissal of employee

One of the Slumber staff, Mr X, was dismissed by Slumber after HIP had given notice to terminate the contract with Slumber and whilst negotiations were ongoing with Dormir. Mr X is owed two months' back pay and unpaid holiday.

Against whom can Mr X bring a claim, and where, if Mr X is a UK national based in Belgium?

Article 9 of CBA no 32*bis* protects the rights of employees against dismissal, where the only reason is the transfer, both towards the transferor and towards the transferee.

There is solidarity between the transferor and the transferee for the debts existing at the time of the transfer (CBA 32*bis*, art 8). If a dismissal takes effect on or immediately before the transfer and/or when it is connected to the transfer, the transferee and the transferor are in solidum liable for the redundancy payment.

In the event of an individual claim against a cross-border transfer of business, the competent jurisdiction must be determined following the rules of Council Regulation (EC) 44/2001 of 22 December 2000. According to s 5 (jurisdiction over individual contracts of employment), an employer domiciled in a member state may be sued:

–   before the courts of the member state where the employer is domiciled (ie where he has his registered office); or

–   in another member state;

– before the courts of the place where the employee usually carries out his work or in the courts of the last place where he did so; or

– if the employee does not or did not habitually carry out his work in one country, before the courts of the place where the business which hired the employee is or was situated.

5. Transfer of employee outside the UK

Mr Y (the marketing director) has been vital to the success of Slumber and has been responsible for many successful ideas. Dormir would like to retain his services and move him to Dormir's headquarters in Belgium. Mr Y has no wish to live in Belgium.

(a) **How does TUPE impact on Mr Y: is he obliged to transfer against his will?**

(UK ONLY TO ANSWER)

(b) **What is the law on objection to a transfer in Belgium?**

CBA no 32*bis* does not provide a rule that allows the employee to refuse a change of employer, in accordance with the case law of the ECJ, which decided that the employee should have the possibility to refuse the transfer of his employment contract to the transferee (Motif 36, ECJ, 24 January 2002, (2002) JTT 185; Motif 34, ECJ, 7 March 1996, (1996) JTT 165). This means that the CBA is deficient in this respect.

However, if the working conditions are substantially changed after the transfer, the employee could consider that the employer acted as if he terminated the employment contract with the employee (being a substantial change in working conditions to the detriment of the employee).

The change of the working place (to another country) is considered as a substantial change in working conditions to the detriment of the employee according to case law, except when the business is transferred to the employee's country of origin.

(c) **Can Mr Y claim constructive dismissal on the basis that he would be expected to work and be based in Belgium and this is nowhere near his home?**

(UK TO ANSWER, BUT PLEASE COMMENT)

Answer

Possibly – if being expected to work and be based abroad amounts to a substantial change in working conditions and is to the employee's detriment.

Comment: According to art 10 of CBA no 32*bis* the employment contract will be considered as terminated by the employer if substantial changes to his working conditions are made.

If there is no mobility clause in the employment contract, relocation may not be lawful. Even if there is a mobility clause in the contract, there can be difficulties enforcing it, depending on the facts.

6. Dormir's business strategy

What is the best way of structuring the transfer of the hotels to Dormir from the Belgian perspective? Would you advise Dormir to set up a subsidiary company registered in the UK specifically to purchase Slumber and thereby avoid any cross-border element?

It must be taken into consideration that CBA no 32*bis* is applicable to any employer who falls within the scope of the Law of 5 December 1968 on collective bargaining agreements and joint committees. This Law applies to any employer located in the Belgian territory, even if he is a foreigner. If only the transferee is located in Belgium, only he will have to comply with the existing CBA, and thus also CBA no 32*bis*. If only the transferor is located in Belgium, only he will have to comply with CBA no 32*bis*. If both are located outside Belgium, CBA no 32*bis* will not apply.

The question whether it should be advisable to avoid any cross border element will depend on whether the applicable law (in the present case, presumably, UK law) is more favourable to Dormir than the Belgian CBA no 32*bis*.

K3.2 Case study 2
(Production moves from one EU country to another EU country; physical move)

Alpha Incorporated is a multinational car tyre manufacturing and distribution business based in Europe. Alpha's headquarters are in the UK. Alpha has tyre plants in Belgium, Germany and France. Each of the tyre plants is a wholly owned and independently operated subsidiary of Alpha. Alpha has a European Works Council.

The subsidiary in Belgium is Beta. Beta employs about 250 employees, mostly in the direct production of tyres. The employees are on standard basic contracts which do not contain any mobility clauses. Due to increased competition from cheaper producers in the Far East, Alpha is having to reduce its own production costs. Beta has the highest production costs of all Alpha's European operations. Alpha has decided to end the production of tyres in Belgium and move production to Gamma, another subsidiary not far away but across the national border in France which has more modern plant and equipment. Beta will continue to exist, but as a sales and marketing organisation only, with about 30 staff.

Most of Beta's tyre-making plant and machinery is transferred to Gamma, but Gamma will only need an extra 125 staff to increase its output to the required level to supply Beta's market. Those employees from Beta who are required to work for Gamma will be expected to accept the terms and conditions and working practices of the Gamma plant, which are very different from those in operation at the Beta plant. For example, Gamma pays its employees considerably lower hourly wages and they work longer hours than those at Beta. Gamma does not want to pay more to the employees transferred to it from Beta than it does to its current employees. Gamma operates a different type of pension scheme.

1. Does this transaction constitute a 'business transfer'?

(a) **As Beta's tyre-making plant and machinery have transferred to Gamma, will this constitute a business transfer under the Acquired Rights Directive implementing legislation of Belgium ('business transfer')?**

Probably yes.

CBA no 32*bis* applies to undertakings which are located in Belgium at the time of the transfer. Beta is situated in Belgium at the time of the transfer.

Although the changes are intra-group, between subsidiaries of Alpha, this does not necessarily affect the fact that there is a change of employer. Relevant transfers can occur between subsidiaries: in *Allen v Amalgamated Construction Co Ltd* [2000] IRLR 119, the European Court of Justice held that two subsidiaries were distinct legal entities, despite having the same management and administration within the parent company.

To be considered as a transfer, it is necessary that there is an economic entity that retains its identity after the transfer.

(b) **Does it make any difference to whether this is a business transfer if employees of Beta transfer across to Gamma?**

The transfer of employees to Gamma is not a conclusive factor, but a factor to consider in ascertaining whether there has been a business transfer.

(c) **Can the transfer of plant and machinery coupled with the transfer of half the employees (125) constitute a business transfer under Belgian legislation if the other 125 employees are dismissed prior to the transfer?**

Yes. The number of transferred employees is not conclusive. The key factor is whether there is an economic entity which retains its identity after the transfer.

According to the case law of the European Court of Justice, the new employer must take over every employee.

If the employees are dismissed prior to the transfer, the dismissed employees are no longer employees of Beta. This means that they do not have to be taken over (provided it could not be argued that their dismissal is linked to the transfer).

(d) Does the fact that the business will transfer to a different country make any difference to whether this is a business transfer?

No, the fact that the business will be transferred to another country does not affect the qualification of the transaction as a business transfer (if the transaction is examined from a Belgian point of view).

(e) Is Belgian business transfer law concerned with the actual distance moved (irrespective of whether this means a change of country)?

Article 10 of CBA no 32*bis* stipulates that if the transfer is followed by a substantial change in the working conditions to the disadvantage of the employee, the employment contract will be considered as being terminated by the employer.

The workplace could be considered as an essential element of the employment contract and as a working condition of the employee. If it is unilaterally changed because of the transfer, the employee could consider that his employment contract has been terminated.

2. Relocation, but no business transfer

(a) Assuming the move does NOT constitute a business transfer (because the business of Beta does not adequately retain its identity) but instead is deemed to be a straightforward relocation, are any of Beta's employees obliged or entitled to transfer?

If this does not constitute a transfer, the Beta employees are in principle not obliged or entitled to transfer.

Since there is no transfer, there is no prohibition for the employer to dismiss some employees because of the relocation. As far as the rules regarding dismissal of employees are concerned, the employer can dismiss his employees.

On the other hand, the question whether the employees are obliged to relocate will depend on the importance (distance) of the relocation and whether the relocation can be considered as an important change of an essential element of the employment contract of the employees concerned. This will, amongst other elements, depend on the terms of the employment contract.

(b) If employees do nevertheless relocate, what will happen to their employment contracts? Will these continue, or will Gamma be entitled to provide new contracts?

If there is no transfer in the sense of CBA no 32*bis*, the contracts will not automatically transfer to Gamma.

In theory, two situations are possible:

- Beta terminates the employment contracts of its employees and Gamma provides new contracts.

- Beta and Gamma negotiate the transfer of some contracts, but then the employment conditions should be maintained or the consent of the employees will be necessary to change them.

(c) **What will be the law applicable to the contracts of the employees who relocate?**

The contracts will be governed by the law chosen in the employment contract, except for the mandatory provisions.

In the absence of a choice, the rules contained in the Rome Convention of 19 June 1980 will be applicable.

3. Dismissals

(a) **Assuming that the move does constitute a business transfer:**

(i) **are any dismissals in connection with the transfer lawful?**

The transfer as such does not constitute a reason to dismiss. In case of a transfer, employees can only be dismissed for serious cause, or for technical or economic reasons (CBA no 32*bis*, art 9).

According to CBA no 32*bis*, both the transferor and the transferee are responsible for the debts and contracts that exist at the moment of the transfer. This means that an unlawfully dismissed employee can start an action against the two companies. If the employment contract of an employee is ended shortly before or after the transfer, both employers can be held responsible for the existing debts.

(ii) **what are the rights and remedies (including applicable law and appropriate jurisdiction) of any employees dismissed:**

a. **before the transfer?**

If the dismissal is not linked to the transfer, the normal rules with regard to dismissal will be applicable. A notice period or indemnity will be due by the transferor.

According to the European Court of Justice, the contract of employment with the employee 'unlawfully dismissed' by the transferor shortly before the transfer must be regarded as still existing even if the 'dismissed' employee has not been taken on after the transfer of the undertaking. In other words, the dismissal will have no effect.

The fact that the contract should be regarded as still existing is an important difference with Belgian law. According to Belgian redundancy legislation, a dismissal (even when unlawful) always terminates an employment contract immediately and definitively. The employee can claim for the payment of a severance indemnity.

There are no particular penalties if the transferor dismisses an employee without complying with art 9 of CBA no 32*bis*. However, the employees could (try to) claim damages for unfair dismissal if the employees are dismissed by Beta because of the transfer.

b.   after the transfer?

If the dismissal is not linked to the transfer, the normal rules with regard to dismissal will be applicable. A notice period or indemnity will be due by the transferee.

There are no particular penalties if the transferee dismisses an employee without complying with art 9 of CBA no 32*bis*. However, the employees could claim damages for unfair dismissal if they are dismissed because of the transfer.

It should be mentioned that in Belgium the disregarding of collective bargaining agreements by the employer is a criminal offence. However, there are no examples in Belgian case law where employers have been found guilty of such criminal offences.

(b)   Would these rights and remedies change if this was not a business transfer?

If this is not a business transfer the employees would not fall within the scope of CBA no 32*bis*. The dismissal will be effective and a notice period or indemnity will be due. The employee will, however, not be entitled to the possible extra damages.

4. European Works Council and other employees' representatives

(a)   Will Alpha be required to inform and consult the European Works Council about the transfer or any redundancies?

The European Works Council is competent for information and consultation on issues that concern at least two establishments in different member states. Amongst others, these issues can be the structure of the undertaking or group and substantial changes concerning the organisation. According to art 27 of CBA no 62, the EWC should deal with the information and consultation with regard to matters that concern at least two groups of undertakings in different member states. This is the case in the present case study.

According to art 37 of CBA no 62, the undertaking or controlling undertaking must communicate to the employees' appointed representatives, general information concerning the interests of employees and information relating more specifically to those aspects of the activities of the undertaking or group of undertakings which affect the employees' interests.

(b) **Are any other employee representatives required to be involved in the transfer or any redundancies (ie at national or local level)?**

The works council should also be informed. In the absence of a works council, the trade union delegation should be informed. For undertakings having no works council or trade union delegation, CBA no 32*bis* stipulates that the employees should be *informed* about the details of the transfer.

5. Collective agreements

What is the effect of the business transfer on any collective agreements affecting Beta's employees?

According to art 20 of the Law of 5 December 1968 on collective bargaining agreements and joint committees, the new employer must respect the collective bargaining agreements that were applicable to the former employer, until their effect ceases.

After their expiry, these CBAs will continue to apply to the employment contracts (except if the contracts expressly provide otherwise): their provisions are deemed to be incorporated into the individual employment contract. There is controversy about the question whether such rules would apply to CBAs concluded within the joint committee, where the joint committee of the (new) employer is different after the transfer. The automatic transfer of terms and conditions does not apply to old age, invalidity, and pension benefits payable under schemes supplementing the official social security system. However, if the system is contained in a CBA, the transferee must maintain it. For other schemes, if the new employer decides not to maintain the schemes, authorities consider that the employees must be granted similar benefits instead of the schemes.

According to art 37, § 2, al 1 of the Law of 28 April 2003 on complementary pensions, a transfer cannot result in the diminution of the acquired pension reserves (at the time of the transfer) of the members. This article also stipulates that a change of joint committee cannot result in the reduction of pension commitments, unless the procedure of introduction or modification of a pension plan is respected. Specific rules apply with regard to the introduction and modification of a pension plan, depending on the kind of pension plan.

6. Change of terms and conditions

(a) **If this is a business transfer, how can Gamma lawfully harmonise employment contracts and change the terms and conditions of the employees currently on the more generous Beta contracts of employment?**

The working conditions of the employees concerned have to be maintained in the event of a transfer. Gamma cannot change the working conditions unilaterally. Gamma can only change the terms and conditions with the employees' consent. In the case of a transfer where a large number of employees is concerned, it could be an option to negotiate the modification of the working conditions with the employees' representatives.

(b) **If this is a business transfer, can Gamma reduce the wages of the former Beta employees?**

The new employer should respect and maintain the working conditions of the transferred employees. The wages are an important working condition. This means that the wages cannot be reduced unilaterally by the transferee. Any reduction of the wages will require the consent of the employees to be lawful.

Article 10 of CBA no 32*bis* stipulates that if the transfer is followed by a substantial change in the working conditions to the disadvantage of the employee, the employment contract will be considered as being terminated by the employer.

(c) **If this is a business transfer, what will happen to the former Beta employees as regards their private pension arrangements?**

The automatic transfer of the employment conditions does not apply to pension benefits payable under schemes supplementing the official social security system. However, if the system is contained in a CBA, the transferee must maintain it. For other schemes, if the new employer decides not to maintain the schemes, some authorities consider that the employees must be granted similar benefits instead of the schemes, since the advantage of a pension benefit should be considered as being part of the remuneration (which should be maintained after the transfer).

(d) **Is it easier to change terms and conditions of employment if the changes are made six months after the transfer?**

The protection guaranteed by CBA no 32*bis* is not limited in time. So changes made in connection with the transfer will be unlawful.

The transferor, however, cannot be held liable for the debts arising after the transfer.

K3.3 Case study 3
(Outsourcing of an ancillary activity to a non-EU country)

A large multinational (ABC) based in Belgium has decided to outsource its entire internal IT function to a third party provider in Romania, as the costs of hiring competent IT personnel in Romania are far lower than in Belgium, largely because wages are so much lower. At present 200 employees are employed by ABC in its IT function at ABC in Belgium. It is anticipated that exactly the same IT function will be required in Romania with approximately the same number of people required to run it. There will be no difference in the service or approach for those requiring IT assistance and even the internal telephone number will be automatically diverted. The Romanian third party provider has no assets or presence in Belgium.

1. Business transfer

Will this be a business transfer within the scope of Belgian law applying ARD?

Yes, this could be considered as a business transfer:

- there is a transfer of a part of a company that can be seen as an economic entity;
- there is a change of employer;
- by contract;
- the identity of the transferred company is maintained after the transfer.

2. Effect on employees

(a) What will happen to the employees currently employed in the IT function at ABC? Will they transfer across?

As Romania is not part (yet) of the EU, the EU Directives are not applicable in Romania. CBA no 32*bis* is not applicable outside Belgium. CBA no 32*bis* will be applicable to the Belgian company (ABC). This means that there will in principle be an automatic transfer of the employees, a prohibition on dismissal because of the transfer and an obligation to inform (and consult).

It is possible and very likely that the employees will not agree on the change of location. They could claim that there has been a change of an essential element of the employment contract (place of work).

Belgian courts could consider that the place of work is an essential element of the contract. If there is a(n) (important) change of location, the employee can consider that the employer has terminated his employment contract. The termination will probably be considered 'in connection with the transfer', so an action for unfair dismissal could be possible.

Some employment contracts stipulate that the place of work is not an essential element of the contract. However, this will only be one factor, amongst others, in deciding whether there is a substantial change of an essential element of the employment contract.

(b) If the employees do transfer, what will the applicable law be for their employment contracts with the third party provider? Where can they make any claims?

If the employment contracts contain a clause with regard to the applicable law, the law chosen by the parties will in principle continue to apply. Probably, this choice will not avoid the application of the mandatory provisions of the law of the country where the contract is executed (in this case Romania). The claims will probably be filed in Romania or in Belgium.

3. Data protection

Will there be special data protection issues on the transfer of knowledge and information outside Belgium to Romania?

Yes.

The Law of 8 December 1992 concerning the privacy of persons, as modified by the European Directive 95/94/EC of 24 October 1995, contains a Chapter VI that forbids the transfer of personal data to countries outside the EC.

According to art 21 of the Law:

'Personal data shall not be transferred to a country outside the European Community unless that country ensures an adequate level of protection.'

To determine whether the protection level is adequate, all circumstances should be taken into consideration. The law provides some determining factors such as the sort of information, the purpose and the duration of the processing of the data.

The transfer of data to Romania will only be possible if Romania can ensure an adequate level of protection. If not, the transfer of data will still be possible, if one of the conditions of art 22, § 1 of the Law of 8 December 1992 is respected.

Article 22 of the Law provides that in a number of cases (six) no adequate level of protection is required. Examples are: (1) express consent is given by the employee to transfer personal data; (2) the information is vital for the execution of a contract between the concerned person and the person responsible for the processing of the data, etc.

4. Transfer to India

Please comment on any differences there would be to your answers if the function was transferred to India rather than Romania.

India is not an EU country. The obligations of the Directives and CBA no 32*bis* should be respected by the (Belgian) transferor. The Indian company (transferee) is not required to respect the EU Directives.

The transfer of data to India will only be possible if India can ensure an adequate level of protection. If not, the transfer of data will still be possible, if one of the conditions of art 22, § 1 of the Law of 8 December 1992 is respected.

Article 22 of the Law provides that in a number of cases (six) no adequate level of protection is required. Examples are: (1) express consent is given by the employee to transfer personal data; (2) the information is vital for the execution of a contract between the concerned person and the person responsible for the processing of the data, etc.

K4 Additional information

K4.1 Website

Practical information: http://www.meta.fgov.be

K4.2 Books

W Van Eeckhoutte *Sociaal Compendium Arbeidsrecht*, Kluwer

Guide de la réglementation sociale pour les entreprises, Partena, Kluwer

L France

Nicolas de Sevin
Caroline Froger-Michon
Catherine Delanoë-Daoud

LI Business transfers

LI.I Background

Jurisdictional issues

Principle: the automatic transfer to the new employer of all employment contracts and liabilities linked to the transferred activity.

The principle of the automatic transfer of all employees linked to a transferred business is set out in art L 122–12 § 2 of the French Labour Code, which provides that: 'wherever a change in the legal situation of the employer occurs, such as a successor in interest, sale, merger, transformation of the going business, or incorporation of the business, all employment contracts in effect on the day of the change remain in effect.'

This provision was enacted by a Law of 19 July 1928, initially inspired by German law, and the text itself has never been amended since then. However, its interpretation by French case law has evolved considerably over the decades.

Article L 122–12 § 2 is a derogation from the general principle of Civil Law set out in art 1165 of the French Civil Code, pursuant to which a contract is binding only upon the signatory parties to the agreement. By virtue of art L 122–12 § 2, the employment contract entered into between an employee and employer X automatically becomes binding upon employer Y whenever the business of X is transferred to Y, without Y having to sign the contract or agree to such transfer.

The purpose of art L 122–12 § 2 is to avoid the transfer in itself constituting a reason to terminate the employment contracts relating to the business transferred: it does not, however, prevent the new employer from amending or even terminating the employment contracts, wherever the new employer's economic and financial situation so require.

Council Directive 77/187/EEC obliged French judges to modify several aspects of interpretation of art L 122–12 § 2. Some areas of discrepancy still exist today, as outlined in this chapter.

Also further to the 1977 Directive, the French Parliament enacted art L 122–12-1 (Law of 28 June 1983) providing for the automatic transfer to the new employer of the previous employer's *liabilities* towards its employees (except in cases of bankruptcy or the substitution of employers without any agreement signed between the transferee and the transferor).

Cross-border issues

The consequences of business transfers for employees are dealt with both at a European and national level. The European and the French rules have the common objective of securing the employees' protection in the event of a business transfer by ensuring the maintenance of their employment contracts and related rights.

In France, the principles of Directive 77/187/EEC appear in art L 122–12 of the Labour Code. This article provides for an automatic transfer of the employees' employment contracts, 'wherever a change in the legal situation of the employer occurs, such as a successor in interest, sale, merger, transformation of the going business, or incorporation of the business'.

It is usually considered that the European Directive does not supersede national regulations. The rationale is that a directive is only binding as to the result to be achieved by the member states to which it is directed, the national authorities being able to decide upon the method and form of implementation. As a consequence, the Acquired Rights Directive 2001/23/EC only aims at harmonising the rules on business transfers by stating general principles to be transposed at a national level by the member states, but each European country remains free to adopt its own rules.

Therefore, according to this first analysis, the European Directive does not expressly enable cross-border transfers of employment contracts.

Certain law professors – in particular Patrick Morvan (RJS 8–9/04) – seem to consider that art L 122–12 should also be applicable to European cross-border transfers, on the basis that the Directive could be directly applicable. This reasoning is based on the fact that French courts must apply art L 122–12 in line with the Directive and the decisions of the European Court of Justice ('ECJ'). As a consequence, they consider that this principle of *conform interpretation* leads in practice to the immediate and unconditional applicability of Directive 2001/23/EC to national regulations and therefore that the Directive should govern European transfers.

However, this position is quite debatable. Indeed, in practice, such legal construction raises the problem of the conservation of the entity's identity (see *L1.3* below) and, anyway, has not been confirmed by case law so far. At the present time, there is one decision of the French Supreme Court that may lead to the conclusion that art L 122–12 does not apply to cross-border transfers, although this case was not expressly dealing with this specific issue. The court ruled in this case of a cross-border relocation that the transfer of business to another country leads to the elimination of the employees' positions in France, and therefore to their dismissal for economic reasons (Supreme Court, 5 April 1995). A further implication of this decision is that the employment contracts are not transferred to the foreign company.

This 1995 decision was made about a transfer to Brazil. To the authors' knowledge, no similar decision has been reached about a relocation to an EU country. However, we believe that the same rationale would apply and, so far, no overruling court decision has been made.

L1.2 Identifying a relevant transfer

Article L 122–12 § 2 does not give a restrictive definition of a relevant transfer: the list of legal transactions covered by the definition is preceded with the wording 'such as' (*notamment*) which allowed case law to interpret it very broadly and apply it to such 'non-listed' transactions as business leases (*location-gérance*), sub-contracts, franchises, service contracts, etc.

French case law on art L 122–12 § 2 has evolved and changed considerably since 1928. It has been progressively adapted to the Directives and the case law of the ECJ.

Pursuant to the simultaneous decisions *SA Nîmoise de tauromachie et de spectacles v Bodrero Sereu* and *Société d'exploitation du Touring Club de Paris-Ouest, Société Les Campings d'Ile-de-France v Appart et Schwindling*[1], in 1990 the French Supreme Court (sitting in Plenary Session) definitively stated as a matter of principle that, in accordance with both art L 122–12 § 2 and the European Directive, the automatic transfer of employment contracts applies wherever the transferred activity:

(a)   is an economic entity with its own identity; and

(b)   is continued as such after the transfer.

In *Pink v Sté Castorama*[2], the French Supreme Court added the concept of 'autonomous' to characterise the economic entity of art L 122–12 § 2.

In two further decisions, *SA Sonevie v Fédération nationale des transports CGT*[3] and *Sté générale de sécurité v Figlia*[4], the French Supreme Court clarified that the automatic transfer rule of art L 122–12 § 2 applies even in the absence of any legal relationship (*lien de droit*) between the successive employers, ie in cases of a change relating to the successive sub-contractors, franchisees or operators of a leased business.

The 'autonomous economic entity' is now defined by French case law as 'an organisation with its own dedicated personnel and tangible and/or intangible assets, which carries out an economic activity having specific goals of its own' (see *Mutuelle Générale de l'Éducation Nationale (MGEN) v CPAM de Paris*[5]; *Sté Perrier Vittel France v comité d'établissement Perrier de Vergeze*[6]; *SA GT Centre Ouest v Barro*[7]). This implies that:

–   the economic entity must be autonomous (ie it may be separated from the company on the basis of its organisation, its hierarchy, its special-ised personnel, its geographical situation and/or its equipment, as opposed to an activity spread out through the whole company);

–   the entity must be transferred (ie there is an actual transfer of employees and assets);

– the entity must be kept as such (ie it should not, after the transfer, be immediately broken up and instantly disappear within the organisation of the transferee).

The French judgments seem to be more restrictive than the European judgments in cases where the 'economic entity' is composed only of a workforce, without tangible or intangible assets being transferred. While the ECJ considers that a community of employees with common activities may in itself constitute an economic entity that automatically transfers to the new operator of the business[8], it appears that the French court is reluctant to apply art L 122–12 § 2 in cases where no tangible (eg premises, equipment, inventory, tools, etc) or intangible (eg goodwill, licence, commercial lease, etc) assets are transferred at all:

– In *Bizzari v Sté Force Majeure*[9] and *Sté Air France v Lamoine*[10], where a company outsourced specific technical services to a sub-contractor using the company's premises and equipment, and subsequently decided to take back such activity; the sub-contractor's employees were denied the right to an 'automatic transfer' of their contracts to the company.

– In *Sarl CIR Médical v Tellie*[11], where there was a change of transportation company, the second company was not obliged to take over the drivers of the first company, as no trucks, buses or ambulances, nor any other tangible or intangible assets, were transferred from the first to the second transportation company.

However, the position of the French Supreme Court seems to vary depending on the particular circumstances of each case: for example, in *SA Serca v Vasseur*[12], the court ruled that a community of qualified employees assigned to a specific marketing and promotion activity constituted an 'autonomous economic entity', so that the company which had actually hired 200 out of the 213 qualified employees should have taken over all 213 existing employment contracts (together with the employees' continuity of service) pursuant to art L 122–12 § 2, regardless of the fact that no tangible or intangible assets were transferred.

This decision is similar to the jurisprudence of the ECJ, which concludes that in sectors of activity using mostly manpower, the economic entity's identity is maintained if the new employer not only continues such activity but also takes over most of the employees dedicated to this activity. In such a case the transfer can qualify as a business transfer even though no assets are transferred.

The French Supreme Court appears to have a more restrictive interpretation of art L 122–12 § 2 in cases of outsourcing by a large company: for example, in *Sté Perrier Vittel France v comité d'établissement Perrier de Vergeze*[13], the court held that the automatic transfer rule does not apply in a situation where a company outsources one of its activities (in this case, a workshop of transport pallets) which does not have a highly qualified or trained personnel attached to it, nor any specific means or an economic purpose of its own. Such asset-stripping of the company's activities obliges the employer to keep the employees dedicated to the outsourced activity, and cannot oblige the subcontractor to take them over.

1   Supreme Court, 16 March 1990.
2   Supreme Court, 26 September 1990.
3   Supreme Court, 6 November 1991.
4   Supreme Court, 12 December 1991.
5   Supreme Court, 7 July 1998.
6   Supreme Court, 18 July 2000.
7   Supreme Court, 30 April 2002.
8   Joined Cases C-127/96, C-229/96 and C-74/97: *Hernandez Vidal SA v Gomez Perez* [1998] ECR I-8179, ECJ.
9   Supreme Court, 19 July 2000.
10 Supreme Court, 17 December 2002.
11 Supreme Court, 25 June 2002.
12 Supreme Court, 24 September 2002.
13 Supreme Court, 18 July 2000.

L1.3 Affected employees

Wherever the two criteria outlined above are satisfied (ie (a) an autonomous economic entity (b) keeping its identity after the transfer of business), the transfer of the employment contracts applies as of right, as a matter of public policy, and is enforceable both vis-à-vis the successive employers and with respect to the employees concerned. This means that:

–   employers cannot agree to bypass art L 122–12;

–   employees cannot refuse to follow the new employer (such refusal would, at least, be a 'real and serious reason' for the employer to dismiss the employee);

–   employment agreements are continued as such, without any modification.

The transfer applies to those employees exclusively or essentially dedicated[1] to the transferred activity, and whose employment contracts are in effect at the time of the transfer (ie all employment contracts, including fixed term employment contracts, and any contracts suspended for any reason such as maternity, parental or sickness leave). Any employees on secondment at another company at the time of the transfer will also be transferred to the new employer, provided that they are nonetheless dedicated to the activity transferred (eg in a world-wide group, where an employee is posted to another company of the group).

1   According to the most recent case law of the French Supreme Court, employees working partly in the undertaking transferred and partly in another part of the (same overall) business can claim that they should transfer and benefit from part-time employment within the transferee after the transfer (Supreme Court, 2 May 2001, *Evenas-Baro v SA Sonauto*: a case involving an employee working 40 per cent of his time for the transferred activity).

Corporate officers

Under French law, corporate officers (*mandataires sociaux*) do not benefit from the protected status of employees. Indeed, corporate officers are not performing their duties under an employment contract but according to a corporate mandate that is given to them by the company. As a result, they do not benefit from the automatic transfer principle of art L 122–12 § 2, unless they combine their corporate mandate with an employment contract in the company: this should be checked in each particular case.

Protected employees

Wherever a business is transferred only in part (as opposed to as a whole), the transfer of any 'protected' employee is subject to obtaining the prior authorisation of the labour inspector. Such prior authorisation should be requested at least 15 days in advance of the transfer, as the labour inspector requires a minimum period of 15 days to make enquiries and ascertain that the transfer of the protected employee(s) is not driven by discriminatory reasons.

Protected employees include, in particular, trade union representatives (including former representatives, for 12 months after the end of their mandate), members of a works council, members of an industrial tribunal, employee delegates, and candidates at any election of employee representatives (if elections are being organised in the company).

L1.4 Effects of the transfer

The transferee has to take over the existing employment contracts as they are, without any modification. For example, the transferee cannot impose a trial period on the employees transferred[1].

1   Supreme Court, 13 November 2001, *SARL Airporc viandes v Pagnon.*

Right to object

When art L 122–12 is applicable, the employees' employment contracts automatically transfer to the successor, as a matter of public policy. Therefore, the employees should not have the right to object to the automatic transfer of their employment contracts. This has been confirmed by case law on several occasions. For example, in *Juchereau v Association Espoir*[1], the Supreme Court held that an employee who had been informed several weeks in advance of the transfer of his employment contract by virtue of art L 122–12 § 2, and who refused to come to work, committed serious misconduct (*faute grave*), allowing his new employer to dismiss him without any notice or indemnity whatsoever.

It should be noted that an isolated decision made by the Paris Court of Appeal on 26 September 2000 acknowledged the right of the employee to object to the automatic transfer rule. The actual significance of this particular decision is, however, uncertain and the Supreme Court has recently reasserted that an employee cannot object to his transfer (*Voisin v Gauthier ès qual*[2]).

1   Supreme Court, 25 October 2000.
2   Supreme Court, 11 March 2003.

Sharing out liabilities

Except if agreed otherwise by the parties, art L 122–12-1 of the Labour Code provides (as a result of the transposition of Council Directive 2001/23/EC) that in the case of a transfer of business the new employer must bear the previous employer's obligations as from *the date of the actual transfer*. The previous employer must reimburse the sums thus paid by the new employer. The transfer must not be detrimental to the employees, ie they should have only one creditor.

The principle set by art L 122–12-1 has, however, given rise to numerous case law decisions, in order to determine which financial obligations are due on the transfer date and shall thus be transferred to the new employer. This is especially the case for deferred payments or rights that are acquired over a certain period of time such as paid vacation, 13th-month payments and bonuses. The principles set by case law in this respect are as follows.

Dismissal indemnities

With regard to indemnities owed to employees on notice at the date of transfer (ie employees who received their dismissal notification, but who remained on the payroll until the end of their notice period), there is very little case law on this specific issue. According to an old decision of the Supreme Court, it has been ruled that the dismissal indemnity owed to the dismissed employee must be paid by the transferor, since he is responsible for the termination of the employment contract, even if the contract remains in force after the transfer for the duration of the employee's notice period[1].

1   Supreme Court, 16 December 1982, *Sté civile immobilière Domaine de Saclas v Burguère.*

Paid vacation indemnity

The new employer is responsible for the payment of all paid vacation accrued during the annual acquisition period (in France, employees acquire rights to paid vacation each month during a reference year which runs from 1 June until 31 May of any given year). His payment cannot be limited to the paid vacation accrued after the transfer.

Bonuses and premiums

If the right to a bonus or premium arises after the transfer, the new employer is responsible for the payment of the entire bonus. For example, a year-end bonus must be paid in whole by the new employer if this debt is incurred after the transfer (*Bardot v Dugail*[1]).

Likewise, it has been ruled that a Christmas bonus payable in December had to be paid by the new employer when the transfer of undertakings took place in November (*Société Eurest collectivités v Kern*[2]).

If the right to a bonus arises before the transfer but its payment remains outstanding at the date of the transfer, the new employer is also responsible for its payment.

Therefore, when a transfer of business occurs, it is always wise to review the existing collective agreements to make a list of the employees' deferred entitlements and check the date of payment of such sums. Depending on the facts, it may be necessary to provide for a specific clause in the transfer agreement dealing with the distribution of liabilities.

1   Supreme Court, 5 November 1987.
2   Supreme Court, 30 May 1980.

Consequences for applicable collective agreements

Collective bargaining agreements

As regards collective bargaining agreements (*conventions collectives et accords collectifs de branche*), ie agreements entered into with trade union representatives at national or regional level, a distinction must be made between cases:

– where the business transfer does not imply a change in the applicable collective bargaining agreement (ie if both companies are subject to the same collective bargaining agreement), when there is no specific procedure to be followed; and

– where the business transfer does imply a change in the applicable collective bargaining agreement, when the following specific procedure applies.

Company agreements

Agreements entered into with trade union representatives at a company level are subject to a specific procedure.

According to the Labour Code, any collective bargaining agreements applicable at the time of a transfer of business subject to art L 122–12 § 2 are automatically 'terminated' by virtue of the transfer and the collective agreements applicable within the transferee become immediately applicable. The former collective agreements will, however, continue to be applicable during a temporary 'survival period' of 15 months (that is, a maximum of 12 months + 3 months' notice period) after the effective transfer. During the 15-month period:

– the new employer has to negotiate with the trade union representatives, in order to try to obtain an agreement allowing for the harmonisation of the benefits and status of all its employees;

– as long as the 'harmonisation agreement' has not been reached, the transferred employees may claim to benefit from both the collective agreement temporarily transferred from their former company, and the collective agreement applicable within their new company (the benefits of both collective agreements do not cumulate, but the employees may benefit, within the same category of benefits, from those that are more favourable, in each of the collective agreements).

If a 'harmonisation agreement' is reached, it applies immediately. If, however, no agreement is reached by the end of the 15-month period, the collective agreements of the former employer cease to apply. In this case, the transferred employees will keep only those individual benefits which they had actually received before the transfer (such as a seniority bonus): 'individually acquired benefits' will be incorporated automatically as part of their employment contract. Conversely, the transferred employees will lose any 'virtual' collective benefits provided by the former collective agreement, such as the dismissal indemnity.

Other collective agreements

Agreements entered into with employee representatives other than trade union representatives, in-house customs (*usages*) and unilateral commitments by the employer are, according to case law, transferred automatically, together with the employment contracts, and the new employer must respect them, except when he decides to initiate a procedure of termination thereof, which implies:

(a) drafting a detailed list of all such collective agreements, customs and commitments which the new employer wishes to terminate;

(b) informing all employee representatives;

(c) informing all employees concerned in writing; and

(d) giving reasonable termination notice (usually between three and six months).

Profit-sharing agreements

Profit-sharing agreements are, in principle, transferred as of right, in particular where their calculation methods cannot apply within the transferee. In this case, the new employer must initiate a negotiation with the trade union representatives, in order to agree the terms of a replacement agreement.

As regards 'legal profit-sharing' (*participation*), which is the mandatory profit-sharing set by French law for any company with more than 50 employees, the negotiation should be initiated within six months of the end of the fiscal year during which the transfer took place.

As regards 'in-house profit-sharing' (*intéressement*), which is a non-mandatory profit-sharing agreement entered into for a duration of three years, the negotiation should be initiated within six months after the transfer.

L1.5 Dismissal of employees

Although no legal provision expressly prohibits a dismissal procedure being initiated by the transferor before the transfer of activity, in practice it is highly inadvisable to do so, as the courts generally consider that such dismissals are a fraud on the automatic transfer rule. Indeed, case law considers that an economic dismissal notified by the transferor on the grounds of a business transfer is null and void (*Maldonado v SA Fina France*[1] and *Voisin v Gauthier ès qual*[2]).

In particular, according to the French Supreme Court, the intention of the transferee not to take over all or some of the employees connected to the transferred activity *is not* a 'real and serious reason' for the transferor to dismiss the relevant employees (*Lubat v Sarrailh*[3] and *Reali v Laborde*[4]).

Any employee whose employment is terminated by the transferor in breach of art L 122–12 has a 'right of option'. He may lodge a claim to ask either for the continuation of his employment contract or the payment of damages for abusive dismissal.

With respect to employee representatives, the judge may *impose* their re-integration by the new operator of the transferred activity.

Note, however, that no legal provision prohibits dismissals being carried out by the transferee after the transfer has taken place, provided the transferee:

(a)   can prove the 'real and serious' reasons for such dismissal[5];

(b)   complies with the applicable procedure; and

(c)   pays the appropriate dismissal payments.

Although any lay-offs should be carried out by the transferee *after* the transfer, the indemnities related to such lay-offs (ie the notice period indemnity, the paid vacation indemnity and the dismissal indemnity based on seniority) may be shared out between the transferor and the transferee.

1   Supreme Court, 20 March2002.
2   Supreme Court, 11 March 2003.
3   Supreme Court, 17 July 1990.
4   Supreme Court, 9 April 2002.
5   This implies, inter alia, that there is no fraud relating to art L 122–12: ie the employees should not be able to prove that the dismissal was planned and agreed by the parties to the transfer even before the transfer took place. In this respect, it has been recently ruled that the change in the employee's remuneration agreed on the date of the transfer is fraudulent (Supreme Court, 9 March 2004, *Parfus v CGEA d'Annecy*).

L1.6 Harmonisation and variation of contract

While a business transfer is not in itself a valid reason to modify transferred employment contracts, the transferee may, prior to the transfer, modify the employment contracts under exactly the same conditions as the transferor could. In practice, it is highly advisable for the transferee to transfer the employment contracts as they are, and to start discussing or implementing modifications only *after* the transfer transaction is completed (*SA Onet propreté v Mullor*[1]). However, such modifications must not be made with the intention of avoiding the application of art L 122–12 provisions. In practice, a major amendment of the employment contract occurring concurrently with or immediately after the transfer is thus rather questionable. For example, it has recently been ruled that a change in an employee's remuneration agreed on the date of the transfer is fraudulent (*Parfus v CGEA d'Annecy*[2]).

Under French law, amending an employee's terms and conditions requires a distinction between two types of changes:

–   a mere change in the working conditions, which the employer may impose on employees as part of his power to organise and manage the workforce in the company's best interests;

–   a modification of an element of the employment contract, which is subject to the employee's prior agreement (ie an amendment should be signed by both parties).

In the second case, should the employee refuse the modification, there are only two alternatives left to the employer: either he keeps the original employment contract, or he takes the decision to dismiss the employee (leading to difficulties in being able to justify the 'real and serious reasons' which required the employer to make the proposed change).

1   Supreme Court, 20 October 1999.
2   Supreme Court, 9 March 2004.

L1.7 Duty to inform and consult

According to art L 432–1 of the Labour Code, the works council (*Comité d'Entreprise*)[1] must be *consulted with prior* to any final decision being made by the company's management regarding the organisation, the general operation and/or the management of the business.

The works council must be given *written* information on the contemplated decision, which must be as detailed as possible to enable it to give an opinion. The information must be forwarded within a reasonable time period before the consultation meeting with the employer's representative. As a rule of thumb, a 'reasonable' time period would be a minimum three to four weeks before the date scheduled for the consultation meeting.

The written information provided to the works council for consultation purposes should include:

–   the reasons for the contemplated transfer of business;

–   the legal conditions of such transfer;

–   the contemplated time schedule;

–   the target organisation of the activity concerned, after the transfer;

–   the consequences of such transfer on the employees concerned, ie with respect to employment agreements, collective bargaining agreements, in-house agreements, company policies, profit-sharing, retirement funds and health benefits, employee representative bodies, etc.

In addition, according to art L 321–4 of the French Labour Code, the works council must be informed and consulted prior to the implementation of economic dismissals.

1   Or, if applicable, the Central Works Council (*Comité Central d'Entreprise*) and the Local Works Councils (*Comités d'Etablissement*).

L2 Redundancy

L2.1 Background

According to art L 321–1 of the French Labour Code, a dismissal on economic grounds is 'a dismissal decided by the employer for one or more reasons that are not related to the employee, which results from *the elimination or transformation of a position or a substantial modification to the employment contract*, notably due to economic difficulties or technical changes'. Moreover, the Supreme Court has added another reason for dismissal on economic grounds to this definition: a company restructuring decided by the employer in order to safeguard the competitiveness of the company or the group sector of activity (eg in a pharmaceutical group, there can be two sectors of activity – the chemical sector of activity and that of the pharmacy).

According to this definition, in order for the dismissal to be valid, the employer must prove the following:

(a)   The elimination or transformation of the position: the position must be eliminated, which means that the dismissed employee cannot be replaced.

(b)   The economic difficulties encountered: in order for these difficulties to qualify as a valid ground for dismissal, they must be real and sufficiently serious at the time the dismissal takes place. These difficulties must be assessed on a company level or, when the company belongs to a group, at the level of the group sector of activity. In the case of a world-wide group, all companies belonging to the same sector of activity, even those located abroad, must be taken into consideration to assess the financial difficulties.

(c)   If the elimination or transformation of the position is not justified by the company's economic and financial difficulties or by technological changes, the grounds justifying the dismissal will only be considered to be real and serious if the dismissal is carried out to safeguard the company's competitiveness. Moreover, when the company belongs to a group, the need to safeguard the competitiveness must be assessed at the level of the sector of activity of the group both on the French market and abroad. However, in practice, evidencing such difficulties is often problematic.

L2.2 Redundancy payments

Redundancy payments should be calculated as provided by the Labour Code or by the applicable collective bargaining agreement, if any. As mentioned above, should any dismissals be notified within 15 months after the transfer, the employees may choose to receive the indemnities as provided either by the collective agreements of the transferor, or by the collective agreements of the transferee.

Notice period

The notice period is a period of time during which the contract remains in force after the employee has been notified of his/her dismissal. During the notice period, both parties continue to perform their obligations, but the employee is usually entitled to two hours off per day to look for a new job. The employer may also decide to release the dismissed employee from the obligation to work in the company during all or part of the notice period.

The notice period begins to run on the day of first delivery of the dismissal letter. The minimum notice period results either from the Labour Code, the applicable collective bargaining agreement, if any, or the employment contract itself. The minimum duration of the notice period is determined by the Labour Code as follows:

- for employees with less than six months of seniority the law refers to the applicable collective labour agreement;

- for employees with seniority between six months and two years, it is at least one month, subject to any collective or contractual provision more favourable to the employee;

- for employees with more than two years' seniority, it is at least two months, subject to any collective or contractual provision more favourable to the employee.

It should be noted that executive employees (*cadres*) are generally entitled to three months' notice – some top executives may even be entitled to six months pursuant to their individual employment contract.

Paid vacation

The dismissed employees must be paid an indemnity corresponding to their accrued rights to paid vacation. Under French labour law, this is usually calculated on the basis of 2.5 days per month of 'effective' work (for the purposes of this rule, an effective month of work is defined as four workweeks, or 24 days of work). The reference period for the purpose of calculating paid vacation is usually 1 June of the previous year to 31 May of the current year. Paid vacation rights continue accruing during the notice period, even if the notice is not actually worked.

Severance indemnity

In addition to the notice period indemnity and outstanding holiday pay, the Labour Code (art L 122–9) provides for a minimum severance indemnity to be paid to employees with more than two years of seniority. In the case of a dismissal for economic reasons, this indemnity is equal to 2/10 of the employee's average gross monthly salary per year of seniority. It is increased by 2/15 per year of seniority above 10 years.

The collective labour agreements applicable to the company, if any, and/or the individual employment agreements, generally provide for higher severance indemnities (regardless of any additional damages for unfair dismissal, if applicable).

Non-competition indemnity

Some employment contracts may include a post-termination non-competition clause, which triggers the payment of a specific non-competition indemnity to the benefit of the employees concerned.

Costs associated with the implementation of redeployment leave

Certain companies dismissing employees for economic reasons must implement so-called 'redeployment leave' (*congé de reclassement*)[1]. This leave is a training and outplacement programme organised by the employer, which lasts between four and nine months and which is to help the employee find new employment. According to the Law dated 17 January 2002, this obligation applies to the following groups and companies:

– A company with more than 1,000 employees in France.

– A group with its registered office in France, subject to the provisions relating to the implementation of a group works council, where the group (ie the sum of the various companies composing the group) employs at least 1,000 employees in Europe.

– A group subject to the obligation of implementing a European Works Council (ie a group (i) with at least 1,000 employees in Europe and (ii) with at least one entity employing more than 150 employees in at least two different European member states), where the company's registered office or that of the 'dominating' company (ie the company controlling the other companies of the group) is located in France, or a representative of the French company has been appointed to the European Works Council, or the company with the largest workforce is located in France.

However, in a ministerial circular dated 15 April 2003, the Labour Minister seems to have extended the scope of this obligation, since this text indicates that redeployment leave should be applied by:

- all companies with more than 1,000 employees in France; and

- all companies or groups employing more than 1,000 people in Europe with at least one entity employing more than 150 employees in at least two different European member states.

No reference is made regarding the other conditions stated by the Law dated 17 January 2002 (eg the location of the registered office of the dominating company, etc). Therefore, there is an ambiguity as to the scope of this obligation even if it could be argued that a simple ministerial circular cannot amend a Law.

If the company falls within the scope of redeployment leave, and if the employee decides to apply to this programme, an assessment of the employees' skills (*bilan d'évaluation*) will be carried out in order to determine which training courses may be required. The employer, in the light of this assessment, determines the length of the leave (between four and nine months). The employee benefits from the necessary training and outplacement measures during his/her notice period and afterwards. The notice period is therefore suspended until the end of the leave. For the duration of this redeployment leave the employee is entitled to full pay during the period corresponding to his/her notice period. He/she is then entitled to a special indemnity amounting to at least 65 per cent of his/her previous salary.

1   Companies exempted from the implementation of redeployment leave are nonetheless subject to another programme, called *Pré-PARE*. This programme is implemented by the French Unemployment Fund. This programme does not entail additional costs for the company.

Specific contribution relating to dismissal of an employee over 50 years of age

Article L 321–13 of the Labour Code provides that the dismissal of an employee of at least 50 years of age subjects the employer to the payment of a contribution (*contribution Delalande*) to the French Unemployment Fund (*Assédic*). The amount to be paid to the Unemployment Fund varies from two to 12 months of salary depending on (i) the size of the Company and (ii) the employee's age at the date of his/her dismissal.

The employer may, however, be exempted from paying this contribution in some cases, listed by law (eg the first dismissal in a 12-month period of an employee aged at least 50).

Costs associated with the implementation of a job preservation plan

Finally, it should be noted that the above dismissal indemnities are the 'minimum' amounts set by law and the applicable collective bargaining agreement(s), if any. These costs are associated with any economic dismissal implemented by any company whatsoever (with the exception of the costs associated with redeployment leave, which is applicable to certain companies only).

However, in the case of a collective redundancy procedure concerning at least 10 employees in a company employing more than 50 employees, the obligation to negotiate a 'job preservation plan' (_plan de sauvegarde de l'emploi_) with the employee representatives generally results in increasing the actual cost by an average six to 12 months per employee concerned (excluding any possible damages awarded afterwards by a court to the dismissed employee). Indeed, such a job preservation plan must provide for measures aimed at avoiding the employees' dismissal (eg outplacement, redeployment support, training programmes, mobility support, and financial incentives), which are rather expensive.

L2.3 Settlement agreements

The statutory period of limitation for employees' claims is five years for any claim relating to a payment of salary, and 30 years for any claim relating to the payment of indemnities (such as damages for unfair dismissal). Where employers wish to prevent or to put an end to any potential dispute, they may consider entering into individual settlement agreements (_transactions_) with the employees dismissed (or at least with those where there is a risk of dispute), whereby the employees waive any claim in exchange for an additional payment as a settlement indemnity (_indemnité transactionelle_).

Such a settlement agreement cannot be concluded before the completion of the formal dismissal procedure described in this chapter (and, for protected employees, after the delivery of formal authorisation from the labour inspector).

Finally, this settlement indemnity is paid _over and above_ the amounts provided by law and the applicable collective bargaining agreement (see _L2.2_ above). The payment of these additional damages is, however, under certain conditions, subject to a favourable tax treatment (income tax and social security contributions).

L2.4 The duty to inform and consult prior to redundancy

The time schedule for a collective dismissal procedure under French law depends, inter alia:

- on the number of employees whose position is eliminated, or is modified (eg change in the contractual place of work, change in the employee's contractual duties, etc); the essential difference is whether two to nine employees, or at least 10 employees are concerned;

- on the size of the company (less than, or at least 50 employees);

- on the existing employee representative bodies (employee delegates, works council, European Works Council, etc);

– on the works council's decision to be assisted by an expert accountant.

A chart at *L4.1* below summarises the procedure applicable in the case of a dismissal of 10 to 100 employees, in a company with a Central Works Council ('CCE') and a local works council ('CE'), with the employees' representatives appointing an expert.

Basically, the implementation of economic dismissal requires the prior information and consultation of the works council. To this end, the works council members must be provided with written and detailed information on the proposed restructuring. During this consultation process, the works council may be assisted by a chartered accountant.

Consultation of the works council implies a consultation on (i) the economic rationale justifying the contemplated dismissal and (ii) the dismissal pro-gramme. Indeed, the content of the job preservation plan must be discussed with the works council. This often gives rise to bargaining negotiations, during which the staff representatives frequently threaten to withhold their opinion if the company does not increase the measures provided for by the job preservation plan.

At the end of the consultation process, the works council must give an opinion on the project. This opinion can be positive or negative, but does not amount to a right of veto. No final decision regarding the contemplated dismissals can be taken before getting this opinion. Therefore, in practice, this process is rather long, and staff representatives may use the lack of information provided to them to refuse the issuance of an opinion and thus delay the overall process. Indeed, any litigation arising during this consulta-tion process can postpone the consultation process for several weeks.

During the consultation process, the works council must also be consulted on the so-called 'selection criteria'. Indeed, in order to identify those employees to be dismissed, the employer has to take into account the ranking criteria set by law (and by the applicable collective bargaining agreement, if any), namely: family situation, seniority, particulars making it difficult for the employee to find another job (eg disability, age), and professional skills.

An employer may give more weight to one or more factors, and/or add other (non-discriminatory) criteria, provided all statutory criteria are taken into consideration and discussed with the employee representatives. The criteria must be applied at the level of a given professional category. A 'professional category' should include all employees performing similar functions, which require the same professional training (*Sté des Grands magasins de la Samari-taine v Comité d'entreprise de la société des Grands magasins de la Samaritaine*[1]). To this end, the employer must take into consideration the functions actually performed by the employee.

1   Supreme Court, 13 February 1997.

L2.5 Offer of alternative work

Under French law, the employer has an obligation to make its 'best efforts' to try to find alternative employment for any employee whose dismissal is contemplated, *prior* to notification of the dismissal.

The scope of this obligation covers the company itself, as well as all companies belonging to the same group, even those companies located outside France (where the company is part of an international group), provided (i) their business and activities make it possible to offer alternative positions to the employees dismissed in France and (ii) no local regulation prevents such hiring (work permits, special prohibition). The French company does not have an obligation to find alternative positions, but to do its best efforts in this regard: whenever the French employer is unable to prove that such efforts have been made, the courts will necessarily consider that the dismissal is abusive. Accordingly, it is essential that the French company should keep written evidence of its deployment efforts (such as copies of the written request sent to the HR managers of the other companies in the group, enclosing the employees' CVs or current job descriptions).

Form of the offer

The offer must be made in writing and must be precise. This means that the redeployment offer should at least indicate the (i) job title, (ii) name of the employer, (iii) working place, (iv) law governing the employment contract, (v) type of contract (fixed term or indefinite term), (vi) salary.

Refusal of the offer

The employee can refuse the redeployment proposal(s) made to him. In this case, if no other position can be proposed to the employee, the employer may proceed with the employee's dismissal for economic reasons.

Rehiring priority

It should be noted that the redeployment obligation differs from the obligation to offer any available position during one year following dismissal (so-called 'rehiring priority').

Indeed, for one year after the dismissal has been notified to the employee, the employee may benefit (subject to informing the company about his intention to benefit therefrom) from a priority right on any position made available in the company, which corresponds to his professional skills or to any new competence acquired by the employee after the dismissal (provided the company has been informed thereof).

L2.6 Unfair redundancy

The indemnities discussed at *L2.2* above must be paid, even if the employer has complied with all of the substantive and procedural requirements set by French labour law. However, if the dismissal is not justified by a valid reason (*cause*), or if the company fails to comply with the dismissal procedure set by the Labour Code, the dismissed employees are entitled to the following additional indemnities.

Penalties for non-compliance with the dismissal process

If a dismissal takes place without the legal procedure being respected, the court can award damages to the employee for the loss thus suffered, with a maximum of one month of salary.

Damages for abusive dismissal

In the event the dismissal is deemed abusive due to the absence of a legitimate ('real and serious') cause, the court may order the payment of damages.

The amount of damages to be awarded depends both on the employee's seniority and the size of the company:

– Employees having more than two years of seniority in a company with more than 11 employees are entitled to damages amounting to *at least* six months of their salary. A higher amount may, however, be granted in consideration of the loss suffered by the employee. For example, the employees' age, family situation, seniority, ability to find another job, period of unemployment since his/her termination will be taken into consideration to assess the amount of damages to be granted. There is no maximum as to the damages that may be awarded, although it is rare for awards to be above two years of salary.

– Employees having less than two years of seniority or employees employed in a company with less than 11 employees are also entitled to damages, but the law does not provide for a minimum award. In this case, the amount of damages will be exclusively determined by consideration of the actual loss suffered by the employee.

The damages for 'abusive dismissal' are due in addition to the severance indemnities referred to above. In addition, the employer must reimburse to the Unemployment Fund all or part of the unemployment allowances paid to the employee dismissed abusively, up to a maximum six months of allowances per employee concerned.

With regard to dismissal for economic reasons, note that if the company cannot justify (i) a real and serious economic cause as defined by the Labour Code and case law and/or (ii) the impossibility of finding another position within the group for the employee made redundant, then the dismissal is deemed abusive.

L3 Case studies

L3.1 Case study 1
(Acquisition of a 'business' situated in another EU state; asset deal; no relocation)

Slumber Ltd, a hotel management company incorporated in the UK based in Manchester, UK, has been in financial difficulties for some time. Slumber operates nine exclusive hotels in the main British cities (London, Manchester, Birmingham, Leeds, Glasgow, Edinburgh, Liverpool, Cardiff and Bristol) under the 'Slumber' brand. Slumber is 100 per cent owned by UK hotel chain Ezeroom plc, also incorporated in the UK. Each hotel has about 50 staff: five in management, 20 in the restaurant and 25 in house service. Slumber does not own the hotels itself; instead it has a seven-year management agreement with Hotel Investment plc ('HIP'), the owner of the hotels, which is incorporated and based in London, UK. Under this contract Slumber runs the fully equipped hotels on its own risk and has to pay a fixed fee to HIP.

In its central management centre in Manchester, Slumber has another 30 staff. These are 10 managers (including Marketing, Managing, Finance, Sales and Operations Directors) and 20 secretaries, clerks and administrators.

A number of staff are members of the trade union, The Association of Hotel Workers ('AHW'), which has been formally recognised by Slumber as having bargaining rights for hourly paid hotel staff. This is a particularly active union and there is a collective agreement in force. Due to increasing staff costs and the declining demand for expensive hotel accommodation, Slumber is making bigger and bigger operating losses. Slumber is obliged to cut jobs in all the hotels and thus dismisses 40 members of staff as redundant. As a consequence, the service worsens and customer complaints become more frequent. When the board of HIP realises how serious the situation has become, it starts to look for a new operator of its hotels.

Some weeks later, while Slumber is still operating the hotels, a French company is found which seems able to manage the hotels in a much more profitable way for HIP than Slumber. The company, which is called Dormir, is based in Paris but has already gathered some experience of running hotels in the UK. It operates hotels under the 'Dormir' brand. The board of HIP enters into discussions with Dormir for it to replace Slumber as manager of the hotels.

1. Acquisition of the hotels

It is anticipated that Dormir will want to manage all nine of the hotels under a single management agreement with HIP.

(a) **Would this be a business transfer (defined as a transfer within the meaning of TUPE) under UK law?**

(ONLY TO BE ANSWERED BY UK CONTRIBUTOR)

(b) **Even though Slumber will not transfer any of its activities to France, would the acquisition of the hotels in this way constitute a business transfer under French law?**

Answer

No. Even though Dormir is a French company, French law would not be applicable in this case.

Legal reasoning

(1) The proposed transaction would take place in the UK and would presumably only involve employees under a UK employment contract.

Under French law, the employment contract of an employee performing his duties in another country is normally governed by the law of that host country. Therefore, in accordance with this territoriality principle, this transaction should fall within the scope of UK law only, irrespective of the fact that Dormir is a French company.

(2) If French Law was applicable, this transaction could qualify as a business transfer under art L 122–12 of the Labour Code.

As stated at *L1.1* above, according to art L 122–12, 'wherever a change in the legal situation of the employer occurs, such as a successor in interest, sale, merger, transformation of the going business (*fonds de commerce*), or incorporation of the business, all employment contracts in effect on the day of the change remain in effect.' In practice, this covers a large variety of transactions.

Under French law, a business transfer implies that the transferred activity is an economic entity with its own identity, which is continued as such after the transfer.

This definition of a business transfer requires a case by case analysis. Overall, the French Supreme Court considers that a transfer of business, as defined by art L 122–12 of the Labour Code, necessarily requires the transfer of operating assets (either tangible or intangible).

In the present case, the transaction will not entail the transfer of tangible assets to Dormir, since all tangible assets (hotels and related equipment) belong to HIP. However, Dormir will continue to operate the nine hotels as before, in the same premises.

The contemplated transaction between HIP, Slumber and Dormir can in fact be compared to a change of provider.

In this type of situation, whereas the ECJ considers that there may be a business transfer even if no tangible asset is transferred by the former service provider to the new provider (*Abler v Sodexho MM Catering Betriebsgesellschaft mbH*: C-340/01 [2004] IRLR 168, ECJ), the French Supreme Court still requires the actual transfer of operating assets in order for the transaction to qualify as a business transfer (Supreme Court, 18 February 2004).

However, French case law has provided for an exception to this requirement, when the successor performs the *same activity within the same premises*. Indeed, the French Supreme Court ruled that the continuation of the same activity on the same premises is sufficient for the transfer to qualify as a business transfer even if no tangible asset is transferred (Supreme Court, 27 June 1990, *Joly v Holiday Inn*).

As a result, if French law was applicable, in the light of this particular case law and subject to a further analysis of the circumstances surrounding the contemplated transfer, it could be considered that such transfer amounts to a business transfer entailing the transfer of the employment contracts to Dormir.

(c)   **Would it make any difference to whether this constituted a business transfer, under TUPE, if Dormir only wanted to manage the six English hotels (excluding the hotels in Glasgow, Edinburgh and Cardiff)?**

(ONLY TO BE ANSWERED BY UK CONTRIBUTOR)

(d)   **Would it make any difference to your answer to (b) above if Dormir only wanted to manage six hotels (for example only the English hotels, excluding those in Scotland and Wales, ie the hotels in Glasgow, Edinburgh and Cardiff)?**

Answer

No.

Legal reasoning

(1)   As in (**b**), even if Dormir is a French company, French law would not be applicable in this restructuring and therefore this transaction would not fall within the scope of art L 122–12 of the Labour Code.

(2)   Assuming that French law was nevertheless applicable, this transaction could qualify as a business transfer provided that the hotels thus transferred qualify as an 'autonomous economic entity'. According to French case law, an 'autonomous economic entity' is defined as an organisation with its own dedicated personnel and tangible and/or intangible assets, which carries out an economic activity having specific goals of its own. This implies that:

–   the economic entity can be separated (from the company) on the basis of its organisation, its hierarchy, its specialised personnel, its geographical situation and/or its equipment;

- the entity is transferred, ie there is an actual transfer of employees and assets;

- the entity is kept as such, ie it should not, after the transfer, be immediately broken up and instantly disappear within the organisation of the successor.

In the present case, an in-depth analysis of the factual situation would thus be essential to determine if the hotels are managed globally as a unique entity or if each hotel is managed separately. Indeed, if the hotels are managed globally, the transfer of the six hotels would probably result in a split of the entity's activity and lead to the inapplicability of art L 122–12.

2. Employees who work only partly in the business

What is the position of those staff who work partly in Slumber and partly in Ezeroom? For example, the human resources director of Slumber is also the human resources director of Ezeroom and he has his employment agreement with Ezeroom. He spends approximately 40 per cent of his time dealing with Slumber's personnel matters and the remainder of his time on the human resources affairs of Ezeroom.

(a) **If this is a TUPE transfer, can he be said to have transferred under TUPE in the UK?**

(UK CONTRIBUTOR TO ANSWER)

(b) **What is the law on employees who work only partly in the undertaking to be transferred in France?**

Under French law, when a transfer qualifies as a business transfer the employment contracts of the employees exclusively or essentially dedicated to the transferred activity are automatically transferred to the new employer. This rule applies to all types of employment contracts, including fixed-term employment contracts, and any contracts suspended for any reason whatsoever, such as maternity, parental or sickness leave.

French case law considers that where there is an art L 122–12 business transfer, the employment contracts of employees working partly for the transferred activity must be partially transferred to the new employer for the part corresponding to said transferred activity (French Supreme Court, 2 May 2001). In theory, this solution leads to these employees having two employers, which in practice creates real difficulties. In practice, the transferee and the transferor try to deal with the situation of these employees by dedicating them totally to the business thus transferred. However, this may require the prior and express consent of the employee.

3. Staff who work outside the UK in another EU country

It transpires that some Slumber central management staff are actually working and based in France already. Two are French nationals.

(a) **Would these staff transfer to Dormir under TUPE if there was a TUPE transfer?**

(TO BE ANSWERED BY UK CONTRIBUTOR. PLEASE COMMENT ON UK RESPONSE)

Answer

In theory yes, although this would depend on a number of factors, including their contracts of employment.

Legal reasoning

TUPE applies to undertakings or parts of undertakings situated in the UK immediately prior to transfer. These employees work for and are employed by Slumber, the undertaking to be transferred, but they are simply based in France. The undertaking of Slumber is situated in the UK immediately before the transfer (even if some staff work outside the UK) therefore members of Slumber central management who are working in France will technically transfer. The important point is that TUPE in principle applies to undertakings or a part of an undertaking which is situated in the UK immediately before the transfer. The fact that some of the employees are not actually located in the UK is irrelevant.

Difficulties may arise in practice. For example, the employees may no longer be required to continue working in the same place and there may be potential breaches of contract. If their employment is terminated, this is likely to be in connection with the transfer and potentially unfair. Whether or not they have claims in the UK, or indeed in France, will depend on conflicts of laws issues (see Chapter D).

Comment: The situation of these two employees should be analysed very precisely. Indeed, as per the Rome Convention, their employment contracts are most certainly governed by French law, ie the law of the country in which these employees habitually carry out their work. The fact that they are of French nationality is irrelevant.

Therefore, if the conditions set by art L 122–12 for the contemplated transfer qualify as a business transfer, then art L 122–12 would be applicable to these two employees, which would theoretically trigger the automatic transfer of their employment contracts to Dormir.

However, given the circumstances, this is rather doubtful, although no case law exists on this specific issue. Indeed, the application of art L 122–12 to these two employees would require that (i) Slumber's activity in France (ie the activity performed by these two French employees) constitutes in itself an autonomous economic entity, and that (ii) the transaction entails a transfer of operating resources, which is unlikely here.

(b) **Would the position be different if there was a branch office of Ezeroom in France, which directly employed these staff?**

(UK TO ANSWER, BUT PLEASE COMMENT)

Answer

The position may be the same.

Legal reasoning

TUPE is likely to apply if the branch office qualifies as an associated employer and the employees are 'assigned' (Botzen v Rotterdamsche Droogdok Maatschappij BV: 186/83 [1985] ECR 519, ECJ) to Slumber (in other words, they carry out all their functions for Slumber which is their de facto employer). In such a case the courts are likely to pierce the corporate veil and treat Slumber as the employer for those purposes.

Comment: Likewise, the employment contracts of these two employees would most certainly be governed by French law, in accordance with the Rome Convention. However, we believe that there is no art L 122–12 issue here, since no transfer will take place between Ezeroom and Dormir.

4. Dismissal of employee

One of the Slumber staff, Mr X, was dismissed by Slumber after HIP had given notice to terminate the contract with Slumber and whilst negotiations were ongoing with Dormir. Mr X is owed two months' back pay and unpaid holiday.

Against whom can Mr X bring a claim, and where, if Mr X is a UK national based in France?

Assuming that Mr X performs his job in France, his employment contract is most certainly governed by French law, as per the Rome Convention (ie the law of the country in which he habitually carries out his work). The fact that he is a UK national is irrelevant.

However, art L 122–12 would probably not be applicable to him for the following reasons:

– As indicated before, art L 122–12 does not apply to cross-border transfers.

– Therefore, the only case where this article would be applicable to Mr X would be if Slumber's activity in France itself constituted an autonomous economic entity. This is unlikely, although no case law exists on this specific issue.

Assuming, however, that art L 122–12 would be applicable, Mr X could lodge his claim against either Slumber or Dormir, depending on the grounds of such action and on the date it is lodged.

As per art 5 of Council Regulation (EC) 44/2001, such claim could be lodged either in the UK (Slumber's headquarters) or in France (Dormir's headquarters).

Legal reasoning

Assuming that art L 122–12 would apply:

(1)   Article L 122–12-1 of the Labour Code provides that, in the case of a transfer of business, the new employer must honour the previous employer's obligations *as from the date of the actual transfer*. Therefore, all salaries due before the transfer but which remain outstanding on the date of the transfer must be borne by the new employer. The previous employer must then reimburse the sums thus paid by the new employer. The purpose of this is that the transfer of business must not be detrimental to the employees. Indeed, thanks to this option, employees are allowed to bring their claim against either their new or former employer. It is often easier for them to contact their former employer (whom they know well). In fact, this principle creates a sort of 'joint liability' between the successive employers with respect to any debts and liabilities relating to the period of employment prior to the transfer, the transferred employees being entitled to recover all payments either from their former employer, its successor, or both. The successive employers must then deal with possible reimbursements between them, without the employee being involved.

However, this principle does not apply when the transfer takes place after a liquidation or when there is no transfer agreement between the successive employers (eg successive service providers). In this case, the employee must turn to his former employer to obtain the payment of any sum relating to the period of employment before the transfer.

(2)   The principle set by art L 122–12-1 has given rise to numerous case law decisions, in order to determine which financial obligations are due on the transfer date and should thus be transferred to the new employer. This is especially the case for deferred payments or rights that are acquired over a certain period of time but which become payable at a later date, such as paid vacation. In this respect, case law has ruled that the new employer is responsible for the payment of all paid vacation accrued during the annual acquisition period, and not only for the paid vacation accrued after the transfer.

Therefore, in order to determine who is responsible for the payment of a debt, it is necessary to check the date of payment of such sums.

(3)   It is important to note that case law considers that an *economic* dismissal notified by the transferor on the occasion of a business transfer is null

and void (Supreme Court, 20 March 2002, *Maldonado v SA Fina France* and 11 March 2003, *Voisin v Gauthier ès qual*).

In this case, the employee unlawfully dismissed has a 'right of option'. He may lodge a claim against either the new employer to ask for the continuation of his employment contract *or* against his former employer in order to obtain damages for wrongful dismissal.

Conversely, French provisions on business transfers do not prevent an employer from dismissing an employee on *personal* grounds (eg gross misconduct) provided that such dismissal has no link with the transfer. This means that there must be no fraudulent agreement between the successive employers aimed at avoiding the application of art L 122–12.

Conclusion

Under French law, the distribution of liability between the successive employers is a complex area where each case will turn on its facts.

In the present case, there will be no transfer agreement between Slumber and Dormir. If art L 122–12 was applicable, Mr X should turn to Slumber to obtain the payment of his two months' back pay and unpaid holiday as per art L 122–12-1 of the Labour Code.

However, Mr X could also lodge a claim against Dormir on the basis that his dismissal is null and void if he could demonstrate that he has been dismissed in order to bypass the automatic transfer rule set by art L 122–12.

5. Transfer of employee outside the UK

Mr Y (the marketing director) has been vital to the success of Slumber and has been responsible for many successful ideas. Dormir would like to retain his services and move him to Dormir's headquarters in Paris. Mr Y has no wish to live in France.

(a) **How does TUPE impact on Mr Y: is he obliged to transfer against his will?**

(UK ONLY TO ANSWER)

(b) **What is the law on objection to a transfer in France?**

Under French law, the amendment of the employee's place of work is governed by the following principles:

(1) If the employment contract *does not include a mobility clause*, the employer must get the employee's prior agreement, except when the new place of work is located in the same 'geographical area'.

If the new place of work is located in a different geographical area and the employee refuses to move, such a refusal will not be considered as a valid ground for dismissal. Therefore, in this case, the employer will have the choice:

– to keep the employee within the same premises; or

–   to dismiss the employee (however, in this case the dismissal will necessarily have to be based on economic reasons, since the employee's refusal will not amount to a breach of his/her contract).

This means that the employer will have to demonstrate that the move is justified by a valid economic reason, as defined by French law. In this respect, it should be noted that when the company belongs to a group, the economic reason must be assessed at the level of the group both in France and abroad.

(2)   If the employment contract *includes a mobility clause*, by which the employee agrees that his/her place of work may be changed from time to time by the company, the employer may, under certain conditions, amend his/her working place without his/her prior agreement being requested. In this case, the employee's refusal to move may be considered as a breach of his/her employment obligations and lead to his/her dismissal on personal (as opposed to economic) grounds.

However, the validity of such a mobility clause is subject to certain conditions. In particular, the mobility clause must be justified by the employee's functions and the company's interests. The clause must also be proportionate. Finally, the employer must act in good faith when enforcing such a clause.

Recent case law decisions have invalidated excessive or unconditional mobility clauses. In particular, the Supreme Court (19 May 2004) recently ruled that a limitless mobility clause is null and void. Therefore, given recent case law developments, the validity of a clause providing for international mobility is rather debatable, but no specific court decision has been made on this issue so far.

(c)   **Can Mr Y claim constructive dismissal on the basis that he would be expected to work and be based in France and this is nowhere near his home?**

(UK TO ANSWER, BUT PLEASE COMMENT)

Answer

Possibly, if this amounts to a fundamental breach of his contract or if being expected to work and be based abroad amounts to a substantial change in working conditions and is to the employee's detriment.

Legal reasoning

In addition to general common law tests for constructive dismissal, reg 5(5) provides that an employee has the right 'to terminate his contract of employment without notice if a substantial change is made in his working conditions to his detriment'. It is important therefore that the change is substantial and to the employee's detriment. Such a claim is likely to lie against the transferee (Dormir). Only in rare circumstances such as where the transferor (Slumber) has not been open with the employee about the change in working conditions is a claim likely to succeed against the transferor (Slumber). Case law is of importance here.

In Merckx and Neuhuys v Ford Motors Co Belgium SA [1996] IRLR 467, Anfo Motors SA transferred its Ford dealership to an independent dealer. There was no transfer of assets and only 14 out of Anfo's 60 employees were taken on. The ECJ identified a community right to claim constructive dismissal where there was a 'substantial change in working conditions to the detriment of the employee' because of the transfer.

In Rossiter v Pendragon [2002] IRLR 483, Mr Rossiter argued that he had suffered a detriment through changes in the calculation of commission, that his holiday pay was no longer based on commission and that he was made to assume lesser duties. The Court of Appeal held that in order to claim constructive dismissal there would have to be a repudiatory breach of contract, which there was not in this case.

The use of mobility clauses is limited in long-distance transfers, as the test for redundancy is where the employee actually carries out his work.

Comment: Under French law, if Dormir was to relocate Mr Y without complying with the rules described above (prior agreement or valid mobility clause), he could lodge a case for constructive dismissal due to this breach of contract on the basis that Dormir did not comply with its contractual obligations.

6. Dormir's business strategy

What is the best way of structuring the transfer of the hotels to Dormir from a French perspective? Would you advise Dormir to set up a subsidiary company registered in the UK specifically to purchase Slumber and thereby avoid any cross-border element?

As far as French labour law is concerned, the creation of a subsidiary company registered in the UK specifically to purchase Slumber would have no impact, since French labour law would basically not apply to the contemplated restructuring.

L3.2 Case study 2
(Production moves from one EU country to another EU country; physical move)

Alpha Incorporated is a multinational car tyre manufacturing and distribution business based in Europe. Alpha's headquarters are in the UK. Alpha has tyre plants in France, Germany and the UK. Each of the tyre plants is a wholly owned and independently operated subsidiary of Alpha. Alpha has a European Works Council.

The subsidiary in France is Beta. Beta employs about 250 employees, mostly in the direct production of tyres. The employees are on standard basic contracts which do not contain any mobility clauses. Due to increased competition from cheaper producers in the Far East, Alpha is having to reduce its own production costs. Beta has the highest production costs of all Alpha's European operations. Alpha has decided to end the production of tyres in France and move production to Gamma, another subsidiary not far away but across the national border in Germany which has more modern plant and equipment. Beta will continue to exist, but as a sales and marketing organisation only, with about 30 staff.

Most of Beta's tyre-making plant and machinery is transferred to Gamma, but Gamma will only need an extra 125 staff to increase its output to the required level to supply Beta's market. Those employees from Beta who are required to work for Gamma will be expected to accept the terms and conditions and working practices of the Gamma plant, which are very different from those in operation at the Beta plant. For example, Gamma pays its employees considerably lower hourly wages and they work longer hours than those at Beta. Gamma does not want to pay more to the employees transferred to it from Beta than it does to its current employees. Gamma operates a different type of pension scheme.

1. Does this transaction constitute a 'business transfer'?

(a) **As Beta's tyre-making plant and machinery have transferred to Gamma, will this constitute a business transfer under the Acquired Rights Directive implementing legislation of France?**

Answer

No.

Legal reasoning

(1) In France, art L 122–12 of the Labour Code provides for an automatic transfer of the employees' employment contracts, 'wherever a change in the legal situation of the employer occurs, such as a successor in interest, sale, merger, transformation of the going business, or incorporation of the business'. (Please refer to *Case study 1* at *L3.1* above. This wording is in fact the actual translation of the Labour Code's article. A complete description of the mechanism provided for by this article is detailed at **L1** above).

Under French law, a business transfer implies that the transferred activity is an 'autonomous economic entity', ie an economic entity with its own identity, which is continued as such after the transfer.

However, it is essential to highlight that, so far, the transfer rule provided by art L 122–12 only applies to business transfers that take place in France. In fact, currently the prevailing analysis leads to the conclusion that art L 122–12 does not apply to cross-border transfers.

In this respect, the French Supreme Court ruled, in a decision dated 5 April 1995, that a cross-border relocation does not result in the transfer of the employees' employment contracts. Indeed, in that case, the Supreme Court concluded that the transfer of business to another country leads to the elimination of the employees' positions in France and therefore to their dismissal for economic reasons.

This 1995 decision was made about a transfer to Brazil. To our knowledge, no similar decision has been made about a relocation in an EU country. However, we believe that the same rationale would apply and, so far, no overruling court decision has been rendered.

(2) For the purposes of this case study, if we were to assume that art L 122–12 is applicable (ie if Beta's activity was relocated in another French area) this restructuring may qualify as a business transfer.

In this case, the application of art L 122–12 would imply that the production of tyres constitutes in itself an 'autonomous economic entity'. This means that the transfer of the production activity would have to meet the following requirements:

–   An actual transfer of assets, which seems to be the case here (transfer of Beta's machinery).

–   The application of art L 122–12 would also imply that the production activity can be separated from Beta's other activities on the basis of its organisation, its hierarchy, its dedicated personnel, its geographical situation and/or its equipment.

–   Finally, the application of art L 122–12 would require that the entity is kept as such, ie it should not, after the transfer, be broken down and disappear immediately within Gamma's organisation.

(b)   Does it make any difference to whether this is a business transfer if employees of Beta transfer across to Gamma?

Answer

No.

Legal reasoning

(1) For the reasons described above, French law on business transfers would not be applicable, irrespective of the fact that all employees are to be transferred to Gamma.

(2) In contrast, if art L 122–12 was likely to apply to this situation, the transfer of employees would be a criterion to be taken into account to determine if the transfer qualifies as a business transfer, without such criterion being exclusive.

Indeed, French case law is now in line with the European jurisprudence, which takes into account, amongst other criteria, that of the number of employees transferred (see *Süzen v Zehnacker*: C-13/95 [1997] ECR I-1259) ECJ and *Hernandez Vidal SA v Gomez Perez* [1998] ECR I-8179, ECJ).

In fact, the French Supreme Court used to be quite hesitant about this criterion. For example, it has been ruled that the mechanism set by art L 122–12 was not applicable to a transfer where the successor contractually agreed to keep 80 per cent of the workforce, since the other criteria (in particular that of the transfer of assets) were not satisfied (Supreme Court, 6 November 1991, *SA Sonevie v Fédération nationale des transports CGT*). However, the position has evolved since then. Indeed, in *SA GT Centre Ouest v Barro*, 30 April 2002, the Supreme Court ruled that art L 122–12 is applicable in a situation where only few assets were transferred but 200 specialised employees (out of 213) were retained by the successor to perform the same activity.

(c) **Can the transfer of plant and machinery coupled with the transfer of half the employees (125) constitute a business transfer under French legislation if the other 125 employees are dismissed prior to the transfer?**

(1) For the reasons explained above, this situation would not fall within the scope of art L 122–12 of the French Labour Code, since the activity is relocated outside France.

(2) If the transfer was to take place in France, this transfer could qualify as a business transfer governed by art L 122–12 of the Labour Code, provided that the conditions mentioned above (see the response to question 1(a) above) are met. In this respect, a limited transfer of employees does not prevent a business transfer and the application of art L 122–12, if the employees thus transferred are the ones dedicated to the transferred activity.

Furthermore, it should be noted that when the conditions set by art L 122–12 are met, all employment contracts connected to the transferred economic entity are automatically assigned to the successor. Consequently, under French law, a business transfer does not constitute a valid ground for dismissal, and any dismissal notified by the transferor on the occasion of a business transfer is null and void (Supreme Court, 20 March 2002, *Maldonado v SA Fina France* and 11 March 2003, *Voisin v Gauthier ès qual*).

Therefore, in the present situation, if the 250 employees were dedicated to the transferred activity (ie tyre production), they should *all* be transferred to Gamma, in accordance with art L 122–12 of the Labour Code. Should Gamma breach this principle, these employees could ask for the continuation of their employment contract within Gamma, or for the allocation of damages.

(d) **Does the fact that the business will transfer to a different country make any difference to whether this is a business transfer?**

This is indeed a key issue. At present, art L 122–12 of the French Labour Code relating to business transfers does not apply to cross-border transfers.

(e) **Is French business transfer law concerned with the actual distance moved (irrespective of whether this means a change of country)?**

Answer

Not really. Provided that the relocation takes place in France, the actual distance is not an issue to be considered for the application of art L 122–12 of the Labour Code. Nevertheless, distance can raise important issues after the transfer.

Legal reasoning

When the conditions set by art L 122–12 are met, the relevant employment contracts are *automatically* transferred to the new employer, without the distance being taken into account.

However, this transfer may subsequently entail a modification of the employees' place of work and, as the case may be, of their employment contract.

Depending on the importance of this change, on the contents of the employees' employment contracts and/or the provisions of the applicable collective bargaining agreement, such a modification may lead to the dismissal of the transferred employee. In this case, the dismissal will have to be conducted by the new employer after the actual transfer.

The main criterion to be considered is that of the 'geographical area'.

If the new place of work is located in a different geographical area and if the employee's employment contract does not contain a valid mobility clause, such an amendment requires the prior agreement of the employee. If the employee refuses such a modification, the successor has the following choice: to maintain the employee's place of work or to dismiss him. In the second case, since the employee's refusal does not constitute a valid ground for dismissal, the successor will have to justify a real and serious economic cause of dismissal. However, in practice, this is often difficult given French requirements regarding the economic cause of a dismissal.

If the new place of work is located in the 'same geographical area', case law considers that this change is only a modification in the employee's conditions of employment. In this case, the employee cannot refuse this change, even if his/her employment contract does not include a mobility clause. Such refusal amounts to a gross fault and can lead to the employee's dismissal on personal grounds (Douai Court of Appeal, 22 September 2000; Supreme Court, 16 December 1998).

The main difficulty lies in the fact that case law does not provide for a definition of the 'geographical area' to be taken into account. Therefore, a case by case analysis is always required.

2. Relocation, but no business transfer

(a) **Assuming the move does NOT constitute a business transfer (because the business of Beta does not adequately retain its identity) but instead is deemed to be a straightforward relocation, are any of Beta's employees obliged or entitled to transfer?**

Answer

No, none of Beta's employees are obliged or entitled to transfer.

Legal reasoning

(1)   If the conditions set by art L 122–12 are not met, then the automatic transfer rule does not apply, and the successor is not obliged to take on any employees. This will be the case here, since art L 122–12 does not apply to cross-border transfers.

As a consequence, if the production employees at Beta cannot be redeployed, they will have to be dismissed for economic reasons due to the elimination of their jobs.

However, in order for such dismissals to be valid, Beta will have to do its utmost to redeploy the employees *before* notifying the dismissals. To this end, all redeployment alternatives will have to be sought within Beta's other activities (sales and marketing) and within the entire Alpha group, even abroad. In practice, this means that any relevant positions available within Gamma (which is also a subsidiary of Alpha) will have to be offered to these employees. It is only if they refuse such proposal, and if there are no other positions available, that they may be dismissed for economic reasons.

In any case, this restructuring process will have to be conducted in accordance with French requirements, in particular with respect to the information and consultation procedure with the works council (see *L1.7* and *L2.4* above).

(2)   It should be noted that when a transfer does not qualify as a business transfer according to art L 122–12 of the Labour Code, the successive employers may nonetheless agree on its conventional application. Note that under French law successive employers may, with each employee's consent, decide that art L 122–12 is applicable even when the conditions set for such application are not met. In this case,

the transfer of the employee's employment contract is not automatic and each employee must consent to the continuation of his/her employment contract with the successor.

(3) Finally, in certain sectors of activity, some collective agreements provide for the automatic transfer of the employment contracts to the successor even when the conditions set by art L 122–12 are not fulfilled.

(b) **If employees do nevertheless relocate, what will happen to their employment contracts? Will these continue, or will Gamma be entitled to provide new contracts?**

Answer

The employees' employment contracts may be amended, or Gamma may provide them with new contracts.

Legal reasoning

When the relocation does not qualify as a business transfer, but the parties nevertheless decide to apply art L 122–12 on a voluntary basis, the employment contracts should in theory be transferred as they stand to the successor. However, the transfer agreement may provide for overriding provisions and state that the employment contracts will be amended, or that some of their provisions will not transfer.

(c) **What will be the law applicable to the contracts of the employees who relocate?**

Answer

It will depend on the provisions of the employment contracts.

Legal reasoning

Since art L 122–12 does not apply to cross-border transfers, the employment contracts will only be transferred if (i) the parties agree upon such a transfer, or (ii) if they are transferred as a result of the employees' redeployment within the transferee (see response to question 2(a) above).

In this case, the parties will decide on the applicable law in the light of the principles set by the Rome Convention, that is to say:

- the law of their choice (with the limit provided by art 6.1 of the Rome Convention, which states that such a choice cannot result in depriving the employee of the protection afforded to him by the mandatory rules of the law which would be applicable in the absence of choice), or

- in the absence of choice, German law (the law of the country in which these employees will habitually carry out their work).

3. Dismissals

(a) Assuming that the move does constitute a business transfer:

(i) are any dismissals in connection with the transfer lawful?

As indicated above, under French law, this transaction would not entail the application of art L 122–12 related to business transfer, since this rule does not apply to cross-border transfers. Therefore, the contemplated transaction would not trigger an automatic transfer of the employees' employment contract to Gamma.

As a consequence, Beta would probably have to dismiss these employees on the grounds that their position has been eliminated. In this respect, in order for these dismissals to be lawful, Beta will have to be able to demonstrate that it had real and serious economic reasons justifying such dismissals and that no alternative positions could be offered to these employees either within Beta or within the Alpha group. Beta would also have to comply with the procedural requirements, especially those relating to the information and consultation of the staff representatives.

Assuming that the transfer would qualify as a business transfer under art L 122–12 (as would probably be the case if this transfer was to take place in France only), the employees' employment contracts would automatically be transferred to the successor, as a matter of public policy. In this case, any dismissal in connection with the transfer would be considered to be null and void. As a consequence, the employee could ask for the continuation of his contract, or the payment of damages.

(ii) what are the rights and remedies (including applicable law and appropriate jurisdiction) of any employees dismissed:

a. before the transfer?

Assuming that art L 122–12 would not be applicable to this cross-border transfer, the only action that could be lodged by the employees would consist in challenging their economic dismissal by Beta, on the basis that their employer did not comply with the provisions relating to economic dismissals (eg non-compliance with the dismissal procedure, lack of a real and serious economic cause, non-compliance with his redeployment obligation). In this case, they could claim damages for unfair dismissal. They would have no action against Gamma.

If art L 122–12 is applicable to this transaction, any economic dismissal notified in connection with the transfer would be null and void. In this case, the dismissed employee would have a 'right of option'. He could lodge a claim against the new employer (Gamma) to ask for the continuation of his employment contract *or* against his former employer (Beta) in order to obtain damages for wrongful dismissal.

b. after the transfer?

As before the transfer, assuming that art L 122–12 would not be applicable to this cross-border transfer, the only action that could be taken by the employees would consist in challenging their economic dismissal by Beta, on the basis that their employer did not comply with the provisions relating to economic dismissals. They could only claim damages for unfair dismissal. They would have no action against Gamma.

If art L 122–12 is applicable to this transaction, the employees' employment contracts would automatically transfer to the successor. However, art L 122–12 does not protect the employees from a dismissal by the successor. The application of art L 122–12 nevertheless has financial consequences in terms of severance indemnities. The successor must indeed honour the length of service acquired by the employees with their former company when calculating their legal entitlement.

(b) Would these rights and remedies change if this was not a business transfer?

If we consider that the transaction does not constitute a business transfer (which would be the case under French law, anyway), the employees could challenge their economic dismissal by Beta, contending that their employer did not comply with the provisions relating to economic dismissals (eg non-compliance with the dismissal procedure, lack of a real and serious economic cause, non-compliance with his redeployment obligation). In this case, they could claim damages for unfair dismissal.

4. European Works Council and other employees' representatives

(a) Will Alpha be required to inform and consult the European Works Council about the transfer or any redundancies?

Answer

Probably, depending on the European Works Council's by-laws.

Legal reasoning

The need to inform and/or consult with the European Works Council will basically depend on the contents of its by-laws. Indeed, the agreement implementing the European Works Council generally indicates which sorts of transactions (relocation, closure of business, collective redundancies etc) are likely to be discussed with it.

When the European Works Council has been implemented as per the subsidiary regime[1] (see the European Works Council Directive 94/45/EC and art L 439–12 of the Labour Code), the competence of the European Works Council covers information and consultation on matters of a transnational nature, ie involving several countries. The European Works Council's information and consultation rights include in particular all transnational issues relating to the structure, economic and financial situation, substantial changes concerning organisation, transfers of production, closures of undertakings, establishments or important parts thereof, and collective redundancies.

In the present case, the transaction will involve Beta (a French company) and Gamma (a German subsidiary of Alpha). It is thus of a transnational nature and will give rise to a discussion with the European Works Council. This procedure may be limited to simple information or further discussions (consultation) with the European Works Council. The scope of the European Works Council's rights will be determined by its by-laws or by the agreement that led to its implementation.

(b) **Are any other employee representatives required to be involved in the transfer or any redundancies (ie at national or local level)?**

Answer

Yes.

Legal reasoning

Beta's staff representatives (ie the works council or, if applicable, the Central Works Council (*Comité Central d'Entreprise*) and the Local Works Councils (*Comités d'Etablissement*)) will have to be informed and consulted on the proposed restructuring.

Indeed, according to art L 432–1 of the French Labour Code, the works council must be informed and consulted with on (i) any projects relating to the organisation or the running of the company, and especially on any measures that are likely to affect the number or the structure of the workforce, and on (ii) any modification of the company's economic or legal organisation (in particular, in case of divestment, merger etc).

Moreover, according to art L 321–4 of the French Labour Code, the works council must be informed and consulted prior to the implementation of economic dismissals. To this end, the works council members must be given written information on the proposed restructuring, which must be as detailed as possible to enable them to give an opinion on this project. Finally, sufficient time must be allowed for them to consider the project.

1　A subsidiary regime applies when the employer refuses to negotiate with the Special Negotiating Body or when no agreement between the employer and the Special Negotiating Body has been reached.

5. Collective agreements

What is the effect of the business transfer on any collective agreements affecting Beta's employees?

(1) Since the transfer of production to Gamma will not entail the application of art L 122–12, there will be no direct impact on collective agreements, which will not be transferred and will thus remain within Beta.

(2) If we were to assume that art L 122–12 is applicable to this transaction, the successor would have to comply with the following rules.

COLLECTIVE BARGAINING AGREEMENTS

With respect to agreements entered into with trade union representatives at national, regional and/or company level, according to the Labour Code, any collective bargaining agreements applicable at the time of a transfer of business subject to art L 122–12 are automatically 'terminated' by virtue of the transfer, and the collective agreements applicable by the transferee become immediately applicable. The former collective agreements will, however, continue to apply during a temporary 'survival period' of 15 months maximum after the effective transfer. During this period, the transferred employees would continue to benefit from the advantages provided by these agreements together with the collective agreement applicable within their new company (the benefits of both collective agreements do not cumulate, but the employees may choose, within the same category of benefits, those that are more favourable to them considered globally, in each of the collective agreements) (see *L1.4* above).

Meanwhile, the new employer would have to negotiate with the trade union representatives, in order to try to reach an agreement allowing for the harmonisation of the benefits and status of all its employees. If a so-called 'harmonisation agreement' is reached, the survival period would terminate immediately on the same date and the new provisions would become enforceable. If no agreement was reached at the end of the survival (15-month period), the collective agreements of the former employer would cease to apply. In this case, the transferred employees would only keep individual *acquired* benefits (such as a seniority bonus), which would be incorporated automatically as part of their employment contract.

IN-HOUSE CUSTOMS (*USAGES*) AND UNILATERAL COMMITMENTS BY THE EMPLOYER

According to case law, these would transferred automatically, and would thus be enforceable against the new employer. The new employer would, however, be able to initiate a procedure to terminate them.

6. Change of terms and conditions

(a) **If this is a business transfer, how can Gamma lawfully harmonise employment contracts and change the terms and conditions of the employees currently on the more generous Beta contracts of employment?**

(1) Under French law, since the transfer of production to Gamma will not qualify as a business transfer entailing the application of art L 122–12, the transfer of the employees' employment contracts will be subject to their prior agreement. Any amendment to their current employment contracts will thus result from the parties' negotiations, and nothing will prevent Gamma from proposing less generous provisions.

(2) If art L 122–12 is applicable to this transfer, the employment contracts would be transferred as they stand in accordance with the principles set by the ECJ. Consequently, Gamma would not be allowed to set a modification of the employment contracts as a condition for the contracts to be transferred.

However, *after the transfer*, the successor would be able to propose, like any other employer, a modification of the employees' employment contracts, provided that such proposal is not intended to by-pass the principle set by art L 122–12.

In this case, the proposal could be less favourable than the previous contractual provisions. It would have to be made in accordance with the general principles governing the amendment of employment contracts, in particular the prior agreement of the employee. Basically, this would require the signature of the employee to an amendment to his/her employment contract.

If the employee were to refuse the proposed modification, the employer would have the following choice: to keep the original employment contract or to dismiss the employee. However, when the employer chooses the second solution, he must demonstrate that the proposed modification is justified by a 'real and serious economic cause' which in practice is rather difficult under the French Labour Code. For example, it has been ruled that the economic dismissal notified to an employee further to his refusal to accept an amendment to his remuneration is abusive, as the employer was not able to demonstrate that the proposed modification was necessary to safeguard the company's competitiveness (Supreme Court, 25 June 1997).

Finally, it should be noted that if the successor were to contemplate the modification of at least 10 employment contracts, a job preservation plan would have to be implemented, which is a detailed process.

(b) **If this is a business transfer, can Gamma reduce the wages of the former Beta employees?**

The legal reasoning described under question 6(a) would also apply. Therefore, subject to the conditions set out above, Gamma would be able to reduce the wages of the former Beta employees, to the extent that the level of remuneration remained consistent with the provisions of the applicable collective bargaining agreements.

(c)   **If this is a business transfer, what will happen to the former Beta employees as regards their private pension arrangements?**

(1)   Since the transfer of production to Gamma will not entail the application of art L 122–12, employees will remain within Beta and, therefore, there will be no direct impact on their pension arrangements. Under French law, regular pensions are governed at a national level, under a specific regime, which is partially managed by the French government. Additional pension agreements may be allowed to certain employees on top of the legal and national pension regime. In the present situation, since art L 122–12 will not be applicable, the employee's employment contracts and associated pensions rights will remain with Beta, which will not be transferred and will thus remain within Beta.

(2)   If we were to assume that art L 122–12 is applicable to this transaction and, therefore, if the employees were to be transferred to Gamma, very specific rules would apply. Basically, in France, two pension schemes are provided to the employees: the basic scheme and the so-called complementary scheme. The basic scheme is governed at a national level and is thus not affected by business transfers. Employees' rights are kept *and follow them*. The complementary scheme is governed by very precise rules, which ensure the preservation of the employees' rights when a business transfer occurs.

Moreover, certain employees (top executives, senior managers etc) may also benefit from additional pension arrangements. The consequences of a business transfer on these types of arrangements must be analysed on a case by case basis, depending on the legal source and the contents of the arrangements.

(d)   **Is it easier to change terms and conditions of employment if the changes are made six months after the transfer?**

Answer

Assuming that art L 122–12 is applicable, it is not easier. However, it is recommended that a certain period of time should elapse between the transfer and any changes.

Legal reasoning

The amendment of the employment contracts cannot be a condition of the transfer and may only occur after the actual transfer. Therefore, as long as such amendment is subsequent to the transfer, there is no legal need for a 'cooling period' to be respected before proposing such modifications to the employees. However, such modifications must not be made with the intention of avoiding the application of art L 122–12 provisions. In practice, a major amendment of the employment contract occurring concurrently to or immediately after the transfer is thus rather questionable. For example, it has recently been ruled that a change in an employee's remuneration agreed on the date of the transfer is fraudulent (Supreme Court, 9 March 2004, *Parfus v CGEA d'Annecy*).

L3.3 Case study 3
(Outsourcing of an ancillary activity to a non-EU country)

A large multinational (ABC) based in France has decided to outsource its entire internal IT function to a third party provider in Romania, as the costs of hiring competent IT personnel in Romania are far lower than in France, largely because wages are so much lower. At present 200 employees are employed by ABC in its IT function in France. It is anticipated that exactly the same IT function will be required in Romania with approximately the same number of people required to run it. There will be no difference in the service or approach for those requiring IT assistance and even the internal telephone number will be automatically diverted. The Romanian third party provider has no assets or presence in France.

1. Business transfer

Will this be a business transfer within the scope of French law applying the ARD?

Answer

No.

Legal reasoning

In France, art L 122–12 of the Labour Code provides for an automatic transfer of the employees' employment contracts, 'wherever a change in the legal situation of the employer occurs, such as a successor in interest, sale, merger, transformation of the going business, or incorporation of the business'.

Under French law, a business transfer implies that the transferred activity is an 'autonomous economic entity', ie an economic entity with its own identity, which is continued as such after the transfer.

However, as indicated in *Case study 2* at *L3.2* above, it is essential to highlight that, so far, the transfer rule provided by art L 122–12 only applies to business transfers that take place in France. In fact, the current position of the French Supreme Court leads to a conclusion that this article does not apply to cross-border business transfers.

In this respect, the French Supreme Court ruled in a decision dated 5 April 1995, that a cross-border relocation does not result in the transfer of the employees' employment contracts. Indeed, in that case, the court concluded that the transfer of business to another country leads to the elimination of the employees' positions in France and therefore to their dismissal for economic reasons.

Conclusion

Therefore, the outsourcing of ABC's IT functions in Romania will not trigger the application of the French business transfer rules, but will instead result in the elimination of the French employees' jobs.

2. Effect on employees

(a) **What will happen to the employees currently employed in the IT function at ABC? Will they transfer across?**

Answer

No.

Legal reasoning

As per the legal reasoning stated in question **1** above, their positions within ABC will be eliminated as a result of this outsourcing. Therefore, ABC will have to do its utmost to redeploy these employees either in France or abroad (since ABC is a multinational company). If no alternative positions can be proposed to them, ABC will have to follow a dismissal procedure for economic reasons.

In order for these dismissals to be valid, ABC will have to demonstrate that it has a real and serious economic reason justifying the dismissals. This means that ABC will have to demonstrate one of the following:

- That it is in economic difficulties. In order for these difficulties to qualify as a valid ground for dismissal, they must be real and sufficiently serious at the time the dismissal takes place. These difficulties must be assessed on a company level or, when the company belongs to a group, at the level of its sector of activity. In the case of a worldwide group, all companies belonging to the same sector of activity, even those located abroad must be taken into consideration to assess the financial difficulties.

- That the elimination of these positions is necessary for the company to safeguard its competitiveness. When a company belongs to a group, the need to safeguard the competitiveness must be assessed at the level of the sector of activity of the group both on the French market and abroad.

(b) **If the employees do transfer, what will the applicable law be for their employment contracts with the third party provider? Where can they make any claims?**

Since art L 122–12 will not be applicable to this transaction, if employees do transfer to Romania, it will necessarily be on a voluntary basis. Therefore, the applicable law will basically depend on the parties' decision: they may decide that French law will continue to be applicable or they may enter into a new contract governed by Romanian law.

If these employees have claims against ABC concerning their former employment contracts, they will have to bring their claims before the relevant French industrial tribunal.

In theory, all claims related to their new relationship with the Romanian provider will be governed by Romanian law.

3. Data protection

Will there be special data protection issues on the transfer of knowledge and information outside France to Romania?

The French 1978 Act has recently been modified (Act of 7 August 2004) to comply with EC Directive 95/46/EC on the protection of individuals with regard to the processing of personal data and on the free movement of such data. Article 69 of the 1978 Act implements into French law art 26 of the Directive. Under those texts, the cross-border transfer of personal data to countries which do not ensure an adequate level of protection is prohibited unless the data subject has given his express consent.

Romania is not a member state of the EU. Therefore, it will be necessary to be certain that it ensures an adequate level of protection. If Romania does not ensure such protection, prior agreement to the transfer must be obtained from the data subjects.

4. Transfer to India

Please comment on any differences there would be to your answers if the function was transferred to India rather than Romania.

There would be no differences to the answers above.

L4 Additional information

L4.1 Appendix

The following is a tentative calendar applicable in the case of a dismissal of 10 to 100 employees, in a company with a Central Works Council ('CCE') and a local works council ('CE'), with the employees' representatives[1] appointing an expert[2], subject to overriding provisions set by the applicable collective bargaining agreement.

- Depending on the facts: information and consultation of the European Works Council and/or of the Group Works Council (according to the timeframe provided by their by-laws).
- Drafting of a memorandum detailing the economic and financial reasons for the contemplated reorganisation and, if appropriate, the drafting of a Job Preservation Plan.
- Search for alternative positions within the company and the group (in France and abroad).

Day	• Convocation of the CCE/CE to the first information/consultation meeting on (i) the reorganisation project (*Livre IV* of the Labour Code) and the economic/financial reasons thereof and (ii) on the contemplated dismissals (*Livre III* of the Labour Code)[3].
	• The following documents must be communicated by the employer:
	– agenda for the first meeting;
	– memorandum detailing in particular: (i) the economic and financial reasons for the contemplated reorganisation, (ii) the grounds justifying the dismissals, (iii) the professional categories likely to be impacted by the restructuring, (iv) the selection criteria to be used to determine the employees to be dismissed, (v) the expected calendar for the implementation of the restructuring;
	– first draft of the contemplated Job Preservation Plan, which must provide for measures aiming at the employees' redeployment.
	• A copy of the above documents must be sent by registered mail to the competent Labour Administration ('DDTE').
D + 15[4]	• First information/consultation meeting with the CCE/CE on (i) the reorganisation project (*Livre IV* of the Labour Code) and (ii) on the contemplated dismissals (*Livre III* of the Labour Code).
	• Designation of an Expert by the CCE/CE.
D + 16 (at the earliest)	• Notification of the dismissal project to the DDTE.
	• Information of the DDTE on the nomination of an Expert Accountant, and on the date scheduled for the second meeting with the CCE/CE.
	• Request to the Unemployment Fund for *Pré-Pare* forms[5].
D + 20	Convocation of the CCE/CE to a second meeting on the reorganisation and the contemplated dismissals.

D + 35[6]	<ul><li>Second meeting with CCE/CE on (i) the reorganisation (*Livre IV*) and (ii) on the contemplated dismissals (*Livre III* of the Labour Code).</li><li>Presentation by the expert accountant of his report.</li><li>Motivated answers by the employer to the observations and suggestions made by the CCE/CE and, if applicable, to the alternative reorganisation proposals communicated by the CCE/CE.</li></ul>
D + 36	<ul><li>Convocation of the CCE/CE to the third information/consultation meeting.</li><li>Information to the DDTE on the date scheduled for the third meeting with the CCE/CE.</li></ul>
D + 49[7]	<ul><li>Third information and consultation meeting with the CCE/CE on (i) the reorganisation (*Livre IV*) and (ii) on the contemplated dismissals (*Livre III* of the Labour Code).</li><li>In-depth examination of the Job Preservation Plan.</li><li>CCE/CE gives its formal opinions both on the economic reasons for the dismissal *and* the draft Job Preservation Plan.</li></ul>
D + 50	<ul><li>Notification of the minutes to the DDTE together with the list of employees whose dismissal is contemplated + any amendments made to the documents previously sent.</li><li>Individual information given to non-protected employees relating to (i) redeployment leave (*congé de reclassement*) and (ii) the *Pré-Pare* programme (see *L2.2*).</li><li>Notification of individual redeployment/outplacement offers, allowing the employee a reasonable delay to apply for alternative positions (usually 15 days).</li></ul>
D + 57[8]	End of the checking period allowed to the DDTE as per art L 321–7 al 4 of the Labour Code.
D + 65	Last day for the employees to accept an alternative position (when a 15-day thinking period has been allowed to them).

D + 66[9] (at the earliest)	Notification of dismissals (registered letter with acknowledgment of receipt) sent to those employees who could not be deployed within the company or the group. Proposal of redeployment leaves (*congés de reclassement*) and *Pré-Pare* programmes. Information about the rehiring priority (the letter must indicate to the employee that s/he has a right to be hired for any position suiting his/her skills, made available in the company).
D + 75	Last day for the employee to apply for redeployment leave.
D + 75 + 4–9 months	End of the redeployment leaves.
D + 67 + 12 months	End of employees' rehiring priority.
	Follow-up of the Job Preservation Plan (information of the works council on a regular basis).

1   This draft timetable does not take into account the litigation procedures that may be initiated by the employee representatives.

2   This draft timetable does not include the specific procedure applicable to 'protected employees'. This specific procedure implies in particular: (i) a pre-dismissal meeting, (ii) the prior consultation of the works council and (iii) the prior authorisation of the labour inspector.

3   This draft timetable provides for the information and consultation of the staff representatives both on the restructuring and on the dismissal plan (simultaneously). However, under certain circumstances, the company may prefer conducting a separate consultation process on the restructuring project, before starting the consultation on the dismissal plan.

4   The Labour Code provides for a specific interval between the convocation (calling of the meeting) and the meeting (three days for the CE and eight days for the CEE). However, in order to allow sufficient time for the CCE/CE to review the documents, a 15-day delay is common.

5   The *Pré-Pare* programme is a redeployment programme implemented by the French Unemployment Fund. In order for the dismissed employees to benefit from this programme, the employer must provide them with a specific application form.

6   The second meeting must take place between 20 and 22 days after the first meeting.

7   Where the restructuring involves less than 100 dismissals, the third meeting must take place, at the latest, 14 days after the second meeting.

8   Plus 21 days (starting the day after the second meeting with the CCE/CE).

9   44 days at the earliest after the notification to the DDTE of the dismissal plan and, in any case, after the end of the thinking period allowed to the employee to accept an alternative job.

10   Eight days from the reception of the dismissal letter.

M Germany

Dr Barbara Bittmann
Astrid Wellhöner, LLM Eur
Dr Wolfgang Schmiedl

MI Business transfers

MI.I Background

General comments

Even before the first European Directive on business transfers in 1977 there was a statutory provision in the Federal Republic of Germany, the purpose of which was to protect employees in the event of a change in the ownership of a business. Section 613A of the German Civil Code is still the central employment law provision applicable to business transfers. The provision has, however, been amended on several occasions since its introduction in 1972 during the transposition of EC directives on business transfers. Where the transfer of a business or part of a business takes place by way of merger, spin-off or transfer of assets as a whole or a part thereof (unlike the classical transfer of individual assets, 'asset deal'), and thereby by way of a universal legal succession (*Gesamtrechtsnachfolge*), the provisions of the Reorganisation Act (*Umwandlungsgesetz*) also apply. The Works Council Constitution Act (*Betriebsverfassungsgesetz*) is also often of particular importance to a company restructuring. It contains extensive information and participation rights for the works council, should one exist.

Relationship between European Community law and German law

European Union directives, including the Directives on business transfers of 1977, 1998 and 2001, do not have direct and mandatory effect in the member states, but must be transposed into the national laws in order to have effect both for and against their citizens, and the companies registered therein. All three Directives on business transfers were transposed by the German legislator. In addition, the principle of interpretation in line with directives applies. Particular significance is attributed to the decisions of the European Court of Justice in this respect.

Jurisdictional issues

Employment law in Germany is standardised to a large extent. Only very few areas are regulated differently in the individual Federal States. This standardised employment law (including s 613A of the German Civil Code) also applies to transfers of businesses and parts of a business; the special regulations for the new Federal States (former GDR) expired on 31 December 1998. However, there can be regional differences, in particular if the rights and obligations arising from the employment relationship are regulated by collective bargaining agreements. Collective bargaining agreements are widely used in Germany. Most collective bargaining agreements are not only applied in a specific field, but also in a specific territory described further in the collective bargaining agreement.

Where the facts show links to the law of another state, perhaps because the business is sold to a foreign company and is relocated abroad, the question is raised as to which law applies to the transfer of a business or part of a business. Which national law is invoked is decided through the German provisions of international private law. German international private law is codified to a large extent by the Introductory Law to the German Civil Code (*Einführungsgesetz zum Bürgerlichen Gesetzbuch*), which adopted the EC Treaty of 19 June 1980 on the law applicable to contractual obligations ('EC Contractual Obligations Treaty').

In principle, the employer and the employee are free to decide which law will apply to the employment contract (principle of free choice of law)[1]. However, there is an important restriction to this principle. The choice of law must not lead to a situation where the employee loses the mandatory protection which he would be afforded by statute under the applicable jurisdiction in the absence of a choice of law[2]. In the absence of a choice of law, the law of the state in which the employee usually fulfils his employment contract applies, even if he is sent to another state temporarily[3]. If the employment relationship is characterised by the fact that the employee usually works in several states (eg flight attendant), the location of the branch which employs the employee determines the applicable state law[4]. However, this does not apply if, seen as a whole, the employment relationship has closer associations with another state, in which case the law of that state will apply.

The question of the applicable law requires special attention in the case of the cross-border transfer of a business. The Federal Employment Court (*Bundesarbeitsgericht*)[5] has decided that the applicable law in a cross-border transfer of a business is that which governs the employment relationship itself. It does not depend on the registered place of the business sold or the law governing the agreement between the former and the new owner (eg company purchase agreement). This case law corresponds to prevalent legal opinion. Therefore, unless there is a provision in the contract to the contrary, generally speaking, the law of the state in which the employee usually works will apply.

The following points remain very much unclear:

–   the extent to which the relocation of a business or part of a business abroad influences whether this constitutes a business (or part of a business) transfer within the meaning of s 613A of the German Civil Code[6];

–   what consequences a business (or a part business) transfer has, and in particular whether the employee is obliged to continue his employment at the new location, and what measures the employer can take in this respect[7];

– whether the employee can be dismissed[8];

– whether in the event of continued employment the law which applied to the former employment relationship continues to apply[9];

– the effects of the cross-border relocation on existing collective bargaining agreements and works agreements, and the activity of any works council[10].

1   Article 27(1) of the Introductory Law to the German Civil Code.
2   Article 30(1) of the Introductory Law to the German Civil Code.
3   Article 30(2) no 1 of the Introductory Law to the German Civil Code.
4   Article 30(2) no 2 of the Introductory Law to the German Civil Code.
5   Federal Employment Court of 29 October 1992, DB 1993, 743.
6   See *M1.2* below.
7   See *M1.6* below.
8   See *M1.5* below.
9   See *M1.4* below.
10 See *M1.4* and *M1.6*.

M1.2 Identifying a relevant transfer

Change of ownership

Only the legal consequences of a transfer of a business or part of a business are regulated by s 613A of the German Civil Code. The prerequisites are set by case law. The first prerequisite for a transfer of a business or part of a business is a change in its ownership. There must, therefore, be a change in the entity which has organisational and managerial control of employment matters. Where the legal form of an owner of a business changes, or where the shareholders change, this does not constitute a 'change of ownership'.

Transfer of an economic unit

In 1997, the Federal Employment Court radically changed the prerequisites for the transfer of a business or part of a business. Until then, the main factor was whether the purchaser had assumed the significant material and/or immaterial operational means of a business or part of a business. The European Court of Justice, on the other hand, has always placed the term 'economic unit' (which must be transferred whilst retaining its identity) in the foreground. When assessing this issue, all of the facts characterising the procedure concerned must be taken into account[1]. The Federal Employment Court adopted the case law of the European Court of Justice for the first time on 22 May 1997[2].

An economic unit is characterised as an independent, definable organised unit. When reviewing whether the economic unit being transferred has retained its identity, the European Court of Justice and the Federal Employment Court, in accordance with current case law, must consider the following seven criteria established by the European Court of Justice in *Spijkers v Gebroeders Benedik Abattoir CV*: 24/85 [1986] 2 CMLR 296, ECJ:

– the type of company or business concerned;

– whether or not material operating means (eg buildings, machines, raw materials) are transferred;

– the value of the immaterial operating means, such as know-how and the existence of intellectual property rights existing at the time of transfer;

– whether or not the core personnel are assumed by the new owner;

– whether or not the customers are transferred;

– the degree of similarity between the activity carried out before and after the transfer;

– the duration of any interruption of activity.

The above list is not exhaustive (eg the question of whether any existing employment organisation or operating methods are assumed can also be of assistance).

1   Current case law of the European Court of Justice since *Spijkers v Gebroeders Benedik Abattoir CV*: 24/85 [1986] 2 CMLR 296, ECJ.
2   Federal Employment Court of 22 May 1997, NZA 1997, 1050.

The difference between pure functional succession and a business transfer

Following the *Christel Schmidt* decision of the European Court of Justice in 1994[1], it was feared that the continuation of the activity (functional succession) was sufficient to constitute a business transfer. Since then, however, both the European Court of Justice and the Federal Employment Court have made it clear that further criteria must be satisfied, regarding the assumption of significant operating means, the employment organisation, the working methods and/or a significant proportion of the personnel[2].

1   C-392/92: *Schmidt v Spar und Leihkasse der früheren Ämter Bordesholm, Kiel und Cronshagen* [1994] ECR I-1311, ECJ.
2   For example, C-13/95: *Süzen v Zehnacker Gebäudereinigung GmbH Krankenhausservice* [1997] ECR I-1259, ECJ.

The difference between closure of business and a business transfer

The difference between a business transfer and a closure of business is of particular significance. In a business transfer, the employees are transferred; upon the closure of business their employment can usually be terminated for operational reasons. A business transfer requires the actual continuation of the operational activities and is precluded by a considerable interruption thereof. Furthermore, a closure requires both a serious and final decision on behalf of the employer, ie the business or part of the business concerned is to be abandoned for an undetermined, but not economically inconsiderable, period of time, and the closure must have already taken on a tangible form.

Relocation of the business

Relocations, even those abroad, can constitute a business (or part business) transfer under s 613A of the German Civil Code, though some local courts have even held that a substantial relocation can lead to the loss of the economic unit's identity, with the effect that this does not constitute a business transfer[1]. However, these decisions are not consistent with the case law of the Federal Employment Court[2]. A review as to whether a transfer of business or part of a business constitutes a business transfer must be based upon a consistent set of criteria.

Whether the purchaser assumes a significant proportion of the personnel is of particular importance. The Federal Employment Court held in 1987, prior to a number of radical changes in case law, that where a significant number of the employees is not prepared to relocate, this will not be a business transfer[3]. On the basis of this decision, it is sometimes concluded that business relocations abroad mostly constitute a closure of business rather than a business transfer, since normally – with the exception of relocation near a border – the majority of the personnel will not be prepared to move as required. This goes too far, however. Rather, each case should be viewed on its individual facts.

1   See Nuremberg Regional Employment Court of 26 August 1996, 7 Sa 981/95; LAGE German Civil Code, s 613A(51) (distance of 25 km); and Cologne Regional Employment Court of 12 June 1997, 5 Sa 362/97 (distance of more than 200 km).
2   Federal Employment Court of 20 April 1989 (relocation from Berlin to Lyon, France), DB 1989, 2334; also Frankfurt Regional Employment Court of 27 February 2003, 11 Sa 799/02 (possible relocation from a town near the Austrian border to Austria); c f also Berlin Regional Employment Court of 18 September 1998, 6 Sa 53/98 (possible relocation 80 km away in the Czech Republic).
3   Federal Employment Court of 12 February 1987, AP No 67 on s 613A of the German Civil Code; also Düsseldorf Regional Employment Court of 16 February 1995, NZA-RR 1996, 241 (possible relocation to England).

Transfer by means of legal transaction

A business (or part business) transfer within the meaning of s 613A of the German Civil Code does not only apply to the classic transfer of assets (asset deal). Rather, a merger, spin-off or transfer of assets as a whole or in part in accordance with the Reorganisation Act (*Umwandlungsgesetz*) can also be a (part) business transfer. This has been recognised for some time by the courts and has now been clarified again by the legislator[1]. The legal nature of the agreement is insignificant where its aim is to transfer a functioning business or part of a business. This applies equally to purchase and lease agreements as well as to gifts, legacies, articles of association and partnership agreements.

1   Section 324 of the Reorganisation Act (*Umwandlungsgesetz*).

M1.3 Affected employees

General comments

Section 613A of the German Civil Code applies to all employment relation-ships existing at the time of the business transfer. The provision also applies to key employees, though not to members of corporate bodies, eg directors (*Geschäftsführer*) of limited liability companies (*Gesellschaften mit beschränkter Haftung*), or directors (*Vorstände*) of stock corporations (*Aktiengesellschaften*). It does not apply to freelance workers, service workers or commercial agents either.

If the employment relationship has already ended prior to the business transfer, s 613A will not apply. The purchaser will not therefore have to fulfil the pension claims of employees who retired before the business transfer.

In the case of hiring out employees, it must be determined whether the hirer has the official permit which is usually required[1]. If the hirer does not have the required official permit, an employment relationship between the employee hired out and the borrowing party is implied by law[2], with the consequence that the employment relationship is affected by a business transfer of the company at which the temporary employee is currently working. If the hirer has the required official permit, the employment relationship remains unaffected.

1   Section 1 of the Temporary Employment Act (*Arbeitnehmerüberlassungsgesetz*).
2   Temporary Employment Act, s 10.

Allocation of the employees

If the prerequisites for a business (or part business) transfer are fulfilled, the employment relationships of the affected employees will be transferred to the business or part business in question. Allocation can be difficult if a company is only selling one of several businesses, or only one part of a business. This applies, in particular, to employees who work in several parts of a business and to 'overhead functions' such as personnel, IT and accounting. The Federal Employment Court has held that, where an employee works for several businesses or parts of a business, it depends, first and foremost, on the wishes of those concerned. Alternatively, the key focus or main emphasis of the activity is the decisive factor.

M1.4 Effects of the transfer

General comments

Where a business or part of a business is transferred within the meaning of s 613A of the German Civil Code, the employment relationships of the personnel allocated to the business or part of a business are transferred to the purchaser by operation of law. The employment relationship is transferred while retaining all rights and obligations[1]. The length of service of the employee at the vendor is retained in his relationship with the purchaser. As a result of the transfer of the business or part of the business, the purchaser takes the place of the former employer, and is liable for all claims of the employee arising from the employment relationship.

In cross-border business transfers which include a relocation of the business, it must be established whether the law which applies to the existing employment relationship will continue to apply in future, or whether the domestic law of the new business location will apply. It is predominantly held that an employee should be able to rely on the law that was applicable on the signing of his employment contract continuing throughout the duration of his employment[2], and in particular with regard to the issue of any notices of termination (*Beendigungskündigungen*) and of any notices of termination pending a change of contract (*Änderungskündigungen*) which are not 'due to the transfer of business' but are connected therewith. However, where there has been a long-term unconditional employment at the foreign business location (as opposed to an unconditional commencement of work), it is implied that the employee is subjecting himself to the law of the new business location and accepts the foreign jurisdiction. The Federal Employment Court has not yet clarified this.

As far as the rights and obligations under the German Works Council Constitution Act (*Betriebsverfassungsgesetz*) are concerned, it has been decided that the Act will not apply to a business which is now located abroad. The principle of territoriality applies, under which Works Council Constitution Act issues are judged, in principle, by the law of the location in which the business is situated[3]. The same must apply to the provisions of employment protection (eg maternity leave, youth work protection, risk protection, maximum working hours regulation)[4]. Unless the respective collective bargaining agreement states to the contrary, the local law governing the employment to which the employment relationship and collective bargaining agreement relates will also apply to future collective bargaining agreements[5]. This remains a disputed topic, though an often-neglected one.

A business (or part business) transfer does not completely release the former employer from liability. Rather, he is jointly and severally liable with the new owner for all claims which arose prior to the transfer of the business or part of the business and which became due within one year[6]. However, the former employer is the sole liable party vis-à-vis all employees who left the company before the business transfer, for example, with respect to the fulfilment of pension obligations.

1   German Civil Code, s 613A(1).

2   Leuchten, FA 2002, 138; Kreitner, Anmerkung zu BAG of 20 April 1989, AP No 81 on s 613A of the German Civil Code; also Feudner, NZA 1999, 1184 with further proof.

3   Feudner, NZA 1999, 1184; Staudinger-Magnus, German Civil Code, 2002, art 30 margin no 265.

4   See Feudner, NZA 1999, 1184 with further proof.

5   Staudinger-Magnus, German Civil Code, 2002, art 30 margin no 251 et seq.

6   German Civil Code, s 613A(2).

Effects of the business transfer on collective bargaining agreements

Numerous rights and obligations between employer and employee are regulated in practice by collective bargaining agreements. A collective bargaining agreement is an agreement between one or more trade unions and an employers' association ('association collective bargaining agreement') or with an individual employer ('in-house collective bargaining agreement').

To the extent that collective bargaining agreements contain legal norms which concern the content, conclusion or termination of employment relationships, they apply directly, and with mandatory effect, to all employers and employees bound by the collective bargaining agreement and who fall within its scope of application[1]. The members of the parties to the collective bargaining agreement (ie the employers' association and the trade union) are bound by the collective bargaining agreement and, in addition, so is every employer who enters a collective bargaining agreement[2]. The territorial, professional and personal scope of application of a collective bargaining agreement is determined by the individual agreement. Furthermore, the German Minister for the Economy and Employment may declare a collective bargaining agreement to be generally binding[3]. Generally binding collective bargaining agreements apply, within their scope of application, directly and with mandatory effect to all, regardless of whether they are members of a respective party to the agreement. Furthermore, in employment contracts there are often clauses which declare certain collective bargaining agreements applicable.

Collective bargaining agreement provisions (in addition to provisions in works agreements – see below) can continue to apply in two ways after the transfer of a business or part of a business: on a collective level (ie as legal norms of a collective bargaining agreement with their associated peculiarities regulated in the Collective Bargaining Agreements Act) or, by virtue of transformations, on an individual level (ie as an integral part of the individual employment contract). In the latter case, in principle, nothing more applies to the (former) provisions of the collective bargaining agreement than to other individual provisions of the employment contract. The type of continued application is of particular importance in relation to the extent to which an amendment to the corresponding provisions is permissible after a business (or part business) transfer.

With respect to the effects of a business (or part business) transfer on rights arising from collective bargaining agreements, it is necessary to distinguish between the type of transfer and the basis on which the collective bargaining agreements were applied at the vendor. The associated questions are very complex and cannot be dealt with further here. In the case of a cross-border transfer of business, if the business is simultaneously relocated abroad, the collective bargaining agreement provisions do not usually continue to apply on a collective level, but become an integral part of the individual employment contract[4].

1   Section 4 of the Collective Bargaining Agreements Act (*Tarifvertragsgesetz*).

2   Collective Bargaining Agreements Act, s 3.
3   Collective Bargaining Agreements Act, s 5.
4   Also Feudner, NZA 1999, 1184 with further proof.

Effects of the transfer of business on works agreements

In addition to collective bargaining agreements, works agreements can regulate the legal relationship between employer and employee. A works agreement is an agreement between the employer and the works council. Like collective bargaining agreements, works agreements have direct and mandatory application[1]. Works agreements apply, in principle, to all employees of the respective business to the extent that the works agreement does not determine otherwise. Key employees and members of corporate bodies are excepted, however[2].

The implications of a business (or part business) transfer on the rights arising from a works agreement are very complex and cannot be dealt with further here. Unlike in the case of rights under a collective bargaining agreement, the type of business (or part business) transfer is not significant. The decisive factor is rather whether the business identity is essentially retained. Again, a notional distinction must be made between continued application on a collective level and continued application on an individual level.

It is still very unclear whether, in a cross-border business transfer, it is possible to continue to apply works agreements on a collective level, or whether – as is usual in the case of collective bargaining agreement provisions – corresponding provisions can be assumed by the individual employment contracts. In principle, the German Works Council Constitution Act, in accordance with the principle of territoriality, stops at Germany's borders. However, it is conceivable that works agreements will continue to apply abroad in accordance with the local co-determination law, to the extent that the country recognises co-determination[3]. In this case, the foreign law will require a statutory instrument which corresponds to that of the German works agreement.

1   Section 77(4) of the Works Council Constitution Act (*Betriebsverfassungsgesetz*).
2   See Works Council Constitution Act, s 5.
3   Feudner, NZA 1999, 1184.

Effects on the activity of the works council

The following applies under the German Works Council Constitution Act as far as the legality of the works council is concerned: where the whole business is transferred, in principle, any existing works council remains in office, though this does not apply if a completely hived-off business is integrated into the business of the purchaser. In such cases, the (former) works council only has a 'remaining mandate' which entitles it to carry out those tasks which are associated with the dissolution of the business as a consequence of the integration[1]. These include, in particular, negotiations regarding a so-called Reconciliation of Interests and Social Plan.

If, on the other hand, only a part of a business is transferred, the former works council will remain in office to its full extent for a transitional period ('interim mandate')[2]. It therefore continues to be responsible for a certain period of time for all co-determination matters, as before, which concern the parts of the business which had been previously allocated to it. There is such an interim mandate except where the part business is integrated into a business of the purchaser for which there is already a works council. It ends as soon as a new works council is elected for the transferred part of the business, or after the expiry of six months, unless this period is extended.

According to the principle of territoriality which determines the scope of the German Works Council Constitution Act, the works council loses its office in the event that the business or part of a business is relocated abroad without an interim mandate[3]. Where relocation abroad takes place before the conclusion of a Social Plan, the works council is probably still entitled to negotiate according to the remaining mandate.

1   Works Council Constitution Act, s 21B.
2   Works Council Constitution Act, s 21A.
3   Feudner, NZA 1999, 1189.

Right to object

The transfer of the employees to the purchaser takes place by operation of law without the consent of the employees being required. However, over and above the European specifications, the employee does have the right to object to the transfer of his employment relationship[1]. The objection must be made in writing, and within one month of receipt of notification, which the former employer or the purchaser of the business or part business is obliged to make[2]. German legislation has gone beyond the European specifications, and requires each individual employee to be informed in writing prior to the business transfer[3]. Since 1 April 2002, employees affected by a business (or part business) transfer must be informed of the following aspects of the transaction by their employers:

–   the date or planned date of the transfer;

–   the reason for the transfer;

–   the legal, economic and social ramifications of the transfer for the employees; and

–   the prospective measures to be taken with respect to the employees.

The deadline for objection declarations from the employees against the business (or part business) transfer will only begin to run once the employees have been properly and fully informed.

1   German Civil Code, s 613A(6).
2   German Civil Code, s 613A(5).
3   German Civil Code, s 613A(5).

MI.5 Dismissal of employees

General comments

Unlawful dismissals are invalid. In the event of an unlawful dismissal, the employee can demand that he continues to be employed, and is not restricted to claiming for compensation or similar. He cannot, however, unrestrictedly invoke the invalidity of his dismissal. Rather, he is obliged to file a claim at the Employment Court within three weeks of receipt of the written notice of dismissal[1]. Otherwise the dismissal will be deemed valid.

1   Section 4 of the Protection against Dismissal Act (*Kündigungsschutzgesetz*).

Prohibition of dismissal on account of the transfer of business

The law prohibits all dismissals 'on account of the business (or part business) transfer', irrespective of whether they are issued by the former employer or the new owner. Employees cannot, therefore, be dismissed on the ground that the purchaser is only assuming the business in a trimmed down form. Employees can be dismissed on other grounds, however[1], eg those that are personal or conduct-related or which relate to operational requirements other than the business transfer as such (eg relocation, reorganisation of the business, rationalisation measures).

1   German Civil Code, s 613A(4).

MI.6 Harmonisation and variation of contract

General comments

Various mechanisms can be employed to transfer former employment conditions after a restructuring. These various mechanisms can cause different employment conditions to apply. As far as the rights and obligations arising from works agreements and collective bargaining agreements are concerned, there will be some harmonisation by operation of law, subject to certain preconditions, where corresponding regulations apply to the purchaser. To a certain extent, the new owner can also take various measures to create harmonisation. It is often incorrectly assumed in practice that no amendments at all may be made to the detriment of the employees during the first year after the business (or part business) transfer. The one-year period only applies to those provisions which were components of a collective bargaining agreement or a works agreement, and became components of the individual employment contracts as a result of the business (or part business) transfer[1]. In addition, there are several exceptions to this principle[2].

1   German Civil Code, s 613A(1), sentence 2.
2   German Civil Code, s 613A(1), sentences 3 and 4.

Statutory harmonisation

In principle, rights and obligations arising from works agreements and collective bargaining agreements, which have been transformed into provisions of the individual employment contracts, can be altered even within one year of the business transfer to the extent that they are regulated at the purchaser by legal norms in another collective bargaining agreement or works agreement[1]. This is not only true of agreements which exist at the purchaser at the time of the business transfer, but also applies to those concluded after the transfer. However, according to the Federal Employment Court, a collective bargaining agreement with the purchaser only prevails if both parties (ie the assumed employees and the purchaser itself) are bound by the collective bargaining agreement. Either the collective bargaining agreement is binding by virtue of the purchaser's membership of the respective employers' association, or by virtue of a generally binding declaration by the German Minister for the Economy and Employment, or the employer itself is a party to the collective bargaining agreement.

The extent to which foreign collective agreements can replace rights and obligations transformed into provisions of the individual contracts is still very unclear. In principle, there is nothing to suggest that this is not possible. However, the precondition must be that the foreign collective agreement is comparable in its function to a German collective bargaining agreement or a German works agreement[2].

Special principles apply to works pension schemes because of the necessity to observe rules relating to the protection of confidence.

1   German Civil Code, s 613A(1), sentence 3.
2   Also Feudner, NZA 1999, 1184 (for collective bargaining agreements).

Harmonisation through works agreements or in-house collective bargaining agreements

To the extent that German works council constitution law and German collective bargaining law apply, the following is true.

Works agreements are only suitable for the harmonisation of employment conditions subject to certain preconditions. To the extent that employees are entitled to rights arising from a works agreement, these rights can be withdrawn in accordance with general rules. Therefore, in the case of continued application of the former works agreement on a collective level, the existing works agreements can be terminated or cancelled by mutual agreement with the works council. Alternatively, new works agreements can be entered into to replace the former works agreements with which employment conditions are harmonised. Again, special rules apply to works pension schemes. Furthermore, to the extent that employees have been granted rights in their employment contract, the so-called favourability principle applies: this means that a works agreement can only suppress those individual clauses which are less favourable to the employee. With respect to rights and obligations regulated at the vendor in collective bargaining agreements and/or works agreements, and which were transformed as a result of the transfer of business, the favourability principle does not apply.

Harmonisation of employment conditions can, in certain circumstances, also be achieved through an in-house collective bargaining agreement. With regard to the individual employment contract, only harmonisation 'for the better' is possible (due to the favourability principle)[1], except where the rights and obligations were regulated at the vendor in collective bargaining agreements and/or works agreements and were transformed as a result of the business transfer.

1   Collective Bargaining Agreements Act, s 4(3).

Negative company practice

Claims which have resulted from company practice at the former owner also transfer to the purchaser. According to recent decisions of the Federal Employment Court (*Bundesarbeitsgericht*), a company practice can be cancelled by a contrary, new, less favourable company practice for the employees. The precondition for this is that the employer does not make a payment, which it has made in the past on the basis of company practice, at least three times and thereby communicates to the employees that it no longer feels bound by its obligation to make the payment. The employees concerned may not have objected to this changed practice. The cancellation of existing rights through a negative company practice is in practice, therefore, difficult to enforce.

Amending a contract

Harmonisation of differing employment conditions can, in principle, also be achieved through amending contracts with the individual employees. The employees affected by the planned amendment must, however, consent to it. Section 613A of the German Civil Code also has the purpose of protecting employees from amended contracts that are less favourable. These will be invalid if the amendment is made within the framework of a business transfer, and provided the less favourable employment condition is without objective grounds (eg for the purpose of maintaining jobs). The Federal Employment Court sets very strict standards in this respect.

It must also be noted that rights resulting from the continued application of a works agreement on a collective level may only be waived with the consent of the works council[1]. If the rights arising from works agreements continue to apply on an individual level, they can only be amended after the expiry of one year from the date of the business transfer by way of amending a contract to the detriment of the employee[2]. A similar situation applies to collective bargaining agreements. To the extent that rights and obligations arising from continued application of a collective bargaining agreement on a collective level are to be changed, only an amendment 'for the better' is permissible, as departures from collective bargaining agreements must not be to the employee's disadvantage[3]. With regard to rights and obligations arising from a collective bargaining agreement which continue to apply on an individual level, the one-year amendment ban (mentioned above) applies.

If the business (or part business) transfer is accompanied by a relocation of the business or part business abroad, an amendment to the employment contract with respect to the location where the employee is to provide his services is usually necessary. Many employment contracts contain a provision according to which the employee is only employed in a particular location, ie the location of the company or branch. This may also arise from the facts. However, even without such a provision, relocation abroad is, in principle, not possible without the consent of the employee. This applies even if the employment contract expressly provides that the employee can be transferred to another location. The relocation in this case is restricted to the Federal Republic of Germany. Provisions in employment contracts which expressly provide for relocation abroad are rare, and usually only apply to managerial staff of international groups. Where the employee does not consent, even implicitly (eg by unreservedly commencing work at a new location), to the amendment to the contract, the purchaser must issue a notice of termination pending a change of contract (*Änderungskündigung*).

1   Works Council Constitution Act, s 77(4).
2   German Civil Code, s 613A(1), sentence 2.
3   Collective Bargaining Agreements Act, s 4(3).

Notice of termination pending a change of contract

The final means of harmonising employment conditions is to issue a notice of termination pending a change of contract (*Änderungskündigung*). However, in order to be valid, such notices of termination must satisfy the requirements of the Protection against Dismissal Act (*Kündigungsschutzgesetz*). A termination pending a change of contract is not justified by an employer's desire to harmonise employment conditions. The Federal Employment Court sets very strict standards here. Furthermore, as far as claims arising from works agreements and collective bargaining agreements are concerned, the same restrictions must be observed with regard to amending contracts.

A notice of termination pending a change of contract is usually also necessary where the employee does not consent to relocation abroad, unless his employment contract contains a valid clause which also provides for such relocation.

M1.7 Duty to inform and consult

German law contains numerous provisions which, in the case of restructuring, require the employees or the employee representatives to be informed and/or consulted. Of particular note are the necessity to:

–   inform the employees involved in a business (or part business) transfer in accordance with s 613A(5) of the German Civil Code;

–   consult the works council and/or the representative body for executive staff before issuing a dismissal in accordance with s 102 of the Works Council Constitution Act or s 31, para 2 of the Representative Bodies for Executive Staff Act (*Sprecherausschussgesetz*);

–   inform the works council prior to any hiring, classification, re-classification and transfer of a non-executive employee pursuant to s 99 of the Works Council Constitution Act;

–   inform the representative body for executive staff before the intended hiring or modifying of the duties of, or transferring of, an executive pursuant to s 31, para 1 of the Representative Bodies for Executive Staff Act;

–   inform the works council in the event of 'operational changes', including negotiations regarding a Reconciliation of Interests and a Social Plan in accordance with s 111 et seq of the Works Council Constitution Act;

–   inform the works council about any collective dismissals in accordance with s 17 of the Protection against Dismissal Act;

–   inform the works council about any merger, spin-off or transfer of assets in whole or in part pursuant to the Reorganisation Act;

–   inform and consult the European Works Council pursuant to ss 32 and 33 of the European Works Council Act (*Europäisches Betriebsräte-Gesetz*); and

–   inform the economic affairs committee about the economic matters of the company in accordance with s 106 of the Works Council Constitution Act.

The duty to inform the employees in the case of a business (or part business) transfer has already been addressed in connection with the employees' right of objection[1]. An overview of the participation of the works council, the European Works Council and/or the Economic Affairs Committee in personnel, social and economic matters is treated in a separate chapter[2]. The same applies to the treatment of the information and participation rights of the works council in the case of collective dismissals[3].

If the transfer of a business or part of a business is by way of a merger, spin-off or transfer of assets in whole or in part by way of universal legal succession (*Gesamtrechtsnachfolge*) in accordance with the Reorganisation Act (as opposed to a transfer of individual assets by way of an 'asset deal'), the works council must be sent the corresponding corporate law agreement (merger agreement, spin-off or transfer agreement), or a draft thereof, at least one month before the date of the shareholders' meeting which will resolve on its consent[4]. Informing the works council is one of several prerequisites for the required register entry.

It should be noted that the above-mentioned information and consultation obligations vis-à-vis employees and employee representatives exist concurrently. All provisions must always be satisfied.

1   See the comments at *M1.4*.
2   See the comments at *M2.6*.
3   See the comments at *M2.1–M2.6*.
4   Reorganisation Act, ss 5(3), 126(3), 176 and 177.

M1.8 Transfer of business in insolvency

General comments

The current Directive on business transfers applies in the framework of insolvency proceedings if and where the respective member state makes such provision[1]. In Germany, the determinative provisions on business transfers, namely s 613A of the German Civil Code apply, in principle, also to a sale of a business or part of a business by the insolvency administrator. There are, however, a few peculiarities to consider in this respect.

1   Directive 2001/23/EC, art 5.

Reduction of liability

If the business transfer takes place after the commencement of insolvency proceedings, the purchaser will only be liable for those claims which are generated after the commencement of the insolvency proceedings. As regards the works pension scheme, this liability privilege means that the purchaser assumes the pension obligations vis-à-vis the employees. In the event of a pension claim, however, it is only liable for the part of the works pension claim which was earned after the commencement of insolvency proceedings. Where the claims to works pension or works pension expectancies already existed on commencement of insolvency proceedings, however, the *Pensionssicherungsverein* (special instrument for safeguarding pensions), an institution ensuring insolvency insurance, is liable.

Right of dismissal

Insolvency as such does not permit any dismissals for operational reasons, though an associated reorganisation would do so. If the employment relationship has already been terminated by the former employer or the insolvency administrator, and if the purchaser assumes the business in insolvency proceedings whilst the notice periods are still running, the employees do not – unlike outside of insolvency proceedings – have a claim to re-employment against the purchaser. Furthermore, the Insolvency Act (*Insolvenzordnung*) provides for alleviation of certain restrictions with respect to the notice periods to be observed, the court review, and the burden of illustration and proof as to the validity of the dismissal.

M2 Redundancy

M2.1 Background

In the case of cross-border redundancies, the first question to answer is which law is applicable in the event of a dispute. German private international law is governed by the Introductory Law to the German Civil Code (*Einführungsgesetz zum Bürgerlichen Gesetzbuch*). The EC Convention of 19 June 1980 on the law applicable to contractual obligations has been incorporated into the Introductory Law to the German Civil Code. The Rome Convention of 19 June 1980 is therefore not directly applicable in the Federal Republic of Germany.

The parties to the employment contract can, in principle, choose which law is to apply to the employment contract (employment contract regime). If the parties have not provided for this in the employment contract, the contract will be subject to the law of the state in which the employee usually carries out his work. If the nature of the work is such that the employee does not, as a rule, carry out his work in one location (eg flight personnel), the applicable law is the law of the branch of the company which employs the person.

If the employment contract regime is subject to German law, then the German rules on protection against dismissal are applicable. The 'general protection' of the Protection against Dismissal Act[1] does not belong to the essential principles of German law (*ordre publique*), nor to the provisions of German law which mandatorily override the law which applies to the contract[2].

Irrespective of the law which applies to the employment relationship, the German provisions regarding 'special protection' against dismissal apply with mandatory effect to certain employees. These are:

- collective dismissals;

- pregnant women, mothers and those on parental leave;

- disabled persons;

- works council members;

- trainees.

This special protection from dismissal even applies to employees in Germany if the employment relationship is subject to another law owing to a choice of law.

Redundancy law in Germany is covered domestically by the Protection against Dismissal Act (*Kündigungsschutzgesetz*). If the Protection against Dismissal Act applies (see *M2.2*), termination of the employment contract will require 'social justification'. An employee can be dismissed if there are urgent operational reasons (*dringende betriebliche Erfordernisse*). In comparison to English law, for example, German law does not provide a legal definition of redundancy. The employer is obliged to try to avoid the dismissal beforehand, eg by offering the employee another vacant position. If there are several employees doing more or less the same job who could be dismissed, the employer must make the decision on the basis of age, length of service, maintenance obligations and any disability. Employees whose continued employment would be in the legitimate interest of the company (either because of their qualifications or work performance, or in order to ensure a balanced staff structure) may be excluded from this selection by the employer. The employee must, within three weeks, file an action at the Employment Courts for a ruling that the written dismissal is invalid. If he fails to do this, the dismissal will be deemed to be valid even if the notice of termination did not comply with German legal requirements[3]. If the dismissal is 'socially unjustified' or invalid for other reasons, the dismissed employee must continue to be employed under the same conditions.

Dismissals on economic grounds often concern a large number of employees (collective dismissals). Germany has special rules regarding collective dismissals. These rules, however, do not relate to substantive conditions (see *M2.2* below) but merely to procedural requirements (see *M2.4* below). The Collective Redundancies Directives are transposed in Germany by Chapter 3 of the Protection against Dismissal Act, ss 17–22[4]. The Collective Redundancies Directive 1998 consolidates the previous Directives of 1975 and 1992 and adds little to them. German law did not need to be adjusted in this respect. In addition to the Protection against Dismissal Act's regulation of employee representatives' participation in the case of collective dismissals, the following statutory law should also be consulted: the Works Council Constitution Act (*Betriebsverfassungsgesetz*), the Representative Bodies for Executive Staff Act (*Sprecherausschussgesetz*)[5], and the European Works Council Act (*Europäisches Betriebsräte-Gesetz*)[6].

1   Sections 1–14 of the Protection against Dismissal Act (*Kündigungsschutzgesetz*).
2   Federal Employment Court, decision of 24 August 1989, DB 1990, 1666.
3   Protection against Dismissal Act, ss 4 and 7.
4   The provisions regarding dismissals requiring notification in the Protection against Dismissal Act were completely reworded through implementation of the Collective Redundancies Directive 1975 by the Second Act Amending the Protection against Dismissal Act of 27 April 1978 (Federal Gazette 1978 I 550, in force since 30 April 1978) and adjusted to the European regulations as a result of the Collective Redundancies Directive 1992 by the Act Adjusting Employment Law Provisions to EC Law of 20 July 1995 (Federal Gazette 1995 I 946, in force since 28 July 1995).
5   Representative Bodies for Executive Staff Act, s 32.
6   European Works Council Act, ss 32–33.

M2.2 Dismissal for urgent operational reasons

Notice of termination

A dismissal must be *in writing*[1], and will be rendered void by a failure to comply with the formal requirements. It is desirable that the notice of dismissal is handed to the employee in person, or delivered to him by courier.

The date of handing over the written notice of dismissal is of great significance with regard to the notice period and the deadline for appeals.

1   German Civil Code, s 623.

Notice periods and termination dates

The law specifies the minimum notice which must be observed in all cases[1]. The length of this minimum notice period depends on the employee's length of service. The employment contract or the collective bargaining agreement can, however, stipulate a longer notice period or an expiry date which is more favourable to the employee.

If the statutory notice periods apply to the *employees*, there is a notice period of four weeks terminating on either the fifteenth day or at the end of a month. This period is then extended when the *employer* gives notice, in accordance with the length of the employee's service. The minimum notice periods under statute are as follows:

Length of service	Notice period and expiry date
Probationary period (up to six months, if agreed)	14 days to expire on any day
Less than two years' continuous employment	Four weeks' notice to the fifteenth or the end of a calendar month
At least two but less than five years' continuous employment	One month to the end of a calendar month
At least five but less than eight years' continuous employment	Two months to the end of a calendar month
At least eight but less than 10 years' continuous employment	Three months to the end of a calendar month
At least 10 but less than 12 years' continuous employment	Four months to the end of a calendar month
At least 12 but less than 15 years' continuous employment	Five months to the end of a calendar month
At least 15 but less than 20 years' continuous employment	Six months to the end of a calendar month
20 or more years' continuous employment	Seven months to the end of a calendar month

If the minimum statutory notice period is not observed, the dismissal is valid but will not take effect until the end of the statutory notice period.

1   German Civil Code, s 622.

Special protection against dismissal

In certain circumstances, termination is only permissible in extraordinary cases, and is often only permissible with the prior consent of the relevant public authority. Lack of permission will automatically result in an invalid dismissal. The most important examples are:

- pregnancy, maternity and parental leave[1];

- membership of the works council[2];

- disabled employees[3];

- apprentices[4];

- collective bargaining agreements[5].

1   Maternity Leave Act, s 9; Federal Education Allowance Act, s 18.
2   Protection against Dismissal Act, s 15; Works Council Constitution Act, s 103.
3   Sections 85 and 91 of the Social Security Code IX.
4   Vocational Training Act, s 15.
5   Numerous collective bargaining agreements provide that the employment relationships of older employees can only be terminated for good cause after a certain number of years of service.

General protection against dismissal: application of the Protection against Dismissal Act (*Kündigungsschutzgesetz*)

The employer's ability to terminate an employment contract is restricted by the Protection against Dismissal Act, which applies if:

(i)   the employee has been employed for *more than six months*;

(ii) the business regularly employs *more than 10 employees* excluding trainees[1].

The determining factor for the application of the Protection against Dismissal Act is the *number of employees employed by a business located in Germany*. An employee is not protected by the Protection against Dismissal Act where, under the employment contract, he or she ordinarily works outside Germany.

In addition, there are certain exclusions, eg members of a company's board of directors (*Vorstand*) and directors (*Geschäftsführer*) of limited liability companies.

If the Protection against Dismissal Act applies, termination of any employment contract requires 'social justification'. The employer must have a valid reason for dismissal. In a cross-border dismissal the employer must also have 'urgent operational reasons'. The burden of proof in establishing urgent operational reasons is borne by the employer.

1   Protection against Dismissal Act, s 23. The threshold was increased with effect from 1 January 2004 (formerly: more than five employees). However, this only applies to new appointments commencing after that date. Those already employed in a business with more than five but no more than 10 employees are still protected against dismissal.

Urgent operational reasons

A dismissal is 'socially unjustified' if it is not the result of urgent operational reasons which preclude the continued employment of the employee[1].

How the business is structured is at the discretion of the company. A job is lost when the company cannot or no longer wishes to continue its business as it has in the past. The loss of positions is therefore the result of a corporate decision made following the changed employment needs. A corporate decision refers to the corporate policy of the management and not to the employer's decision to dismiss employees, though the implementation of the corporate decision may indeed lead to the loss of employment. Whether a corporate decision requiring the termination of employment contracts has been made must be reviewed by the Employment Courts. The Employment Courts will not consider the justification for, or reasonableness of, the corporate decision itself, but it will intervene where a decision is clearly unobjective, illogical or arbitrary (misuse control).

A dismissal can be for *internal* or *external* operational reasons.

1   Protection against Dismissal Act, s 1(2).

Internal operational reasons

A dismissal for internal operational reasons is 'socially justified' if the employer decides on an internal organisational measure, which has the result that one or more employees are no longer required. This covers corporate decisions such as:

–   rationalisation measures;

–   reorganisation or restriction of production;

–   closure of the business.

According to case law, the corporate decision can be to work with fewer staff in the long term, causing an increase in the performance of the (reduced) staff. This increased performance (*Leistungsverdichtung*) is the desired aim and the resulting necessary changes must have been taken into account. The employment of personnel is a matter of free corporate decision.

External operational reasons

External operational reasons are, for example:

–   lack of work; or

–   drop in turnover.

The operational reasons are not usually the direct and sole result of economic developments (drop in production, etc), but are the result of a decision made by the employer on the basis of economic developments or fiscal considerations (corporate decisions, internal operational reasons).

Lack of possibilities for continued employment

A dismissal will only be justified if the continued employment of the employee in another position in the business or company is not possible[1]. The possibilities of continued employment must be reviewed at company level. So far, the Federal Employment Court (*Bundesarbeitsgericht*) has left open whether, subject to certain preconditions, there is always or only in exceptional cases a duty to continue to employ the employee within the group and whether this can, as a result, render the dismissal invalid. However, it has definitely dismissed the social incompatibility of a dismissal where the employer does not have sufficient legal, or actual, possibilities to enforce the employee's continued employment by a third party company[2].

Both the employer and the employee must objectively view the continued employment to be possible and reasonable. There must be either a vacant comparable (equivalent) position or a vacant position on different (less favourable) terms. Secondly, the employee must have the necessary skills and knowledge. A position is deemed to be vacant if it is not filled upon the receipt of the notice of dismissal, or if it is vacant upon the expiry of the notice period. The employee has a right to continue his employment in a vacant position even if this is only possible after a reasonable amount of additional training or re-training[3]. If a comparable vacant position is available, then the employer must redeploy the employee accordingly. Employment in a vacant position on different (less favourable) terms takes precedence over a final dismissal (*Beendigungskündigung*). This may be implemented by way of a notice of termination pending a change of contract (*Änderungskündigung*).

1   Protection against Dismissal Act, s 1(2).
2   Federal Employment Court, decision of 21 February 2002, BB 2002, 2335.
3   Protection against Dismissal Act, s 1(2).

Social selection

The dismissal is 'socially unjustified', and therefore invalid, if the employer does not, or does not sufficiently, take into account the employee's number of years of service, age, maintenance obligations and any disability. These criteria rank equally and must be 'sufficiently' considered by the employer, who therefore has a certain amount of scope for evaluation. In the case of numerous dismissals the employer can, alternatively, use a points scheme which takes into account the selection criteria, though he must carry out an individual final review following the selection on the basis of the points scheme. If a collective bargaining agreement or a works agreement stipulates how the social criteria are to be valued in relation to each other, only gross errors in the valuation will be reviewed by the Employment Court[1].

Who is to be included in the social selection is determined, first and foremost, by the characteristics of the job performed. This does not only apply where jobs are identical, but also to jobs which the employee would carry out on account of his experience and training. A short introductory period being required would not preclude such comparability. Two jobs are not comparable where the employer cannot unilaterally move or redeploy the employee to the other job.

Employees whose continued employment is in the legitimate interest of the business (*Leistungsträger*), in particular on account of their knowledge, ability and performance or to ensure a balanced personnel structure in the business, must not be included in the social selection[2]. The interests of the socially weaker employee must be weighed up against the operational interest in excluding the *Leistungsträger*: the stronger the social interest, the better the reasons must be for excluding the *Leistungsträger*.

The social selection must also be observed in collective dismissals. It can lead to many practical difficulties where parts of businesses are closed but others continue.

Where there is a works council and an operational change within the meaning of s 111 of the Works Council Constitution Act (*Betriebsverfassungs-gesetz*) is planned[3], the employees to be dismissed can be referred to by name in the Reconciliation of Interests to be concluded ('list of names'). This possibility is of practical relevance in cases where only part of a business is closed or relocated abroad but another part is continued. In this case, the law assumes that the dismissal is the result of urgent operational reasons. The social selection of the employees can only be reviewed in this case with respect to gross errors[4]. The social selection only contains gross errors if disproportionate consideration was apportioned to the criteria of age, years of service, maintenance obligations, or disability.

1   Protection against Dismissal Act, s 1(4).
2   Protection against Dismissal Act, s 1(3).
3   See *M2.6* below.
4   Protection against Dismissal Act, s 1(5).

M2.3 The duty to inform and consult prior to redundancy

If there is a works council, it must be heard before every dismissal[1]. According to recent decisions of the Federal Employment Court (*Bunde-sarbeitsgericht*), a dismissal will not only be invalid if the works council has not been informed, but also where the employer has not properly observed its information obligation, in particular where it has not provided sufficiently detailed information.

The employer must inform the works council of the details of the employee to be dismissed, the number of years of service, the type of dismissal (with or without notice period, pending a change of contract) and the reasons for dismissal. The aim of the consultation procedure, over and above simple notification, is to give the works council the opportunity to comment on the proposed dismissal. The employer is obliged to inform the works council of the reasons for the proposed dismissal, including a detailed account of the facts. The facts detailed must be sufficiently comprehensive for the works council to be able to review the reasons for the dismissal and to get a picture of the situation without the need for further investigation.

1   Works Council Constitution Act, s 102.

Court review

The Employment Court must fully review whether a corporate decision was made and whether this necessitated the employee's dismissal. However, the corporate decision must not be reviewed with respect to its necessity, objective justification or its purposefulness. The Employment Court will not consider the justification for, or reasonableness of, the corporate decision itself, but it will intervene where a decision is clearly unobjective, illogical or arbitrary.

The Employment Court will consider the time at which the notice of dismissal is received, and whether the reason for dismissal (eg loss of employment requirement) existed at this time. The principles of alternate burden of proof apply. Firstly, the employer must illustrate how the corporate decision is to be implemented. It is then up to the employee to illustrate why this decision is clearly unobjective, illogical or arbitrary. Only then must the employer provide further information. Where, upon the receipt of the notice of dismissal, continued employment remains possible, but the decision to terminate the contract has already been made, it depends on whether the employee can be dispensed with upon expiry of the notice period. This is assumed to be the case when at the time the notice of termination is issued, it can be expected that the operational reason for the dismissal will exist upon expiry of the notice period. The decision underlying the prognosis must, however, have already been made. This means that dismissal owing to closure of a business is not justified if the closure has merely been considered or planned, but has not yet been implemented.

The principles of alternate burden of proof also apply to social selection. First, the employee must dispute that the social selection is correct. If the employee disputes the correctness of the social selection, and names other employees who are apparently less worthy of protection, he must, in the event of a dispute, prove this. Only if he is not in a position to comment on the social selection, and therefore requests that he be informed by the employer of the reasons for its selection, does the burden of proof first pass to the employer. Upon providing the information, the full burden of illustration will pass back to the employee.

If the dismissal is 'socially unjustified' or invalid for other reasons, the Employment Court will determine that the employment did not end on the date of termination. The employee will continue to be employed under the former conditions. If the court decision is only made after expiry of the notice period, as is often the case, the employer is obliged to make back-payments to the employee in respect of remuneration from when the notice period expired.

M2.4 Collective dismissals, including redundancies

Scope of application

Considerable reduction of personnel can, according to case law of the Federal Employment Court constitute a business restriction[1], and thereby activate the co-determination right of the works council in economic matters[2]. The guidelines for this are the thresholds for collective dismissals requiring notification. In the case of large businesses, the Federal Employment Court only accepts a business restriction where five per cent of the employees are dismissed. If the thresholds are exceeded, the employer must negotiate with the competent works council regarding a Reconciliation of Interests and a Social Plan. This co-determination right of the works council exists alongside a participation right with respect to the proposed collective dismissal.

The information and consultation procedure for collective dismissals only applies to businesses which usually have more than 20 employees[3]. Not only businesses under private law, but also businesses – in this respect German law goes beyond the Collective Redundancies Directive 98/59/EC – which are managed by public administration authorities and pursue economic purposes[4] (in particular, public undertakings such as transport companies and hospitals) are covered. Seasonal businesses with high fluctuation and purely seasonal businesses are not covered, however[5], as the dismissals are the result of the nature of the businesses[6]. This exception is covered by art 1(2)(a) of the Directive.

The term 'business' is not defined in the Collective Redundancies Directive itself. According to recent decisions of the European Court of Justice[7], a 'business' is a unit to which employees affected by the dismissal belong for the purpose of fulfilling their duties. A 'business', according to the definition, does not require a management which can make collective redundancies itself. The common German understanding of the term 'business'[8] differs from this, however, and is based on the uniform management apparatus as a constitutive characteristic. The term 'business' in s 17 of the Protection against Dismissal Act must therefore be interpreted within the meaning of the case law of the ECJ in conformity with the Directive; the management is of less importance.

Section 17 of the Protection against Dismissal Act protects the employees. Although under German law key employees are also, in principle, subject to general protection from dismissal, s 17(5) of the Protection against Dismissal Act excludes 'operations managers and similar key persons exercising management functions insofar as they have the authority to independently appoint or dismiss employees' from protection from collective redundancies. Such an exception is not provided for by EC Directive 98/59/EC. German law therefore infringes Community law in this respect. Owing to the fact that the EC Directive has not been fully implemented, it is impossible to review the German law by way of preliminary ruling proceedings. Since EC directives do not apply directly to private parties, key employees wrongfully excluded from the scope of protection may simply file a claim against the Federal Republic of Germany, subject to narrowly-defined preconditions, to compensate them for the inadequate transposition of the Directive.

1   Works Council Constitution Act, s 111.

2   See *M2.6* below.
3   Protection against Dismissal Act, s 17(1).
4   Protection against Dismissal Act, s 23(2).
5   Seasonal businesses operate all year round but with seasonal influxes (eg hotels); purely seasonal businesses only operate for a few months of the year (eg outdoor pools).
6   Protection against Dismissal Act, s 22(1).
7   C-449/93: *Rockfon AS v Specialarbejderforbundet i Danmark* [1995] ECR I-4291, ECJ.
8   A business is an organisational unit within which an employer, on his own or with its employees, follows certain working processes on a permanent basis with the assistance of technical and immaterial means, and which is not limited to satisfying its own requirements.

Determinative threshold value

The employer must notify the Employment Agency (*Agentur für Arbeit*) prior to the dismissal of:

–   more than five employees in businesses which usually have more than 20 and fewer than 60 employees;

–   10 per cent of the employees or more than 25 employees in businesses which usually have at least 60 and fewer than 500 employees;

–   at least 30 employees in businesses which usually have at least 500 employees,

within 30 calendar days. Other terminations which are invoked by the employer (ie under a settlement agreement) are considered to be equivalent to a dismissal[1].

Under German law the reason for the dismissal is insignificant. Not only dismissals for operational reasons but also dismissals owing to misconduct or incapacity come under collective dismissal protection. In this respect, German law goes beyond the Collective Redundancies Directive, which only covers dismissals which are not the responsibility of the employee. The Federal Employment Court holds that, 'dismissal' within the meaning of ss 17–18 of the Protection against Dismissal Act is not the notice of dismissal but the actual termination of employment[2]. Decisive for the notification duty is therefore not the time that notice is given, but the actual enforcement of the dismissal (expiry of notice period)[3]. Therefore, upon the issuing of the notice of dismissal, a final decision on the notification requirement is not possible. Where the number of dismissals does not initially reach the threshold mentioned above, a subsequent notification duty may arise if later dismissals cause the statutory thresholds to be exceeded.

1   Protection against Dismissal Act, s 17(1).
2   The Employment Court of Berlin referred the question to the European Court of Justice, decision of 14 January 2004, EzA-SD 10/2004.
3   Federal Employment Court, decision of 13 April 2000, DB 2000, 2175.

Information and consultation obligation

The Collective Redundancies Directive demands that employee representatives are informed and consulted. It leaves the determination of who are to be employee representatives up to national law (art 1(1)(b)).

German law provides for a works council to be established at businesses of the sizes covered by the EC Directive (see s 1 of the Works Council Constitution Act (*Betriebsverfassungsgesetz*)). However, the establishment of a works council is not obligatory in Germany and requires the corresponding initiative of the employees.

If there is a works council, the employer must inform it in due time about a planned collective dismissal for which notification is necessary. The German legislator has not further defined 'in due time'. However, it is clear that the works council should be involved from a time when it still has the possibility of having an influence. The works council must be informed in writing and the notification must contain certain information, in particular:

– the reasons for the planned dismissals;

– the number and the occupational groups of the employees to be dismissed;

– the number and the occupational group of the employees regularly employed;

– the period of time over which these dismissals are to take place;

– the intended criteria for the selection of the employees to be dismissed;

– the intended criteria for calculating any severance payments.

The employer and the works council must, in particular, discuss the possibilities for avoiding or limiting dismissals or alleviating their effects. This information obligation described in the Protection against Dismissal Act is also required by the EC Directive.

There is no substitute for a works council under German law (for example, in the form of participation by the trade unions represented in the business). In Germany the employees are entitled to establish a works council at any time, even against the wishes of the employer. If they choose not to, this is their responsibility.

It has already been mentioned that the Collective Dismissals Directive covers key employees but that German law excludes certain key employees from collective dismissal protection (see *M2.4* above). Those employees who belong to the broader circle of key employees within the meaning of s 5(3) of the Works Council Constitution Act (*Betriebsverfassungsgesetz*) are not represented by the works council and cannot ask to be represented by it. Their employee representation is the representative body for executive staff and is regulated in its own act, the Representative Bodies for Executive Staff Act (*Sprecherausschussgesetz*). However, the representative body for executive staff is not mentioned in s 17 of the Protection against Dismissal Act. This national regulation deficiency must therefore be corrected in conformity with the Directive to the extent that the employer must perform its legal information and consultation obligations vis-à-vis the representative body for executive staff[1].

For the informing of, and consultation with, a European Works Council in the case of cross-border collective dismissals (these are already available when a decision on redundancies is made in another member state) special provisions apply[2] which implement the minimum standard of the European Works Council Directive 94/45/EC. The participation rights of the European Works Council are rather weak in Germany and of little practical relevance[3]. The informing of, and consultation with, the European Works Council in cross-border cases does not replace the informing of, and consultation with, German employee representatives in cases of collective dismissals.

1   Wissmann, RdA 1998, 221 (224).
2   European Works Council Act, s 32(2) and s 33(1).
3   See *M2.6* below.

Notification duty and waiting period for dismissals

In addition to the information and consultation procedure, the employer must notify in writing the Employment Agency (*Agentur für Arbeit*) about the planned collective dismissals[1]. Pre-printed forms for this are available from the Employment Agency. Any comments of the works council must be attached to the notification, otherwise it is ineffective. A Reconciliation of Interests with a list of names replaces the comments by the works council[2].

Only after effective notification and expiry of the waiting period of one month (*Entlassungssperre*) from receipt of the notification[3] can the dismissals become effective. Before expiry of the one-month waiting period, dismissals are only effective with the express consent of the Employment Agency. However, the waiting period can be extended by the Employment Agency to a maximum of two months[4]. The dismissals must be made within 90 days of expiry of the waiting period, otherwise a further notification will be required.

1   Protection against Dismissal Act, s 17(3).
2   Protection against Dismissal Act, s 1(5).
3   Protection against Dismissal Act, s 18(1).
4   Protection against Dismissal Act, s 18(2).

Sanctions in the case of infringement of the notification duty and/or the information and consultation obligation

German law does not expressly provide for an infringement of the notification and/or the information and consultation obligation. One has to go back to case law and to existing provisions, in particular those on operational changes. Whether German law contains sufficient sanctions for the infringement of the requirements of the Collective Redundancies Directive is disputed. The sanction possibilities are deficient in scope and intensity.

Article 6 of the Collective Redundancies Directive contains procedural requirements to be fulfilled by the EU member states: the employee representatives and/or the employees must have the opportunity to enter into administrative and/or court proceedings regarding the enforcement of obligations arising from the Directive. The Directive does not provide for an express substantive sanction. In this case, the principles established by the

European Court of Justice apply to the *effet utile* of Community law. If a Community law directive does not contain any particular sanctions when its provisions are infringed, or if it refers to national legal and administrative law, the member states are obliged, pursuant to art 5 of the EC Convention, to take all suitable measures to ensure the effective application of Community law. However, in doing so the member states, with which the choice of sanctions remains, must ensure that Community law infringements are punished in accordance with objective and procedural legal rules which correspond to national laws in type and extent. Further, the sanctions must be effective, relative and of a deterrent nature[1].

The Federal Employment Court has differentiated between the issue of the notice of dismissal and the dismissal itself, ie the actual termination of the employment relationship. There is only a duty to notify the actual dismissal pursuant to s 17 of the Protection against Dismissal Act. According to recent decisions of the Federal Employment Court[2], a failure to make, or making an incorrect collective dismissal notification leads to ineffectiveness of the dismissal as a purely practical measure, but not to ineffectiveness of the notice of termination itself. German law lacks a provision automatically linking the ineffectiveness of a collective dismissal notification to the ineffectiveness of the notice of termination[3]. If, at the intended time of the dismissal, the necessary consent of the Employment Agency has not been granted, a waiting period for dismissals begins irrespective of the effectiveness under private law of the dismissal. The dismissal is only then ineffective if the employee appeals under s 18 of the Protection against Dismissal Act.

Whether a notice of termination as a one-sided declaration of intent is effective or ineffective depends on other provisions, ie the general protection against dismissal (see *M2.2* above). The special rules on collective dismissals only determine – first and foremost in the public interest as opposed to the interest of the individual employee – that the notice period for effective dismissal under private law depends also on a decision by the Employment Agency. The Employment Courts are bound by non-appealable acts of administration in the same way as they are bound by negative clearance certificates from the Employment Agency. If, as a result of the notification from the Employment Agency, it is determined that the dismissal may not take place at the time set out in the notice of termination, the legal situation is the same as if the employee had been effectively dismissed but the notice period under statute, collective bargaining agreement, etc were longer than that observed. The dismissal cannot then take place at the proposed time, but only on expiry of the waiting period. If the employer does not continue to employ the employee, then the employer is regarded as not having accepted the work performance. He is obliged to pay the contractual remuneration.

There are doubts in numerous respects as to whether the sanction 'ineffectiveness of the dismissal' is sufficient to ensure the principle of the *effet utile* of Community law.

Under German law it is (so far) restricted solely to the notification duty towards the Employment Agency which is, above all, in the public interest.

Since effective notification requires the works council to have been informed (otherwise its comments cannot be attached to the notification), the information duty vis-à-vis the works council is, at least indirectly, covered by the sanction. Infringements by the employer of the consultation duty pursuant to s 17(2) of the Protection against Dismissal Act, on the other hand, are not covered.

In order for the sanction to be effective, the works council ought to be given the opportunity to ensure that its participation rights (information and consultation) are observed. In this respect the Directive is generous and requires either for the employees or the employee representatives a procedure regarding the enforcement of the obligations arising from the Directive. However, German law does not grant the works council any possible methods of procedure. According to current case law, the dismissal does not automatically become ineffective, but a claim of ineffectiveness (within three weeks of receipt of the notice of dismissal!)[4] must be asserted by the employee. This individual claim cannot be made by the works council. The sanction is therefore very weak if only a few or even none of the employees concerned object to the lack of, or an incorrect collective dismissal notification, even if this is due to the fact that relevant information was not provided.

1   See, for insufficiency of sanctions under English law under the Collective Redundancies Directive, the decision in C-383/92: *European Commission v United Kingdom* [1994] ECR I-2479, ECJ.
2   Federal Employment Court, decision of 24 October 1996, DB 1997, 630; decision of 11 March 1999, DB 1999, 1274; decision of 13 April 2000, DB 2000, 2175.
3   This is not so, for example, in the case of not, or not properly consulting the works council before issuing a dismissal. Pursuant to s 102(1) of the Works Council Constitution Act, this infringement is always automatically linked to ineffectiveness of the notice of dismissal.
4   Protection against Dismissal Act, s 4.

Compensation for detrimental effects of dismissal (*Nachteilsausgleich*)

The Protection against Dismissal Act does not provide for any special severance regulations in the case of collective dismissals. The general regulations apply (see *M2.5* below).

As already mentioned, the clear majority of collective dismissals are also operational changes within the meaning of s 111 of the Works Council Constitution Act (*Betriebsverfassungsgesetz*) for which a Reconciliation of Interests (*Interessenausgleich*) is necessary. In the framework of the negotiations regarding the Reconciliation of Interests, the works council is informed about the planned collective dismissals and consulted about whether, and how, dismissals are to be made, with the aim of reaching an agreement. However, the consultation regarding the 'social accompanying measures' provided for in art 2(2) of the Collective Redundancies Directive is not a subject of the Reconciliation of Interests. It is, from a German perspective, the subject of the Social Plan. To the extent that this can be enforced[1], the consultation right of the works council is secured. However, for the purposes of the enforceability of the Social Plan in cases of simple personnel reduction, German law requires relatively high dismissal numbers in comparison to the Collective Redundancies Directive. The following table clarifies this.

Size of business	Notification duty pursuant to Protection against Dismissal Act, s 17 in the case of ... dismissals	Enforceable Social Plan in accordance with Works Council Constitution Act, s 112A in the case of ... dismissals
More than 20 but less than 60 employees	More than five employees	20% or at least six employees
At least 60 but less than 250 employees	10% or more than 25 employees	20% or at least 37 employees
At least 250 but less than 500 employees	10% or more than 25 employees	15% or at least 60 employees
At least 500 employees	30 or more employees	10% or at least 60 employees

Due to the incongruency of the determinative thresholds, only some of the collective dismissals covered by the Directive are covered by an *enforceable* Social Plan.

Employees who are dismissed for operational reasons can demand a severance payment if the employer has not attempted to conclude a Reconciliation of Interests with the works council, as 'compensation for detrimental effects of dismissal' (*Nachteilsausgleich*)[2]. According to the Federal Employment Court, compensation for detrimental effects of dismissal is a sanction for infringements of the Works Council Constitution Act by an employer which has not satisfied its statutory consultation duty in the case of operational changes. Depending on the age of the employee concerned, the severance payment must be an amount of up to 18 monthly salary payments[3].

The practical effect and deterrent nature of compensation for detrimental effects of dismissal (*Nachteilsausgleich*) is questioned by the fact that the Federal Employment Court regards statutory compensation for the detrimental effects of dismissal as requiring set-off against the severance payments arising from Social Plans[4]. The employer is therefore not even mildly or slightly punished by this 'sanction' unless – and only to this extent – the compensation for detrimental effects of dismissal which it is ordered to pay exceeds the Social Plan severance payment otherwise owed to the employee[5]. With respect to the effectiveness of the sanction – even if it is covered by the Directive – the fact that the claim for compensation for detrimental effects of dismissal must be asserted by the employee concerned, despite the fact that it is the infringement of the participation rights of the works council, must be judged critically.

1   Works Council Constitution Act, s 112 and s 112A.
2   Works Council Constitution Act, s 113(1), (3).
3   Protection against Dismissal Act, s 10, by analogy.
4   Federal Employment Court, decision of 13 June 1989, BAGE 62, 88. The question of whether the Collective Redundancies Directive requires the exclusion of the setting off of a social plan severance payment against the statutory compensation for detrimental effects of dismissal for an effective sanction for an infringement of the consultation duties in the case of collective dismissals regulated by the Directive was recently expressly left open by the Federal Employment Court because, in its view, the consultation duty required by the Directive had definitely been fulfilled in the case in question (Federal Employment Court, decision of 20 November 2001, DB 2002, 950).
5   The decision in C-383/92: *European Commission v United Kingdom* [1994] ECR I-2479, ECJ regarded a 'severance payment' (protective award) provided for under English law and to be paid owing to infringement of information and consultation duties, which completely or partly replaced the amounts owed by the employer to the employee on the basis of the employment contract or as a result of this contract having been terminated, as an insufficient sanction.

Right of the works council to require the employer to refrain from making collective dismissals

The most effective sanction upon the employer's infringement of the information and consultation obligation would without doubt be if the works council were entitled to a right to require the employer to refrain from making the collective dismissals until fulfilment of these obligations. However, such a right is disputed in German legal commentary, and there are contradictory decisions in case law. The Federal Employment Court has not yet ruled on this matter.

M2.5 Statutory severance payment

Entitlement

The Law reforming the employment market (*Gesetz zu Reformen am Arbeitsmarkt*) of 24 December 2003 introduced for the first time in Germany a statutory severance payment for dismissals for operational reasons[1]. However, the severance payment claim only results if the employer desires it. A requirement is that the employer states in the notice of dismissal:

(i)   that the dismissal is based on urgent operational reasons; and

(ii) that the employee can request the severance payment if he lets the deadline expire without asserting a claim.

If the dismissed employee does not assert a claim within the three-week period, with which he asserts the invalidity of the dismissal, the employee is entitled to the statutory severance payment on expiry of the notice period. This new regulation has not yet been tested. However, it can be expected that employees will regard the employer's comment as a 'first severance payment offer' and assert a claim anyway, hoping to either be able to keep their jobs or to achieve a higher severance payment.

1   Protection against Dismissal Act, s 1A.

Calculation

The amount of the severance payment is regulated with mandatory effect by law[1]. It amounts to 0.5 of a monthly salary payment for each year of service. A period of more than six months must be rounded up to a year when ascertaining the duration of the employment. There is no provision for capping the severance payment with respect to its amount.

1   Protection against Dismissal Act, s 1A(2).

Other compensation

Claims to severance payments can also result from a Social Plan. The amount of these severance payments is negotiated with the works council, taking into account the age and number of years of service of the respective employees.

If the employer makes an operational change without having attempted to conclude a Reconciliation of Interests with the works council, the employees dismissed have a statutory right to compensation for detrimental effects of dismissal (see *M2.4* above).

In practice, many court proceedings following an employee's dismissal are settled through severance payments. The amount of the severance payment is freely negotiated between the parties, taking into account the employee's prospects of success in the proceedings. The calculation of the severance payment is usually, in practice, based on the rule of thumb: 0.5 gross monthly salary payments per year of service.

M2.6 Works co-determination in Germany

General comments

In Germany there is a very extensive system of works co-determination by employees. The participation of employees in private companies is regulated by the Works Council Constitution Act (*Betriebsverfassungsgesetz*). The participation rights of executive employees are set out in the Representative Bodies for Executive Staff Act (*Sprecherausschussgesetz*), whilst the participation rights of employees in authorities or public sector enterprises are regulated by the Staff Representation Act (*Bundespersonalvertretungsgesetz*) containing general provisions. Individual participation rights are regulated by the Staff Representation Acts (*Personalvertretungsgesetze*) of the 16 Federal States.

The main provision regulating works co-determination is the Works Council Constitution Act. Where the employees of a business have opted to elect a works council, this works council will be involved in social, personnel and economic matters.

Works constitution bodies

Works council

Under the Works Council Constitution Act the application of participation rights requires the appointment of a works council. The establishment of a works council is the sole responsibility of the personnel. If the personnel do not opt to elect a works council, their co-determination rights under the Works Council Constitution Act cannot be enforced against the employer. The term 'business' – as opposed to a 'company' – is deemed to be the organisational unit within which an employer alone, or together with his employees works with the aid of technical and immaterial means on a long-term basis. The main component therefore is, first and foremost, the unit of organisation, ie the use and organisation of human working capacity by a uniform managing body. Works councils can be established in all businesses in which there are at least five permanent employees entitled to vote, three of whom can be elected[1]. All employees of the works over the age of 18 are eligible to vote if they have been employed for more than three months[2]. All employees entitled to vote who have been with the employer for six months are eligible for election[3]. Members of corporate bodies of legal entities[4] and executive employees are not employees under the Works Council Constitution Act[5].

A part of the business is considered to be independent if it is at a distance from the main business or is independent with respect to its role and organisation[6]. An independent works council must be elected in such a case. However, only one works council must be elected if it is a 'joint business'. A joint business is when two companies jointly use and uniformly manage the same employees and operational means[7].

German works council constitution law requires a business to be maintained in Germany. Provided this is the case, works councils can therefore also be elected in businesses belonging to foreign companies.

In small businesses of up to 20 employees entitled to vote, the works council consists of one person. In businesses of 21 or more employees entitled to vote, the works council is a body with three or more members[8]. The works council is, in principle, responsible for all participation rights under the Works Council Constitution Act.

Where a company has several works councils, the establishment of a Central Works Council is prescribed by statute as a representative body of the employees on a company level[9]. As a matter of principle, each works council elects two members as representatives on the 'central works council'; differing provisions are possible through collective bargaining agreements or works agreements. The central works council is responsible for exercising the participation rights under the Works Council Constitution Act. Competency may be transferred if the central works council is instructed by the individual works councils to deal with a matter[10]. The central works council is competent from the outset for matters concerning the entire company, and which cannot be regulated by the individual works councils[11]. It is often very difficult to determine when this criterion has been fulfilled. This creates considerable legal uncertainty, particularly in the case of company-wide restructuring. In principle, the individual works councils may even be competent with regards to a business restructuring.

The prevailing view is that a central works council must be established at company level as a matter of principle at foreign companies even if the domicile of the company is situated outside of Germany. However, the preconditions which must be fulfilled in the individual case are disputed and have not yet been clarified by a court decision.

Where there are several central works councils in a group, these may establish a 'group works council' at group level. In principle, the same competency regulations apply to the group works council as to the central works council. The group works council deals with matters with which it has been instructed by the individual central works councils[12], or with matters which concern the entire group and which cannot be regulated by the individual central works councils within their companies[13].

It is disputed as to which preconditions apply to the establishment of a group works council of a foreign group parent company with its domicile outside Germany, and this has not yet been clarified by a court decision. Prevailing legal opinion holds that at least one independent subgroup with its own management apparatus should exist in Germany.

1   Works Council Constitution Act, s 1(1).
2   Works Council Constitution Act, s 7.
3   Works Council Constitution Act, s 8.
4   Works Council Constitution Act, s 5(2).
5   Works Council Constitution Act, s 5(3).
6   Works Council Constitution Act, s 4(1).
7   Works Council Constitution Act, s 1(2).
8   See Works Council Constitution Act, s 9 on the size of works councils.
9   See Works Council Constitution Act, s 47 et seq.
10 Works Council Constitution Act, s 50(2).
11 Works Council Constitution Act, s 50(1).
12 Works Council Constitution Act, s 58(2).
13 Works Council Constitution Act, s 58(1).

Economic affairs committee

An economic affairs committee (*Wirtschaftsausschuss*) must be established in companies which regularly employ more than 100 employees. Its task is to consult with the employer on economic matters, and to inform the works council accordingly. The economic affairs committee is only an advisory works constitution body which, with the exception of certain information rights, cannot exercise any independent participation rights. Indeed, it is actually only an auxiliary body of the works council and serves to fulfil works council duties, whilst consisting of at least three, and a maximum of seven, members of the company. At least one must be a works council member[1]. The members of the economic affairs committee are elected by the central works council, should one exist, or by the works council for its term of office, and can be removed by the appointing body at any time[2].

1   Works Council Constitution Act, s 107(1).
2   Works Council Constitution Act, s 107(2).

Conciliation Board

A difference of opinion between the employer and works constitution bodies may not be settled by court action under German law. Rather, a special organ, the Conciliation Board, resolves internal works conflicts. However, the Conciliation Board is not responsible for clarifying whether there is an individual participation right. The Conciliation Board can only determine the content of an agreement between the employer and the respective works constitution body where the application of a co-determination right is not disputed. The Conciliation Board's decision does not preclude legal recourse to the Employment Court for a subsequent review[1]. A type of internal works preliminary proceedings therefore takes place before the Conciliation Board.

In certain participation matters, in particular regarding co-determination rights in social matters, the decision of the Conciliation Board replaces the agreement between employer and the respective works constitution body. The decision therefore applies with mandatory effect to all employees at the affected business.

The Conciliation Board consists of an equal number of representatives elected by the employer and employees and an impartial chairman[2]. The members need not belong to the business. If there is no agreement on the number of members, the Employment Court decides. The Employment Court is also responsible for appointing an impartial chairman where he is not appointed by mutual consent of the employer and the respective works constitution body.

1   Works Council Constitution Act, s 76(7).
2   Works Council Constitution Act, s 76(2).

Participation rights

Co-determination in social matters

The works council, or in individual cases the central or group works council, has an extremely strong position in 'social matters'[1]. These matters requiring co-determination include, in particular, the conduct of the employees in the business; the distribution of the weekly working hours over the individual days of the week; the requirement to work overtime and short-time work (*Kurzarbeit*); the establishment of general principles on holidays and holiday plans; determining the holiday dates of the individual employees in the event of a dispute between the employer and the employee concerned; introduction and use of technical installations with a view to monitoring the conduct of the employees; organisation of works bodies and questions pertaining to the wage structure of the business, including the determination of performance-based remuneration. In these social matters, the works constitution body has a real co-determination right. If the works council does not grant its consent to a desired decision of the employer, the employer must call the Conciliation Board, which will decide with binding effect on the planned measure[2]. The co-determination right of the works council is not dispensed with in urgent cases. This is of particular significance in the case of an instruction to work overtime. Where there are no frame agreements, the works council must agree to every single hour of overtime. If in a social matter the co-determination right of the works council is infringed, a measure ordered by the employer against the employees is invalid, and it may be ignored.

1   See the catalogue of the individual co-determination matters in s 87(1) of the Works Council Constitution Act.
2   Works Council Constitution Act, s 87(2).

Co-determination in personnel matters

The works council also has strong co-determination rights in personnel matters. The employer must first inform the works council about personnel planning[1]. It must discuss with the works council the nature and scope of the necessary measures[2]. The works council can further demand that vacant positions are first advertised within the business before they are filled[3]. The works council must consent to individual personnel measures[4]. Appointments, classifications in collective bargaining salary groups and redeployment are therefore only permitted with the consent of the works council. However, the employer may circumvent the need for this consent by applying to the Employment Court. Finally, the works council must be consulted before every dismissal[5]. If the works council objects to a dismissal, it is not rendered invalid. However, the employee may retain a right to continued employment after the expiry of the notice period until the court proceedings following the dismissal are over. A dismissal will be invalid, however, if the works council was not consulted, or was insufficiently consulted prior to the dismissal being issued.

1   Works Council Constitution Act, s 92(1).
2   Works Council Constitution Act, s 92(1).
3   Works Council Constitution Act, s 93.
4   Works Council Constitution Act, s 99(1).
5   Works Council Constitution Act, s 102(1).

Co-determination in economic matters

To the extent that an economic affairs committee has been established at a company, this committee must be informed in detail by the company about economic matters[1]. Pursuant to the Works Council Constitution Act, the economic matters which require notification include, in particular:

–   the economic and financial situation of the company;

–   the level of production and turnover;

–   rationalisation measures;

– the introduction of new working methods;

– the restriction and closure of businesses or parts thereof;

– the relocation of businesses or parts thereof;

– the merger or spin-off of companies or businesses;

– change in the organisation of the business;

– and all other procedures and proposals which could significantly affect the interests of the employees of the company.

Therefore the economic affairs committee must be informed in due time and in detail about a business transfer planned by the employer.

Irrespective of these notification obligations, however, according to the far-reaching German Works Council Constitution Act, economic matters are generally in the ambit of the company and are not subject to co-determination. 'Operational changes' provide an exception, however, and have considerable practical implications for restructuring and business transfers. The employer must discuss in due time and in detail any planned operational changes with the works council in businesses with more than 20 employees eligible to vote[2]. Operational changes pursuant to the Works Council Constitution Act are[3]:

– restriction and closure of the whole business or significant parts thereof;

– relocation of the whole business or significant parts thereof;

– merger with other businesses or spin-off of businesses;

– fundamental change in the organisation of the business, the purpose of the business or the operating installations;

– introduction of fundamentally new working methods and production methods.

According to case law, an operational change within the meaning of a restriction of the business includes reductions in personnel without any further restructurings[4]. However, the number of employees dismissed must exceed a certain proportion of the employees at the business. Case law states that this is based on the specifications governing the notification requirement in the case of collective dismissals.

Case law also states that there is no operational change upon a business transfer. In this respect, the employees are protected by s 613A of the German Civil Code which leads to the statutory transfer of the existing employees to the new owner[5]. However, there can be an operational change in connection with a business transfer for the part of a business transferred, if this is connected with further measures such as relocation of the place of business. There will be an operational change, however, if the hive-off of part of a business in connection with a business transfer has implications for the remaining employees, eg the restriction of the business or a change in production methods.

Upon a business transfer, the employer must negotiate with the competent works council regarding a Reconciliation of Interests (*Interessenausgleich*) and a Social Plan (*Sozialplan*)[6]. A Reconciliation of Interests is an agreement between the employer and the competent works council clarifying whether, and how, a planned operational change is to be implemented. The Reconciliation of Interests therefore concerns all aspects of the implementation of the operational change. The Reconciliation of Interests is an agreement between the employer and the works council which has no direct effect on the individual employee as such. However, if an employer makes operational changes without attempting to conclude a Reconciliation of Interests with the works council, the employees who are dismissed or who suffer other economic disadvantages have a right to 'compensation for detrimental effects of dismissal' (*Nachteilsausgleich*) to be determined by the Employment Court[7]. The Reconciliation of Interests cannot be enforced by the competent works council. Though the Conciliation Board can be called upon, it cannot determine a binding Reconciliation of Interests. Unlike the Reconciliation of Interests, the works council can enforce the conclusion of a Social Plan. Where the employer and respective works council fail to reach an agreement, the Conciliation Board decides bindingly on the content of a Social Plan[8]. The Social Plan contains provisions to compensate for, and alleviate the economic effects which the employees suffer as a result of the operational change. First and foremost, it concerns the financial claims of the employees concerned in the form of severance payments for the lost positions or less favourable conditions.

The information and participation obligations also take effect if the decision to make an operational change in an international company is made by the foreign parent company of the German company. The German company must then request the necessary information from the parent company.

1   Works Council Constitution Act, s 105.
2   Works Council Constitution Act, s 111, sentence 1.
3   Works Council Constitution Act, s 111, sentence 3.
4   See Richardi *Works Council Constitution Act* (8th edn, 2002), s 111, margin no 70 et seq.
5   See Federal Employment Court of 21 October 1980, AP No 8 on s 111 of the Works Council Constitution Act 1972, Richardi *Works Council Constitution Act* (8th edn, 2002), s 111, margin no 132 et seq.
6   Works Council Constitution Act, s 112(1).
7   Works Council Constitution Act, s 113.
8   Works Council Constitution Act, s 112(4).

Transposition requirement of the Information and Consultation Directive 2002/14/EC on notifying and consulting the employees

The deadline for transposition of Directive 2002/14/EC into national law for Germany is 23 March 2005, and it has not yet been transposed. Corresponding legislation proposals have not yet been made either. Legal commentary has only addressed the question of the transposition of Directive 2002/14/EC in a few cases[1]. It is generally held that the standard of the Directive has already been realised by the German Works Council Constitution Act. The only thing which is problematic is that the three participation rights contained in art 4(2) of the Directive are spread across a number of individual provisions in the German Works Council Constitution Act. However, a rationalisation of German co-determination matters has not been announced. According to art 1(1), the aim of the Directive is merely to provide a general framework of minimum standards governing the right to be informed and consulted. Therefore the national legislator is not prohibited from determining more far-reaching participation rights or from dividing these between individual provisions. However, it remains problematic that under German law there is a notification obligation vis-à-vis the economic affairs committee in economic matters. The view that notification in the light of Directive 2002/14/EC must be directly to the works council cannot be accepted[2]. According to art 2 of the Directive, employee representatives are those representatives of the employees provided for in individual national provisions. Under the European law *effet utile* principle which is set out in art 1(2) of the Directive, it is simply necessary that the participation rights of the Directive can be exercised effectively. This is indisputedly the case as far as the duties of economic affairs committees are concerned. However, action must be taken with respect to the requirements for the establishment of an economic affairs committee. Under German law an economic affairs committee can only be established in companies with more than 100 employees. In this respect, the German legislator must adjust this threshold in line with the requirements of art 3(1) of the Directive.

1   See Deinert, NZA 1999, 800 et seq; Giesen, RdA 2000, 298 et seq; Reichold, NZA 2003, 298 et seq.
2   See Reichold, NZA 2003, 298, 299.

European Works Council

Background

Directive 94/45/EC on the 'Establishment of a European Works Council or a Procedure in Community Scale Undertakings and Community Scale Groups of Undertakings for the Purposes of Informing and Consulting Employees' was transposed by the Act on European Works Councils (*Gesetz über Europäische Betriebsräte*) of 28 October 1996[1] which came into force on 1 November 1996. The deadline for implementation of 22 September 1996 was almost met.

The European Works Council Act was amended by the Act of 22 December 1999 to implement Directive 97/74/EC of the Council of 15 December 1997. This extended Directive 94/45/EC to the United Kingdom and came into force on 31 December 1999.

1   Federal Gazette 1996 I 1548.

European Works Council by agreement

The primary aim of the European Works Council Act is to ensure that the cross-border co-operation of employees is guaranteed as a matter of principle by an agreement between the central company management and a special negotiating body representing the employees. Only if such an agreement has not been reached voluntarily is a European Works Council established by operation of law.

The special negotiating body's role is to negotiate and conclude with the central management an agreement regarding a cross-border information process and hearings[1]. The central management and the special negotiating body are completely free to structure the cross-border information process and the process for hearing employees as they wish[2]. They may provide for the establishment of a European Works Council or they may agree on a decentralised information and hearing process. The only precondition is that the agreement provides for cross-border information and hearing of employees and extends to all employees employed in the member states in which the company or the company group is located. The special negotiating body will also have to ensure that each member state is represented by at least one employee in the framework of the agreement, and that those member states which have the largest number of employees have additional representatives. The strongest form of transnational co-operation is the hearing. A 'hearing' is defined as 'an exchange of opinion and the establishment of dialogue between employee representatives and central management'[3].

1   European Works Council Act, s 8(1).
2   European Works Council Act, s 17.
3   European Works Council Act, s 1(4).

European Works Council by operation of law

If a solution is not reached, a European Works Council is formed by operation of law. This is the case if central management refuses to enter into negotiations within six months of the application, if agreement has not been reached within three years of the application, or if central management or the special negotiating body prior to this declare that negotiations have failed[1]. The European Works Council is a permanent establishment without any fixed period of office. The membership of the European Works Council is restricted to four years.

The competence of the European Works Council established by operation of law is restricted to matters which have cross-border effects[2]. In particular, this includes economic matters where they affect the company or the company group as a whole, or at least two establishments or companies in various member states.

Central management must inform the European Works Council once per calendar year as to the development of the business and perspectives of the company or company group operating EU-wide, and must allow the European Works Council a hearing on these matters[3].

The European Works Council, in addition to a right to be informed and heard on a regular basis, is granted further co-determination rights by operation of law in extraordinary circumstances, such as a business transfer or a company closure causing collective dismissals and seriously jeopardising employees' interests[4]. The management must inform the European Works Council without undue delay of such extraordinary circumstances, providing it with the necessary documents and giving it an audience on request and, in principle, allowing sufficient time for its proposals and concerns to be taken into consideration.

As far as can be ascertained, the co-determination rights of European Works Councils did not used to be the subject of German jurisdiction. European Works Councils are usually established on the basis of agreements with a special negotiating body. Should disputes arise in connection with the involvement of a European Works Council, recourse to the Employment Courts is available. If the co-determination rights of a European Works Council by operation of law are infringed, this is a regulatory offence subject to a maximum fine of €15,000.00[5].

1   European Works Council Act, s 21(1).
2   European Works Council Act, s 31.
3   European Works Council Act, s 32.
4   European Works Council Act, s 33.
5   European Works Council Act, s 45.

M3 Case studies

M3.1 Case study 1
(Acquisition of a 'business' situated in another EU state; asset deal; no relocation)

Slumber Ltd, a hotel management company incorporated in the UK and based in Manchester, UK, has been in financial difficulties for some time. Slumber operates nine exclusive hotels in the main British cities (London, Manchester, Birmingham, Leeds, Glasgow, Edinburgh, Liverpool, Cardiff and Bristol) under the 'Slumber' brand. Slumber is 100 per cent owned by UK hotel chain Ezeroom plc, also incorporated in the UK. Each hotel has about 50 staff: five in management, 20 in the restaurant and 25 in house service. Slumber does not own the hotels itself; instead it has a seven-year management agreement with Hotel Investment plc ('HIP'), the owner of the hotels, which is incorporated and based in London, UK. Under this contract Slumber runs the fully equipped hotels on its own risk and has to pay a fixed fee to HIP.

In its central management centre in Manchester, Slumber has another 30 staff. These are 10 managers (including Marketing, Managing, Finance, Sales and Operations Directors) and 20 secretaries, clerks and administrators.

A number of staff are members of the trade union, The Association of Hotel Workers ('AHW'), which has been formally recognised by Slumber as having bargaining rights for hourly paid hotel staff. This is a particularly active union and there is a collective agreement in force. Due to increasing staff costs and the declining demand for expensive hotel accommodation, Slumber is making bigger and bigger operating losses. Slumber is obliged to cut jobs in all the hotels and thus dismisses 40 members of staff as redundant. As a consequence, the service worsens and customer complaints become more frequent. When the board of HIP realises how serious the situation has become, it starts to look for a new operator of its hotels.

Some weeks later, while Slumber is still operating the hotels, a German company is found which seems able to manage the hotels in a much more profitable way for HIP than Slumber. The company, which is called Dormir, is based in Berlin but has already gathered some experience of running hotels in the UK. It operates hotels under the 'Dormir' brand. The board of HIP enters into discussions with Dormir for it to replace Slumber as manager of the hotels.

1. Acquisition of the hotels

It is anticipated that Dormir will want to manage all nine of the hotels under a single management agreement with HIP.

(a) **Would this be a business transfer (defined as a transfer within the meaning of TUPE) under UK law?**

(ONLY TO BE ANSWERED BY UK CONTRIBUTOR)

(b) **Even though Slumber will not transfer any of its activities to Germany, would the acquisition of the hotels in this way constitute a business transfer under German law?**

Answer

If German law is applicable here, this could constitute a business transfer under s 613A of the German Civil Code, depending on the facts of the case.

Legal reasoning

Where a scenario suggests links to the laws of another state, perhaps because the business is being sold to a foreign company, the question of which country's laws apply to the business transfer is raised. Pursuant to the current case law of the Federal Employment Court, a business transfer is subject to the laws of the state which also apply to the employment relationship itself (employment contract statute). Only if the employment contract statute leads to the application of German law, will German law be applicable to the business transfer (s 613A of the German Civil Code).

In principle, the laws of the state in which the employee usually carries out his work in fulfilment of his employment contract apply to the employment relationship.

Since the hotel staff and Slumber employees all work in England, their employment relationships will be governed by English law. If the German company, Dormir, acquires the assets of Slumber, English law will determine the fate of the employment relationships.

If the situation were reversed, with an English company acquiring the German Slumber by way of an asset deal, German law would apply. Whether this would constitute a business transfer under s 613A of the German Civil Code would depend on the seven criteria (see *M1.2* above) established by the European Court of Justice and applied by the Federal Employment Court (*Bundesarbeitsgericht*). One would therefore need to consider whether an independent business unit is transferred that retains its identity after the transfer.

Conclusion

If Dormir acquires all of Slumber's assets and if Dormir enters into all management agreements with HIP in order to continue to operate the nine hotels as before, this constitutes a transfer of an economic unit which retains its identity after the transfer. If German law were to apply, this would constitute a business transfer under s 613A of the German Civil Code.

(c) **Would it make any difference to whether this constituted a business transfer, under TUPE, if Dormir only wanted to manage the six English hotels (excluding the hotels in Glasgow, Edinburgh and Cardiff)?**

(ONLY TO BE ANSWERED BY UK CONTRIBUTOR)

(d) **Would it make any difference to your answer to (b) above if Dormir only wanted to manage six hotels (for example only the English hotels, excluding those in Scotland and Wales, ie the hotels in Glasgow, Edinburgh and Cardiff)?**

Answer

This would not make any difference in terms of the criteria for a (part) business transfer.

Legal reasoning

If Dormir were to enter into only six of the management agreements in the framework of an asset deal, this could constitute a transfer of part of a business. Section 613A of the German Civil Code applies to the transfer of a 'business or part of a business'. In either case, there must be an 'economic unit' which is transferred. This, of course, depends on the facts.

2. Employees who work only partly in the business

What is the position of those staff who work partly in Slumber and partly in Ezeroom? For example, the human resources director of Slumber is also the human resources director of Ezeroom and he has his employment agreement with Ezeroom. He spends approximately 40 per cent of his time dealing with Slumber's personnel matters and the remainder of his time on the human resources affairs of Ezeroom.

(a) **If this is a TUPE transfer, can he be said to have transferred under TUPE in the UK?**

(UK CONTRIBUTOR TO ANSWER)

(b) **What is the law on employees who work only partly in the undertaking to be transferred in Germany?**

Answer

Under German law, the human resources director of Ezeroom would not automatically be transferred to the party acquiring the business.

Legal reasoning

The change of employer required by s 613A of the German Civil Code relates to all employment relationships in existence at the time of the business transfer, to the extent that they were with the former owner of the business. The *legal* affiliation to the business or part of the business being transferred and not the actual employment is therefore determinative. The human resources director has an employment contract with Ezeroom. However, the business of Slumber is the subject of the business transfer. The fact that the human resources director spends a significant amount of his time working for Slumber is irrelevant. As a result of the business transfer, a significant number of his duties will cease to exist, which might justify, inter alia, a dismissal pending a change of contract for urgent operational reasons.

Difficult allocation problems arise if a company sells only one of several businesses or only one part of a business (eg the human resources director works for business A and business B, but only business B is transferred). Only those employees who can be allocated to the part of the business being transferred are transferred. Allocation can be particularly difficult in the case of employees who work in several parts of the same business and for 'overhead functions' (ie personnel, IT, accounting, purchasing). If no agreement is reached between the parties, it depends first and foremost on the main focus of the employee's work.

3. Staff who work outside the UK in another EU country

It transpires that some Slumber central management staff are actually working and based in France already. Two are French nationals.

(a)   Would these staff transfer to Dormir under TUPE if there was a TUPE transfer?

(TO BE ANSWERED BY UK CONTRIBUTOR. PLEASE COMMENT ON UK RESPONSE)

Answer

In theory yes, although this would depend on a number of factors, including their contracts of employment.

Legal reasoning

TUPE applies to undertakings or parts of undertakings situated in the UK immediately prior to transfer. These employees work for and are employed by Slumber, the undertaking to be transferred, but they are simply based in France. The undertaking of Slumber is situated in the UK immediately before the transfer (even if some staff work outside the UK): therefore members of Slumber central management who are working in France will technically transfer. The important point is that TUPE in principle applies to undertakings or a part of an undertaking which is situated in the UK immediately before the transfer. The fact that some of the employees are not actually located in the UK is irrelevant.

*Difficulties may arise in practice. For example, the employees may no longer be required to continue working in the same place and there may be potential breaches of contract. If their employment is terminated, this is likely to be in connection with the transfer, and potentially unfair. Whether or not they have claims in the UK, or indeed in France, will depend on conflicts of laws issues (see Chapter **D**).*

Comment: In this case, the employment contracts of the two French employees would transfer under German law too, in so far as German law applies to them. This can, for example, be the case if the parties to the employment contract have chosen the application of German law, or the French nationals have only been sent to France temporarily. Where there is no choice of law, however, the law of the state where the employee usually works (France) applies, with the effect that the possible transfer of his/her employment contract by means of a business transfer is no longer subject to German law.

(b)   Would the position be different if there was a branch office of Ezeroom in Germany, which directly employed these staff?

(UK TO ANSWER, BUT PLEASE COMMENT)

Answer

The position may be the same.

Legal reasoning

TUPE is likely to apply if the branch office qualifies as an associated employer and the employees are 'assigned' (Botzen v Rotterdamsche Droogdok Maatschappij BV: 186/83 [1985] ECR 519, ECJ) to Slumber (ie they carry out all their functions for Slumber, who is their de facto employer). In such a case the courts are likely to pierce the corporate veil and treat Slumber as the employer for those purposes.

Comment: If the employment contracts are with a legally independent subsidiary of Ezeroom in Germany, they would not automatically transfer to Dormir. The two French nationals are not 'assigned' to the business of Slumber being transferred, since their employment contracts are with Ezeroom. The fact that they actually work for Slumber in France is irrelevant from a legal point of view.

4. Dismissal of employee

One of the Slumber staff, Mr X, was dismissed by Slumber after HIP had given notice to terminate the contract with Slumber and whilst negotiations were ongoing with Dormir. Mr X is owed two months' back pay and unpaid holiday.

Against whom can Mr X bring a claim, and where, if Mr X is a UK national based in Germany?

Answer

Mr X can file a claim against Slumber for payment of two months' back pay and unpaid holiday and for a determination that the dismissal is invalid. Mr X can file this claim at the registered office of Slumber in England (Council Regulation (EC) 44/2001, art 19(1) read with art 60) or at its usual workplace (art 19(2)(a)), ie in Germany. Mr X can choose in which country to bring the claim against Slumber.

The parties can only agree a place of jurisdiction after a dispute has commenced (Council Regulation (EC) 44/2001, art 21).

Moreover, Mr X can file a claim against Dormir for continued employment owing to the business transfer and for back pay and unpaid holiday once the negotiations come to a close. This claim must be filed at the registered office of the company in Germany (Council Regulation (EC) 44/2001, art 19(4)).

Legal reasoning

In all EU member states, Council Regulation (EC) 44/2001 on Jurisdiction and the Recognition and Enforcement of Judgments in Civil and Commercial Matters applies directly and uniformly. It takes precedence over national civil procedural law (see Chapter **D**).

5. Transfer of employee outside the UK

Mr Y (the marketing director) has been vital to the success of Slumber and has been responsible for many successful ideas. Dormir would like to retain his services and move him to Dormir's headquarters in Germany. Mr Y has no wish to live in Germany.

(a)　**How does TUPE impact on Mr Y: is he obliged to transfer against his will?**

(UK ONLY TO ANSWER)

(b)　**What is the law on objection to a transfer in Germany?**

In the case of a business transfer, the transfer of the employment contract to the purchaser is by operation of law, ie the employee's consent is not required. However, the Federal Employment Court (*Bundesarbeitsgericht*) has for some time recognised the right of the employee to object to the transfer of his employment contract. This principle is now enshrined in law. Mr Y could therefore object to the transfer of his employment contract, with the effect that he remains a Slumber employee.

If the employee objects to the transfer of his employment contract, this does not automatically justify a dismissal for urgent operational reasons, the general principles for which must still be observed (ie grounds for dismissal, social selection). In certain circumstances, this can lead to another employee not directly affected by the transfer of the business having to be dismissed first, and the employee who objected to the transfer remaining with the company.

In certain circumstances, an objection to the transfer of the business would not be necessary, since Dormir cannot unilaterally demand that Mr Y relocate abroad (to Germany) (see response to question 5(c) below).

(c)　**Can Mr Y claim constructive dismissal on the basis that he would be expected to work and be based in another EU country and this is nowhere near his home?**

(UK TO ANSWER, BUT PLEASE COMMENT)

Answer

Possibly – if this amounts to a fundamental breach of his contract or if being expected to work and be based abroad amounts to a substantial change in working conditions and is to the employee's detriment.

Legal reasoning

In addition to general common law tests for constructive dismissal, reg 5(5) provides that an employee has the right 'to terminate his contract of employment without notice if a substantial change is made in his working conditions to his detriment'. It is important, therefore, that the change is substantial and to the employee's detriment. Such a claim is likely to lie against the transferee (Dormir). Only in rare circumstances, such as where the transferor (Slumber) has not been open with the employee about the change in working conditions, is a claim likely to succeed again the transferor (Slumber). Case law is of importance here.

In Merckx and Neuhuys v Ford Motors Co Belgium SA: C-171/94 [1996] ECR I-1253, [1996] IRLR 467, Anfo Motors SA transferred its Ford dealership to an independent dealer. There was no transfer of assets and only 14 out of Anfo's 60 employees were taken on. The ECJ identified a community right to claim constructive dismissal where there was a 'substantial change in working conditions to the detriment of the employee' because of the transfer.

In Rossiter v Pendragon [2002] IRLR 483, Mr Rossiter argued that he had suffered a detriment through changes in the calculation of commission, that his holiday pay was no longer based on commission, and that he was made to assume lesser duties. The Court of Appeal held that in order to claim constructive dismissal there would have to be a repudiatory breach of contract, which there was not in this case.

The use of mobility clauses is limited in long-distance transfers, as the test for redundancy (see above) is where the employee actually carries out his work.

Comment: If the business transfer results in the relocation of the business or part of the business abroad, an amendment to the employment contract with respect to the employee's place of work is usually necessary. According to the Federal Employment Court (*Bundesarbeitsgericht*), relocations abroad require the consent of the employee. This even applies if the employment contract contains a mobility clause. In such a case, the mobility clause is restricted to the Federal Republic of Germany. Mobility clauses which also provide for relocation abroad are rare and usually only apply to managerial staff of international groups.

If the employee does not consent to the amendment of his employment contract with respect to his place of work, the party acquiring the business (Dormir) must issue a dismissal pending a change of contract (*Änderungskündigung*).

6. Dormir's business strategy

What is the best way of structuring the transfer of the hotels to Dormir from a German perspective? Would you advise Dormir to set up a subsidiary company registered in the UK specifically to purchase Slumber and thereby avoid any cross-border element?

A company acquiring a business must consider a number of factors, particularly where there is a cross-border element. The applicable law is of particular importance in determining whether the transfer constitutes the transfer of a business and whether the employment contracts are transferred to the purchaser. The Rome Convention provides a common framework for all member states of the European Union. However, many details of cross-border business transfers have to be clarified by case law. Therefore, parties acquiring and selling businesses require a greater level of planning and advice.

M3.2 Case study 2
(Production moves from one EU country to another EU country; physical move)

Alpha Incorporated is a multinational car tyre manufacturing and distribution business based in Europe. Alpha's headquarters are in the UK. Alpha has tyre plants in the UK, Germany, and France. Each of the tyre plants is a wholly owned and independently operated subsidiary of Alpha. Alpha has a European Works Council.

The subsidiary in Germany is Beta. Beta employs about 250 employees, mostly in the direct production of tyres. The employees are on standard basic contracts which do not contain any mobility clauses. Due to increased competition from cheaper producers in the Far East, Alpha is having to reduce its own production costs. Beta has the highest production costs of all Alpha's European operations. Alpha has decided to end the production of tyres in Germany and move production to Gamma, another subsidiary not far away but across the national border in France which has more modern plant and equipment. Beta will continue to exist, but as a sales and marketing organisation only, with about 30 staff.

Most of Beta's tyre-making plant and machinery is transferred to Gamma, but Gamma will only need an extra 125 staff to increase its output to the required level to supply Beta's market. Those employees from Beta who are required to work for Gamma will be expected to accept the terms and conditions and working practices of the Gamma plant, which are very different from those in operation at the Beta plant. For example, Gamma pays its employees considerably lower hourly wages and they work longer hours than those at Beta. Gamma does not want to pay more to the employees transferred to it from Beta than it does to its current employees. In addition, Beta has an occupational pension scheme for its German staff. Gamma operates a different type of pension scheme.

1. Does this transaction constitute a 'business transfer'?

(a) As Beta's tyre-making plant and machinery have transferred to Gamma, will this constitute a business transfer under the Acquired Rights Directive implementing legislation of Germany?

Answer

Under certain circumstances, yes. However, this would depend on the facts of the case.

Legal reasoning

A transfer of a business within the meaning of s 613A of the German Civil Code is said to occur when a new legal entity continues to operate an 'economic unit' that retains its identity in that entity's hands. Whether the new owner acquires an essentially unchanged 'business' depends on the facts of the case. The decisive factors include, in particular, the nature of the business concerned; whether any operational equipment is transferred; what happens to any buildings or moveable assets owned by the business, as well as their value and significance; whether any immaterial operating means or the existing organisation of the business are assumed; the degree of similarity between the business activities of the new owner and those of the former owner; whether the workforce continues to be employed; whether customer and supplier relationships are transferred; and the length of any interruption to the business activities carried out by the business. It is necessary, even upon the acquisition of part of a business, that the 'economic unit' in question retains its identity.

The transfer of a business or part of a business can also take place where the business or part of a business is relocated abroad. Relocation abroad does not mean that the closure of a business in Germany and the re-establishment of that business abroad can be assumed. Whether a particular case constitutes the transfer of a business or part of a business depends on the same criteria as all other cases. In the case of the relocation of a production business it depends, in particular, on whether the operating means are to be transferred; whether production is to be continued at the new location with the same employment organisation and operating methods; and whether only parts of the business are to be sold, which are to be integrated into the operational organisation of the purchaser at various production sites.

In the above example, the transfer is by way of an asset deal and over 125 employees are transferred. Provided production is continued at Gamma with the same employment organisation, this is likely to constitute the transfer of a business. On the other hand, the fact that 125 employees should be sufficient to maintain production for the German market suggests that the employment organisation at Gamma will be significantly changed, with the consequence that the identity of the production part of the business may not be retained.

Conclusion

Whether this constitutes the transfer of a business cannot be conclusively ascertained without further details.

(b) **Does it make any difference to whether this is a business transfer if employees of Beta transfer across to Gamma?**

Answer

In principle, no, as the transfer of employees is the legal *consequence* of the transfer of a business. However, the transfer of the workforce to the new owner is one of seven criteria which would suggest a business transfer has taken place.

Legal reasoning

The transfer of (part of) a business is assumed if, and to the extent that, the specific 'economic unit' retains its original identity with the purchaser. The European Court of Justice and the Federal Employment Court (*Bundesarbeitsgericht*) look to seven criteria to determine whether the transfer of a business has taken place, including whether or not the core workforce is assumed by the new owner. There are no clear boundaries in this respect. Rather, it depends on whether the purchaser assumes a significant proportion of the personnel in terms of number and expertise.

If an overall review of the seven criteria justifies the assumption that a business transfer has taken place, the employees are transferred to the purchaser of the business by virtue of law, even if the purchaser does not want to assume any of the staff. This is the legal consequence of the transfer of a business.

(c) **Can the transfer of plant and machinery coupled with the transfer of half the employees (125) constitute a business transfer under German legislation if the other 125 employees are dismissed prior to the transfer?**

Answer

Yes, this can also constitute a business transfer.

Legal reasoning

The vendor is not prevented from carrying out rationalisation measures or from issuing dismissals for operational reasons before the transfer. Whether or not there is a business transfer depends solely on whether the transferred business (reduced in size) retains its identity after the transfer.

(d) **Does the fact that the business will transfer to a different country make any difference to whether this is a business transfer?**

Answer

In principle, no.

Legal reasoning

The transfer of a business can also take place where the business or part of the business is relocated abroad (see response to question 1(a) above).

Although their decisions do not correspond with the case law of the Federal Employment Court (*Bundesarbeitsgericht*), a few Regional Employment Courts have held that a business's identity is lost upon relocation abroad, with the consequence that there can be no transfer of that business. However, in 1987, the Federal Employment Court held that the identity of a business is lost if a significant number of its employees are not prepared to continue their employment abroad. In such a case, the staff community is dissolved, with the consequence that it is regarded as the closure of the business and not a business transfer. It is debatable whether this ruling still applies (see *M1.2* above).

(e) **Is German transfer law concerned with the actual distance moved (irrespective of whether this means a change of country)?**

Answer

In principle, no.

Legal reasoning

The criteria used to determine whether a transfer constitutes a business transfer apply equally in the case of a relocation.

However, where a business is sold and relocated, it is necessary to establish whether a closure or a transfer of that business has taken place. The Federal Employment Court (*Bundesarbeitsgericht*) held in 1987 that the identity of a business is lost if a significant number of its employees refuse to continue their employment abroad. However, it should be noted that the Federal Employment Court has significantly changed its case law on business transfers since then. It is therefore debatable whether this ruling still applies (see *M1.2* above). If the relocation does not constitute a transfer of the business, employees who regard the relocation of their jobs as positive cannot rely upon s 613A of the German Civil Code. They are not entitled to transfer.

2. Relocation, but no business transfer

(a) **Assuming the move does NOT constitute a business transfer (because the business of Beta does not adequately retain its identity) but instead is deemed to be a straightforward relocation, are any of Beta's employees obliged or entitled to transfer?**

Answer

No, none of Beta's employees are obliged or entitled to transfer.

Legal reasoning

The employees are only obliged or entitled to transfer if the move constitutes a business transfer within the meaning of s 613A of the German Civil Code.

If there is no business transfer, Gamma is not obliged to employ any of Beta's employees. Beta employees therefore have no claims for re-appointment against Gamma. If production at Beta is closed down completely and there are no further employment opportunities for the production employees at Beta, they can legitimately be dismissed for urgent operational reasons. Beta cannot force a change of employer upon the production employees by way of a dismissal pending a change of contract (*Änderungskundigung*). Beta must observe the general principles of protection from dismissal, ie dismissal for urgent operational reasons, proper social selection, no further employment opportunities at Beta. Moreover, the participation rights of any works council must be observed. In cases of mass dismissals, the Employment Agency must be notified.

(b) If employees do nevertheless relocate, what will happen to their employment contracts? Will these continue, or will Gamma be entitled to provide new contracts?

Answer

Gamma is entitled to provide new contracts.

Legal reasoning

The transferring employees do not come under the protection of s 613A of the German Civil Code. Only upon a business transfer do former employment contracts remain valid. If Gamma takes on employees where there has not been a business transfer, their terms and conditions of employment can be negotiated. Gamma can therefore offer them its usual terms and conditions of employment, even if they are worse than those offered by Beta. However, the employees concerned are not obliged to accept the terms and conditions offered by Gamma. If they do not, they will continue to be employed by Beta and their employment contracts can be terminated for urgent operational reasons, where appropriate.

(c) What will be the law applicable to the contracts of the employees who relocate?

Answer

This depends on the terms and conditions of the employment contracts.

Legal reasoning

In the employees' new employment contracts with Gamma, the parties can agree upon the applicable law, eg German law. However, such agreement cannot override the mandatory provisions of French law (ie the usual place of work).

In the absence of a choice of law, the contracts of employment will be governed by the law of the country in which the employees habitually carry out their work in performance of the contracts, ie French law will apply.

3. Dismissals

(a) Assuming that the move does constitute a business transfer:

  (i)   are any dismissals in connection with the transfer lawful?

Answer

All dismissals 'on account of the transfer of a business or part of a business', irrespective of whether they are issued by the former employer or the new owner, are invalid. However, dismissals for 'other reasons' (according to the Protection against Dismissal Act, dismissals for urgent operational reasons, and for reasons related to the person or conduct of the employee) may be lawful.

Legal reasoning

If the motive for a dismissal is exclusively the impending transfer of a business, the dismissal is invalid pursuant to s 613A(4) of the German Civil Code and the employee can demand continued employment with his employer. This prohibition on dismissals in connection with business transfers is intended to prevent the vendor or the purchaser from 'cherry picking' employees. The aim of s 613A is the continuation of employment relationships.

However, dismissals in connection with a change of owner, in terms of time and matter, can legitimately be made provided they are 'socially justified' in accordance with the Protection against Dismissal Act (*Kündigungsschutzgesetz*). The owner of a business can legitimately carry out rationalisation measures to improve it before a sale and may issue dismissals for operational reasons. A purchaser can also issue dismissals for operational reasons after the transfer of business, owing to the effects of synergies and rationalisation measures. In the case of the purchase of an insolvent business, the Federal Employment Court (*Bundesarbeits-gericht*) recently declared that dismissals for operational reasons by the vendor in anticipation of a restructuring concept of the purchaser were valid.

(ii) **what are the rights and remedies (including applicable law and appropriate jurisdiction) of any employees dismissed:**

a. **before the transfer?**

Where there is no choice of law, German law will apply to the Beta employees (ie the law of the regular place of work). If Beta dismisses any employees, those employees can contest the validity of their dismissals by filing claims at the German Employment Courts.

Dismissals at Beta before the business transfer are not excluded per se. However, such dismissals will be invalid if the sole motive behind them is the business transfer itself, or if they are not 'socially justified' by operational reasons or by reasons related to the person or conduct of the employees under the Protection against Dismissal Act. Where a business transfer is imminent, the employer must take care when restructuring its business to avoid any resulting dismissals being regarded as invalid pursuant to s 613A(4) of the German Civil Code. An employee who is invalidly dismissed can demand to be re-employed. However, the employee must file a claim in this regard at the competent Employment Court within three weeks of receipt of the written notice of dismissal. Should he fail to do so, the dismissal will be valid.

The statutory severance claim recently introduced in Germany in relation to dismissals for operational reasons will only apply if the employer so desires, and requires a notice of dismissal to contain certain statements (see *M2.5* above). Severance claims can also result from a Social Plan or, as is often the case in practice, they are the outcome of court settlements between the parties.

b. after the transfer?

It is widely assumed that German law continues to apply to an employee's contract of employment after a business transfer, unless a prolonged period of work abroad suggests that he accepts the foreign law and jurisdiction as applying to his contract. The Federal Employment Court (*Bundesarbeitsgericht*) has not yet ruled on this matter (see *M1.4* above).

The purchaser may legitimately dismiss employees for operational reasons (eg synergy or rationalisation measures), even after a business transfer. Such dismissals are subject to the same statutory restrictions as apply in general to dismissals for operational reasons. The dismissals must therefore be 'socially justified' under the Protection against Dismissal Act.

A mistake that is often made in practice is the assumption that a dismissal issued by a purchaser within one year of a business transfer is invalid. This is not the case. Dismissals by a purchaser for operational reasons after a business transfer are not subject to any time restrictions.

(b) Would these rights and remedies change if this was not a business transfer?

Answer

No.

Legal reasoning

Even if this were not a business transfer, the dismissals by Beta would still have to be 'socially justified' under the Protection against Dismissal Act (see *M2.2* above). If the dismissals are not 'socially justified' (for example, if there is no operational reason for them, or if the 'social selection' is incorrect) they will be invalid. In such cases, the employee can demand that they continue their employment with Beta.

If Gamma voluntarily takes on Beta employees and later dismisses them, the validity of these dismissals will be subject to French law, as the law of the country in which the employees usually carry out their work. If German law were to apply after the business transfer, any dismissals would have to be 'socially justified' under the Protection against Dismissal Act.

4. European Works Council and other employees' representatives

(a) Will Alpha be required to inform and consult the European Works Council about the transfer or any redundancies?

Answer

Yes.

Legal reasoning

Pursuant to s 33 of the European Works Council Act, a European Works Council must be informed about, and provided with the necessary documents detailing, any extraordinary circumstances which are likely to have considerable effects on employees' interests. Such 'extraordinary circumstances' include the relocation of a company, business or significant part of a business, the closure of a company, business or part of a business, and collective redundancies. European Works Councils must be heard in such circumstances.

An agreement establishing a European Works Council in a particular workplace may contain further provisions in relation to consultation.

Conclusion

As there is a European Works Council in place, Alpha will be required to inform and consult it in relation to the cross-border transfer and any redundancies it plans to make.

(b) Are any other employee representatives required to be involved in the transfer or any redundancies (ie at national or local level)?

Answer

Yes, employee representatives must be involved in the decision-making processes in relation to both the transfer and any redundancies.

Legal reasoning

TRANSFERS

Economic affairs committees must be established in all companies that regularly employ more than 100 permanent employees. Economic affairs committees advise employers and inform works councils. They must be informed in good time and in detail about any restriction or closure of a business or part of a business, relocation of a business or part of a business, rationalisation projects, etc (see *M2.6* above).

The relocation of a whole business or of significant parts of a business, the closure of a whole business or of significant parts of a business and fundamental changes to the operational organisation of a whole business, or of significant parts of a business, are all regarded as 'operational changes' (see *M2.6* above). Upon a business transfer, Beta is obliged to inform and consult the works council with respect to the planned operational changes. A Reconciliation of Interests in relation to the operational changes must be concluded in writing between Beta and the works council. A Social Plan would serve to compensate for or to alleviate the economic disadvantages which the employees might incur as a result of the planned operational changes.

COLLECTIVE REDUNDANCIES

If the thresholds for collective redundancies are exceeded (see *M2.2* above), an employer is obliged to inform any works council that is in place in writing of the reasons for the planned redundancies, the number and the occupational groups of the employees to be made redundant, the number and the occupational groups of the employees normally employed, the period during which the redundancies are to take place, the intended criteria for selection of the employees to be made redundant and the criteria provided for the calculation of any severance payments. This notification usually takes place at the same time as negotiations in relation to a Reconciliation of Interests and a Social Plan.

INDIVIDUAL REDUNDANCIES

A works council must also be heard before any individual redundancies are carried out (see *M2.2* above).

5. Collective agreements

What is the effect of the business transfer on any collective agreements affecting Beta's employees?

Upon a business (or part of a business) transfer under s 613A of the German Civil Code, the employment contracts of the personnel assigned to the business (or part of a business) are automatically transferred with all rights and duties to the purchaser. The purchaser takes the place of the former employer.

The effects of a business (or part business) transfer on rights regulated by collective agreements (ie collective bargaining agreements and works agreements) are very complex, even where the transfer takes place in Germany (see *M1.4* above). Upon a cross-border business transfer where the business is simultaneously relocated abroad, the provisions of any collective agreement that applied whilst the business was owned by the vendor do not continue to apply in their former collective agreement form, but become an integral part of the employment contracts between the transferring employees and the purchaser. The provisions therefore continue to apply on an individual level. Moreover, they cannot be amended to the detriment of the transferring employees within the first year of the business transfer. However, this restriction on amendment does not apply if the rights and obligations concerned are regulated by another collective bargaining agreement at the purchaser. Unfortunately, the extent to which a foreign (eg French) collective agreement can impact upon the German collective agreement provisions in individual employment contracts following a cross-border business transfer is still very unclear.

6. Change of terms and conditions

(a) **If this is a business transfer, how can Gamma lawfully harmonise employment contracts and change the terms and conditions of the employees currently on the more generous Beta contracts of employment?**

Answer

Changing terms and conditions of employment is very difficult.

Legal reasoning

The various mechanisms that exist to facilitate the continued application of former terms and conditions of employment following a business transfer can lead to different terms and conditions applying within one business (in this case, Gamma).

German law does provide for a certain amount of harmonisation in relation to rights and duties under works agreements and collective bargaining agreements following a business transfer if corresponding agreements are in place at the purchaser. It is also conceivable that a new owner might wish to implement measures to harmonise rights and duties, either by mutual amendment to employment contracts or by dismissals pending changes of contract (*Änderungskündigung*).

The Federal Employment Court (*Bundesarbeitsgericht*) has held that any amendments made to contracts that provide less favourable employment conditions for employees without objective grounds (eg for the purpose of maintaining jobs), are invalid.

Moreover, the original rights and duties regulated by collective agreements that continue to apply on an individual level after a business transfer can only be amended to the detriment of the employee after a period of one year has passed.

If a business transfer results in the relocation of the business abroad, amendments to the transferring employees' contracts of employment to this effect (change of work location) are usually necessary.

If an employee is unwilling to come to a mutual agreement, an employer may issue a dismissal pending a change of contract (*Änderungskündigung*). However, in order to be valid, dismissals pending a change of contract must satisfy the requirements of the Protection against Dismissal Act (*Kündigungsschutzgesetz*). Such dismissals can only be made for reasons relating to the person or the conduct of the employee, or for operational reasons. A dismissal pending a change of contract will not be justified by an employer's desire to harmonise employment conditions. Further, the restriction on amendments within the first year of a business transfer must be observed, and any rights and duties arising from works agreements or collective bargaining agreements will continue to apply on an individual level.

A dismissal pending a change of contract will also be necessary if the business is to be relocated abroad and an employee does not consent to his place of work being changed.

Any works council in place must be heard before a dismissal pending a change of contract is carried out.

(b) **If this is a business transfer, can Gamma reduce the wages of the former Beta employees?**

Answer

It would be extremely difficult for Gamma to reduce the employees' wages.

Legal reasoning

The principles applying to the harmonisation of employment conditions, set out in the response to question **6(a)** above, also apply to wage reductions. As it will not generally be possible to mutually agree a wage reduction, a dismissal pending a change of contract must be issued. The Federal Employment Court (*Bundesarbeitsgericht*) has repeatedly held that a wage reduction with the intention of harmonising employment conditions within a workforce is subject to very strict standards and is only possible in exceptional circumstances. Here, Gamma would need to be in an economically precarious situation and fear that, if the employment conditions were not adjusted, jobs would be lost and dismissals would be unavoidable.

(c) **If this is a business transfer, what will happen to the former Beta employees as regards their private pension arrangements?**

Upon a business transfer, the commitment to a works pension scheme granted by the vendor – since it is also part of the employment relationship – is transferred to the purchaser. Whether the purchaser can legitimately change the pension commitment or cancel it completely depends on its legal basis. In any case, certain peculiarities must be observed for reasons of fidelity.

(d) Is it easier to change terms and conditions of employment if the changes are made six months after the transfer?

Answer

No.

Legal reasoning

The rights and duties arising from collective bargaining agreements and works agreements that are transformed into individual employment contract provisions may only be changed to the detriment of the employee after the expiry of a period of one-year following a business transfer. The preconditions for such an amendment to the employment conditions to be valid remain unchanged (ie an amendment to the contract or a socially justified dismissal pending a change of contract is necessary).

M3.3 Case study 3
(Outsourcing of an ancillary activity to a non-EU country)

A large multinational (ABC) based in Germany has decided to outsource its entire internal IT function to a third party provider in Romania, as the costs of hiring competent IT personnel in Romania are far lower than in Germany, largely because wages are so much lower. At present 200 employees are employed by ABC in its IT function in Germany. It is anticipated that exactly the same IT function will be required in Romania with approximately the same number of people required to run it. There will be no difference in the service or approach for those requiring IT assistance and even the internal telephone number will be automatically diverted. The Romanian third party provider has no assets or presence in Germany.

1. Business transfer

Will this be a business transfer within the scope of Germany's law applying the ARD?

Answer

No, this will not be a business transfer under s 613A of the German Civil Code. This is a pure continuation of the business activity (functional succession).

Legal reasoning

It was held by the European Court of Justice in *Süzen v Zehnacker Gebäudereinigung GmbH Krankenhausservice*: C-13/95 [1997] ECR I-1259, ECJ that a 'unit may not be understood as mere activity'. The Federal Employment Court (*Bundesarbeitsgericht*) has since implemented this decision. The decisive characteristic of a business transfer is the further use of an already existing employment organisation, which was set up by the former owner of the business on a permanent basis for a particular operational purpose ('identity of the economic unit'). A mere activity cannot be considered an economic unit in this sense. A business transfer therefore requires further criteria to be satisfied, such as the assumption of significant operational means, the employment organisation, the working methods and/or a significant number of personnel of the organisation.

2. Effect on employees

(a)   **What will happen to the employees currently employed in the IT function at ABC? Will they transfer across?**

Answer

These employees are not transferred by operation of law to the IT provider in Romania. ABC can terminate the employment contracts for operational reasons owing to a part closure of the business.

Legal reasoning

Since the requirements of a business transfer under s 613A of the German Civil Code are not fulfilled, the employment contracts are not transferred by operation of law to the Romanian IT provider. The employees currently employed in the IT function remain employees of ABC. However, ABC has outsourced the IT functions, ie there are no longer any jobs for the employees who formerly worked in this department. ABC can therefore terminate the employment contracts for urgent operational reasons. For the terminations to be 'socially justified' under the Protection against Dismissal Act, ABC must first review whether it would be possible to continue to employ these employees at the company, on different terms if appropriate. Only if this is not possible can terminations be carried out.

(b)   **If the employees do transfer, what will the applicable law be for their employment contracts with the third party provider? Where can they make any claims?**

Answer

The parties can, in principle, choose which law is to apply to their employment contracts. If no such choice of law has been made, the employment contract is determined in accordance with the relevant provisions of Romanian private international law.

Legal reasoning

It must first be determined whether the employment contract entered into with ABC states the applicable law. If this is the case, the employment contract will be subject to the law agreed between the parties. However, the mandatory law of the place of work will apply to the employees. If, on the other hand, the parties have not expressly agreed a choice of law, the law to which the employment contract is subject is determined in accordance with the relevant provisions of private international law. In the event of a dispute, therefore, a judge must base his decision on the provisions of private international law which apply to his country. In a dispute before a Romanian court the question of applicable law would have to be judged in accordance with Romanian private international law.

The question of the international jurisdiction of German employment courts is decided in accordance with the general procedural provisions of Germany. German employment courts have local jurisdiction first and foremost at the registered place of business of the employer or the place where the work is carried out. In the present case, a claim could only be filed before a German employment court, therefore, whilst the IT people carry out their function in Germany, ie until the transfer of business. After that time, the jurisdiction of the Romanian courts must be judged on the basis of Romanian national law.

3. Data protection

Will there be special data protection issues on the transfer of knowledge and information outside Germany to Romania?

Answer

A transfer of personal data would only be lawful under certain conditions.

Legal reasoning

There will be data protection issues in relation to the transfer of knowledge and information to Romania. A transfer of personal data to countries outside the EU is only permitted if there is evidence of a suitable level of data protection, or if the person concerned has expressly consented to the transfer of his data to a country outside the EU[1]. The EU Commission has ascertained in this respect that there is only a sufficient level of data protection under the EC Data Protection Directive in Switzerland and Hungary and, with restrictions, in Canada. A sufficient level of data protection can be established in the USA if an American company subjects itself to the 'safe harbour principles' of the American Department of Commerce.

1   Federal Data Protection Act, s 4C(1).

4. Transfer to India

Please comment on any differences there would be to your answers if the function was transferred to India rather than Romania.

Answer

There would be no difference to the given responses.

Legal reasoning

The situation is identical whether the transfer of the IT function is to India or to Romania. However, the following is worth noting: that even if the Indian IT provider assumes the operational means and employees of the IT function, it is unlikely that this will constitute a business transfer under s 613A of the German Civil Code. The Federal Employment Court (*Bundesarbeitsgericht*) held in 1987 that the identity of a business is lost if a significant number of its employees refuse to continue their employment abroad (see *M1.2* above). In practice, the majority of the workforce is unlikely to be prepared to work in India. Therefore, the business in Germany may close. In this case, ABC may be entitled to dismiss the employees of the IT department for urgent operational reasons.

M4 Additional information

M4.1 Useful websites

Federal Ministry of Economics and Labour (*Bundesministerium für Wirtschaft und Arbeit* – 'BMWA'):
http://www.bmwa.bund.de/Navigation/root.html

Federal Employment Court (*Bundesarbeitsgericht*) with press releases
http://www.bundesarbeitsgericht.de/

Federal Employment Agency (*Bundesagentur für Arbeit*)
http://www.arbeitsagentur.de

European Court of Justice
http://www.curia.eu.int/de/content/juris/index.htm

EUR-Lex – The Portal to European Union Law
http://europa.eu.int/eur-lex/en/index.html

M4.2   Protection against Dismissal Act

Kündigungsschutzgesetz (KSchG)

Protection against Dismissal Act

Erster Abschnitt
Allgemeiner Kündigungsschutz

Chapter 1
General protection against dismissal

§ 1 Sozial ungerechtfertigte Kündigungen

1 Socially unjustified dismissals

(1)   Die Kündigung des Arbeitsverhältnisses gegenüber einem Arbeitnehmer, dessen Arbeitsverhältnis in demselben Betrieb oder Unternehmen ohne Unterbrechung länger als sechs Monate bestanden hat, ist rechtsunwirksam, wenn sie sozial ungerechtfertigt ist.

(1)   The termination of the employment relationship of an employee who has been employed in the same business or the same company without interruption for more than six months is legally invalid if it is socially unjustified.

(2)   Sozial ungerechtfertigt ist die Kündigung, wenn sie nicht durch Gründe, die in der Person oder in dem Verhalten des Arbeitnehmers liegen, oder durch dringende betriebliche Erfordernisse, die einer Weiterbeschäftigung des Arbeitnehmers in diesem Betrieb entgegenstehen, bedingt ist. Die Kündigung ist auch sozial ungerechtfertigt, wenn

(2)   A dismissal is socially unjustified if it is not due to reasons related to the person or the conduct of the employee, or to urgent operational reasons which preclude the continued employment of the employee in the business. The termination is also socially unjustified if:

1.   in Betrieben des privaten Rechts

1.   in private law businesses

a.   die Kündigung gegen eine Richtlinie nach § 95 des Betriebsverfassungsgesetzes verstößt,

a.   the termination violates a guideline pursuant to s 95 of the Works Council Constitution Act,

b.	der Arbeitnehmer an einem anderen Arbeitsplatz in demselben Betrieb oder in einem anderen Betrieb des Unternehmens weiterbeschäftigt werden kann		b.	the employee can continue to be employed in another position in the same business or in another business of the company

und der Betriebsrat oder eine andere nach dem Betriebsverfassungsgesetz insoweit zuständige Vertretung der Arbeitnehmer aus einem dieser Gründe der Kündigung innerhalb der Frist des § 102 Abs 2 Satz 1 des Betriebsverfassungsgesetzes schriftlich widersprochen hat,

and the works council or another competent representative body of the employees under the Works Council Constitution Act has objected in writing to the dismissal for one of these reasons within the period set forth in s 102(2), sentence 1 of the Works Council Constitution Act,

2. in Betrieben und Verwaltungen des öffentlichen Rechts

2. in public sector businesses and public administrations

    a. die Kündigung gegen eine Richtlinie über die personelle Auswahl bei Kündigungen verstößt,

    a. the termination violates a guideline regarding the selection of personnel for dismissal,

    b. der Arbeitnehmer an einem anderen Arbeitsplatz in derselben Dienststelle oder in einer anderen Dienststelle desselben Verwaltungszweigs an demselben Dienstort einschließlich seines Einzugsgebiets weiterbeschäftigt werden kann

    b. the employee can continue to be employed in another position in the same office or in another office of the same administrative branch in the same locality or its catchment area

und die zuständige Personalvertretung aus einem dieser Gründe fristgerecht gegen die Kündigung Einwendungen erhoben hat, es sei denn, daß die Stufenvertretung in der Verhandlung mit der übergeordneten Dienststelle die Einwendungen nicht aufrechterhalten hat.

Satz 2 gilt entsprechend, wenn die Weiterbeschäftigung des Arbeitnehmers nach zumutbaren Umschulungs- oder Fortbildungsmaßnahmen oder eine Weiterbeschäftigung des Arbeitnehmers unter geänderten Arbeitsbedingungen möglich ist und der Arbeitnehmer sein Einverständnis hiermit erklärt hat. Der Arbeitgeber hat die Tatsachen zu beweisen, die die Kündigung bedingen.

and the competent employee representative body has raised objections to the dismissal in due time for one of these reasons, unless a superior representative body in negotiations with a superior office has not upheld these objections.

Sentence 2 applies accordingly if the continued employment of the employee is possible after a reasonable amount of re-training or additional training under modified working conditions and the employee has given his consent. The employer bears the burden of proving the facts which caused the dismissal.

(3) Ist einem Arbeitnehmer aus dringenden betrieblichen Erfordernissen im Sinne des Absatzes 2 gekündigt worden, so ist die Kündigung trotzdem sozial ungerechtfertigt, wenn der Arbeitgeber bei der Auswahl des Arbeitnehmers die Dauer der Betriebszugehörigkeit, das Lebensalter, die Unterhaltspflichten und die Schwerbehinderung des Arbeitnehmers nicht oder nicht ausreichend berücksichtigt hat; auf Verlangen des Arbeitnehmers hat der Arbeitgeber dem Arbeitnehmer die Gründe anzugeben, die zu der getroffenen sozialen Auswahl geführt haben. In die soziale Auswahl nach Satz 1 sind Arbeitnehmer nicht einzubeziehen, deren Weiterbeschäftigung, insbesondere wegen ihrer Kenntnisse, Fähigkeiten und Leistungen oder zur Sicherung einer ausgewogenen Personalstruktur des Betriebes im berechtigten betrieblichen Interesse liegt. Der Arbeitnehmer hat die Tatsachen zu beweisen, die die Kündigung als sozial ungerechtfertigt im Sinne des Satzes 1 erscheinen lassen.

(3) Where an employee is dismissed owing to urgent operational reasons within the meaning of (2), the dismissal is nevertheless held to be socially unjustified if, in selecting the employee, the employer has not, or has not sufficiently, considered the number of years of service, the age, the maintenance obligations and any disability of the employee; at the employee's request, the employer must inform the employee of the reasons on which the selection in question was made. Employees whose continued employment is in the legitimate interest of the business, in particular on account of their knowledge, ability and performance or to ensure a balanced personnel structure in the business, must not be included in the social selection. The employee bears the burden of proving the facts which make the dismissal appear to be socially unjustified within the meaning of sentence 1.

(4) Ist in einem Tarifvertrag, in einer Betriebsvereinbarung nach § 95 des Betriebsverfassungsgesetzes oder in einer entsprechenden Richtlinie nach den Personalvertretungsgesetzen festgelegt, wie die sozialen Gesichtspunkte nach Abs 3 Satz 1 im Verhältnis zueinander zu bewerten sind, so kann die Bewertung nur auf grobe Fehlerhaftigkeit überprüft werden.

(4) Where a collective bargaining agreement, a works agreement pursuant to s 95 of the Works Council Constitution Act or a corresponding guideline under the laws governing personnel representation stipulates how the social factors pursuant to para (3), sentence 1 should be valued in relation to each other, the valuation can only be reviewed with respect to gross errors.

(5) Sind bei einer Kündigung aufgrund einer Betriebsänderung nach § 111 des Betriebsverfassungs-gesetzes die Arbeitnehmer, denen gekündigt werden soll, in einem Interessenausgleich zwischen Arbeitgeber und Betriebsrat namentlich bezeichnet, so wird vermutet, dass die Kündigung durch dringende betriebliche Erfordernisse im Sinne des Abs 2 bedingt ist. Die soziale Auswahl der Arbeitnehmer kann nur auf grobe Fehlerhaftigkeit überprüft werden. Die Sätze 1 und 2 gelten nicht, soweit sich die Sachlage nach Zustandekommen des Interessenausgleichs wesentlich geändert hat. Der Interessenausgleich nach Satz 1 ersetzt die Stellungsnahme des Betriebsrates nach § 17 Abs 3 Satz 2.

(5) If in the case of dismissal for operational reasons pursuant to s 111 of the Works Council Constitution Act the employees to be dismissed are named in a reconciliation of interests between the employer and the works council it is assumed that the dismissal is for urgent operations reasons within the meaning of para (2). The social selection of the employees can only be reviewed with respect to gross errors. Sentences 1 and 2 shall not apply if the situation has fundamentally changed since the reconciliation of interests was concluded. The reconciliation of interests pursuant to sentence 1 replaces the comments of the works council pursuant to s 17(3), sentence 2.

§ 1A Abfindungsanspruch bei betriebsbedingter Kündigung

(1)   Kündigt der Arbeitgeber wegen dringender betrieblicher Erfordernisse nach § 1 Abs 2 Satz 1 und erhebt der Arbeitnehmer bis zum Ablauf der Frist des § 4 Satz 1 keine Klage auf Feststellung, dass das Arbeitsverhältnis durch die Kündigung nicht aufgelöst ist, hat der Arbeitnehmer mit dem Ablauf der Kündigungsfrist Anspruch auf eine Abfindung. Der Anspruch setzt den Hinweis des Arbeitgebers in der Kündigungserklärung voraus, dass die Kündigung auf dringende betriebliche Erfordernisse gestützt ist und der Arbeitnehmer bei Verstreichenlassen der Klagefrist die Abfindung beanspruchen kann.

(2)   Die Höhe der Abfindung beträgt 0,5 Monatsverdienste für jedes Jahr des Bestehens des Arbeitsverhältnisses. § 10 Abs 3 gilt entsprechend. Bei der Ermittlung der Dauer des Arbeitsverhältnisses ist ein Zeitraum von mehr als sechs Monaten auf ein volles Jahr aufzurunden.

1A Claim to a severance payment in the case of dismissal for operational reasons

(1)   If the employer dismisses an employee for urgent operational reasons pursuant to s 1(2), sentence 1 and if the employee does not submit an action for a ruling that the employment relationship has not been terminated by the notice of termination by the deadline pursuant to s 4(1), the employee has the right to a severance payment after expiry of the notice period. The claim depends on notification by the employer in the notice of termination that the dismissal is for urgent operational reasons and the employee is entitled to the severance payment once the deadline for claims has expired.

(2)   The amount of the severance payment is 0.5 of a monthly salary for each year of service with the employer. s 10(3) applies accordingly. A period of more than six months must be rounded up to a year for the purpose of ascertaining the number of years of service.

§ 2 Änderungskündigung

Kündigt der Arbeitgeber das Arbeitsverhältnis und bietet er dem Arbeitnehmer im Zusammenhang mit der Kündigung die Fortsetzung des Arbeitsverhältnisses zu geänderten Arbeitsbedingungen an, so kann der Arbeitnehmer dieses Angebot unter dem Vorbehalt annehmen, dass die Änderung der Arbeitsbedingungen nicht sozial ungerechtfertigt ist (§ 1 Abs 2 Satz 1–3, Abs 3 Satz 1 und 2). Diesen Vorbehalt muss der Arbeitnehmer dem Arbeitgeber innerhalb der Kündigungsfrist, spätestens jedoch innerhalb von drei Wochen nach Zugang der Kündigung erklären.

§ 4 Anrufung des Arbeitsgerichtes

Will ein Arbeitnehmer geltend machen, dass eine Kündigung sozial ungerechtfertigt ist oder aus anderen Gründen rechtsunwirksam ist, so muss er innerhalb von drei Wochen nach Zugang der schriftlichen Kündigung Klage beim Arbeitsgericht auf Feststellung erheben, dass das Arbeitsverhältnis durch die Kündigung nicht aufgelöst ist. (...)

§ 7 Wirksamwerden der Kündigung

Wird die Rechtsunwirksamkeit einer Kündigung nicht rechtzeitig geltend gemacht (§ 4 Satz 1, §§ 5 und 6), so gilt die Kündigung als von Anfang an rechtswirksam; ein von Arbeitnehmer nach § 2 erklärter Vorbehalt erlischt.

2 Notice of dismissal pending change of contract

If the employer terminates the employment relationship and if it offers the employee continued employment at changed conditions in connection with the termination, the employee can accept this offer subject to the proviso that the change in the employment conditions is not socially unjustified (s 1(2), sentences 1–3; s 1(3), sentences 1 and 2). The employee must declare this proviso to the employer within the notice period, at the latest, however, within three weeks of receipt of the notice of termination.

4 Appeal to the Employment Court

If an employee wants to assert that a dismissal is socially unjustified or invalid for other reasons he must file an action at the employment courts for a ruling that the employment relationship has not been terminated by the dismissal within three weeks of receipt of the written notice. (...)

7 Effectiveness of the dismissal

Where the invalidity of a socially unjustified dismissal is not asserted in due time (s 4. sentence 1; ss 5 and 6) the dismissal is considered to be valid from the start; any reservation declared by the employee pursuant to s 2 is cancelled.

Dritter Abschnitt *Anzeigepflichtige Entlassungen*	Chapter 3 *Dismissals requiring notification*
§ 17 Anzeigepflicht	**17 Duty of notification**
(1) Der Arbeitgeber ist verpflichtet, der Agentur für Arbeit Anzeige zu erstatten, bevor er	(1) The employer shall notify the Employment Agency within 30 calendar days prior to dismissing:
1. in Betrieben mit in der Regel mehr als 20 und weniger als 60 Arbeitnehmern mehr als 5 Arbeitnehmer,	1. more than five employees in businesses which regularly employ more than 20 and fewer than 60 employees,
2. in Betrieben mit in der Regel mindestens 60 und weniger als 500 Arbeitnehmern 10 vom Hundert der im Betrieb regelmäßig beschäftigten Arbeitnehmer oder aber mehr als 25 Arbeitnehmer,	2. 10 per cent of the employees regularly employed or more than 25 employees in businesses with at least 60 and fewer than 500 employees,
3. in Betrieben mit in der Regel mindestens 500 Arbeitnehmern mindestens 30 Arbeitnehmer	3. at least 30 employees in businesses which regularly employ at least 500 employees.
innerhalb von 30 Kalendertagen entläßt. Den Entlassungen stehen andere Beendigungen des Arbeitsverhältnisses gleich, die vom Arbeitgeber veranlaßt werden.	These dismissals shall be treated the same as other terminations of the employment relationship which are brought about by the employer.
(2) Beabsichtigt der Arbeitgeber, nach Absatz 1 anzeigepflichtige Entlassungen vorzunehmen, hat er dem Betriebsrat rechtzeitig die zweckdienlichen Auskünfte zu erteilen und ihn schriftlich insbesondere zu unterrichten über	(2) Where an employer intends to make dismissals which are notifiable pursuant to para (1), he must inform the Works Council in writing and in a timely manner of, in particular,
1. die Gründe für die geplanten Entlassungen,	1. the reasons for the planned dismissals,

2.   die Zahl und die Berufsgruppen der zu entlassenden Arbeitnehmer,

2.   the number and occupational group of the employees to be dismissed,

3.   die Zahl und die Berufsgruppen der in der Regel beschäftigten Arbeitnehmer,

3.   the number and occupational group of the employees regularly employed,

4.   den Zeitraum, in dem die Entlassungen vorgenommen werden sollen,

4.   the period of time over which these dismissals are to take place,

5.   die vorgesehenen Kriterien für die Auswahl der zu entlassenden Arbeitnehmer,

5.   the intended criteria for the selection of the employees to be dismissed,

6.   die für die Berechnung etwaiger Abfindungen vorgesehenen Kriterien.

6.   the criteria for calculating any severance payments.

Arbeitgeber und Betriebsrat haben insbesondere die Möglichkeiten zu beraten, Entlassungen zu vermeiden oder einzuschränken und ihre Folgen zu mildern.

The employer and the Works Council shall, in particular, have the opportunity to discuss ways in which the dismissals can be prevented or limited and how their consequences can be mitigated.

(3)   Der Arbeitgeber hat gleichzeitig der Agentur für Arbeit eine Abschrift der Mitteilung an den Betriebsrat zuzuleiten; sie muß zumindest die in Absatz 2 Satz 1 Nr 1 bis 5 vorgeschriebenen Angaben enthalten. Die Anzeige nach Absatz 1 ist schriftlich unter Beifügung der Stellungnahme des Betriebsrats zu den Entlassungen zu erstatten. Liegt eine Stellungnahme des Betriebsrats nicht vor, so ist die Anzeige wirksam, wenn der Arbeitgeber glaubhaft macht, daß er den Betriebsrat mindestens zwei Wochen vor Erstattung der Anzeige nach Absatz 2 Satz 1 unterrichtet hat, und er den Stand der Beratungen darlegt. Die Anzeige muß Angaben über den Namen des Arbeitgebers, den Sitz und die Art des Betriebes enthalten, ferner die Gründe für die geplanten Entlassungen, die Zahl und die Berufsgruppen der zu entlassenden und der in der Regel beschäftigten Arbeitnehmer, den Zeitraum, in dem die Entlassungen vorgenommen werden sollen und die vorgesehenen Kriteren für die Auswahl der zu entlassenden Arbeitnehmer. In der Anzeige sollen ferner im Einvernehmen mit dem Betriebsrat für die Arbeitsvermittlung Angaben über Geschlecht, Alter, Beruf und Staatsangehörigkeit der zu entlassenden Arbeitnehmer gemacht werden. Der Arbeitgeber hat dem Betriebsrat eine Abschrift der Anzeige zuzuleiten.

(3)   At the same time, the employer must send to the Employment Agency a copy of the notification to the Works Council. This notification must at least contain the information set forth in para (2), sentence 1, nos 1–5 above. The notification pursuant to para (1) must be in writing and include the Works Council's comments regarding the dismissals. Where the Works Council has not given its comments, the notification shall still be effective if the employer can demonstrate that he informed the Works Council at least two weeks prior to submitting the notification pursuant to para (2), sentence 1 and it describes the status of the discussions between the employer and the Works Council. The notification shall give the employer's name, the domicile and nature of the business, the reason for the planned dismissals, the number and occupational group of employees to be dismissed and of those regularly employed, the period of time over which the dismissals are to take place and the intended criteria for the selection of the employees to be dismissed. Further, in agreement with the Works Council, the notification should state the sex, age, occupation and nationality of the employees to be dismissed, for use by the Employment Agency. The employer shall send a copy of the notification to the Works Council.

Der Betriebsrat kann gegenüber der Agentur für Arbeit weitere Stellungnahmen abgeben. Er hat dem Arbeitgeber eine Abschrift der Stellungnahme zuzuleiten.

The Works Council may submit further comments to the Employment Agency. It shall send the employer a copy of such comments.

(3A) Die Auskunfts-, Beratungs- und Anzeigepflichten nach den Absätzen 1 bis 3 gelten auch dann, wenn die Entscheidung über die Entlassungen von einem den Arbeitgeber beherrschenden Unternehmen getroffen wurde. Der Arbeitgeber kann sich nicht darauf berufen, daß das für die Entlassungen verantwortliche Unternehmen die notwendigen Auskünfte nicht übermittelt hat.

(3A) The duty to provide information, to consult with the Works Council and to notify the Employment Agency pursuant to paras (1) to (3) shall apply even if the decision on the dismissals was made by a company controlling the employer. The employer cannot avoid his obligations under this provision by arguing that the company responsible for the dismissals did not convey the necessary information.

(4) Das Recht zur fristlosen Entlassung bleibt unberührt. Fristlose Entlassungen werden bei Berechnung der Mindestzahl der Entlassungen nach Absatz 1 nicht mitgerechnet.

(4) The right of employers to carry out dismissals without notice shall remain unaffected. Dismissals without notice shall not be counted in the calculation of the minimum number of dismissals pursuant to para (1).

(5) Als Arbeitnehmer im Sinne dieser Vorschrift gelten nicht

(5) The following shall not be deemed to be employees within the meaning of this provision:

1. in Betrieben einer juristischen Person die Mitglieder des Organs, das zur gesetzlichen Vertretung der juristischen Person berufen ist,

1. in businesses of a legal entity, members of the body appointed to legally represent that legal entity,

2. in Betrieben einer Personengesamtheit die durch Gesetz, Satzung oder Gesellschaftsvertrag zur Vertretung der Personengesamtheit berufenen Personen,

2. in businesses of a partnership, the persons appointed by law or in the partnership agreement to represent the partnership,

3. Geschäftsführer, Betriebsleiter und ähnliche leitende Personen, soweit diese zur selbständigen Einstellung oder Entlassung von Arbeitnehmern berechtigt sind.

3. directors, operations managers and similar persons exercising management functions insofar as they have the authority to independently appoint or dismiss employees.

§ 18 Entlassungssperre

18 Waiting period for dismissal

(1) Entlassungen, die nach § 17 anzuzeigen sind, werden vor Ablauf eines Monats nach Eingang der Anzeige bei der Agentur für Arbeit nur mit dessen Zustimmung wirksam; die Zustimmung kann auch rückwirkend bis zum Tage der Antragstellung erteilt werden.

(1) Dismissals which require notification pursuant to s 17 shall only become effective sooner than one month from the date of receipt of the notification by the Employment Agency with its consent; such consent may also be granted with retroactive effect as of the date of application.

(2) Die Agentur für Arbeit kann im Einzelfall bestimmen, daß die Entlassungen nicht vor Ablauf von längstens zwei Monaten nach Eingang der Anzeige wirksam werden.

(2) The Employment Agency may, in individual cases, determine that dismissals shall not become effective before a maximum period of two months has elapsed following the date on which the Employment Agency received the notification.

(3) (*weggefallen*)

(3) (*repealed*)

(4) Soweit die Entlassungen nicht innerhalb von 90 Tagen nach dem Zeitpunkt, zu dem sie nach den Absätzen 1 und 2 zulässig sind, durchgeführt werden, bedarf es unter den Voraussetzungen des § 17 Abs 1 einer erneuten Anzeige.

(4) If the dismissals are not carried out within a period of 90 days following the date on which they became permissible pursuant to paras (1) and (2), a new notification must be made which conforms to the requirements of s 17(1).

M4.3   *Civil Code, s 613A*

Bürgerliches Gesetzbuch	**Civil Code**
§ 613A Rechte und Pflichten bei Betriebsübergang	**613A Rights and obligations upon the transfer of a business**

(1)   Geht ein Betrieb oder Betriebsteil durch Rechtsgeschäft auf einen anderen Inhaber über, so tritt dieser in die Rechte und Pflichten aus den im Zeitpunkt des Übergangs bestehenden Arbeitsverhältnissen ein. Sind diese Rechte und Pflichten durch Rechtsnormen eines Tarifvertrags oder durch eine Betriebsvereinbarung geregelt, so werden sie Inhalt des Arbeitsverhältnisses zwischen dem neuen Inhaber und dem Arbeitnehmer und dürfen nicht vor Ablauf eines Jahres nach dem Zeitpunkt des Übergangs zum Nachteil des Arbeitnehmers geändert werden. Satz 2 gilt nicht, wenn die Rechte und Pflichten bei dem neuen Inhaber durch Rechtsnormen eines anderen Tarifvertrags oder durch eine andere Betriebsvereinbarung geregelt werden. Vor Ablauf der Frist nach Satz 2 können die Rechte und Pflichten geändert werden, wenn der Tarifvertrag oder die Betriebsvereinbarung nicht mehr gilt oder bei fehlender beiderseitiger Tarifgebundenheit im Geltungsbereich eines anderen Tarifvertrags dessen Anwendung zwischen dem neuen Inhaber und dem Arbeitnehmer vereinbart wird.

(1)   Where a business or part of a business is transferred to another owner by means of a legal transaction, the new owner enters into the rights and obligations arising from the employment relationships in existence at the time of transfer. Where these rights and obligations are regulated by means of legal standards set in a collective bargaining agreement or by a works agreement, they shall become an integral part of the employment relationship between the new owner and the employee and may not be altered to the detriment of the employee until a period of one year has elapsed since the date of the transfer. Sentence 2 shall not apply if the rights and obligations arising from the employment relationship with the new owner are regulated by means of legal standards set in another collective bargaining agreement or another works agreement. The rights and obligations may be altered prior to the expiry of the period pursuant to sentence 2 if the collective bargaining agreement or the works agreement has ceased to exist, or if neither party is bound to a collective bargaining agreement, within the scope of application of another collective bargaining agreement, the application of which is agreed upon between the new owner and the employee.

(2)   Der bisherige Arbeitgeber haftet neben dem neuen Inhaber für Verpflichtungen nach Absatz 1, soweit sie vor dem Zeitpunkt des Übergangs entstanden sind und vor Ablauf von einem Jahr nach diesem Zeitpunkt fällig werden, als Gesamtschuldner. Werden solche Verpflichtungen nach dem Zeitpunkt des Übergangs fällig, so haftet der bisherige Arbeitgeber für sie jedoch nur in dem Umfang, der dem im Zeitpunkt des Übergangs abgelaufenen Teil ihres Bemessungszeitraums entspricht.

(2)   The former employer shall be jointly and severally liable, together with the new owner, for those obligations pursuant to para (1) which arise prior to the date of transfer and those which become due before one year after that date has elapsed since the date of transfer. However, where such obligations become due after the date of transfer, the previous employer shall be liable only for the fraction of the total liability that arose from the period prior to the transfer date.

(3)   Absatz 2 gilt nicht, wenn eine juristische Person oder eine Personenhandelsgesellschaft durch Umwandlung erlischt.

(3)   Paragraph (2) shall not apply if a legal entity or commercial partnership ceases to exist by virtue of merger, spin-off or transformation.

(4)   Die Kündigung des Arbeitsverhältnisses eines Arbeitnehmers durch den bisherigen Arbeitgeber oder durch den neuen Inhaber wegen des Übergangs eines Betriebs oder eines Betriebsteils ist unwirksam. Das Recht zur Kündigung des Arbeitsverhältnisses aus anderen Gründen bleibt unberührt.

(4)   Any termination of an employee's employment relationship by the former employer or the new owner on account of the transfer of a business, or part of a business, shall be invalid. The right to terminate the employment relationship for other reasons remains unaffected.

(5)   Der bisherige Arbeitgeber oder der neue Inhaber hat die von einem Übergang betroffenen Arbeitnehmer vor dem Übergang in Textform zu unterrichten über:

(5)   The former employer or the new owner shall inform the employees affected by a transfer in writing prior to the transfer of:

1.   den Zeitpunkt oder den geplanten Zeitpunkt des Übergangs,

1.   the planned date of the transfer,

2.   den Grund für den Übergang,

2.   the reason for the transfer,

3. die rechtlichen, wirtschaftlichen und sozialen Folgen des Übergangs für die Arbeitnehmer und

3. the legal, economic and social ramifications of the transfer for the employees and

4. die hinsichtlich der Arbeitnehmer in Aussicht genommenen Maßnahmen.

4. the prospective measures to be taken with respect to the employees.

(6) Der Arbeitnehmer kann dem Übergang des Arbeitsverhältnisses innerhalb eines Monats nach Zugang der Unterrichtung nach Absatz 5 schriftlich widersprechen. Der Widerspruch kann gegenüber dem bisherigen Arbeitgeber oder dem neuen Inhaber erklärt werden.

(6) An employee may object to the transfer of the employment relationship in writing within one month of receiving the notification pursuant to para (5). The objection may be made to the former employer or the new owner.

M4.4 Works Council Constitution Act

Betriebsverfassungsgesetz (BetrVG)	Works Council Constitution Act

Zweiter Unterabschnitt
Betriebsänderungen

Subchapter 2
Operational changes

§ 111 Betriebsänderungen

111 Operational changes

In Unternehmen mit in der Regel mehr als zwanzig wahlberechtigten Arbeitnehmern hat der Unternehmer den Betriebsrat über geplante Betriebsänderungen, die wesentliche Nachteile für die Belegschaft oder erhebliche Teile der Belegschaft zur Folge haben können, rechtzeitig und umfassend zu unterrichten und die geplanten Betriebsänderungen mit dem Betriebsrat zu beraten. Der Betriebsrat kann in Unternehmen mit mehr als 300 Arbeitnehmern zu seiner Unterstützung einen Berater hinzuziehen; § 80 Abs 4 gilt entsprechend; im Übrigen bleibt § 80 Abs 3 unberührt. Als Betriebsänderungen im Sinne des Satzes 1 gelten:

In companies which regularly employ more than 20 employees who are eligible to vote, the owner shall promptly and comprehensively inform the Works Council of planned operational changes which could result in significant disadvantages for the personnel or a considerable part of the personnel, and confer with the Works Council with respect to the planned operational changes. In companies with over 300 employees, the Works Council may engage a consultant to assist; s 80(4) applies accordingly; s 80(3) remains unaffected. Operational changes within the meaning of sentence 1 include:

1. Einschränkung und Stillegung des ganzen Betriebs oder von wesentlichen Betriebsteilen,

1. A reduction in or closure of the entire business or significant parts thereof;

2. Verlegung des ganzen Betriebs oder von wesentlichen Betriebsteilen,

2. a relocation of the business or considerable parts thereof;

3. Zusammenschluss mit anderen Betrieben oder die Spaltung von Betrieben,

3. an amalgamation with other businesses or a separation of businesses;

4. grundlegende Änderungen der Betriebsorganisation, des Betriebszwecks oder der Betriebsanlagen,

4. fundamental changes in the organisation, purpose or operating installations of the business;

5. Einführung grundlegend neuer Arbeitsmethoden und Fertigungsverfahren.

5. the introduction of fundamentally new working methods and production processes.

§ 112 Interessenausgleich über die Betriebsänderung, Sozialplan

112 Reconciliation of interests with respect to operational change; Social Plan

(1) Kommt zwischen Unternehmer und Betriebsrat ein Interessenausgleich über die geplante Betriebsänderung zustande, so ist dieser schriftlich niederzulegen und vom Unternehmer und Betriebsrat zu unterschreiben. Das Gleiche gilt für eine Einigung über den Ausgleich oder die Milderung der wirtschaftlichen Nachteile, die den Arbeitnehmern infolge der geplanten Betriebsänderung entstehen (Sozialplan). Der Sozialplan hat die Wirkung einer Betriebsvereinbarung. § 77 Abs 3 ist auf den Sozialplan nicht anzuwenden.

(1) If a reconciliation of interests is agreed between the owner and the Works Council with regard to planned operational changes, this shall be recorded in writing and be signed by the owner and the Works Council. The same applies to an agreement with regard to a settlement or the mitigation of financial disadvantages that the employees will suffer as a result of the planned operational changes ('Social Plan'). The Social Plan shall have the effect of a works agreement. s 77(3) does not apply to the Social Plan.

(2) Kommt ein Interessenausgleich über die geplante Betriebsänderung oder eine Einigung über den Sozialplan nicht zustande, so können der Unternehmer oder der Betriebsrat den Vorstand der Bundesagentur für Arbeit um Vermittlung ersuchen, der Vorstand kann die Aufgabe auf andere Bedienstete der Bundesagentur für Arbeit übertragen. Erfolgt kein Vermittlungsersuchen oder bleibt der Vermittlungsversuch ergebnislos, so können der Unternehmer oder der Betriebsrat die Einigungsstelle anrufen.

(2) If a reconciliation of interests with regard to the planned operational changes or an agreement on a Social Plan cannot be achieved, the owner or the Works Council may call upon the Board of the Federal Employment Agency to mediate; the Board may instruct other employees of the Federal Employment Agency to mediate on its behalf. If this does not happen or if the attempt to mediate fails, the owner or the Works Council may appeal to the Conciliation Board.

Auf Ersuchen des Vorsitzenden der Einigungsstelle nimmt ein Mitglied des Vorstands der Bundesagentur für Arbeit oder ein vom Vorstand der Bundesagentur für Arbeit benannter Bediensteter der Bundesagentur für Arbeit an der Verhandlung teil.

(3) Unternehmer und Betriebsrat sollen der Einigungsstelle Vorschläge zur Beilegung der Meinungsverschiedenheiten über den Interessenausgleich und den Sozialplan machen. Die Einigungsstelle hat eine Einigung der Parteien zu versuchen. Kommt eine Einigung zustande, so ist sie schriftlich niederzulegen und von den Parteien und vom Vorsitzenden zu unterschreiben.

At the request of the Conciliation Board's chairman, a member of the Board of the Federal Employment Agency or a Federal Employment Agency employee appointed by the Board, shall participate in the negotiations.

(3) The owner and the Works Council shall make suggestions to the Conciliation Board to resolve any differences of opinion on the reconciliation of interests and the Social Plan. The Conciliation Board shall encourage the parties to reach an agreement. If no agreement is reached, this fact shall be recorded in writing and signed by the parties and the chairman of the Conciliation Board.

(4) Kommt eine Einigung über den Sozialplan nicht zustande, so entscheidet die Einigungsstelle über die Aufstellung eines Sozialplans. Der Spruch der Einigungsstelle ersetzt die Einigung zwischen Arbeitgeber und Betriebsrat.

(4) If no agreement on the Social Plan is reached, the Conciliation Board shall decide on the establishment of the Social Plan. The Conciliation Board's decision shall replace any agreement between the employer and the Works Council.

(5) Die Einigungsstelle hat bei ihrer Entscheidung nach Absatz 4 sowohl die sozialen Belange der betroffenen Arbeitnehmer zu berücksichtigen als auch auf die wirtschaftliche Vertretbarkeit ihrer Entscheidung für das Unternehmen zu achten. Dabei hat die Einigungsstelle sich im Rahmen billigen Ermessens insbesondere von folgenden Grundsätzen leiten zu lassen:

(5) In making its decision pursuant to para (4), the Conciliation Board shall consider the social concerns of the affected employees as well as the economic feasibility of its decision for the company. The Conciliation Board shall, at its reasonable discretion, particularly be guided by the following principles:

1. Sie soll beim Ausgleich oder bei der Milderung wirtschaftlicher Nachteile, insbesondere durch Einkommensminderung, Wegfall von Sonderleistungen oder Verlust von Anwartschaften auf betriebliche Altersversorgung, Umzugskosten oder erhöhte Fahrtkosten, Leistungen vorsehen, die in der Regel den Gegebenheiten des Einzelfalles Rechnung tragen.

1. When compensating for or mitigating financial disadvantages, in particular those resulting from loss of income, fringe benefits or expectancies in company pension plans, from removal costs or increased travel costs, it should provide for benefits which generally take the individual's circumstances into account.

2. Sie hat die Aussichten der betroffenen Arbeitnehmer auf dem Arbeitsmarkt zu berücksichtigen. Sie soll Arbeitnehmer von Leistungen ausschließen, die in einem zumutbaren Arbeitsverhältnis im selben Betrieb oder in einem anderen Betrieb des Unternehmens oder eines zum Konzern gehörenden Unternehmens weiterbeschäftigt werden können und die Weiterbeschäftigung ablehnen; die mögliche Weiterbeschäftigung an einem anderen Ort begründet für sich allein nicht die Unzumutbarkeit.

2. It must consider the affected employee's prospects on the employment market. It should exclude from any benefits employees who could be further employed and who reject continued and reasonable employment in the same business or in a different business of the company or in companies belonging to the group; continued employment in a different place of work shall not be deemed to be unreasonable for that reason alone.

2A. Sie soll insbesondere die im Dritten Buch des Sozialgesetzbuches vorgesehenen Förderungsmögli-chkeiten zur Vermeidung von Arbeitslosigkeit berücksichtigen.

2A. In particular, it should take into consideration the possibilities for advancement in order to prevent unemployment that are set out in the Third Book of the Social Security Code.

3. Sie hat bei der Bemessung des Gesamtbetrages der Sozialplanleistungen darauf zu achten, dass der Fortbestand des Unternehmens oder die nach Durchführung der Betriebsänderung verbleibenden Arbeitsplätze nicht gefährdet werden.

3. When calculating the total amount of the Social Plan benefits, it shall ensure that the continued existence of the company or the jobs remaining after the execution of the operational changes will not be endangered.

§ 112A Erzwingbarer Sozialplan bei Personalabbau, Neugründungen

(1) Besteht eine geplante Betriebsänderung im Sinne des § 111 Satz 3 Nr 1 allein in der Entlassung von Arbeitnehmern, so findet § 112 Abs 4 und 5 nur Anwendung, wenn

1. in Betrieben mit in der Regel weniger als 60 Arbeitnehmern 20 vom Hundert der regelmäßig beschäftigten Arbeitnehmer, aber mindestens 6 Arbeitnehmer,

2. in Betrieben mit in der Regel mindestens 60 und weniger als 250 Arbeitnehmern 20 vom Hundert der regelmäßig beschäftigten Arbeitnehmer oder mindestens 37 Arbeitnehmer,

3. in Betrieben mit in der Regel mindestens 250 und weniger als 500 Arbeitnehmern 15 vom Hundert der regelmäßig beschäftigten Arbeitnehmer oder mindestens 60 Arbeitnehmer,

4. in Betrieben mit in der Regel mindestens 500 Arbeitnehmern 10 vom Hundert der regelmäßig beschäftigten Arbeitnehmer, aber mindestens 60 Arbeitnehmer

112A Compulsory Social Plan due to redundancy; new formations

(1) If a planned operational change within the meaning of s 111, sentence 3, no 1 consists solely of the dismissal of employees, s 112(4) and (5) shall only apply if:

1. in businesses which regularly employ less than 60 employees, 20% of the regular employees, but at least six employees,

2. in businesses which regularly employ at least 60 and less than 250 employees, 20% of the regular employees or at least 37 employees,

3. in businesses which regularly employ at least 250 and less than 500 employees, 15% of the regular employees or at least 60 employees,

4. in businesses which regularly employ at least 500 employees, 10% of the regular employees, but at least 60 employees

aus betriebsbedingten Gründen entlassen werden sollen. Als Entlassung gilt auch das vom Arbeitgeber aus Gründen der Betriebsänderung veranlasste Ausscheiden von Arbeitnehmern auf Grund von Aufhebungsverträgen.

are to be dismissed for operational reasons. If the employer instigates the departure of an employee on the basis of a termination agreement, this shall also be deemed to be a dismissal due to operational changes.

(2) § 112 Abs 4 und 5 findet keine Anwendung auf Betriebe eines Unternehmens in den ersten vier Jahren nach seiner Gründung. Dies gilt nicht für Neugründungen im Zusammenhang mit der rechtlichen Umstrukturierung von Unternehmen und Konzernen. Maßgebend für den Zeitpunkt der Gründung ist die Aufnahme einer Erwerbstätigkeit, die nach § 138 der Abgabenordnung dem Finanzamt mitzuteilen ist.

(2) Section 112(4) and (5) shall not apply to the businesses of a company during the first four years of its establishment. This shall not apply to new formations in connection with the legal restructuring of a company or a group. The commencement of business operations, which must be reported to the Tax Authority pursuant to s 138 of the General Tax Code is decisive for determining the time of formation.

§ 113 Nachteilsausgleich

113 Compensation for detrimental effects of dismissal

(1) Weicht der Unternehmer von einem Interessenausgleich über die geplante Betriebsänderung ohne zwingenden Grund ab, so können Arbeitnehmer, die infolge dieser Abweichung entlassen werden, beim Arbeitsgericht Klage erheben mit dem Antrag, den Arbeitgeber zur Zahlung von Abfindungen zu verurteilen; § 10 des Kündigungsschutzgesetzes gilt entsprechend.

(1) Where the owner deviates from a reconciliation of interests with regard to the planned operational changes without a compelling reason, the employees who have been dismissed as a result of this deviation may file complaints with the Employment Court, petitioning it to order the employer to make severance payments; s 10 of the Protection Against Dismissals Act shall apply accordingly.

(2) Erleiden Arbeitnehmer infolge einer Abweichung nach Absatz 1 andere wirtschaftliche Nachteile, so hat der Unternehmer diese Nachteile bis zu einem Zeitraum von zwölf Monaten auszugleichen.

(2) If employees incur other financial disadvantages as a result of a deviation pursuant to para (1), the owner shall compensate them for these disadvantages within a period of twelve months.

(3) Die Absätze 1 und 2 gelten entsprechend, wenn der Unternehmer eine geplante Betriebsänderung nach § 111 durchführt, ohne über sie einen Interessenausgleich mit dem Betriebrat versucht zu haben, und infolge der Maßnahme Arbeitnehmer entlassen werden oder andere wirtschaftliche Nachteile erleiden.

(3) Paragraphs (1) and (2) apply accordingly if the company executes a planned operational change pursuant to s 111 without attempting to reach a reconciliation of interests with the Works Council and, as a result of this operational change, employees are dismissed or incur other financial disadvantages.

N Hungary

Gabriella Ormai
Péter K Bán

N1 Business transfers

N1.1 Background

Introduction

Succession in contractual relationships is generally possible in every modern legal system. The legal problems in relation to business transfers emerged much later in Hungary than in the European Community – where EC Directive 77/187/EEC was enacted in the late 1970s. The issues in this regard only became apparent in Hungary with the onset of the privatisation process at the start of the 1990s. Before that, the overwhelming majority of the population were public sector employees, so the influence of the State and the lack of a functioning market economy had a considerable effect on employment regulations. The bottom line was that there was only one employer in Hungary, and so the concept of a business transfer had little meaning.

The privatisation process changed everything. In the early 1990s, all forms of what we now call a 'business transfer' had appeared, eg the sale of a plant, the sale of part of a business, and the distribution of the core assets of big state-owned enterprises to various legal personalities. The turbulent nature of these changes meant that Hungarian legislation lagged behind the needs of reality. According to the long-held employment law tradition in Hungary, an employment relationship is close and personal – an intimate relationship which requires trust between employers and employees to be maintained. It can be argued that such a personal relationship does not allow any succession at all: it would be strange if a sick employee could send his or her nephew to the workplace to carry out his or her duties. Further, it could be said that an employee decides to work for a particular employer for a good reason and, therefore, the identity of the employer matters in the same way.

In the absence of legal rules, traditions or case law in relation to business transfers, the first years of privatisation resulted in turmoil: in some cases, employment contracts were terminated; in others, they were renegotiated. The same was true of collective bargaining agreements, which often had very favourable terms for employees, so that new owners tried to get rid of them as quickly as possible. The situation only changed officially in 1997, when the Hungarian Parliament stepped in to harmonise Act XXII of 1992 on the Hungarian Labour Code ('Labour Code') with the requirements of the European Union. In Hungary, the law treats a business transfer as a special case where the employment contract is modified without the formal consent of the parties being required.

Currently, the Labour Code enshrines the three main principles of contemporary EC rules on the protection of workers' acquired rights in the case of a transfer of undertakings:

- automatic transfer of employment relationships by virtue of the transfer itself (Labour Code, s 85/A(2));

- protection against dismissal (the business transfer cannot be a cause for dismissal (Labour Code, s 89(4)); and

- employees and/or their representatives must be consulted before the transfer actually takes place (Labour Code, s 85/B(1)–(5)).

Jurisdictional issues

There are some features of the Hungarian business transfer rules that may differ from the rules in other jurisdictions. First, breach of the information and consultation obligations affects the validity of a transfer only if there is a recognised trade union at the transferor employer or if there is a duly elected works council. In the absence of these, the failure of the transferor and transferee employers to consult is a lex imperfecta – if a court finds there has been a breach of the duty to inform and consult the employees, there is no express sanction available.

Furthermore, employees in senior managerial positions are not excluded from the scope of the transfer rules. Moreover, since s 188(1) of the Labour Code defines the category of senior executives very narrowly, there is relatively strong protection from dismissal for all transferred employees.

There is no express statutory list of criteria to identify business transfers, which leaves courts open to interpret the scope of the transfer of undertakings rules broadly. As Hungary is now a member of the EU, one can expect Hungarian courts to take the case law of the European Court of Justice (the 'ECJ') into consideration in the future and apply the list of criteria established in *Spijkers*[1].

Currently, the Labour Code only covers employment in the territory of Hungary and the secondment of employees who regularly conduct their activities in Hungary. Therefore, the transfer rules in the Labour Code do not have any extraterritorial effect, either in the territory of the European Community or in other countries outside the borders of Hungary. However, Directive 2001/23/EC, which currently regulates business transfers within the European Community, provides that cross-border transactions within its territory can fall within the scope of the definition of a transfer of an undertaking. Therefore, the Hungarian Labour Code will have to be amended to comply with the EC rules. However, there are no amendments pending before the Hungarian Parliament to change the current situation and there are no published cases from the Hungarian Supreme Court ('Supreme Court') on this subject matter.

According to the conflict of laws rules of Law Decree No 13 of 1979 on Private International Law (the 'Conflict of Laws Rules'), parties can choose which law is applicable to their employment contract. If no such choice is made, the lex loci laboris rule (the rule that provides that the law in the place where the employee habitually carries out his work applies to his contract of employment) has to be applied. These are the same rules as those enshrined in the Rome Convention of 1980 on the law applicable to contractual obligations. Notwithstanding that parties are free to choose the law applicable to their employment contracts, in the absence of a foreign element, choice of law clauses are hard to justify before courts. According to the Rome Convention, where there is no foreign element, the parties cannot deviate from the mandatory rules of the country which has all the connecting elements to the relevant transaction. The Supreme Court has yet to confirm whether it considers the business transfer rules are mandatory rules of Hungarian law, in accordance with the local Conflict of Laws Rules.

Since its accession to the EU, Council Regulation (EC) 44/2001 of 22 December 2000 on jurisdiction and the recognition and enforcement of judgments in civil and commercial matters (the 'Jurisdiction Regulation'), has been in force in Hungary. According to the Jurisdiction Regulation, courts in the member state where the defendant is domiciled will have jurisdiction to hear and decide legal controversies with regard to that defendant. This rule is supplemented by arts 18 and 19 of the Jurisdiction Regulation, whereby an employee may sue in the place where he/she habitually carried out his/her work. This rule will have particular importance if national laws differ in their treatment of cross-border business transfers – particularly as most civil law legal systems do not recognise the common law concept of forum non conveniens (which allows a court to decline its own jurisdiction because the courts in another jurisdiction can more conveniently try a case).

1   See the judgment of the ECJ of 18 March 1986, Case 24/85: *Jozef Maria Antonius Spijkers v Gebroeders Benedik Abbatoir CV et Alfred Benedik en Zonen BV* [1986] ECR 1119.

N1.2 Identifying a relevant transfer

Ruling no 154 of the labour law *collegium* of the Supreme Court

As has been seen above, the concept of a business transfer is relatively new to Hungarian law. The privatisation boom of the early 1990s left this whole issue unregulated, and the problems were exacerbated by the system imposed by the old, socialist-era labour code, Act II of 1967 on the Labour Code ('the 1967 Labour Code').

The Supreme Court cut the Gordian knot in September 1992 by issuing ruling no 154 of the labour law *collegium* of the Supreme Court ('MK 154')[1]. This decision introduced the concept of a business transfer into Hungarian law without formal legislative support. Decisions of a Supreme Court *collegium* are binding on all lower courts in the country. The long-lasting impact of MK 154 clearly shows that, even though Hungary has a civil law system where precedents are not recognised as a formal source of law, de facto the decisions of the Supreme Court operate in the same way as common law precedents.

MK 154 filled a yawning gap in Hungarian jurisprudence. It established the concept of a business transfer in Hungarian employment law for the first time and distinguished it from the concept of a legal succession under civil law contract and company law, thereby reaffirming the broader interpretation of legal succession for the purposes of employment law.

MK 154 quickly gained acceptance from the lower courts, especially since it could be applied retroactively, unlike a formal act of Parliament. This, of course, raised concerns as to whether the decision conformed to the constitutional principle that legislative acts should not have retroactive effect.

According to MK 154, if a business transfer (*munkáltatói jogutódlás*) occurs, this does not affect the existence of the relevant employment relationships. Employment relationships in such a situation are deemed continuous, and the period before the transfer has to be taken into account when seniority and all seniority-based benefits, like notice periods and severance payments, are being assessed. According to the Supreme Court, there is no need for any formal transfer agreement between the new employer and the employee following a transfer. Moreover, the rules of the so-called 'transfer agreements' under the 1967 Labour Code were deemed to be immaterial in the context of a business transfer and, therefore, could not be applied.

A little background to the concept of 'transfer agreements' (*áthelyezési megállapodás*) is crucial to understanding the motives behind MK 154. A transfer agreement was an atypical contract in the 1967 Labour Code: a tripartite agreement between the employee and two employers, whereby the transferee employer agreed to employ the employee while taking into account the time spent with the previous employer for the calculation of seniority but not the calculation of severance pay. By virtue of a transfer agreement, the employee's previous employment was terminated. The *ratio* behind this concept was to make restructuring in the privatisation process possible, without the need to make considerable severance payments to employees who had had long employment relationships with the transferor (usually a socialist-era state conglomerate). However, the Supreme Court acted contrary to the 1967 Labour Code, especially by giving MK 154 retroactive effect.

Formal legal succession rarely occurred during the privatisation process in Hungary, since buyers usually set up a Special Purpose Vehicle ('SPV') that bought only the assets of the state-owned company and continued its operations. In MK 154, the Supreme Court gave a wide interpretation to the term 'business transfer', which closely resembled the one adopted by Directive 77/187/EEC. According to MK 154, a business transfer occurs on either:

(i)   a succession based on the law; or

(ii) a transfer of the whole or part of a business by sale, lease or contribution to a different business organisation, provided that the transferee takes the place of the transferor.

1   See 1 Bírósági Határozatok (Supreme Court Rulings) 1993.

Supreme Court decision no 398/1993

The scope of the term 'business transfer' has been gradually extended by the Supreme Court. The first published decision that applied MK 154 was in 1993, shortly after the decision itself was issued. Supreme Court decision no 398/1993 was clearly a contra legem verdict, but one that was in perfect harmony with the business transfer rules that had been established by MK 154. The plaintiff in this case initiated a lawsuit for a severance payment after his employment was terminated in 1992. He claimed that there had been a business transfer between the state-owned merchandising company and a newly incorporated company to which the plaintiff was transferred by virtue of a 'transfer agreement' (*áthelyezési megállapodás*) in 1990. The defendant company relied on s 209 of the Labour Code, which stipulated that, in the case of a 'transfer agreement', the calculation of seniority starts at the time of that transfer agreement, so that the plaintiff was not entitled to a severance payment.

The Supreme Court ruled that, if it was found that there had been a business transfer between the transferor and the transferee company, the employment relationship would be deemed to be continuous, such that the transfer agreement would be invalid. The Supreme Court, while assessing whether the business transfer rules applied to the facts of the case, took into consideration that:

(i)   the transferor company was one of the transferee's founders, as it had moved a considerable amount of assets, both tangible and intangible, to the transferee company;

(ii) the registered office of the transferee and the transferor were the same; and

(iii) the plaintiff carried out his work using assets that were actually transferred from the transferor to the transferee.

The Supreme Court quashed the lower court's initial decision and referred the case back for determination in accordance with the principles it had set out.

Supreme Court decision no 708/1993

In decision no 708/1993, the Supreme Court went further than decision no 398/1993, when it established that a 'transfer agreement' does not play a role where there is a simultaneous transfer of an undertaking between transferor and transferee employers. In this case, the Supreme Court established that there had been a transfer of an undertaking since the plaintiff:

(i)   worked at the same place;

(ii) for the same salary; and

(iii) had similar tasks, before and after the transfer.

The court held that it was clear that the business was transferred as a going concern and that its activities continued unchanged. The decision used similar criteria to those applied in the *Spijkers* case[1].

1   Case 24/85: *Jozef Maria Antonius Spijkers v Gebroeders Benedik Abbatoir CV et Alfred Benedik en Zonen BV* [1986] ECR 1119.

Supreme Court decision no 403/1993

Decision no 403/1993 held that there had been a business transfer on the basis of an ownership-based criterion. Such a factor is not usually decisive in practice, as is shown by its absence from the list of criteria in *Spijkers*[1]. However, in this instance, the Supreme Court ruled that there was a business transfer solely on the basis that the transferor owned 100 per cent of the shares in the transferee.

The ownership-based criterion could work the other way around as well: it is easy to foresee a scenario in which a company tries to reorganise in such a way that valuable or useful assets are put into a separate company for further operation, and the original company is left to become insolvent in order to free up the remaining valuable assets. In these circumstances, under the current Labour Code, as we will see in *N1.5*, an employee may turn to his/her previous employer for a severance payment or payment during his/her notice period.

In case no 403/1993, because the employee objected to the transfer and was accordingly dismissed, the Supreme Court ruled that he was not entitled to the increased severance payment stipulated by a collective bargaining agreement with the transferor. This decision implicitly raised the question of whether there is a right for employees to object to business transfers.

1   Case 24/85: *Jozef Maria Antonius Spijkers v Gebroeders Benedik Abbatoir CV et Alfred Benedik en Zonen BV* [1986] ECR 1119.

Act LI of 1997

Act LI of 1997 was enacted to implement the employment law-related directives of the European Communitiy, as part of Hungary's efforts to create a legal system which conforms to the *acquis communautaire*.

The basic idea behind the Act was to sanction court practice and the case law stemming from MK 154 by inserting a new chapter into the Labour Code on the transfer of undertakings. This new chapter, s 85/A, together with s 209(2), defined a transfer of an undertaking as:

–   a succession based on the law; or

–   a transfer or take-over by way of a lease, a sale of assets, a transfer of assets to a company for shares or quota, or by way of another method of transferring an employer's separate and organised group of material and non-material resources (eg a business unit, a plant, a business, a shop, a site, a workplace or a part thereof) to another organisation, with the intention that the operation of the business is continued or resumed, employing the workforce of the transferor on the same or similar terms and conditions.

The new chapter was put into Part III of the Labour Code (Part III contains the rules on individual employment contracts), notably amongst the rules which govern the amendment of employment contracts. In the majority of cases, succession by law means a merger or the winding-up of a company in accordance with Act CXLIV of 1997 on Business Associations (the 'Companies Act'). If the employer is a private entity, the successor becomes party to the relevant employment contracts – there is no exemption to this rule under Hungarian law, unlike in other civil law jurisdictions in Europe.

The recent amendment to the business transfer rules – Act XX of 2003

Directive 2001/23/EC on the safeguarding of employees' rights in the event of a transfer of an undertaking or business, or part of an undertaking or business, was implemented into Hungarian employment law by Act XX of 2003, with an effective date of 1 July 2003.

The amendment brought some transparency by moving the definition of a transfer of an undertaking into the unified s 85/A of the Labour Code. The new definition became broader than it was under Act LI of 1997: according to the new s 85/A(1) of the Labour Code, a transfer of an undertaking is either:

–   a succession by virtue of the law (see above); or

–   when an independent unit (such as a strategic business unit, a plant, a shop, a division, a workplace, or any section of these) or the material and non-material assets of an employer are transferred by agreement to an organisation or person falling within the scope of the Labour Code, for the further operation or restarting of the relevant business, if such a transfer takes place within the framework of a sale, exchange, lease, or capital contribution for a business association.

The amendment corrected a serious defect within the old definition in s 209 of the Labour Code by deleting the condition that employees perform their duties on the same, or similar, terms and conditions before and after the transfer. It cannot be denied that this is usually the case in a business transfer scenario, but continued employment on similar terms and conditions is no longer a precondition of a business transfer in Hungary.

The new definition contains an important addition, that the unit is to be 'transferred by agreement to an organisation or person falling within the scope of the Labour Code', which was not applied before. The Labour Code only covers employment relationships between private parties and excludes relationships where the State or any State agency is involved. These relationships are regulated by separate acts of Parliament, such as Act XXIII of 1992 on Civil Servants (the 'Civil Service Act') and Act XXXIII of 1992 on Public Servants (the 'Public Servants Act'). To deal with this situation, the Labour Code now contains separate provisions on the transfer of employees into the public sector, as well as on the transfer of employees from the public sector to private companies.

N1.3 'Employees' and 'affected employees'

Employees

The Labour Code does not directly define who is an 'employee'. However, it does establish that an employment relationship is created by a contract of employment. Consequently, the Labour Code applies to all relationships that are created on the basis of a contract of employment. The term 'employee' has to be interpreted restrictively: a consultant or an agency worker, and even an employee of a different company on secondment who does not have a formal employment agreement, cannot be considered an employee. As a result of this, such persons do not transfer automatically in the case of a transfer of an undertaking, and the guarantee described in N1.4 below does not apply to them.

Affected employees

In a transfer of an undertaking scenario, it is evident that only those employees who are employed by the transferor at the time of the transfer are affected. The Acquired Rights Directive 2001/23/EC contains no definition of who should be considered an 'employee', so the interpretation of this is a task for the national courts. It is most likely that, following accession, the Hungarian courts will stick to the current interpretation of the word 'employee' and exclude consultants and even temporary agency workers from the scope of the protection offered by the business transfer rules of the Labour Code.

Service or consultancy agreements may be reclassified by the Hungarian courts if they show the characteristics of an employment agreement. In practice, an employment relationship may be distinguished from a civil law agency relationship on the basis of several criteria. According to decision no 99/1997 of the Hungarian Supreme Court, all legal relationships must be judged on the basis of their content and not on the formal terms and conditions of the underlying contract. The courts will decide this question on a case-by-case basis, paying particular attention to the scope of the employee's work.

If the relationship between the parties satisfies the criteria of an employment relationship, as described below, they cannot validly execute an agency or consultancy agreement instead. If a Hungarian court establishes that a service contract is, in fact, an employment contract, it has the power to declare this with retroactive effect, stretching back to the date on which the parties entered into the 'service agreement'.

N1.4 Effects of the transfer

Transfer of public servants

As described above, the legal regulations in Hungary applicable to public sector employees (ie public servants and civil servants) are different from the regime applicable to the employees of private companies. According to the Public Servants Act 1992, the appointment of public servants affected by the transfer of an undertaking or part of an undertaking, irrespective of its actual form, ceases as at the date of the transfer, provided that the new employer falls within the scope of the Labour Code. All non-public legal persons (ie companies, foundations, etc) are subject to the Labour Code. Contrary to the normal transfer of business rules, the rights and obligations arising from the relationships of the public servants concerned do not automatically transfer to the new employer – it is obliged to engage in an 'offering mechanism'.

In such a situation, the transferor has a duty to inform the public servants who will be affected by the transfer, at least 30 days beforehand, of:

(i)   the reasons for;

(ii)   the date of; and

(iii)   the legal, economical and social consequences of the transfer.

The transferor also has a duty to consult and negotiate with the representatives of the public servants who will be affected by the transfer, in relation to its consequences and the mitigation of any possible harmful effects.

Thirty days before the date of the transfer, the new employer must notify the public servants who will be affected of the terms and conditions of their future employment contracts. In formulating its offer, the new employer is restricted in only two ways:

(i)   the wage of the public servant cannot be lower than it previously was, taking into account all his/her allowances and other benefits under his/her appointment; and

(ii)   if the public servant's appointment was for an indefinite term, the employment contract cannot be concluded for a finite term.

If the public servant agrees to work for the transferee, it is under an obligation to conclude an employment contract with him/her in accordance with its previous offer. If the public servant refuses the offer, his/her public service status is terminated as at the date of the transfer and he/she is entitled to severance payment. All the years spent as a public servant are taken into account for the purposes of calculating all seniority-related benefits, as if they had been spent in an employment relationship with the new, private sector employer.

Transfer of civil servants

The regime applicable to civil servants utilises a similar 'offering mechanism' to the one in the Public Servants Act 1992, described at *N1.4* above. The transferor must notify the affected civil servants no later than 60 days before the date of the transfer and communicate to them all the relevant information, including the terms and conditions of their new employment contracts.

If a civil servant accepts the terms and conditions communicated to him/her by the private company participating in the transfer, he/she will be automatically transferred as at the date of the transfer. The same limitations on the new employer's offer as are outlined above in respect of public servants apply in the case of civil servants.

Civil servants' seniority calculations, with the exception of the calculation of notice periods and redundancy pay (see below), are measured by adding the time spent as a civil servant to the duration of employment with the new employer. The notice periods and redundancy payments to which transferred civil servants will be entitled will be much longer than those applicable to private sector employees, as the duration of the notice periods and the amount of the severance payments stipulated by the Civil Service Act 1992 must be added to those to which the employee is entitled under his/her employment contract. This serves to make the termination of employment contracts with former civil servants by the transferee very expensive.

Transfer to the public sector

The transfer rules in the Labour Code contain a different regime for when employees are transferred from the private to the public sector, ie to an organisation that falls within the scope of the Public Servants Act 1992 or the Civil Service Act 1992. In such a situation, the employment relationship ceases to exist de jure as at the date of the transfer. The new employer – a public body – has to offer an appointment to the employee and communicate the terms and conditions of such appointment.

These terms and conditions are crucial, since the salary of civil and public servants is decided by law and not by negotiated agreements. Therefore, it is difficult to ensure that employees are transferred to the public sector on the same terms and conditions. The Labour Code provides a one-sided solution. The salary of the employee as a public servant cannot be lower than his/her basic salary under his/her previous employment agreement. However, this is not the case if the employee has been transferred to the public sector as a civil servant. Here, the Labour Code sets a 20 per cent threshold – if the basic salary of the employee in the private sector was more than 20 per cent higher than the amount he/she will be entitled to under the Civil Service Act, the difference above the 20 per cent threshold cannot be taken into account.

If the employee objects to the transfer to the public sector, he/she will be entitled to a severance payment and remuneration during his/her notice period, provided he/she has accumulated sufficient seniority.

N1.5 Safeguarding of employees' rights

Automatic transfer of rights and obligations

Upon legal succession, the rights and obligations arising from an employment relationship transfer from the 'legal predecessor' to the 'legal successor'. The 'legal predecessor' (or transferor) is obliged to inform the 'legal successor' (or transferee) of these rights and obligations. However, the employees' use of these rights to enforce claims is not affected if the transferor does not meet this obligation to inform. An employee, however, can choose against whom he/she wishes to seek enforcement for claims originating before the date of the transfer, due to the joint and several liability of the transferor and the transferee, as described below.

An employee's period of employment is deemed to be continuous, particularly with regard to the length of the notice period and the amount of the severance payment to which he/she is entitled (Act LI of 1997 rejected the distinction made in the original business transfer concept between notice periods and severance payments as benefits tied to seniority). There is no need to enter into a new employment agreement or to modify the existing agreement – this is only required if the transferee wishes to modify the terms and conditions of the employment relationship.

Right to object

The right of an employee to object to, and the need for an employee to consent to, a transfer of an undertaking were topics of a Supreme Court decision in 1995 – before the formal legislative adoption of the business transfer regime in the Labour Code in 1997. Supreme Court Decision No 375/1995 upheld the verdict of the Court of Appeal. The Court of Appeal held, inter alia, that legal succession for employment law purposes is established by the fact of a business transfer, with no need to secure the employee's consent to it. The decision established the main guideline for judicial practice in assessing whether there has been a transfer of an undertaking:

> 'it shall be considered a business transfer within the terms of employment law if the transferee de facto replaces the transferor and employs the transferred employee. In assessing whether there was a business transfer, courts must consider only the circumstances of the transaction itself – it is irrelevant whether the employee consented to the business transfer or not.'

Liability for redundancy pay

The Labour Code distinguishes between two types of liability with regard to transferred employees:

–   Liability for debts and damages incurred prior to the date of the business transfer, provided that such claims are enforced within one year of the transfer. This liability is joint and several and does not depend on any further conditions, such as the surety described below. After the one-year period, only the transferee can be held liable within the general limitation period, which is three years in Hungary (s 11(1)–(4) of the Labour Code).

–   Liability incurred if an employee is dismissed by the transferee within one year of the date of the transfer, for reasons connected with its operations or because a period of fixed-term employment has ended. In these situations, the transferor is liable, as a surety, for the employee's redundancy pay upon the termination of the employment relationship. However, this liability is conditional – the transferor is only liable if:

(i)   the transferor;

(ii)   a company controlled by the transferor;

(iii)   the majority owner of the transferor; or

(iv)   a company in which the majority owner of the transferor has a majority shareholding,

together hold more than 50 per cent of the voting shares in the transferee.

Protection from dismissal

As explained above, the fact of a business transfer is not, of itself, an acceptable reason for dismissing employees. However, in reality, this rule does not offer much protection to employees. Commentaries on the Labour Code suggest that dismissals associated with business transfers may be justified if they are for 'operational reasons'. An operational reason is one that is related to an economic, technical or organisational issue with regard to an employer. A corporate restructuring is one example of a potential 'operational reason', but could trigger mass redundancy rules if the number of dismissed employees reached the prescribed levels.

Collective agreements

One of the fundamental problems with MK 154 was that it did not address the survival of the mandate of a works council, the recognised or 'representative' status of a trade union in a particular workplace or, most notably, the effect of a business transfer on existing collective bargaining agreements. Because of this, its application has been burdened by many questions and criticisms.

The situation became more blurred when the Supreme Court published its controversial Decision No 175/2000, where it held that the rights and obligations arising from a collective agreement survive a business transfer, such that employees may enforce them against their new employers.

The decision opened the floodgates of litigation and had very serious implications on existing cases. Moreover, it raised a lot of questions: How long can a collective agreement be applied to a transferred employee? Is a modification to a collective agreement by the transferee valid in relation to the transferred employees? What happens if the transferor also has a collective agreement in place? These questions were only answered with the introduction of Act XX of 2003 on the amendment of the Labour Code. The new rules harmonised the Labour Code with the Acquired Rights Directive 2001/23/EC.

According to the current rules of the Labour Code, if a transferor was party to a collective agreement before the transfer, the transferee is bound by the work conditions (not including working time regulations) prescribed by that collective agreement. However, this only applies to employees transferred to the transferee within one year of the date of transfer.

The situation is different if the transferee is also party to a collective agreement. In this scenario, the transferred employees benefit from being able to 'cherry-pick' from both collective agreements, with the more favourable provisions being applicable to them. However, this choice is not available to transferred employees where the transferee enters into a collective agreement after the date of the transfer: in these circumstances, only the new collective agreement will govern their employment relationships.

A collective agreement entered into by the transferor will not apply to transferred employees if it ceases to apply within one year of the transfer, either because a new collective agreement replaces it or because its term expires.

N1.6 Variation of contract

As mentioned above, the employment contracts of the transferred employees transfer on the same terms and conditions. However, it is not always possible for a transferee to achieve this. For example, the transferor may have provided private health or pension insurance, where the transferee does not have such policies in place. Hungarian law does not offer an express solution to this problem, except in the case of a change in the employee's place of work, as described below.

The only substantial solution is for a transferee to propose a formal amendment to the original employment contract. If the employee refuses, which is not common in reality, the situation becomes very delicate. On the one hand, the transferee cannot terminate the employment contract on ordinary notice solely because an employee has objected to its amendment. On the other hand, the transferee cannot be expected to shoulder a disproportionate burden by creating policies especially for the benefit of a small group of transferred employees. This raises the issue of discrimination as well – should the existing employees of the transferee have less favourable working conditions, solely because the transferred employees are entitled to enjoy the same terms and conditions they had prior to the transfer?

As regards an employee's place of work, the Labour Code does not require the formal modification of his/her employment contract where his/her employer has moved its operations to another location, so long as an unreasonable and disproportionate burden is not placed on the employee.

N1.7 Duty to inform and consult

Employee information and consultation is treated as a priority by the Labour Code: the representatives of the affected employees must be informed of the date or the planned date of the legal succession, the reason(s) for the legal succession and its legal, economic and social consequences at least 15 days beforehand. Further, they must also be consulted on other planned measures that will affect the employees participating in the transfer.

A consultation must be held with the representatives of the affected employees to discuss the key principles behind the 'measures', the steps that will be taken to avoid any detrimental consequences and the means by which any unavoidable detrimental consequences can be mitigated.

A breach of the consultation obligations affects the validity of a business transfer, only if there is a recognised trade union or a duly elected works council in place. In the absence of a recognised trade union or a works council, the failure of the transferor and the transferee to consult does not have a sanction (in this regard, the Labour Code is a lex imperfecta – if a court establishes that there has been a breach of the duty to inform and consult employees, there are no legal consequences).

The duty to consult with the representatives of the affected employees must be complied with by both the transferor and the transferee, who are jointly liable for ensuring that the necessary consultations take place before a business transfer. A failure to consult is not excused by the fact that the decisions relating to the transfer were taken by a parent company or another group company – even if there is a global-level transfer, consultations must be conducted on a local level.

Civil servants are under a strict duty of obedience to the State and are not, therefore, allowed to bargain collectively or be trade union members. Thus, there is no duty to consult with the representatives of civil servants before a transfer.

N2 Redundancy

N2.1 Background

As a general rule, an employment relationship can only be terminated in the circumstances and in the manner provided for in the Labour Code. It sets out a finite list of the possible methods of terminating an employment contract. It is not possible for parties to deviate from these methods, even though Hungarian law recognises that employers and employees can enter into settlement agreements to terminate employment relationships.

Automatic termination

The employment relationship can, in certain cases, be terminated automatically. Such cases are *not* considered to be redundancy situations, so the employee does not receive redundancy payment or severance based upon seniority. An employment relationship ends automatically upon the death of an employee, upon the dissolution of the employer where there is no legal successor (after the end of a liquidation process), or upon the expiration of a fixed-term contract. Since this is a 'closed' list, it is not possible to provide for situations in the employment contract where the employment contract ends automatically outside the above without being a redundancy. Please note, when a company is dissolved, the Labour Code orders that, notwithstanding the fact that it is not a formal redundancy, the employee shall be paid the same benefits as in the case of an ordinary dismissal. Therefore, one may argue that this is a quasi-redundancy situation – a fact hard to question.

Notice

An employer must generally justify dismissing an employee, although there are some cases where a reason is not required. In Hungary, there is no such concept as 'employment-at-will', where a contract of employment may be terminated at any time, by either the employer or the employee, without cause.

An employment contract may be terminated with immediate effect during a trial period, either by the employee or the employer. In such a case, there is no need to give a reason. However, the parties must stipulate the trial period in an employment contract and it must not last longer than three months. Moreover, the extension of the trial period is explicitly forbidden.

There is also no requirement to provide a reason where the dismissed employee is a 'statutory executive' in accordance with s 188 of the Labour Code. There is similarly no requirement to give a reason for a dismissal if the employee has reached retirement age, has acquired the right to retire before the official retirement age, or receives a disability allowance.

Ordinary notice

The most common way of terminating an employment contract is by 'ordinary termination'. An ordinary termination must be justified by the employer – and this justification has to satisfy four substantial criteria in order to be acceptable. If the employer is obliged to justify the termination of an employment contract because it does not fall within the exceptions given under 'Notice' above, and it does so without a legal reason, the dismissal will be considered 'unfair' and the employer will have to pay damages to the employee.

A letter giving notice of dismissal must be in writing and must provide the employee with information regarding the manner and deadline by which he/she can seek a legal remedy against unlawful termination of his/her employment contract (ie filing a statement of claim alleging unlawful termination within 30 days of termination).

A letter of notice is considered valid only if it has been duly signed by a person who has authority to terminate the employment relationship – the Labour Code calls such persons those 'entitled to exercise employer's rights'. According to the Labour Code, someone exercising 'employer's rights' is entitled to establish and terminate employment relationships, to apply legal sanctions in the event of any failure to comply with obligations arising from an employment relationship and to establish liability for damages. Delegation is only possible under limited circumstances: employers have to notify employees which body or person exercises (or fulfils) the employer's rights (and obligations) originating from the employment relationship. If the employer's rights are not exercised by the body or person authorised to do so and notified to the employees, its actions are invalid, unless the employee(s) concerned should reasonably have been aware of the authority of the acting person/body from the circumstances. Because these rules are considered to be imperative, any deviation from them will be invalid. Thus, if the 'wrong' person signs the notice letter, it is considered invalid irrespective of its actual content.

The reasons for the termination of an employment relationship must be:

(i)   real;

(ii)   substantial;

(iii)   clear; and

(iv)   cannot be an *abus de droit*.

Reality

If there is a dispute in this regard, the burden of proof is on the employer to establish the validity of the facts which served as the basis for the dismissal. The case law in this area limits the facts which serve as the basis for the dismissal to those expressly mentioned in the notice letter itself.

Substantiality

The reason(s) for the termination must be sufficiently substantial to justify it. The criterion of substantiality is both a subjective and an objective test: it is always a question of balancing the facts of the case against the test of proportionality (ie whether the consequences of the employee's acts are proportionate to the termination of his/her employment) and reasonableness (ie whether, in the circumstances, the employer can reasonably be expected to continue to employ the employee).

Clearness

The requirement of clearness means that the notice letter must clearly detail the reason(s) for the dismissal. For example, it is not sufficient for the employer to simply say that the the employment relationship is being terminated for non-performance – the notice in such a situation must also state why the employer feels the employee's performance was unsatisfactory.

Abuse of rights

This long-standing civil law principle is often raised in unfair dismissal litigation. For example, it is unfair to dismiss an employee under a pretext, if the employee proves that he/she has raised a complaint of discrimination, or as a retaliation for union acitivities, even if the reasons themselves are sufficient to justify the dismissal on the basis of the above.

Before an employee can be dismissed on grounds of his/her performance or conduct (ie personal reasons), he/she must be given an opportunity to defend himself/herself against the allegations made by the employer. This is not the case if the reason for the dismissal relates to the employer's business (eg corporate restructuring or the rationalisation of the employer's processes). The economic rationale behind an employer's decision(s) in this regard cannot be questioned before the courts, which makes redundancies based on organisational restructuring extremely hard for employees to challenge.

The employment contracts of employees who will reach their official pensionable age within five years of their dismissal can only be terminated in particularly justified cases. However, this is not an absolute protection – in such cases, the courts have to rigorously scrutinise the substantiality of the reasons given by the employer for the termination.

Extraordinary notice

Employment contracts can be terminated in writing by way of an 'extraordinary notice' only in a limited number of cases. According to s 96 of the Labour Code, a party to an employment contract may terminate it with extraordinary notice if:

– the other party acts in a manner which wilfully or with gross negligence breaches his/her main employment obligations; or

–   the other party behaves in a manner that makes the continuation of the employment relationship impossible.

An extraordinary dismissal notice filed by an employer must contain information on the method and deadline of any legal remedy available for alleged unlawful termination. Unlike in the case of an ordinary notice, an employee filing an extraordinary notice must justify it by satisfying the critera of reality, substantiality and clearness discussed above. An employee may only terminate his/her employment contract on extraordinary notice if the employer commits a fundamental breach of contract, such as not paying his/her salary or engaging in discriminatory conduct.

Employment contracts and collective agreements may stipulate the circumstances in which the parties are entitled to terminate the employment contract on extraordinary notice. These circumstances, however, must still fall within the stipulations referred to above.

There is a very strict time limit during which the right to terminate an employment contract on extraordinary notice must be exercised. The 'subjective' time limit (that of 15 days) starts when the person exercising the employer's rights becomes aware of the employee's breach. If the employer's rights over the relevant employee are exercised by a body (eg a Board of Directors), then the 15-day time limit starts on the date on which the body is expressly informed of the reason for the termination. However, it should be noted that there is also a one-year objective limitation period in relation to extraordinary notices.

Different rules relating to fixed-term employment contracts

If an employer terminates an employment contract for a finite period before the contract term has expired, the employee is entitled to receive a payment equal to his average earnings for a maximum period of one year or, if the outstanding term of the contract is less than one year, a payment equal to his average earnings for such outstanding period. The rules relating to ordinary notices do not apply in such situations. A party is, however, free to terminate a fixed-term employment contract with extraordinary notice where there has been a serious breach of that contract by the other party. Such employment contracts may also be terminated by way of settlement agreements.

Protection of trade union officials

The dismissal on ordinary notice of an employee holding a position within a trade union, or the transfer of such an official to another workplace, requires the consent of the relevant trade union.

Before an employer can dismiss such a person on an extraordinary basis, it must seek the opinion of the relevant trade union. Officials are entitled to this protection for the duration of their term of office, plus a period of one year after it ceases, provided they held the position for at least six months.

Mass redundancies

The dismissal of a certain number of employees on operational grounds is subject to special rules, in accordance with Directive 1998/59/EC. The application of these rules is triggered:

–   for an employer with between 21 and 99 employees, by the dismissal of at least 10 employees;

–   for an employer with between 100 and 299 employees, by the dismissal of at least 10 per cent of the employees; and

–   for an employer with at least 300 employees, by the dismissal of at least 30 employees.

This is subject to the employer terminating the employment contracts of such employees within the same 30-day period. All methods of termination, including termination by common consent, count towards the calculations in this regard. If these thresholds are reached at individual sites, rather than across the employer's entire operation, this will still constitute a group dismissal.

Before making a decision about a group dismissal, an employer must initiate a consultation process with the works council. If there is no works council in place, then a commission consisting of representatives of trade unions (if any) and representatives of the affected employees, must be consulted. The consultation must cover the reason(s) for the group dismissal, any methods that could be employed to prevent the dismissal and any means of mitigating the consequences of the dismissal and reducing the number of employees affected by it.

At least seven days before holding the consultation, the employer must inform the employee representatives in writing of the reasons for the planned group dismissal, as well as the number of employees likely to be affected, broken down according to their positions. The consultation must be initiated at least 15 days prior to the decision relating to the group dismissal being made.

In the course of the consultation, the employer must inform the employee representatives in writing of:

–   the planned schedule for the group dismissal;

–   the selection criteria for the employees to be dismissed; and

–   the proposed provision of benefits for the dismissed employees, insofar as they differ from the benefits specified by law or in a collective agreement, and how such benefits will be calculated.

If the employer and the representatives of the employees conclude an agreement in the course of the consultation, such agreement must be evidenced in writing and must be notified to the relevant Labour Centre.

Once the employer has made its decision relating to the group dismissal, it must, at least 30 days prior to notifying the employees of the ordinary termination of their employment contracts, inform the employee representatives and the Labour Centre. The termination of the employees' employment contracts is void if the employer does not comply with the notification rules. Non-compliance with the rules relating to prior consultation with employee representatives will currently only entitle the works council or trade union to make a claim to court for a declaration that a breach has occurred, thus making the dismissals void. As a consequence, if there is no trade union or works council in place, then a failure by an employer to consult in these circumstances will have no practical consequences.

Protection against dismissal

Notwithstanding the provisions mentioned above, it is unlawful for an employer to dismiss a non-executive employee on ordinary notice during, and for a certain period after, the following occurrences:

–   illness;

–   a period of sick pay for looking after ill children or close relatives;

–   pregnancy, for three months after giving birth and during unpaid holiday for child-care; and

–   national service.

If the periods of protection referred to above exceed 15 days, then no notice of termination may be given for another 15 days after the employee returns to work. If the period of protection exceeds 30 days, then the period during which no notice of termination may be given is extended to 30 days. However, the prohibition against dismissal during these periods of protection does not apply if the employee has reached retirement age, has the right to retire before the official retirement age, or receives disability allowance.

Different rules pertaining to executives

The Labour Code differentiates between 'regular' employees and 'executive officers'. In accordance with the Labour Code, an employer may terminate an executive employee's contract without having to give reasons for doing so. However, this rule applies only to 'statutory executive employees'. By law, only the chief executive of a company and his/her deputy constitute 'statutory executives'.

In an employment contract, an employer may state that an employee is to be considered a designated executive officer. Such an employee will be considered an executive in relation to some, but not all, of the rules applicable to senior executives. Most notably, the right to terminate his/her employment contract on ordinary notice without having to give reasons will not be applicable to such an employee. Thus, an employer wishing to terminate such an employee's employment contract must comply with the same rules as in the case of non-executive employees, and any termination notice must satisfy the requirements of reality, substantiality and clearness.

The objective deadline with regard to extraordinary termination is extended to three years for both 'statutory' and 'designated' executives, instead of the one-year term applicable to other employees.

N2.2 Redundancy payments

Severance

Employees who are dismissed on ordinary notice after more than three years' service must be paid one month's salary as a redundancy payment. This payment increases in size according to the number of years' service, up to a maximum of six months' salary after 25 years of service. However, the parties may stipulate in an employment contract that the employee is entitled to a more substantial severance payment. The severance payment must be paid as a lump sum on the employee's last day at work.

Notice period

The period of ordinary notice must be at least 30 days. Longer periods may be stipulated in employment contracts, but these cannot exceed one year. The 30-day notice period will be prolonged, depending on the duration of the employment relationship in question. It is extended by five days after three years in service, 15 days after five years' service, 20 days after eight years' service, 25 days after 10 years' service, 30 days after 15 years' service, 40 days after 18 years' service and 60 days after 20 years' service. As is the case with severance payments, the parties are free to stipulate longer notice periods, although they cannot exceed one year.

If an employee is dismissed on ordinary notice, he/she must be exempted from performing work for at least half of the notice period. This rule does not apply if the employee terminates his/her employment contract – in this case, the employee must work for the whole notice period.

N2.3 Settlement agreements

Settlement agreements are popular methods of terminating employment relationships for a number of reasons. They can be applied to all forms of employment relationship, irrespective of whether they are for fixed or undetermined terms. The parties are free to stipulate when they want to terminate their employment relationship. Since settlement agreements are not unilateral notices, there are fewer restrictions in relation to them. Although an employee who enters into a settlement agreement cannot claim either compensation for the relevant notice period or a severance payment, the parties do stipulate that the employee receives compensation in exchange for entering into the agreement in the vast majority of cases.

A settlement agreement must be put in writing. Moreover, the intention of the parties to terminate the employment relationship on an agreed date must be unequivocal. Since a settlement agreement is a contract, it cannot be challenged before the courts on the same basis as a termination notice, as it does not contain the reasons for the employee's dismissal. Thus, from an employer's point of view, settlement agreements can be viewed as the 'safest' way to terminate employment relationships.

Notwithstanding the above, it is possible to challenge a settlement agreement. However, the scope for review is very limited and a party may only challenge a settlement agreement:

–   if that party was mistaken about an imperative fact or circumstance at the time the agreement was concluded, provided that such mistake was caused or could have been recognised by the other party;

–   if both parties entered into the agreement under the same erroneous assumption; or

–   if the agreement was concluded under unlawful duress.

The term 'duress' in the Labour Code is defined as a threat of illegal personal or material loss directed to the threatened person or one of his/her relatives. According to the decision of the Supreme Court no 50/1998, a party declaring that he/she will initiate legal proceedings against another party does not constitute such a threat.

There is a limitation period for challenging settlement agreements. The statutory subjective time limit is 30 days. According to the Labour Code, the 30-day period starts when the aggrieved party recognises their mistake or when the illegal coercion ends. However, a court will not entertain any claim made more than six months after a settlement agreement is concluded.

If an employee contests a settlement agreement, the burden of proof is on him/her to prove the unlawfulness of the termination (eg that he/she signed the agreement under duress or he/she was misled by his/her employer).

N2.4 Remedies for unfair dismissal

If a final and binding judgment of a court of law establishes that the employer has breached the rules of the Labour Code in the course of the dismissal, and hence the employer has unlawfully dismissed the employee, the primary remedy available is reinstatement, meaning that the employee must be re-employed in his/her original position. The court may also decide, upon the request of the employer, not to reinstate the employee in his/her original position if the further employment of the employee 'cannot be expected' from the employer. Since courts are bound to the motions of the parties, reinstatements are exceptionally rare in Hungary, notwithstanding the relatively large number of lawsuits initiated for unfair dismissal. This is understandable, since usually the relationship between the employer and the employee has so much deteriorated that in most cases it is not reasonable to 'expect' the employer to continue the employment relationship.

If the employee does not wish to be reinstated or the court does not reinstate the employee upon the employer's request, the court will have to order the employer to pay a quasi-penalty to the employee, which can be an amount between his/her two months' and 12 months' average earnings, in addition to the normal redundancy payment. The court may freely determine the amount of the penalty between such limits. It is relatively rare that a court awards 12 months' salary as a compensation, except in exceptional cases such as racial discrimination or discrimination against pregnant women.

Furthermore, the employee must be reimbursed for lost earnings and other damage incurred. Earnings and damages, which have been recovered by the employee from other sources, do not need to be reimbursed by the employer. This consequence of the unfair dismissal verdict is often much more severe than the penalty described above. The reason is that the employment is only terminated at the date of the final and binding court verdict, which can be years after the original termination – for which period the employer has to pay salary as well as default interest. If the employee finds a new job, then the damages constitute only the difference between the two salaries – provided that the new salary is lower than the one enjoyed in the job where the employee has been made redundant.

However, the court may decide on the amount to be reimbursed at its discretion, taking into consideration all the circumstances of the case, and the employee is obliged to mitigate his damages under general civil law rules. In other words, the employee may claim non-pecuniary damages as well, eg because his professional reputation has been undermined due to the unfair dismissal. Currently, Hungarian courts are very reluctant to award such damages and, even if they do so, the amounts are usually not significant. Although the Labour Code clearly states the employee's duty to mitigate damages, this is not a strict requirement, since courts usually do not require employees to prove that they took reasonable efforts to mitigate damages.

N3 Case studies

N3.1 Case study 1
(Acquisition of a 'business' situated in another EU state; asset deal; no relocation)

As Hungary has only recently joined the EU, the position will be unclear until the effect of the adoption of EU legislation can be ascertained.

N3.2 Case study 2
(Production moves from one EU country to another EU country; physical move)

As Hungary has only recently joined the EU, the position will be unclear until the effect of the adoption of EU legislation can be ascertained.

N3.3 Case study 3
(Outsourcing of an ancillary activity to a non-EU country)

A large multinational based in Hungary (ABC) has decided to outsource its entire internal IT function to a third party provider in Romania, as the costs of hiring IT personnel in Romania are far lower than in Hungary, largely because wages are so much lower. At present, 200 employees are employed by ABC in its IT function in Hungary. It is anticipated that exactly the same IT function will be required in Romania with approximately the same number of people required to run it. There will be no difference in the service or approach for those requiring IT assistance and even the internal telephone number will be automatically diverted. The Romanian third party provider has no assets or presence in Hungary.

1. Business transfer

Will this be a business transfer within the scope of Hungarian law applying ARD?

Act XXII of 1992 on the Hungarian Labour Code ('Labour Code') adopts a definition of 'transfer of an undertaking' which is very similar to that used in Council Directive 2001/23/EC (the 'Acquired Rights Directive'); it also adopts a very similar approach and level of protection. Notwithstanding this, the scenario described above would not constitute a business transfer under the Labour Code.

Under s 85/A of the Labour Code, a transfer of an undertaking can be: (i) a succession by virtue of a legal regulation; or (ii) a transfer by agreement of an independent unit (such as a strategic business unit, plant, shop, division, workplace, or any part thereof) or the material and non-material assets of an employer to an organisation or person falling within the scope of the Hungarian Labour Code, for further operation or to enable operations to re-start, provided such a transfer takes place within the framework of a sale, exchange, lease or capital contribution for a business association.

The Labour Code *only* covers transactions between companies that employ workers in the territory of the Republic of Hungary. Consequently, a cross-border transaction of the kind described above would not be considered a transfer of an undertaking under Hungarian law. Currently, there are no amendments regarding the Labour Code pending before the Hungarian

Parliament that would change this situation. In addition, there are no published judgments of the Supreme Court on the issue of cross-border transfers.

The Acquired Rights Directive clearly provides that a cross-border trans-action within the European Community can fall within the definition of a 'transfer of an undertaking'. Following Hungary's accession to the European Union on 1 May 2004, the Hungarian Parliament is obliged to adopt legislation that conforms to the Acquired Rights Directive. If it fails to do so and, as a result, an employee cannot rely on provisions equivalent to those within the Acquired Rights Directive, the Hungarian State may incur liability before the European Court of Justice (the 'ECJ').

2. Effect on employees

(a) **What will happen to the employees currently employed in the IT function at ABC? Will they transfer across?**

As the scenario described above would not constitute a transfer of an undertaking under the Labour Code, employees currently employed in the IT function of ABC could be validly dismissed as part of a re-organisation. They would not transfer across to the third party provider in Romania automatically.

However, if the Labour Code is amended in accordance with the Acquired Rights Directive to encompass cross-border transfers, or a preliminary ruling of the ECJ states that the Acquired Rights Directive overrides the rules of the Labour Code, the employees currently employed in the IT function of ABC will be automatically transferred to the third party provider in Romania on the same terms and conditions.

(b) **If the employees do transfer, what will the applicable law be for their employment contracts with the third party provider? Where can they make any claims?**

Under the Hungarian conflict of laws rules of Law Decree No 13 of 1979, parties can choose the law applicable to their employment contract. If no such choice were made within the contracts of employment of the employees in the scenario, the lex loci laboris rule (the rule whereby an employee is subject to the legislation of the country in which he habitually carries out his work) would have to be applied. Accordingly, if the employees transferred in such a situation, Romanian law would be the applicable law for their contracts with the third party provider in relation to work carried out in Romania.

The place where the employees would be able to make claims would depend on the nature of their claims. If a claim were connected with an employee's employment in Hungary, he/she could make a claim before the Hungarian courts. The courts would have jurisdiction on the basis of the defendant's domicile (ie the domicile of the previous employer).

If a claim were connected with an employee's employment in Romania, the employee could only make a claim in Romania. In the event that the Romanian employer refused to recognise the transfer, an employee could bring claims in both Hungary and Romania, since the country of the employee's last place of work would be Hungary.

If an employee were made redundant within one year of the transfer for any reasons connected to the operation of the transferee, the Hungarian transferor would be liable as a suretor. The employee could choose where he/she wished to make a claim – in Hungary or Romania. A Hungarian court would entertain such a claim, as the forum non conveniens doctrine (the doctrine that a court will decline to hear a dispute when it can be better or more conveniently settled in a foreign forum) is not known in Hungarian law.

Since the Labour Code remained unchanged following 1 May 2004, if a Hungarian court refuses to entertain an employee's claim in these circumstances, the employee could initiate a claim against the Hungarian State before the ECJ for failure to adopt the Acquired Rights Directive before accession to the EU.

3. Data protection

Will there be special data protection issues on the transfer of knowledge and information outside Hungary to Romania?

Under Hungarian data protection principles, personal data can generally only be transferred domestically with the consent of the data subject. Depending on the circumstances, consent can be implied, although not where the data transferred can be characterised as sensitive. For example, consent would be implied where 'non-sensitive' personal data in relation to the employment relationship is transferred within the organisation of an employer or to a related company. However, according to s 85/A(3) of the Labour Code, a transferor must inform a transferee of the rights and obligations stemming from the relevant employment relationships, prior to a business transfer taking place. This rule, in our opinion, is clearly a legal mandate for transferors to disclose personal information relating to their employees to transferees in connection with the transfer of undertakings.

Under Act LXIII of 1992 on the Protection of Personal Data (the 'Data Protection Act'), data transfers between EU member states must be treated the same as domestic data transfers under Hungarian law, following accession.

If the Labour Code were amended to include cross-border transfers, so that the above scenario would constitute a 'business transfer' under Hungarian law, the relevant employment contracts would be transferred automatically at the date of the transfer, so that the Romanian company would become the employees' employer. Accordingly, the Romanian company would have implied consent, as an employer, to handle personal data in relation to the employees.

4. Transfer to India

Please comment on any differences there would be to your answers if the function was transferred to India rather than Romania.

As India is not part of the European Union, a transfer of functions there would not be considered a transfer of an undertaking under Hungarian law. Accordingly, the employees would not be transferred automatically on the same terms and conditions.

Personal data in relation to these employees could only validly be transferred to India if the relevant Indian legislation complied with the requirements of the EU data protection regulations.

N4 Additional information

N4.1 Key websites

Ministry of Justice
(*Igazságügyi Minisztérium*)
http://www.im.hu/

Ministry of Foreign Affairs
http://www.kulugyminiszterium.hu/Kulugyminiszterium/en/

The Hungarian Parliament
http://www.mkogy.hu/parl_en.htm

Ministry of Employment and Labour
(*Foglalkoztatáspolitikai és Munkaügyi Minisztérium*)
http://www.fmm.gov.hu

National Employment Service
http://www.afsz.hu

National Labour Registry
http://www.emma185.hu/

National Labour Inspectorate
http://www.ommf.hu

National Employment Foundation
(*Országos Foglalkoztatási Közalapítvány*)
http://www.ofa.hu/

National ILO Council of Hungary
www.nilo.hu

Labour Mediation and Arbitration Service
http://www.fmm.gov.hu/mkdsz/english/index_english.html

The Constitutional Court of the Republic of Hungary
(*Magyar Köztársaság Alkotmánybírósága*)
http://www.mkab.hu/en/enmain.htm

N4.2 Key books and articles

The authors have no knowledge of any useful English-language books or articles on Hungarian employment law.

O Italy

Massimo Donna

O1 Business transfers

O1.1 Background

The regulation of employees' rights in the event of a transfer of business is contained in art 2112 of the Italian Civil Code (hereinafter referred to as the 'Transfer of Business Regulation'), which has been substantially modified over the last few years in order to make it compliant with the relevant EU legislation. The Transfer of Business Regulation has now been modified by Legislative Decree no 276 of 10 September 2003, implementing Law no 30 of 14 February 2003.

Jurisdiction and applicable law

Italy is one of the signatories of the Convention of Rome of 1980 on the law applicable to contractual obligations. According to art 6 of the Convention, contracts of employment are governed 'by the law of the country in which the employee habitually carries out his work performance of the country, even if he is temporarily employed in another country'. The transferor's and transferee's obligations in the case of a transfer of business according to the Transfer of Business Regulation shall be considered contractual obligations, as they are a direct consequence of the work relationships existing between the relevant employees and the business to be transferred. Article 6 will consequently apply to all those disputes arising from the transfer of a business located in Italy (immediately before the same transfer) between the transferor, the transferee and the employees involved in the transfer.

Territorial jurisdiction within Italy

The territorial jurisdiction of the Employment Courts within Italy shall be determined according to one of the criteria set by art 413 of the Italian Code of Civil Procedure: (i) the place where the work relationship was established; (ii) the place where the business is located; or (iii–iv) the place of the subsidiary of the business where the employee carries out or was carrying out his activity at the moment of the termination of the work relationship.

O1.2 Identifying a relevant transfer

Notion of 'business'

The meaning of 'business' for the purpose of the application of the Transfer of Business Regulation has always been controversial in Italy.

First of all, it should be pointed out that the notion of business (*azienda*) for the purpose of the Transfer of Business Regulation is absolutely different from its meaning according to art 2555 of the Italian Civil Code, which provides a definition of business for corporate and commercial purposes ('... a complex of goods organised by the entrepreneur for the management of the enterprise').

Indeed, for the purpose of the Transfer of Business Regulation, 'business' shall mean an 'economic and organised entity' whose identity pre-exists the transfer and maintains its autonomy at the completion of the transfer.

Notion of business ownership

For the purposes of the Transfer of Business Regulation, the notion of business ownership is wide. In fact, with business ownership one can refer to a number of different situations such as property, *usufruct*[1] or tenancy of the assets and goods constituting the business; 'ownership' of the goodwill; client ownership, etc.

1   The right of enjoying a thing, the property of which is vested in another, and to draw from the same all the profit, utility and advantage which it may produce, provided it be without altering the substance of the thing.

Notion of transfer of business

General principle

Starting from the second half of the 1980s, the Italian Supreme Court (*Suprema Corte di Cassazione*) has been stating that, in order for the Transfer of Business Regulation to apply, it should not be considered whether all assets and goods constituting the business have been transferred, but whether or not the transferee has been put in the position of 'substituting' for the transferor in his relations with third parties, and particularly with clients, as a consequence of the transfer[1].

1   Italian Supreme Court, no 1829/1986. See also Italian Supreme Court, nos 1921/1981, 7338/1986 and 3167/1990.

Application of the 'Spijkers criteria'

In the judgment of the *Spijkers* case, the European Court of Justice ('ECJ') set the following criteria for a transfer of business to subsist: (i) the type of the undertaking or business; (ii) whether tangible assets were transferred; (iii) the value of intangible assets at the time of the transfer; (iv) whether the majority of employees were taken on by the new owner; (v) whether customers were transferred; (vi) the degree of similarity between the activities carried on before and after the transfer; and, finally, (vii) the period, if any, during which those activities were suspended as a result of the transfer.

(i)   Even if the *Spijkers* judgment itself is not expressly mentioned in the case law of the Italian Supreme Court, in judgment no 11622/2002, the criteria as set out in the ECJ judgment are clearly mentioned and even in the same order. In particular, the Italian Supreme Court stated in this judgment that trade unions cannot be considered businesses for the purpose of the Transfer of Business Regulation because unions are neither profit-oriented entities nor entities organised on an economical basis. Furthermore, in judgment no 5550/2000, the Italian Supreme Court clearly stated that, for the purpose of the Transfer of Business Regulation, the involved entities have to carry out organised activities aimed at the production and/or trade of goods for a profit or at least economical orientation. In this regard, the Council of State (Italy's highest administrative court) has stated that both the transferor and the transferee must be entities carrying out organised activities aimed at the production and/or trade of goods for a profit or at least economical orientation, so that the Transfer of Business Regulation does not apply in the case of the succession of a private entity to a public entity in the performance of a public service.

(ii) With regard to the tangible assets of the transferred business, the Italian Supreme Court has stated that, for the purpose of the Transfer of Business Regulation, their transfer certainly represents an important hint of the actual existence of a business transfer.

(iii) The case law of the courts of first instance and of appeal has specified that intangible assets include patents, copyrights and goodwill, which is not only limited to the relationship with customers, but also with collaborators, suppliers, etc.

(iv) In fact, further to the latest amendments to the Transfer of Business Regulation, it seems likely that the mere transfer of a number of employees may be considered a business transfer. In the past, in order for a business transfer to exist, tangible and/or intangible assets had to be transferred together with employees.

(v) According to the Italian Supreme Court, the transferred business must preserve its identity.

Transfer of Business Regulation cases

The Transfer of Business Regulation specifically applies in the following circumstances:

(a) *Sale of business*.

(b) *Usufruct of business*, as expressly provided by the Transfer of Business Regulation.

(c) *Lease of business*, as expressly provided by the Transfer of Business Regulation. More specifically, the Italian Supreme Court has stated that:

    (i) at the end of the lease period, when the business is transferred back from the tenant to the owner, the Transfer of Business Regulation will also apply, should the owner perform the same economic activities that were carried out by the tenant;

(ii) if, at the end of the lease period, the owner leases the business to a different tenant, the Transfer of Business Regulation will apply, should the new tenant perform the same economic activities that were carried out by the previous tenant.

(d) *Franchising agreement*: the Italian Supreme Court[1] has ruled that the Transfer of Business Regulation applies also in the event of a substitution of the franchisee by the franchiser.

(e) *Mergers and acquisitions*: the new version of the Transfer of Business Regulation expressly envisages a *merger* as a typical example of a transfer of business. In contrast, no mention of acquisitions is made.

Some observers consider company acquisitions as 'universal successions': the new company arising from the acquisition would, in fact, automatically be given all the previous rights and duties of the buyer and of the acquired company. Other observers consider that a company acquisition is essentially a mere modification of the relevant deeds of incorporation and bylaws. According to this theory, the employees of the acquired company would not be granted the guarantees provided by the Transfer of Business Regulation.

Surprisingly, the Italian Supreme Court[2] has partially agreed with the theory of the 'modification of the deeds of incorporation' set out above. The court has, in fact, stated that, should the new company arising from the acquisition continue to perform its productive activity in the same location where it was performed before the acquisition, there is no transfer of business, and the Transfer of Business Regulation would not apply.

(f) *Company split*: according to art 2504*septies* of the Italian Civil Code, a company split can consist of the transfer of the company's assets (or part of the assets) to existing entity/entities or new entity/entities set up ad hoc followed by the transfer of the relevant shares or quotas to the shareholders or quota holders of the 'mother company'.

In judgment no 9897/1998 the Italian Supreme Court ruled that even a company split may be covered by the Transfer of Business Regulation if it is verified that the business has been transferred, totally or partially, to a different owner.

1   Decision no 2200/1998.
2   Decision no 6177/1996.

Notion of 'transfer of part of a business' (*trasferimento di ramo di azienda*)

The notion of 'transfer of part of a business' is certainly one of the most controversial under Italian law. Indeed, when the Transfer of Business Regulation was recently modified, the unions remarked that it could be used to evade the strict requirements relating to individual (and collective) dismissals. The unions were concerned that big companies would transfer their redundant employees to smaller entities, which could more easily dismiss the (transferred) employees. This is because, under Italian law, employees of entities with more than 15 employees have the right to be reinstated should the termination of their employment be considered unjustified, while in the same circumstances employees of entities with 15 or fewer employees only have the right to receive compensation for their loss of employment.

Possibly the most controversial issue relating to the transfer of part of a business is the determination of whether it can consist of the mere transfer of a number of employees from one employer to another. On this point, the Italian Supreme Court's case law has not been clear (see below).

In cases 10701/2002 and 10761/2002 *(Alcatel/Pllb)*, the Italian Supreme Court had to decide whether the transaction in question could be defined as the transfer of part of a business by Alcatel. In fact, Alcatel had outsourced an 'instruments' maintenance' service including a number of departments with different functions. Some of the transferred employees objected, claiming that the outsourced service was not autonomous, but absolutely collateral to Alcatel's core business and that, therefore, the transaction should not have been regulated by the Transfer of Business Regulation. On such occasions, the Italian Supreme Court held that, for the purpose of the application of the Transfer of Business Regulation, 'part of a business' should mean an 'economic activity', *even if it consisted of only employees*, if those employees, because of their shared background and expertise, could jointly perform their working activities with the new employer. To sum up, in these circumstances the Italian Supreme Court stated that even a mere transfer of employees, if specific requirements are met, may constitute a transfer of part of a business.

In cases 14961/2002 and 15105/2002 *(Ansaldo Energia/Manital Consorzio)*, the Italian Supreme Court completely overruled its previous position. The court held that, in order for the Transfer of Business Regulation to apply, the transferred business must include those material and/or immaterial assets included by art 2555 of the Italian Civil Code in the definition of business *(azienda)*. Therefore, in such circumstances, it was held that a mere transfer of employees, even if specific requirements are met, will *not* constitute a transfer of part of a business.

It should be noted that the decision in the *Ansaldo/Manital* cases can be explained by the Italian Supreme Court's concern that the transferor may artificially group a number of redundant employees together in order to transfer them as a part of a business to a smaller entity, and therefore, as indicated above, deprive them of any statutory protection against unfair dismissal. It should also be pointed out here, as it will be further explained below, that, should the Transfer of Business Regulation apply, employees have no right to oppose the transfer. It is therefore clear that it is much easier for the employer to group a number of redundant employees together in an 'artificial' part of the business and transfer it to a smaller transferee, rather than to transfer the employees' work contracts to another employer. In this event, in fact, the consent of the transferred employees will be needed.

In the light of the above, it seems that with the decision in *Ansaldo/Manital* the Italian Supreme Court has tried to prevent a 'simulated' transfer of part of a business by stating the necessity of a transfer of some of the transferor's assets together with the employees.

Further to the amendment of the Transfer of Business Regulation by Legislative Decree no 276 of 10 September 2003, implementing Law no 30 of 14 February 2003, the position of the Italian Supreme Court on the transfer of part of a business is expected to change substantially. In fact, the Transfer of Business Regulation now states that: 'The provisions of this Article also apply to the transfer of part of a business, this part being a functionally autonomous entity of an economic and organised activity, identified (as autonomous) by the parties at the moment of the Transfer'. According to this new wording, it seems that the entity to be transferred is to be identified by the parties at the moment of the transfer, meaning that the entity does not have to exist before the transfer.

O1.3 Affected employees

As mentioned above, according to the Transfer of Business Regulation, in the case of a transfer of business, the work relationships of the employees will continue with the transferee.

According to the ECJ, the definition of employee is provided by the relevant national legislation[1]. In Italy, for the purpose of the Transfer of Business Regulation, it is considered that an 'employee' is whoever has entered into a work agreement with the transferor.

The so-called collaborators (*collaboratori coordinati e continuativi* or, according to the wording of Law no 30/2003 which substantially changed the Labour legislation in Italy, *lavoratori a progetto*[2]) are not granted any protection by the Transfer of Business Regulation, while employees who have entered into an 'entry agreement' (*contratto di inserimento*[3]) are covered by the Transfer of Business Regulation.

1   Under art 409 of the Italian Code of Civil Procedure: '... other relationship of collaboration (which) consists of a continuing and co-ordinated provision of services, mostly of a personal character, even if not subordinate'.
2   Legislative Decree no 276/2003 has integrated this provision of the Italian Code of Civil Procedure, by stating that, such 'collaborations' shall be aimed at a 'project or work-programme'. Any illegal utilisation of the collaborators would lead to the transformation of such collaboration into an employment contract of undetermined (permanent) duration.
3   The *contratto di inserimento* is aimed at introducing (or re-introducing) a number of determined categories of workers to the job market, through the implementation of an individual project for the adjustment of the worker's professional skills to a specific work context.

O1.4 Effects of the transfer

Safeguarding employees' rights

In the last few years, the determination of which of the transferred employees' rights have to be safeguarded on the occasion of a transfer of business has been controversial in Italy. However, generally speaking, all transferred employees' rights deriving from both their individual and collective work contacts shall be preserved. Thus, employees shall retain their rights to fringe benefits and salary levels (deriving from their individual contract) and longer notice periods according to their collective bargaining contracts.

Collective contract rights

According to art 2112 of the Italian Civil Code:

> '... the transferee shall grant to the transferred employees those economic and working conditions provided by the collective contracts entered into both at national, local and company level in force at the moment of the transfer, till their expiry date unless they are substituted with different collective contracts applicable to the transferee's business. Such substitution is possible only with collective contracts of the same standard ...'[1].

In the past few years, the interpretation of this provision has been controversial in Italy.

Some commentators considered that the transferor's collective agreement should have applied to the transferred employees unless a new collective contract was entered into with the transferee (so-called 'harmonisation contracts').

Other commentators considered that the transferor's collective agreement should have applied to the transferred employees, unless the transferee applied a collective contract of the same standard (entered into respectively at national, local or company level).

In judgment no 9545/1999 the Italian Supreme Court definitively opted for this second opinion, stating that the transferor's collective agreement shall apply to the transferred employees only if the transferee does not apply any collective contract.

1 Please note that this is a non-literal translation.

Statutory economic rights

Under art 2112 of the Italian Civil Code, it is expressly provided that transferred employees are entitled to the same economic treatment they had before the transfer under their individual employment agreement.

Progressive rights

It has been clarified by the Italian Supreme Court that only fully matured rights shall be transferred as a consequence of the transfer of a business. Progressive rights (ie new rights which may arise for employees, such as the right to pay rises depending on length of service (so-called 'scatti di anzianita') envisaged in the collective contract applied by a transferor) shall not transfer.

Fringe benefits

While it is clear and not controversial that transferred employees shall retain their right to fringe benefits, it has been made clear that they shall not retain the right to those particular fringe benefits which were previously granted for work-related reasons in the event that the new employer changes their duties (within the limits set by art 2103 of the Italian Civil Code, according to which employees cannot be assigned duties or an employment status inferior to what was agreed in their individual employment agreement). For example, when a company car is assigned because of the particular duties to be performed by the employee, if the new employer change the employee's duties, assigning him to new functions not involving the need to move/relocate in the territory, he shall lose his right to the company car.

Joint liability of transferor and transferee

Under the Transfer of Business Regulation, the transferor and the transferee are jointly liable for all the employer's financial obligations existing at the time of the transfer vis-à-vis the employees.

Such joint liability only operates with regard to the transferor's financial obligations vis-à-vis the transferred employees existing at the moment of the transfer. Therefore, any such financial obligations originating after the transfer and relevant to the work relationship between the transferee and the transferred employees are not covered by such joint liability.

Consequently, transferred employees are entitled to enforce financial obligations, which the transferor has with them, also with the transferee, and the transferee is obliged to make any such relevant payment. The transferee is then entitled to require the transferor to reimburse the amount of money paid.

In the past few years, it has been controversial whether the right to require the transferee which has payments to employees still outstanding at the moment of transfer applies only to employees transferred to the transferee, or any employees, including those who had not continued their working relationship with the transferee. Eventually, the Italian Supreme Court stated that only the transferred employees are entitled to enforce outstanding payments against the transferee[1].

Under the Transfer of Business Regulation, transferred employees may waive their right to enforce their financial rights against the transferor. Under these circumstances, the transferee is solely responsible for such financial obligations. In order to grant the interested employees a high degree of protection, it has been provided that such waivers must be formalised before the local Employment Office. Waivers must be executed according to the procedures set out in arts 410 and 411 of the Italian Code of Civil Procedure. Once the waivers are executed, the transferred employees are entitled to enforce their financial rights only against the transferee and not against the transferor.

According to art 1655 of the Italian Civil Code, an *appalto* ('service agreement') contract is a contract by means of which one party is paid to perform a particular job or to provide a particular service with its own equipment and at its own management's risk. According to the Transfer of Business Regulation, should the transferor enter into an *appalto* agreement with the transferee, the performance of which is completed using the transferred part of the business, if the transferor-contractor does not fulfil his salary obligations to his employees, those employees are entitled to claim the amount of money they are owed also against the transferee, within the limit of the amount of money that the transferee owes to the transferor-contractor at the moment at which the employees' claim is brought.

1   Italian Supreme Court, case no 12889/1997.

Employees' rights to non-statutory benefits

The Transfer of Business Regulation does not make any reference to maintaining, after the transfer, any rights arising from private pension schemes. On this point, readers should be reminded that art 3, para 4(a) of the Acquired Rights Directive 2001/23/EC states that:

> 'Unless Member States provide otherwise, paragraphs 1 and 3 [of art 3 of the same Directive – Safeguarding of employees' rights] shall not apply in relation to employees' rights to old age, invalidity or survivors' benefits under supplementary company or intercompany pension schemes outside the statutory social security schemes in Member States'.

Notwithstanding this, under para 4(b), it is stated that:

> 'Even where they do not provide in accordance with subparagraph (a) that paragraphs 1 and 3 apply in relation to such rights, Member States shall adopt the measures necessary to protect the interests of employees and of persons no longer employed in the transferor's business at the time of the transfer in respect of rights conferring on them immediate or prospective entitlement to old age benefits, including survivor's benefits, under supplementary schemes referred to in subparagraph (a).'

It has been argued that, as the Transfer of Business Regulation does not expressly exclude rights enshrined in supplementary pension schemes from the field of application of the Transfer of Business Regulation, transferred employees should preserve them in the new job with the transferee.

Recently, a distinction has been proposed based upon whether the relevant pension fund is, or is not, a legal entity according to Italian law:

(i) If the relevant pension fund is a separate legal entity, with respect to pension benefits payments and their management, the employees refer exclusively to the same fund, with no involvement of the employer. In this case, the Transfer of Business Regulation would not apply.

(ii) If, on the other hand, the relevant pension fund is not a legal entity, the pension scheme should be considered part of the work agreement in force between the employer and the employee: the Transfer of Business Regulation will, consequently, apply.

Right to object

Under the Transfer of Business Regulation, should his working conditions substantially change as a result of the transfer, the transferred employee may resign within three months of the transfer.

The 'substantial change' in working conditions can be related to working time, location or functions. At the moment of the resignation, the employee shall have the right to be paid an 'in lieu of notice indemnification', according to art 2119 of the Italian Civil Code. It should be noted that notice periods in Italy are set both by individual and collective contracts.

Apart from the right to resign, no general right to object is acknowledged for employees in the event of a business transfer.

Liability for redundancy pay

According to art 2120 of the Italian Civil Code, in any case of termination of employment, the terminated employee shall have the right to a severance payment (*Trattamento di Fine Rapporto* or 'TFR'). Under Italian law, the amount of the severance payment is determined by accruing, on an annual basis, an amount of money equal to the annual salary divided by 13.5 (ie the relevant amount is approximately 7.40 per cent of the relevant annual salary).

In the past, it has been controversial whether the transferee should be held responsible for the portion of the TFR of the transferred employees relevant to the period prior to the transfer. Nowadays, even if some courts keep on stating the contrary, it has been made clear that the transferee is responsible for the whole amount of the TFR, including the portion relevant to the period prior to the transfer.

O1.5 Dismissal of employees

According to the Transfer of Business Regulation, the transfer of business does not in itself constitute a justifiable reason for dismissal. The Italian Supreme Court has interpreted this provision as meaning that the termination of employment, which may be carried out in the event of a transfer of business, is legal when it is justified by a reason(s) totally autonomous and independent from the transfer of business to be carried out.

Such interpretation is also consistent with the content of the Acquired Rights Directive 2001/23/EC, according to which:

> 'The transfer of the undertaking, business or part of the undertaking or business shall not in itself constitute grounds for dismissal by the transferor or the transferee. This provision shall not stand in the way of dismissals that may take place for economic, technical or organisational reasons entailing changes in the workforce (the so called "ETO reasons")'.

In the past, Italian courts have held that, if the transferee requested the transferor to reduce the workforce prior to the transfer, this could be considered an ETO reason. However, in recent years, the courts have viewed this slightly differently. Although the jurisprudence of the Italian Supreme Court is not unambiguous on this point, commentators have been quite unanimous in not considering the above as a valid ETO reason.

Should the transferor terminate the employment of a number of employees who will then be re-employed with a new different contract by the transferee, the termination shall be considered void, as it is performed in order to elude the provisions of law (as set out below).

O1.6 Variation of contract

Under art 2112 of the Italian Civil Code, transferred employees are entitled to the same economic treatment they had before the transfer under both their individual employment agreement and the collective agreements applicable to the transferor.

Collective contracts rights

According to art 2112 of the Italian Civil Code:

> '... the transferee shall grant to the transferred employees those economic and working conditions provided by the collective contracts entered into both at national, local and company level in force at the moment of the transfer, till their expiry date unless they are substituted with different collective contracts applicable to the transferee's business. Such substitution is possible only with collective contracts of the same standard ...'[1].

As mentioned above, in judgment no 9545/1999 the Italian Supreme Court definitively stated that the transferor's collective agreement shall apply to the transferred employees only if the transferee does not apply any collective contract.

---

1   Please note that this is a non-literal translation.

Harmonisation

In order to harmonise employment contracts, the transferee may apply a collective contract of the same standard as the one applied by the transferor before the transfer. In some cases, the transferee may propose to his employees to enter into new 'harmonisation contracts'. Such contracts are not expressly envisaged by law; and their content may substantially change from case to case. In any case, normally the relevant unions play an important role in the negotiation procedure.

O1.7 Duty to inform and consult

According to art 47 of Law no 428/90, if the transferor has more than 15 employees, it must carry out an information and consultation procedure with the unions. In this respect, it should be noted that, in order to determine the size (in terms of the number of employees) of the transferor, all employees should be taken into consideration, including those with fixed-term contracts, entry contracts (*contratti di inserimento*), etc.

The transferor and the transferee should give notice to the unions at least 25 days before the 'reference date' of the transfer. According to Legislative Decree no 18/2001 (which has amended the Transfer of Business Regulation), the reference date is either the date of signature of the transfer agreement, the date of signature of the preliminary contract of transfer or, if these documents are not applicable, any agreements which are aimed at the transfer and are binding upon both parties.

In fixing such a strict time limit for notification to the unions, it is evident that the intention of the Italian legislator was to give the unions an actual negotiating power with the management of the transferor and transferee, to be exercised prior to the implementation of the transfer of the business. Notwithstanding this, it should be pointed out that such a strict provision, obliging the parties to disclose to the unions their intention to transfer before any binding agreement is signed, may engender serious problems for the potential transferor and transferee from a confidential and competitive point of view. In fact, even though the unions will be bound by a confidentiality obligation, their internal structure, often not strictly hierarchically organised, may make such an obligation difficult to implement.

With specific reference to companies' mergers and spin-offs, the case law is not clear. In some cases it has been held that the notification to the unions should be carried out 25 days before the merger (or spin-off) has been approved by the company's board of directors and, in other cases, it has been claimed that the 25 days should be counted backward starting from the shareholders' resolution in relation to the merger and/or company split.

The notice must be served with the following unions' representative bodies:

–   United Representative Bodies of the unions in the business/

establishment to be transferred (*Rappresentanze Sindacali Unitarie* ('RSU'); *Rappresentanze Sindacali Aziendali* ('RSA'));

– unions of the relevant professional category which have signed the collective agreement applicable in the businesses involved in the transfer; or

– should any RSUs (or RSAs) not be established in the relevant entities, the notice should be filed with the most representative unions of the relevant category.

The notice shall contain the following information:

– Reasons for the transfer of business.

– Legal, economic and social consequences for the employees.

– Possible measures to be taken in respect of the employees.

Within seven days of receiving the notice, the relevant unions are entitled to require the management of both the transferor and the transferee to give a joint assessment of the situation (*esame congiunto*). The parties to the transfer (ie the transferor and the transferee) shall start the consultation/information procedure within seven days of the request of the unions. Should the consultation not be over within 10 days from the starting date, it shall be considered completed.

Should the above procedure not be followed, totally or partially, the relevant unions are entitled to file a complaint with the local Employment Court according to art 28 of Law no 300/70. Within two days of the filing, the court may grant an injunction against the transferor and the transferee, ordering them to stop any 'anti-union conduct', ie ordering them to follow the above information/consultation procedure. Criminal consequences may follow for non-compliance with such an order.

O1.8 Transfer of the business of an undertaking in financial distress

When an undertaking is in financial distress, the sale of one or more businesses may represent the only opportunity of guaranteeing its continued presence in the market and of preserving the employment of its employees. Therefore, in order to make the businesses of the troubled undertaking more attractive to possible buyers, the Italian legislator has allowed, under defined circumstances, the derogation of the Transfer of Business Regulation, but with specific regard given to the transferred employees' rights.

In particular, the derogation of the general provisions of the Transfer of Business Regulation applies in the following cases:

– if the Ministry of Labour and Social Policies has declared a status of crisis in relation to the business/businesses or part/parts of the business to be transferred; or

– if the transferring entity has been declared bankrupt or subjected to one of the bankruptcy procedures envisaged by Italian law (*omologazione di concordato prreventivo consistente nella cessione dei beni, emanazione del provvedimento di liquidazione coatta amministrativa, amministrazione straordinaria*); or

–   if the transferring entity has reached an agreement concerning the maintenance, even partial, of the employment of its employees as follows:

   •   such agreement shall be entered into between the management of the transferor and the relevant unions;

   •   the involved unions shall be the work councils (*Rappresentanze Sindacali Aziendali* ('RSA') or *Rappresentanze Sindacali Unitarie* ('RSU')) and/or the most representative unions on a national basis which have signed the collective agreement applicable in the business to be transferred;

   •   should only some of the employees be transferred to another entity (the transferee) and the remaining employees be dismissed, the agreement shall set out the *criteria* to be used to select the employees to be dismissed;

   •   should such criteria not be agreed with the unions, the statutory criteria (length of service, family burden and ETO reasons) will apply;

   •   in the past few years, the right of the unions to enter into agreements concerning the termination criteria, which also affect employees who are not members of the same unions, has been questioned. The Italian Constitutional Court, with judgment no 268 of 1994, has definitively stated that unions are entitled to enter into such agreements.

Should the conditions above apply, the Transfer of Business Regulation does not apply. Consequently:

–   the employees to be 'transferred' shall, basically, be dismissed and re-employed by the transferee, but the collective agreement which previously applied to their employment will not apply to them in their new employment and, as a result, economic conditions of the employment may substantially change; and

–   the 'transferred' employees will not benefit from the joint liability of the transferor and the transferee for the transferor's financial obligations vis-à-vis the employees.

The employees of the transferred business in financial distress who are not being transferred to the transferee have the right to be recruited in preference to other candidates, should the transferee want to hire new employees within one year from the date of the transfer. Such employees will not benefit by the guarantees set by the Transfer of Business Regulation.

Should the transferee not give preference to the former employees of the transferred business if new positions arise in that one-year period, such employees will be entitled to damages.

O2 Redundancy

O2.1 Background

Under Italian law, employers with more than 15 employees must go through an information/consultation procedure with the unions should they want to dismiss five or more employees, in the same establishment or in different establishments located in the same province, within a time period of 120 days, as a consequence of a reduction or of a transformation of production or of work activity.

With regard to the characteristics of the employer, note that, under Law no 223/1991, the collective dismissal regulation used to apply to profit-oriented businesses only. The collective dismissal regulation, consequently, did not apply to non-profit entities.

Law no 14/2003 expressly empowered the government to issue a Legislative Decree in order to fully implement in Italy Directive 98/59/EC, which does not distinguish between profit and non-profit entities for the purposes of the application of the collective dismissal regulation. Therefore, recently, by way of Legislative Decree no 110/2004, the application of the collective dismissal regulation has been extended to non-profit entities.

O2.2 Collective dismissal

In order for the collective dismissal regulation to apply, the number of employments to be terminated must be at least five. This number refers to the initial intention expressed by the employer in the notification to the unions, which actually starts the collective dismissal procedure.

Such number, however, can be reduced following performance of the mass dismissal procedure. In fact, within the consultation with the unions (so-called '*esame congiunto*': see below), the parties may agree that some of the employees to be dismissed be sent on secondment to different businesses and/or be given a different professional status, even lower than that originally agreed in their individual employment agreements.

The collective dismissal procedure must be carried out also if the employer stops its activity and, therefore, dismisses all its employees.

With regard to the employees to be taken into consideration in order to determine the size (in terms of the number of employees) of the employer and, consequently, whether the mass dismissal procedure applies, first of all it should be noted that managers (*dirigenti*) are not affected by such procedure and, therefore, should not be calculated for its purposes.

At present, it is still not clear whether apprentices and employees hired with entry contracts (*contratti di ingresso*) have to be taken into account for such purposes. In fact, while the Labour Ministry seems to consider that they do have to be taken into account (Ministry of Labour and Social Policies circular letter no 62/1996), many commentators do not agree with that opinion. It should be noted anyway that according to the most recent employment courts' case law, apprentices must be taken into account when determining the number of employees in a company (as mentioned above, the mass dismissal procedure can be carried out only if the employer has more than 15 employees), but their termination does not fall within the collective dismissal procedure.

O2.3 The duty to inform and consult prior to redundancy

The intention to proceed with a collective dismissal as defined above must be notified to the relevant unions, which are as follows:

–   United Representative Bodies of unions in the relevant business/ establishment (*Rappresentanze Sindacali Unitarie; Rappresentanze Sindacali Aziendali*);

–   unions of the relevant professional category which have signed the collective agreement applicable in the undertaking which is proceeding with the transfer; or

–   should any RSUs (or RSAs) not be established in the relevant entities, the notice should be filed with the most representative unions of the relevant category.

The notification to the unions shall contain the following elements:

–   reasons for the collective dismissal;

–   technical, organisational and production reasons which prevent the employer avoiding the collective dismissal;

–   number, professional allocation and professional characteristics of the employees to be dismissed and of the employees habitually working for the relevant undertaking;

–   time schedule of the mass dismissal; and

–   possible measures which the employer intends to take in order to deal with the social consequences of the mass dismissal.

A copy of the above notification shall be lodged with the local Employment Office.

Within seven days of the notification above, if requested to do so by the unions, the employer must meet the same unions in order to jointly examine the reasons which make the redundancies necessary and to assess the possibility of utilising some of the affected employees in other productive units/establishments, even with other more flexible employment contracts. Other social measures may be agreed.

In the past, it has been controversial whether agreements entered into with the unions are binding only on those employees who are members of the same unions or for all the affected employees. In decision no 268/1994 the Italian Constitutional Court eventually stated that the selection criteria agreed with the unions bind all the employees, including those who are not members of the relevant unions. Most commentators interpret this ruling as an implicit extension of the efficacy of any aspects of such agreements with regard to all the affected employees.

The information/consultation procedure with the unions must end within 45 days (23 days if the number of employees to be dismissed is fewer than 10) of the notification to the unions. Should no agreement be reached with the unions, the local Employment Office must be formally notified. In this event, the Employment Office may start a further consultation stage with the employer and the unions. This stage may have a maximum duration of 30 days (15 days if the number of employees to be dismissed is fewer than 10) starting from the date of notification to the Employment Office.

The selection of the employees to be dismissed shall be carried out by the employer on a fair and non-discriminatory basis. Italian law provides the relevant objective criteria. They are:

- Family burdens.

- Length of service.

- Technical, organisational and productive needs of the employer.

It is easy to understand that such strict statutory criteria, where the technical and economic needs of the employer form only one criterion out of three, may cause significant trouble for the employer, who may as a consequence easily be excluded from any 'power of selection'. It is therefore paramount for the employer to reach an agreement with the unions, during the information/consultation procedure, in order to set 'termination criteria' that are different from those stipulated by Italian law.

Once the procedure with the unions (and with the Employment Office) is completed, the employer is entitled to commence the mass dismissal by giving notice to each affected employee individually in writing. The affected employees shall have the right to their notice period, as provided by the relevant individual and collective employment agreements. A list of the dismissed employees must be notified to the local Employment Office.

The termination notice to be addressed to each employee need not necessarily contain the reasons for the termination, as such reasons have been widely discussed with the unions within the information/consultation procedure.

O2.4 Unfair redundancy

Should the employees consider that the selection criteria have not been followed and, consequently, that they should not have not been dismissed, they can appeal the termination within 60 days of receiving the notice. Should the Employment Court acknowledge the violation of the selection criteria, the relevant employees will be reinstated.

In this respect, please note that the employer can terminate a number of employees equal to those who have been reinstated following the appeal, by the subsequent proper application of the selection criteria. On the other hand, should the collective dismissal be considered void by reason of a violation of the procedure (other than violation of the selection criteria), the whole procedure should be re-started by the employer.

The employment of pregnant women cannot be terminated within a collective dismissal procedure. Such prohibition starts from the beginning of the pregnancy up to the date of the first anniversary from birth. In addition, women cannot be dismissed when they get married and, specifically in the period from the publishing of the banns, up to one year after the celebration of the wedding.

O3 Case studies

O3.1 Case study I
(Acquisition of a 'business' situated in another EU state; asset deal; no relocation)

Slumber Ltd, a hotel management company incorporated in the UK and based in Manchester, UK, has been in financial difficulties for some time. Slumber operates nine exclusive hotels in the main British cities (London, Manchester, Birmingham, Leeds, Glasgow, Edinburgh, Liverpool, Cardiff and Bristol) under the 'Slumber' brand. Slumber is 100 per cent owned by UK hotel chain Ezeroom plc, also incorporated in the UK. Each hotel has about 50 staff: five in management, 20 in the restaurant and 25 in house service. Slumber does not own the hotels itself; instead it has a seven-year management agreement with Hotel Investment plc ('HIP'), the owner of the hotels, which is incorporated and based in London, UK. Under this contract Slumber runs the fully equipped hotels on its own risk and has to pay a fixed fee to HIP.

In its central management centre in Manchester, Slumber has another 30 staff. These are 10 managers (including Marketing, Managing, Finance, Sales and Operations Directors) and 20 secretaries, clerks and administrators.

A number of staff are members of the trade union, The Association of Hotel Workers ('AHW'), which has been formally recognised by Slumber as having bargaining rights for hourly paid hotel staff. This is a particularly active union and there is a collective agreement in force. Due to increasing staff costs and the declining demand for expensive hotel accommodation, Slumber is making bigger and bigger operating losses. Slumber is obliged to cut jobs in all the hotels and thus dismisses 40 members of staff as redundant. As a consequence, the service worsens and customer complaints become more frequent. When the board of HIP realises how serious the situation has become, it starts to look for a new operator of its hotels.

Some weeks later, while Slumber is still operating, an Italian company is found which seems able to manage the hotels in a much more profitable way for HIP than Slumber. The company, which is called Dormir, is based in Rome but has already gathered some experience of running hotels in the UK. It operates hotels under the 'Dormir' brand. The board of HIP enters into discussions with Dormir for it to replace Slumber as manager of the hotels.

1. Acquisition of the hotels

It is anticipated that Dormir will want to manage all nine of the hotels under a single management agreement with HIP.

(a) **Would this be a business transfer (defined as a transfer within the meaning of TUPE) under UK law?**

(ONLY TO BE ANSWERED BY UK CONTRIBUTOR)

(b) **Even though Slumber will not transfer any of its activities to Italy, would the acquisition of the hotels in this way constitute a business transfer under Italian law?**

If Slumber does not transfer any of its activities to Italy, Italian law would not apply.

Legal reasoning

In fact, as the transferred business is located in the UK, the transferor is a company incorporated under UK law and the employees affected by the transfer are located in the UK and have employment contracts regulated under UK law, there is no connection with Italy and, consequently, no opportunity to apply Italian law.

(c) **Would it make any difference to whether this constituted a business transfer, under TUPE, if Dormir only wanted to manage the six English hotels (excluding the hotels in Glasgow, Edinburgh and Cardiff)?**

(ONLY TO BE ANSWERED BY UK CONTRIBUTOR)

(d) **Would it make any difference to your answer to (b) above if Dormir only wanted to manage six hotels (for example only the English hotels, excluding those in Scotland and Wales, ie the hotels in Glasgow, Edinburgh and Cardiff)?**

No, it would not make any difference.

Legal reasoning

Please refer to legal reasoning under 1(b) above.

2. Employees who work only partly in the business

What is the position of those staff that work partly in Slumber and partly in Ezeroom? For example, the human resources director of Slumber is also the human resources director of Ezeroom and he has his employment agreement with Ezeroom. He spends approximately 40 per cent of his time dealing with Slumber's personnel matters and the remainder of his time on the human resources affairs of Ezeroom.

(a)   **If this is a TUPE transfer, can he be said to have transferred under TUPE in the UK?**

(UK CONTRIBUTOR TO ANSWER)

(b)   **What is the law on employees who work only partly in the undertaking to be transferred in Italy?**

There are no specific legal provisions present under Italian law, nor is specific case law on this subject available. Generally speaking, the formal criterion will apply and the employees will be considered as employed by the company with which they have entered into an employment agreement.

3. Staff who work outside the UK in another EU country

It transpires that some Slumber central management staff are actually working and based in Italy. Two are Italian nationals.

(a)   **Would these staff transfer to Dormir under TUPE if there was a TUPE transfer?**

(UK CONTRIBUTOR TO ANSWER THIS. PLEASE COMMENT ON UK RESPONSE)

Answer

In theory yes, although this would depend on a number of factors, including their contracts of employment.

Legal reasoning

TUPE applies to undertakings or parts of undertakings situated in the UK immediately prior to transfer. These employees work for and are employed by Slumber, the undertaking to be transferred, but they are simply based in Italy. The undertaking of Slumber is situated in the UK immediately before the transfer (even if some staff work outside the UK); therefore, members of Slumber central management who are working in Italy will technically transfer. The important point is that TUPE, in principle, applies to undertakings or a part of an undertaking situated in the UK immediately before the transfer. The fact that some of the employees are not actually located in the UK is irrelevant.

*Difficulties may arise in practice and, for example, the employees may no longer be required to continue working in the same place. If their employment is terminated this is likely to be in connection with the transfer and be potentially unfair. Whether or not they have claims in the UK or indeed in Italy will depend on conflicts of laws issues: see Chapter **D**.*

Comment: The same consideration may apply should Slumber be incorporated under Italian law.

(b) **Would the position be different if there was a branch office of Ezeroom in Italy, which directly employed these staff?**

(UK TO ANSWER, BUT PLEASE COMMENT)

Answer

The position may be the same.

Legal reasoning

TUPE is likely to apply if the branch office qualifies as an associated employer and the employees are 'assigned' (Case 186/83: Botzen v Rotterdamsche Droogdok Maatschappij BV [1985] ECR 519, ECJ) to Slumber (ie they carry out all their functions for Slumber, who is their de facto employer). In such a case the courts are likely to pierce the corporate veil and treat Slumber as the employer for those purposes.

Comment: In Italy, generally speaking, the formal criterion will apply, so that the employees will be considered as employed by the company with which they have entered into an employment agreement.

4. Dismissal of employee

One of the Slumber staff, Mr X, was dismissed by Slumber after HIP had given notice to terminate the contract with Slumber and whilst negotiations were ongoing with Dormir. Mr X is owed two months' back pay and unpaid holiday.

Against whom can Mr X bring a claim, and where, if Mr X is a UK national based in Italy?

Mr X can certainly bring a claim against Slumber. Should Mr X be a UK national based in Italy, the claim can be brought either in Italy or in the UK.

Legal reasoning

According to art 6 of the 1980 Rome Convention on applicable law, Mr X's claim can be brought both at the location where the working activity has been actually carried out (Italy) and at the location where the office is of the business which hired the same employee (UK).

5. Transfer of employee outside the UK

Mr Y (the marketing director) has been vital to the success of Slumber and has been responsible for many successful ideas. Dormir would like to retain his services and move him to Dormir's headquarters in Italy. Mr Y has no wish to live in Italy.

(a)   **How does TUPE impact on Mr Y: is he obliged to transfer against his will?**

(UK ONLY TO ANSWER)

(b)   **What is the law on objection to a transfer in Italy?**

Under Italian law, in the case of a business transfer, the affected employees have no right to object to the transfer. According to art 2112 of the Italian Civil Code, the transferred employee can resign within three months of the business transfer, should his work conditions change substantially.

(c)   **Can Mr Y claim constructive dismissal on the basis that he would be expected to work and be based in Italy and this is nowhere near his home?**

(UK TO ANSWER, BUT PLEASE COMMENT)

Answer

Possibly – if being expected to work and be based abroad amounts to a substantial change in working conditions and is to the employee's detriment.

Legal reasoning

Regulation 5(5) provides that an employee has the right 'to terminate his contract of employment without notice if a substantial change is made in his working conditions to his detriment'. It is important therefore that the change is substantial and to the employee's detriment. Such a claim is likely to lie against the transferee (Dormir) and only in rare circumstances, eg where the transferor (Slumber) has not been open with the employee about the change in working conditions, is a claim likely to succeed again the transferor (Slumber). Case law is of importance here.

In Merckx and Neuhuys v Ford Motors Co Belgium SA [1996] IRLR 467, Anfo Motors SA transferred its Ford dealership to an independent dealer. There was no transfer of assets and only 14 out of Anfo's 60 employees were taken on. The ECJ identified a community right to claim constructive dismissal where there was a 'substantial change in working conditions to the detriment of the employee' because of the transfer.

In Rossiter v Pendragon [2002] IRLR 483, Mr Rossiter argued that he had suffered a detriment through changes in the calculation of commission, that his holiday pay was no longer based on commission and he was made to assume lesser duties. The Court of Appeal held that in order to claim constructive dismissal, there would have to be a repudiatory breach of contract, which there was not in this case.

If there is no mobility clause in a contract of employment, relocation may not be lawful. Even if there is a mobility clause in the contract, there can be difficulties enforcing it, depending on the facts.

Comment: According to art 2112 of the Italian Civil Code, the transferred employee can resign within three months of the business transfer, should his work conditions change substantially. The employee will have the right to PILON (payment in lieu of notice).

6. Dormir's business strategy

What is the best way of structuring the transfer of the hotels to Dormir from Italy's perspective? Would you advise Dormir to set up a subsidiary company registered in the UK specifically to purchase Slumber and thereby avoid any cross-border element?

This could be an opportunity. Tax aspects should be examined, though.

O3.2 Case study 2
(Production moves from one EU country to another EU country; physical move)

Alpha Incorporated is a multinational car tyre manufacturing and distribution business based in Europe. Alpha's headquarters are in the UK. Alpha has tyre plants in the UK, Italy and France. Each of the tyre plants is a wholly owned and independently operated subsidiary of Alpha. Alpha has a European Works Council.

The subsidiary in Italy is Beta. Beta employs about 250 employees, mostly in the direct production of tyres. The employees are on standard basic contracts which do not contain any mobility clauses. Due to increased competition from cheaper producers in the Far East, Alpha is having to reduce its own production costs. Beta has the highest production costs of all Alpha's European operations. Alpha has decided to end the production of tyres in Italy and move production to Gamma, another subsidiary not far away but across the national boarder in France which has more modern plant and equipment. Beta will continue to exist, but as a sales and marketing organisation only, with about 30 staff.

Most of Beta's tyre-making plant and machinery is transferred to Gamma, but Gamma will only need an extra 125 staff to increase its output to the required level to supply Beta's market. Those employees from Beta who are required to work for Gamma will be expected to accept the terms and conditions and working practices of the Gamma plant, which are very different from those in operation at the Beta plant. For example, Gamma pays its employees considerably lower hourly wages and they work longer hours than those at Beta. Gamma does not want to pay more to the employees transferred to it from Beta than it does to its current employees. In addition, Beta has an occupational pension scheme for its Italian staff. Gamma operates a different type of pension scheme.

1. Does this transaction constitute a 'business transfer'?

(a) **As Beta's tyre-making plant and machinery have transferred to Gamma, will this constitute a business transfer under the Acquired Rights Directive implementing legislation of Italy?**

Yes.

Legal reasoning

According to art 2112 of the Italian Civil Code, implementing the ARD Directive in Italy, '... for the purposes of this article, transfer of business is any operation that, further to contractual transfer or merger, has as a consequence the change in the ownership of an economic and organised activity, profit or non profit, pre-existing to the transfer and which preserves its identity ...'[1].

In the present case Beta plant and machinery are transferred to Beta together with part of Beta's employees. It is therefore a classic case of transfer of assets and employees aimed at continuing the same economic activities in a different location. In other words, the business which Beta used to carry out in Italy will now be continued in France, therefore preserving its identity.

1   Please note that this is a non-literal translation.

(b) **Does it make any difference to whether this is a business transfer if employees of Beta transfer across to Gamma?**

The transfer of employees is not a necessary requirement for a transfer of business to exist. However, from a labour law point of view, the case would not be very interesting, should no employees be transferred. Besides, it should be pointed out that under Italian law the notion of 'business transfer' is much wider for the purposes of labour law than for the purposes of general commercial law.

Legal reasoning

The commercial discipline of business transfers is regulated under arts 2555–2562 of the Italian Civil Code, a set of provisions regulating in detail all commercial aspects of such operations such as liabilities/guarantees, etc.

All labour-related aspects of business transfers are regulated under art 2112 of the Italian Civil Code.

(c) **Can the transfer of plant and machinery coupled with the transfer of half the employees (125) constitute a business transfer under Italian legislation if the other 125 employees are dismissed prior to the transfer?**

Yes. In order to minimise the risk of the redundancies being seen as connected to the business transfer, and therefore illegal, a practical approach is that the 125 redundant employees should be terminated at least a few months prior to the business transfer, so that there is no immediate connection with the transfer.

However, the Italian Employment Courts might check the reasons for the terminations under a number of different headings, including the question of timing, in order to verify whether they should be considered connected to the business transfer.

In order for the termination to be legal, valid and effective (please be aware that under Italian law illegal employment terminations are often considered ineffective), Beta should be able to prove that the terminations carried out are not connected in any way to the business transfer and so would have been justified under Italian law even if no transfer had been carried out.

Legal reasoning

According to art 2112 of the Italian Civil Code, business transfer itself does not constitute a justifiable reason for termination of employment. However, both parties to a business transfer may carry out those dismissals which are allowed under Italian law, if they are not connected with a transfer.

(d) **Does the fact that the business will transfer to a different country make any difference to whether this is a business transfer?**

No.

Legal reasoning

Under Italian law, no specific provision has been made with regard to trans-national business transfers. Therefore, the Italian business transfer regulations should apply in the present case. Notwithstanding this, a number of practical problems arise, such as the implementation of the transferee's joint liability with regard to the transferor's financial obligations to the transferred employees; the determination of the collective contract of the same standard to be applied to the transferred employees, etc.

(e) **Is Italian business transfer law concerned with the actual distance moved (irrespective of whether this means a change of country)?**

No. However, a number of considerations need to be taken into account.

Legal reasoning

Should the business be transferred outside Italy, problems may arise with regard to different implementations of the ARD Directive in each country. Obviously, even more relevant problems may arise should the business be transferred outside the European Union, where the ARD Directive is not effective/binding.

2. Relocation, but no business transfer

(a)   **Assuming the move does NOT constitute a business transfer (because the business of Beta does not adequately retain its identity) but instead is deemed to be a straightforward relocation, are any of Beta's employees obliged or entitled to transfer?**

    (i)   Under Italian law, even in the absence of an express mobility clause, employees may be transferred to a different productive unit in a different location within the same legal entity. In order for the employer to be entitled to transfer the employee to a different entity of the same group, it is therefore advisable to insert a provision specifying that the relocation can be carried out within different entities of the same group ('Group Mobility Clause'). Notwithstanding this, it is very likely that a transfer to a different country will be opposed by most of the involved employees.

    (ii)   On the other hand, should Beta decide to relocate the business to France, this could be a justifiable reason for proceeding with a collective dismissal. In this case, under the information/consultation procedure with the unions, a certain number of employees may be entitled to transfer. Italian law provides that under the information/consultation procedure with the unions (to be carried out prior to the collective dismissals), it can be agreed that some of the employees may avoid termination and be transferred on secondment to a different company. In this respect, it should be noted that no time limit is envisaged for such secondment.

Legal reasoning

    (i)   According to art 2103 of the Italian Civil Code, even if no mobility clause is present in the contract, employees can be transferred to a different productive unit in a different location within the same legal entity for justifiable technical, production or organisational reasons.

    Affected employees are entitled to oppose the transfer, claiming the non-existence of such reasons.

(ii) Under Italian law, in the case of mass dismissals, the unions' representatives may require the holding of a joint assessment of the business situation with the employer's management (*esame congiunto*). During the *esame congiunto*, the opportunity/possibility for a number of employees to be transferred/seconded to another business will be taken into consideration. Should it be possible, this will certainly make a potential agreement with the unions easier with all the subsequent consequences in terms of favourable industrial relations.

(b) If employees do nevertheless relocate, what will happen to their employment contracts? Will these continue, or will Gamma be entitled to provide new contracts?

(i) Should they be transferred to Gamma (Gamma being part of the same legal entity as Beta under Italian Law), according to art 2103 of the Italian Civil Code they will be entitled to preserve their economic and working conditions.

(ii) Should they be transferred to Gamma within a mass dismissal procedure, different work conditions may be negotiated and agreed during the *esame congiunto*.

Legal reasoning

(i) The transfer to another establishment/productive unit within the same entity is not in itself a justifiable reason to proceed with changes to employment agreements.

(ii) Please refer to legal reasoning under **2(a)** above.

(c) What will be the law applicable to the contracts of the employees who relocate?

In the case of a transfer of employees under art 2103 of the Italian Civil Code (transfer to a different productive unit within the same legal entity) or in the case of an intra-group transfer (with a Group Mobility Clause), the employment agreements of the relevant employees will continue to be regulated by Italian law.

In any other circumstances, the 1980 Rome Convention on applicable law for contractual obligations will apply and French law would consequently regulate the relevant employment agreements.

3. Dismissals

(a) Assuming the move does constitute a business transfer:

(i) **are any dismissals in connection with the transfer lawful?**

No.

Legal reasoning

According to art 2112 of the Italian Civil Code, the business transfer does not in itself constitute a justifiable reason for termination of employment, but both parties of a business transfer may nevertheless carry out those dismissals which are allowed under Italian law if they not connected with the transfer.

(ii) what are the rights and remedies (including applicable law and appropriate jurisdiction) of any employees dismissed:

a. before the transfer?

Ordinary remedies: depending on the size of the transferor, the dismissed employee may request re-instatement (if the transferor has more than 15 employees) or re-engagement (if the transferor has 15 or fewer employees) plus compensation.

b. after the transfer?

The same remedies as before the transfer. In this case, and depending also on the actual content of any single claims, such remedies can be used against both the transferor and the transferee.

(b) Would these rights and remedies change if this was not a business transfer?

Yes. If it is not a business transfer but a collective dismissal, the relevant procedure must be carried out. For further details about this procedure, see **O2.2–O2.3**.

4. European Works Council and other employees' representatives

(a) Will Alpha be required to inform and consult the European Works Council about the transfer or any redundancies?

It depends on the act of constitution of the EWC.

Legal reasoning

In fact, Legislative Decree no 74/2002, implementing the European Works Councils Directive 94/45/EC, does not contain any provision relating to such obligations. Specific information/consultation procedures with the EWC in the event of business transfers and/or redundancies can be provided in the act of constitution of the relevant EWC, but are not statutorily provided.

(b) Are any other employee representatives required to be involved in the transfer or any redundancies (ie at national or local level)?

Yes. In both cases work councils (or, if not existing, the representatives of the most representative unions) are involved in information/consultation procedures.

Legal reasoning

In the case of the transfer of business, an information/consultation procedure must be carried out according to art 47 of Law no 428/1990.

In the case of mass dismissal, the information/consultation procedure to be carried out is regulated under Law no 223/1991.

5. Collective agreements

What is the effect of the business transfer on any collective agreements affecting Beta's employees?

Beta's employees have the right to the working and wages conditions envisaged by the collective agreements – agreed either at national, local or company level – which applied when they used to work for the transferor.

Collective agreements applied to the transferee's business before the business transfer may be applied to the transferred employees, if they are collective agreements of the same standard (agreed at national, local or company level) as those that applied to the transferor before the transfer.

Legal reasoning

According to art 2112 of the Italian Civil Code:

> '... the transferee shall grant to the transferred employees those economic and working conditions provided by the collective contracts entered into both at national, local and company level in force at the moment of the transfer, till their expiry date unless they are substituted with different collective contracts applicable to the transferee's business. Such substitution is possible only with collective contracts of the same standard ...'[1].

In the past few years, the interpretation of this provision has been controversial in Italy.

Some commentators considered that the transferor's collective agreement should have applied to the transferred employees unless a new collective contract was entered into with the transferee after the transfer (so-called 'harmonisation contracts').

Other commentators considered that the transferor's collective agreement should have applied to the transferred employees, unless the transferee applied a collective contract of the same standard (entered into at national, local or company level).

In judgment no 9545/1999 the Italian Supreme Court definitively opted for the second opinion, stating that the transferor's collective agreement shall apply to the transferred employees only if the transferee does not apply any collective contract.

1   Please note that this is a non-literal translation.

6. Change of terms and conditions

(a) **If this is a business transfer, how can Gamma lawfully harmonise employment contracts and change the terms and conditions of the employees currently on the more generous Beta contracts of employment?**

Generally speaking, transferred employees are entitled to the same economic treatment as they had before the transfer.

Even automatic salary increases envisaged by the applicable collective contract are due, unless it is possible to apply the transferee's collective contract with different provisions. In order to harmonise employment contracts, the transferee may apply a collective contract of the same standard as the one applied by the transferor before the transfer. In some cases, the transferee may propose to his employees to enter into new 'harmonisation contracts'. Such contracts are not expressly envisaged by law; and their content may substantially change from case to case. In any case, normally the relevant unions play an important role in the negotiation procedure.

Legal reasoning

Under art 2112 of the Italian Civil Code, it is provided that transferred employees are entitled to the same economic treatment as they had before the transfer under their individual employment agreement.

In addition, according to the same legal provision, the transferred employees are granted those same rights envisaged by the collective contracts made with the transferor. Automatic pay increases linked to length of service envisaged by collective contracts will apply, unless the applicable collective contracts are changed.

(b) **If this is a business transfer, can Gamma reduce the wages of the former Beta employees?**

Wages cannot be reduced.

Legal reasoning

Please refer to the legal reasoning under **6(a)** above.

(c) **If this is a business transfer, what will happen to the former Beta employees as regards their private pension arrangements?**

No specific provision exists at present under Italian law. This subject is very controversial in Italy.

Legal reasoning

No specific provision is present under Italian law.

It should be noted that, in any event, a number of agreements establishing pension schemes provide that, in the case of a business transfer, the transferred employees are entitled, upon specific approval of the transferee and only if the transferee has no occupational pension scheme, to continue their contributions with the transferor's pension scheme.

In addition, some commentators consider that, if the pension arrangements are included in the employment agreement, they should be considered as part of the salary and, subsequently, the transferee should guarantee their continuation.

Indeed, pension arrangements are often included in collective agreements reached at company level, and therefore they may be changed by the transferee on the conditions reviewed above.

(d) **Is it easier to change terms and conditions of employment if the changes are made six months after the transfer?**

In a trans-national transfer of business, it will depend on the law of the location of the transferee (in this case, French law).

O3.3 Case study 3
(Outsourcing of an ancillary activity to a non-EU country)

A large multinational (ABC) based in Italy has decided to outsource its entire internal IT function to a third party provider in Romania, as the costs of hiring competent IT personnel in Romania are far lower than in Italy, largely because wages are so much lower. At present 200 employees are employed by ABC in its IT function in Italy. It is anticipated that exactly the same IT function will be required in Romania with approximately the same number of people required to run it. There will be no difference in the service or approach for those requiring IT assistance and even the internal telephone number will be automatically diverted. The Romanian third party provider has no assets or presence in Italy.

1. Will this be a business transfer within the scope of Italian law?

The issue is still very controversial in Italy. First of all it should be said that in Italy outsourcing (or, in Italian *esternalizzazione*) means a wide range of operations, some very different from the others.

(i) The outsourcing can be carried out by transferring the tangible and/or intangible assets to another entity together with the employees of the relevant transferred function. This would be the case if ABC Italy transferred to Romania those assets necessary to carry out the IT function (computers, switchboards, etc) together with those employees formerly working in Italy in the IT department. In this case, the outsourcing would constitute a transfer of part of a business and would be covered by the Transfer of Business Regulation.

(ii) The outsourcing may also be carried out by a contract by which the IT functions are carried out by a separate entity according to the provisions of art 1655 of the Italian Civil Code (a so-called 'appalto' contract).

(iii)   It should also be stressed that the transfer of part of a business is often accompanied by the signature of service agreement contract. It is, in fact, quite common that the transferor enters into a service agreement with the transferee, which is then executed with the transferred part of the business.

Legal reasoning

(i)   According to art 2112 of the Italian Civil Code, implementing the ARD Directive in Italy:

> '... for the purposes of this article, transfer of business is any operation that, further to contractual transfer or merger, has as a consequence the change in the ownership of an economic and organised activity, profit or non profit, pre-existing to the transfer and which preserves its identity ... The provisions of this article also apply to the transfer of part of a business, meant as a part functionally autonomous of an economically organised activity, identified as such by the transferor and transferee at the moment of the transfer'[1].

(ii)   According to art 1655 of the Italian Civil Code, the appalto contract ('service agreement') is a contract by which one party is paid to perform a particular work or to provide a particular service with its own resources organisation and at its own risk. This would be the case if ABC Italy entered into a contract with a specialised IT firm in Romania in order for it to carry out the IT function and without transferring any assets and/or employees to the said entity.

(iii)   It is also important to point out that, according to the last paragraph of art 2112 of the Italian Civil Code, should the transferor enter into a service agreement with the transferee, the performance of which is carried out by the transferred part of the business, if the transferor-contractor does not fulfil his legal salary obligations with his employees, those employees will be entitled to claim the amount of money they are owed also against the transferee, within the limit of the amount of money that the transferee owes to the transferor-contractor at the moment at which the employees' claim is brought.

1   Please note that it is a non-literal translation.

2. Effect on employees

(a) What will happen to the employees currently employed in the IT function at ABC? Will they transfer across?

Theoretically speaking, should the operation be considered a transfer of part of a business, the relevant employees should be transferred to the non-EU country. A number of problems may arise.

Legal reasoning

The transferee, as an entity incorporated under the law of a non-EU country, shall not be bound either by the ARD Directive or by the Italian Transfer of Business Regulation. This means that, just to take an example, the transferee's joint liability for the transferor's financial obligations vis-à-vis the transferred employees would not apply (if not provided for under the law of Romania).

(b) **If the employees do transfer, what will the applicable law be for their employment contracts with the third party provider? Where can they make any claims?**

According to international private law. Claims relating to the transfer procedure may be brought in Italian courts.

Legal reasoning

Should the employee be transferred, the applicable law will be determined according to the principles of international private law. The transferred employees may, in any event, bring a claim against the transferor in Italy if they consider the transfer procedure not legally carried out. Italian Employment Courts also have jurisdiction for any claim put by the unions in relation to the transfer of business information/consultation procedure.

3. Data protection

Will there be special data protection issues on the transfer of knowledge and information outside Italy to Romania?

Yes.

Legal reasoning

Italian data protection regulations submit the transfer of personal and/or sensitive information outside the EU to a number of strict requirements and conditions.

4. Transfer to India

Please comment on any differences there would be to your answers if the function was transferred to India rather than Romania.

There are no significant legal differences, as neither Romania nor India is a member of the European Union.

P The Netherlands

Jos Pothof
Solveigh Bijkerk-Verbruggen
Rachida el Johari

PI Business transfers

PI.1 Background

Cross-border transactions can result in international legal relationships between the parties.

From the point of view of labour law, international private law will then play a role, with international conventions, national legislation and national case law all playing their part.

PI.2 Identifying a relevant transfer

The rights of employees when an undertaking is transferred are laid down in Dutch legislation in Book 7, ss 662–666 of the Dutch Civil Code ('BW'), in s 14A of the Collective Bargaining Agreements Act (*Wet op de Collectieve Arbeidsovereenkomst* ('WCAO')) and s 2(a) of the Collective Bargaining Agreements (Declaration of Universally Binding and Non-binding Status) Act (*Wet op het algemeen verbindend en het onverbindend verklaren van bepalingen van collectieve arbeidsovereenkomsten* ('WAVV')).

After definitions of the terms 'employee', 'transfer' and 'economic entity' are set out in BW, Book 7, s 662, the key rules on the safeguarding of employees' rights in the event of the transfer of an undertaking are laid down in Book 7, s 663: the rights and obligations under contracts of employment, which existed for the transferor at the time of the transfer, pass to the transferee.

BW, Book 7, s 664 deals with pension commitments.

BW, Book 7, s 665 allows the employment contract to be dissolved by the court on the application of the employee, if the transfer results in a change of working conditions to the detriment of the employee. If the employment contract is dissolved on the basis of this section in connection with BW, Book 7, s 685, the employee may be awarded compensation. In this case the termination of the contract is assumed to be due to a reason for which the employer is accountable. (See *P2.1* on the different ways of terminating employment contracts and *P2.2* for the calculation of the amount of the compensation).

BW, Book 7, s 665(a) lays down the conditions under which the employer must provide information to its employees who are involved in the transfer of the company.

Lastly, BW, Book 7, s 666 provides that the aforementioned provisions do not apply to the transfer of an undertaking if the employer is declared to be in a state of bankruptcy and the undertaking is part of the liquidation assets.

It can be gathered from these provisions that the Dutch legislator did not choose to incorporate all the provisions of Directive 98/50/EC, which are voluntary in nature, into Dutch legislation. Dutch legislation was first amended by the Act of 18 April 2002, implementing Directive 98/50/EC, and that Act took effect on 1 July 2002. Directive 98/50/EC, with changes to the numbering, was followed by Directive 2001/23/EC.

Scope

The sections are applicable to the transfer of an undertaking as a result of either an agreement, a merger or a split of a whole of an organised structure, intended to carry out a corporate activity, whether or not its purpose is primarily economic. Besides being the result of an agreement, that transfer can also be the result of a merger or a split. These forms of transfer are regulated in Title 7 of Book 2 of the Dutch Civil Code (*Burgerlijk Wetboek* ('BW')), and should be distinguished from the terms '*share merger*' and '*share split*', through which only the control of the undertaking changes; in that case there is no change of employer.

A relevant transfer must involve the transfer of an economic entity, and that term should be construed widely. It encompasses every service or institution, aimed at producing or delivering goods or providing services, whether the profit motive is or is not important. An establishment or branch establishment also falls under this term, according to BW, Book 7, s 662(3).

The transfer is effected on the same date as that on which the transferee actually has the necessary operating resources at its disposal. So there can be some difference in time. Nevertheless, the determining factor is the date of the actual transfer.

P1.3 Affected employees

Book 7, s 662 of the Dutch Civil Code (BW) indicates that the provisions on the protection of employees' rights on the transfer of an undertaking also apply to those employees who perform work in an undertaking maintained by the State, province, municipality, water board or any other public body.

In the Netherlands, civil servants are excluded from employment law, as regulated in the Dutch Civil Code. Non-civil servants, who have a civil law employment contract with the government, are protected by BW, Book 7, s 662, as they fall under the definition in Directive 98/50/EC, which provides that an 'employee' shall mean any person who is protected as an employee under national employment law.

In the event of the transfer of the business of a public service, the employees will be transferred to the transferee, but not the civil servants.

The position of the Dutch legislator is in line with two decisions of the European Court of Justice, given on 14 September 2000 (C-343/98: *Collino and Chiappero v Telecom Italia SpA* [2000] ECR I-6659, ECJ) and on 26 September 2000 (C-175/99: *Mayeur v APIM* [2000] ECR I-7755, ECJ).

As stated, an important criterion is that the employee has a contract of employment with the employer/transferor. The place where his or her actual work is done is not important in this context. For example, a seconded employee will also be transferred if the company of his or her employer is transferred. Conversely, the seconded employee would not be transferred if the company where he or she actually performed the work were transferred to a third party.

P1.4 Effects of the transfer

The safeguarding of rights and obligations (Dutch Civil Code, Book 7, s 663)

This section provides explicitly that through the transfer of an undertaking, rights and obligations of the employee pass to the transferee by operation of law. However, for one year after the transfer, in addition to the transferee, the transferor is jointly and severally liable for compliance with the obligations under the contract of employment which arose before the transfer date.

In the framework of the transfer of rights and obligations as stipulated in the existing employment contract between the employee and the transferor, the transferee will have to settle any outstanding debt to such an employee. The transferee will therefore have to pay out any as yet unpaid salary as well as unused days' holiday, and also any redundancy pay granted by the transferor to the employee. The transferee will have to comply with these obligations, albeit that the transferee who has paid a debt to an employee which dates from before the transfer may claim repayment of that debt from the transferor (BW, Book 6, ss 10 and 12).

Therefore, the rights and obligations include the salary applicable to the employee, the number of days' holiday, an overtime allowance, the number of years' service, as accumulated at the transferor: in short, the whole of the rights and obligations arising from the contract of employment. Only existing rights and obligations will be transferred. No consideration is given to future expectations. Those rights and obligations can ensue from the contract of employment and/or from the Collective Bargaining Agreement ('CBA') governing the legal relationship of the parties.

Section 14(a) of the Collective Bargaining Agreements Act (WCAO) and s 2(a) of the Collective Bargaining Agreements (Declaration of Universally Binding and Non-binding Status) Act (WAVV) apply to the rights and obligations ensuing from a CBA applicable to the parties' legal relationship.

The former section provides that through the transfer of an undertaking within the meaning of BW, Book 7, s 662, the rights and obligations ensuing from employment law provisions of a CBA, which are binding on the transferor, pass to the transferee by operation of law.

The aforementioned rights and obligations terminate at the time the transferee is bound by a CBA concluded after the date of transfer of the undertaking, and becomes required on that basis to comply with those provisions. The rights and obligations also terminate as soon as the CBA applicable at the time of the transfer expires.

Section 2(a) of the WAVV provides that through the transfer of an undertaking within the meaning of BW, Book 7, s 662 (and arising from a declaration that the CBA is generally binding), all existing rights and obligations pass to the transferee by operation of law. This Act is intended to allow CBAs to apply also to employers and employees who are not associated with the parties to the CBA.

In this way, the same effect is achieved collectively as in the individual contract of employment pursuant to Book 7, s 663.

The transferee which is not a party to the transferor's CBA will not be bound by that CBA, but it will have to apply the rights included in it to the employees transferred to it. In practice, therefore, it is possible that the same employer will have to apply two CBAs to two different groups of employees within its company.

The transferee may no longer be bound by the CBA applicable to the employees transferred to it if the transferee itself becomes bound by another CBA. In such an instance, those provisions will apply to all employees within its company without distinction as to their origin.

The transferee will also no longer be bound by a CBA on termination of the transferor's CBA, ie by the expiration of the CBA. In a case like this, the effect of the WAVV is no longer of any importance.

However, the following concepts cause complications: 'direct effect' and 'continued effect' of CBA provisions. The 'direct effect' of a CBA means that the employment conditions included in a CBA have a direct effect on the individual contracts of employment of employees who are not members of a trade union/CBA party.

'Continued effect' means that the employment conditions included in a CBA also remain in force after the end of a CBA between the employer and employee until the time they make other agreements or a new CBA takes force.

It must be concluded from the foregoing that the transferee-employer will be freed from the effect of the CBA provisions, as will the transferor, only if the transferee itself becomes bound by a CBA applicable to all employees, and if that CBA arranges all matters at least to the same standard as was previously the case.

The description of the aforementioned problems for the transferee-employer confronted with one or more applicable CBAs indicates the need for the harmonisation of employment conditions after the transfer of an undertaking.

P1.5 Harmonisation of employment conditions

The possibilities of achieving harmonisation of employment conditions are partly determined by the decision of the European Court of Justice in Case 324/86: *Foreningen af Arbejdsledere i Danmark v Daddy's Dance Hall A/S* [1988] ECR 739, ECJ.

In this case it was decided that employees could not waive the rights conferred on them by the Directive, not even with their consent. It does not matter that, broadly speaking, an employee is on aggregate better off following a business transfer compared to beforehand.

Another question was whether the employee can agree different employment conditions with the transferee after the transfer: it was held that he could. The European Court of Justice adds that the transfer of the undertaking as such could constitute a ground for such change. The court also confirmed this case law in C-209/91: *Rask and Christensen v ISS Kantineservice A/S* [1992] ECR I-5755, ECJ.

The most obvious way to effect a harmonisation of employment conditions is for the employees involved in the transfer to consent to adjustments to the employment conditions with the transferee. Employees will usually be offered a total package of changes, and that total package will then be compared to the former package of employment conditions. If the balance of the difference between those two packages is acceptable to the employees, the adjustment of the employment conditions will be simple to carry out.

In doing so, compensation schemes will have to be used, which could involve a phasing out of existing employment conditions over a certain period, a scheme that neutralises the advantages and disadvantages as far as possible, or a scheme by which salaries are frozen etc.

If the adjustment of employment conditions cannot be effected with the consent of the employees, there is then the possibility of bringing about unilateral changes to employment conditions, to be imposed by the employer. These unilateral changes could be based on Book 7, s 611 of the Dutch Civil Code ('BW'), in which standards for being a good employer and employee are described, and which section is a clear development of the reasonableness and fairness appropriate for the performance of contracts. The Dutch Supreme Court decided that an employee should generally react positively to reasonable proposals by the employer based on a change of circumstances. The employee may only reject such proposals if acceptance of them cannot reasonably be expected of him.

A second possibility could be a so-called unilateral changes clause pursuant to BW, Book 7, s 613.

A link can also be sought with BW, Book 6, s 258, which offers the possibility when employment conditions are changed to request the court to change a contract. If such a request is made, the unforeseen circumstances must be of such a nature that, according to the criteria of reasonableness and fairness, the employer or employee cannot be required to continue the contract unchanged. An example of an unforeseen circumstance is a change in tax law, stating that specific remunerations paid by the employer will no longer be deductible.

Dutch Civil Code, Book 7, s 611

Effecting changes to employment conditions has been possible since the *Taxi Hofman* decision (Hoge Raad [Dutch Supreme Court], 26 June 1998, JAR 1998/199), on the basis of the starting point that the employee should, in general, respond favourably to reasonable proposals by the employer, relating to changed circumstances at work, and the employee can only reject such proposals if he or she cannot reasonably be required to accept them. This rule also applies with respect to changed conditions falling within the employer's scope of risks rather than that of the employee.

The decision of the Hoge Raad therefore means that employees generally have to accept an offer from the employer to change the employment conditions, unless such cannot be required in all reasonableness. To assess such a situation, the concept of reasonableness and fairness will usually have to be interpreted: has there been sufficient consultation, has compensation been offered, etc.

Dutch Civil Code, Book 7, s 613

On the basis of this section, the employer may rely on a unilateral changes clause, which must be included in the contract in writing, if it has such a major interest in the proposed change that, according to the criteria of reasonableness and fairness, the employee's employment conditions will change to his disadvantage.

In this situation a review takes place of that interest on the part of the employee, which, according to the criteria of reasonableness and fairness, should give way to a change. The review will require there to be serious commercial or organisational circumstances, such as a restructuring.

In general, one could say that a harmonisation of employment conditions ensues from commercial circumstances, in the sense that equal remuneration is desired for equal positions. This is mandatory anyway on the basis of case law (the '*Agfa* ruling', Hoge Raad, 8 April 1994, JAR [Employment Case Law] 1994/704).

Dutch Civil Code, Book 6, s 258

On the basis of this section, the court can change a contract of employment on the grounds of unforeseen circumstances, which are of such a nature that, according to the criteria of reasonableness and fairness, the employee cannot be expected to continue the contract unchanged. It is clear that this section requires a tougher review than that referred to in the statutory provisions referred to above.

It is not easy to make changes to employment conditions on the basis of this section, which also provides that a change to the contract of employment cannot be pronounced by the court in so far as, on the basis of the nature of the contract or generally accepted opinion, the unforeseen circumstances should be borne by the party invoking them (see s 258(2)). Changing employment conditions may not meet the criteria of reasonableness and fairness if the reasons for the change are solely for the employer's own benefit, eg changes for economic and/or organisational reasons.

It is often attributable to the employer that it wants harmonisation of employment conditions, the reason being the acquisition of a business. That reason will be attributed to the (new) employer, so it will not usually be easy to rely successfully on that section.

The conclusion must be that harmonisation of employment conditions after the transfer of an undertaking must at least be able to withstand the test of reasonableness and fairness. Therefore, this requires careful consultation with employees about the proposals made in all reasonableness. Phase-out schemes, compensation schemes and suchlike will play an important part here.

Pension in the event of the transfer of an undertaking

Since 1 July 2002, the pension scheme has also become an important factor in the adjustment of Dutch legislation to the European directives. These matters are regulated in Book 7, s 664 of the Dutch Civil Code.

Together with the introduction of this statutory provision, the Pensions and Savings Funds Act (*Pensioen- en Spaarfondsenwet*) was amended, which has resulted in an increase in pension commitments. If the transferring employer has not made any pension commitments to its employees who are involved in the transfer, the transferee is expected to make the same pension commitments to the employees involved in the transfer as it has already made to its other employees. Therefore, the Act introduces a presumption that pension commitments have been made.

This statutory presumption is based on equal treatment of employees in equal situations, and is therefore different from the retention of employment conditions on the transfer of an undertaking. Employment conditions other than pension commitments do, after all, remain unchanged and are only adjusted in the context of harmonisation, whether or not on the basis of a

CBA. In this case, with respect to pensions, there is a statutory presumption which can result in an increase improvement in employment conditions.

There are several exceptions to the main rule in BW, Book 7, s 664 that pensions are to be retained on the transfer of an undertaking. The first exception makes it possible for the transferee to choose when the undertaking is transferred to make the same pension commitments to employees taken over as it had previously made to its own employees. Therefore, in that situation, the pension circumstances for the employees involved in the transfer may change.

If the transferee-employer has different pension schemes for different groups of employees, it may also introduce this differentiation in the choice it makes when the company is transferred. Therefore, if the transferee has one or more pension schemes, it can in all reasonableness carry through such differentiation in the choice it makes of how to deal with this in relation to the new employees involved in the transfer.

Great differences are possible in situations where the transferor has, and the transferee has not, made pension commitments (or vice versa). It may also happen that the transferor has a sectoral pension fund (ie a fund with members in one specific branch only) and the transferee does not (or vice versa).

It is evident that Dutch pension practice has many different schemes, which could lead to different consequences for the employees involved in the transfer of an undertaking.

P2 Redundancy and termination

P2.1 Background

Under Dutch law, if a business is transferred, an employee is automatically transferred to the acquirer and retains his terms of employment. The situation is different if the employee expressly states that he does not want to be transferred. In that case the employment is terminated by operation of law and the employee is deemed to be voluntarily unemployed. This can have implications for any claims the employee may have under social security law. Circumstances can, however, exist as a result of the transfer of the business which make it unreasonable for the employee to be transferred to the acquirer. In such a case the general rules of the law on termination of employment apply in full. If the employee can argue convincingly that he cannot reasonably be required to be employed in the new situation, he can apply for the employment contract to be dissolved. The court may then rule that the employer must pay the employee a reasonable severance payment. Despite the employee's (well-founded) refusal to be transferred and the actual transfer of the business, the employment is not then terminated by operation of law. The employee is not voluntarily unemployed and retains all his social security entitlements.

The law on termination of employment is also relevant if the acquirer is dealing with employees who have stipulated in their employment contracts that Dutch law applies, as after the transfer of the business the (foreign) acquirer must observe the rules of the general law on termination of employment. Finally, the regular law on termination of employment is relevant if, under international private law, Dutch law is declared to apply.

This section concentrates on the situation in which the general Dutch law on termination of employment is being invoked.

> 'An employment contract is a contract under which one party, the employee, undertakes to work in the employ of the other party, the employer, for pay for a certain time.'

This is the definition of an employment contract according to Dutch law (BW, Book 7, s 610(1)). One of the features of an employment contract is that it applies for a 'certain time' and it therefore qualifies as a 'continuing performance contract'. A distinction is subsequently made between a fixed-term employment contract and a contract for an indefinite period. Although the parties are bound by the period for which the contract has been entered into, in certain circumstances termination may be logical or necessary.

Death and passage of time

Firstly, an employment contract logically ends when the employee dies. The employer does, however, have an obligation to make a payment, equivalent to one month's pay, to the employee's surviving relatives (see BW, Book 7, s 674(2)). Secondly, an employment contract ends by operation of law when the time specified in the contract, provided by law or sanctioned by usage, has expired (BW, Book 7, s 667(1)).

Mutual consent

The employment contract can be terminated because the employer and employee decide to terminate it by mutual consent – often with a severance payment. Mutual consent may or may not be recorded in an agreement on legal relations, also called a 'termination agreement'.

Dutch law provides no rules for the form and content of a termination agreement, but the Supreme Court has ruled that the employer must ascertain that the employee's consent is clearly, voluntarily and unambiguously aimed at terminating the employment contract (Supreme Court, 14 January 1983, NJ 1983, 457; Supreme Court, 28 May 1982, NJ 1983, 2; Supreme Court, 20 September 1991, NJ 1991, 785; Joint Court of Justice of the Netherlands Antilles and Aruba, 17 September 2002, NJ 2003, 290).

Under certain circumstances, termination of the employment contract by means of a termination agreement alone can adversely affect the employee's right to a payment, as he or she has 'resigned voluntarily'.

Notice of termination

If only one of the parties wants to terminate the employment contract, one speaks of 'notice of termination' of the contract. An employment contract for an indefinite period is (usually) terminated by notice. There are three grounds for notice of termination: commercial grounds; a difference in perception between the employer and employee on how the employee should or should not perform his job (which is not connected with inadequate performance on the part of the employee); and inadequate performance on the employee's part.

A contract for a fixed period can only be terminated before the expiration of the agreed period by giving notice, if the right to do so has been agreed in writing by both parties.

If an employment contract is terminated by giving notice, the agreed notice period (or, if there is none, the statutory notice period) must be observed.

To give notice of termination the employer needs prior consent from the Central Organisation for Work and Income ('CWI'); the employee does not. The branch of the CWI to which the application must be submitted is regulated in the CWI Working Areas Decree of 7 March 2002, Government Gazette 2002, no 53, p 20. The starting point is that the application be sent to the branch in the CWI working area in which the employee concerned works. The CWI is a government body, which concentrates on the labour market, and whose role is to mediate regarding employment and assess redundancy plans from a preventive point of view. There are 16 CWI offices in the Netherlands.

The procedure via the CWI takes place in writing.

Once an application for consent (application for a dismissal), with detailed supporting arguments, has been submitted by the employer, the employee is given time to put forward a defence to the application submitted by his employer and the documents forming part of it (art 2, para 2 of the Dismissals Decree). Often a single exchange of correspondence is sufficient, but a second may be required. Each party is then given 10 days in which to respond. The periods are minimum periods. They can be extended, if required, by special circumstances. Once the written exchanges have been completed, the CWI is obliged to seek advice from the Dismissals Advisory Committee (art 2, para 5 of the Dismissals Decree), after which the CWI will grant or reject the application. The CWI's decision is irrevocable and not open to appeal. If the dismissal permit is granted, the applicable notice period must be observed, though it can be reduced by one month if this still leaves one month's notice (BW, Book 7, s 671(4)).

The aim of the standard procedure as set out above is to get from application to decision within four to six weeks. If termination by notice is necessary owing to bad commercial conditions, the 'accelerated procedure' can be followed if the application is accompanied by a declaration of no objection (to the notice of termination) from the employee (art 2, para 6 of the Dismissals Decree; Annexe C to the Dismissals Decree includes a 'declaration of no objection' form, which must be completed and signed by the employee). The CWI assesses independently whether the ground for dismissal is correct and subsequently makes a decision as soon as possible. No advice is sought from the Dismissals Advisory Committee and the parties are not heard. In the case of the accelerated procedure the dismissal rules of the Dismissals Decree must, of course, be complied with (these concern compliance with the seniority principle, the principle of proportionality, and research into re-employment and occupational disability owing to illness). In case of doubt the CWI may decide to give the employee an opportunity to put forward a defence.

An employment contract terminated without the consent of the CWI is subject to annulment. This means that the employee has the right to initiate litigation in order for the court to declare the termination null and void. The employee can invoke nullity (art 9 of the BBA (Extraordinary Labour Relations Decree)) until six months after the date of termination. If this is successful, the employment contract is considered not terminated. In that case, the employer must pay the employee his salary over the period from the date on which the employment contract was terminated (without prior consent) up to the date the contract is terminated in compliance with statutory rules. If nullity is not invoked in time (ie within six months) the employment contract is terminated definitively.

The prior consent of the CWI is not required in the case of a valid summary dismissal. Nor is consent required if the employment contract is terminated during the probationary period or as a result of compulsory liquidation (BBA, art 9).

The employer is not allowed to terminate by giving notice in the following cases:

- during the first two years of occupational disability owing to illness (BW, Book 7, s 670(1));

- during pregnancy and a period thereafter (BW, Book 7, s 670(2));

- during military service (BW, Book 7, s 670(3));

- during membership of the works council (BW, Book 7, s 670B);

- because of membership of a trade union or because of trade union activities (BW, Book 7, s 670(5)). NB: Employees are only protected in relation to union activities during working hours if they have the employer's consent for them. No consent is needed for union activities outside working hours. The employee must also not act contrary to the law, the CBA and the obligation to behave as a good employee;

- because of political leave (BW, Book 7, s 670(6) in conjunction with BW, Book 7, s 643);

- because the employee has exercised his or her right to parental leave (BW, Book 7, s 670(7));

- because of a change of ownership of a business (BW, Book 7, s 670(8));

- if the employee is a prospective or former member of the works council (BW, Book 7, s 670A(1)).

The termination prohibitions are mandatory legal provisions. Deviations from them to the employee's disadvantage are only permitted in the case of illness and military service, under a CBA or arrangements governed by public law. If termination of employment is contrary to one of the prohibitions, the employee can request the judge to annul the termination of the contract up to two months after notification.

However, there are exceptions to the prohibitions. They do not apply if the employment contract is terminated during the probationary period, for urgent cause or with the employee's consent, ie in the same circumstances as those in which no CWI consent is required (BW, Book 7, s 670B(1)). Nor do the prohibitions apply when the business or a part of it in which the employee mainly or exclusively works is closed down or ceases, or if the employment contract is terminated by the receiver in a compulsory liquidation, the agreed period expires, or the resolutive condition occurs (parties can agree on a condition, which is stipulated in the employment agreement, to the effect that if the condition occurs the employment contract is considered to be terminated).

Dissolution

As well as by termination or agreement, the employment contract can also be dissolved by the court on the application of either party and at any time. There are two kinds of dissolution: owing to 'serious cause' (BW, Book 7, s 685) and owing to 'a breach of contract' (BW, Book 7, s 686). Dissolution for breach of contract hardly ever occurs in practice and is not covered further in this chapter.

'Serious cause' means, firstly, the circumstances which constitute urgent cause (BW, Book 7, s 685(2)). This can happen if an employer is not sure whether instant dismissal will be held justifiable in court. By submitting an application to dissolve the contract the employer can request the court to dissolve it for urgent cause, as the court is free to determine the ground for dissolution. Secondly, a change of circumstances, such that the employment contract must end on the grounds of equity, is also regarded as serious cause. This ground for dissolution is very wide and can concentrate on unsatisfactory performance by the employee, a disturbed working relationship, or poor business circumstances.

The possibility cannot be excluded that a court, which does not consider that urgent circumstances exist that must result in dissolution of the employment contract, will nevertheless dissolve the employment contract owing to a change of circumstances.

In practice, the dissolution procedure is generally preferred, as it enables the employment contract to be terminated reasonably quickly compared to the CWI procedure. Dissolution does not require a dismissal permit. Even if the CWI refuses to issue a dismissal permit, the court can nevertheless dissolve the employment contract at the request of one of the parties. The CWI assesses the ground for dismissal, while the district court also looks at the method and consequences of the termination of the employment and the interests of both the employee and the employer. The consequences of dismissal are assessed by reference to the circumstances prevailing at the time of dismissal.

In addition, in the case of dissolution by the district court, there is no notice period and the court is not obliged to take account of the termination prohibitions. It is only compelled to ascertain whether the dissolution request is connected with a termination prohibition. It need not, however, attach any consequences to this (Unemployment Insurance Act, s 16(3)).

If the district court grants the dissolution request, the contract is dissolved immediately or later. Dissolution cannot be pronounced retroactively, ie the end of the employment cannot be placed at a time in the past.

Dissolution is final as soon as the district court has pronounced it. No appeal, including an appeal to the Supreme Court, can be brought against the court's decision (BW, Book 7, s 685(11)).

Urgent cause

The final method of terminating the employment contract is 'urgent cause', also referred to in common parlance as 'instant dismissal'. Either party can terminate the employment contract for urgent cause (BW, Book 7, s 677(1)). The employment then ends with immediate effect without notice. Contrary to normal termination, the rules regarding termination prohibitions do not apply and the CWI's consent is not needed. On the other hand, certain requirements must be met:

1 there must be an urgent cause which can be objectively defined;

2 this cause must be such that continuation of the employment contract can no longer reasonably be required;

3 the other party must be notified of the urgent cause;

4 notification must be effected at the same time as termination takes effect.

The law gives a non-exhaustive list of 'urgent causes':

– when the employee, when entering into the contract, misled the employer by producing false or forged testimonials, or gave the employer false information about how his previous employment contract was terminated;

- serious lack of skill or suitability as regards carrying out the work stipulated;

- drunkenness and other dissolute behaviour;

- theft, embezzlement, deception;

- deliberately or recklessly damaging goods;

- deliberately or recklessly endangering himself or others.

P2.2 Redundancy payments

Entitlement

In the case of dissolution on the grounds of a change of circumstances, the court can award a payment to one of the parties (BW, Book 7, s 685(8)). The payment can be awarded to the party against whom the dissolution request has been made, but also to the requesting party. In principle the district court has discretion on whether or not to award a payment and its level, taking into account all the circumstances of the case (Supreme Court, 5 March 1999, NJ 1999, 644, JAR 1999/73). Payments to the employer hardly ever occur. The payment is determined equitably. The award of a payment does not require the existence of financial loss. The payment relates in particular to the consequences of the termination of the employment contract and how it is terminated. The payment does not include amounts owed to the employee which have arisen during the employment, such as back wages and holiday pay entitlements; these must be recovered in separate proceedings.

Calculation

To avoid legal uncertainty and legal inequality regarding the award of severance payments, and given that it is not possible to appeal, a method of calculating the payment has been developed. Payment is calculated using the formula A x B x C. This method of calculation, in which the three factors are multiplied together, is called 'the district court formula'.

'A' stands for the number of the years of service taken into account on the date of dissolution. The years of service are rounded to whole years, eg half a year plus a day counts as a whole year. Years of service before the age of 40 count as 1, years of service between the ages of 40 and 50 as 1.5, and years of service above the age of 50 as 2.

'B' stands for the gross monthly salary, plus fixed permanent and agreed pay components such as holiday allowance, a fixed thirteenth month, structural overtime pay and a fixed shift work allowance. Other pay components only count in special cases. In practice, what is meant by the term 'salary' is often contested.

'C' stands for the adjustment factor. In determining this, the court looks at the degree to which blame for the ground for dissolution can be attributed. If blame lies wholly in the employer's sphere of risk, the adjustment factor is greater than 1.

If dissolution is to a greater or lesser extent attributable to the employee, or if commercial circumstances do not permit a higher payment, the factor C is less than 1. Under the Unemployment Insurance Act, an employee is in principle not entitled to unemployment benefit if his unemployment is voluntary (an employee can be voluntarily unemployed if he or she has insufficiently defended himself against dismissal: Unemployment Insurance Act, s 24(1)(b) and s 27(1)).

If blame is attributable to neither party, the factor C is set at 1. Application of an adjustment factor of one is also referred to as 'blameless dissolution'.

The attribution of blame and all the other special circumstances of the case are thus expressed in the adjustment factor. These special circumstances may include, for example, the very short duration of the employment, a new job in the offing, or whether or not the employee is bound by a competition clause. Plans are currently well advanced to alter these rules so that factor B counts only for 50 per cent and the maximum cannot exceed one year's gross annual salary. The formal legislative path has yet to start. Factor C thus gives the court the freedom to reduce or increase the payment.

P2.3 Settlement agreements

If an employer wants to terminate the employment contract but doubts whether the CWI will consent to dismissal, he or she can start substantive dissolution proceedings before the court. To avoid this, the employer can also choose to make the employee an offer to terminate the employment contract amicably. Though in principle there is no question of mutual consent, the employee may nevertheless be willing to consent if the severance payment is high enough.

In the above cases and on termination by mutual consent, the choice is made of 'pro forma' dissolution via the district court. This means that the employer submits a 'pro forma' application to dissolve the employment contract for serious cause, whereupon the employee only defends himself 'formally'. The parties have taken account of each other's documents before these are submitted to the court. The intention of the parties is that the court should only formally assess the ground for dissolution put to it and the level of the severance payment to be awarded.

In this form of termination the employee will have his Unemployment Insurance Act entitlements safeguarded as much as possible. The agreements made by the parties for that purpose are (nearly) always recorded in an agreement on legal relationships, also called a 'termination agreement'.

The aspects recorded in the termination agreement include agreements connected with the agreed termination date, the severance payment and the settlement of employee benefits. By signing the agreement, the parties grant each other full discharge in respect of the employment contract and the rights and obligations arising under it.

The termination agreement creates a situation in which, in principle, the employee can no longer contest the termination of the contract. By signing the agreement the employee expressly states that he or she has no objection to the termination. As a result, the remedies available to him or her against the consequences of dismissal, invoking irregular or manifestly unreasonable termination, will lapse. To protect employees, the Supreme Court therefore requires the employee's consent to be unambiguous and clear (Hoge Raad, 25 March 1994, NJ 1994, 390, JAR 1994/92 (*Ritico*); Hoge Raad, 19 April 1996, JAR 1996/116). For the employer this creates a duty of care and a duty to examine the matter. He must ascertain that the employee is aware of the termination and any consequences of it.

P2.4 The duty to inform and consult prior to redundancy

Directive 98/59/EC and its implementation in Dutch law

The directives on employee participation have been implemented in various Dutch Acts of Parliament whose purpose is to guarantee various forms of employee participation, firstly by the trade unions concerned and secondly by the employees themselves in a works council context.

The obligation to set up a works council and involve it in the company's decision-making is regulated in the Works Councils Act ('WCA'), which first came into being on 4 May 1950 on the initiative of the Dutch business community. The main purpose of Directive 98/59/EC, however, is to guarantee trade unions participation in decision-making. This was implemented in the Collective Redundancy (Notification) Act ('CRNA'), which came into being on 24 March 1976 immediately following the Directive. The CRNA was altered in 1994 in connection with the revision of the Directive.

Because the content of the Dutch legislation has broadly grown in line with the content of the European legislation, the government has not always thought it necessary to implement the various directives separately. For example, the WCA had just been thoroughly revised at the time Directive 98/59/EC was published and, according to the Dutch government, this made it superfluous to implement the Directive separately in the WCA. Incidentally, the Directive has in fact been explicitly implemented, especially in the area of the transfer of a business, in other Acts of Parliament (Bulletin of Acts and Decrees 2002, no 215).

Finally, Dutch law includes specific rules of conduct relating to business mergers. The Merger Code was drawn up by the Social and Economic

Council ('SEC'), a co-operative body consisting of employers' and employees' representatives. The Code is, in fact, a form of self-regulation for the business community. It sets out specific rules regarding consultation with, and participation by, trade unions in relation to mergers and takeovers. These consultative powers were drawn up on the basis of the Directive and are an extension of the employee consultation guaranteed by the CRNA.

Appropriate representatives

Representatives of the employees

The Directive prescribes that 'representatives of employees' are entitled to be involved in the decision to effect collective redundancy and in its implementation. The term 'representatives of employees' refers in this context to the trade unions. Section 13 of the CRNA implements the Directive by means of the obligations which the employer has towards the trade unions in the context of collective redundancy. The section states that an employer who intends to terminate the employment of at least 20 employees working in an area of operation, at one or more times within a three-month period, must notify the interested 'associations of employees' in writing for the purposes of timely consultation.

In the case of mergers, this obligation is fleshed out in greater detail in s 4 of the Decree on the Rules relating to Mergers of the Social and Economic Council, which regulates procedure and consultation in the event of a merger or takeover. A trade union must be involved in discussions concerning a restructuring if the trade union is an association of employees which includes among its members people who work in the company; if its object by virtue of its statutes is to look after the interests of its members as employees; and if the employer has been aware of it as a legal person for two years. Section 2 of the WCA states the purpose of setting up a works council, namely to consult with and represent the people working for the company.

The works council and employee representation

In the area of employee participation, Dutch law has a Works Councils Act and also a European Works Councils Act which was drawn up on the basis of European Directive 94/45/EC. The Acts cover different areas: the scope of the Works Councils Act is purely national, while the European Works Councils Act applies only to businesses which have locations in more than one European country. The aim in both cases is to provide a platform for employee participation. The complicating factors caused by the fact that European works councils involve more than one legal system are largely overcome by the Directive's implementation in national law and the specific rules relating to Dutch employees who are subject to the Directive and their specific rights.

A business which for two years has had an average of at least 150 employees in at least two member states and an average of 1,000 employees in the member states as a whole falls within the scope of the European Works Councils Act. The European Works Council's powers are confined to the provision of information and consultation on the matters which are relevant to the whole business with a community dimension or the whole group with a community dimension, or to at least two locations or businesses of the group in different member states. The information and consultation concerns the structure of the community business or group, its financial and economic position, the presumed development of its activities, and a limited list of subjects which are set out in s 19 of the European Works Councils Act.

An undertaking in which as a rule at least 50 people are employed is obliged to set up a works council (WCA, s 2). An employer with fewer than 50 employees but more than 10 can also set up employee representation (s 35(c)).

A works council is involved in a wide range of subjects. Employee representation has powers only in respect of main aspects. A works council's tools are the right of approval, the right to be consulted, and the right of initiative (ie the right to start discussions on subjects as set out in WCA, s 23.2 and s 28). The works council is also entitled to written information, which it needs to fulfil its role properly (WCA, s 30). Both consultative bodies have a right of approval regarding the company's social policy and the right to be consulted in the financial, commercial and business management areas (ss 25–30). This includes, among other areas, everything that relates to the company's financial and commercial housekeeping, the annual report and accounts (s 31(a)), and information about the social policy (s 31(b)).

The information to which a works council is unreservedly entitled by reason of its general right of information and on which it is allowed to give advice is that connected with a planned collective redundancy decision. The advice in this context relates, inter alia, to whether the undertaking has taken sufficient account of the consequences which the planned measures have for the employees, and whether sufficient measures have been taken to mitigate them as far as possible.

The legally prescribed 'consultation' of the trade unions, as prescribed by CRNA, s 3, relates at least to the possibilities of avoiding collective redundancies or reducing their number. In addition, the consultation also relates to reviewing the possibility of mitigating their consequences, eg by taking social assistance measures, contributing to re-employment, or retraining the redundant employees. The undertaking and the trade unions are supposed to reach agreement on the number of redundancies and to draw up a redundancy plan supported by both parties.

In the case of a merger, the undertaking gives the trade unions an opportunity to voice their opinion on the employees' interests which are at stake in relation to the merger, one of the areas covered being the basis of measures to prevent, eliminate or reduce any adverse consequences for employees, including financial contributions (s 4 of the Rules relating to Mergers).

Involvement of the competent authority

The CRNA prescribes that an employer who intends to terminate the employment of at least 20 employees working in a Centre for Work and Income ('CWI') area, at one or more times within a three-month period, must notify the CWI in its area of operation in writing of its intention to do so. The area of a CWI is the criterion for deciding whether a person working in a particular region belongs among the 20 employees who are being made redundant in a three-month period.

The notification includes the considerations which have led to the collective redundancy plan. The employer must also state the basis on which the employees are surplus to requirements, and one aspect of this is a breakdown by occupation or job, a breakdown by sex, the number of people usually employed, the date or dates on which the employer plans to terminate the employment, and the selection criteria for the employees facing redundancy (CRNA, s 4(2)).

Time period

The request for advice must be submitted to the works council in a timely manner. This requirement arises from European Directive 94/45/EC, the Rules Relating to Mergers and the WCA. The WCA states on this topic that the advice must be requested at such a time that it can have a real effect on the decision to be taken. This timeliness requirement is one of the most disputed questions in employee participation since, despite all the legal cases which have taken place concerning it, the timing of a request for advice has to be considered afresh in each case.

The timely involvement of the trade unions is enforced by the duty imposed by the CWI to observe a month's statutory delay after the notification to the trade unions and the CWI itself (CRNA, s 6). The rationale for this statutory delay is to enable the CWI to seek financial or other solutions, e g by means of re-employment or training. If the notification shows that the works council has not been asked for advice and the trade unions have not yet been invited for consultation, the CWI will not process the application until the request for advice has been made, or the unions have been invited for consultation.

The Rules relating to Mergers prescribe that the parties involved in the merger should ask the trade unions' opinion at a time when it can have a real impact on whether or not the merger comes about, and the conditions on which it does so.

Failure to comply

The WCA provides a number of measures which the works council can take, and which are intended to enable the works council to impose its influence on decisions by the managing director. If the undertaking takes a decision, which is not or not wholly in accordance with the works council's *advice*, he must observe a month's statutory delay before implementing his decision

(WCA, s 25(6)). For a month after the decision, the works council can lodge an appeal with the Enterprise Section of the Amsterdam Court of Appeal. The Enterprise Section can oblige the undertaking to withdraw the decision wholly or partly. It can also instruct the undertaking to reverse certain consequences of the decision, or can prohibit it from carrying out actions or having third parties carry out actions in implementation of the decision or parts of it (WCA, s 26). This possibility of appeal also applies if the works council has issued no advice because it has not been asked for it, or because it has not been able to issue advice.

The CRNA has no active sanctions, only a suspension of the obligations of the CRNA. The handling of redundancy applications on which no decision has yet been taken is suspended until the notification has been effected. Subsequently, an additional month's statutory delay is imposed, and the CWI therefore observes not one but two months' delay before the requests are assessed for consent (CRNA, s 7).

The Rules relating to Mergers include a procedure for a disputes committee whose members and powers are regulated in the Decree itself (Rules relating to Mergers, s 17 et seq). All disputes which have to do with one or more merger parties' failure to observe, or failure to observe properly, the Rules relating to Mergers can be brought before the committee by an employees' association or another party involved in the merger (Rules relating to Mergers, s 18). The most severe sanction which the disputes committee can impose for non-compliance with the rules is the disclosure of its opinion (s 32). In the most extreme case this can be in the form of a press release.

Notifying redundancies

The process and the rules which apply specifically to collective redundancy are laid down in the Acts of Parliament and regulations discussed above; the WCA which regulates the works council's employee participation; the CRNA, in which the rights of the trade unions and the involvement of the CWI are officially laid down; and the Rules relating to Mergers, which set out the specific rules applying between the companies and trade unions involved in the event of a merger.

Notification of trade unions and the competent authority

An employer who intends to terminate the employment of at least 20 people must report this to the interested employees' associations so that timely consultation can take place (CRNA, s 3). This section regulates the trade unions' fundamental right to be involved in, and consulted on, the collective redundancy plan, in accordance with the Directive.

Besides the consultation, the employer is obliged to report the intended redundancies to the Centre for Work and Income, in its area of operation concerned. If at least five requests to dissolve employment contracts have been submitted to the district court for an economic reason for employees who work in the same region, these are part of the collective redundancy.

After the notification, the CWI observes a month's statutory delay. In exceptional cases the statutory delay is disregarded, if observing it would jeopardise the employees' re-employment or the continued existence of the jobs. The statutory delay is also not observed if the notification from the employer is supported by a declaration from the trade unions which are interested parties that they have been consulted and agree to the redundancies (CRNA, s 6).

If, on expiry of the month's statutory delay, the CWI is asked for consent to dismiss the employees who, according to the employer, are eligible for redundancy, the CWI applies the Dismissals Decree as a guideline for the redundancy criteria to be applied. In the case of collective redundancy, an employee can apply the seniority principle to each age group, so that the age structure of the group proposed for redundancy is a reflection of the whole staff complement. Only exceptionally is deviation from the seniority principle possible, eg if an employee has special skills.

Social plan

It is virtually always the norm that employers who wish to implement a restructuring draw up a social plan to regulate collectively its consequences for the employees concerned. There is no legal provision that makes drawing up a social plan obligatory. This obligation can, at most, be derived from the duty to consult the trade unions, and an employer also generally regards himself as morally bound to do so. In addition, the collectivity of a social plan has the effect that employees in identical situations are dealt with identically, without each individual case having to be put to the court or the CWI, with proceedings being conducted to the bitter end.

The discussion partners in the sequence for a social plan to come into being are primarily the trade unions. On behalf of the employees they represent, they are party to the plan and in fact by means of it they bind all the employees. Because they are involved in the creation of the plan and the negotiations have been conducted by them, a court will readily take the view that the interests of individual employees have been sufficiently covered at that stage, and an individual employee will have little chance of success if he contests the conditions of the termination of his employment in dissolution proceedings by virtue of BW, Book 7, s 685, or in manifestly unreasonable redundancy proceedings by virtue of BW, Book 7, s 681 after the termination of the employment contract by giving notice. This is particularly so if the works council has given a favourable recommendation regarding the social plan.

Collective termination of employment contract

If all the legal conditions for collective redundancy have been met, the employer can request the CWI's consent, in accordance with the Dismissals Decree, to terminate the contracts of the employees who have been declared superfluous to requirements. On receipt of this consent, the employer gives notice of termination of the employment contract to take effect at the end of the month, with due observance of the notice period. Under the social plan, obligations such as out-placement, a benefit top-up or training measures can still arise for the employer after the end of the employment.

The other ordinary way of terminating employment, the dissolution procedure via the district court, is strongly discouraged by the judiciary, as the procedure is considered too individual and the district court does not have all the background information required to give a sound judgment. Nor does the judiciary consider that it has the capacity that would be required to give a large number of substantive decisions.

Nevertheless, it does sometimes happen in practice that individual employment contracts are terminated by means of a formal dissolution procedure. In that case the payment awarded by the court is prescribed by the social plan. A small number of actions will still be substantive, however, as one can virtually rule out the assumption that all employees will always acquiesce in the outcome of the social plan in their situation.

Conclusion

The group termination of employment contracts and the employee participation in this process are guaranteed in the CRNA, the WCA and, for the business community, the Rules relating to Mergers. The rules in their entirety largely provide a more or less comprehensive employee participation system. Their different scope, sphere of application, status and sanction possibilities, however, create great diversity, so that situations can still arise in which it is the intention of the Directive to provide protection, but Dutch legislation does not provide it sufficiently. An example of this is the regulation that the government must create the possibility of appeal for situations in which trade unions think they have been insufficiently involved in a restructuring. This possibility of appeal is only required within the business community and specifically in the form of a disputes committee. It is doubtful whether the Directive refers to this kind of proceeding, since it is probably not an adequate regular appeal provided by the government, as intended by the Directive. The CRNA does not have an adequate possibility of appeal of this kind. The Dutch government has seen no reason, however, to prepare new legislation further to the most recent directives, and therefore at present a Dutch employee has less protection than that to which he is entitled according to European Directive 94/45/EC.

P2.5 Offer of alternative work

In certain circumstances, an employee cannot continue to work in his original job at the company. This can happen if the employee performs inadequately, or in the event of restructuring or occupational disability. When this is ascertained, the employer can offer the employee other suitable work. According to law, suitable work is: '... any work geared to the employee's powers and skills, unless he or she cannot be required to accept it for reasons of a physical, mental or social nature' (BW, Book 7, s 658A(3)). The employer must check whether the employee can be offered another suitable job in his business and must promote the employee's placement in such a job. There is no trial period connected to alternative work.

An employee who rejects an offer of alternative and suitable work jeopardises the continuation of his employment. Furthermore, the employee could also jeopardise his entitlement to unemployment benefits because the CWI might consider his unemployment to be the result of his own fault.

P2.6 Unfair redundancy

Manifestly unreasonable dismissal

If one of the parties terminates the employment contract contrary to the law, the collective bargaining agreement or the employment contract, the other party can bring proceedings before the district court, invoking 'manifestly unreasonable dismissal' (BW, Book 7, s 681). The employee can then claim reinstatement or severance pay. The court will regard a dismissal as 'manifestly unreasonable' if a party acting reasonably could not have terminated the contract. An employee can claim reinstatement or severance pay on the grounds of manifest unreasonableness until six months after termination of the contract.

The law mentions a number of examples of manifestly unreasonable dismissal, including the following:

– dismissal effected without stating the reasons, or giving a false reason;

– dismissal where, taking into account the arrangements made for the employee and his opportunities for finding other suitable work, the consequences for him of termination are too serious compared to the employer's interest in terminating the employment.

Termination of the employment during the probationary period and instant dismissal are not manifestly unfair.

P3 Case studies

P3.1 Case study 1
(Acquisition of a 'business' situated in another EU state; asset deal; no relocation)

Slumber Ltd, a hotel management company incorporated in the UK and based in Manchester, UK, has been in financial difficulties for some time. Slumber operates nine exclusive hotels in the main British cities (London, Manchester, Birmingham, Leeds, Glasgow, Edinburgh, Liverpool, Cardiff and Bristol) under the 'Slumber' brand. Slumber is 100 per cent owned by UK hotel chain Ezeroom plc, also incorporated in the UK. Each hotel has about 50 staff: five in management, 20 in the restaurant and 25 in house service. Slumber does not own the hotels itself; instead it has a seven-year management agreement with Hotel Investment plc ('HIP'), the owner of the hotels, which is incorporated and based in London, UK. Under this contract Slumber runs the fully equipped hotels on its own risk and has to pay a fixed fee to HIP.

In its central management centre in Manchester, Slumber has another 30 staff. These are 10 managers (including Marketing, Managing, Finance, Sales and Operations Directors) and 20 secretaries, clerks and administrators.

A number of staff are members of the trade union, The Association of Hotel Workers ('AHW'), which has been formally recognised by Slumber as having bargaining rights for hourly paid hotel staff. This is a particularly active union and there is a collective agreement in force. Due to increasing staff costs and the declining demand for expensive hotel accommodation, Slumber is making bigger and bigger operating losses. Slumber is obliged to cut jobs in all the hotels and thus dismisses 40 members of staff as redundant. As a consequence, the service worsens and customer complaints become more frequent. When the board of HIP realises how serious the situation has become, it starts to look for a new operator of its hotels.

Some weeks later, while Slumber is still operating the hotels, a Dutch company is found which seems able to manage the hotels in a much more profitable way for HIP than Slumber. The company, which is called Dormir, is based in Amsterdam but has already gathered some experience of running hotels in the UK. It operates hotels under the 'Dormir' brand. The board of HIP enters into discussions with Dormir for it to replace Slumber as manager of the hotels.

1. Acquisition of the hotels

It is anticipated that Dormir will want to manage all nine of the hotels under a single management agreement with HIP.

(a)   **Would this be a business transfer (defined as a transfer within the meaning of TUPE) under UK law?**

   (ONLY TO BE ANSWERED BY UK CONTRIBUTOR)

(b)   **Even though Slumber will not transfer any of its activities to the Netherlands, would the acquisition of the hotels in this way constitute a business transfer under Dutch law?**

   Answer

   Yes.

   Legal reasoning

Section 662 of Book 7 of the Civil Code (Directive 77/187/EEC, art 1(1)) provides that it applies to the transfer of businesses, locations or parts of them to another employer as a result of a transfer pursuant to an agreement or merger.

This is a question of the transfer of business activities, examples of which are the transfer of buildings, plant and machinery, customers, licences, know-how, goodwill, etc.

The purpose of the Directive is to ensure the continuity of the employment relationships which exist in the context of an economic entity, including on a change of owner. The decisive criterion regarding whether there is a transfer within the meaning of the Directive is therefore whether the identity of the entity concerned is retained, which is shown in particular by the fact that its operations are continued or resumed by the new owner. In the *Spijkers* judgment of 1986, the European Court of Justice ruled that a number of factors are relevant in answering the question of whether there is a business transfer. It is a question of the nature of the business or location concerned, whether tangible assets such as buildings and movable property are being transferred, the value of the intangible assets at the time of the transfer, whether the new employer is taking over virtually all the members of staff, or the customers are being transferred, or the activities carried on before and after the transfer correspond with each other, and the length of any interruption in those activities. The *Süzen* judgment introduced the distinction between labour-intensive and non-labour-intensive activities. This means that there is a business transfer within the meaning of the Directive if the acquirer takes over a substantial proportion – in terms of numbers and expertise – of the seller's staff. See *Spijkers v Gebroeders Benedik Abattoir CV*: 24/85 [1986] ECR 1119, points 11 and 12; and *Süzen v Zehnacker*: C-13/95 [1997] ECR I-1259, point 10.

Case C-340/01: *Carlito Abler v Sodexho MM Catering Gesellschaft mbH* [2004] IRLR 168, ECJ concerned a (renewed) outsourcing of activities, and the question whether this constituted a business transfer. At the end of 1990 the Wien-Speising Hospital ('WS') concluded a catering agreement with Sanrest, under which Sanrest took on all catering activities for the hospital by providing meals and drinks for the personnel and patients. The meals had to be prepared in the hospital's work areas. Sanrest's obligations included preparing the menus it had drawn up itself, purchasing the products, transporting the meals to the various departments within the hospital, serving meals in the corporate restaurant, running the hospital cafeteria, clearing away and washing up the dishes, and cleaning the areas used. The hospital made the areas available, as well as the water, energy supply and the necessary kitchen equipment such as ovens and dishwashers. Sanrest was liable for any damage to and/or loss of this kitchen equipment. As a result of a disagreement between the hospital and Sanrest in the summer of 1998, the hospital eventually terminated the catering agreement. In November 1999 the hospital awarded all catering services to Sodexho. Sodexho refused to take over moveable equipment/stock and personnel of Sanrest, nor did it receive the cost calculations, menus, diets, recipes and experience reports from Sanrest. However, Sodexho was working in the same areas that the hospital had made available at the time to Sanrest, and it was using the same kitchen equipment. In a letter dated 15 November 1999, Sanrest terminated the employment contracts with the personnel that it had taken on in the hospital. A number of these employees (Abler et al) instigated a claim in this respect at the Arbeits- und Sozialgericht, to have their employment contract with Sanrest continued by Sodexho under the Austrian Arbeitsvertragrechts- Anpassungsgesetz, based on Council Directive 77/187/EEC concerning the transfer of business establishments.

Ultimately, the European Court of Justice ruled that the transfer of the kitchen and kitchen equipment was crucial. In fact, *Sodexho* mirrors its reasoning in *Liskojärvi v Oy Liikenne Ab*: C-172/99 [2001] IRLR 171: no transfer of essential assets, therefore no business transfer. If essential material assets are indeed transferred, this is enough to indicate that the business has retained its identity. Furthermore, the circumstance that the material assets taken over by the new business were not the property of its predecessor but were made available by the client does not lead to the conclusion that there is no business transfer.

Conclusion

HIP is terminating the existing management agreement with Slumber. The management of its nine fully furnished and equipped hotels is to be awarded to Dormir. Based on the *Sodexho* ruling, it is likely that this constitutes a business transfer within the meaning of the Directive. Furthermore, Dormir is taking over all the employees of the nine hotels, although according to the court in *Sodexho* this is not of crucial significance. In addition, based on ECJ case law, it is not necessary for the applicability of the Directive that there be a direct contractual link between the transferor and the acquirer. The Directive applies whenever, in the context of the contractual relations, a change occurs in the natural or legal person who is responsible for running the business and who enters into obligations vis-à-vis the business's employees.

(c) **Would it make any difference to whether this constituted a business transfer, under TUPE, if Dormir only wanted to manage the six English hotels (excluding the hotels in Glasgow, Edinburgh and Cardiff)?**

(ONLY TO BE ANSWERED BY UK CONTRIBUTOR)

(d) **Would it make any difference to your answer to (b) above if Dormir only wanted to manage six hotels (for example only the**

English hotels, excluding those in Scotland and Wales, ie the hotels in Glasgow, Edinburgh and Cardiff)?

Answer

No.

Legal reasoning

If each of the nine hotels constitutes an individual entity and Dormir decides only to take over the management of six of the nine, this will constitute a business transfer within the meaning of the Directive. Even when the nine hotels together form a single entity, this will constitute a business transfer within the meaning of the Directive, since BW, Book 7, s 662 provides that the Directive also applies to the transfer of parts of businesses. Here too, however, it is still a condition that the parts to be transferred can retain their identity and continue to exist as an independent economic entity. As it must be assumed that the hotels to be taken over will retain their identity and function and each hotel can continue to exist as a separate economic entity, it is very probable that one is dealing here with a business transfer, despite three of the nine hotels being sold off. The requirement that the business should retain its identity is set out in BW, Book 7, s 662(2) (and see: *Spijkers v Gebroeders Benedik Abattoir CV*: 24/85 [1986] ECR 1119, ECJ and C-340/01: *Carlito Abler v Sodexho MM Catering Gesellschaft mbH* [2004] IRLR 168, ECJ).

2. Employees who work only partly in the business

What is the position of those staff who work partly in Slumber and partly in Ezeroom? For example, the human resources director of Slumber is also the human resources director of Ezeroom and he has his employment agreement with Ezeroom. He spends approximately 40 per cent of his time dealing with Slumber's personnel matters and the remainder of his time on the human resources affairs of Ezeroom.

(a) **If this is a TUPE transfer, can he be said to have transferred under TUPE in the UK?**

(UK CONTRIBUTOR TO ANSWER)

(b) **What is the law on employees who work only partly in the undertaking to be transferred in the Netherlands?**

The employee's transfer to the acquirer always requires the employee to have an employment contract by virtue of BW, Book 7, s 610 with the seller whose business is being transferred. Employees in a group, who are employed by the parent company but actually work for one or more subsidiaries, are not transferred when these subsidiaries are transferred. Since the HR Director has an employment contract with Ezeroom, the transfer has no consequences for his position as an employee. After all, his formal employer is not a party to the transfer and therefore remains the same, namely Ezeroom.

If it has to be assumed that the HR Director had an employment contract with Slumber, on the basis of which he works for the nine (or a few) hotels, his employment contract with Slumber will be continued with Dormir on the basis of the Directive. However, this is not the case if the HR Director has an employment contract with Slumber Head Office, since this is not being transferred.

Dutch law does not distinguish between full-time and part-time employees. Employees who are employed part-time by the seller on the basis of an employment contract are transferred to the acquirer just like the full-timers, and of course on the same terms, including the number of working hours as agreed in the employment contract with the seller.

3. Staff who work outside the UK in another EU country

It transpires that some Slumber central management staff are actually working and based in the Netherlands already. Two are Dutch nationals.

(a) **Would these staff transfer to Dormir under TUPE if there was a TUPE transfer?**

Answer

In theory yes, although this would depend on a number of factors, including their contracts of employment.

Legal reasoning

TUPE applies to undertakings or parts of undertakings situated in the UK immediately prior to transfer. These employees work for and are employed by Slumber, the undertaking to be transferred, but they are simply based in the Netherlands. The undertaking of Slumber is situated in the UK immediately before the transfer (even if some staff work outside the UK): therefore members of Slumber central management who are working in the Netherlands will technically transfer. The important point is that TUPE in principle applies to undertakings or a part of an undertaking which is situated in the UK immediately before the transfer. The fact that some of the employees are not actually located in the UK is irrelevant.

*Difficulties may arise in practice. For example, the employees may no longer be required to continue working in the same place and there may be potential breaches of contract. If their employment is terminated, this is likely to be in connection with the transfer, and potentially unfair. Whether or not they have claims in the UK, or indeed in the Netherlands, will depend on conflicts of laws issues (see Chapter **D**).*

(b) **Would the position be different if there was a branch office of Ezeroom in the Netherlands, which directly employed these staff?**

Answer

The position may be the same.

Legal reasoning

TUPE is likely to apply if the branch office qualifies as an associated employer and the employees are 'assigned' (Botzen v Rotterdamsche Droogdok Maatschappij BV: 186/83 [1985] ECR 519, ECJ) to Slumber (ie they carry out all their functions for Slumber, who is their de facto employer). In such a case the courts are likely to pierce the corporate veil and treat Slumber as the employer for those purposes.

Comment: If a Dutch business is wholly owned by a foreign legal entity, which is not residing in the Netherlands, it is considered a branch office. As a branch office is not a legal entity under Dutch law, it cannot employ any staff directly on its own behalf. In such a situation Slumber would be considered the employer of all employees of the Dutch branch office. A transfer of business due to the purchase of Slumber by Dormir would mean that the branch office employees would automatically transfer to the acquirer, ie Dormir (BW, Book 7, s 662).

If Slumber had a subsidiary in the Netherlands incorporated under Dutch law, it would be possible for it to directly employ staff, subject to Dutch employment law. In that case, the subsidiary, a Dutch legal entity, is the employer. In order to transfer staff directly employed by the subsidiary in the Netherlands to Dormir, Dormir should also purchase the subsidiary (asset deal). Then Dormir would be the new employer of the (former) subsidiary's employees. Furthermore, the decisive criterion regarding whether there is a transfer within the meaning of the Directive must be met. The decisive criterion is whether the identity of the entity concerned is retained, which is shown in particular by the fact that its operations are continued or resumed by the new owner.

If Dormir does not purchase the subsidiary, the employees will not transfer to Dormir.

4. Dismissal of employee

One of the Slumber staff, Mr X, was dismissed by Slumber after HIP had given notice to terminate the contract with Slumber and whilst negotiations were ongoing with Dormir. Mr X is owed two months' back pay and unpaid holiday.

Against whom can Mr X bring a claim, and where, if Mr X is a UK national based in the Netherlands?

Answer

Slumber.

Legal reasoning

Mr X was evidently dismissed before the business was transferred.

If Mr X's dismissal was not connected with the intention to transfer the business, only Slumber is liable to Mr X as regards the claim for payment of arrears of wages and holidays not taken. This is because Mr X had an employment contract with Slumber.

The European Court of Justice has decided that, according to the EC Directive relating to the transfer of a business, the acquirer is not liable for claims for holiday pay and the compensation of employees who were no longer employed by the business at the time of the transfer (NJ 1985/901: *Wendelboe*:19/83 [1985] ECR 457, ECJ; and C-209/91: *Rask and Christensen v ISS Kantineservice A/S* [1992] ECR I-5755, ECJ). Under Dutch law it follows from BW, Book 7, s 663 that the acquirer is not liable for liabilities of the transferring party towards employees with whom there was no longer an employment contract at the time of the transfer.

If the dismissal of Mr X was connected with the transfer of business, the dismissal would be null and void under BW, Book 7, s 663. The European Court of Justice ruled that such a dismissal is contrary to the Directive and therefore not permitted (NJ 1990/247: *Bork* 15 June 1988, ECJ). Employees who are dismissed before and because of the transfer are considered to be employed by the acquirer. The seller's liability in that case would be limited to those obligations which exist at the time of the transfer. The former employer is not liable for obligations relating to work done by the employee after the transfer. Also, the liability of the old employer is limited to a period of one year prior to the transfer. With this rule in the last sentence of s 663 of Book 7 of the Civil Code, the Dutch legislator has made use of the option which the EC Directive provides in art 3(1). The employee therefore has a choice as regards amounts owed by his former employer. For a year after the transfer he can claim from his old employer, but he can also choose to claim from the acquirer. Once that year has expired, the employee can still claim against the acquirer, but no longer against the seller. The joint and several liability was included to protect the employee; the one-year period was intended to limit the time for which a claim can be made by the employee against the seller. It is not the intention that the rule should infringe the legal relationship between the acquirer and the seller, and this means that an acquirer who has paid a debt to an employee for which the seller was liable and obliged to contribute before the transfer can claim repayment from the seller, regardless of whether or not the one-year period has expired.

Assuming that Dutch law is applicable and that Mr X was dismissed due to the (intended) business transfer, he will be able to instigate legal proceedings against both Slumber and Dormir. Based on Dutch law, the writ of summons must be submitted to the court in the domicile of the defendant. Assuming that Dormir does not have offices in the UK, this would mean that Mr X could instigate proceedings either in the UK or in the Netherlands, unless of course the employment contract designates a particular court. In that case, the court concerned will be exclusively competent to hear the case and any dispute relating to that agreement.

5. Transfer of employee outside the UK

Mr Y (the marketing director) has been vital to the success of Slumber and has been responsible for many successful ideas. Dormir would like to retain his services and move him to Dormir's headquarters in the Netherlands. Mr Y has no wish to live in the Netherlands.

(a) **How does TUPE impact on Mr Y: is he obliged to transfer against his will?**

(UK ONLY TO ANSWER)

(b) **What is the law on objection to a transfer in the Netherlands?**

Assuming that there is a transfer of a business as referred to in the Directive and that Dutch law applies, the unambiguous refusal of the employee concerned to be transferred results in the termination of the employment by operation of law.

A refusal by the employee to join the acquirer does not mean that the employment contract with the seller continues. The employment contract with the seller ends by operation of law at the time of the transfer (BW, Book 7, s 663). If in connection with the transfer a change occurs in the circumstances to the detriment of the employee, as a result of which it cannot reasonably be expected of the employee that his employment should be continued with the acquirer, this is at the risk of the (new) employer (BW, Book 7, ss 665 and 685). This means that a reasonable severance payment must be made to the employee, at the employer's expense.

(c) **Can Mr Y claim constructive dismissal on the basis that he would be expected to work and be based in the Netherlands and this is nowhere near his home?**

Answer

Possibly – if this amounts to a fundamental breach of his contract, or if being expected to work and be based abroad amounts to a substantial change in working conditions and is to the employee's detriment.

Comment: Under Dutch law it is very likely that Mr Y can claim constructive dismissal. The actual distance involved in the transfer has no effect on whether a business transfer arises.

Furthermore, if the employment contract with the old employer states that the place of work of Mr Y is the UK, a refusal to move to the Netherlands probably would not be a refusal to transfer. In that case Mr Y is considered to have transferred to the new employer under the same employment conditions as he had with Slumber. There is no obligation to accept relocation. Especially not if the distance between home and workplace which is deemed to be unreasonably great can be a reason for the employee to have the employment contract dissolved by the district court. Formally an application of this kind can only be made after the transfer to the new employer. If the contract is ordered to be dissolved for that reason, liability for the dissolution rests with the acquirer. In a case of this kind the district court can award the employee a reasonable severance payment, to be paid by his (new) employer.

6. Dormir's business strategy

What is the best way of structuring the transfer of the hotels to Dormir from the perspective of the Netherlands? Would you advise Dormir to set up a subsidiary company registered in the UK specifically to purchase Slumber and thereby avoid any cross-border element?

Answer

No.

Legal reasoning

If Dormir takes over the management of the hotels and this were to mean the transfer of a business, the only result of this will be that Dormir will be regarded as the employer from the time of transfer. Dormir will be bound by the employment contracts and their terms, as entered into with the original employer. There will be no question of relocating the hotels or changing the services they provide. The employees will also continue to do the same work. The takeover by Dormir will therefore have no practical implications for the running of the hotels.

The situation would be no different if Dormir specifically incorporated an English subsidiary for the purpose of taking over the management of the hotels. In that case too, the subsidiary, as the employer, would be bound by the rules arising from the Directive, and would thus also be bound by the employment contracts and the terms set out in them.

A cross-border element with which Dormir could be faced, without the intervention of an English subsidiary, is that it would have to take legal action in England and under English law in the event of any dispute with employees.

Conclusion

Incorporating a subsidiary under English law will make no significant contribution to preventing cross-border issues, particularly as there are no cross-border issues which are so negative that they need to be avoided. We would not advise Dormir to incorporate a subsidiary in the UK.

P3.2 Case study 2
(Production moves from one EU country to another EU country; physical move)

Alpha Incorporated is a multinational car tyre manufacturing and distribution business based in Europe. Alpha's headquarters are in the UK. Alpha has tyre plants in the UK, the Netherlands and Germany. Each of the tyre plants is a wholly owned and independently operated subsidiary of Alpha. Alpha has a European Works Council.

The subsidiary in the Netherlands is Beta. Beta employs about 250 employees, mostly in the direct production of tyres. The employees are on standard basic contracts which do not contain any mobility clauses. Due to increased competition from cheaper producers in the Far East, Alpha is having to reduce its own production costs. Beta has the highest production costs of all Alpha's European operations. Alpha has decided to end the production of tyres in the Netherlands and move production to Gamma, another subsidiary not far away but across the national border in Germany which has more modern plant and equipment. Beta will continue to exist, but as a sales and marketing organisation only, with about 30 staff.

Most of Beta's tyre-making plant and machinery is transferred to Gamma, but Gamma will only need an extra 125 staff to increase its output to the required level to supply Beta's market. Those employees from Beta who are required to work for Gamma will be expected to accept the terms and conditions and working practices of the Gamma plant, which are very different from those in operation at the Beta plant. For example, Gamma pays its employees considerably lower hourly wages and they work longer hours than those at Beta. Gamma does not want to pay more to the employees transferred to it from Beta than it does to its current employees. In addition, Beta has an occupational pension scheme for its Dutch staff. Gamma operates a different type of pension scheme.

1. Does this transaction constitute a 'business transfer'?

(a) **As Beta's tyre-making plant and machinery have transferred to Gamma, will this constitute a business transfer under the Acquired Rights Directive implementing legislation of the Netherlands ('business transfer')?**

Answer

Yes.

Legal reasoning

Article 1(1) of Directive 77/187/EC provides that it applies to the transfer of enterprises, branches or parts thereof to another undertaking as a result of a transfer further to an agreement or merger.

The purpose of the Directive is to ensure the continuity of the employment relationships which exist in the framework of an economic entity, including on a change of ownership. The decisive criterion regarding whether there is a transfer within the meaning of the Directive is therefore whether the identity of the entity concerned is retained, shown in particular by the fact that its operations are continued or resumed. See in this context the judgments of the European Court of Justice in *Spijkers v Gebroeders Benedik Abattoir CV*: 24/85 [1986] ECR 1119, points 11 and 12; and *Süzen v Zehnacker*: C-13/95 [1997] ECR I-1259, point 10.

The Directive can only be applied, however, if the transfer relates to an economic entity organised on a long-term basis whose activities are not confined to carrying out a specific job. The concept of an entity therefore refers to an organised body of persons and assets by means of which an economic activity with its own objectives can be carried on. This requirement seems to be fulfilled in the specific case (Case C-340/01: *Carlito Abler v Sodexho MM Catering Gesellschaft mbH* [2004] IRLR 168, ECJ)).

To determine whether the conditions for the transfer of an economic entity organised on a long-term basis have been fulfilled, all the actual circumstances characterising the transaction concerned, such as the nature of the enterprise or branch concerned, whether tangible assets such as buildings and movable property are being transferred, the value of the intangible assets at the time of the transfer, whether the new employer is taking over virtually all the employees, whether the customers are being transferred, the extent to which the activities carried out before and after the transfer correspond, and the duration of any interruption in those activities must be taken into account. All these factors, however, are only constituent aspects of the overall investigation to be carried out and must not therefore be assessed separately: *Spijkers* judgment, point 13; and *Süzen* judgment, point 14.

Conclusion

Based on the above, and depending greatly on the circumstances, it is likely that under Dutch law this case will involve a business transfer as referred to in BW, Book 7, s 662.

(b) **Does it make any difference to whether this is a business transfer if employees of Beta transfer across to Gamma?**

Answer

No.

Legal reasoning

Assuming that the choice of whether or not to transfer lies with the Beta employees themselves, the answer to this question would have to be in the negative. Whether or not all or some of the employees transfer is one of the many actual constituent aspects on the basis of which one can determine whether one is dealing with the transfer of an economic entity organised on a long-term basis. This specific aspect will not in itself be decisive regarding whether or not a business transfer is involved, as it may be that a large proportion or all of the Beta employees refuse to transfer, as they would be expected to relocate to another country. Despite their refusal to transfer, if the conditions set out by the Directive and BW, Book 7, s 662 are fulfilled, there may nevertheless be a business transfer. See the judgments of the ECJ in *Spijkers v Gebroeders Benedik Abattoir CV*: 24/85 [1986] ECR 1119, point 13; and *Süzen v Zehnacker*: C-13/95 [1997] ECR I-1259, point 14.

(c) **Can the transfer of plant and machinery coupled with the transfer of half the employees (125) constitute a business transfer under Dutch legislation if the other 125 employees are dismissed prior to the transfer?**

Answer

Yes.

Legal reasoning

The transfer of plant and machinery coupled with the transfer of half the employees can nevertheless constitute a business transfer. Dismissals in the period prior to the business transfer do not detract from the fact that if the transfer criteria within the meaning of the Directive are fulfilled there will be a business transfer as referred to in BW, Book 7, s 662. Here, too, it boils down to whether there is a transfer of an economic entity organised on a long-term basis whose activities are not confined to carrying out a specific job. The concept of an entity thus refers to an organised body of people and assets by means of which an economic activity with its own objectives can be carried on (*Süzen v Zehnacker*: C-13/95 [1997] ECR I-1259).

To determine whether the conditions for the transfer of an economic entity organised on a long-term basis have been fulfilled, account must be taken of all the actual circumstances characterising the transaction concerned, such as the nature of the business or location concerned, whether tangible assets such as buildings and movable property are being transferred, the value of the intangible assets at the time of the transfer, whether the new employer is taking over virtually all the members of staff, whether the customers are being transferred, the extent to which the activities carried on before and after the transfer correspond with each other, and the length of any interruption in those activities (C-340/01: *Carlito Abler v Sodexho MM Catering Gesellschaft mbH* [2004] IRLR 168, ECJ).

Conclusion

The dismissal of 125 employees before the business is transferred means that all the remaining 125 employees are now transferred to the acquirer. Combined with the transfer of the plant and machinery, in principle this will be assumed to constitute a business transfer. The employees are then deemed to have joined Gamma, retaining their terms and conditions of employment.

In the context of this question, even if none of the remaining 125 employees wish to transfer, one is still dealing with a business transfer since, as already stated, it is irrelevant how many or what proportion of the employees transfers. It is, of course, assumed that the criteria specified in the European Court of Justice cases concerning *Spijkers*, *Süzen* and *Sodexho* have been fulfilled.

(d) **Does the fact that the business will transfer to a different country make any difference to whether this is a business transfer?**

Answer

No.

Legal reasoning

From a formal point of view the Directive is applicable as soon as the business to be transferred has been established in an EU member state immediately prior to the transfer. Article 3(1) of the Directive (implemented under BW, Book 7, s 663) provides that, as a result of the transfer, the rights and obligations arising for the seller under the employment contract or employment relationship existing at the time of the transfer pass to the acquirer. Country borders are irrelevant in this context. According to the preamble to the Directive, its purpose is not only to protect employees from the consequences of the transfer of the enterprise, but also to facilitate the establishment of enterprises in other countries. In this context it is in principle therefore not surprising that a cross-border transfer does not stand in the way of the Directive's applicability.

(e) **Is Dutch business transfer law concerned with the actual distance moved (irrespective of whether this means a change of country)?**

Answer

No.

Legal reasoning

The actual distance involved in the transfer has no effect on whether a business transfer arises, though a distance between home and workplace which is deemed to be unreasonably great can be a reason for the employee to have the employment contract dissolved by the district court. An application of this kind can only be made after the transfer to the new employer. If the contract is ordered to be dissolved for that reason, the reason is imputed to the employer. In a case of this kind the district court can award the employee a reasonable severance payment, to be paid by his (new) employer.

2. Relocation, but no business transfer

(a) **Assuming the move does NOT constitute a business transfer (because the business of Beta does not adequately retain its identity) but instead is deemed to be a straightforward relocation, are any of Beta's employees obliged or entitled to transfer?**

Answer

No.

Legal reasoning

If it is to be assumed that, in the context of its relocation to Gamma, Beta will terminate its business *or a part thereof* in the Netherlands, the consequence of this is that all the employees *or those employees working in the part of the business that is terminated* must be dismissed. As there are 250 employees, this constitutes collective redundancy, which will proceed according to the general rules of Dutch law on the termination of employment via the Centre for Work and Income or the district court. As at that time the employees cannot derive any rights from the provisions regarding business transfers and therefore do not enjoy the protection provided by the Directive, there can be no question of their employment continuing. Beta's employees cannot be obliged to join Gamma, nor can they insist that they be taken on by Gamma. Of course, Gamma is at liberty to offer contracts to the employees or some of them; this will constitute new employment with a new employer.

Conclusion

If Beta ends its business in the Netherlands and the criteria for a business transfer as stated in *Spijkers v Gebroeders Benedik Abattoir CV*: 24/85 [1986] ECR 1119 and later in *Carlito Abler v Sodexho MM Catering Gesellschaft mbH*: C-340/01 [2004] IRLR 168, ECJ) are not met, the employees concerned will be neither obliged nor entitled to join Gamma.

(b) **If employees do nevertheless relocate, what will happen to their employment contracts? Will these continue, or will Gamma be entitled to provide new contracts?**

Answer

Gamma is entitled to provide new contracts.

Legal reasoning

If it is to be assumed that there are employees who join Gamma, because Beta has terminated its business and there is no business transfer, then under Dutch law on the termination of employment the Dutch employment contract with Beta must be terminated. Gamma must then offer Beta's former employees new employment contracts. This can be done according to the law of the country where the work will be done after the termination, but Gamma can of course agree a different choice of law with the individual employees.

If these employees join Gamma on the grounds of a business transfer, then in principle Gamma will have to employ them on the basis of their existing employment contract. Gamma is at liberty, however, to offer a new contract to the employees who have been taken over. It is then up to the employees to decide whether or not to accept the new contract; Gamma cannot oblige them to do so.

(c)   **What will be the law applicable to the contracts of the employees who relocate?**

The applicable law is international private law. It is a matter here of a transfer of rights and obligations to the employee. Conflict rules regarding contracts can be found in the European Convention on the Law Applicable to Contractual Obligations. The formal scope of application of this Convention is universal and it applies to commitments under a contract where a choice has to be made from the laws of different countries. In this case one is dealing with a transfer of rights and obligations arising from an employment contract. According to the Convention, the contract is governed by the law which the parties have chosen (art 3(1)) or, if no choice of law has been made, by the law of the country with which it is most closely connected (art 4(1)). For an employment contract art 6 of the Convention gives a special conflict rule which differs from these main rules: the law of the country where the employee normally carries out his work in performance of the contract applies, unless the whole body of circumstances shows that the employment contract is more closely connected with a different country.

Conclusion

We are assuming here a situation in which Beta has ceased its business in the Netherlands, and Gamma offers new employment contracts to the (former) employees of Beta who were made redundant in the Netherlands according to the regular law on the termination of employment, and who want to join Gamma. In that situation Gamma will probably opt for its national legislation, but a choice by both parties of any other legal system is of course also possible. If no express choice of law is made, then by reference to actual circumstances a link will be sought with the law most closely connected with the employment relationship. In particular cases, this will most probably be that of the country where the work is actually carried out.

If the employees transfer in the context of a business transfer as referred to in the Directive, in principle the law agreed in the employment contract will apply. If no choice of law has been made, then (again) based on the actual circumstances the law of the country to which Beta has relocated will probably be declared to apply.

3. Dismissals

(a) Assuming the move does constitute a business transfer:

(i) are any dismissals in connection with the transfer lawful?

Article 4(1) of the Directive provides that the transfer of the business, branch or part of the business or branch is not in itself reason for either the *seller* or the *acquirer* to dismiss employees. The provision is not, however, an obstacle to redundancies for economic, technical or organisational reasons which involve changes in the number of jobs.

Dismissals before or after the transfer, with due observance of the applicable rules, which are connected with or prompted by the business transfer only, will be null and void on the grounds contained in BW, Book 7, s 663. In its judgment in NJ 1990/247: *Bork* 15 June 1988, ECJ, the European Court of Justice ruled that such dismissals are contrary to the Directive and that employees dismissed before the transfer are deemed to be employed by the business at the time it is transferred.

(ii) what are the rights and remedies (including applicable law and appropriate jurisdiction) of any employees dismissed before and after the transfer?

Assuming that the Beta employees who were dismissed before the transfer have Dutch employment contracts which are subject to Dutch law, they will be able to turn to the Dutch district court. To invoke nullity of the dismissal, the employees are not bound by the normal six-month period specified in art 9 of the Extraordinary Labour Relations Decree ('BBA') (Supreme Court, 29 December 1995, JAR 1996/29: *Buyck/Van den Ameele*). Nullity by virtue of BW, Book 7, s 663 prevails over the ground for nullity by virtue of BBA, art 9. In a case of that kind the employees can bring an action to recover back wages, claiming continued payment of wages in full until the time the employment contract has been legally terminated, or claim re-employment with payment of wages for the months when the employer did not enable them to carry out their duties. The competent court is the court where the employee normally carried out his duties or the domicile of the defendant (ie the new employer), at the employee's discretion.

If no clear choice of law has been made, the applicable law will be decided by reference to the EVO and the EEX (Convention on the Jurisdiction and Enforcement of Judgments in Civil and Commercial Matters).

(b) Would these rights and remedies change if this was not a business transfer?

Answer

No.

Legal reasoning

If there is no business transfer, the extraordinary circumstance as given in BW, Book 7, s 663 lapses, since at that moment the redundancy protection in the context of a business transfer does not apply. One must therefore fall back on the general law on the termination of employment. Given the facts in this case, the redundancy will most probably have to be based on commercial grounds. The redundancy can be effected via the CWI or the district court. If the employer does not follow the applicable procedures in full, there is a danger that the notice of dismissal will be declared null and void. If there is a voidable dismissal, in the first place a period of six months will apply under BBA, art 9 within which the employees must claim annulment of the dismissal. It is possible now also to claim re-employment and bring an action to recover back wages. These options are not just connected with the voiding of an employee's dismissal in the context of the transfer of a business, but apply generally.

4. European Works Council and other employees' representatives

(a) Will Alpha be required to inform and consult the European Works Council about the transfer or any redundancies?

The powers of the European Works Council are limited to the provision of information and consultation on the matters which are relevant to the whole business and have a community dimension; or the whole group and have a community dimension; or businesses in different member states. The minimum requirement is that at least two of the group's branches or businesses in different member states should be involved (European Works Councils Act, s 19(1)). The answer is then that the European Works Council must indeed be concerned with the transfer, since it concerns two of Alpha's locations in different countries.

The European Works Council must be informed and consulted about a wide range of topics, including for example: substantial changes in the organisation; the transfer, reorganisation or closure of businesses, branches or significant parts of them; and the situation and trends regarding jobs and collective redundancy (European Works Councils

Act, s 19(2)). These topics, which refer to the ending of production activities in the Netherlands and the transfer of the employees from Beta to Gamma, fall within the framework of the European Works Council. The European Works Council must therefore be informed and consulted about the transfer and about the dismissal of one or more employees due to the transfer.

(b) **Are any other employee representatives required to be involved in the transfer or any redundancies (ie at national or local level)?**

A Dutch employer who intends to terminate the jobs of at least 20 employees working in a working area at one or more locations at times within a three-month period must report this in writing to the interested employees' associations so that timely consultation can take place (Collective Redundancy (Notification) Act, s 3). 'Associations of employees' means trade unions, which must be consulted on the need for and extent of the collective redundancy. The term 'consultation' is misleading; the intention is that agreement should be reached on the number of redundancies and the redundancy terms. Consultation focuses specifically on the collective redundancy and on the need to effect it. Joint efforts must be made to take steps which reduce the consequences of the redundancies as far as possible. The trade unions are not asked for their opinion on the policy decision to shift production to another country and all the decisions connected with that.

5. Collective agreements

What is the effect of the business transfer on any collective agreements affecting Beta's employees?

In principle, employees' rights and obligations arising from a collective agreement are also transferred to the acquirer. If the employment conditions have (also) been recorded in a collective agreement which has been declared to apply, whether or not it is mandatory, then the terms and conditions of employment of the collective agreement will also be transferred by operation of law. This means that the seller's collective agreement which applies at the time of the takeover continues to apply to employees who have been transferred to the acquirer. The collective agreement applies until it expires, or the acquirer is bound by a new agreement (which has been declared to be mandatory). Only then is it possible for another collective agreement, which applies to the acquirer, to apply also to the employees who have transferred. Pensions are an exception to this, however: see question **6(c)**. All this is set out in detail at **P1**.

6. Change of terms and conditions

(a) **If this is a business transfer, how can Gamma lawfully harmonise employment contracts and change the terms and conditions of the employees currently on the more generous Beta contracts of employment?**

Gamma is located outside the Netherlands. In principle, therefore, this question can only be answered on the basis of the law applying to Gamma. Supposing that Gamma were subject to Dutch law, in principle it would not be entitled to make changes to the employment conditions.

See in this context the judgment of the European Court of Justice in 324/86: *Foreningen af Arbejdsledere i Danmark v Daddy's Dance Hall A/S* [1988] ECR 739, ECJ, in which it was decided that employees could not waive the rights conferred on them by the Directive, not even with their consent. It does not matter that, broadly speaking, an employee is on aggregate better off following a business transfer compared to beforehand.

Another consideration was that the employee can agree different employment conditions with the transferee after the transfer. The European Court of Justice adds that the transfer of the undertaking of itself could constitute a ground for such change. The European Court of Justice also confirmed this view in C-209/91: *Rask and Christensen v ISS Kantineservice A/S* [1992] ECR I-5755, ECJ.

The most obvious way to effect a harmonisation of employment conditions is the method by which the employees involved in the transfer consent to adjustments to the employment conditions with the transferee. Employees will usually be offered a total package of changes, and that total package will then be compared to the former package of employment conditions. If the balance of the difference between those two packages is acceptable to the employees, the adjustment of the employment conditions will be simple to carry out.

In doing so, compensation schemes will have to be used, which could involve a type of phasing out of existing employment conditions over a certain period, a scheme that neutralises the advantages and disadvantages as far as possible, or a scheme by which salaries are frozen, etc.

If the changes to employment conditions cannot be effected with the consent of the employees, there is then the possibility to bring about unilateral changes to employment conditions, imposed by the employer. These unilateral changes could be based on BW, Book 7, s 611, in which standards for being a good employer and employee are described, and which section is a clear development of the reasonableness and fairness requirement appropriate for the performance of contracts.

A second possibility could be a so-called unilateral changes clause pursuant to BW, Book 7, s 613.

A link can also be sought with BW, Book 6, s 258, which offers the possibility when employment conditions are changed to request the court to change a contract. If such a request is made, the unforeseen circumstances must be of such a nature that, according to the criteria of reasonableness and fairness, the employee cannot be required to continue the contract unchanged.

(b) **If this is a business transfer, can Gamma reduce the wages of the former Beta employees?**

Answer

In principle, no.

Legal reasoning

Under Dutch law a change in salary to the employees' detriment would not be allowed. A change in salary might be possible in certain circumstances with due observance of what is stated under **6(a)** above. Conditions can be laid down, however: eg a reasonable period in which this change can take place, compensation via other employee benefits which apply, and so on. This is known as the pluses and minuses principle.

In C-209/91: *Rask and Christensen v ISS Kantineservice A/S* [1992] ECR I-5755, ECJ, it was ruled that if national law does not stand in the way of a negative change in the employment conditions, particularly as regards pay, such a change is not forbidden merely because the business has now been transferred and the contract has been entered into with the new employer. Such a change may not be made at the time of the transfer, nor may the transfer be the reason for it.

(c) **If this is a business transfer, what will happen to the former Beta employees as regards their private pension arrangements?**

Here, too, an answer must be given on the basis of the law applying to Gamma.

Since 1 July 2002, the pension scheme has also become important for the adjustment of Dutch legislation to the European Directive. These matters are regulated in BW, Book 7, s 664.

Together with the introduction of this statutory provision, the Pensions and Savings Funds Act (*Pensioen- en Spaarfondsenwet*) was amended, which has resulted in an increase in pension commitments. If the transferring employer has not made any pension commitments to its employees who are involved in the transfer, the transferee is expected to make the same pension commitments to the employees involved in the transfer as it has already made to its other employees. Therefore, the Act introduces a presumption that pension commitments have been made.

This statutory presumption is based on equal treatment of employees in equal situations, and is therefore different from the retention of employment conditions on the transfer of an undertaking. Employment conditions other than pension commitments do, after all, remain unchanged and are only adjusted in the context of harmonisation, whether or not on the basis of a collective agreement. In this case, with respect to pensions, there is a statutory presumption which can result in an increase in employment conditions.

There are several exceptions to the main rule in BW, Book 7, s 664 that pensions are to be retained on the transfer of an undertaking. The first exception makes it possible for the transferee to choose, when the undertaking is transferred, to make the same pension commitments to employees taken over as it had previously made to its own employees. Therefore, in that situation, the pension circumstances for the employees involved in the transfer may change.

If the transferee-employer has different pension schemes for different groups of employees, it may also introduce this differentiation in the choice it makes when the company is transferred. Therefore, if the transferee has one or more pension schemes, it can in all reasonableness carry through such differentiation in the choice it makes of how to deal with this in relation to the new employees involved in the transfer.

Great differences are possible in situations where the transferor has, and the transferee has not, made pension commitments or vice versa. It may also happen that the transferor has a sectoral pension fund (ie a fund with members in one specific branch only) and the transferee does not, or vice versa.

It is evident that Dutch pension practice has many different schemes, which could lead to different consequences for the employees involved in the transfer of an undertaking.

Summary

The main rule is BW, Book 7, s 663: the employee's rights and duties are transferred by operation of law at the time of transfer.

Under BW, Book 7, s 664 this basic rule also applies from 1 July 2002 to the pension rights guaranteed in the Pension and Savings Funds Act, broadly speaking as follows:

1 if the seller of the business has no pension scheme but the acquirer does, the acquirer's pension scheme applies from the transfer;

2 if the seller of the business has a pension scheme but the acquirer does not, the seller's pension scheme continues to apply from the time of transfer;

3 if the seller of the business has a pension scheme and so does the acquirer, the seller's or acquirer's pension scheme applies, at the acquirer's option, from the time of transfer.

What happens to the pension rights of the Beta employees who have transferred thus depends on the actual circumstances.

(d) **Is it easier to change terms and conditions of employment if the changes are made six months after the transfer?**

Answer

In all likelihood, yes.

Legal reasoning

Dutch law has not made use of the option provided in the Directive to reduce the period for which the employment terms must be maintained. The Directive also states that if use is made of this option, the period must not be less than one year. This was confirmed in the judgment in C-209/91: *Rask and Christensen v ISS Kantineservice A/S* [1992] ECR I-5755, ECJ.

The passage of time during which it turns out that there is inequality in employment conditions for different groups of employees in the same business can nevertheless hasten harmonisation, as what reasons could continue to apply year after year which would justify this (legal) inequality? It must be possible to achieve harmonisation by applying standards of reasonableness and fairness (the pluses and minuses principle).

Where groups of employees are involved, existing consultation structures with a works council and/or trade unions will play a role.

If the intended harmonisation concerns an individual employee or a very small group of employees, the changes must be made subject to the test of BW, Book 7, s 611 (good employment practice and being a good employee), s 613 (unilateral changes clause), or s 258 (unforeseen circumstances).

P3.3 Case study 3
(Outsourcing of an ancillary activity to a non-EU country)

A large multinational (ABC) based in the Netherlands has decided to outsource its entire internal IT function to a third party provider in Romania, as the costs of hiring competent IT personnel in Romania are far lower than in the Netherlands, largely because wages are so much lower. At present 200 employees are employed by ABC in its IT function in the Netherlands. It is anticipated that exactly the same IT function will be required in Romania with approximately the same number of people required to run it. There will be no difference in the service or approach for those requiring IT assistance and even the internal telephone number will be automatically diverted. The Romanian third party provider has no assets or presence in the Netherlands.

1. Business transfer

Will this be a business transfer within the scope of Dutch law applying ARD?

Answer

Yes.

Legal reasoning

In this case, part of the business is being hived off, ie outsourced. As far as the present case shows, this part will retain its identity. As ABC is bound by the Directive, the rules in the context of the transfer of a business will also now apply, as the Directive applies to the transfer of enterprises, branches or parts of enterprises or branches to another undertaking as a result of a transfer further to an agreement or merger, where the branch to be transferred or the part of the enterprise to be transferred is in an EC member state at the time of the transfer.

Conclusion

Formally, the Directive applies if the business being transferred is established in an EC member state. Although Romania is not a member of the EC, the Directive applies. In practice, however, it is unlikely that the Directive will be implemented in full, as an acquirer who is not an EC member will be able to reject the applicability of the Directive. This encourages closure, with the dismissal of the employees at the Dutch branch concerned, and transfer will then take place. In cases such as these, practice proves stronger than formal doctrine.

2. Effect on employees

(a) **What will happen to the employees currently employed in the IT function at ABC? Will they transfer across?**

Answer

Yes.

Legal reasoning

In a formal sense the employees are automatically transferred to the acquirer. The intention of the Directive, and hence of BW, Book 7, s 663, is that in principle the employees should by operation of law become employed by the acquirer, retaining the terms of their employment, unless they expressly and unambiguously state that they are not prepared to become employed by the acquirer, in which case the employment contract is terminated by operation of law.

It can happen, however, that the transfer of employees comes up against practical objections, and that the individual employee can therefore not be expected to relocate to Romania. In that case the employer (seller) must seek a solution with the employee. This will often probably proceed to formal dissolution via the district court, the employee being awarded a severance payment.

(b) **If the employees do transfer, what will the applicable law be for their employment contracts with the third party provider? Where can they make any claims?**

Here, too, one must look at whether a specific choice of law has been agreed. If not, it will be necessary to assess, on the basis of international private law, which law applies. The close connection requirement plays a large role here.

Under BW, Book 7, s 663, the seller's liability is limited to those obligations which exist at the time of the transfer. The old employer is not liable for obligations relating to the work which the employee does after the transfer. The old employer's liability is also limited to a period of one year. The employee therefore has a choice regarding sums owed by his old employer. For a year after the transfer he can claim them from his old employer, but he can also choose to claim them from the acquirer. Once that year has expired, he can still claim against the acquirer, but no longer against the seller. An acquirer who has paid a debt to an employee, for which the seller was liable and obliged to contribute before the transfer, can make a claim for repayment against the seller, regardless of whether or not the one-year period has expired.

3. Data protection

Will there be special data protection issues on the transfer of knowledge and information outside the Netherlands to Romania?

Personal data are processed according to law and in a proper and careful manner (Personal Data Protection Act, s 6). Personal data are collected for specific, expressly described and justifiable purposes (s 7). The personal data may only be processed if the person concerned has given his unambiguous consent, or the data are required to implement an agreement to which the person concerned is a party, or are needed to comply with a statutory obligation to which the responsible person is subject (s 8). The data on the employee may be processed by the employer by reason of the fact that there is an agreement between the parties. The processing of the data may be a necessary consequence of the agreement; this is so in the case of an employment contract, too.

The transfer of a business is a legal fact which permits the transfer of personal data. By entering into an employment contract the employee accepts that his employer will hold his personal data. As a logical consequence of this, any new employer who acquires the undertaking pursuant to the Directive will also be given the employee's implicit consent to hold data.

It is irrelevant to whether a transfer of personal data is permitted whether the acquirer is a Dutch business or a foreign one. Personal data may also not be processed in a way which is irreconcilable with that for which it was obtained.

Hence, personal data can only be processed for the purpose for which the personal data was obtained; this applies equally to the acquirer.

4. Transfer to India

Please comment on any differences there would be to your answers if the function was transferred to India rather than Romania.

Answer

There do not appear to be significant differences.

Legal reasoning

Formally the Directive continues to apply, since ABC is established in the Netherlands, which is an EC state. In theory, therefore, this would involve the transfer of an enterprise, with the employees automatically being transferred to the new employer in India.

India is not subject to EC law, so it is unlikely that the acquirer will consent to take over all the employees and retain their agreed terms and conditions of employment. Nor is it inconceivable that employees will not want to relocate to India. In practice, this will mean that individual arrangements will have to be agreed with the employees concerned. The most obvious result is that the employment contract is terminated by being formally dissolved, with the award of a severance payment. In this way an employee keeps his entitlements to any Unemployment Insurance Act benefit.

It is not wholly clear, however, how cases of this kind will be resolved in practice. Another possibility, which is also completely theoretical, is to assume that the enterprise is being terminated. For the ABC employees this would mean that they will be made redundant on the basis of Dutch law. As 200 employees are involved, this will be a collective redundancy, for which there are specific redundancy rules, discussed above.

Conclusion

In a formal sense a transfer of the enterprise to India will not change the answers.

Q Spain

Francisco Fernández

Q1 Business transfers

Q1.1 Background

Directive 98/50/EC, which modified Directive 77/187/EEC on the approximation of the laws of the member states relating to the safeguarding of employees' rights in the event of transfers of undertakings, businesses or parts of businesses, has been implemented into Spanish legislation by Law 12/2001 of 9 July, on urgent measures to reform the work market in order to increase employment and improve its quality. Although Directive 2001/23/EC has not yet been implemented in Spain, its principles have to be taken into consideration.

A transfer of business is regulated by art 44 of the Spanish Employment Law (*Estatuto de los Trabajadores*) ('SEL'), which includes the modifications provided by the above-mentioned Law 12/2001 of 9 July.

The principles regarding a transfer of business established in the Directives are governed in Spanish law by means of SEL, art 44. After the legal reform carried out in 2001, the law on transfers was not modified substantially. However, precise solutions to controversial unresolved matters have been introduced in this article, and new sections have been introduced to cover procedural issues and information.

Therefore, even though art 44 has been amended, the regulations that had been in force regarding transfers have not been altered substantially. There is now clarification on several points, even the literal transcription of many parts of the Directive. Therefore, most case law that had arisen from the prior regulation may still be considered valid and applicable.

Directive 2001/23/EC establishes that it shall apply to public and private undertakings engaged in economic activities, whether or not they are operating for gain. According to the Directive, an administrative reorganisation of public administrative authorities, or the transfer of administrative functions between public administrative authorities, is not a transfer within the meaning of the Directive.

On the other hand, SEL, art 44 does not specify what types of undertakings are included in its scope of application. However, SEL, art 1.3(a) excludes government employees and civil servants from its application. The Public Function Statute governs these personnel. Additionally, SEL does not govern the relationship between the state, autonomous communities, or local administrative authorities and their personnel, not considered strictly civil servants, that render services to them. In such cases, administrative law or statutory rulings will apply to such relationships, ie statutory personnel (*personal estatutario*). Nonetheless, despite the fact that these relationships have an administrative nature, conflicts are usually referred to social jurisdiction.

Notwithstanding the above, civil service departments or public administrative authorities may enter, as employers, into employment contracts governed by the SEL in specific cases as provided by law.

According to SEL, art 44, a transfer of business exists when the transfer involves an economic entity, which maintains its identity as a group of means, organised to carry out an economic activity. Any change in the ownership of a company, work centre or autonomous production unit does not, on its own, terminate the employment relationship. The new employer is subrogated to the old employer in respect of employment and social security rights and obligations, including pension commitments.

As mentioned above, the transfer does not of itself terminate employment contracts and, consequently, any termination of an employment contract must be based on the general reasons provided by SEL.

Sale by order of the court (*venta judicial*) of all or part of the company must be considered, from the legal point of view, as a transfer of a business when the sale includes all the necessary elements and assets to be able to continue the ordinary course of the company's business. In the event that a new employer decides not to continue or suspends the activity of the previous employer, he must follow the procedure established for redundancies (SEL, art 51.11).

Under Spanish law, certain groups of employees fall within the ambit of a special regulation, due to the specific characteristics of their employment relationship. That is the case of senior executives (*altos directivos*). Royal Decree 1382/1985 of 1 August regulates the special employment relationship of senior executives.

This special employment relationship is characterised by the reciprocal duty of trust and confidence that exists between the senior executive and the company due to the duties that are inherent to his/her position. Senior executives have powers inherent to the ownership of the company: they are included in the framework of fundamental and strategic decisions; their powers are linked to the general targets of the business entity and are applied to the whole company or to functional areas of utmost importance for the company. Furthermore, senior executives carry out their powers with total autonomy, responsibility and independence, only limited by the guidelines of the company's government and management bodies.

Article 10.3 of the Royal Decree provides that in the event of a transfer of a business, or an important change in the ownership of the company that implies a change in the management bodies or in the nature of the company's principal activity, senior executives may terminate their employment contracts. In such a case, they will receive the severance payment agreed in the employment contract or, if there is no such agreement, seven days' of salary per year of service, with a limit of six months, provided that the termination takes place within three months after the changes.

However, art 44, which regulates the ordinary employment relationship, does not allow ordinary employees to terminate their employment contract receiving severance payment in the event of a transfer of a business that complies with the legal requirements.

Furthermore, most case law has stated that subrogation by virtue of SEL, art 44 is not applicable in the case of senior executives, unless it is agreed in the contract, since the Royal Decree does not refer to art 44.

Spanish case law has also established that agreements for severance payments ('golden parachute clauses') between the employer and senior executives are obligatory for the old employer, but it is possible that, taking into consideration the specific characteristics of each agreement, they cannot be imposed on the new employer after the transfer of the business.

Q1.2 Identifying a relevant transfer

In order to determine whether the transfer of business regulations apply, the requirements set out in SEL, art 44 and Spanish case law must be met. As mentioned above, art 44 refers to the transfer of a business as affecting an economic entity that maintains its identity as a group of means organised in order to carry out an economic activity.

The lack of legislative precision has been substituted by a vast body of case law that attempts to determine and identify the concept of 'business' referred to in SEL, art 44 in order to identify the cases where the transfer of business regulations must be applied.

Subrogation by virtue of SEL, art 44 requires the transfer of all essential assets of the undertaking, business (or parts of the undertaking or business that may qualify as an autonomous production unit) and the continuity of the operation of the business or undertaking by the transferee. The transferee will take on the liabilities and obligations of the transferor in respect of the employees.

Three types of transfer of business are permitted. Subrogation takes place not only when transferring an entire company, but also when a single work centre or even an independent production unit is transferred. It includes all business possibilities, which involve the continuation of the activity by the new employer, provided that the transferred activity forms a productive and economic unit with sufficient autonomy to carry out services and activities and that the performance of the services is continued from the time the transfer becomes effective.

Legal subrogation does not apply when there is a mere transfer of the business premises and not the business itself, nor when the transferred material assets are not connected with the activity. Furthermore, case law has established that SEL, art 44 does not apply in the event of a mere transfer of shares, or when the transfer relates to the activity itself without any assets to support it.

Jurisdictional issues

Spanish case law requires, in particular, two elements to constitute a transfer of a business. In the first place, there must be a transfer of the effective ownership of an undertaking, business or part of an undertaking or business. This means that the new employer obtains the effective ownership and assumes all the acquired rights of the employees, including pension commitments. Secondly, case law requires the transfer of tangible assets, such as buildings and movable property that are necessary to carry out the activity.

European case law differs from Spanish case law since it has introduced, in some cases, a flexible meaning to the transfer of a business. The European Court of Justice introduced in some decisions a new definition of 'business' that allows the identification of the business, at least in certain production sectors (in which the activity rests basically in the employees' labour without requiring any specific material elements), with the group of employees that carry out the activity. Indeed, in some court decisions the ECJ found the existence of a transfer of a business when the employees were transferred but no material assets were transferred. This point of view contrasts radically with the general interpretations of 'business' and 'transfer' as understood by the Spanish Supreme Court.

The Spanish Supreme Court considers that the application of the transfer of business regulations depends on the effective transfer of tangible assets (ie machinery, technical equipment, etc), while the ECJ maintains a more flexible and broad interpretation, taking into consideration different elements and circumstances.

The Spanish Supreme Court considers the economic entity to be the business as an entire organisational structure, including personal and material elements.

Even though the Spanish Supreme Court has not adopted the European interpretation, some of the Spanish lower courts, such as the High Court of Justice of Castilla-La Mancha, in a judgment of 30 January 1999 (AS 1999, 162), have followed the European view on a transfer of a business, constituting a departure from previous Spanish rulings on this matter.

In the above-mentioned judgment, the court held that the activity of the employees was not based on any operational and technical resources and assets and, consequently, the transfer of the employees alone justified the application of SEL, art 44 regarding the transfer of a business. In this case, the activity of the employees consisted in giving support to physically and mentally handicapped people at their homes. The infrastructure behind the activity was not the deciding factor in determining whether there was a transfer of a business. The court found that the business transfer itself took place by the transfer of the employees, and no transfer of assets was required in this case.

Nonetheless, there are plenty of examples where Spanish case law has been reluctant to accept the transfer of a business where there is solely a transfer of staff. The Supreme Court held in a judgment of 29 February 2000 that there is no effective transfer of a business when there is no effective change in the business ownership and no transfer of tangible assets in order to continue the activity. The facts of this judgment were as follows: the company, I. LAE, was in charge of the ground control for passengers and airplanes. The Spanish Airports and Aerial Navigation public body ('AENA') invited tenders to pass that work to a second concessionaire. Notwithstanding this, I. LAE would also still carry out the service. Many employees from I. LAE were transferred to the new company that would assume the ground control. The employees had not given their consent to be assigned to a new employer. The Supreme Court held that in this case there had not been a transfer of a business and that another company had started to provide services that previously had been provided by I. LAE as a monopoly. The court based its decision on the fact that I. LAE had not transferred its infrastructure and necessary assets to the new company in order to permit it to continue with the service.

Case law has provided that in the event of administrative concessions for public services, the transfer of business regulations shall apply when the business that operates with the original concessionaire is accompanied by the transfer of the material infrastructure that is necessary to continue with the business as an autonomous production unit.

Q1.3 Employees and affected employees

Under Spanish law, employees are defined in SEL, art 1.1, which states that the law applies to employees who voluntarily provide paid services for an individual or legal entity, called the employer, and are under its management, organisation and control.

In relation to employees affected by a transfer of business, they will be those whose employment relationships are linked to the business, undertaking, or part of the business or undertaking that is transferred.

However, parts of the Spanish doctrine, following modern trends, consider that the affected employees are not only those who will be assigned a new employer, but also the employees who were already rendering services to the transferee and those who will remain in the transferor's company in the event of a partial transfer of business.

When the wording of SEL, art 44 defines the change of ownership, it not only refers to the transfer of a business or company but also includes the work centre, since a company may be formed by one or several work centres in which several autonomous production units can co-exist.

According to SEL, art 1.5, the work centre may be defined as a production unit with a specific organisation which is registered before the labour authorities. An 'autonomous production unit' has been defined by case law as the clearly differentiated work centre or operational unit that constitutes a socio-economic unit of production.

Q1.4 Effects of the transfer

The principal aim of Spanish regulation of transfers of business is the protection of employees, guaranteeing the maintenance of their employment and their rights.

According to SEL, art 44.1, any change in the ownership of a company, work centre or autonomous production unit does not, of itself, terminate the labour relationship. The new employer is subrogated in the labour and social security rights and obligations of the previous employer, including pension commitments.

Directive 2001/23/EC contemplates what happens before and after the transfer in relation to who assumes pending obligations. Indeed, the Directive stipulates that, after the date of the transfer, the transferor and transferee shall be jointly and severally liable in respect of obligations that arose before the date of the transfer.

In accordance with the European rules, SEL, art 44.3 provides that, in the case of transfers that occur through 'inter vivos' acts, the transferee and transferor are jointly and severally liable for a period of three years for unsatisfied labour obligations which accrued before the transfer. Compliance with obligations dated before the change of employer is set out in order to avoid any damage to employees' rights.

Joint and several liability does not arise in the event of transfer 'mortis causa'.

Spanish employment law also foresees the case of obligations that arise after the date of the transfer. In the event that the transfer is considered as a crime by a court (see below), the transferee and transferor are also jointly and severally liable for obligations which occur after the transfer.

Title XV of the Spanish Criminal Code, 'Crimes against the rights of employees', and in particular art 311.1, provides that those who, by means of deceit, fraud or abuse, impose on the employees in their service, labour and social security conditions that undermine their rights as recognised by law, collective agreements or employment contract, shall be punished with imprisonment and a fine.

Furthermore, according to art 311.2 of the Criminal Code, the same sanctions shall be imposed on those employers who, in the event of a transfer of business, consciously maintain the aforementioned conditions imposed by third parties.

A transfer shall only be considered as a criminal offence when it is established by an unappealable judgment from the criminal jurisdiction, although these cases are highly exceptional.

Collective agreements

A collective labour agreement, which applies to the transferred company, work centre or autonomous production unit at the time of a transfer, continues to apply to the affected employees unless otherwise agreed (once the transfer is completed) between the transferee and the employees' representatives. This application is maintained until the collective labour agreement expires or until a new collective agreement comes into force and applies to the transferred economic entity.

SEL, art 44 does not oblige the new employer to maintain indefinitely the working conditions provided by the collective agreement which applies to the transferred company at the time of transfer. Through a new collective agreement entered into after the transfer and through the negotiation with the employees' representatives, working conditions may be harmonised. However, it may be necessary to compensate employees for the pre-existing, more beneficial collective conditions.

Employees' representatives

In relation to the employees' representatives, SEL, art 44 provides that in the event that the transferred company, work centre or autonomous production unit maintains its autonomy, the change of employer does not imply that the employees' representatives will no longer assume their functions. Indeed, they continue carrying out their functions as employees' representatives under the same conditions that existed before the transfer.

Social Security

In relation to the Spanish Social Security system, transfers of businesses or undertakings create different obligations. It is necessary to determine who is responsible for the possible breach of the obligation to pay the Social Security contributions.

In the event of a change in the company's owner, it is compulsory to carry out a new registration or note in the employer's Social Security registry. Registration has to be requested within the six days following the transfer.

The transferee is jointly and severally liable with the transferor or his/her heirs or assigns for the payment of Social Security contributions corresponding to the employees and for the payment of any benefits which arose before the transfer when the original employer was responsible for that payment.

Right to object

The subrogation imposed by SEL, art 44 in the event of a transfer of a business obliges the new employer to be subrogated in the labour and Social

Security rights and obligations of the previous one. Consequently, the employees are also obliged to accept the new employer.

As a general rule, if SEL, art 44 applies, the employees are not entitled to refuse the transfer. Furthermore, the employees are not entitled to terminate their employment contracts and receive a severance payment for the termination. The transfer must not affect the rights and obligations of the employees, and the affected employees must accept the transfer.

Notwithstanding the above, in the event that the transfer of business implies certain labour measures in relation to the employees, such as collective relocations or collective modifications in working conditions, the transferor and the transferee must respect what is established in SEL, arts 40.2 and 41.4. Article 40 of the Spanish Employment Law, which regulates the employees' geographical mobility, requires the existence of economic, technical, organisational or production reasons in order to justify the company's decision to relocate. In the case of collective relocation, the employer is obliged to have a consultation period with the employees' representatives. Once the consultation period is finished, with agreement or without such agreement between the parties, the employer must communicate to the employees his decision regarding the relocation, with a notice period of 30 days.

The employees have the right to opt:

–   to accept the transfer, in which case the employees are entitled to receive an economic compensation for the expenses incurred within the limits provided by the collective labour agreement; or

–   to terminate their employment contracts, receiving a severance payment of 20 days of salary per year of service, with a maximum payment of 12 months of salary.

Employees also have the right to bring a claim challenging the company's decision before a competent jurisdiction. Collective claims are also possible.

SEL, art 41 provides similar consequences in the event of substantial modifications in working conditions. In this case, the maximum limit for severance payment is nine months of salary.

If the transfer of business regulations do not apply, employees are entitled to refuse the change of employer and even request the termination of their employment contracts, receiving the severance payment established for unfair dismissals. The employees' consent is necessary in these cases. If an employee refuses a change of employer and, nevertheless, the employer decides to transfer his/her employment contract, this could be considered as a dismissal that, for lack of justification, will be considered as unfair and entitle the employee to receive the legal severance compensation.

The Supreme Court, in the above-mentioned judgment of 29 February 2000 (see *Q1.2*), has followed this interpretation. If there is no transfer of business,

SEL, art 44 does not apply and, consequently, subrogation cannot be imposed on employees. Since there is no transfer, the employer cannot force the employees to transfer from one company to another, since this fact would imply a novation of the contract through a change of employer, and this cannot be done without the employees' consent.

Q1.5 Dismissal of employees

According to SEL, art 44.1, any change in the ownership of a company, work centre or autonomous production unit does not, of itself, terminate the labour relationship, and the new employer is subrogated in the labour and Social Security rights and obligations of the previous one, including pension commitments.

Indeed, the mere fact of a transfer does not terminate the employment contracts. Therefore, any termination of an employment contract must be based on the general causes provided by SEL, such as disciplinary reasons, economic, technical, organisational or production reasons. In the event the dismissal is considered as unfair, the employee would be entitled to the legal severance payment for unfair dismissals, which is 45 days of salary per year of service with a maximum limit of 42 months.

A transfer cannot be a ground for a dismissal and the employment contracts are continued and assumed by the transferee, which is the new employer. Therefore, the seniority of the transferred employees shall be maintained and respected.

The new employer must take on the obligations and liabilities of the previous employer and, consequently, is obliged to assume the employment contracts entered into between the transferred employees and the previous employer.

The above-mentioned subrogation operates *ope legis*, and possible agreements between transferor and transferee do not prevail over it.

The severance payment for unfair dismissal has to be calculated taking into account the employee's seniority with the prior employer. In the case of a dismissal based solely on the transfer and without any adequate legal reason, the employee is entitled to claim for unfair dismissal within a period of 20 days following the date of dismissal.

It is an essential requirement for subrogation that the employment relationships have not been terminated before the transfer.

The subrogation affects any employment contract, provided that it has not been declared void.

Q1.6 Harmonisation and variation of contractual terms and conditions

As discussed above, SEL, art 44.1 establishes that the new employer is subrogated in the labour and Social Security rights and obligations of the previous one, including pension commitments.

However, case law has established that SEL, art 44 does not oblige the new employer to maintain indefinitely the working conditions provided by the collective agreement which applies to the transferred company at the time of the transfer. Through a new collective agreement after the transfer and the negotiation with the employees' representatives, working conditions may be harmonised. However, it may be necessary to compensate the employees for the previous, more beneficial collective conditions.

If the transferor or transferee plans to adopt labour measures in relation to the employees (dismissals, relocations, modifications on working conditions, etc) on the transfer of a business, it is obliged not only to inform but also to negotiate with the employees' representatives. In these cases, it is obliged to enter into a consultation period with the employees' representatives concerning the possible measures that can be adopted and how they will affect the employees (see *Q1.4*).

Q1.7 Duty to inform and consult

The duty to inform and consult has been an aspect that had never been sufficiently regulated under Spanish law until the new wording of SEL, art 44 established by the above-mentioned Law 12/2001. The current regulations provide that transferee and transferor are obliged to inform the employees' representatives; therefore, both of them are responsible for compliance with that duty.

According to Royal Decree 5/2000 of 4 August concerning Infractions and Sanctions in the Social Order, the breach of the duty to inform the employees' representatives in the event of a transfer of business established in SEL, art 44.6 is considered to be a serious infraction from the labour point of view.

The recipients of the information are the representatives of the employees affected by the transfer. In the event that the company does not have employees' representatives, the transferee and transferor must inform directly the employees who may be affected by the transfer.

The rule assumes that the information shall be provided in writing in accordance with the legal rights concerning the employer's duties to inform the personnel delegates (SEL, art 62), works committees (SEL, art 64) and union delegates (Law of Syndicalism Freedom, art 10.3).

The transferee and the transferor have the obligation to inform the employees' representatives on the following issues:

–   The date of the transfer.

–   The reasons for undertaking such a measure.

–   Legal, economic and social consequences for the employees.

–   The planned measures in relation to the employees.

The transferor is obliged to provide the above-mentioned information sufficiently in advance of the transfer taking place. The transferee is also obliged to provide the information sufficiently in advance of the transfer and, in any case, before the employees are affected in their employment and work conditions.

In the event of mergers and demergers of companies, the transferor and the transferee must provide the mentioned information at the time of the call to the general shareholders' meetings that have to adopt the resolutions.

If the transferor or the transferee plans to adopt labour measures (dismissals, relocations, modifications, etc) in relation to the employees on the occasion of a transfer of business, they are obliged not only to inform but also to negotiate with the employees' representatives. Indeed, in these cases, they are obliged to enter into consultation with the employees' representatives concerning the possible measures that can be adopted and how they will affect the employees. The consultation period has to be completed before the implementation of the measures. During the consultation period, the parties must negotiate according to the principle of good faith ('bona fide') in order to obtain a favourable agreement between the employer and the employees.

In the event that the labour measures to be adopted consist of collective changes in the working conditions or geographic mobility that implies collective relocation of employees, the transferor and transferee must enter into consultation with the employees' representatives and comply with the procedural requirements established for these specific cases in SEL, arts 40.2 and 41.4.

Both articles establish similar consultation periods in the event that the employer wishes to carry out collective relocation or collective modification of labour conditions. The minimum duration for the consultation period with the employees' representatives is 15 days. Once that period has finished, whether an agreement has been reached or not, the employer must provide the affected employees with 30 days' notice of the measures that will be implemented. In such a case the employees are entitled to opt between accepting the transfer, or terminating their employment contracts, receiving a severance payment equivalent to 20 days of salary per year of service, with a maximum of 12 months of salary in the event of relocation and nine months of salary where there are substantial modifications.

The duties to inform and consult also apply in the case of a group of companies or similar organisations. Indeed, the information obligation also applies whether the decision regarding the transfer of business has been adopted by the transferor and the transferee or by the companies that control them. In this case, the transferor and transferee cannot allege insufficient information from the company that has adopted the transfer decision. Consequently, the employer is responsible, in any case, for the performance of the legal duties to inform and consult with the employees or their representatives.

Q2 Redundancy

Q2.1 Background

Collective dismissals are regulated by SEL, art 51 and Royal Decree 43/1996 of 19 January, which approve the regulation of collective dismissals (*Procedimientos de Regulación de Empleo*) and administrative performance in collective relocations. These rules include the fundamental contents of the European Directives in this matter (Directives 75/129/EEC and 92/56/EEC derogated by Directive 98/59/EC on the approximation of the laws of the member states relating to collective redundancies).

Under Spanish law, in order to determine whether the collective dismissal regulation applies, it is compulsory to take into consideration three elements: its causes, quantitative requirements and temporal requirements.

According to SEL, art 51, collective dismissal occurs when, within a period of 90 days, termination of employment contracts based on economic, technical, organisational or production reasons affects at least the following number of employees:

– 10 employees in companies with fewer than 100 employees;

– 10 per cent of the company's employees in companies that have between 100 and 300 employees;

– 30 employees in companies with 300 or more employees.

Collective dismissal also exists when termination affects all the company's employees, provided that there are more than five affected employees and termination is based on the total cessation of the company's activity for the above-mentioned reasons.

Causes

SEL contemplates two types of reasons for collective dismissals:

– Economic reasons: when the termination of the employment contracts contributes to improving the negative economic situation of the company in order to guarantee, if possible, its viability.

– Technical, organisational, or productive reasons: when the termination helps to guarantee the company's viability and employment in the company through a more effective utilisation of its resources.

Jurisdictional issues

Spanish case law has established that the negative economic situation has to be real and effective. The High Court of Justice of Galicia in a judgment of 2 February 2001 rejected the existence of a negative economic situation in a notary's office due to the temporal illness of the notary in charge of the business. The business went through a period of economic difficulties, but the activity was recovering its normal course of business due to the progressive return of the notary to the facilities. On the other hand, the High Court of Justice of Andalucía in a judgment of 11 November 1998 established that the fact that the company had been suffering economic losses during the previous three years and eviction from the work facilities due to the non-payment of rents is enough to certify a negative economic situation.

Negative economic situations that have been suffered in the past cannot justify a collective dismissal once the situation has passed.

It is not necessary that the collective dismissal guarantees the total recovery of the business. The High Court of Justice of Navarra in a ruling of 20 September 2001 stated that the collective dismissal does not have to ensure the complete recovery of the business and that it is enough to adopt measures that are necessary to guarantee partial recovery. However, it is always for the employer to prove how the termination of contracts will encourage progressive recovery in the future.

In the case of companies that form part of a group of companies, case law has considered that the economic, technical, organisational or production reasons have to be established within the group and not solely taking into consideration the subsidiary where the employees carry out their services.

General procedure

In order to carry out a collective dismissal, the employer has to obtain an authorisation from the Spanish Labour Authority. Collective dismissal without the mentioned authorisation is void and the employer is obliged to reinstate the employees in their positions, paying them the salaries not received..

The procedure begins with the employer's application to the Labour Authority. Simultaneously, the employer must open in writing a consultation period with the employees' legal representatives.

The company may communicate the commencement of the procedure for collective dismissal to its employees, but this should never be understood as a communication of dismissal. Case law has established that the communication to employees regarding the company's intention to initiate a collective dismissal does not constitute a dismissal, provided that the company retains its employees with their employment contracts and salaries and complies with its social security obligations.

The employees, through their representatives, are also entitled to commence the procedure for collective dismissal when they believe that non-commencement of the procedure by the employer might cause them irreparable damage. In this case, they will only need to submit to the Labour Authority the necessary report stating the reasons for the application, any evidence that can prove the aforementioned damages, the communication made to the employer informing him/her that they have applied for the procedure to the Labour Authority, and any response and documents returned from the employer.

Once the consultation period is finished, the employer must notify this to the Labour Authority, stating the outcome. The consultation period may terminate with or without an agreement between the parties.

In the event that an agreement is reached, the Labour Authority might authorise such agreement and the termination of the employment contracts, unless it has been reached by means of fraud, coercion or circumvention of the law. In such a case, the Labour Authority will refer the matter to the Social Court.

The agreement reached between the parties is binding and has legal force between them. The Labour Authority must rule on the agreement within a period of 15 days, and the measure shall implicitly be understood to be authorised, if there has been no resolution. Once an agreement has been reached between the employer and the employees' representatives, any employee's dissent is not legally taken into account.

If no agreement is reached between the parties, the Labour Authority shall consider the employer's application within the 15 days following the end of the consultation period. Among the different alternatives the Labour Authority has, it may either opt to authorise the termination of the contracts or deny such termination if the company has not provided sufficient evidence to support it. A partial authorisation is also an alternative.

If the Labour Authority has not provided any written decision within a period of 15 days, it is understood that termination of the employment contracts is authorised.

Unless the collective dismissal affects all the employees of the company, the employees' representatives have priority to be the last employees to be affected by a collective dismissal. Other categories of employees do not benefit from this priority. The Spanish Supreme Court in a ruling dated 11 June 2001 stated that mentally and physically handicapped employees, and any other employees who are disabled in some way, do not benefit from the priority to continue in the company, since the benefit of the law is restricted to employees' representatives.

The Insolvency Law (Ley Concursal)

The Spanish Parliament has recently passed the Insolvency Law 22/2003 of 9 July (*Ley Concursal*), which contains provisions regarding collective dismissal in the case of bankrupted companies. Indeed, the Insolvency Law, which will come into force on 1 September 2004, introduces changes in the procedure described above.

In accordance with the Insolvency Law, the competent body to decide on collective dismissal in the event of insolvent companies shall no longer be the

Labour Authority but the Mercantile Judge (*Juez de lo Mercantil*) created by the Law for matters dealing with insolvency procedures.

The Law establishes that the Insolvency Administration, the bankrupted employer or the employees' representatives may request the Mercantile Judge to open the procedure. Once the application is accepted, the judge shall commence a consultation period between the employees' representatives and the Insolvency Administration.

After the consultation period, the result is communicated to the Mercantile Judge who will request the Labour Authority to issue a report so that he may resolve the issues in a proper manner. This decision may be appealed before the Social Courts.

Therefore, even though the Mercantile Judge has been substituted for the Labour Authority in the case of insolvent companies, employees' representatives still maintain their role in the procedures for collective dismissal.

The Insolvency Law also provides that with regard to the special employment relationship of senior executives, the severance payment agreed in their employment contracts may be reduced by the Mercantile Judge, while respecting the legal limits established for collective dismissals (20 days of salary per year of service, with a maximum limit of 12 months of salary).

Q2.2 Redundancy payments

Those employees whose employment contract terminates under the terms contemplated in SEL, art 51 (collective dismissals) are entitled to receive a severance payment equivalent to 20 days of salary per year of service, with a maximum limit of 12 months of salary.

Through individual or collective agreement, the parties may establish a higher amount for the redundancy payment.

The severance payment has to be paid by the employer simultaneously with the adoption of the decision to terminate.

Q2.3 Settlement agreements

Although SEL, art 51.8 provides the statutory redundancy payment discussed above, it is possible that the severance payment to be paid to the affected employees is one agreed during the consultation period.

In the event that the Labour Authority determines that the agreement has been reached on the basis of fraud, misconduct, coercion or circumvention of law, it must refer the matter to the Social Courts in order to allow them to decide whether it should be judged to be null and void.

Q2.4 The duty to inform and consult prior to redundancy

At the same time as the employer lodges the application for collective dismissal before the Labour Authority, the employer must commence a consultation period with the employees' legal representatives, in writing and accompanied by the necessary documents to justify the reasons for such a measure. A copy of the documentation has to be lodged before the Labour Authority.

Appropriate representatives

The company and the employees, through their representatives, are entitled to take part in the collective dismissal procedure. If there are no employees' representatives in the company, the employees themselves are entitled to intervene in the procedure. However, if the company has 10 or more employees, they must appoint a maximum of five representatives before the Labour Authority.

The works committee is also entitled to negotiate while its term of office is in force, and until new elections.

Trade unions that represent the majority of members of the works committee may negotiate with the company in order to reach agreements that may terminate the collective dismissal procedure.

In the case of companies with a number of work centres and employees' organisations, consultation may be carried out with the inter-centre works committee, provided that its rules allow for this.

Time period

The minimum duration for the consultation period is 30 days. In the case of companies with fewer than 50 employees, the minimum duration for the consultation period is 15 days.

In the event that the parties reach an agreement to be presented to the Labour Authority before the expiration of the mentioned minimum periods, it is understood that the consultation period is terminated.

Spanish law does not provide a maximum duration for the consultation period.

Information required

During the consultation period, each party must negotiate in good faith. The negotiations shall contemplate the reasons that have motivated the situation and the possibility of avoiding or reducing the effects of collective dismissal. The parties must participate in creating solutions to reduce the consequences for the affected employees and to facilitate the continuity and viability of the company.

The negotiations maintained during the consultation period must be reflected in minutes and, in any case, in the final minutes comprehensive of all the negotiations documents and reports that have been analysed.

The Labour Authority may request reports from different institutions in order to be able to properly reach its decision.

The employer must include the following information:

– A report explaining the reasons that justify the collective dismissal, including all the documents the employer considers necessary to justify such a measure. If the reason is economic, the employer must include financial documents and reports that have been subject to audit and that prove the financial evolution of the company during the last three years. If the causes are productive, organisational or technical, the employer must include any plans, programmes and technical reports to justify the dismissals.

– The number and professional category of the employees who have been employed during the last year; the number of employees that will be affected by the dismissal; the criteria that have been used to select them; the estimated period during which the dismissals would take place.

– In companies with 50 or more employees, the employer must formulate a social plan that contemplates the measures adopted or foreseen by the company in order to avoid or to reduce the effects of the collective dismissal for the affected employees. Such measures include, among others, those specially aimed at the readjustment or reorganisation of the employees and their possible integration into different positions in the company or group of companies, as well as those that favour the maintenance of indefinite employment contracts or redistribution of the working day between the affected employees.

– An application document addressed to the employees' representatives requesting from them a report about the planned collective dismissal.

– If more than 50 per cent of the company's employees are affected, the employer must inform the employees' representatives and the Labour Authority about any sale of the company's assets, unless it constitutes the usual economic traffic of the company.

Failure to comply

In the event that the Labour Authority decides that the employer has not submitted a relevant document, it will grant a period of 10 days in order for this to be lodged.

In the event that the employer does not respect the minimum requirements provided by SEL, art 51 for collective dismissal procedures, e g the obligatory consultation period with the employees' representatives or referring the necessary documents to the Labour Authority, the latter shall not authorise such dismissals and, consequently, they will be void.

According to Royal Decree 5/2000 of 4 August concerning Infractions and Sanctions in the Social Order, the breach of the rights of employees' representatives and personnel delegates in matters regarding the legally established information and consultation obligations of the employers is considered to be a serious infringement from the labour point of view.

Q2.5 Offer of alternative work

In the case of an employer's offer of an alternative position, it is necessary to take into account SEL, arts 40 and 41 which regulate the employees' geographic mobility, and substantial modifications of working conditions, respectively.

Both articles require the existence of economic, technical, organisational or production reasons in order to justify a company's decision of relocation. The employees have the right to opt between two possibilities:

– to accept the transfer, in which case the employees are entitled to receive an economic compensation for the expenses incurred within the limits provided by the collective labour agreement; or

– to terminate their employment contracts, receiving a severance payment of 20 days of salary per year of service with a maximum payment of 12 months of salary in the event of relocation and nine months of salary where there is a substantial modification in working conditions.

Employees also have the right to bring a claim on the company's decision before the competent jurisdiction. Collective claims are also possible.

Q2.6 Unfair redundancy

Automatic unfairness

In the event that the Labour Authority does not authorise the collective dismissal, the employer shall not be entitled to dismiss the employees, the collective dismissal will be considered void and the employer will be obliged to reinstate the employees, paying the salaries not received by the employees during the corresponding period.

Q3 Case studies

Q3.1 Case study 1
(Acquisition of a 'business' situated in another EU state; asset deal; no relocation)

Slumber Ltd, a hotel management company incorporated in the UK and based in Manchester, UK, has been in financial difficulties for some time. Slumber operates nine exclusive hotels in the main British cities (London, Manchester, Birmingham, Leeds, Glasgow, Edinburgh, Liverpool, Cardiff and Bristol) under the 'Slumber' brand. Slumber is 100 per cent owned by UK hotel chain Ezeroom plc, also incorporated in the UK. Each hotel has about 50 staff: five in management, 20 in the restaurant and 25 in house service. Slumber does not own the hotels itself; instead it has a seven-year management agreement with Hotel Investment plc ('HIP'), the owner of the hotels, which is incorporated and based in London, UK. Under this contract Slumber runs the fully equipped hotels on its own risk and has to pay a fixed fee to HIP.

In its central management centre in Manchester, Slumber has another 30 staff. These are 10 managers (including Marketing, Managing, Finance, Sales and Operations Directors) and 20 secretaries, clerks and administrators.

A number of staff are members of the trade union, The Association of Hotel Workers ('AHW'), which has been formally recognised by Slumber as having bargaining rights for hourly paid hotel staff. This is a particularly active union and there is a collective agreement in force. Due to increasing staff costs and the declining demand for expensive hotel accommodation, Slumber is making bigger and bigger operating losses. Slumber is obliged to cut jobs in all the hotels and thus dismisses 40 members of staff as redundant. As a consequence, the service worsens and customer complaints become more frequent. When the board of HIP realises how serious the situation has become, it starts to look for a new operator of its hotels.

Some weeks later, while Slumber is still operating the hotels, a Spanish company is found which seems able to manage the hotels in a much more profitable way for HIP than Slumber. The company, which is called Dormir, is based in Madrid, but has already gathered some experience of running hotels in the UK. It operates hotels under the 'Dormir' brand. The board of HIP enters into discussions with Dormir for it to replace Slumber as manager of the hotels.

1. Acquisition of the hotels

It is anticipated that Dormir will want to manage all nine of the hotels under a single management agreement with HIP.

(a) **Would this be a business transfer (defined as a transfer within the meaning of TUPE) under UK law?**

(ONLY TO BE ANSWERED BY UK CONTRIBUTOR)

(b) **Even though Slumber will not transfer any of its activities to Spain, would the acquisition of the hotels in this way constitute a business transfer under Spanish law?**

Answer

Probably. It depends on the facts.

Legal reasoning

From the Spanish point of view, art 44 of the Spanish Employment Law ('SEL') refers to the transfer of business as affecting an economic entity that maintains its identity as a group of means organised in order to carry out an economic activity. Moreover, subrogation by virtue of art 44 requires the transfer of the essential assets of the undertaking, business, or parts of the undertaking or business that may be qualified as an autonomous production unit, and the continuity of the operation of the business by the transferee.

Consequently, in the event that Slumber terminates the activity in the hotels, transferring to Dormir an actual work centre with the necessary tangible assets and the necessary personnel to continue the activity, under Spanish law (if it applies to this case), this could be considered as a transfer of a business.

(c)   **Would it make any difference to whether this constituted a business transfer, under TUPE, if Dormir only wanted to manage the English hotels (excluding the hotels in Glasgow, Edinburgh and Cardiff)?**

(ONLY TO BE ANSWERED BY UK CONTRIBUTOR)

(d)   **Would it make any difference to your answer to (b) above if Dormir only wanted to manage six hotels (for example only the English hotels, excluding those in Scotland and Wales, i e the hotels in Glasgow, Edinburgh and Cardiff)?**

Answer

No.

Legal reasoning

Under Spanish law, subrogation takes place not only when the transfer affects an entire company, but also when a single work centre or even an independent production unit is transferred.

2. Employees who work only partly in the business

What is the position of those staff who work partly in Slumber and partly in Ezeroom? For example, the human resources director of Slumber is also the human resources director of Ezeroom and he has his employment agreement with Ezeroom. He spends approximately 40 per cent of his time dealing with Slumber's personnel matters and the remainder of his time on the human resources affairs of Ezeroom.

(a)   **If this is a TUPE transfer, can he be said to have transferred under TUPE in the UK?**

(UK CONTRIBUTOR TO ANSWER)

(b)   **What is the law on employees who work only partly in the undertaking to be transferred in Spain?**

SEL, art 44 does not differentiate between different kinds of employment contract. The new employer is subrogated in the employment and social security rights and obligations of the previous one, including pension commitments, independently of the kind of employment contract of each employee.

3. Staff who work outside the UK in another EU country

It transpires that some Slumber central management staff are actually working and based in Spain already. Two are Spanish nationals.

(a) **Would these staff transfer to Dormir under TUPE if there was a TUPE transfer?**

(UK TO ANSWER, BUT PLEASE COMMENT)

Answer

In theory yes, although this would depend on a number of factors including their contracts of employment.

Comment: It would be necessary to analyse whether Spanish law is applicable to the employees based in Spain and, if it is, whether they are affected by the transfer, assuming that they are an essential part of the transfer for the purposes of assuring the continuity of the activity by Dormir. In practice, it could also depend on the result of the negotiation procedure.

(b) **Would the position be different if there was a branch of Ezeroom in Spain, which directly employed these staff?**

(UK TO ANSWER, BUT PLEASE COMMENT)

Answer

The position may be the same.

Comment: In this case, in all probability Spanish law would be applicable to their employment contracts, since the actual employer would be the Spanish office.

4. Dismissal of employee

One of the Slumber staff, Mr X, was dismissed by Slumber after HIP had given notice to terminate the contract with Slumber and whilst negotiations were ongoing with Dormir. Mr X is owed two months' back pay and unpaid holiday.

Against whom can Mr X bring a claim, and where, if Mr X is a UK national based in Spain?

Answer

Mr X can bring a claim against both Slumber and Dormir before Spanish courts.

Legal reasoning

Although, according to SEL, art 44, the transferee and the transferor are jointly and severally liable for a period of three years for unsatisfied labour obligations dating before the transfer, Mr X should bring the claim against his employer that is carrying out the dismissal. Since the dismissal takes place before the transfer is effective, the employer is Slumber. However, in practice, it is possible for the employee to bring the claim against both companies.

The European Regulation (EC) 44/2001 of 22 December 2000 provides that an employer domiciled in a member state may be sued in the courts of the member state where he is domiciled, in the courts for the place where the employee habitually carries out his work, or in the courts for the last place where he did so.

5. Transfer of employee outside the UK

Mr Y (the marketing director) has been vital to the success of Slumber and has been responsible for many successful ideas. Dormir would like to retain his services and move him to Dormir's headquarters in Spain. Mr Y has no wish to live in Spain.

(a)   **How does TUPE impact on Mr Y: is he obliged to transfer against his will?**

(UK ONLY TO ANSWER)

(b)   **What is the law on objection to a transfer in Spain?**

If the transfer of business regulation applies, the employee is obliged to accept the new employer. Indeed, if SEL, art 44 applies, the employee is not entitled to refuse the transfer. If the transfer of business regulation does not apply, employees are entitled to refuse the change of employer and even request termination of their employment contracts, receiving the severance payment established for unfair dismissals.

However, if the transfer implies labour measures in relation to the employees, a consultation period is necessary. Moreover, SEL, art 40, which regulates the employees' geographic mobility, and art 41, which regulates substantial modifications in working conditions, provide that the employee is entitled to terminate his employment contract, receiving a severance payment of 20 days' salary per year of service, with a maximum payment of 12 months' salary in the case of relocation. He can also bring a claim on the company's decision before the competent jurisdiction. Consequently, under Spanish law he would be able to refuse the relocation to Spain unless an agreement is reached between the parties.

(c)   **Can Mr Y claim constructive dismissal on the basis that he would be expected to work and be based in Spain and this is nowhere near his home?**

(UK TO ANSWER, BUT PLEASE COMMENT)

Answer

Possibly – if being expected to work and be based abroad amounts to a substantial change in working conditions and is to the employee's detriment.

Comment: According to Spanish law, an employee may apply for termination of his employment contract before social jurisdiction in some cases: substantial modifications in working conditions which are detrimental to the employee's professional training or his dignity; the continued delay or non-payment of the employee's salary; any other serious breach of the employer's obligations. In these cases, the employee may be entitled to the legal severance pay established for disciplinary dismissal which is declared unfair.

Relocation must be based on economic, technical, organisational or production reasons. Furthermore, the employee is entitled to opt between accepting the relocation, or terminating his contract and receiving a severance payment equivalent to 20 days of salary per year of services up to a maximum of 12 months of salary.

6. Dormir's business strategy

What is the best way of structuring the transfer of the hotels to Dormir from Spain's perspective? Would you advise Dormir to set up a subsidiary company registered in the UK specifically to purchase Slumber and thereby avoid any cross-border element?

A priori and taking into consideration the Spanish labour legislation, we do not foresee any labour implication.

Q3.2 Case study 2
(Production moves from one EU country to another EU country; physical move)

Alpha Incorporated is a multinational car tyre manufacturing and distribution business based in Europe. Alpha's headquarters are in Italy. Alpha has tyre plants in Spain, Italy and France. Each of the tyre plants is a wholly owned and independently operated subsidiary of Alpha. Alpha has a European Works Council.

The subsidiary in Spain is Beta. Beta employs about 250 employees, mostly in the direct production of tyres. The employees are on standard basic contracts which do not contain any mobility clauses. Due to increased competition from cheaper producers in the Far East, Alpha is having to reduce its own production costs. Beta has the highest production costs of all Alpha's European operations. Alpha has decided to end the production of tyres in Spain and move production to Gamma, another subsidiary in nearby France which has more modern plant and equipment, and lower labour costs. Beta will continue to exist, but as a sales and marketing organisation only, with about 30 staff.

Most of Beta's tyre-making plant and machinery is transferred to Gamma, but Gamma will only need an extra 125 staff to increase its output to the required level to supply Beta's market. Those employees from Beta who are required to work for Gamma will be expected to accept the terms and conditions and working practices of the Gamma plant, which are very different from those in operation at the Beta plant. For example, Gamma pays its employees considerably lower hourly wages and they work longer hours than those at Beta. Gamma does not want to pay more to the employees transferred to it from Beta than it does for its current employees. In addition, Beta has an occupational pension scheme for its Spanish staff. Gamma operates a different type of pension scheme.

1. Does this transaction constitute a 'business transfer'?

(a)   **As Beta's tyre-making plant and machinery have transferred to Gamma, will this constitute a business transfer under the Acquired Rights Directive implementing legislation of Spain?**

Answer

Probably yes, if the legal conditions required for a business transfer are complied with.

Legal reasoning

Under Spanish law, a transfer of business exists when it affects an economic entity that maintains its identity as a group of means organised in order to carry out an economic activity. An 'autonomous production unit' has been defined by case law as the work centre or the clearly differentiated operative unit that constitutes a socio-economic unit of production. Accordingly, what is being transferred is an autonomous production unit (the tyre-making plant and machinery), since Beta will continue existing for sales and marketing purposes.

The transfer of business regulation applies if the essential assets, infrastructure and the staff that is necessary to develop the business are transferred. In other words, the tyre-making plant and machinery must be transferred as a whole production unit, including all the elements that are necessary to continue operating in the market. Therefore, the principal elements that Spanish case law requires to consider this a 'transfer of business' seem to be complied with: (i) the transfer of the effective ownership (Gamma will assume the position of new employer); and (ii) the transfer of tangible assets and employees to continue the activity.

(b)   **Does it make any difference to whether this is a business transfer if employees of Beta transfer across to Gamma?**

Answer

No.

Legal reasoning

If the requirements set out by SEL, art 44 and the case law are complied with, the transfer of a business exists independently of the fact that the employees of Beta transfer across to Gamma. This fact does not change the juridical concept of a transfer of a business if this is a transfer of an economic entity that maintains its identity as a group of means organised to carry out the economic activity.

(c) **Can the transfer of plant and machinery coupled with the transfer of half the employees (125) constitute a business transfer under Spanish legislation if the other 125 employees are dismissed prior to the transfer?**

Answer

Probably yes.

Legal reasoning

Spanish case law requires the transfer of the personal and material elements that are necessary to carry out the activity. A transfer cannot be a ground for dismissal. Therefore, all the employees who are necessary for the tyre-making plant must be considered as part of the whole production unit and must be included in the transaction. However, if the dismissals that take place prior to the transfer are not connected with the transfer itself and they are based on the legal causes provided by law (economic, production, technical or organisational reasons), and comply with the legal requirements established by SEL, art 51 for collective dismissals (including the corresponding agreement with the employees' representatives and the authorisation of the Spanish Labour Authority), dismissals may be considered fair. In this case, those dismissals would not have to be considered as part of the business transfer.

(d) **Does the fact that the business will transfer to a different country make any difference to whether this is a business transfer?**

Answer

No.

Legal reasoning

SEL, art 44 does not contain any provision regarding transfer to a different country. Consequently, since Spanish law applies to the employment relationship of the affected employees, the fact that the business will transfer to a different country does not affect the consideration of transfer, since the principal target of art 44 is the protection of employees and guaranteeing the maintenance of their employment relationships and their rights.

(e) **Is Spanish transfer law concerned with the actual distance moved (irrespective of whether this means a change of country)?**

Answer

No.

Legal reasoning

Article 44 of the Spanish Employment Law, which regulates the transfer of a business, does not contain any particular stipulation regarding the actual distance moved or the circumstance of a change of country.

2. Relocation, but no business transfer

(a) **Assuming the move does NOT constitute a business transfer (because the business of Beta does not adequately retain its identity) but instead is deemed to be a straightforward relocation, are any of Beta's employees obliged or entitled to relocate?**

Answer

No.

Legal reasoning

Article 40 of the Spanish Employment Law, which regulates the employees' geographic mobility, requires the existence of economic, technical, organisational or production reasons in order to justify the company's decision to relocate. In this specific case, there is a collective relocation (since it affects at least 10 per cent of the employees in a company that has between 100 and 300 employees, provided that relocations take place within a period of 90 days). The employer is obliged to open a consultation period with the employees' representatives. Once the consultation period is terminated, with or without agreement between the parties, the employer must communicate to the employees his decision regarding the relocation, with a notice period of 30 days.

The employees have the right to opt between two possibilities:

● to accept the transfer, in which case employees are entitled to receive an economic compensation for the expenses incurred within the limits provided by the Collective Labour Agreement; or

● to terminate their employment contracts, receiving a severance payment of 20 days of salary per year of service, with a maximum payment of 12 months' salary.

Employees also have the right to bring a claim on the company's decision before the competent jurisdiction. Collective claims are also possible.

The above-mentioned SEL, art 40 regulates the relocation, as the transfer to a different work centre of the same company implies a change in the employee's residence. However, in this case the relocation takes place to a different company but within the same group of companies. Indeed, notwithstanding the fact that there is a group of companies, each plant is a subsidiary wholly owned and independent from Alpha. In any case, the employees' acceptance is necessary for the relocation.

(b) **If employees do nevertheless relocate, what will happen to their employment contracts? Will these continue, or will Gamma be entitled to provide new contracts?**

Answer

Yes. Through the necessary negotiation the parties would decide the future of the contracts.

Legal reasoning

Gamma may be entitled to provide new contracts. However, it has to be done through negotiation with the employees' representatives.

(c) **What will be the law applicable to the contracts of the employees who relocate?**

Answer

It depends on the provisions of the employment contracts.

Legal reasoning

The Rome Convention of 19 June 1980, regarding the law applicable to contractual obligations establishes in art 3 that the law chosen by the parties will govern the contracts. However, art 6.1 sets out a limit on the parties' freedom to choose the applicable law, confirming that this choice in employment contracts 'shall not have the result of depriving the employee of the protection afforded to him by the mandatory rules of the law which would be applicable under Article 6 paragraph 2 in the absence of choice'.

Article 6.2 provides that, in the absence of choice by the parties, the employment contract is governed by the law of the country in which the employee habitually carries out his work in performance of his contract, even if he is temporarily employed in another country or, in the event that the employee does not carry out his work in a single country, the law of the country in which the place of business through which he was engaged is situated, unless it appears from the circumstances as a whole that the employment contract is more closely connected with another country, in which case the law of that other country applies.

As a general rule, Spanish case law has established that the protection of employees' rights implies the obligation to analyse each specific case in order to apply the rule which is more beneficial for the employees.

(Better Law: a general principle which implies that, in the event of conflict, the most favourable rule for the employee's rights will be applicable.)

3. Dismissals

(a) **Assuming that the move does constitute a business transfer:**

(i) **are any dismissals in connection with the transfer lawful?**

Answer

No. Under Spanish law a transfer cannot be a ground for a dismissal.

Legal reasoning

According to SEL, art 44.1, any change in the ownership of a company, work centre or autonomous production unit does not itself terminate the labour relationships, and the new employer is subrogated in the labour and social security rights and obligations of the previous one, including pension commitments. Consequently, a transfer cannot be a ground for a dismissal. Any termination of an employment contract must be based on the general causes provided by SEL. The new employer is obliged to assume the position of the previous employer and, consequently, is obliged to assume the employment contracts entered into between the transferred employees and the previous employer.

Therefore, any dismissal in connection with the transfer would be declared unfair. Furthermore, since this is a case of collective dismissal, if the employer does not respect the compulsory requirements established by SEL, art 51 (ie the consultation period, authorisation from the Labour Authority, etc), the termination of the employment contracts would be declared void. Since the dismissals are connected with the transfer, the Labour Authority shall not authorise the dismissals and the employer will not be entitled to terminate the employment contracts. In these cases, through negotiation, the employer may try to reach an agreement with the employees' representatives in order to ease the procedure.

(ii) **what are the rights and remedies (including applicable law and appropriate jurisdiction) of any employees dismissed:**

a. **before the transfer?**

In order to carry out a collective dismissal the employer has to respect the compulsory procedure and requirements of SEL, art 51. The employer has to obtain an authorisation from the Spanish Labour Authority. Collective dismissal without such prior authorisation is void. The procedure begins with the employer's application to the Labour Authority. Simultaneously, the employer is obliged to open in writing a consultation period with the employees' representatives.

Those employees whose employment contract terminates under the terms contemplated in SEL, art 51 are entitled to receive a severance payment equivalent to 20 days of salary per year of service, with a maximum limit of 12 months' salary. However, through individual or collective agreement reached during the consultation period, the parties may establish a higher amount for redundancy payments. In the event that the dismissals are in connection with the transfer, or do not comply with the compulsory requirements of SEL, art 51, the Labour Authority will not authorise the collective dismissal and the employer will not be entitled to dismiss the employees. In this case the collective dismissal will be considered void and the employer shall be obliged to reinstate the employees, paying the salaries not received by the employees during the corresponding period.

In relation to the applicable law and appropriate jurisdiction, in the absence of choice by the parties in the employment contracts, since the employees are rendering their services in Spain, Spanish law shall apply and Spanish jurisdiction shall be competent.

b. after the transfer?

A priori, the same rights and remedies would apply after the transfer. The new employer is obliged to assume the position of the previous employer and, consequently, is obliged to assume the employment contracts entered into between the transferred employees and the previous employer (including seniority, eventual salary improvements, etc). The new employer assumes all the employment obligations with the affected employees. However, in practice, it is necessary to analyse each specific employment contract. The principal target of Spanish regulation for the transfer of a business is the protection of employees, and guaranteeing the maintenance of their employment relationship and their rights. SEL, art 44.3 provides that both transferee and transferor are jointly and severally liable during a period of three years for unsatisfied labour obligations dated before the transfer.

The law applicable to the contract will be that chosen by the parties and, in the absence of choice, the law of the country where the employee habitually carries out his/her work. Article 19 of European Regulation (EC) 44/2001 of 22 December 2000 provides that an employer domiciled in a member state may be sued in the courts of the member state where he is domiciled, or in the courts for the place where the employee habitually carries out his work, or in the courts for the last place where he did so.

(b) Would these rights and remedies change if this was not a business transfer?

Answer

No.

Legal reasoning

A priori, the rights and remedies do not change. However, by negotiation and agreement with the employees' representatives it is possible to agree higher amounts in order to ease or make the procedure possible. For information purposes, according to SEL, art 56, the severance payment an employee is entitled to in the case of a disciplinary dismissal being declared unfair is equivalent to 45 days of salary per year of service, with a limit of 42 months' salary.

4. European Works Council and other employees' representatives

(a) Will Alpha be required to inform and consult the European Works Council about the transfer or any redundancies?

Answer

Probably, yes. It would depend on the alternative procedure of information and consultation established by the community-scale group of undertakings. In any case, Beta, as the actual employer, would be required to inform and consult.

Legal reasoning

Law 44/1999 of 29 November, which modifies Law 10/1997 of 24 April concerning the rights of information and consultation of employees in companies and groups of companies with a European dimension, has implemented the European Directives on Work Councils into Spanish legislation. From the provisions of these laws, the European Works Council must be informed and consulted sufficiently in advance about the transfers, redundancies or any other measures that may affect the employees.

(b) Are any other employee representatives required to be involved in the transfer or any redundancies (ie at national or local level)?

Answer

Yes.

Legal reasoning

The transferor and transferee are obliged to inform the local employees' representatives (personnel delegates, works council, union representatives) on: the date of the transfer; the reasons for undertaking such a measure; the legal, economic and social consequences for the employees; and the planned measures. If the transferor or the transferee plans to adopt labour measures in relation to the employees, they are not only obliged to inform but also to negotiate with the employees' representatives. A consultation period, therefore, must be opened.

In collective dismissals the employer is also obliged to open in writing a consultation period with the employees' representatives.

5. Collective agreements

What is the effect of the business transfer on any collective agreements affecting Beta's employees?

The conditions provided for by the Collective Labour Agreement that applies to Beta's employees before the transfer must be respected until a new one comes into force and is applicable. According to Spanish law, the Collective Labour Agreement, which is applicable to the transferred company, work centre or autonomous production unit at the time of transfer, continues to apply to the affected employees unless otherwise agreed, once the transfer is completed, between the transferee and the employees' representatives until it expires or a new collective agreement applicable to the transferred economic entity is in force.

6. Change of terms and conditions

(a) **If this is a business transfer, how can Gamma lawfully harmonise employment contracts and change the terms and conditions of the employees currently on the more generous Beta contracts of employment?**

Answer

It depends on whether or not an agreement with employees' representatives is reached.

Legal reasoning

Gamma is subrogated in the labour and social security rights and obligations of Beta regarding the transferred employees, including pension commitments. However, case law has established that the labour conditions may be harmonised through an agreement with the employees' representatives. In practice, these issues are resolved through sometimes-difficult negotiations with the representatives in order to reach an agreement that permits harmonisation of the working conditions. Moreover, case law has also established that SEL, art 44 does not oblige the new employer to maintain indefinitely the working conditions provided by the collective agreement applicable to the transferred company at the time of transfer. Through a new collective agreement after the transfer and negotiation with the employees' representatives, working conditions may be harmonised. However, it may be necessary to provide compensation for the pre-existing, more beneficial collective conditions not acquired in a private capacity.

(b)   **If this is a business transfer, can Gamma reduce the wages of the former Beta employees?**

Answer

It depends on whether an agreement with employees' representatives is reached, but it is difficult in practice to reduce the wages.

Legal reasoning

As discussed above, through negotiations with the employees' representatives a new collective agreement may apply to the transferred employees specifying a reduction in wages in order to harmonise the conditions. However, in practice, it would be very difficult for employees to accept the situation of a change in their country of residence with a reduced wage. Indeed, according to SEL, art 44, in the event that the transfer of business implies labour measures in relation to the employees such as collective relocations or collective changes in working conditions, the transferor and the transferee must respect the provisions of SEL, art 40.2 (geographical mobility) and art 41.4 (substantial modifications in working conditions). These articles provide employees with the possibility of terminating the employment contract and receiving a severance payment of 20 days of salary per year of service, with a maximum of 12 months' salary in the event of relocation and nine months' salary where there are substantial modifications. Case law shows that the employer may resort to SEL, art 41 in order to reduce the salary improvements (TSJ Madrid, 9–6–96).

(c)   **If this is a business transfer, what will happen to the former Beta employees as regards their private pension arrangements?**

A priori, any pension arrangements must be respected by Gamma, since SEL, art 44 has specifically contemplated this case. The new employer is subrogated in the labour and social security rights and obligations of the previous one, including pension commitments. However, through negotiations with the representatives, pension arrangements may be also harmonised.

(d)   **Is it easier to change terms and conditions of employment if the changes are made six months after the transfer?**

Taking into consideration the above comments, it will depend on the course of negotiations and the difficulties encountered in each specific case.

Q3.3 Case study 3
(Outsourcing of an ancillary activity to a non-EU country)

A large multinational (ABC) based in Spain has decided to outsource its entire internal IT function to a third party provider in Romania, as the costs of hiring competent IT personnel in Romania are far lower than in Spain, largely because wages are so much lower. At present 200 employees are employed by ABC in its IT function in Spain. It is anticipated that exactly the same IT function will be required in Romania with approximately the same number of people required to run it. There will be no difference in the service or approach for those requiring IT assistance and even the internal telephone number will be automatically diverted. The Romanian third party provider has no assets or presence in Spain.

1. Business transfer

Will this be a business transfer within the scope of Spanish law applying ARD?

Answer

Not necessarily.

Legal reasoning

It will depend on whether in this specific case of outsourcing, where the strategic use of outside resources is to perform the IT activity traditionally handled by internal staff and resources, the requirements that SEL, art 44 and the Spanish case law require in order to consider this a transfer of business are complied with.

Indeed, for this specific case to be considered a transfer of business under Spanish law, it would be compulsory to transfer the employees and the essential assets necessary to continue carrying out the activity, provided that the IT function is considered as an autonomous production unit that after the transfer maintains its identity. According to the information provided, those requirements do not seem to be complied with.

However, it is important to mention that, although the Spanish Supreme Court considers that the application of the transfer of business regulation depends on the effective transfer of tangible assets (ie machinery, technical equipments, etc), lower courts (ie the High Court of Justice of Castilla-La Mancha, the High Court of Justice of Galicia, etc) have accepted in specific cases a new definition of the concept of 'business' that permits the business to be identified, at least in certain productive sectors (in which the activity rests basically in the employees' labour without requiring specific material elements), with the group of employees that carry out the activity.

2. Effect on employees

(a) **What will happen to the employees currently employed in the IT function at ABC? Will they transfer across?**

Answer

Assuming that in this specific case of outsourcing SEL, art 44 does not apply, employees do not automatically transfer and, in any case, their consent would be necessary.

Legal reasoning

The employees' acceptance is necessary. If the transfer implies labour measures in relation to the employees such as collective relocations or collective changes in working conditions, the transferor and the transferee must respect the provisions of SEL, art 40.2 (geographic mobility) and art 41.4 (substantial modifications in working conditions). Both articles require the existence of economic, technical, organisational or production reasons in order to justify the company's decision to relocate, and the employer is obliged to open a consultation period with the employees' representatives.

The employees have the right to opt between accepting the transfer, or terminating their employment contracts and receiving a severance payment of 20 days of salary per year of service, with a maximum payment of 12 months' salary in the event of relocation and 9 months' where there are substantial modifications.

Employees also have the right to bring a claim challenging the company's decision before the competent jurisdiction. Collective claims are also possible.

Assuming that this is not a transfer of business, SEL, art 51, which regulates the procedure for collective dismissals, would apply. The employer would have to obtain an authorisation from the Spanish Labour Authority. Collective dismissal without prior authorisation is void. The procedure would begin with the employer's application to the Labour Authority. Simultaneously, the employer would be obliged to open in writing a consultation period with the employees' representatives. Assuming that in this case there is not a legal cause (economic, organisational, technical or production), the Labour Authority would not authorise the dismissals and any termination would be declared void. The solution in practice would be to try to reach an agreement with the employees' representatives.

(b) **If the employees do transfer, what will the applicable law be for their employment contracts with the third party provider? Where can they make any claims?**

Answer

The employees who render services for ABC Spain presumably have contracts that are governed by Spanish law.

Legal reasoning

According to art 10.6 of the Spanish Civil Code, the obligations derived from the employment contract will be governed by the law chosen by the parties or, in default of election, the law of the country where the employee usually carries out his/her work.

However, in the event that a conflict arises between the parties, it is possible that the court would require a comparison between the chosen law and the law corresponding to the country where the employee habitually carries out his work. In this case the most favourable law for the employee in each specific situation shall apply (Better Law: a general principle that implies the application of the most beneficial rule for the employees' rights).

In relation to the place where the employees can make any claims, according to art 25 of the Spanish Judicial Power Organic Law, Spanish courts will be competent when the services have been rendered in Spain or the contract has been entered into in Spain; when the defendant is domiciled in Spain or has an agency, branch or delegation in Spain; or when the employee and the employer have Spanish nationality although the services have been rendered in another country.

3. Data protection

Will there be special data protection issues on the transfer of knowledge and information outside Spain to Romania?

Answer

Yes. An authorisation from the Spanish Agency of Data Protection would be required.

Legal reasoning

According to Organic Law 15/1999 of 13 December concerning personal data protection, the general principle is that in order to carry out an international transfer of data, it is necessary that the country of reception of the data has national legislation regarding protection of data similar to the Spanish legislation. That protection will be verified by the Spanish Agency of Data Protection, taking into consideration, among others, the following circumstances: the nature of the data, the aim of the transfer, the original country and the country of reception, professional rules, etc.

The Decree of 2 February 1995 establishes the countries that are considered to have national regulations regarding data protection similar to the Spanish one, and Romania is not included.

4. Transfer to India

Please comment on any differences there would be to your answers if the function was transferred to India rather than Romania.

In relation to data protection issues on the transfer of knowledge and information outside Spain, India is not included in the Decree of 2 February 1995 or the Decree of 31 July 1998 that establish the countries with data protection similar to that in the Spanish legislation. Therefore, in order to transfer knowledge and information to this country, prior written authorisation from the Agency of Data Protection would be required.

However, art 34 of Organic Law 15/1999 of 13 December concerning personal data protection establishes some cases in which the prior authorisation from the Agency of Data Protection is not required: eg transfer of data by virtue of bilateral treaties signed by Spain; when the transfer is necessary for medical prevention or diagnosis; when the affected party has given unequivocal consent to transfer the data; when the transfer is made to any member state of the European Union, etc.

R Switzerland

Dr Stefan Gerster LLM
Dr Matthias Leemann LLM

R1 Business transfers

R1.1 Background

General issues

The transfer of 'employment relationships' due to business transfers is essentially dealt with in art 333 of the Swiss Code of Obligations ('CO')[1]: see *R1.2*. The provision stipulates that where there is a transfer of a business or a part thereof, the employment relationships between the transferring party and its employees are automatically transferred to the acquiring party with all rights and obligations (see *R4.2*), unless the employees object to the transferring (see *R2.4*).

Before the enactment of CO, art 333, the right of an employer to enjoy the job performance of an employee could be assigned to a third party if so agreed upon in the employment contract, or if such assignment arose 'from the circumstances'. The latter condition was considered as fulfilled by the relevant case law whenever the employment contract was construed as having been concluded with the employer as a particular business, rather than as a particular person. This analysis was based on the idea that, in those cases, the employee provided his services to the business rather than its proprietor. Accordingly, in the case of business transfers involving such employees, the employment relationships were deemed to be transferred as a whole to the acquiring party on the basis of a tacit tripartite agreement. An employee's consent was assumed if and when he continued to work without objecting, after the business had been transferred.

This construct of a tacit agreement between the parties was no longer needed following the enactment of the former version of CO, art 333 in 1971, which provided for the automatic transfer of employment relationships in such a situation. A further reform in 1993 – after Switzerland had declined accession to the European Economic Area ('EEA') in a referendum – brought the provision more in line with the corresponding EU law (at the time the EC Acquired Rights Directive 77/187/EEC). The transfer of the employment contract no longer requires the consent, tacit or otherwise, of the party acquiring the business. In addition, provisions regarding the applicability of collective employment agreements as well as the information and consultation of employees were introduced.

This historical background is important in understanding the essential features of the Swiss law governing business transfers. The fact that the enactment of the provisions now in force was, to a large extent, driven by the desire to adapt Swiss law in accordance with EU law plays an important role in understanding the law in this area. As the case law of the Swiss Federal Supreme Court indicates, the relevant EU law and its developments have to be considered when interpreting Swiss law on business transfers[2].

1   Schweizerisches Obligationenrecht vom 30 März 1911 (SR 220).
      Transfer of Employment Relationship [unofficial informal translation]:
      Article 333 CO (Effects)
      1   If the employer transfers a business or a part thereof to a third party, the employment relationship is transferred to the acquirer, including all rights and obligations as at the date of the transfer, unless the employee declines the transfer.
      1*bis* If a collective employment agreement applies to the employment relationship transferred, the acquirer shall comply with it for one year from the date of transfer, unless it expires earlier or is terminated by notice.
      2   In the case of an employee declining to transfer to the acquirer, the employment relationship shall be terminated upon expiry of the legal notice period; the acquirer and the employee shall be bound to perform their duties under the employment contract until such date.
      3   The previous employer and the acquirer shall be jointly and severally liable for an employee's claims that have become due prior to the transfer, and those which will later become due until the date upon which the employment relationship could have validly been terminated, or the date upon which it is terminated by the employee declining to transfer.
      4   The employer is not entitled to transfer the rights from an employment relationship to a third party unless otherwise agreed upon, or if it arises from the circumstances.
2   For example, see the Decision of the Swiss Federal Supreme Court ('BGE') of 25 March 2003, BGE *129* III 335 at 350 et seq, Consideration ('C') 6.

R1.2   Identifying a relevant transfer

The Swiss Code of Obligations does not define the term 'business transfer' and there are very few court decisions dealing with the matter. Since the current text of CO, art 333 was aimed at adapting Swiss law to accord with the applicable EU law, the case law of the European Court of Justice ('ECJ') needs to be considered when interpreting the provision[1]. A *relevant transfer* takes place only where a business is passed on *to a third party* while the *identity* of that business is retained. The Swiss Federal Supreme Court has stated that there is *no need for a legal relationship between the transferor and the transferee*. The fact that the running of the business is continued or taken up by the transferee will suffice. The requirement of a *relevant transfer* is fulfilled, for example, if the owner of a restaurant facility terminates the contract concluded with the manager of the restaurant in order to enter into a new contract with another manager[2]. In this situation, the employment relationships pass from the first to the second restaurant manager.

Article 333 of the Swiss Code of Obligations thus covers different types of transactions. The decisive criterion for a *relevant transfer* is the change in the identity of the employer and not the change in the identity of an employed manager or the executive body of a legal entity. The fact, for example, that the business of an individual enterprise is put into a joint-stock company triggers CO, art 333, even if the former employer obtains all shares in this company. On the other hand, CO, art 333 does not apply in the case of a sale of all the shares of a joint-stock company that carries on a business, as, from a legal perspective, the company continues to be the employer.

A *business*, within the meaning of CO, art 333, is defined as a self-contained organisational unit designed to operate on a continuing basis. According to the Swiss Federal Supreme Court, CO, art 333 only applies on the transfer of a business if the organisational unit retains its essential identity (ie its purpose, organisation and individual character). This has to be assessed taking into consideration all the facts and circumstances characterising the relevant transaction. It is therefore crucial that the same, or at least similar, business activities are actually continued or taken up by the transferee, irrespective of the legal basis (lease, sale, donation, etc) on which the business is transferred. As already mentioned, a legal relationship between the transferor and the transferee is not required. The Swiss courts have not yet dealt with the question of whether CO, art 333 also applies to transfers involving non-profit organisations or public services. However, it should be mentioned that the recently enacted Swiss Merger Act[3] applies by analogy to mergers, changes of corporate form and transfers of assets and liabilities involving public bodies. Accordingly, CO, art 333, to which the Swiss Merger Act refers with regard to the transfer of employment relationships, would also be applicable to such transactions.

The question of whether CO, art 333 also applies to business transfers by virtue of universal succession (merger, succession, etc) has been a controversial one in Swiss legal doctrine. The majority of commentators feel that the scope of the provision is limited, such that it does not apply to corporate transactions such as mergers, where the acquirer is bound by individual, as well as collective, employment agreements by virtue of universal succession. However, the Swiss Merger Act, which came into force in July 2004, now declares that CO, art 333 is applicable with regard to mergers, spin-offs, and transfers of assets and liabilities[4].

As the wording of CO, art 333 does not mention insolvency, it is debatable whether the provision applies to business transfers which take place after the transferor has been adjudicated bankrupt. Some scholars are of the opinion that the provision applies equally to business transfers arising out of bankruptcy situations, while others hold the view that CO, art 333 is not applicable in such cases.

The Swiss Federal Supreme Court has recently decided that the joint and several liability of the transferee for employees' claims which arose prior to the transfer (as per para 3 of CO, art 333), does not apply to transfers out of bankrupt estates[5]. However, the court explicitly left open the question of whether the general rule of CO, art 333, para 1 (ie the transfer of the employment relationship) is applicable to such transfers in the first place.

1   BGE *127* V 187 C 4b.
2   BGE *123* III 468 C 3a.
3   Bundesgesetz über Fusion, Spaltung, Umwandlung und Vermögensübertragung (Fusions-gesetz, FusG) vom 3 Oktober 2003.
4   See art 27, para 1 (Merger); art 49, para 1 (Spin-off); and art 76, para 1 (Transfer of Assets and Liabilities) of the Swiss Merger Act.
5   BGE *129* III 335 et seq.

RI.3 Affected employees

The implications of business transfers with regard to employees are dealt with in CO, art 333, which forms part of the provisions on employment contracts (CO, art 319 et seq). The article does not explicitly define who is, and who is not, to be considered an *employee*. An employee within the meaning of CO, art 319 is someone who obliges himself, by means of a contract based on private law, to perform work in an employer's service for payment. The employment relationships of federal, cantonal or municipal government personnel, on the other hand, are subject to the public law of the respective entity.

Temporary workers have employment contracts with temporary employment companies and not with the clients they actually work for. Therefore, their employment relationships are only of concern with regard to CO, art 333 if the businesses of the temporary employment companies by which they are employed, are transferred.

With regard to cases where only part of a business is transferred, the Swiss Federal Supreme Court has not yet decided upon the question of whether the activities actually performed by the employees prior to the transfer have to be taken into consideration, or whether it is the employees' formal attachment to a particular department that is the crucial consideration.

RI.4 Effects of the transfer

The effects of a business transfer as per CO, art 333 are essentially threefold. Firstly, the employment relationships are automatically transferred to the transferee, with all rights and obligations, unless an employee objects to this (paras 1 and 2). Secondly, if a collective employment agreement applies to an employment relationship that is transferred, the acquiring party is bound by it for one year, unless it expires earlier or is terminated by notice (para 1*bis*). Thirdly, the previous employer and the acquiring party are jointly and severally liable for employees' claims that become due prior to the transfer, and those which become due until the date upon which the employment relationship could have validly been terminated, or the date upon which it is terminated by the employees declining to transfer (para 3). The latter provision is mandatory and agreements, provisions of standard employment contracts, and collective employment agreements deviating from its terms, are null and void.

The employment relationship is maintained upon transfer and continues to exist with all rights and obligations in place. The beginning of the employment relationship with the former employer remains decisive when determining the rights of the parties by reference to the duration of the contractual relationship (eg duty to pay the salary in the case of an employee's faultless prevention from working[1], notice periods[2], period in which termination is barred[3], etc).

Article 333 of the Swiss Code of Obligations does not expressly mention that the working conditions in place prior to the transfer need to be maintained. The fact that the employment relationship continues upon transfer implies, however, that the working conditions should remain unchanged. However, it should be mentioned that, under Swiss law, nothing prevents the acquiring party from terminating the employment contracts transferred, if the employees do not agree to their amendment (ie in general, Swiss law does not prevent employers from terminating employment relationships at will).

1   CO, art 324a.
2   CO, art 335b and 335c.
3   CO, art 336c and 336d.

Right to object

Generally, the transfer of the contractual relationship to the acquiring party is in the interest of the employee, as various rights (such as the right to vacation, severance pay, the right to receive salary from the employer in the event that the employee is faultlessly prevented from working, the right to notice, etc) depend on the duration of the employment relationship. If, however, the employee prefers to decline the transfer, he can do so within one month of the date he first learnt about the business transfer (CO, art 335b, para 1, by analogy). After this period, the employee is deemed to have tacitly waived his right to object.

Where the employee utilises his right to object to a transfer, the employment relationship is terminated upon expiry of the legal notice period. Until such date, both the acquiring party and the employee are bound to perform their contractual duties (CO, art 333, para 2). Unlike the employee, the employer does not have such a right to object, and can disengage himself only by terminating the employment contract with the employee. Exceptionally, as has been decided by a cantonal court, the new employer may also have the right to decline the transfer if the employee is a key member of staff and the personal relationship between employer and employee is vital (such as in the case of a professional coach of a football club). Also, in this case, the employment relationship would be terminated upon expiry of the statutory notice period (CO, art 333, para 2).

R1.5 Dismissal of employees

Although the reform of CO, art 333 in 1993 was aimed at bringing Swiss employment law in line with EU developments, the enactment of the provision did not enhance the protection for employees against unfair dismissal. The transfer of employment relationships as per CO, art 333, para 1 does not, in principle, prevent the transferor from terminating employment contracts prior to the business transfer or the transferee from dismissing employees after the transfer has taken place. However, if the former terminates an employment contract purely because of the business transfer (ie in order to circumvent the effects of CO, art 333), the notice is invalid[1]. Furthermore, special rules against unfair dismissal apply in respect of employees' representatives[2].

A particular feature of Swiss employment law is the fact that employment contracts for an indefinite period of time can – apart from certain dismissals which are always considered abusive (eg for reasons of personal characteristics such as race, sexual orientation, age, etc, or because of lawful union activities) – be terminated for any reason[3]. Both the employer and the employee can terminate the contract without having to establish that it was for a specific reason, such as economic, technical or organisational ones.

1   BGE *127* V 194 C 7; the decision leaves open the question of what the consequences of such a dismissal would be, ie whether the employment relationship would be upheld or whether the dismissal would merely be considered abusive, which would nonetheless dissolve the contract and lead to an indemnity payment to the employee.
2   CO, art 336, para 3 provides that the dismissal by the acquiring party of an employee who lost his mandate as an elected employee representative due to the business transfer is considered unfair if the dismissal notice is given during the period the mandate would have lasted if the employment relationship had not been transferred.
3   After the expiry of a probation period, an employment relationship may be terminated as per CO, art 335c during the first year of service with a notice period of one month, in the second, and up to and including the ninth year, with a notice period of two months, and thereafter with a notice period of three months.

R1.6 Variation of contract

Alterations to contractual terms and conditions require the mutual consent of the parties. In general, even minor alterations to contractual terms and conditions are implemented by consent. Where no consent is given, the party that intends changing the terms of the employment contract must terminate the existing contract in order to negotiate the modified terms of the new contract.

As both parties can, in principle, freely terminate the employment contract before or after the business transfer has taken place, the acquirer is not prevented from terminating employment relationships in order to negotiate new contracts on the basis of changed contractual terms[1]. However, such notice of termination pending a change of contract (*Änderungskündigung*) must be based on a practical reason[2]. A notice lacks such a reason, and is therefore considered abusive, if there are no operational or business reasons for the proposed change in salaries and working conditions[3]. To a certain extent, the harmonisation of the contractual terms and conditions of the combined business may lawfully be considered a practical reason.

1   See BGE *114* II 353.
2   BGE *123* III 250 et seq, C 3b.
3   BGE *123* III 251 C 3b.

R1.7 Duty to inform and consult

In order to enable employees to take a well-informed decision with regard to their right to object to a transfer (see CO, art 333, para 1), CO, art 333a, para 1[1] provides that employers have a duty to inform. Accordingly, if an employer transfers a business or a part thereof to a third party, the employees' representatives or, if there are none, the employees, shall be informed in good time prior to the transfer of the following:

- the reason for the transfer; and

- the legal, economic and social consequences of the transfer for the employees.

In addition, CO, art 333a, para 2 provides that employers have a duty to consult: if, as a result of the proposed transfer, measures affecting the employees are planned (eg dismissals or transfers of certain employees, wage cuts, etc), the employees' representatives (or, if there are none, the employees) must be consulted in good time prior to a decision being taken on these measures. It is the employer who proposes the respective measures who is under the obligation to consult (ie either the transferor or the transferee, as the case may be). The consultation process must include a right for the employees or their representatives to be heard. Accordingly, any decision about the planned measures is not admissible before the employees have had the chance to give their opinion on the matter. The consultation process must take place early enough to give the employer the opportunity to consider the proposals of the employees.

However, any proposals made by employees or their representatives do not in any way bind the employer. The latter's freedom to decide on how he wishes to proceed is therefore not restricted by the duty to consult.

If the employer fails to comply with his duties to inform and consult, the relevant business transfer, as well as the measures taken in this regard, remain effective, although he may be liable to pay damages for breach of contract, as per CO, art 97.

The newly enacted Swiss Merger Act contains provisions which refer to a duty to inform and consult in the case of business transfers[2]. Accordingly, with respect to mergers there is a duty on the merging companies to consult on intended measures which may affect the employees[3]. Moreover, the Act provides for specific sanctions for breach of this duty: in particular, employee representatives can seek a court injunction to prevent the entry of the respective transaction in the commercial register[4].

1   CO, art 333a (Consultation with the Employees' Representation) [unofficial informal translation]:
    1 If the employer transfers a business or a part thereof to a third party, the employees' representation or, if there is none, the employees, shall be informed in good time prior to the transfer of:
        a.the reason for the transfer;
        b.the legal, economic and social consequences of the transfer for the employees.
    2 If, as a result of the transfer, measures affecting the employees are planned, the employees' representation or, if there is none, the employees, shall be consulted in good time prior to a decision being taken on these measures.
2   See art 28, para 1 (Merger); art 50 (Spin-Off); and art 77, para 1 (Transfer of Assets and Liabilities) of the Swiss Merger Act.

3   Article 28 of the Swiss Merger Act, which refers to CO, art 333a.
4   See Swiss Merger Act, art 28, para 3; art 50; and art 77, para 2.

R1.8 Proposed developments

A parliamentary initiative aims to extend the protection of CO, art 333 in favour of current employees. The initiative aims to make the provision equally applicable to transactions analogous to business transfers, such as mergers or the creation of rescue companies under composition proceedings to avoid compulsory liquidation.

As mentioned above, the Swiss Merger Act, which came into force in July 2004, declares CO, art 333 to be applicable with regard to mergers, spin-offs, and transfers of assets and liabilities. The controversy surrounding the applicability of CO, art 333 to such transactions has thereby been resolved.

R2   Redundancy

R2.1 Background

In Switzerland, redundancy law is distinct from the application of CO, art 333. In principle, the termination of an employment relationship for reasons unrelated to the individual characteristics of the employee (eg due to the actual or intended closure of the business in relation to which the employee is employed) is not, as such, considered unfair or abusive. However, Swiss law provides for special rules regarding collective redundancies.

Under CO, art 335d, collective dismissals are defined as notices of termination given by an employer within 30 days, for reasons unrelated to the individual characteristics of the employees and which affect:

–   at least 10 employees in enterprises usually employing more than 20 and less than 100 persons;

–   at least 10 per cent of all employees in enterprises usually employing more than 100 and less than 300 persons; or

–   at least 30 employees in enterprises usually employing at least 300 persons.

The provisions governing collective dismissals are also applicable to employment relationships for a fixed period of time, if they are terminated before the expiry of the agreed period[1]. They further apply to apprentices as well as volunteers.

1   CO, art 335e, para 1.

R2.2 Redundancy payments

There is no system of statutory redundancy payments for employees who have been dismissed by reason of redundancy in Switzerland. A payment is due only where the termination notice was abusive (eg because of failure to inform or consult as per CO, art 336, para 2c). In the latter case, the payment may not exceed the sum of two months' pay (CO, art 336a, para 3).

R2.3 Alternative agreements

Although the duty to inform and consult employees or their representatives is not mentioned in the list of mandatory provisions in CO, arts 361 and 362, it is a duty that can only be modified to the advantage of employees. Conceivably, an individual or collective employment agreement could therefore contain provisions which are more favourable to employees than are required by law, such as a contractual penalty for failure to consult, or the assurance of financial benefits in the event of redundancy.

R2.4 The duty to inform and consult prior to redundancy

An employer planning collective dismissals must consult with the employees' representatives or, if there are none, with the employees[1]. In doing so, he must give them the opportunity to make suggestions as to how to avoid the proposed dismissals or to limit the number of dismissals needed and to alleviate their consequences[2].

1   CO, art 335f, para 1.
2   CO, art 335f, para 2.

Appropriate representatives

In the context of the employer's duty to inform and consult, the appropriate representatives in enterprises with at least 50 employees, as per the Federal Act on the Information and Consultation of Employees in Enterprises[1], are (optional) employee representatives. Where no such representation exists, each employee is individually entitled to be informed and consulted by his employer.

1   Bundesgesetz über die Information und Mitsprache der Arbeitnehmerinnen und Arbeitnehmer in den Betrieben (Mitwirkungsgesetz) vom 17 Dezember 1993 (SR 822.14).

Time period

The Swiss Code of Obligations does not provide for a specific time period in relation to the duty to inform and consult. According to CO, art 335f, para 1, the employer must initiate consultation as soon as he 'plans' collective dismissals[1]. In order for the required consultation to fulfil its purpose, it must in any case take place before the decision to dismiss the employees has been made[2]. In the context of mergers, the consultation must take place before the merger agreement has been accepted by the relevant body of the respective company[3].

The employer may set a deadline for a response from the employees/ employee representatives, combined with the warning that the right to be consulted will be waived if they fail to respond within the deadline. The employees must, however, have enough time in order to process the information they are given by the employer, as well as to formulate responses and convey them to him. The appropriateness of the deadline set by an employer depends on the circumstances of the individual case, in particular the complexity of the issues raised and the urgency of the measures planned[4]. An employer can only ever fix a deadline after he has provided sufficient information.

1   BGE *123* III 180 C 4a.
2   BGE *123* III 180 C 4a.
3   Article 28, para 2 of the Swiss Merger Act.
4   BGE *123* III 181 et seq, C 4b and c; in the present case 24 hours were considered as absolutely insufficient; while the Swiss Federal Supreme Court left open the question what period would have been appropriate, it stated that four to six weeks (as asserted by the claimant) were considerably too long.

Information required

The employer is under an obligation to provide all pertinent information to the employees' representatives. In any case, he must provide information to them in writing on the following issues[1]:

– the reasons for the proposed collective dismissals;

– the number of employees it is proposed will be dismissed;

– the number of persons usually employed; and

– the time period within which it is proposed the notifications of the dismissals will be given.

1   CO, art 335f, para 3.

Meaningful consultation

The purpose of the consultation process is to enable employees to exert an influence on the decisions of their employers. Employees should therefore have the opportunity to convey their suggestions or alternative solutions to their employer, before he takes a final decision on proposed collective dismissals. According to one (controversial) view in Swiss legal doctrine, the employer must give reasons if he rejects the propositions put forward by employees.

The right of employees to be consulted is limited to the measures planned by their employer. The employer is not, however, bound by any suggestions or alternative solutions proposed by the employees.

Failure to comply

The right of employees to information and consultation can be enforced by way of execution, based on cantonal procedural law.

If notices of termination are given in connection with a collective dismissal, without prior consultation with employees, the dismissals are considered abusive[1]. In such a situation, the employer is liable to make a payment, the amount of which may not exceed two months' gross pay for the employee[2]; this payment is designed to be punitive.

1   CO, art 336, para 2c.
2   CO, art 336a, para 3.

The employer's defence

There is no general defence in Swiss law under which an employer can be excused for failing to comply with his duty to consult, even if there are special circumstances which render it impractical for him to do so. However, when considering the time period granted by the employer for employees or employees' representatives to respond to his proposals as part of the consultation process, the courts have taken the urgency of the planned collective dismissals into account.

However, CO, art 335e, para 2 states that the provisions governing collective dismissals do not apply to the termination of business operations as a result of a court order, as, in such a case, the continuation of employment relationships is beyond the control of the employer. This rule applies, in particular, in the event that the employer is declared bankrupt.

Notifying redundancies to the Cantonal Labour Office

The Cantonal Labour Office must be sent copies of the information provided by the employer to his employees or employee representatives[1]. The Labour Office is further involved in the procedure relating to collective redundancies: it must be notified of the results of the consultation process and will seek solutions to the problems arising in relation to the planned collective dismissals[2].

If an employer has given notices of termination to employees as part of a collective dismissal, the employment relationships will end 30 days after notification of the same to the Cantonal Labour Office, unless the terminations become effective at a later time in accordance with contractual or legal provisions[3].

1   CO, art 335f, para 4.
2   See CO, art 335g.
3   See CO, art 335g, para 4.

R2.5 Offer of alternative work

The concept of an 'offer of alternative work' is unknown in Swiss law. However, the parties are free to agree on a new contract in order to continue the employment relationship after notice of termination has been given by the employer.

R2.6 Unfair redundancy

A dismissal is considered abusive by statute if notice of termination was given in connection with collective dismissals, without prior consultation with the employees or their representatives[1]. Nevertheless, such a termination is valid. However, the employer would be liable to make a payment, the amount of which may not exceed two months' gross pay for the employee[2].

The fact that a dismissal was for reason of redundancy as such, however, is not considered abusive. Even if the employment relationship is terminated for a reason that is deemed abusive by statute (eg because the employee exercises a constitutional right or because the employee belongs to an employees' association), the contract is terminated, with the employer liable to make a payment.

1   CO, art 336, para 2c.
2   CO, art 336a, para 3.

R3   Case studies

R3.1   Case study 1
(Acquisition of a 'business' situated in an EU state; asset deal; no relocation)

Slumber Ltd, a hotel management company incorporated in the UK and based in Manchester, UK, has been in financial difficulties for some time. Slumber operates nine exclusive hotels in the main British cities (London, Manchester, Birmingham, Leeds, Glasgow, Edinburgh, Liverpool, Cardiff and Bristol) under the 'Slumber' brand. Slumber is 100 per cent owned by UK hotel chain, Ezeroom plc, also incorporated in the UK. Each hotel has about 50 staff: five in management, 20 in the restaurant and 25 in house service. Slumber does not own the hotels itself; instead it has a seven-year management agreement with Hotel Investment plc ('HIP'), the owner of the hotels, which is incorporated and based in London, UK. Under this contract Slumber runs the fully equipped hotels on its own risk and has to pay a fixed fee to HIP.

In its central management centre in Manchester, Slumber has another 30 staff. These are 10 managers (including Marketing, Managing, Finance, Sales and Operations Directors) and 20 secretaries, clerks and administrators.

A number of staff are members of the trade union, The Association of Hotel Workers (AHW), which has been formally recognised by Slumber as having bargaining rights for hourly paid hotel staff. This is a particularly active union and there is a collective agreement in force. Due to increasing staff costs and the declining demand for expensive hotel accommodation, Slumber is making bigger and bigger operating losses. Slumber is obliged to cut jobs in all the hotels and thus dismisses 40 members of staff as redundant. As a consequence, the service worsens and customer complaints become more frequent. When the board of HIP realises how serious the situation has become, it starts to look for a new operator of its hotels.

Some weeks later, while Slumber is still operating, a Swiss company is found which seems able to manage the hotels in a much more profitable way for HIP than Slumber. The company, which is called Dormir, is based in Berne, but has already gathered some experience of running hotels in the UK. The board of HIP enters into discussions with Dormir for it to replace Slumber as manager of the hotels.

1. Acquisition of the hotels

It is anticipated that Dormir will want to manage all nine of the hotels under a single management agreement with HIP.

(a) **Would this be a business transfer (defined as a transfer within the meaning of TUPE) under UK law?**

(ONLY TO BE ANSWERED BY UK CONTRIBUTOR)

(b) **Even though Slumber will not transfer any of its activities to Switzerland, would the acquisition of the hotels in this way constitute a business transfer under Swiss law?**

The implications of business transfers with regard to employment relationships under Swiss law are dealt with in art 333 of the Swiss Code of Obligations ('CO'). This provision does not define the term *business transfer* and there is little case law on this matter. In particular, there is no case law in Switzerland on cross-border business transfers.

As the management of the hotels would be transferred to Dormir (ie a legal entity different from Slumber Ltd), an important precondition of CO, art 333 would be fulfilled, as a *relevant transfer* can only take place where a business is passed on to a third party. According to Swiss case law and legal doctrine, a *relevant transfer* occurs if the identity of a business, in terms of purpose, organisation and individual character, is maintained. Accordingly, the crucial question is whether the business retains its identity following the transfer. To assess this, all the facts and circumstances characterising the transaction must be considered. It is crucial that the same, or at least similar, business activities are continued or taken up by the transferee following the transfer, irrespective of the legal basis (eg by lease or sale) on which the transferee can dispose of the means of production. According to the Swiss Federal Supreme Court, there is no need for a legal relationship between the transferor and the transferee.

Based on these principles and the relevant case law, the acquisition of the hotels by Dormir would probably constitute a business transfer under Swiss law. However, it must be noted that the relevant Swiss law would only apply to the transfer if the employment contracts were governed by Swiss law. This is rather unlikely in the circumstances, and conceivably mandatory UK law would be applicable.

(c) **Would it make any difference to whether this constituted a** business transfer, under TUPE, if Dormir only wanted to manage the six English hotels (excluding the hotels in Glasgow, Edinburgh and Cardiff)?

(ONLY TO BE ANSWERED BY UK CONTRIBUTOR)

(d) Would it make any difference to your answer to (b) above if Dormir only wanted to manage six hotels (for example only the English hotels, excluding those in Scotland and Wales, ie the hotels in Glasgow, Edinburgh and Cardiff)?

CO, art 333, para 1 explicitly states that the transfer of a part of a business is sufficient to constitute a *relevant transfer*. There would not therefore be any difference to the answer to (b) above in these circumstances.

2. Employees who work only partly in the business

What is the position of those staff that work partly in Slumber and partly in Ezeroom? For example, the human resources director of Slumber is also the human resources director of Ezeroom and he has his employment agreement with Ezeroom. He spends approximately 40 per cent of his time dealing with Slumber's personnel matters and the remainder of his time on the human resources affairs of Ezeroom.

(a) If this is a TUPE transfer, can he be said to have transferred under TUPE in the UK?

(UK CONTRIBUTOR TO ANSWER)

(b) What is the law on employees who work only partly in the undertaking to be transferred in Switzerland?

The employee must organisationally be part of the respective business, in order for his employment contract to be transferred. If only a part of a business is transferred, CO, art 333 applies to all employees who are exclusively, or at least mainly, active in that part of the business.

If an employee works only partly in the undertaking which is to be transferred, but does not have an employment contract with this entity, his employment relationship would not be affected by the transfer of the undertaking, as his employment relationship would continue to be with his employer.

3. Staff who work outside the UK in a non-EU country

It transpires that some Slumber central management staff are actually working and based in Switzerland. Two are Swiss nationals.

(a) Would these staff transfer to Dormir under TUPE if there was a TUPE transfer?

(UK CONTRIBUTOR TO ANSWER THIS. PLEASE COMMENT ON UK RESPONSE)

Answer

In theory yes, although this would depend on a number of factors, including their contracts of employment.

Legal reasoning

TUPE applies to undertakings or parts of undertakings situated in the UK immediately prior to transfer. These employees work for, and are employed by, Slumber, the undertaking to be transferred, but they are simply based in Switzerland. The undertaking of Slumber is situated in the UK immediately before the transfer (even if some staff work outside the UK); therefore members of Slumber central management who are working in Switzerland will technically transfer. The important point is that TUPE, in principle, applies to undertakings or a part of an undertaking situated in the UK immediately before the transfer. The fact that some of the employees are not actually located in the UK is irrelevant.

*Difficulties may arise in practice and, for example, the employees may no longer be required to continue working in the same place. If their employment is terminated this is likely to be in connection with the transfer and potentially unfair. Whether or not they have claims in the UK or indeed in Switzerland will depend on conflicts of laws issues: see Chapter **D**.*

Comment: Under Swiss law, the transaction would only affect the employment relationships if they were governed by Swiss law. It is thus mainly an issue of conflicts of laws. As the central management staff habitually carry out their work in Switzerland, their employment agreements would be governed by Swiss law, unless the parties had declared English law to be applicable (art 121 of the Swiss Private International Law Act). The contracts would thus transfer to Dormir under CO, art 333.

(b) **Would the position be different if there was a branch office of Ezeroom in Switzerland, which directly employed these staff?**

(UK TO ANSWER, BUT PLEASE COMMENT)

Answer

The position may be the same.

Legal reasoning

TUPE is likely to apply if the branch office qualifies as an associated employer and the employees are 'assigned' (Case 186/83: Botzen v Rotterdamsche Droogdok Maatschappij BV [1985] ECR 519, ECJ) to Slumber (ie they carry out all their functions for Slumber, who is their de facto employer). In such a case, the courts are likely to pierce the corporate veil and treat Slumber as the employer for those purposes.

Comment: As the branch office would be part of Ezeroom, the company would still be the employer. Whether the employment relationships would be transferred under Swiss law would depend on whether they are governed by Swiss employment law (see comment to question 3(a) above).

4. Dismissal of employee

One of the Slumber staff, Mr X, was dismissed by Slumber after HIP had given notice to terminate the contract with Slumber and whilst negotiations were ongoing with Dormir. Mr X is owed two months' back pay and unpaid holiday.

Against whom can Mr X bring a claim, and where, if Mr X is a UK national based in Switzerland?

The transfer of employment relationships as per CO, art 333, para 1 does not, in principle, prevent the transferor from terminating employment contracts prior to the business transfer. However, if he terminates the employment contracts purely in connection with the business transfer (ie in order to circumvent CO, art 333), any notice issued in this regard would be invalid. However, the Swiss Federal Supreme Court has left open the question of what the consequences of such a dismissal would be (BGE *127* V 194 C 7).

Mr X could certainly bring a claim against Slumber. Possibly, he may also be able to bring a claim against Dormir, if the dismissal was regarded as a means to circumvent the effects of CO, art 333 (under the principle of the joint and several liability of the transferee as per CO, art 333, para 3).

Claims against Slumber could be made in the UK, based on art 2 and art 5(1) of the Lugano Convention. Claims against Swiss-based Dormir could possibly be made in Switzerland (based on art 2 of the Lugano Convention) or in the UK (under art 5(1) of the Lugano Convention).

5. Transfer of employee outside the UK

Mr Y (the marketing director) has been vital to the success of Slumber and has been responsible for many successful ideas. Dormir would like to retain his services and move him to Dormir's headquarters in Switzerland. Mr Y has no wish to live in Switzerland.

(a)   How does TUPE impact on Mr Y: is he obliged to transfer against his will?

(UK ONLY TO ANSWER)

(b)   What is the law on objection to a transfer in Switzerland?

Employees have the right to decline to transfer to a new employer on a business transfer. To do so, they must indicate that they object within one month of the date they first learn about the business transfer. After this period, they are deemed to have tacitly waived their right to object.

If an employee exercises his right to object, the employment relationship is terminated upon expiry of the legal notice period. Until such date, both the transferee and the employee are bound to perform their contractual duties (CO, art 333, para 2). Unlike the employee, the transferee does not have such right to object, and can disengage himself only by terminating the employment contract.

(c) **Can Mr Y claim constructive dismissal on the basis that he would be expected to work and be based in Switzerland and this is nowhere near his home?**

(UK TO ANSWER, BUT PLEASE COMMENT)

Answer

Possibly – if being expected to work and be based abroad amounts to a substantial change in working conditions and is to the employee's detriment.

Legal reasoning

Regulation 5(5) provides that an employee has the right 'to terminate his contract of employment without notice if a substantial change is made in his working conditions to his detriment'. It is important therefore that the change is substantial and to the employee's detriment. Such a claim is likely to lie against the transferee (Dormir) and only in rare circumstances such as where the transferor (Slumber) has not been open with the employee about the change in working conditions is a claim likely to succeed again the transferor (Slumber). Case law is of importance here.

In Merckx and Neuhuys v Ford Motors Co Belgium SA [1996] IRLR 467, Anfo Motors SA transferred its Ford dealership to an independent dealer. There was no transfer of assets and only 14 out of Anfo's 60 employees were taken on. The ECJ identified a community right to claim constructive dismissal where there was a 'substantial change in working conditions to the detriment of the employee' because of the transfer.

In Rossiter v Pendragon [2002] IRLR 483, Mr Rossiter argued that he had suffered a detriment through changes in the calculation of commission, that his holiday pay was no longer based on commission and he was made to assume lesser duties. The Court of Appeal held that in order to claim constructive dismissal there would have to be a repudiatory breach of contract, which there was not in this case.

If there is no mobility clause in a contract of employment, relocation may not be lawful. Even if there is a mobility clause in the contract, there can be difficulties enforcing it, depending on the facts.

If an employer ceases to carry on business at a particular place and recommences business elsewhere, an employee who is dismissed will normally be redundant. If the employer requires an employee to transfer to the new business location and there is no mobility clause in the employment contract which expressly provides for this, then the transfer may amount to a repudiatory breach of contract, which may entitle the employee to resign and claim constructive dismissal.

In Bass Leisure Ltd v Thomas [1994] IRLR 104, the Employment Appeal Tribunal considered mobility clauses. It held that a factual, rather than contractual, approach concerning mobility clauses has been taken to geographical mobility for redundancy purposes.

A similar approach in High Table Ltd v Horst [1997] IRLR 513 was adopted by the Court of Appeal, which agreed with the decision in Bass Leisure Ltd, stating that the place where the employee was employed was to be established by factual enquiry.

In the absence of an express mobility clause in the contract of employment, an employee who is required to relocate may be entitled to claim a redundancy payment (even if the new place of work is relatively near). However, an offer of employment at a different location may amount to an offer of suitable alternative employment, and if the employee unreasonably refuses this, then in those circumstances he may lose the right to claim a redundancy payment.

As Mr Y has no mobility clause in his contract, he may therefore be able to claim constructive dismissal.

Comment: It may be assumed that the Slumber and Mr Y had implicitly agreed on the employee's place of work. If so, Dormir would not be permitted to give instructions as per CO, art 321d, unless the employee's performance of work at another place was reasonably required because of an urgent operational need. Due in part to the considerable distance between the UK and Switzerland, this requirement would probably not be fulfilled in the present case.

If the parties cannot agree on a new place of work for the employee, the employer is bound by the terms of the employment contract. However, the employer could give a notice of termination pending a change of contract (*Änderungskündigung*).

6. Dormir's business strategy

What is the best way of structuring the transfer of the hotels to Dormir from Switzerland's perspective? Would you advise Dormir to set up a subsidiary company registered in the UK specifically to purchase Slumber and thereby avoid any cross-border element?

A number of issues would need to be considered in order to reach a decision on this matter. As the relevant employment contracts would most probably not be governed by Swiss employment law, the decision would not primarily be made based on the rules of Swiss law regarding business transfers.

R3.2 Case study 2
(Production moves from a non-EU country to an EU country; physical move)

Alpha Incorporated is a multinational car tyre manufacturing and distribution business based in Europe. Alpha's headquarters are in France. Alpha has tyre plants in Switzerland, Germany and France. Each of the tyre plants is a wholly owned and independently operated subsidiary of Alpha. Alpha has a European Works Council.

The subsidiary in Switzerland is Beta. Beta employs about 250 employees, mostly in the direct production of tyres. The employees are on standard basic contracts which do not contain any mobility clauses. Due to increased competition from cheaper producers in the Far East, Alpha is having to reduce its own production costs. Beta has the highest production costs of all Alpha's European operations. Alpha has decided to end the production of tyres in Switzerland and move production to Gamma, another subsidiary not too far away but across the national border in Germany, which has more modern plant and equipment. Beta will continue to exist, but as a sales and marketing organisation only, with about 30 staff.

Most of Beta's tyre-making plant and machinery is transferred to Gamma, but Gamma will only need an extra 125 staff to increase its output to the required level to supply Beta's market. Those employees from Beta who are required to work for Gamma will be expected to accept the terms and conditions and working practices of the Gamma plant, which are very different from those in operation at the Beta plant. For example, Gamma pays its employees considerably lower hourly wages and they work longer hours than those at Beta. Gamma does not want to pay more to the employees transferred to it from Beta than it does for its current employees. Gamma operates a different type of pension scheme.

1. Does this transaction constitute a 'business transfer'?

(a) **As Beta's tyre-making plant and machinery have transferred to Gamma, will this constitute a business transfer under Swiss law?**

The implications of a business transfer with regard to employment relationships are dealt with in art 333 of the Swiss Code of Obligations ('CO'). The provision does not define the term *business transfer*, and there is little case law on this matter. In particular, there is no case law on cross-border business transfers.

As the plant and machinery have transferred to Gamma (ie a legal entity different from Beta), an important precondition of CO, art 333 has been fulfilled, as a *relevant transfer* can only take place where the business is passed on to a third party. According to Swiss case law and legal doctrine, there is a *relevant transfer* if the identity of the business with regard to organisation, purpose and character is maintained after the transfer. Accordingly, the crucial question is whether the business has retained its identity. Whilst the transfer of the plant and machinery indicates that a transfer has taken place, the situation as a whole needs to be considered to assess whether the identity of the business has been maintained. Due in part to the fact that there is little Swiss case law in this area, a Swiss judge having to decide this matter would also need to consider the relevant case law of the European Court of Justice.

(b)   Does it make any difference to whether this is a business transfer if employees of Beta transfer across to Gamma?

The transfer of employees is another important element when assessing the question of whether there has been a business transfer within the meaning of CO, art 333, para 1.

(c)   Can the transfer of plant and machinery coupled with the transfer of half the employees (125) constitute a business transfer under Swiss legislation if the other 125 employees are dismissed prior to the transfer?

The transfer of plant and machinery together with the transfer of a considerable part of the workforce can constitute a business transfer within the meaning of CO, art 333, para 1.

(d)   Does the fact that the business will transfer to a different country make any difference to whether this is a business transfer?

The fact that the transfer is across a national border does not, of itself, make a difference to the determination of whether there has been a business transfer.

(e)   Is Swiss business transfer law concerned with the actual distance moved (irrespective of whether this means a change of country)?

There is no case law in Switzerland regarding the implications of the actual distance moved, as regards a transfer. Conceivably, it may have an effect on the question of whether the identity of the business has been retained following transfer.

2. Relocation, but no business transfer

(a)   Assuming the move does NOT constitute a business transfer (because the business of Beta does not adequately retain its identity) but instead is deemed to be a straightforward relocation, are any of Beta's employees obliged or entitled to transfer?

If the move does not constitute a business transfer within the meaning of CO, art 333, para 1, the relevant employment relationships are not transferred. Accordingly, Beta's employees are neither entitled nor obliged to transfer to Gamma.

(b)   If employees do nevertheless relocate, what will happen to their

employment contracts? Will these continue, or will Gamma be entitled to provide new contracts?

The employment relationships will transfer in this situation provided all three parties agree. Such tripartite agreements may take place tacitly (ie there may be an assignment from Beta to Gamma and deemed consent by the employees if they continue to work without objection after the business has been relocated). However, the transfer of the existing employment contracts will not take place if Gamma provides new agreements for the employees, as it is entitled to do.

(c) **What will be the law applicable to the contracts of the employees who relocate?**

In Switzerland, the conflicts of laws rules are contained in the Swiss Private International Law Act ('SPILA'). According to SPILA, art 121, para 1, employment contracts are governed by the law of the state in which the employee habitually carries out his work. Accordingly, from a Swiss conflicts of laws perspective, German law will apply to the employment contracts of the employees who transfer. As per SPILA art 121, para 3, the parties may theoretically agree that Swiss law be applicable to the employment contracts, provided the respective employees continue to be habitually resident in Switzerland. However, a German court would apply the German conflicts of laws rules, which might lead to a different result.

3. Dismissals

(a) **Assuming the move does constitute a business transfer:**

(i) **are any dismissals in connection with the transfer lawful?**

Swiss business transfer law (ie CO, art 333 et seq) does not enhance employees' protection against dismissal. It does not, in principle, prevent the transferor from terminating employment relationships prior to a business transfer, nor the transferee from dismissing employees after a business transfer.

However, if the transferor terminates an employment contract purely in connection with a business transfer and in the interests of the acquirer, the termination notice is invalid according to the Swiss Federal Supreme Court[1]. However, the court left open the question as to what the consequences of such a dismissal would be.

A particular feature of Swiss labour law is the fact that employment contracts can, in principle, be terminated for any reason. Accordingly, the above-mentioned limitation must be interpreted narrowly. Therefore, the dismissal of half of Beta's workforce would only be inadmissible if the dismissals were exclusively because of the transfer, in order to avoid the consequences of CO, art 333, para 1 (ie the transfer of the employment relationships). Conceivably, in the light of the very liberal approach of Swiss labour law with respect to termination, the dismissals might be valid to the extent that there are specific (eg economic) reasons for them. It should be mentioned that, due to the number of dismissals involved, the provisions regarding collective dismissals (CO, art 335d et seq) would have to be complied with.

Finally, CO, art 336, para 3 provides that the dismissal by an acquiring party of an employee who, due to the business transfer, lost his mandate as an elected employee representative, is considered unfair if the termination notice is given during the period the mandate would have lasted if the employment relationship had not been transferred. Such dismissal would still be effective, but Gamma would become liable to make a payment.

(ii) **what are the rights and remedies (including applicable law and appropriate jurisdiction) of any employees dismissed:**

a. **before the transfer?**

The Swiss Federal Supreme Court left open the question of what the consequences of such an inadmissible dismissal would be. In any case, the previous employer and the acquiring party would be jointly and severally liable for the claims of employees which became due before the transfer and which become due during a certain period following the transfer (CO, art 333, para 3).

Under the Swiss Act on Jurisdiction, the courts in Beta's domicile and, if different, the courts of the place where the employee habitually carries out his work, would have jurisdiction to decide matters in this regard. According to SPILA, art 121, para 1, Swiss law would be applicable, unless the parties had agreed that a different law should apply.

A claim against Gamma could be brought in Germany in accordance with art 2 of the Lugano Convention or, alternatively, at the place where the employee habitually carries out his work, as per art 5(1) of the Lugano Convention. A German court would apply the relevant law in accordance with German conflicts of laws rules.

b. **after the transfer?**

To the extent Swiss law applies in this situation, Gamma would not be prevented from dismissing the employees, provided it complies with the provision on collective dismissals (CO, art 335d et seq).

(b) **Would these rights and remedies change if this was not a business transfer?**

If this was not a business transfer, CO, art 333 would not apply and there could be no limitation regarding dismissals in circumvention of the provision. The dismissals would therefore certainly be permitted under Swiss law. However, the requirements relating to collective dismissals (CO, art 335d et seq) would still have to be met.

1   BGE *127* V 194 C 7.

4. European Works Council and other employees' representatives

(a)   Will Alpha be required to inform and consult the European Works Council about the transfer or any redundancies?

There is no obligation under Swiss law to inform or consult a European Works Council.

(b)   Are any other employee representatives required to be involved in the transfer or any redundancies (ie at national or local level)?

The employees' representatives or, if there are none, the employees of Beta would have to be informed and consulted prior to the transfer (CO, art 333a). They would also have to be involved in the redundancies as per CO, art 335f.

5. Collective agreements

What is the effect of the business transfer on any collective agreements affecting Beta's employees?

The ambit of collective agreements is generally subject to the principle of territoriality. Accordingly, they are applicable within the territory for which the parties to the collective agreement are responsible according to their respective articles of association. As the field of activity of the trade unions has in general been limited to Swiss territory, the effects of collective agreements are limited to Switzerland. Therefore, Gamma is not bound by the terms of the collective employment agreement.

6. Change of terms and conditions

(a)   If this is a business transfer, how can Gamma lawfully harmonise employment contracts and change the terms and conditions of the employees currently on the more generous Beta contracts of employment?

As far as Swiss law is concerned, Gamma would be able to harmonise the contracts by means of a notice of termination pending a change of contract ('Änderungskündigung'). It would be able to negotiate new terms in this way, provided there are practical reasons for doing so and the notice is not abusive. As there would be obvious business reasons for Gamma changing the contractual terms, it could lawfully harmonise the employment contracts under Swiss law. There may, however, be mandatory rules under German law which have to be complied with, in any case.

(b)   If this is a business transfer, can Gamma reduce the wages of the former Beta employees?

The above-mentioned explanation (see **6(a)**) would apply equally to changes in the wages of the former Beta employees.

(c)   If this is a business transfer, what will happen to the former Beta employees as regards their private pension arrangements?

The employees would be entitled to the amount accrued on the date that their contracts are terminated; it would be transferred to a blocked account of their choice. If they decided to emigrate to Germany, they would be entitled to have the accrued sum paid out to them.

(d)   Is it easier to change terms and conditions of employment if the changes are made six months after the transfer?

This does not appear to make any difference.

R3.3 Case study 3
(Outsourcing of an ancillary activity to another non-EU country)

A large multinational (SwissCo) based in Switzerland has decided to out-source its entire internal IT function to a third party provider in Romania, as the costs of hiring competent IT personnel in Romania are far lower than in Switzerland, largely because wages are so much lower. At present 200 employees are employed by SwissCo in its IT function in Switzerland. It is anticipated that exactly the same IT function will be required in Romania with approximately the same number of people required to run it. There will be no difference in the service or approach for those requiring IT assistance and even the internal telephone number will be automatically diverted. The Romanian third party provider has no assets or presence in Switzerland.

1. Business transfer

Will this be a business transfer within the scope of Swiss business transfer legislation?

As SwissCo will be transferring only an *activity* to the third party provider, the latter will merely be a *functional successor*, who has to perform a specific task. Accordingly, the outsourcing of the IT function would not be considered a business transfer under Swiss law, unless substantial means of production and employees are also transferred to Romania.

2. Effect on employees

(a)   What will happen to the employees currently employed in the IT function at SwissCo? Will they transfer across?

As the transfer would not constitute a business transfer within the meaning of CO, art 333, para 1, the employment relationships of SwissCo's employees in the IT function would not transfer to the third party provider.

(b)   If the employees do transfer, what will the applicable law be for their employment contracts with the third party provider? Where can they make any claims?

As far as Swiss law is concerned, the courts in SwissCo's domicile would have jurisdiction with regard to claims against the company. According to SPILA, art 121, para 1, Swiss law would be applicable as long as the employees continued to work in Switzerland. Thereafter, Romanian law would apply. Claims against the third party provider would have to be made in Romania under the conflicts of laws rules applicable there.

3. Data protection

Will there be special data protection issues on the transfer of knowledge and information outside Switzerland to Romania?

Special rules apply with regard to cross-border data flows. In particular, two requirements of Swiss data protection law need to be complied with:

1)   According to art 6, para 1 of the Swiss Data Protection Act ('SDPA'), no personal data may be transferred abroad if the personal privacy of the persons affected could be seriously endangered, and this is particularly so in cases where there would be a failure to provide protection equivalent to that provided under Swiss law.

SwissCo will therefore have to make sure that any personal data will be protected in Romania to a level comparable with that in Switzerland. If Romanian data protection laws do not meet Swiss standards, the employees could possibly enforce their rights in this regard on a contractual basis. If this is not possible either, the employees concerned may be asked to waive their rights under data protection legislation.

2)   According to SDPA, art 6, para 2, SwissCo would have to notify the Federal Data Protection Commissioner before it transmitted data to Romania in cases where: (i) there is no legal obligation to disclose the data; and (ii) the persons affected would have no knowledge of the transmission. There are, however, various exceptions to this obligation (eg where the persons concerned have been notified beforehand).

4. Transfer to India

Please comment on any differences there would be to your answers if the function was transferred to India rather than Romania.

There do not appear to be significant legal differences.

R4 Additional information

R4.1   Key websites

State Secretariat for Economic Affairs (general information on labour in Switzerland):
http://www.seco.admin.ch/themen/arbeit/index.html?lang=de

Office for Economic Affairs and Labour of the Canton of Zurich (information on collective redundancies):
http://www.awa.zh.ch/personalverantwortliche/rav/massenentlassung.asp

Information on the Swiss Merger Act:
http://www.fusg.ch

R4.2   Key books and articles

Manfred Rehbinder and Wolfgang Portmann 'CO 333 et seq' in Honsell, Vogt and Wiegand (eds) *Obligationenrecht I, Basler Kommentar zum Schweizerischen Privatrecht* (3rd edn, 2003) Basel/Geneva/Munich

Urs Wickihalder 'Arbeitsrechtliche Aspekte des Outsourcing' in Weber, Berger and Auf der Maur *IT-Outsourcing* (Zurich 2003), pp 153–91

S United Kingdom

Susan Mayne

S1 Business transfers

S1.1 Introduction

Since 1993, there has been a significant increase in the number of mergers and acquisitions throughout Europe[1]. In 1998, 7,600 Europe-based companies were involved in mergers and acquisitions ('M&As') and cross-border mergers as a percentage of M&As involving Europe-based companies as a whole have steadily increased since 1990, reaching 49.9 per cent in 1998. According to the United Nations Conference on Trade and Development (UNCTAD)[2], the value of cross-border mergers in Europe increased in 1999 by 83 per cent and acquisition-related sales and purchases increased by 75 per cent, reaching totals of US$345 billion and US$498 billion respectively. The EU accounted for almost half of all global cross-border M&A-related sales, and 70 per cent of all purchases. EU companies were involved in all but one of 1999's 10 largest cross-border M&As. The UK accounts for 25 per cent of all EU cross-border M&A transactions[3].

Despite these impressive statistics showing lively activity in cross-border M&As, there are numerous difficult issues involving national laws applying the EC Acquired Rights Directive 77/187/EEC (the 'ARD') in a cross-border context.

1   European Commission 'Mergers and Acquisitions' in *European Economy*, supplement A, no 21, February 1999.
2   UNCTAD 'World Investment Report 2000: Cross-Border Mergers and Acquisitions and Development', October 2000.
3   See European Industrial Relations Observatory (EIRO) at http://www.eiro.eurofound. eu.int/.

S1.2 Background to TUPE

The controversial Transfer of Undertakings (Protection of Employment) Regulations 1981 ('TUPE') were passed to implement the ARD, which sought to 'provide for the protection of employees in the event of a change of employer in particular to ensure that their rights are safeguarded' (see also the 1998 Directive 98/50/EEC). Before the ARD was implemented in the UK, the sale of a business as a 'going concern' resulted in the dismissal of the its employees by reason of redundancy. The new owner of the business was free to re-employ all, some, or none of the employees on whatever contract terms could be agreed. The employees were equally free to accept or reject any offer he made. The ARD's twin features (the prohibition of dismissal in connection with business transfers, and the requirement that both the employees and the new owner of a business continue to honour employment contracts previously negotiated) were a big departure from the common law concept of freedom of contract.

The ARD has been re-enacted and replaced by the Business Transfers Directive 2001/23/EC (together 'the Directives'). The amended TUPE Regulations are compliant with the 2001 Directive, but we are awaiting revised regulations to take advantage of some of the flexibility it offers as an option, and to make other, domestically inspired, changes to the current position. The Government has stated that it is possible that the commencement of the new regulations may not take place until 2005.

Both the ARD and TUPE are concerned with safeguarding employees' employment in a transferring business, yet neither directly deals with the situation where an undertaking or business transfers to another jurisdiction, even though this appears to have been contemplated prior to the drafting of the ARD. However, neither TUPE nor the ARD is expressly framed in terms of cross-border application, and the ARD draws no express distinction between cross-border and purely national transfers. Consequently, the law in this area is left in something of a vacuum. It is also fair to say that when the ARD and TUPE were originally introduced (in 1977 and 1981 respectively) cross-border transfers were rare in practice, in contrast to the position today (see *S1.1* above).

Consequently, the ARD is concerned with the common application of its principles within each jurisdiction, rather than addressing the transfer of an economic entity from one country to another.

The European Commission had originally planned that the ARD would have cross-border effect. The 1974 Commission proposal for the Directive contained a provision on the conflict of laws drafted as follows:

'1.   The labour laws of Member States which are applicable to employment relationships prior to the merger or takeover shall also apply after the merger or takeover has taken place.

2.   Paragraph 1 shall not apply where the place of work of the employee is transferred in a valid manner to another Member State or where the application of another body of labour law is concluded with the employee in a valid manner[1].

However, this provision was dropped from the final text of the ARD because it was to be dealt with by a proposed EU Regulation on conflicts of laws in employment matters (see Chapter **D**). This Regulation was itself never adopted. Impracticability and political difficulty may have contributed to this.

The Directives enshrine three basic principles that are adopted by TUPE:

–   automatic transfers of employment upon a business transfer, together with the terms and conditions of contract and collective agreements in relation to those employees transferred (TUPE, regs 5, 6, 7 and 9);

–   special protection against dismissal in connection with a business transfer (TUPE, reg 8);

–   informing and consulting workers' representatives about a business transfer (TUPE, regs 10 and 11).

The ARD provided for a two-year deadline within which member states had to introduce compliant legislation. The intention was that member states would reduce differences between them in relation to the protection they afforded to employees in the context of business transfers. The preamble stated that such differences could have an effect on how the European common market functioned. Since TUPE has been implemented to comply with the ARD, employment tribunals and courts are required to give national laws a purposive construction/interpretation that fully complies with their parent directive. Thus, European cases shape the decisions of UK courts. European law has provided clarification where UK legislation has been ambiguous, and the European Court of Justice (the 'ECJ') has sought to interpret TUPE purposively with the Directives, so that there should be as much consistency as possible.

Further, in the public sector, there is scope for employees to sue the state for failing properly to implement a Directive (a '*Francovich*'[2] claim). The supremacy of EC law above that of individual member states was emphasised in *Marleasing SA v La Commercial Internacional de Alimentacion SA*: C-106/89 [1992] 1 CMLR 305.

EC legislation may also be directly effective in member states. Where a directive is sufficiently clear and unconditional, it may be relied on in UK courts (see Case 43/75: *Defrenne v SABENA (No 2)* [1976] ECR 455).

Significant differences between TUPE and the ARD have, however, arisen. Some of these have since been 'corrected' by case law, the Trade Union Reform and Employment Rights Act 1993 ('TURERA') and the Collective Redundancies and Transfer of Undertakings (Protection of Employment) (Amendment) Regulations 1995 (the 'Collective Redundancies Regulations').

Through its case law, the ECJ has highlighted a number of ways in which the TUPE Regulations, as originally drafted, failed to give full effect to the ARD. In particular, the TUPE Regulations originally excluded transfers of undertakings that were 'not in the nature of a commercial venture' – an exclusion which the ECJ held was inconsistent with the ARD in *Dr Sophie Redmond Stichting v Hendrikus Bartol*: C-29/91 [1992] ECR I-3189, [1992] IRLR 366. This provision, which placed charities and other non-profit making organisations outside the remit of the TUPE Regulations, but has since been amended, so that the TUPE Regulations apply to transfers of all undertakings, in accordance with the ARD.

In *EC Commission v United Kingdom* [1994] ICR 664, the European Commission applied, in October 1992, to the ECJ for a declaration that the UK government had failed to fulfil its obligations under art 5 of the EEC Treaty. The European Commission alleged that it had failed in various respects to transpose the ARD correctly into its national law, and challenged the following parts of the TUPE Regulations:

(a) the exclusion of non-commercial ventures – on the grounds that the ARD was not limited to undertakings that operated with a view to making profit;

(b) their limitation to 'situations in which the business transferred is owned by the transferor';

(c) the failure to require the parties to consult with a view to reaching agreement, contrary to art 6(2) of the ARD 77/187/EEC, which requires that a transferor or transferee who is contemplating measures in respect of his employees must consult employee representatives in good time 'with a view to seeking agreement';

(d) the lack of an effective sanction for a breach of the requirements in art 6(1) and (2) of the ARD to inform and consult employee representatives;

(e) the failure to establish a procedure to designate employee representatives where there is no voluntary appointment of such representatives (as there is not in the UK, in the absence of trade union recognition – which is becoming increasingly less prevalent).

The ECJ decided in favour of the European Commission and held that the TUPE Regulations, as they stood, were in breach of the ARD in respect of all five complaints. The above inconsistencies have since been rectified and amended by TURERA and the Collective Redundancies Regulations.

The UK has never adopted art 3(2) of the ARD, which requires work agreements and collective bargaining agreements to be preserved by the transferee for at least a year after a business transfer has taken place. Instead, the TUPE Regulations state that where, at the time of a transfer, there exists a collective agreement with a trade union recognised by the transferor, 'that agreement, in its application in relation to the employee, shall, after the transfer, have effect as if made by or on behalf of the transferee with that trade union ...'. Note, however, that collective agreements in the UK typically have a very different role to those in continental Europe. In particular, UK law presumes that collective agreements are not legally binding between the negotiating parties. Only certain aspects of those agreements may become legally binding, and only then by 'incorporation' into individual employees' contracts of employment. So, perhaps, the UK government of the day saw no need to take advantage of the potential limitation in the ARD.

There is no provision in the ARD itself relating to an employee's right to object to the automatic transfer of his employment upon a business transfer. However, such a right has been recognised through case law, with the interpretation being a matter for member states. The ECJ has held that there is a fundamental right to object but that it is up to member states to provide for the legal consequences of such an objection. Under the TUPE Regulations, an employee's somewhat limited right to object means that, if exercised, his employment terminates but he has no right to claim he has been dismissed by the transferor.

1   Source: Fernando Pereira, DG Employment and Social Affairs, Unit D2 – Labour Law and Work Organisation, November 2002.
2   See *Francovich and Bonifaci v Italy*: C-6, 9/90 [1991] ECR I-5357, [1992] IRLR 84, ECJ.

Jurisdictional issues

There are three particular features of the UK system of employment law that differ significantly from legal systems in other parts of Europe.

(1)   UK law does not declare dismissals void, or delay business transactions until notification/consultation obligations have been met.

(2)   UK employment law does not exclude senior managers from statutory protection against dismissal, discrimination and so on. Senior executives enjoy the same legal rights that other employees do under UK law (such as the right not to be unfairly dismissed and to be consulted via their representatives in relation to redundancy situations, and business transfers).

(3)   TUPE operates to transfer the old employer's liabilities with regard to the transferring employees for injuries or illness caused by their work.

The UK's laws have yet to developed a legal response to the migration of businesses across national borders. The TUPE Regulations are stated to apply to 'a transfer ... of an undertaking situated immediately before the transfer in the UK or a part of one so situated' (TUPE, reg 3(1)). The ARD states that it applies where and insofar as 'the undertaking or business or part of the undertaking or business to be transferred is situated within the territorial scope of the Treaty'. There is nothing in the language of the ARD or TUPE that indicates there cannot be a 'relevant transfer' between the UK and another country. However, in practice TUPE stops at the national boundaries of the UK and does not have extra-territorial effect. Thus, UK employees have no legal right to follow their jobs if the undertaking in relation to which they are employed is transferred abroad. Furthermore, employees can only assert their statutory rights under TUPE (eg to claim unfair dismissal against a non-UK based transferee where they are refused a job following a business transfer) in the UK. This is consistent with UK common law and the UK government's legislative policy of confining UK law to the UK, although the ECJ may in future find that confining the implementing legislation to the UK does not comply with EC law. So UK legislation (including the right to claim unfair dismissal) will not apply to British citizens who are recruited abroad to work for foreign (or even British) businesses outside the UK. Where there is a nexus with a particular country, it is common, in practice, to stipulate in a contract of employment that the law of a particular country. applies purely for the construction and interpretation of that contract. No statutory rights would flow from that provision (see Chapter **D**).

In *Lawson v Serco Ltd* [2004] EWCA Civ 12, [2004] 2 All ER 200 (see *D9.2*), the question of the territorial limits to the jurisdiction of UK employment tribunals was explored. The Court of Appeal concluded that the right not to be unfairly dismissed applied only to 'employment in Great Britain' and that, although the residence of the parties to an employment relationship might be relevant, the emphasis must be on the employment itself. In some cases, a degree of assessment will be necessary to determine whether someone has actually been employed in the UK for the purposes of bringing a claim for unfair dismissal. Pill LJ accepted that a dismissal during a single short absence from Great Britain would not normally exclude an employee from the protection of the Employment Rights Act 1996 ('ERA 1996'). Similarly, a person temporarily posted to work in the UK must be permitted to enforce domestic statutory rights while working here (as required by the EC Directive on Posted Workers 96/71/EC).

Under TUPE, jurisdiction is exercised according to the location of the undertaking being transferred. If the undertaking is based in the UK, TUPE will apply and domestic courts and employment tribunals have jurisdiction over it, or at least of the part based in the UK. Regulation 3(3) states that TUPE will apply notwithstanding that the transfer itself is governed or effected by the laws of a country outside the UK; that persons employed in relation to the undertaking ordinarily work outside the UK; or that the employment of any of such persons is governed by any such other law. In other words, the application of TUPE cannot be avoided in situations where countries outside the UK are involved. Otherwise, British employment law generally applies according to the place of work of the employees (as discussed above). However, the precise application is decided by rules specific to each particular right (eg unfair dismissal, redundancy).

So far as common law is concerned, the Rome Convention of 1980 is given force by the Contracts (Applicable Law) Act 1990 (see Chapter **D**).

S1.3 TUPE: Identifying a 'relevant transfer'

TUPE applies when there is a 'relevant transfer' of a business or a part of a business. It only applies when there is a change in the legal ownership of the business. TUPE does not therefore apply if there has been a simple relocation where ownership remains the same. TUPE also does not apply to a change in the ownership of shares in a company, since the company continues to be owned by its shareholders. There has been much case law in connection with TUPE, particularly in relation to when it actually applies. This depends on whether there is an undertaking (part or whole) which retains its identity after the transfer from transferor to transferee. In the UK, a substantial distance between locations does not generally determine whether TUPE applies, although it may be argued that the business unit has changed its identity as a consequence. However, if there is a change in location, it may be that there is then a redundancy situation, and employees may consequently be made redundant as a result of the transfer (see **S2** below). In such a situation, the question of whether TUPE applies may be rendered irrelevant. Further, if in the course of the transfer, the business changes its character, it may be that it has no longer 'retained its identity' – in which case TUPE will not apply.

A business transfer can be by way of 'sale or by some other disposition or by operation of law' (TUPE, reg 3(2)). This will cover a wide variety of transactions, including outsourcing.

Courts and employment tribunals will look at the substance of any transaction, rather than its form, to establish whether there has been a 'relevant transfer' (a vexed question of fact and law). UK courts will also keep pace with ECJ judgments to define what may constitute a 'relevant transfer'. Examples of possible TUPE transfers include: licences/franchises; inter-group transfers; mergers/acquisitions/joint ventures; and property transactions.

To determine whether a 'relevant transfer' has taken place, employment tribunals ask whether the same work or activity as was being carried out by the transferor before the transfer is being carried out after the transfer. The key issue is whether, having taken a realistic view of the activities in relation to which the relevant employees are involved, there exists a stable[1] (ie not short-term or one-off) economic entity that retains its identity, despite changes (see *Spijkers v Gebroeders Benedik Abattoir CV*: 24/85 [1986] 2 ECR 1119, ECJ). The ECJ's analysis in *Spijkers* remains useful in establishing whether there has been a 'relevant transfer'. An 'economic entity' may consist of activities, assets and employees, although a transferee cannot refuse to take on employees as a means of circumventing TUPE. In certain labour-intensive sectors, an organised group of workers engaged together on a permanent basis may constitute an 'economic entity'[2].

The 'economic entity' does not have to be exactly the same before and after the transfer for TUPE to apply – the crucial question is whether the 'economic entity' has 'retained its identity'.

The Directives and TUPE apply where, following a legal transfer or merger, there is a change in the natural or legal person responsible for carrying on the business who, by virtue of that fact, incurs the obligations of an employer vis-à-vis the employees of the relevant undertaking, regardless of whether ownership of the undertaking is actually transferred.

Following C-13/95: *Süzen v Zehnacker Gebäudereinigung GmbH Krankenhausservice* [1997] IRLR 255, it was thought that if tangible or 'intangible assets' (which might include most of the relevant workforce) did not transfer, there could be no relevant transfer. In C-173/96 and C-247/96: *Hernandez Vidal and Sanchez Hidalgo v Associacion de Servicio Aser,* the ECJ clarified the position by stating that the aim of the ARD was to 'ensure continuity of employment relationship within an economic entity, irrespective of a change of ownership'. Employees in sectors such as cleaning or surveillance, where there is a substantial workforce but few other assets, would not necessarily be excluded from protection under the Directives and TUPE where there was a change in the service provider. However, as the identification of an 'economic entity' that retains its identity is largely a question of fact and degree for an employment tribunal to determine, decisions in this regard are often very difficult to appeal.

There may be a series of transactions. Will these amount to one 'relevant transfer' or a succession of 'relevant transfers'? This is a question of fact: is the transfer effected by one or more of the transactions?[3]

As far as the UK is concerned, cross-border transfers tend to be outsourcings or, as they are increasingly known to distinguish them from outsourcing within the UK, offshorings. Many of the offshoring transfers that take place fall into a 'grey area' and sometimes the offshored business will plainly not constitute an 'undertaking' or an identifiable part of one for the purposes of TUPE. Call centre operations and other 'back office' activities often covered by so-called 'business process outsourcing' may not amount to 'undertakings'. Where these have already been outsourced to a provider within the UK and a further outsource to an offshore location is to take place, there is some debate as to whether they are merely a contract rather than an undertaking or a part of an undertaking. For outsourced operations, there may or may not be a dedicated function to support particular clients. This is a factual issue and enquiry needs to be made to find out about this. If there is no dedicated team, then it is unlikely that there is an 'undertaking' for the purposes of TUPE. Even if there is a dedicated team within an outsourcing centre, it is then necessary to decide whether this is merely a contract or something more substantial. Where the pre-outsourcing activities are provided in-house of the client (eg in the accounting function, the invoicing department, the sales and purchase ledger teams, or in IT support), then these are probably not going to fit the traditional picture of an 'undertaking'.

Even if the existence of an 'undertaking' can be established, in order for TUPE to apply, the entity must retain its identity. It is unlikely that this test would be satisfied in a cross-border transfer where the business is no longer carried out in the original jurisdiction. Further, in such a context, there will not usually be a transfer of tangible assets. In the case of call centres, for example, there will be entirely new facilities in the new location (eg India). Where a 'back office function' (eg processing) is transferred, there are also likely to be major changes. The new function may still require access to data to run payroll and bill processing, but this is likely to be done on terminals in a different country, and the terminals and IT equipment required will almost certainly not be the same as those used in the UK.

The key issue is whether a similarity in the way the work is performed means the undertaking retains its identity. However, there are only so many ways in which call centre and business process outsourcing can be carried out. Of course, on the 'snapshot' test, the function may look the same. In reality, it may be a contract that, in effect or in substance, dictates the form in which the work is to be done by the provider in another jurisdiction.

1   C-48/94: *Rygaard v Stro Molle Akustik A/S* [1996] IRLR 51.
2   C-13/95: *Süzen v Zehnacker Gebäudereinigung GmbH Krankenhausservice* [1997] ECR I-1259, ECJ; see also *Hernandez Vidal v Associacion de Servicio Aser* [1999] IRLR 132 and *Sanchez Hidalgo v Associacion de Servicio Aser* [1999] IRLR 136.
3   *Longden v Ferrari Ltd* [1994] IRLR 157.

S1.4 Affected employees

TUPE protects 'employees', that is, 'any individual who works for another person whether under a contract of service or apprenticeship or otherwise but does not include anyone who provides services under a contract for services' (reg 2(1)). A contract of employment is 'any agreement between an employee and his [or her] employer determining the terms and conditions of his [or her] employment' (reg 2(1)). The employee must be employed by the transferor immediately before (see below) the transfer, in the whole or part of the undertaking transferred, under a contract of employment that would otherwise have been terminated by the transfer.

The Directives provide that employees (ie not other types of worker) should be protected – see *Danmols*: 105/84 [1985] ECR 2639 – but there is no standardised employment protection across the European jurisdiction. The case law of the ECJ makes clear that the reference to 'employment relation-ships' in art 3(1) of the ARD was not intended to extend the Directives' protection to persons who are not regarded as employees within individual member states. The ECJ has determined that it is for domestic courts and tribunals to decide who is, and who is not, an employee. The extended definition in reg 2(1) of TUPE may cover workers supplied to an employer through an employment agency under a contract that is not exactly a contract of employment, but is not a contract for services. Care needs to be taken in deciding whether or not individuals who are presumed not to be employees are, indeed, 'employees' for the purposes of TUPE (see *Governing Body of Clifton Middle School v Askew* [1999] IRLR 708 and *Ralton v Havering Borough Council* [2001] IRLR 738). In *Ralton* the Employment Appeal Tribunal ('EAT') held that 'employment relationship' has no autonomous meaning under EC law.

As stated above, the employee must be employed by the transferor immedi-ately before the transfer in order for reg 5 of TUPE (which transfers employees and their rights and entitlements) to apply. This has been the subject of some conflicting case law (see *Sunley Turiff v Thomson* [1995] IRLR 184 and *Michael Peters v Farnfield & Michael Peters Group* [1995] IRLR 190). In *Duncan Webb Offset (Maidstone) Ltd v Cooper* [1995] IRLR 633, the EAT stated that, on occasion, an employee may not technically be employed by the transferor but nevertheless ought to enjoy the protection of TUPE. The EAT stated:

'Employment Tribunals will be astute to ensure that the provisions of the Regulations are not evaded by devices such as service companies or by complicated group structures which conceal the true position. Thus it may well be possible to say that if a person always and only worked on the business of Company B, then Company A was employing him on behalf of and as agent for Company B. Alternatively, there may be certain circumstances in which Company A might be regarded as a party to the transfer even if not expressly named in the contract for sale. Or on the other hand it may be that the employee remains employed by Company A, who has other work for him to do'.

Employment tribunals will therefore attempt to protect employees when the business in relation to which they work is transferred, even if they are not technically employed by it (ie by interpreting UK law in a purposive way).

Clearly, it may be a problem where only part of a business is being transferred. The test is whether, as a question of fact and degree, a particular employee can be said to have been 'assigned' to the part being transferred. Employment tribunals must keep in mind the purpose of TUPE and the Directives, and the need to prevent complicated corporate structures from getting in the way of a result that gives effect to this.

In *Botzen v Rotterdamsche Droogdok Maatschappij BV*[1], the ECJ ruled that the national courts should ask whether there is a transfer of the part of the undertaking to which employees 'were assigned and which formed the organisation or framework within which their employment relationship took effect'. The fact that an employee also provides services to other parts of a business is not necessarily fatal[2]. The ECJ stated that an employment relationship is 'essentially characterised by the link existing between the employee and the part of the undertaking or business to which he or she is assigned to carry out his or her duties'. In order to decide whether the Directives and reg 5 of TUPE apply 'it is sufficient to establish to which part of the undertaking or business the employee was assigned'. In *Botzen*, the ECJ considered as 'employees' workers in certain general departments of an undertaking including personnel, portering services, general maintenance and administration, which were not themselves transferred. The ECJ held that such employees would not be transferred, even if they performed duties involving the use of assets assigned to the part transferred, or carried out duties for the benefit of that part[3].

One practical problem may be how much importance to attach to the terms of the employment contract in determining an employee's assignment and, in particular, the impact of broad job descriptions and express or implied mobility clauses[4].

The question of assignment is essentially one of fact for employment tribunals to determine. A number of factors need to be considered, including:

–   the amount of time that an employee spends on one part of the business or on others;

–   the amount of value given to each part of the business by the employee;

–   the terms of the contract of employment showing what the employee could be required to do; and

–   how the cost to the employer of the employee's services is allocated between the different parts of the business.

This is a non-exhaustive list (see *Duncan Webb Offset (Maidstone) Ltd v Cooper* above).

1   186/83 [1985] ECR 519, [1986] 2 CMLR 50, ECJ.
2   *Duncan Webb Offset (Maidstone) Ltd v Cooper* [1995] IRLR 633; *Buchanan-Smith v Schleicher & Co International Ltd* [1996] ICR 613.
3   See also *CPL Distribution Ltd v Todd* [2003] IRLR 28.
4   See *Securicor Guarding Ltd v Fraser Security Services Ltd* [1996] IRLR 552.

S1.5 Effects of the transfer

The main effect of reg 5 of TUPE is to transfer outstanding contractual liabilities, rights, duties and obligations (ie all existing contract terms, express and implied, and statutory rights) in respect of employees in the relevant undertaking, from the transferor to the transferee. Non-contractual rights, such as mere permissions or concessions, are not transferred. Thus, for example, any outstanding wages or holiday pay due to the employees is transferred, and will be recoverable by them from the transferee even though it was not their employer at the time the liability was incurred. In effect, the transferee 'steps into the shoes' of the transferor. Tortious liability for misrepresentation will pass to the transferee. (See, however, *Hagen v ICI* [2002] IRLR 31, where the transferor and transferee companies made representations to their employees that they would enjoy broadly comparable pension benefits. These representations were not correct. The High Court held that liability remained with the transferor company, as reg 7 of TUPE excludes the transfer of liabilities relating to an occupational pension scheme). Civil liabilities and personal injuries claims[1] are subject to transfer; whilst criminal liabilities and third party liabilities (eg liabilities owed to the Inland Revenue) remain with the transferor.

As indicated above, reg 7 of TUPE provides that liabilities in respect of occupational pension schemes does not automatically pass to the transferee. The pension exclusion is narrowly construed. In *Beckmann v Dynamo Whicheloe Macfarlane Ltd* [2002] IRLR 578, the ECJ commented:

'early retirement benefits intended to enhance the conditions of such retirement paid in the event of dismissal to employees who have reached a certain age, such as the benefits at issue in the main proceedings, are not old-age invalidity or survivors' benefits ... within the meaning of Article 3(3) ... it is only benefits paid from the time when an employee reaches the end of his normal working life as laid down by the general structure of the pension scheme in question ... that can be classified as old-age benefits, even if they are calculated by reference to the rules for calculating normal pension benefits.'

It therefore appears that any liability to provide benefits on early retirement may transfer under TUPE (see *S1.7* below).

Examples of what may transfer pursuant to TUPE include:

– all collective agreements with any recognised trade union, and recognition itself;

– all rights under, and in connection with, the contract of employment;

– personal injury claims;

– discrimination claims arising from acts carried out before transfer;

– promises in relation to terms of employment given by the transferor;

– claims for unfair dismissal in connection with the transfer; and

– liability in relation to current disciplinary proceedings.

Once reg 5(2) of TUPE has operated to transfer rights, claims and duties to a transferee, it is not possible for a transferring employee to bring a claim against a transferor in respect of a liability that has transferred. Equally, a transferor will no longer be able to assert any right transferred to a transferee in respect of transferred employees.

There are, however, problem areas (eg share options[2] (which may form part of a collateral contract), restrictive covenants[3] and profit-sharing schemes). These may need to be reconsidered in the context of the transferee's business. In *Mitie Managed Services v French* [2002] IRLR 512, employees received benefits under a profit-sharing scheme (approved by the Inland Revenue and paid in shares). The EAT held that the transferee company's obligation was to provide 'participation in a scheme of substantial equivalence but one which is free from unjust, absurd or impossible features'. Restrictive covenants are another difficult area. In *Crédit Suisse First Boston v Padiachy* [1998] IRLR 504, the High Court held that it was unlawful to vary restrictive covenants on a TUPE transfer and that any new covenants were therefore void. But in *Morris Angel & Son v Hollande* [1993] IRLR 169, the Court of Appeal held that reg 5(1) of TUPE should be interpreted purposively, so that an employee who had entered into restrictive covenants referable to the transferor company shortly prior to a 'relevant transfer' was to be treated as lawfully prevented from dealing with clients of the transferred undertaking.

There has also been conflicting case law on the question of liability under reg 10 of TUPE (the obligation to inform and consult employees in relation to a 'relevant transfer'). In *Kerry Foods Ltd v Creber* [2000] IRLR 10, the EAT held that liability under this Regulation did transfer. The Scottish EAT declined to follow this judgment in *TGWU v James McKinnon* [2001] IRLR

597, but in *Alamo Group (Europe) Ltd v Tucker* [2003] IRLR 266, the decision in *Kerry* was followed by the EAT. This means that, at present, liability for the failure of a transferor to inform and consult its staff prior to a 'relevant transfer' will transfer to a transferee.

Regulation 5 of TUPE does not apply where the employee in question is retained by the transferor in another part of the organisation, or has ceased to be employed by the transferor prior to a point in time that could be described as 'immediately before the transfer'.

These words should be interpreted widely to mean 'immediately before the transfer or would have been so employed if he had not been unfairly dismissed by reg 8(1)'. Regulation 8(1) of TUPE provides that a dismissal is automatically unfair if it is in connection with a 'relevant transfer' and does not fall within an exception expressly provided for. Sometimes, however, the transfer of a business does not take place at one point, but over a period of time (see *Astley v Celtec Ltd* [2002] IRLR 629, which has now been referred to the ECJ).

Where there are dismissals connected with a 'relevant transfer' that cannot be justified, the transferee will be primarily liable to compensate the employees who have been affected, which may include a payment in lieu of notice, statutory redundancy payments and compensation for unfair dismissal (since the dismissals will be automatically unfair).

1   See *Bernadone v Pall Mall Services Group Ltd* [1999] IRLR 617 – liability to pay personal injuries claims passed to transferee together with right of transfer of an indemnity from insurers. See also *DJM International v Nicholas* [1996] IRLR 76.
2   *Chapman and Elkin v CPS Computer Group plc* [1987] IRLR 462; *Thompson v ASDA MFI Group plc* [1988] 2 All ER 722.
3   See *Morris Angel & Son Ltd v Hollande* [1993] IRLR 169.

Right to object

In the UK, an employee has a somewhat limited right to object to a transfer (regs 5(4A) and (4B) of TUPE). In essence, the employee's employment terminates, but he is deemed to have resigned and so has no right to claim any compensation from the transferor. The practical outcome is that of a resignation without any legal recourse. An employee who objects in this manner will have no claim for unfair or wrongful dismissal against the transferor or the transferee, although any pre-existing liabilities will remain with the transferor.

However, in *University of Oxford v Humphreys*[1], Mr Humphreys objected to a transfer on the grounds that his prospective new employer would significantly alter the terms and conditions of his employment to his detriment. On transfer, Mr Humphreys brought a claim under reg 5(4A) of TUPE against his old employer for damages for wrongful dismissal on the grounds that, as his contract of employment was going to be changed, the proposed transfer was a constructive dismissal. His claim was upheld by the Court of Appeal, which held that his claim for constructive dismissal was against the transferor and did not transfer to the transferee pursuant to TUPE.

1   [2000] 1 All ER 996, CA.

S1.6 Dismissal of employees

In the UK (in contrast to some other European jurisdictions), a dismissal is never void, even in the context of TUPE. There may be exposure to damages if the dismissal is judged to be unfair, but the dismissal would still be effective. Regulation 8(1) of TUPE affords some protection to employees who may be dismissed in the context of a transfer:

> 'Where either before or after a relevant transfer, any employee of the transferor or transferee is dismissed, that employee shall be treated as unfairly dismissed if the transfer or a reason connected with it is the reason or principal reason for the dismissal.'

Regulation 8 provides that, if the reason, or principal reason, for an employee's dismissal is connected with a 'relevant transfer', his dismissal is automatically unfair. There is no 'cut off point' when sufficient time is judged to have elapsed, after which a dismissal is not regarded as being in connection with a transfer – it is a question of fact and degree that must be decided on a case-by-case basis. This applies to dismissals that take place both before and after the transfer, unless the employer can establish that[1]:

–   the reason was an economic, technical or organisational ('ETO') one; and

–   it entailed changes in the workforce of either the transferor or the transferee[2].

An 'economic' reason might be where demand for an undertaking's products or services has fallen to such an extent that the undertaking's profitability will no longer allow staff to be employed.

A 'technical' reason might be where an undertaking has been employing staff on manually-operated machines and the new owner wishes to use only computerised machinery, with the result that the employees of the undertaking might not have the necessary technical skills to be employed by the transferee or that fewer workers are required following the transfer.

An 'organisational' reason might be where an undertaking at one location is taken over by a transferee at a distant location. In such a case, it might be appropriate to dismiss the staff employed in relation to the undertaking on the grounds that it is not practical to relocate them.

Any argument that an employee has been dismissed for an ETO reason will not usually be sustainable where that employee continues to work for the transferee following a transfer. Further, even if a dismissal does satisfy the above criteria, an employer must still act reasonably in all the circumstances in dismissing the relevant employees. 'Acting reasonably' will involve an employer showing that:

- as much advance warning as is reasonably practicable has been given of an impending redundancy;

- the dismissed employee has been consulted;

- the possibility of alternative employment has been investigated and offered to him; and

- objective and fair selection criteria have been adopted and fairly applied.

Where dismissals are effected prior to or on completion of a transfer, they will not satisfy the requirements of reg 8 of TUPE, unless they are for an ETO reason and are necessary for the running of the business (ie because the transferee needs a reduced workforce). Where a transferor dismisses employees prior to a transfer, so that the transferee can offer re-employment to some or all of them on changed terms and conditions, this will not be regarded as necessary for the running of the business. Rather, the dismissals will be regarded as automatically unfair, with liability in this respect passing to the transferee.

The second requirement of reg 8(2) of TUPE (ie entailing a change in the workforce) must also be satisfied. This means there need to be changes in the overall numbers or functions of the workforce. The unilateral imposition of new terms and conditions of employment does not amount to 'changes in the workforce' while the overall numbers and functions of the workforce remain unchanged[3]. Dismissals or resignations resulting from an employee's refusal to accept changes in his terms and conditions of employment offered by the transferor will be automatically unfair.

1   Regulation 8(2).
2   *Delabole Slate Ltd v Berriman* [1985] IRLR 305; *Crawford v Swinton Insurance Brokers Ltd* [1990] IRLR 42.
3   *Servicepoint Ltd v Clynes* [1989] EAT/154/88.

Liability for redundancy pay

TUPE does not affect the entitlement of dismissed employees to redundancy pay, provided they are entitled to redundancy pay in the normal way. Those employees who are transferred automatically to a transferee under TUPE have no right to claim redundancy pay against their old employer (the transferor), since there is no dismissal (actual or deemed) and therefore no termination of their employment.

If employees are dismissed prior to a transfer for a reason unconnected with it, then they may claim redundancy pay in the normal way against the transferor. In other words, their dismissal must not be mainly or partly as a consequence of the proposed transfer. However, where their dismissal takes effect on or immediately before (and is connected with) a transfer, the obligation to make redundancy payments passes to the transferee.

S1.7 Variation of contract

The ECJ has stated that the ARD provides protection for employees that must be considered 'mandatory'. It is not therefore possible to derogate from the rules in a way that is unfavourable to employees. Employees are not entitled to waive the rights conferred upon them by the ARD, even with their freely given consent. This prohibition applies even if changes that are detrimental to the employee are balanced against changes that are to their advantage, so that the employee is not left in a worse position overall. See also the ECJ's judgment in C-4/01: *Serene Martin v South Bank University* [2004] IRLR 74, which addressed the issue of the transfer of early retirement benefits. The ECJ stated that the statutory protection afforded to employees is a matter of public policy and is therefore independent of the will of the parties.

If an employer dismisses an employee after a 'relevant transfer' for his failure to agree to changes to his terms and conditions of employment, this will automatically be unfair, unless the employer can show that its actions were motivated by an ETO reason entailing changes in the workforce (see above). Even if the employer can show this, the dismissal may still be unfair under the ordinary laws.

If a transferee negotiates with an employee and agrees changes to his terms and conditions of employment, these changes will only be valid if they are unconnected with the transfer, or if the employer can show there was an ETO reason for them entailing a change in the workforce.

If changes to an employee's terms and conditions of employment are in connection with a transfer (and no ETO reason for them can be shown), the variation is ineffective and cannot be relied upon by the employer[1].

In *Merckx and Neuhuys v Ford Motors Co Belgium SA*: C-171/94 [1996] IRLR 467, the ECJ identified a European Community right to claim constructive dismissal where there was a 'substantial change in working conditions to the detriment of the employee' because of the transfer (see also art 4(2) of the ARD). Regulation 5(5) of TUPE provides:

> '[paragraphs (1) and 4(A) above are] without prejudice to any right of an employee arising apart from these regulations to terminate his contract of employment without notice if a substantial change is made in his working conditions to his detriment; but no such right shall arise by reason only that, under that paragraph, the identity of his employer changes unless the employee shows that, in all the circumstances the change is a significant change and is to his detriment.'

However, in *Rossiter v Pendragon* [2002] IRLR 483, the Court of Appeal held that there would still have to be a repudiatory breach of contract, as is normally required under UK law. Employers' concerns about potential changes to terms and conditions of employment are unlikely to constitute a fundamental breach of the implied duty of trust and confidence (see *Sita (GB) Ltd v Burton* [1997] IRLR 501).

1   *Wilson v St Helens Borough Council; Meade and Baxendale v British Fuels Ltd* [1998] IRLR 706, HL; *Crédit Suisse First Boston (Europe) Ltd v Lister* [1998] IRLR 700.

S1.8 Proposed developments

The Department of Trade and Industry (the 'DTI') has announced that new TUPE Regulations will be published in 2004, initially in draft for consultation. The new Regulations may not then come into force until late 2005. The consultation exercise will concentrate on whether the draft Regulations fulfil the stated policy aims. The new TUPE Regulations will primarily codify existing case law and consolidate the provisions of the Directives.

The principal substantive proposed change is for insolvent businesses to take advantage of the relevant provisions in the new Directive. Namely, when an insolvent business (not one in administrative receivership) is transferred :

–   the transferee will be able to agree changes to terms and conditions of employment, subject to the new Directive's safeguards; and

–   liability for arrears of wages will not transfer to the transferee, but will be guaranteed by the state (up to the normal limits for state guarantees in insolvency.

Eventually, the exclusion of occupational pension rights from transfer under TUPE will be removed. In its place provisions will be introduced requiring transferees to match employees' pension contributions up to a maximum of six per cent into stakeholder (or equivalent) pension schemes where previously at least as generous provision was made by transferors.

Draft Directive on Cross-Border Mergers

In June 2004, the DTI published a consultative document on the draft Directive on Cross-Border Mergers. The draft Directive aims to establish common rules across the EU (in a company law context) governing cross-border legal mergers. The objective of the draft Directive is to create a legal framework to enable companies based in different member states to merge. It is not aimed, however, at setting out a unified procedure in relation to employees, and so, to this extent, the use of the draft Directive is limited. However, art 2 of the proposed Directive aims at identifying the law applicable to each of the merging companies in the event of a cross-border merger. Save as otherwise provided by the draft Directive, each company will remain subject to its national law on domestic mergers. In relation to employees, it is stated that the cross-border merger (as defined in the Directive) will remain subject to the relevant provisions that apply in each relevant member state (as harmonised by the ARD and other applicable European legislation). By virtue of this legislation, the change in the identity of the employer that results from the merger or acquisition must have no effect on the contracts of employment or employment relationships in force at the time of the transaction, so that they automatically transfer to the new owner. However, this broad statement of intent does not take into account the situation where an operation closes in one country and subsequently opens in another.

The merging companies (as defined in the draft Directive) must draw up common draft terms for the cross-border merger. The only employment-related point that has to be included in the common draft terms of a cross-border merger is information on the arrangements for employee involvement in decisions taken by the company created by the merger or acquisition. There are no further obligations to include information about other employment issues in the draft terms of cross-border merger (e g about the consequences of the cross-border merger for the employees of the undertakings involved).

Article 14 of the draft Directive deals with the participation of employees in the company created by a cross-border merger. The provisions will have a significant effect on companies considering merging with companies in other European countries that have established systems of employee participation. Employee participation is essentially a system that exists in some member states and gives employees the statutory right to be involved in decision-making at board level. The existing employee participation systems in the member states vary widely. Without considering the 10 new member states, only Belgium, Italy, Spain, Portugal and the UK have no general legislation or widely applicable collective agreements providing for board-level representation in at least some types of company. In France, Greece and Ireland there exists legislation on employee participation only in the public sector. Relatively comprehensive legislation on board-level representation can be found in Austria, Denmark, Finland, Germany, Luxembourg, the Netherlands and Sweden.

With the draft Directive, the European Commission aimed to retain the member states' existing employee participation rights. However, the likely result by far exceeds this objective. For employee participation is not only retained: it is exported to countries that do not currently have such systems. In practice, this means that certain companies will be unable to merge, or face severe disadvantages as opposed to other companies. It seems improbable that a UK-based company considering a merger with a German-based company will accept the fact that half of its one-tier board is filled with employee representatives. And even if this were acceptable, the merged company would run the danger of having to implement a continuous stream of legal amendments that apply to a different member state where employee participation is based on the 'standard rules'.

S1.9 Duty to inform and consult

The Collective Redundancies and Transfer of Undertakings (Protection of Employment) (Amendment) Regulations 1999, SI 1999/1925 (incorporated into ERA 1996) set out the obligation to inform and consult representatives where there is a 'relevant transfer'. The obligations to inform and consult in the context of a TUPE transfer are entirely separate from the obligation to consult in the context of collective redundancies (see *S2.4* below).

The main obligations are that:

- where a business transfer is proposed, employers have to consult with a recognised trade union or, if there is none, with employee representatives (who themselves must be employees);

- employers do not have to set up standing arrangements for employee representatives: they can be elected by employees when a business transfer is proposed (but there are specific rules for election); and

- both the transferor and transferee of a business are required to give certain information to any recognised trade union or elected employee representatives for any employee they represent who is affected by a TUPE transfer (including those who do not actually transfer)[1].

The following information is to be given to the appropriate representatives:

- the fact of the transfer, when it is to take place and the reasons for it;

- the legal, economic and social implications of the transfer for the affected employees;

- the measures that the employer envisages it will take in relation to those employees;

- the measures that the transferee envisages it will take in relation to the affected employees who will become its employees after the transfer; and

- where no such measures are to be taken by the transferor or transferee, then that fact should also be stated.

There is only an obligation to *consult* (as opposed to 'inform', as set out above) if either the transferor or transferee intends to take any 'measures' in relation to its affected employees. In UK law 'consultation' means listening to representatives' representations, considering them and replying to them (with reasons). The obligation is to consult 'with a view to seeking agreement' on those measures. There is no 'numbers' threshold for the requirement to consult where there is a TUPE transfer (contrast this with consultation for collective redundancies: see *S2.4* below).

However, failure to inform and consult results only in financial penalties in the UK. There are no other sanctions, unlike in some other European jurisdictions. Failure to inform or consult entitles a trade union, employee representative, or affected person or persons to make a complaint to an employment tribunal within three months of the completion of the 'relevant transfer'. If a complaint is upheld, the employment tribunal must make a declaration and may order the employer to pay 'appropriate compensation' to the affected employees – but this is subject to a maximum of 13 weeks' (gross) pay per employee[2].

1   Where there is no recognised union and where affected employees fail to elect representatives (having had a genuine opportunity to do so), the employer may (*and should*) fulfil its obligations by providing relevant information directly to affected employees.
2   There is no provision for offset of compensation for failure to consult in the case of collective redundancies and TUPE transfers.

S1.10   European Works Councils

European legislation has strongly influenced information and consultation obligations in the UK in recent years. The EU Directive on the establishment of European Works Councils 94/45/EC (the 'Works Council Directive'), which came into force on 22 September 1996, set in train the introduction of formal information and consultation in the UK. The Works Council Directive aims at unifying employee rights across the European Community in relation to the 'transnational information and consultation of employees'. The Transnational Information and Consultation of Employees Regulations 1999 (the 'Works Council Regulations'), which implement the Works Council Directive in the UK, came into force on 15 January 2000.

The Works Council Directive and the Works Council Regulations set out requirements for informing and consulting employees at a European level in undertakings or groups of undertakings with at least 1,000 employees across the member states and at least 150 employees in each of two or more of those member states. The Works Council Regulations stipulate the steps for negotiating a works council agreement and ancillary issues. It should be noted that the Works Council Regulations mainly deal with establishing the 'special negotiating body' (the 'SNB'), leaving the precise details of works council agreements to be negotiated between the parties. The Schedule to the Works Council Regulations sets out the matters in relation to which a European works council can expect to be informed and consulted. These include: collective redundancies; mergers; the structure, economic and financial situation of the business; the probable trend of employment; investments and substantial changes affecting the organisation; the introduction of new working methods; and cut-backs or closures.

S1.11   Information and Consultation Directive

The EU Directive establishing a general framework for informing and consulting employees 2002/14/EC (the 'Information and Consultation Directive') is discussed in detail in Chapter C. Following a substantial period of consultation, the UK government, which must implement the Information and Consultation Directive by March 2005, published a draft of the Information and Consultation of Employees Regulations 2004 (the 'Information and Consultation Regulations') in July 2004.

Currently, the rights of employees in the UK to receive information and to consult with their management (outside of those employed by large multi-national companies with European Works Councils) are broadly limited to situations involving collective redundancies and transfers of undertakings and to health and safety issues. Accordingly, the UK Government was granted the right to utilise transitional provisions in achieving implementation. The Information and Consultation Regulations therefore provide that, whilst the Information and Consultation Directive will apply to all UK-based organisations with 150 or more employees from March 2005, UK-based companies with 100 or more members of staff will have until March 2007 before they will be covered, and UK-based firms with 50 or more employees have until March 2008 before the Information and Consultation Directive applies to them. Whilst the Directive will apply in the UK to both public and private undertakings carrying out economic activities for gain, it will not apply to firms with fewer than 50 employees. Although the Information and Consultation Directive provides that companies within the member states can enter into voluntary agreements with their employees to establish information and consultation procedures before national implementing legislation is in place, it would appear that relatively few such agreements have been reached in the UK to date.

There is no automatic requirement in the Information and Consultation Regulations for employers to put in place information and consultation procedures. Further, the Information and Consultation Directive does not specify what information and consultation arrangements should be established, and no mention is made of European Works Councils and no default model of information and consultation is included. However, the establishment of a standing body of employee representatives would appear to be implicit. Whilst the Information and Consultation Directive allows for arrangements whereby employers communicate directly with employees, it would appear that these should be additional to, and not instead of, information and consultation procedures. Employers and employees in the UK may agree procedures that are different to those set out in the Information and Consultation Directive and may meet their obligations by means of agreements that pre-date the Information and Consultation Regulations, so long as they are in writing, cover all employees in the undertaking, set out how employees or employee representatives are to be informed and how the employer will seek their views, and have been approved by the employees.

In situations where there are no pre-existing agreements in place, an employer can initiate negotiations under the Information and Consultation Regulations by notifying its employees. Alternatively, an employer is obliged to put procedures in place upon a written request, either direct to the employer to the Central Arbitration Committee (the 'CAC'), from at least 10 per cent of employees of the undertaking (subject to a minimum of 15 and maximum of 2,500). In both cases, the negotiation process with regard to practical arrangements for information and consultation must be initiated within three months and concluded within six months (although the latter time limit can be extended by agreement), with the employer obliged to make arrangements for the employees to appoint or elect negotiating representatives, inform them who has been so elected or appointed, and then invite the representatives to negotiate. The parties to a negotiated agreement can obviously agree the information and consultation arrangements that best suit their needs and circumstances. As with European Works Councils, there are no requirements under the Information and Consultation Regulations as to the contents of negotiated agreements (including the nature, subject matter or timing of information and consultation representatives), or the means of choosing or the identity of information and consultation representatives, which are deemed to be matters for agreement between the employers and negotiating representatives (as is consistent with art 5 of the Information and Consultation Directive). However, negotiated agreements under the Information and Consultation Regulations must cover all the employees in the undertaking, set out the circumstances in which they will be informed and consulted, and be in writing.

In the event of a failure to establish agreed procedures, less flexible statutory provisions (known as 'Standard Information and Consultation Provisions' and based on art 4 of the Directive) will apply. The employer is given a further period of six months in which to arrange for the election of information and consultation representatives and to set up statutory structures (as set out in the Information and Consultation Regulations), before a complaint can be brought and the Standard Information and Consultation Provisions can come into effect. During this period, the employer may still agree a negotiated agreement.

The Information and Consultation Regulations set out minimum standards for information and consultation. These are:

(a)   information on recent and probable development of the undertaking's or establishment's activities and economic situation;

(b)   information and consultation on the situation, structure and probable development of employment within the undertaking and on any anticipatory measures envisaged, especially where there is a threat to employment; and

(c)   information and consultation on decisions likely to lead to substantial changes in work organisation or in contractual relations.

The Information and Consultation Regulations are not specific about the frequency or timing of information and consultation (ie employers must provide information to the information and consultation representatives at an 'appropriate time' to enable them to conduct an adequate study and to prepare for consultation insofar as the company decision-making process is concerned, and consultation on decisions that are likely to lead to substantial changes in work organisation or contractual relations must be carried out 'with a view to reaching agreement' on decisions within the scope of management's powers). The Information and Consultation Regulations do not stipulate the precise issues for information and consultation. However, they provide that employers are not under a duty to give information to representatives where to do so would, according to objective criteria, seriously harm the functioning of the undertaking or be prejudicial to it. Employee representatives can challenge the withholding of information by employers, and employers can impose duties of confidentiality on employee representatives, which could extend beyond their individual terms of office.

Employers can complain of an employer's failure to establish information and consultation procedures to, and employers can dispute whether such an obligation applies before, the CAC. In the event that agreement has been reached by negotiated settlement or the statutory provisions have been applied, disputes about the operation of the procedures may be brought before the CAC. In all of these situations, the CAC can specify steps for an employer to take and/or apply to the EAT for a penalty notice to be issued (such penalty, payable to the Secretary of State, not to exceed £75,000). If, on receipt of an application or complaint under the Information and Consultation Regulations, the CAC is of the opinion that the issue is reasonably likely to be settled by conciliation, it can refer the application or complaint to the Advisory, Conciliation and Arbitration Service ('ACAS'), which will seek to promote a settlement between the parties.

S2 Redundancy

S2.1 Background

Redundancy law is entirely distinct from the application of TUPE. In the UK, redundancy law is in two distinct parts. Individual redundancy situations are covered domestically by ERA 1996. The law on collective redundancy (ie the redundancy of 20 or more employees at one establishment) is contained in the Trade Union Law Reform (Consolidation) Act 1992 ('TULR(C)A 1992'). Individual redundancy and a redundancy situation are defined in s 139 of the Employment Rights Act 1996 as follows:

> 'For the purposes of this Act an employee who is dismissed shall be taken to be dismissed by reason of redundancy if the dismissal is attributable wholly or mainly to –
>
> (a) the fact that his employer has ceased, or intends to cease –
>> (i) to carry on the business for the purposes of which the employee was employed by him, or
>> (ii) to carry on that business in the place where the employee was so employed, or
> (b) the fact that the requirements of that business –
>> (i) for employees to carry out work of a particular kind, or
>> (ii) for employees to carry out work of a particular kind in the place where the employee was employed by the employer,
>> have ceased or diminished or are expected to cease or diminish.'

To be a valid redundancy, the dismissal must be wholly or mainly attributable to the situations defined. To summarise, the three main redundancy situations are:

1.   closure (actual or intended) of the business as a whole;

2.   closure (actual or intended) of the business at a particular workplace; and

3.   diminished requirement for employees to carry out work of a particular kind.

The defined situations are narrowly applied in practice. For example, a reallocation of an employee's duties among other employees in a particular workplace in an attempt to cut costs, without any actual reduction in the volume of work undertaken or number of staff employed, may not constitute a redundancy. Further, if an employee is dismissed because of his or her poor work performance, but a redundancy situation exists in a particular workplace, it may be that the main reason for his or her dismissal is the poor performance. He or she will therefore not have been dismissed for reason of redundancy.

Section 139(1)(a) of ERA 1996 covers situations where the employer has ceased or intends to cease, whether permanently or temporarily and for whatever reason, to carry on the business. A permanent cessation of business will automatically terminate the contracts of those employees employed in relation to the business. A temporary cessation of business may occur in a variety of situations, eg the business may be closed for repairs, or employees may be laid off or kept on short time until business picks up. Both permanent and temporary cessations may entitle an employee to a redundancy payment. There are special rules about redundancy pay in temporary cessations.

An employer may cease to carry on business at a particular workplace. An employee thereby dismissed is still redundant, even if the business recommences elsewhere. Note, for the purposes of this chapter, that TUPE cannot apply in such a situation unless there is a change in the identity of the employer. If an employer requires an employee to transfer to a new location in breach of the terms of his or her contract, this may amount to a repudiatory breach, giving rise to a claim for constructive dismissal by reason of redundancy.

Section 139(1)(b) of ERA 1996 covers three types of situation:

1.   where the requirement for employees to carry out work of a particular kind has ceased or diminished because less of that kind of work is available;

2.   where the requirement for employees in a particular place has ceased or diminished because the work is no longer carried out by employees; and

3.   where the requirement for employees in a particular place has ceased or diminished following a reorganisation resulting in fewer employees doing the same work.

S2.2 Statutory redundancy payment

Entitlement

An employee is potentially entitled to a statutory redundancy payment when he or she has been dismissed by reason of redundancy. To qualify for such a payment, he or she must show that he or she has been dismissed within the definition contained in ERA 1996, s 136(1), ie:

'(a) the contract under which he is employed by the employer is terminated by the employer (whether with or without notice),

(b) he is employed under a contract for a fixed term and that term expires without being renewed under the same contract, or

(c) the employee terminates the contract under which he is employed (with or without notice) in circumstances in which he is entitled to terminate it without notice by reason of the employer's conduct.'

An employee is qualified for a statutory redundancy payment if he or she has been employed continuously for two years at the relevant date (ERA 1996, ss 135, 155) and is at least 20 years of age. The relevant date is determined in accordance with s 145 of ERA 1996 and is usually the effective date of termination of the contract.

Calculation

A statutory redundancy payment is calculated according to age, length of service and the employee's weekly pay. The entitlement is as follows:

(a) half a week's pay for each complete year of employment in which the employee was less than 22 years old;

(b) one week's pay for each complete year of employment in which the employee was less than 41, but not less than 22 years old;

(c) one and a half weeks' pay for each complete year of employment in which the employee was 41 years old or more.

Only years after the employee's 18th birthday count, and a maximum limit of 20 years' service is applied for the purposes of this calculation. Further, a week's pay is subject to a statutory maximum, which is reviewed annually and is currently £270 (from 1 Feb 2004).

If an employer does not make a redundancy payment voluntarily, within six months of the relevant date when it is obliged to do so, the employee must either pursue his or her claim for one by making a written claim for payment to the employer, referring the determination of whether he or she is entitled to a redundancy payment to an employment tribunal, or making an unfair dismissal complaint to an employment tribunal. For the purposes of calcu-lating this six-month period, the relevant date where the employee has worked for a trial period and has left during it is the date of termination of that trial period.

S2.3 Alternative agreements

Section 203 of ERA 1996 makes clear that any provision in an agreement is void if it purports to exclude or limit the operation of the Act or to preclude an employee from presenting a complaint to an employment tribunal. An agreement will similarly be void if it purports to deprive an employee of his or her right to redundancy pay or to a statutory trial period.

However, where a written agreement has been reached between the parties that contains certain mandatory language and the employee has received advice on its terms and effect from a 'relevant independent advisor' (as defined) with appropriate insurance cover, then the agreement will be effective to preclude any claims being brought to an employment tribunal.

S2.4 The duty to inform and consult prior to redundancy

The duty that employers have to consult their employees in the event of collective redundancies is entirely separate from the obligation to inform and consult in the context of a business transfer covered by TUPE (see S1.8 above). The statutory duty to consult trade union representatives or employee representatives where collective redundancies are proposed is separate from the duty to consult the employees themselves on an individual basis. The latter duty is not a statutory one, but failure to comply with it may result in a finding of unfair dismissal. Failure to comply with the statutory obligation to consult collectively may result in an employment tribunal awarding compensation (known as a 'protective award') to the affected employees.

Section 188 of TULR(C)A 1992 sets out the employer's duty to consult appropriate employee representatives where collective redundancies are pro-posed. The 1992 Act has been amended so as to require employers to inform and consult either representatives of a recognised trade union or elected representatives of the affected employees.

The obligation to consult over redundancies arises only where an employer is proposing to dismiss as redundant '20 or more employees at one establish-ment within a period of 90 days or less'. Where an employer proposes redundancies involving 20 or more employees at a particular establishment within the specified period, it will be required to consult all those who are appropriate representatives of any of the employees who may be dismissed.

The meaning of 'proposal' to dismiss in TULR(C)A 1992, s 188 was considered by the EAT in *Scotch Premier Meat Ltd v Burns* [2000] IRLR 639. Here, the employment tribunal considered whether there was a distinction between 'proposing' to dismiss under this section and 'contemplating collective redundancies' under the EC Collective Redundancies Directive 98/59/EC. The EAT upheld the tribunal's decision that the company 'was proposing to dismiss as redundant 20 or more employees', even though it had not reached a final decision as to whether that was the course of action it would take. Once the company had determined on a plan that included two possible scenarios, one of which included dismissals, that constituted a 'proposal' within the meaning of s 188. The EAT rejected the argument that so long as the sale of the business as a 'going concern' was being considered, redundancies were merely 'contemplated' and not 'proposed'. However, it acknowledged that 'contemplated' was far wider than 'proposed', so that it would be difficult to construe 'proposed' as wide enough to cover redundancies that the employer is merely 'contemplating'. In this case, however, there was an intention in the mind of the employer sufficient to fulfil the requirements of s 188. Further, the employees who had accepted voluntary redundancy were entitled to protective awards – they were held to have been dismissed. The EAT held that where the 'whole background to the employee's departure is determination by the employer to close a factory and make the employees inevitably redundant, the fact that some employees accepted a package as a means of effecting that decision does not preclude a finding that they were dismissed'.

The term 'propose' has also been criticised as being in contravention of the intent of Council Directive 75/129/EEC, art 2(1), which provides that an employer should consult in good time when redundancies are 'contemplated'. In *MSF v Refuge Assurance plc* [2002] IRLR 324, the EAT considered the issue of timing for the duty to consult. The obligation pursuant to TULR(C)A 1992 is to consult when an employer 'is proposing to dismiss' 20 or more employees: as highlighted above, this appears to be less strict than the obligation under art 2(1) of the EC Collective Redundancies Directive (ie when the employer 'contemplates' collective redundancies). The EAT decision was that the formulation in TULR(C)A 1992 was not consistent with the Directive: s 188 should not be construed so as to accord with the Directive, because other aspects of UK law were more favourable to employees than the Directive.

Appropriate representatives

'Appropriate representatives' of any employees are: (a) if the employees are of a description in respect of which an independent trade union is recognised by the employer, representatives of the union or, in any other case, (b) employee representatives elected by the employees. Employers who recognise a trade union must consult that union and cannot simply consult other employee representatives.

Employee representatives are defined as employees who have been elected by other employees for the specific purposes of being consulted about proposed dismissals, or have been elected for another purpose and it is appropriate that they be consulted in this regard.

Where there is neither a recognised independent trade union nor are there standing elected employee representatives, the employer must make such arrangements for their election (if the employees want to elect representatives for information and consultation purposes) as are reasonably practical to ensure that the election is fair. In particular, the employer is required:

(a)   to determine that the number of representatives is sufficient to represent all affected employees, having regard to the number and class of the employees;

(b)   to determine the length of office of each representative so that sufficient information can be given to employees, and consultations completed satisfactorily; and

(c)   to allow representatives time off work to train for, and to perform, their functions as representatives.

Time period

Consultation with appropriate representatives must begin in 'good time'. In any event, where the employer proposes to dismiss 100 or more employees at one establishment within a period of 90 days or less, consultation must begin at least 90 days before the first of the dismissals takes effect. Otherwise, consultation must begin at least 30 days before that date.

Information required

Section 188(4) of TULR(C)A 1992 sets out the information that an employer must disclose by delivering it to each of the appropriate representatives, or by sending it to an address notified by them to the employer or, in the case of trade union representatives, by posting the information to the union's head or main office. The information must be in writing and state:

(a)   the reasons for the proposed redundancies;

(b)   the number and descriptions of those employees involved;

(c)   the total number of employees of that description employed by the employer at the establishment;

(d)   the proposed method of selecting the employees who may be dismissed;

(e)   the proposed method of carrying out the dismissals, having due regard to any agreed procedure, and the proposed timing of them; and

(f)   the proposed method of calculating the amount of any redundancy payments to be made (otherwise than in compliance with any statutory obligation) to employees who may be dismissed.

Meaningful consultation

There must be sufficient time available for 'meaningful consultation' to take place. No definition of such consultation is provided in the legislation, but employment tribunals take a dim view of any procedure where it is clear that the employer has no intention of changing a predetermined plan. Consultation must be undertaken by the employer 'with a view to reaching agreement' with the appropriate representatives. It does not matter that agreement is not actually reached. Representatives of all employees who may be affected should be consulted – not just those whom it is proposed to make redundant.

Failure to comply

Where an employer fails to comply with any requirement of s 188 or s 188A of TULR(C)A 1992, a complaint may be made by the trade union, employee representatives, or dismissed employees (as appropriate) to an employment tribunal before the dismissals take effect, or within three months thereafter.

If an employer is found to be in breach of s 188 or s 188A, an employment tribunal has two powers. It must make a declaration to that effect and may make a protective award (a financial penalty) for a 'protected period' (TULR(C)A 1992, s 189(2) and (3)). A 'protected period' is to be as long as the employment tribunal decides is just and equitable, bearing in mind the seriousness of the employer's failure to comply. Case law establishes that it is for each employment tribunal to assess the length of the 'protected period', but a proper approach in a case where there has been no consultation is to start with the maximum period and reduce it only if there are mitigating circumstances justifying a reduction to an extent that the Employment Tribunal considers appropriate[1]. It should be noted that a failure to also consult about a TUPE transfer may result in a financial penalty, which is payable in addition to the protective award.

1   *Susie Radin Ltd v GMB* [2004] IRLR 400.

The employer's defence

Section 188(7) of TULR(C)A 1992 states that, if there are any special circumstances that render it not reasonably practicable for an employer to comply with any of the requirements, that employer should take all such steps towards compliance as are reasonably practicable in the circumstances.

'Special circumstances' must be something exceptional, out of the ordinary, or uncommon (*Clarks of Hove Ltd v Bakers' Union* [1978] ICR 1076). Insolvency and financial disaster may constitute 'special circumstances', but only if the crisis was unforeseen and out of the ordinary. Insolvency in itself is not necessarily exceptional.

Notifying redundancies to the Department of Trade and Industry (DTI)

If an employer proposes to dismiss 20 or more employees at one establishment by reason of redundancy, he or she has a duty under s 193 of TULR(C)A 1992 to notify the DTI in writing on form HR1. This form is available by calling the DTI Orderline (0870 1502500) and some Jobcentres/ Benefits Agencies.

A copy of the notice should be supplied to trade union representatives or employee representatives (as appropriate) who are entitled to be consulted under TULR(C)A 1992, s 188. Section 193(4) states that an employer must, in its notification to the DTI, identify the trade union or employee representative concerned and state the date when consultation with it or them began.

Failure to comply with the requirement of notification to the DTI is a criminal offence, punishable with a fine of up to £5,000 on summary conviction. The defence of 'special circumstances' applies under this section as well (see above).

S2.5 Offer of alternative work

Refusal of the offer

If an employee refuses an offer of new alternative employment (either out of hand or during a trial period – see below), the right to a redundancy payment will be lost if the offer constituted an offer of suitable employment in relation to the employee and his or her refusal of the same was unreasonable; although he or she will still be regarded as having been dismissed for redundancy. If the employee gives no indication of acceptance or refusal, the right to a redundancy payment is lost. If the employee refuses unsuitable employment, or his or her refusal of suitable employment was reasonable, he or she will be treated as having been dismissed by reason of redundancy and will remain entitled to a redundancy payment. The issue of suitability is one that must be judged objectively, while the reasonableness of a refusal to accept a new job is to be considered subjectively from the employee's point of view (*Cambridge & District Co-operative Society Ltd v Ruse* [1993] IRLR 156).

Form of the offer

The offer of new alternative employment need be in no particular form. It need not be in writing, but must be made by the employer or any associated employer and be sufficiently clear for the employee to understand what is being offered. The offer should specify any terms in respect of which the new employment differs from the old, but need not be very detailed. An employer must be careful to ensure that the offer of a job is in clear terms, as a vague promise will not constitute a proper offer. The date on which the new employment is to begin must be stated, unless it is obvious that the new employment continues straight on from the old. The offer need not be made to each individual employee, and a notice on a board may suffice if it is brought to the notice of the relevant employee, is capable of being understood by him or her and is in fact read by him or her (*McCreadie v Thomson and MacIntyre (Patternmakers) Ltd* [1971] 2 All ER 1135).

Where a collective offer of new alternative employment is made to a number of employees, to be accepted by all or none of them, the new jobs must be suitable for all of them. If they are not, there will have been no suitable offer in relation to any of them (*E & J Davis Transport Ltd v Chattaway* [1972] ICR 267).

Statutory trial period

The statutory trial period is mandatory and begins when the employee's original contract of employment ends. It lasts until the end of a four-week period that begins with the date on which the employee starts work under the new contract (ERA 1996, s 138(3)). The new contract must take effect not more than four weeks after the old contract ends (s 138(1)). The trial period arises where there is any difference in the new employment offered, no matter how small that difference may be, and even if the new terms are more favourable to the employee. However, there is no statutory right to a trial period where an employee is re-engaged under the same terms as his or her old contract of employment.

If an employee resigns or gives notice during a trial period, he or she will be treated as having been dismissed for reason of redundancy when the original contract of employment ended (ERA 1996, s 138(4)).

The employer and the employee may agree to extend the trial period for any period beyond the statutory four weeks for the purpose of retraining the employee for his or her new job. Any such extension must be agreed before the employee starts work under his or her new contract of employment, must be in writing, and must specify the date on which the trial period will end, and the terms and conditions of employment that will apply to the employee after the extended trial period has expired (ERA 1996, s 138(3) and (6)). If the above conditions are not met exactly, an employee will not be able to claim a statutory redundancy payment if he or she stays beyond the statutory four-week trial period.

The employer may dismiss the employee or give notice during the trial period for a reason connected with, or arising out of, the change to the renewed, or new, employment, in which case the employee will be treated as having been dismissed when the original contract of employment ended. Such a dismissal will be for reason of redundancy and the employee will receive a statutory redundancy payment. However, where the dismissal is for a reason unconnected with the new employment (eg dismissal for misconduct during the trial period), he or she will not be entitled to a statutory redundancy payment.

S2.6 Unfair redundancy

A 'redundant' employee may claim a statutory redundancy payment against his or her employer and also claim unfair dismissal (by reason of redundancy). The qualifying period to bring a claim for unfair dismissal is one year. Whilst an employee with one year's (but less than two years') employment may bring an unfair dismissal claim, he cannot claim a statutory redundancy payment. A dismissal may be for a genuine redundancy reason, but may be unfair as a result of the way in which it was carried out (for example, if the selection criteria adopted were prejudicial to certain employees, or because of the employer's failure to consult with employees or to give proper consideration to the possibility of providing suitable alternative employment).

A successful unfair dismissal claim may result in an award of reinstatement, re-engagement, or a compensatory payment in addition to any statutory redundancy payment. The limit for compensatory awards for unfair dismissal claims is set annually. The 'basic award' for successful unfair dismissal claims is 'wiped out' by the award of a statutory redundancy payment.

Automatic unfairness

Selection for redundancy may be automatically unfair in certain specified situations. The first is where an employee is selected for redundancy for a 'trade union reason' which falls within s 153 of TULR(C)A 1992. Previously, selection for redundancy in breach of a customary arrangement or agreed procedure was automatically unfair, but this is no longer the case. Where an organisation decides to abandon its usual practice, however, selection for redundancy must still satisfy the test of reasonableness. Care should still be taken, therefore, in deciding the criteria for selection, and objectivity in applying the criteria is still important.

Subsequent legislation has introduced further instances of automatically unfair selection for redundancy, where an employee has been selected for the following reasons:

(a)   because he or she has asserted a statutory right (ERA 1996, s 104);

(b)   because he or she has brought to the employer's attention certain health and safety issues (ERA 1996, s 100);

(c)   because she is pregnant or is taking maternity leave (ERA 1996, s 99);

(d)   because, being a protected or opted-out shop worker or betting worker, he or she refused (or proposed to refuse) to do shop work or betting work on Sunday (ERA 1996, s 101);

(e)   because, being a trustee of an occupational pension scheme, he or she performed (or proposed to perform) functions as such (ERA 1996, s 102);

(f)   because he or she performed (or proposed to perform) functions as an employee representative or candidate for election as such (being such a representative or candidate), or took part in such an election for the purposes of collective redundancies under TULR(C)A 1992 or TUPE;

(g)   because he or she made a protected disclosure within the meaning of the Public Interest Disclosure Act 1998 (ERA 1996, s 103A);

(h)   because he or she asserted certain specified rights under the National Minimum Wage Act 1998 (ERA 1996, s 104A);

(i)   because he or she asserted certain specified rights under the Working Time Regulations 1998 (ERA 1996, s 101A);

(j)   because action was taken and proposed to be taken by and on behalf of the employee to enforce rights or secure benefits under the Tax Credit Act 1999, that employee has been designated by the employer to carry out such activities (ERA 1996, s 100(1)(a)).

An employer must apply fair selection criteria when deciding which employees are to be made redundant where only some employees in a group doing the same work ('the pool') need to be dismissed. Generally speaking, employers may adopt selection criteria that are most suitable for their businesses, but these must be objective criteria and be applied reasonably, fairly and objectively.

Where there is a recognised trade union, it is vital to consider whether any collective agreement records agreed terms, including selection criteria for redundancy. An employee can enforce against his employer the terms of a collective agreement by virtue of TULR(C)A 1992, s 179, if the relevant terms have been expressly or impliedly incorporated into his or her contract of employment. However, unless a collective agreement or contract of employment provides otherwise, redundancy selection criteria in collective agreements are not regarded as having contractual status.

The EAT set out guidelines for selecting employees in *Williams v Compair Maxam Ltd* [1982] IRLR 83:

(a)   Were the selection criteria chosen objectively and applied fairly?

(b)   Were the employees warned and consulted about the redundancy?

(c)   Was the trade union consulted as to the fairest means of dealing with the redundancy?

(d)   Was there any investigation of whether alternative work could be offered?

The EAT said that tribunals should decide, when determining the reasonableness of a selection for redundancy, whether dismissal lay within the range of conduct which a reasonable employer could have adopted.

Once the 'pool' has been fairly defined, the criteria applied for selecting particular employees must also be objective and not merely reflect the subjective opinion of the employer; they must be capable of substantiation and of being supported with evidence and data. There are a number of factors that could be used as a 'reasonable' basis for selection, including performance and ability, attendance records, health, age and personal circumstances.

The criteria for selection must not only be objective but must be reasonably applied. Employment tribunals will be quick to find a dismissal unfair if they believe that an employer has selected an employee for redundancy in order to get rid of him or her for other reasons, even if the criteria used are fair. Employers should, of course, check that factual details are correct.

S3 Case studies

S3.1 Case study 1
(Acquisition of a 'business' situated in another EU state; asset deal; no relocation)

Slumber Ltd, a hotel management company incorporated in the UK and based in Manchester, UK, has been in financial difficulties for some time. Slumber operates nine exclusive hotels in the main British cities (London, Manchester, Birmingham, Leeds, Glasgow, Edinburgh, Liverpool, Cardiff and Bristol) under the 'Slumber' brand. Slumber is 100 per cent owned by UK hotel chain Ezeroom plc, also incorporated in the UK. Each hotel has about 50 staff: five in management, 20 in the restaurant and 25 in house service. Slumber does not own the hotels itself; instead it has a seven-year management agreement with Hotel Investment plc ('HIP'), the owner of the hotels, which is incorporated and based in London, UK. Under this contract Slumber runs the fully equipped hotels on its own risk and has to pay a fixed fee to HIP.

In its central management centre in Manchester, Slumber has another 30 staff. These are 10 managers (including Marketing, Managing, Finance, Sales and Operations Directors) and 20 secretaries, clerks and administrators.

A number of staff are members of the trade union, The Association of Hotel Workers ('AHW'), which has been formally recognised by Slumber as having bargaining rights for hourly paid hotel staff. This is a particularly active union and there is a collective agreement in force. Due to increasing staff costs and the declining demand for expensive hotel accommodation, Slumber is making bigger and bigger operating losses. Slumber is obliged to cut jobs in all the hotels and thus dismisses 40 members of staff as redundant. As a consequence, the service worsens and customer complaints become more frequent. When the board of HIP realises how serious the situation has become, it starts to look for a new operator of its hotels.

Some weeks later, while Slumber is still operating the hotels, a French company is found which seems able to manage the hotels in a much more profitable way for HIP than Slumber. The company, which is called Dormir, is based in Paris but has already gathered some experience of running hotels in the UK. It operates hotels under the 'Dormir' brand. The board of HIP enters into discussions with Dormir for it to replace Slumber as manager of the hotels.

1. Acquisition of the hotels

It is anticipated that Dormir will want to manage all nine of the hotels under a single management agreement with HIP.

(a) **Would this be a business transfer (defined as a transfer within the meaning of TUPE) under UK law?**

Answer

Probably, although this will depend on the facts (eg immediate handover, transfer of bookings etc).

Legal reasoning

As stated at *S1.3*, TUPE applies when there is a 'relevant transfer' of a business or a part thereof. According to reg 3(2) of TUPE, a transfer can be by 'sale or by some other disposition or by operation of law'. This covers a wide variety of transactions, such as franchising and outsourcing, but does not extend to share sales. Accordingly, as this is an asset sale and not a share sale, TUPE will potentially apply.

To determine if there is a relevant transfer, the central issue is whether there is an economic entity that retains its identity following acquisition by Dormir. This is largely a question of fact, and case law is of great assistance.

The leading case is *Spijkers v Gebroeders Benedik Abattoir CV*: 24/85 [1986] 2 CMLR 296, ECJ. Mr Spijkers was the assistant manager of an abattoir. The premises were sold to the respondent in December 1982. The respondent took on all employees except for Mr Spijkers and one other. Mr Spijkers claimed, inter alia, that the respondent company should have provided him with work or compensation. The ECJ held:

> 'It is necessary to determine whether what has been sold is an economic entity which is still in existence, and this will be apparent from the fact that its operation is actually being continued or has been taken over by the new employer, with the same economic or similar activity.'

The ECJ held that factors to be taken into account include the type of undertaking, the similarity of activities before and after the transfer, if any customers transferred, the value of any intangible assets, if and how many staff were taken on, and the duration or any interruption of services.

Conclusion

If Dormir replaces Slumber as manager of the hotels, following the transfer the same business will be operating in the same premises, but in different ownership. Accordingly, the requirements laid down in *Spijkers* are fulfilled and this will amount to a relevant transfer under TUPE.

(b)   **Even though Slumber will not transfer any of its activities to France, would the acquisition of the hotels in this way constitute a business transfer under French law?**

(NOT APPLICABLE TO UK CHAPTER)

(c)   **Would it make any difference to whether this constituted a business transfer, under TUPE, if Dormir only wanted to manage the six English hotels (excluding the hotels in Glasgow, Edinburgh and Cardiff)?**

Answer

There would not be any difference in the application of the law, as the test would be exactly the same. However, different conclusions may be drawn.

Legal reasoning

According to reg 3(1), TUPE applies when there is a relevant transfer of a business *or part* of a business. Therefore the acquisition of only six of the hotels would still mean that TUPE potentially applied to that part which is transferring. The key question would again be whether the six hotels constituted an economic entity which retained its identity following the transfer. The sort of issues which should be explored are whether there are six separate transfers (one for each hotel), or whether the six are a self-contained entity etc.

(d)   **Would it make any difference to your answer to (b) above if Dormir only wanted to manage six hotels (for example only the English hotels, excluding those in Scotland and Wales, ie the hotels in Glasgow, Edinburgh and Cardiff)?**

(NOT APPLICABLE TO UK CHAPTER)

2. Employees who work only partly in the business

What is the position of those staff that work partly in Slumber and partly in Ezeroom? For example, the human resources director of Slumber is also the human resources director of Ezeroom and he has his employment agreement with Ezeroom. He spends approximately 40 per cent of his time dealing with Slumber's personnel matters and the remainder of his time on the human resources affairs of Ezeroom.

(a)   **If this is a TUPE transfer, can he be said to have transferred under TUPE in the UK?**

Answer

Probably not, although this is a complex issue.

Legal reasoning

Case law is of assistance in determining whether or not the HR director transfers. According to the ECJ in *Botzen v Rotterdamsche Droogdok Maatschappij BV*: 186/83 [1986] 2 CMLR 50, the issue is whether there is a transfer of the part of the undertaking to which the employees were 'assigned and which formed the organisation or framework within which their employment relationship took effect'.

In order to decide whether TUPE (in particular, reg 5) applies 'it is sufficient to establish to which part of the undertaking or business the employee was assigned'. This is not necessarily governed by the contract of employment, but depends on the facts. The HR director's contract is with Ezeroom and he spends 60 per cent of his time dealing with the HR affairs of Ezeroom. Accordingly, it appears that he is assigned to Ezeroom, as he devotes most of his time to Ezeroom. However, this is not conclusive.

The question of assignment is one of fact. Guidance on factors to be taken into account was given in *Duncan Webb Offset (Maidstone) Ltd v Cooper* [1995] IRLR 633. These factors include: the amount of time the employee spends on each part of the business (although this is not an issue of whether the employee spends 50 per cent or more of his time in a particular business, but a more complex analysis), the terms of the contract showing what the employee could be required to do as well as the employee's contractual duties, and how the employer's cost of the employee's services is allocated between the different parts of the business, or how the different parts of the business benefit or profit from the employee's work.

The most recent case on assignment in the UK is *CPL Distribution Ltd v Todd* [2003] IRLR 28. Here the Court of Appeal held that a personal assistant was not part of the 'human stock' belonging to a concessionary coal contract which was transferred, even though the majority of her typing work was concerned with concessionary coal.

If, for example, the HR director's time spent on behalf of Ezeroom includes time working on the HR affairs of Ezeroom's subsidiaries and not just Ezeroom itself, and the 40 per cent of his time spent at Slumber is the greatest proportion that he spends on any one business, then he may transfer with Slumber.

Conclusion

This is a complex area where each case will turn on its facts. However, as the human resources manager spends 40 per cent of his time working for Slumber and the remaining 60 per cent working for Ezeroom, this may mean that he is 'assigned' to Ezeroom, although a detailed factual analysis is required. If he is assigned to Ezeroom, then, accordingly, he will not transfer with Slumber.

(b) **What is the law on employees who work only partly in the undertaking to be transferred in France?**

(NOT APPLICABLE TO UK CHAPTER. SEE ANSWER TO QUESTION 2(b) AT *L3.1*)

3. Staff who work outside the UK in another EU country

It transpires that some Slumber central management staff are actually working and based in France. Two are French nationals.

(a) **Would these staff transfer to Dormir under TUPE if there was a TUPE transfer?**

Answer

In theory yes, although this would depend on a number of factors, including their contracts of employment.

Legal reasoning

TUPE applies to undertakings or parts of undertakings situated in the UK immediately prior to transfer. These employees work for and are employed by Slumber, the undertaking to be transferred, but they are simply based in France. The undertaking of Slumber is situated in the UK immediately before the transfer (even if some staff work outside the UK): therefore members of Slumber central management who are working in France will technically transfer. The important point is that TUPE in principle applies to undertakings or a part of an undertaking which is situated in the UK immediately before the transfer. The fact that some of the employees are not actually located in the UK is irrelevant.

Difficulties may arise in practice. For example, the employees may no longer be required to continue working in the same place and there may be potential breaches of contract. If their employment is terminated, this is likely to be in connection with the transfer, and potentially unfair. Whether or not they have claims in the UK, or indeed in France, will depend on conflicts of laws issues (see Chapter **D**).

(b) **Would the position be different if there was a branch office of Ezeroom in France, which directly employed these staff?**

Answer

The position may be the same.

Legal reasoning

TUPE is likely to apply if the branch office qualifies as an associated employer and the employees are 'assigned' (*Botzen v Rotterdamsche Droogdok Maatschappij BV*: 186/83 [1985] ECR 519, ECJ) to Slumber (ie they carry out all their functions for Slumber, who is their de facto employer). In such a case the courts are likely to pierce the corporate veil and treat Slumber as the employer for those purposes.

4. Dismissal of employee

One of the Slumber staff, Mr X, was dismissed by Slumber after HIP had given notice to terminate the contract with Slumber and whilst negotiations were ongoing with Dormir. Mr X is owed two months' back pay and unpaid holiday.

Against whom can Mr X bring a claim, and where, if Mr X is a UK national based in [*the contributor's own country*]?

(NOT APPLICABLE TO UK CHAPTER)

5. Transfer of employee outside the UK

Mr Y (the marketing director) has been vital to the success of Slumber and has been responsible for many successful ideas. Dormir would like to retain his services and move him to Dormir's headquarters in Paris. Mr Y has no wish to live in France.

(a) **How does TUPE impact on Mr Y: is he obliged to transfer against his will?**

Answer

Even if TUPE potentially applies to Mr Y, there are practical difficulties when requiring an individual to transfer outside the UK. An analysis of his contract of employment would be important to check, for example, whether he has a mobility clause covering such a change of place of work (but see below).

Assuming there is no relevant mobility clause and TUPE applies, Mr Y has the right to object to his being transferred.

Legal reasoning

The use of a mobility clause is limited. Whilst an employer can argue that there has been no fundamental breach of contract (because there is a mobility clause) in requiring the employee to relocate, there is still an argument that any termination of employment for refusal to transfer may be a redundancy termination. The test for redundancy is where an employee actually carries out his work. If Mr Y habitually works in the UK and he refuses to transfer outside the UK, any termination of his employment is likely to be for a redundancy reason.

Regulations 5(4A) and (4B) of TUPE give the employee the right to object to the transfer. Regulation 5(4B) provides:

'Where an employee so objects the transfer of the undertaking or part in which he is employed shall operate so as to terminate his contract of employment with the transferor but he shall not be treated for any purpose as having been dismissed by the transferor.'

Mr Y can object but, if he does, his employment terminates and, unless he can argue constructive dismissal, he has no rights against either the transferor or transferee.

Conclusion

Mr Y may object and resign. He will need to show that moving to Dormir's headquarters is a substantial detriment amounting to a constructive dismissal if he is to have any claims against either Slumber or Dormir (see below and see also *University of Oxford v Humphreys* [2000] 1 All ER 996, discussed at *S1.5* above).

(b)   **What is the law on objection to a transfer in France?**

(NOT APPLICABLE TO UK CHAPTER)

(c)   **Can Mr Y claim constructive dismissal on the basis that he would be expected to work and be based in France and this is nowhere near his home?**

Answer

Possibly – if this amounts to a fundamental breach of his contract, or if being expected to work and be based abroad amounts to a substantial change in working conditions and is to the employee's detriment.

Legal reasoning

In addition to general common law tests for constructive dismissal, reg 5(5) provides that an employee has the right 'to terminate his contract of employment without notice if a substantial change is made in his working conditions to his detriment'. It is important, therefore, that the change is substantial and to the employee's detriment. Such a claim is likely to lie against the transferee (Dormir). Only in rare circumstances, such as where the transferor (Slumber) has not been open with the employee about the change in working conditions, is a claim likely to succeed again the transferor (Slumber). Case law is of importance here.

In *Merckx and Neuhuys v Ford Motors Co Belgium SA*: C-171/94 [1996] ECR I-1253, [1996] IRLR 467, Anfo Motors SA transferred its Ford dealership to an independent dealer. There was no transfer of assets and only 14 out of Anfo's 60 employees were taken on. The ECJ identified a community right to claim constructive dismissal where there was a 'substantial change in working conditions to the detriment of the employee' because of the transfer.

In *Rossiter v Pendragon* [2002] IRLR 483, Mr Rossiter argued that he had suffered a detriment through changes in the calculation of commission, that his holiday pay was no longer based on commission, and that he was made to assume lesser duties. The Court of Appeal held that in order to claim constructive dismissal there would have to be a repudiatory breach of contract, which there was not in this case.

The use of mobility clauses is limited in long-distance transfers, as the test for redundancy (see above) is where the employee actually carries out his work.

6. Dormir's business strategy

What is the best way of structuring the transfer of the hotels to Dormir from the French perspective? Would the contributor advise Dormir to set up a subsidiary company registered in the UK specifically to purchase Slumber and thereby avoid any cross-border element?

(NOT FOR UK TO ANSWER – ONLY TO BE ANSWERED BY OTHER CONTRIBUTORS)

S3.2 *Case study 2*
(Production moves from one EU country to another EU country; physical move)

Alpha Incorporated is a multinational car tyre manufacturing and distribution business based in Europe. Alpha's headquarters are in Germany. Alpha has tyre plants in the UK, Germany, and France. Each of the tyre plants is a wholly owned and independently operated subsidiary of Alpha. Alpha has a European Works Council.

The subsidiary in the UK is Beta. Beta employs about 250 employees, mostly in the direct production of tyres. The employees are on standard basic contracts which do not contain any mobility clauses. Due to increased competition from cheaper producers in the Far East, Alpha is having to reduce its own production costs. Beta has the highest production costs of all Alpha's European operations. Alpha has decided to end the production of tyres in the UK and move production to Gamma, another subsidiary not far away but across the national border in France which has more modern plant and equipment. Beta will continue to exist, but as a sales and marketing organisation only, with about 30 staff.

Most of Beta's tyre-making plant and machinery is transferred to Gamma, but Gamma will only need an extra 125 staff to increase its output to the required level to supply Beta's market. Those employees from Beta who are required to work for Gamma will be expected to accept the terms and conditions and working practices of the Gamma plant, which are very different from those in operation at the Beta plant. For example, Gamma pays its employees considerably lower hourly wages and they work longer hours than those at Beta. Gamma does not want to pay more to the employees transferred to it from Beta than it does to its current employees. In addition, Beta has an occupational pension scheme for its UK staff. Gamma operates a different type of pension scheme.

1. Does this transaction constitute a 'business transfer'?

(a)   **As Beta's tyre-making plant and machinery have transferred to Gamma, will this constitute a business transfer under the Acquired Rights Directive implementing legislation of the UK ('business transfer')?**

Answer

Probably yes.

Legal reasoning

Regulation 3(1) of TUPE applies to undertakings which are situated in the United Kingdom immediately before the transfer. Beta is situated in the UK immediately before the transfer.

TUPE applies when there is a 'relevant transfer', defined in reg 3 as being by 'sale or some other disposition or by operation of law'. This covers a wide variety of transactions. However, the form of the transaction is not conclusive: courts and tribunals will look at the substance rather than the form of any transaction to ascertain whether or not there has been a relevant transfer. However, there are some types of transactions, such as share sales, where the regulations will not apply. As this is an 'asset sale', it is likely that this is a 'business transfer' for the purpose of TUPE.

An important point to consider is whether there can be a 'relevant transfer' between the two wholly owned subsidiaries of Alpha: Beta and Gamma. Relevant transfers can occur between subsidiaries: in *Allen v Amalgamated Construction Co Ltd* [2000] IRLR 119, the ECJ held that two subsidiaries were distinct legal entities despite having the same management and administration within the parent company.

Conclusion

This is likely to amount to a 'business transfer' for the purposes of TUPE. However, as there is to be a transfer from one EU country to another EU country, the practical effect may be limited.

(b)   **Does it make any difference to whether this is a business transfer if employees of Beta transfer across to Gamma?**

Answer

Yes, this is one factor to consider in ascertaining whether there has been a business transfer, but it is unlikely to be conclusive.

Legal reasoning

As stated at *S1.3* and in the answer to *Case study 1*, question **1**, a relevant transfer is identified by an economic entity that has retained its identity. The number of employees who transfer assists in determining whether or not there has been a transfer (see *Spijkers v Gebroeders Benedik Abattoir CV*: 24/85 [1986] 2 CMLR 296, ECJ referred to at *S1.3*), although it is not conclusive. Other factors such as the transfer of tangible and intangible assets, the similarity of activities before and after the transfer, and whether any customers have transferred must also be taken into account. In addition, a transferee cannot refuse to take on employees to avoid the effect of TUPE. Even if none of the employees transferred across from Beta to Gamma, this could potentially still amount to a 'relevant transfer' within the meaning of TUPE.

(c) **Can the transfer of plant and machinery coupled with the transfer of half the employees (125) constitute a business transfer under UK legislation if the other 125 employees are dismissed prior to the transfer?**

Answer

Yes, as the test is not how many employees transfer (if any), but whether there is an economic entity which retains its identity.

Legal reasoning

The crucial test is whether or not there is an economic entity that has retained its identity after the transfer. Therefore, as long as the business does not change in any fundamental respects following the transfer, it will be deemed to have retained its identity and the transfer thereby constitutes a relevant transfer, irrespective of how many employees do, or do not, transfer.

(d) **Does the fact that the business will transfer to a different country make any difference to whether this is a business transfer?**

Answer

The strict answer is no, as the test is the same irrespective of where the business transfers. However, a transfer to a different country is relevant – both in determining whether TUPE applies (does/can it retain its identity?) and, if it does apply, what effect it has on employees.

Legal reasoning

Regulation 3(1) states that the Regulations apply to an 'undertaking situated immediately before the transfer in the United Kingdom, or part of one which is so situated'. Difficulties can occur in practice, however. Although TUPE may technically apply, it will be very difficult to enforce all the rights and obligations under TUPE once the business (and employees) transfer. The courts in France, where Gamma is situated, will not recognise TUPE and do not have jurisdiction to enforce it (see Chapter **D**).

(e)   **Is the UK's business transfer law concerned with the actual distance moved (irrespective of whether this means a change of country)?**

Answer

TUPE does not specifically cover this issue and there is no UK case law specifically on this point. UK cases are *not* concerned with relocation generally, although distance does raise some important issues.

Legal reasoning

TUPE applies to undertakings situated in the UK immediately before the transfer. There are no other formal restrictions on its application, and distance is not expressly covered. However, TUPE does not have extra-territorial effect and, as our domestic laws will not apply in other jurisdictions, employees will not be able to enforce their rights under TUPE outside the UK. Therefore, distance may be relevant to the extent that a change in location can be said to change the identity of the business. Even if distance does not affect the strict application of TUPE, it can mean that there is a redundancy situation, as the place of work has changed. As a recognised ETO reason, redundancy can mean that dismissals even in connection with TUPE are fair, and therefore a change in the location of the business can impact on whether employees actually transfer to the new place or are dismissed by reason of redundancy.

The use of a mobility clause is limited. Whilst an employer can argue that there has been no fundamental breach of contract (because there is a mobility clause) in requiring the employee to relocate, there is still an argument that any termination of employment for refusal to transfer may be a redundancy termination. The test for redundancy is where an employee actually carries out his work. If an employee habitually works in the UK and he refuses to transfer to another country, any termination of his employment is likely to be for a redundancy reason.

In *Bass Leisure Ltd v Thomas* [1994] IRLR 104, the Employment Appeal Tribunal considered mobility clauses. It held that a factual, rather than contractual approach should be taken to mobility clauses when considering geographical mobility for redundancy purposes.

A similar approach in *High Table Ltd v Horst* [1997] IRLR 513 was adopted by the Court of Appeal, which agreed with the decision in *Bass Leisure Ltd*, stating that the place where the employee was employed was to be established by factual enquiry.

An offer of employment at a different location may amount to an offer of suitable alternative employment and, if the employee unreasonably refuses this, then in those circumstances he may lose the right to claim a redundancy payment.

2. Relocation, but no business transfer

(a) **Assuming the move does NOT constitute a business transfer (because the business of Beta does not adequately retain its identity) but instead is deemed to be a straightforward relocation, are any of Beta's employees obliged or entitled to transfer?**

Answer

No, none of Beta's employees are obliged or entitled to transfer.

Legal reasoning

As this is not a business transfer, the employees do not enjoy the protection of TUPE, and Gamma is not obliged to take on any of Beta's employees.

If there is not a business transfer, then the position in English law is that Beta's employees are deemed dismissed for reason of redundancy in accordance with s 139(1)(b) of the Employment Rights Act 1996. The employees are not entitled to transfer, although the question does arise whether they should be offered alternative employment as an alternative to redundancy.

In the event that the employees are redundant, Beta will have to comply with its obligations of information and consultation on both an individual and collective level. This will also include the consideration of alternatives, such as offering early retirement, offering voluntary redundancy, redeployment, re-engagement and retraining. As stated at *S2.6*, the employees may claim a statutory redundancy payment from Beta if they had been employed for a period of two years at the date of termination of their employment.

(b) **If employees do nevertheless relocate, what will happen to their employment contracts? Will these continue, or will Gamma be entitled to provide new contracts?**

Answer

Yes, Gamma is entitled to provide new and different contracts of employment.

Legal reasoning

As the employees will not enjoy the protection of TUPE, their employment contracts with Beta will not automatically transfer to Gamma. However, note that if employees do transfer to Gamma they will not be entitled to receive a statutory redundancy payment. This is because, even though they are technically redundant from Beta, their employment does not terminate as they are offered alternative employment with Gamma, an associated employer. As Gamma is an associated employer, continuity of employment is preserved and therefore a statutory redundancy payment is not appropriate.

As a new (albeit associated) employer, Gamma is entitled to provide new contracts of employment. Accordingly, if it wishes to offer reduced terms and conditions, then it has the opportunity of doing so, although of course the employees are not obliged to accept the employment. If the employees do not accept the new employment on revised terms, their employment will terminate in the normal way and statutory redundancy payments may be payable.

Employees offered alternative employment (in the UK) in redundancy situations are entitled to a four-week trial period. If the employee chooses not to proceed with the job during the trial period, he may still be entitled to a statutory redundancy payment, depending on the reason for termination.

(c) **What will be the law applicable to the contracts of the employees who relocate?**

Answer

This depends on the provisions of the contracts of employment.

Legal reasoning

As there is no business transfer, Gamma may require new employees to have contracts governed by French law. It is possible for the contracts to state that English law is the governing law of the contract, but if the employees actually work in France, English law cannot oust the mandatory laws of France.

If employees are dismissed for not accepting this change, this may be an unfair dismissal (constructive or actual) under UK law. Whether or not there is a redundancy depends on the main reason for any dismissal.

3. Dismissals

(a) **Assuming the move does constitute a business transfer:**

   (i) **are any dismissals in connection with the transfer lawful?**

      Answer

      All dismissals in connection with a relevant transfer are unlawful unless they are for an economic, technical or organisational ('ETO') reason, and fairly carried out. Any liabilities covered by TUPE arising from such dismissals will be met by the transferee.

However, if the transferee is not a UK business, TUPE will not have extra-territorial effect, and employees cannot enforce their rights.

Legal reasoning

In England and Wales dismissals are always effective even if they are unlawful. However, there may be a risk of financial compensation if the dismissal is, for example, unfair. Regulation 8(1) provides some protection for employees who are dismissed in connection with a TUPE transfer:

'Where either before or after a relevant transfer, any employee of the transferor or transferee is dismissed, that employee shall be treated as unfairly dismissed if the transfer or a reason connected with it is the reason or principal reason for the dismissal.'

Accordingly, the starting point is that a dismissal for any reason connected with the transfer is unlawful.

However, reg 8(2) qualifies this by providing that the reason or principal reason for the dismissal of employees in connection with the transfer will not be unfair where an ETO reason entails changes in the workforce of either the transferor or the transferee (whichever was the dismisser).

Economic reasons may include dismissals owing to decreased profitability; technical reasons may include where computerised machinery replaces manually operated machines; and organisational reasons may include situations where a business in one location is taken over by another in a distant location and it is not practical to relocate the employees.

Having satisfied an ETO reason, there is a second stage to the process. The employer needs to follow a fair procedure when effecting the dismissals. This depends on the facts.

(ii) **what are the rights and remedies (including applicable law and appropriate jurisdiction) of any employees dismissed:**

a. **before the transfer?**

Dismissals in connection with the transfer effected prior to the transfer will not satisfy the requirements of reg 8 of TUPE unless they are for an ETO reason (as discussed above), and so will be unfair (provided the necessary qualifying conditions for unfair dismissal are met). Employees (with the necessary qualifying service, etc) have a right not to be unfairly dismissed and may therefore pursue a claim for unfair dismissal in an employment tribunal. Beta may decide to dismiss employees before the transfer so that the employees can be offered re-employment by Gamma on reduced terms and conditions. Whilst this would be regarded as automatically unfair, and liability for the dismissals would pass to a transferee if the business were in the UK, as Gamma is in a different jurisdiction employees will not be able to enforce their rights against Gamma.

In *Litster v Forth Dry Dock and Engineering Co Ltd* [1989] 1 All ER 1134, the House of Lords held that the ARD was to be construed purposively so as to offer protection to employees. The appellants were dismissed by the receivers of their insolvent employer. An hour later, the business was acquired by the respondent, who recruited other labour and did not re-engage the appellants. It was held that the appellants would have been employed immediately before the transfer had they not been dismissed for a reason connected with the transfer. Accordingly, the appellants technically transferred to the respondent and were dismissed by it.

Dismissals effected before the transfer are very risky, and employees will have strong claims for unfair dismissal.

b.   after the transfer?

As stated above, if the employees are dismissed in connection with the transfer, then their dismissal will be automatically unfair unless it is for an ETO reason entailing changes in the workforce. Regulation 8(1) provides that 'where either before or after' a relevant transfer employees are dismissed in connection with the transfer, the dismissals are unfair.

Effecting dismissals after the transfer is also risky, although perhaps less so than effecting dismissals before the transfer. It is sometimes easier to argue that the dismissal is *not* in connection with the transfer where dismissals are effected after the transfer than it is to argue this if there are dismissals before the transfer. However, note that there is no intrinsically 'safe' period after a transfer when dismissals are no longer 'in connection' with the transfer. This is a question of fact. For example, a dismissal one hour after the transfer may be fair if it is not connected with the transfer, while a dismissal one year after the transfer may be unfair if it is connected with the transfer.

(b)   Would these rights and remedies change if this was not a business transfer?

Answer

Yes.

Legal reasoning

Any dismissals made prior to the transfer to Gamma are likely to be by reason of redundancy and therefore potentially 'fair'. Accordingly, the employees would be entitled to a statutory redundancy payment if they are qualified to receive it (see above and Chapter **B** which covers both individual and collective redundancy issues). If employees do transfer to Gamma and then there are subsequent dismissals, these dismissals are likely to be subject to French law and French claims.

4. European Works Council and other employees' representatives

(a) Will Alpha be required to inform and consult the European Works Council about the transfer or any redundancies?

Answer

This depends on whether a transfer or redundancies are within the competence of the relevant EWC.

Legal reasoning

Alpha's EWC may have been created by a number of different processes which could affect its scope and competence. For example, if it is the result of a voluntary agreement, then transfers and redundancies may not be part of its remit.

However, if the EWC is subject, for example, to the UK's Transnational Information and Consultation of Employees Regulations 1999, then detailed arrangements for the information and consultation of employees are required. In practice, this would cover transfers and redundancies.

(b) Are any other employee representatives required to be involved in the transfer or any redundancies (ie at national or local level)?

Answer

Yes, employee representatives must be involved in both TUPE transfers and collective redundancies.

Legal reasoning

TUPE TRANSFERS

TUPE places an obligation on employers to inform and consult the appropriate representatives of affected employees. If no representatives are elected, the employer is obliged to provide information only.

The duty to inform and consult will be triggered even if only one employee is affected.

COLLECTIVE REDUNDANCIES

When there are 20 or more redundancies to be made at one establishment within a period of 90 days, as outlined at *S2.4* above, consultation must take place in accordance with the Trade Union and Labour

Relations (Consolidation) Act 1992: s 188 provides that the employer shall consult about the dismissals all the persons who are the 'appropriate representatives' of the affected employees. The same section defines 'appropriate representatives' as trade union representatives (if an independent trade union is recognised) or employee representatives appointed or elected by the affected employees.

Therefore, if there are no elected representatives, the employer is obliged to provide information only to all affected employees.

'Affected employees' are any UK-based employees who may be affected by the proposed dismissals or by measures taken in connection with those dismissals. This does not merely cover those employees who are dismissed by reason of redundancy. For example, following reorganisation of the workforce, retained staff are also likely to be 'affected employees'. The term 'employee' for these purposes is wide and includes any individual working for the employer under a contract of service or apprenticeship or otherwise, but does not include self-employed contractors.

INDIVIDUAL REDUNDANCIES

Individual consultation should also take place. The consultation must be genuine and should explore all ways to avoid redundancies or minimise them.

There is no legislation which governs individual redundancies, but there is case law. In the House of Lords case *Polkey v A E Dayton Services Ltd* [1988] ICR 142, Lord Bridge held:

> 'the employer will normally not act reasonably unless he warns and consults any employees affected or their representative, adopts a fair basis on which to select for redundancy and takes such steps as may be reasonable to avoid or minimise redundancy by redeployment within his own organisation.'

5. Collective agreements

What is the effect of the business transfer on any collective agreements affecting Beta's employees?

According to reg 6 of TUPE, any collective agreement transfers with the employees. However, as unions do not yet operate across national borders, in practice Gamma cannot recognise the collective agreement and it would be lawful to ignore it. However, Gamma may decide to agree to a similar arrangement in France.

6. Change of terms and conditions

(a) **If this is a business transfer, how can Gamma lawfully harmonise employment contracts and change the terms and conditions of the employees currently on the more generous Beta contracts of employment?**

Answer

Under UK law, changing terms and conditions is difficult and cannot be done unless such changes are not connected with the transfer. However, as this is a transfer across national boundaries, it seems that, in practice, Gamma can change and harmonise employment contracts, because the transferred employees are unlikely to be able to rely on UK law or practices.

Legal reasoning

Under UK law, Gamma can only change terms and conditions if such changes are not connected with the transfer, even if the employees consent. Even if the employees consent to the changes, any changes are ineffective.

Under UK law, if Gamma wants to make changes to the employees' terms and conditions, it should wait for an opportunity such as an annual review that is not connected with the transfer. There is no defined period how long Gamma should wait before attempting to introduce the changes, but in practice the longer it waits the better, as it may be easier to argue that the changes are not in connection with the transfer. However, in the final analysis this is a question of fact.

(b) **If this is a business transfer, can Gamma reduce the wages of the former Beta employees?**

Answer

Under UK law, it is extremely difficult for Gamma to reduce the employees' wages. However, as this is a transfer across national boundaries, the transferred employees are unlikely to be able to rely on UK law or practice.

Legal reasoning

If there is a TUPE transfer and if the reason for the reduction in wages is connected with the transfer, Gamma cannot lawfully reduce wages even in the unlikely event that the employees consent. The changes would be ineffective.

Even if the reduction is not connected with the transfer, it will still be extremely difficult for Gamma to do this as a unilateral change. A unilateral reduction in wages is deemed to be a fundamental breach of the employment contract, and so any reduction will require the consent of the employees to be lawful. If the reduction is imposed without consent, then the employees can either claim damages or resign and claim constructive dismissal.

If TUPE does not apply and the employees consent, then a reduction will be lawful. However, if the employees do not consent, they can either claim damages or resign and claim constructive dismissal.

(c)   If this is a business transfer, what will happen to the former Beta employees as regards their private pension arrangements?

Regulation 7 excludes occupational pension schemes (except any provisions which do not relate to old age, invalidity or survivors), so Gamma will not be obliged to provide entry to an occupational scheme which offers the same benefits or like benefits as Beta's occupational scheme did. Accordingly, at present the employees' private pension arrangements will not transfer.

In 2005 it is expected that there will be changes to pensions arrangements, and employees who transfer will have some pension protection. Clauses 203–204 of the Pensions Bill 2004 provide several alternative forms of protection. However, these proposals do not require the transferee to provide identical pension arrangements to those provided by the transferor, and the proposals give the transferee considerable latitude. Where employers make contributions to money purchase or stakeholder schemes it is expected that the transferor will be required to match the employee's contributions up to a maximum of six per cent.

(d)   Is it easier to change terms and conditions of employment if the changes are made six months after the transfer?

Answer

Not necessarily.

Legal reasoning

If the changes are in connection with the transfer, they will be unlawful irrespective of when they are made. Note that theoretically it is lawful to effect the changes the day after the transfer if such changes are not in connection with the transfer. Contrast this with the fact that changes made a year later, but still in connection with the transfer, will be unlawful. The test is whether the changes are 'in connection' with the transfer – not when they are made.

S3.3 Case study 3
(Outsourcing of an ancillary activity to a non-EU country)

A large multinational (ABC) based in England has decided to outsource its entire internal IT function to a third party provider in Romania, as the costs of hiring competent IT personnel in Romania are far lower than in England, largely because wages are so much lower. At present 200 employees are employed by ABC in its IT function in England. It is anticipated that exactly the same IT function will be required in Romania with approximately the same number of people required to run it. There will be no difference in the service or approach for those requiring IT assistance and even the internal telephone number will be automatically diverted. The Romanian third party provider has no assets or presence in England.

1. Business transfer

Will this be a business transfer within the scope of UK law applying ARD?

Answer

Yes, the structure of this outsourcing suggests that, technically, it will be a business transfer and TUPE may apply.

Legal reasoning

It is well established that outsourcing of activities to third party contractors may be caught by TUPE and hence may constitute a business transfer (C-51/00: *Temco Service Industries SA v Samir Imzilyen*, [2002] IRLR 214, ECJ).

The fact that the function is outsourced outside the UK is not necessarily fatal to the application of TUPE within the UK, because the only territorial restriction on TUPE is that it only applies to undertakings which, as we have already seen, are situated in the UK prior to transfer. TUPE does not expressly exclude transfers outside the UK and so potentially it can, at least theoretically, apply to such transfers, although in practice obligations may be restricted to information and consultation issues. Therefore, whilst employees may theoretically have claims in connection with the transfer, these cannot be enforced outside the UK.

The test to establish whether TUPE does in fact apply is whether there is an economic entity that retains its identity after the transfer. This is a difficult issue. The facts stress that the outward identity of the IT function is to be preserved, although of course the function will actually be carried out in a different place, by different systems and by different people. If TUPE is deemed to apply, practical difficulties will arise in relation to the potential transfer or redundancy of employees (see next question).

2. Effect on employees

(a) **What will happen to the employees currently employed in the IT function at ABC? Will they transfer across?**

Answer

If this is a business transfer, then pursuant to TUPE employees should transfer. However, most, if not all, employees will not wish to transfer and their employment will terminate for an ETO reason (redundancy).

Note that, as the transferee will not be subject to UK jurisdiction, there would be practical problems and conflicts of laws issues in trying to enforce the application of TUPE (see Chapter **D**).

Legal reasoning

Although reg 5 of TUPE states that the contract of employment is not terminated by the transfer (of itself) and, accordingly, employees will transfer across, this is not likely to occur in practice. The UK employees will be unlikely to want to relocate to Romania, nor are they likely to be wanted to do so by the transferee. In practice, their employment in the UK will terminate by reason of redundancy (in principle, an ETO reason). To hold otherwise would serve to deny them redundancy pay for refusing to transfer.

If employees are terminated 'in connection with the transfer', the starting point is that the dismissals are automatically unfair. If there is an automatically unfair dismissal, at present it appears there is a lacuna in the law, as such a claim would normally lie against the transferee, ie Romania. Difficulties would then arise, as the transferee is not subject to the jurisdiction of the UK Employment Tribunals and has no assets within the UK for ease of execution of a judgment against it. Unless there is an International Treaty giving reciprocal recognition and enforcement of judgments (which is unlikely to cover employment issues), enforcing any judgments will be very difficult.

Even if the dismissal is fair, for example because it is for a fair reason such as redundancy, even then the liabilities which accrue (such as statutory redundancy pay and notice pay) would lie at the transferee's door and the same difficulties of enforceability apply.

As part of the transfer, indemnities are generally negotiated between the parties so as to address the legal problems and to determine who, for example, pays redundancy costs.

(b) **If the employees do transfer, what will the applicable law be for their employment contracts with the third party provider? Where can they make any claims?**

Answer

This depends on the facts, on the terms of the employment contracts (if any) and domestic statutory/mandatory law.

Legal reasoning

CONTRACTUAL

If the contract does not expressly state the applicable law governing it, then the governing law of the contract is likely to be the law of the country where the employer is based and where the work under the contract is to be performed (eg Romania). However, this is a simplistic answer and a detailed analysis of the home of each of the parties, the place of performance and the place where the contract was made is needed. Please refer to Chapter **D** for further details on this issue.

If the contract specifies a particular law, such law is likely to govern *construction* of the contract only.

STATUTORY

Irrespective of what the contract says, domestic/statutory/mandatory law will apply to the employees, subject to any eligibility criteria applicable (see Chapter **D**).

3. Data protection

Will there be special data protection issues on the transfer of knowledge and information outside the UK to Romania?

Answer

Yes, as Romania is not a member of the EU or the EEA.

Legal reasoning

The United Kingdom has relatively sophisticated data protection provisions contained in the Data Protection Act 1998. Part 1(8) of Sch 1 (The Data Protection Principles) provides that:

'Personal data shall not be transferred to a country or territory outside the European Economic Area unless that country or territory ensures an adequate level of protection for the rights and freedoms of data subjects in relation to the processing of personal data.'

Romania is not a member of either the EU or EEA. Personal data cannot be transferred to Romania unless Romania ensures an adequate level of protection for the rights and freedoms of data subjects in relation to the processing of personal data, or express consent in writing to such transfer is given by the employees. Obtaining the consent of employees can cause difficulties in practice where employers do not want to alert employees, eg of a sale or transfer of the business, at an early stage.

4. Transfer to India

Please comment on any differences there would be to your answers if the function was transferred to India rather than Romania.

In practice there would be no difference to the answers to questions 1 and 2, as the employees' employment would still be likely to terminate by reason of redundancy. Applicable law and jurisdiction issues are likely to cause the most difficulties in practice.

Like Romania, India is not a member of either the EU or EEA. Personal data cannot be transferred to India unless India ensures an adequate level of protection for the rights and freedoms of data subjects in relation to the processing of personal data, or express consent in writing to such transfer is given by the employees. Obtaining the consent of employees can cause difficulties in practice where employers do not want to alert employees, eg of a sale or transfer of the business, at an early stage.

S4 Additional information

S4.1 Useful websites

Department of Trade and Industry
www.dti.gov.uk

DTI Employment Relations
www.dti.gov.uk/ER/empcont.htm

Advisory, Conciliation and Arbitration Service (ACAS)
www.acas.org.uk

Employment Lawyers Association
www.elaweb.org.uk

Butterworths Links Library
www.butterworths.com/cgi-bin/linkscgi.exe

Department for Work and Pensions
www.dwp.gov.uk

Inland Revenue
www.inlandrevenue.gov.uk

Employment Tribunals Service
www.ets.gov.uk

European Court of Human Rights
www.echr.coe.int

European Court of Justice
europa.eu.int/cj/en/index.htm

S4.2 Useful literature

Patrick Elias QC & John Bowers *Transfer of Undertakings: The Legal Pitfalls* (Longman, 1996)

Simon Deakin & Gillian Morris *Labour Law* (Butterworths, 2004)

John Bowers QC, Simon Jeffreys, Brian Napier and Fraser Younson (eds) *Transfer of Undertakings* (Sweet & Maxwell, looseleaf)

Index